Ernst M. Conradie (Ed.)

Creation and Salvation
Volume 2

Studies in Religion and the Environment
Studien zur Religion und Umwelt

published on behalf of the
European Forum for the Study
of Religion and the Environment
by

Sigurd Bergmann

Volume 6

LIT

Creation and Salvation

Volume 2:

A Companion
on Recent Theological Movements

edited by

Ernst M. Conradie

LIT

Cover image:
© Odd J. Marakatt Sivertsen, *Menneskejord – Blå* (Human Earth – Blue), 64 × 54 cm, oil on canvas.
Sami Norwegian painter and writer Odd Sivertsen (b. 1947) explores in a long lasting process the entanglement of nature, man/women and the Divine. His paintings often embed the believers and their liturgy in the sub-arctic landscape at the beach where life and death, nature and culture, creation and salvation meet in one common liberated cosmos.
Cf. http://www.oddsivertsen.no/

∞

Gedruckt auf alterungsbeständigem Werkdruckpapier entsprechend
ANSI Z3948 DIN ISO 9706

Bibliographic information published by the Deutsche Nationalbibliothek
The Deutsche Nationalbibliothek lists this publication in the Deutsche Nationalbibliografie; detailed bibliographic data are available in the Internet at http://dnb.d-nb.de.

ISBN 978-3-643-90137-8

A catalogue record for this book is available from the British Library

Klosbachstr. 107
CH-8032 Zürich
Tel. +41 (0) 44-251 75 05
Fax +41 (0) 44-251 75 06
e-Mail: zuerich@lit-verlag.ch
http://www.lit-verlag.ch

LIT VERLAG Dr. W. Hopf
Berlin 2012
Fresnostr. 2
D-48159 Münster
Tel. +49 (0) 2 51-620 320
Fax +49 (0) 2 51-23 19 72
e-Mail: lit@lit-verlag.de
http://www.lit-verlag.de

Distribution:
In Germany: LIT Verlag Fresnostr. 2, D-48159 Münster
Tel. +49 (0) 2 51-620 32 22, Fax +49 (0) 2 51-922 60 99, e-mail: vertrieb@lit-verlag.de
In Austria: Medienlogistik Pichler-ÖBZ, e-mail: mlo@medien-logistik.at
In Switzerland: B + M Buch- und Medienvertrieb, e-mail: order@buch-medien.ch
In the UK: Global Book Marketing, e-mail: mo@centralbooks.com

Table of Contents

Introduction: Doing Justice to Creation and Salvation

Ernst M. Conradie

Doing Justice to Both Creation and Salvation

Each news report on ecological destruction serves as a reminder of the need for "saving the planet". Every next Conference of the Parties indicates the political difficulties involved in collaborative attempts to do precisely that. As a result there are significant challenges for religious traditions seeking to engage with ecological threats in the public sphere.[1] This applies especially to Christian discourse on ecology. Given the debate on the environmental impact of the Jewish-Christian tradition, any Christian talk about "saving the planet" is likely to be met with suspicion.

Such suspicion requires some intra-Christian reflection on the symbols employed in this regard. This task is addressed in this volume of essays on contemporary theological views on the relationship between creation and salvation. Interpreted in Christian categories, "saving the planet" requires attention to God's work both of creation and of salvation. In the context of Christian ecotheology, there is more or less consensus that the message of salvation in Jesus Christ should not be understood as salvation *from* creation (that which is material, earthly and bodily) but as the salvation *of* creation (again that which is material, earthly and bodily). However, the history of Christian theology suggests that it has been far from easy to do justice both to creation and salvation. Moreover, it is not immediately clear what the phrase "the salvation of creation" could mean. How exactly do God's acts of salvation have an impact on the biological functioning of ecosystems?

The underlying problem is not only relevant in the context of Christian engagement with environmental concerns. It surfaces in other forms in numerous different contexts: How does the gospel relate to our culture? Does the gospel have any significance for discussions on sexual orientation? Is gay good but straight better? What does it mean for the church to be in the world but not "of" the world? What is the relation between church and state? And text and context? How may the language of faithful reflection and the language of scientific reflection be related to each other in such a way that separation and fusion can both be avoided? How is Christianity related to other religious traditions?

One pertinent example of the underlying issue comes from the quest for religious identity in the African context. This is evident from the question raised by Mercy Amba Oduyoye: "Is the God of our redemption the same God of our creation?"[2] This question is born from the African quest for identity. What is the continuity between a pre-Christian African notion of the Creator God and the Christian message of redemption that has taken root in Africa following the work of Western missionaries? Because the earliest Bible translators have used the same word and name for the God of our

---

1 On the theme of religion and ecology in the public sphere, see the volume of essays edited by Heirich Bedford-Strohm and Celia Deane-Drummond (2011). See also Peter Scott's earlier contribution on *A Political Theology of Nature* (2003).

2 See Oduyoye (2000), 75.

ancestors and for the God of Christian proclamation, there appears to be some continuity in this regard, but given the legacy of colonialism, certainly also deep tensions.

Why, then, is it so difficult to do justice to God's work of both creation and salvation? I suggest that four distinct aspects of this problem have to be addressed. Only a very brief description can be provided here:

Firstly, there is the noetic problem of how knowledge of God is possible in the first place. If all notions of what transcends us come from below (from the world of nature), how on earth can we claim to know anything about God? How should the category of God's "revelation" be understood with reference to what we know otherwise about the evolutionary history of the planet? Can a distinction still be made between the "book of nature" and the "book of Scripture" or between "general revelation" and "special revelation"? How can the dangers of natural theology – as represented by a German theology of "blood and soil" and by apartheid theology in South Africa – then be avoided? Linked to the very possibility of God-talk is the question how something happening in the world can be ascribed to God's work (of creation or of salvation). How should one understand the possibility of divine action in the world? This is a highly complex and much-debated question in the context of contemporary dialogue between theology and science.

More specifically, there is a long-standing debate on whether or not knowledge of God as Saviour has a noetic priority over knowledge of God as Creator. Is creation theology in the biblical roots of Christianity merely an extrapolation of experiences of God as Liberator? How is it possible to know God as Creator if we can only speak about "the beginning" by way of social construction? It is not self-evident that the world may indeed be understood as "creation" and not, for example, as the product of randomness, luck, fate, intelligent design or a wicked plot. Indeed, to describe the world as God's own creation and to ascribe it to the work of the triune Creator is a counter-intuitive claim, given the presence of evil and the recognition that pain, suffering and death form a necessary and integral part of the evolution of life on earth. Suffice it to say that contemporary theologies remain deeply divided on these questions and that there are traps all along the way of theological reflection.

Secondly, it is not clear how the message of salvation would make a difference to the world. Is transformation introduced "from above" (through God's Word), or "from below" (through evolutionary processes working through flesh and blood), or both (through a form of *concursus*)? Christian theology continues to struggle with the dualisms of ideas and reality, spirit and matter, soul and body. What does it mean that creation took place by word and that the Word became flesh? Is the gospel not all too easily reduced to words about the Word that became flesh? Alternatively, words may be reduced to nothing more than genes or brain chemistry. How can such reductionism be avoided without falling into the trap of an alienating dualism?

Furthermore, what is it that has to be saved and what is the world to be saved from (if not from humans)? The danger here is that anthropocentric notions of salvation may unwittingly return so that it remains humans that have to be saved from anthropogenic ecological destruction – or worse, that salvation is actually about maintaining industrialised civilisation, continuing with a consumerist culture and safeguarding the benefits of neo-liberal capitalism for some. The task of "saving the future" and discourse on sustainability can easily be reduced to attempts to safeguard one's standard of living as far as possible. Indeed, for many living in a secularised context the concerns over "health" and "security" have functionally replaced the need for Christian discourse on salvation. In response, many others would suggest that salvation refers to the victims of the globalised economy. What has to be saved should be the poor, oppressed and marginalised. They have to be saved from the environmental and economic impact of the powerful (or from the legacy of late-industrialised capitalism). Alternatively, one may widen the scope of the phrase to mean the salvation of all forms of life on earth from anthropogenic ecological destruction. The focus would then still be on the structural consequences of human sin.

The deeper problem is that the notion of salvation can be interpreted in contrasting ways in relation to nature. This is the classic theological problem of the relationship between nature and grace, except that one has to recognise that God's grace cannot be reduced to salvation. There is a "double gratuity" (Joseph Sittler) where both an "original blessing" (Matthew Fox) and liberation from the forces of evil (various forms of liberation theology) are involved. How then does salvific grace affect nature? One approach is to emphasise human sin as the root problem that has to be addressed. In response, a notion of salvation is then proposed that would lead to restoration, replenishing, reinvigoration, reconciliation, reconstruction, renewal, reformation, recapitulation, etc. However, given evolutionary change, history and the stages of development of any organism, it is not clear what such restoration could possibly mean? It can scarcely entail a return to the beginning or to some earlier phase. Some suggest that it may entail a return to the original goal of creation, but is the whole of history then merely aimed at some final destiny? What is the meaning of any one moment in the history of the universe? Another approach is to allow for some form of salvation as elevation. Salvation makes the ennobling of creation possible. This may be described in terms of education, evolution, development, cultural advancement, sanctification or divinisation. Christ is thus portrayed as the highest expression of humanity. The danger here is that such a notion of salvation can easily revert to a denigration of that which is material, bodily and earthly. It can breed contempt for the fragility and mortality of being embodied. The body is good, but the soul is better. Nature is good, but culture is better. Thus the question returns: what are we to be saved from: only sin and the evil consequences of sin, or "natural suffering" or both? Or is salvation to be equated with getting the process of education and "development" back on track? Again, contemporary theological movements are deeply divided over this question.

Thirdly, a different kind of problem emerges when creation is understood as an act of God (*creatio*) and not so much as the outcome of such creativity (*creatura*) – the problem discussed above. Most contemporary theologians are fully aware of the danger of separating or compartmentalising these two acts of God. Neo-Calvinism offers an illustration of this danger. On this basis one may construct certain "orders of creation", including differences of gender, race, caste and species and see those differences as the outcome of God's prior act of creating. Typically, it is presumed that such "orders" were ordained by God "in the beginning", were distorted by the impact of human sin and have to be restored. This leads to a rather naïve view of pre-human history and can easily be married with creationist notions. Such "orders" are deconstructed by others as nothing but social constructions of reality that entrench positions of domination. Note that salvation is then understood as the restoration of the orders that have been described and prescribed.

The opposite danger is one of fusion. Accordingly, God's work of creation and salvation cannot be separated. This is certainly in line with the biblical witnesses. In short, God's work of creation is regarded as "salvific" (establishing some order amidst chaos), while God's work of salvation is regarded as "creative". Such views are certainly attractive and are sometimes radicalised to question any notion of creation "in the beginning" (for example in some forms of process theology). However, upon further reflection, fusion begs intractable questions. What is it that has to be saved? Where does it come from? What is the problem from which the earth has to be saved? Where does that come from? How can such work of salvation be ascribed to God's work? What is the source of such creativity? How, then, is God related to the world, if not as its Creator? On such questions contemporary theologies also remain deeply divided. Liberal, secular and process theologies can argue that God-talk is a symbolic way of talking about human activity or about the world and thus resolve the problem. However, other theologies continue to seek ways of making cosmological sense of God's immanence and transcendence and speak of God as the "ultimate mystery" of the world. Typically, that is understood in terms of God's acts of creation.

Finally, all these problems resurface when the focus shifts towards the identity and character of this God. In trinitarian theology this begs numerous questions regarding the relationships between Father, Son and Spirit. Despite the renaissance of trinitarian theology in the 20th century, it remains far from clear how the work of the Father (the Creator) and that of the Son (the Saviour) is related, even if both creation and salvation are regarded as the work of the triune God. Given the challenges posed by Gnosticism, Manicheism and various other forms of dualism, it has been an immense problem to keep the first and the second articles together. Today these tensions surface in other ways, for example regarding the claims to universality (postmodern critiques) and particularity (the uniqueness of Christ). Likewise, the relationship between the work of the Son and that of the Spirit has been the subject of long-standing ecumenical debates around the *filioque* problem. The relationship between the Father and the Spirit also begs questions regarding the identity of the Spirit (of Christ) in an age where numerous forms of spirituality flourish.

It should be clear from the above that the theme of the relationship between creation and salvation cuts to the very core of any theological position, approach or movement. Moreover, it is scarcely possible to separate one's views on creation and salvation from views on sin, providence, the emergence of humanity, the church and the completion of God's work. At a colloquium hosted at the University of the Western Cape in South Africa in 2007, the question was therefore formulated as "How are they telling the story?",[3] in other words, how is a particular theologian telling the story of God's work, including creation, ongoing creation, the emergence of humanity, providence, salvation, the formation of the church and the completion / fulfilment of God's work? This is an interesting way of formulating the problem but, of course, even more

[3] A selection of these reflections was published in two volumes of the journal *Scriptura*. See Conradie (2008). Several of the authors who contributed to that colloquium contributed the corresponding sections to this volume as well.

complex than when only two aspects of God's work are considered.

The Story behind this Volume

The initiative behind this volume emerged from within the Christian Faith and the Earth project. This is a collaborative research project investigating the content and the significance of the Christian faith from an ecological perspective. The theme of one of the working groups within this project is "How is the Earth to be Saved? Christian Discourse on Creation and Salvation in an Eschatological Perspective".

On the basis of preliminary correspondence within this working group, the following questions that require further reflection (as prompted by ecological concerns) have been identified:

- How is the Christian notion of "salvation" to be understood in the context of environmental threats such as anthropogenic climate change, the loss of biodiversity, pollution and ecological destruction?
- How can the relationship between the Christian doctrines of creation and salvation be articulated in such a way that justice can be done to both?
- How can an escapist eschatology be avoided in order to articulate a vision of hope for the earth itself? How should the content of Christian hope be articulated?
- How, on the basis of responses to such questions, can the notion that the earth itself is to be saved be best articulated? What could the moral and ecological significance of such discourse be?

The first of these questions was explored during a colloquium held at Yale Divinity School, 11-12 December 2008. The papers from that colloquium, together with various responses, were subsequently published in a double volume of the journal *Worldviews: Global Religions, Culture, and Ecology*. The results of such reflections on ecology and soteriology are important for the present volume in one particular way, namely in the use of the word "salvation" in the title. Following rather extensive consultation, it was decided to use "salvation" as a generic English term to refer to a range of soteriological concepts, including liberation, deliverance, redemption, healing, reconciliation, regeneration, reconstruction and many others. As various contributions to this volume illustrate, this decision will remain contested, if only because different theological schools give preference to one of these soteriological metaphors above others. It is certainly the case that the word "redemption" is more often used in conjunction with "creation" than "salvation". However, it is not at all clear how "redemption" and "salvation" may be distinguished from each other. The lack of clarity in this regard is quite remarkable. There are clearly different ways in which these terms are used in relation to each other in different confessional traditions, language groups and geographical contexts.

The *Anchor Bible Dictionary* lists the following Hebrew terms for "salvation" and "redemption": *nasal* (deliver), *palat* (bring to safety), *padah* (redeem, liberate), *malat* (deliver), *ga'al* (buy back, restore), *yasa'* (save in times of distress, rescue). Redemption is required from enemies, the wicked, oppression, death and severe penalties. It lists the following Greek terms: the verb *sozo* (save, keep from harm, rescue, liberate) and the noun *soteria*, *ruomai* (rescue), *agorazo* (to buy back, redeem), the verb *lytroo* (to pay a ransom, release, buying a slave in order to give him or her freedom) and the noun *apolytrosis* (redemption). It has no entry for "reconciliation" (*katalasso*)! The wealth of biblical terminology prompts further theological reflection. However, given the overlapping connotations between these terms, the varied ways in which they are used in particular biblical texts and the theological (over)extension of their metaphorical meaning, it is scarcely possible to base distinctions in contemporary soteriological reflection on the biblical witnesses or to draw on the etymological roots of such terminology in order to establish their meaning for today.

On this basis, the relationship between creation and salvation, i.e. the second of the above questions, can be explored. This has led to planning towards two volumes of essays on the ways in which the relationship between creation and salvation has been understood in the history of Christian theology, in different contexts. The first volume offers a mosaic of reflections on classic Christian theologians and theological movements. It includes essays by Svein Rise on Irenaeus, Denis Edwards on Athanasius, Sigurd Bergmann on Gregory of Nazianz, Scott Dunham on Augustine, Elizabeth Theokritoff on Maximus, Mary Grey on medieval female mystics, Ilia Delio on the Franciscan tradition, William French on Aquinas, Paul Santmire on Martin Luther and Ernst Conradie on John Calvin.

This present volume may be described as a "companion" regarding the various ways in which the relationship between creation and salvation is understood in contemporary theological movements. Since the immediate roots of some of these theological movements have to be understood in terms of developments in the 20th century, at least, but in some cases also the late 19th century, the word "recent" that is used is deliberately somewhat vague. This does require further clarification on the structure of the volume and the planning behind it.

The Structure of the Volume

The task addressed in this volume is a highly complex one. Given the ecumenical scope of the inquiry and the intercontinental nature of the collaboration involved in this project, it soon became almost encyclopaedic in nature and could easily have lost its particular focus without careful planning.

The selection of relevant chapters to be included in this volume followed a consultative process within the working group of the Christian Faith and the Earth project mentioned above and thereafter with an expanding number of participants. The same applied to the selection of relevant sections within each chapter. To contain the volume somewhat, it was decided to restrict each section to around 2500 words and then to consider suggestions for the number of sections to be included in each chapter.

Three selection criteria were employed in this regard, more or less in order of priority. First, the question was whether the position of a particular theologian or theological movement holds promise for contemporary attempts to do justice to God's work both of salvation and of creation – especially in the context of ecotheology, but also in several other contexts where the significance of the message of salvation for that which is material, bodily and earthly is at stake. Second, the question was whether a particular theologian's position is recognised to be highly influential, at least in a particular context and tradition. Such influence would not necessary be beneficial (e.g. in terms of ecological sustainability), it may also have been used in destructive ways and would then be challenged by others. In that case, it would still be important to understand the theological motif underlying such a position, if only to recognise the dangers in this regard. Third, considerations in terms of confessional traditions, geographic contexts, theological schools, gender and race each played a role in the selection of chapters and relevant sections.

Of course numerous other sections could have been added to a volume of this nature. One example is the influence of American expressions of creationism and of fundamentalism. Given the selection criteria, these movements are certainly highly influential and (one may argue) ecologically destructive, but hardly attractive for attempts to do justice to both creation and salvation. Likewise, Pentecostalism is undoubtedly highly influential, especially in altering current discourse on salvation, but it is not immediately clear where one may find exponents that can aid a Christian understanding of God's work of salvation *and* creation. In chapter 12 a section on African Pentecostalism is included.

Another example is the absence of a chapter on the Anglican tradition. Given the intense environmental engagement within the Anglican Communion, it would be worthwhile to explore the sources of inspiration behind that. However, the organising principles employed to map the terrain are not only confessional or thematic, but also contextual and geographic. On this basis sections on Arthur Peacocke and John Polkinghorne are included in chapter 6 on science and theology. Likewise, there are contributions on several Methodist theologians in chapter 7 on process theology and on the Anabaptist tradition in chapter 9 which explores "North American Perspectives from the Margins". Cross-references are found in many of the concluding sections.

It should also be noted that Roman Catholic theologies feature in several of the chapters. Feminist perspectives are brought into play in most of the chapters, not only in the chapter 8 on Western ecofeminist theologies. Issues around justice, peace and a sustainable society are addressed throughout, whether explicitly or implicitly.

A number of further clarifications regarding the selection criteria are necessary:

- The use of English as medium of communication imposed some restrictions, although attempts were made not to standardise the use of English too much so that different voices (if you like, different English accents) from different contexts might still be heard in the text.
- While this volume is situated primarily in terms of Christian ecotheology, the selection of theologians considered was not made in terms of their direct involvement in debates on ecotheology. In the concluding section of each chapter, contributions to ecotheology were noted in terms of "further developments'.
- An editorial decision had to be made regarding those scholars who are currently contributing to debates in Christian ecotheology and whose positions have already become influential. The situation is that many of these theologians were asked to contribute sections or edit chapters, which meant that they would then have needed to write about themselves. To avoid that, it was decided to focus on those scholars whose positions have reached some maturity, typically beyond retirement age. Admittedly, this was not possible in the case of emerging theological movements, but

in those cases the relevant sections do not carry the name of a particular person. Where necessary and appropriate, further exceptions were considered. Again, the concluding section of each chapter on "further developments" allowed an opportunity to mention the more recent contributions.

The identification of suitable authors for each section was done in consultation with the chapter editors. The more than fifty contributors to this volume, from at least twenty-four countries of origin, bear witness to the complexity of this process, but also to the rich diversity that such collaborative work facilitates. Of course, the emphasis was on scholarly expertise on the work of a particular theologian or theological movement. In several cases this entails a lifetime of scholarship. Indeed, this is required to capture the position of theologians like Bavinck, Barth, Noordmans, Van Ruler and Moltmann – to use examples from the chapter on reformed theology only.

It is nevertheless interesting to observe that there are several cases where a contemporary scholar writes about a theologian in another part of the world. Thus Lai Pan-chiu from China writes about Paul Tillich, Pauliina Kainulainen from Finland writes about Yvone Gebara, Denis Edwards from Australia writes about Karl Rahner, Celia Deane-Drummond, now based in the USA, writes about Sergii Bulgakov, Anné Verhoef from South Africa writes about Robert Jenson and several South African feminist scholars reflect on the positions of their North Atlantic colleagues. This is actually a refreshing demonstration of the possibility of ecumenical dialogue and solidarity.

The same structure is used in most of the chapters, namely an introduction by the chapter editor(s), which provides same background to the particular theological movements, a number of sections on individual theologians or theological movements or reflections on a particular challenge, followed by a final section on further, more recent developments within the movement covered in the particular chapter.

A Note on Bibliographic Aspects

Any one of the sections included in this volume could be expanded towards a full monograph. In fact, contributors have been encouraged to do just that elsewhere.[4] The difficult question that most contributors thus had to face was how to condense the position of a scholar, who has perhaps written a few million words, into 2500 words, without losing the nuances of that scholar's position. In order to use the available space, contributors were encouraged to minimise (but not avoid) quotations and references (although there are several exceptions), but also to include a list of recommended readings besides the specific works that were referred to in the text. The repetition of bibliographic details was avoided as far as possible. Where such bibliographic details form part of the narrative of the argument it is not repeated under the subheading "References and Recommended Reading". Where numerous references to a standard work of a particular author are included, page references are provided in the text with an explanation in a footnote at the first instance of such references.

---

4 See, for example, the volume of essays on Abraham Kuyper's legacy (Conradie 2011b) which preceded work on the two volumes on creation and salvation published by LIT Verlag. I have also completed a monograph on the same theme with reference to the reformed tradition of Swiss, Dutch and German origin and the reception of that tradition in the South African context.

References and Recommended Reading

Bedford-Strohm, H. & Deane-Drummond, C.E. (eds.) (2011), *Religion and Ecology in the Public Sphere*, London / New York: T & T Clark International.

Conradie, Ernst M. (ed.) (2008a), "How are They Telling the Story?", *Scriptura*, Vol. 97, 1-136.

--- (ed.) (2008b), "How are They Telling the Story?", *Scriptura*, Vol. 98, 137-243.

--- (ed.) (2011a), *Creation and Salvation: A Mosaic of Essays on Selected Classic Christian Theologians*, Berlin: LIT.

--- (ed.) (2011b), *Creation and Salvation: Dialogue on Abraham Kuyper's Legacy for Contemporary Ecotheology*, Leiden: Brill.

Conradie, Ernst M. and Jenkins, Willis (eds.) (2010), *Ecology and Christian Soteriology*, Special issue of *Worldviews: Global Religions, Culture, and Ecology*, Vol. 14, 2-3, 107-265.

Oduyoye, Amba (2000), *Hearing and Knowing: Theological Reflections on Christianity in Africa*, Maryknoll: Orbis.

Scott, P. (2003), *A Political Theology of Nature*, Cambridge: Cambridge University Press.

Ernst M. Conradie

1. Eastern Christian Thought

Edited by Oliver Smith and Elizabeth Theokritoff

Introduction

The Eastern Christian tradition is characterised both by continuity with the early church and by considerable creativity in elaborating this heritage in recent centuries. An important role in this process was played by representatives of Russian religious thought; although some of their ideas are often placed without the purview of Orthodoxy, these thinkers drew on a shared and ancient tradition, which informed and moulded their reflections.

Tradition and creative re-appropriation are both very evident in the theology of creation and salvation. The Eastern tradition has typically thought in terms of what Panayiotis Nellas calls the "great axis" of creation-deification, rather than a truncated schema of fall-redemption. The incarnation, death and resurrection of Christ are seen as central for the entire cosmos, not just humanity: the Creator Word comes in order to fulfil the purpose of his creation. This is expressed in the patristic concept of deification (*theosis*) – the Word "became a human being in order that he might deify us in himself" (Athanasius) – as well as in the conviction that matter can be sanctified, emphasised alike by early Fathers and modern Orthodox thought. This vision of creation for the sake of salvation, worked out most fully by St Maximus the Confessor, provides the structure for much contemporary Orthodox thinking. The uncreated light of Mount Tabor as witnessed in the transfiguration, interpreted with further help from Palamite teaching on the essence-energy distinction and Hesychastic practice, would become the core paradigmatic model of the Eastern view of a transfigured creation.

The transmission of this tradition has been neither smooth nor linear, however. After some three centuries during which Orthodox theology was heavily dominated by Western categories of thought, the beginnings of a modern revival may be traced to the work of St Nicodemus of the Holy Mountain (1749-1809). His enormously influential *Philokalia* (translated almost immediately into Russian) includes extensive passages from Palamas as well as Maximus, who influenced him profoundly. Although sustained scholarly engagement with the work of these figures, so central to contemporary Orthodox thought, would await the 20th century, through Nicodemus they began to reinvigorate spiritual life from the early 19th century onwards, beginning with a monastic revival in Moldavia and Russia.

All this represented the backdrop to the intellectual movement located in Orthodox Russia in the early 19th century, which would prove so important for modern Eastern Christian thinking on creation. Yet at this stage it was no more than this – a backdrop, against which the imported ideas of Western philosophy, first of the French Enlightenment and then, more productively, of German idealism in the shape of Schelling and Hegel, would play out alongside the esoteric writings of masons and mystics such as Jacob Boehme. It would be many years before the patristic legacy of the East would receive its due alongside these and sundry other sources, despite a Russian revival of patristic scholarship at the same time and the appearance of gifted church hierarchs such as Metropolitans Platon (Levshin) and Filaret (of Moscow). Nevertheless, the reception of the products of Western thinking by a predominantly Orthodox culture created a unique symbiosis whereby new ideas were interpreted under an ancient hermeneutic or else old concepts were moulded into novel forms.

The quest for an original mode of philosophising (in early 19th-century Russia, the word *samobytnost'*, "originality", was something of a mantra) would locate itself in an ever-expanding series of binaries: Western philosophy versus Eastern wisdom; Orthodoxy versus Catholicism / Protestantism; atomisation versus wholeness. It is somewhat ironic that Vladimir Soloviev, the first great synthesiser of such binaries, himself became the object of great division after his death in 1900. A mark of Soloviev's ambiguity as founder of an independent philosophical-theological tradition is that even his followers (often characterised as "sophiologists") related to his legacy with a certain ambivalence. Sergii Bulgakov, while continuing to plough the same broad furrow as his predecessor, would talk about the "fateful incursion of carnal sensuality into the spiritual realm",[1] which he observed in Soloviev's visionary, eroticised philosophy of Sophia, or divine Wisdom. For both Bulgakov and Pavel Florensky, the two most notable theologians of the post-revolutionary period, however, there remained an irreducible veracity to Soloviev's envisionings of Sophia, which they continued to hold under the Christological lens of theanthropy (*bogochelovechestvo*) – the union of divine and human natures in Christ. Whatever the character of the sophiological strand in Russian religious thought, then, the Russian Sophia was never intended as an annexation to, far less a departure from, Orthodoxy. Indeed, she represented less an original theological principle than a certain matrix, a place of mediation in which were held, often in an inscrutable way, the contradictory properties of a life lived between temporality and eternity. She contains within herself the paradoxical identity-in-difference of a fallen creation which, as Paul has it, "groans in labour pains until now", and a world redeemed at its core under the kingship of Christ.

Despite the attempted corrective given by later Russian sophiologists to Soloviev's original vision, a fissure was to open up toward the middle of the 20th century between his followers, on the one hand, and representatives of the so-called neo-patristic synthesis, on the other. Foremost among these latter was Vladimir Lossky, who was suspicious of the preceding momentum of Russian theology (in 1935, Bulgakov's sophiological Christology was condemned by the Moscow Patriarchate, although it fell short of the criterion of heresy) and its alleged propensity for rationalistic theorising on the nature of the divine and its relation to the creaturely. Despite these differences, Lossky agreed with the sophiologists' ecclesiological vision of the cosmos, emphasising that the world is created in order to participate in divine life. Georges Florovsky, the other prominent figure in this movement, would signal an even greater break with the sophiologists. Where Bulgakov stressed ontological continuity between Creator and creation, Florovsky moved in the other direction, arguing for a radical discontinuity between the two.

Academic debate over the Orthodoxy or otherwise of these two camps continues to the present day, although interest in all currents of Russian theological thought can now be observed both within and outside the church. Sophiology itself, despite some

[1] Bulgakov (2003), 357.

notable exceptions, has had little resonance within the Orthodox world, receiving instead more attention from Catholic and Protestant theologians. Nevertheless, much contemporary Orthodox thinking continues to strive for the kind of synthesis the sophiologists sought, finding in patristic writings and the liturgical and monastic traditions that wholeness and integrality that are the defining marks of the tradition. Responding to the creativity of Russian theologians, the second half of the 20th century has seen several notable thinkers from outside the Russian tradition. Dumitru Stăniloae has only recently begun to receive the attention he merits through translation of his works from the original Romanian. Stăniloae's dual emphasis on *creatio ex nihilo* and the ultimate deification of the created order shares much with Lossky, yet the Romanian makes more explicit perhaps than any earlier thinker that salvation in the Christian view concerns not the isolated individual, nor humanity as a whole, but humanity ontologically united with all creation. In Stăniloae, the cosmology of the Christian East, notably that of Maximus and Palamas, receives significant elaboration in the light of modernity. His patristic scholarship has influenced Greek theology largely thanks to Panayiotis Nellas, who explores the theology of deification and argues strongly that the incarnation represents the very goal of creation, irrespective of human sin.

John Zizioulas's metaphysics of relation continues to be influential in current environmental debate from the theological perspective. His stress on the absence of connection with God except through the person, while resonating with the oft-overlooked figure of Lev Karsavin, differs not only from thinkers who owe something to Bulgakov, but also from those influenced by the monastic tradition. Zizioulas's development of the concept of personhood is echoed in the work of Christos Yannaras, one of whose principal concerns has been the overcoming of the Western "myth of subjectivity" and the attainment of a renewed personal sphere of relation free of the atomised individuality of the modern era. Through his liturgical understanding of humanity's role within creation as given in the Holy Communion, he envisages the human assent to Christ's assumption of our nature as effecting the communication of the Word to all created matter. Even for these strongly personalist theologians, therefore, human personhood clearly administers the salvation of all of creation.

References and Recommended Reading

Bulgakov, Sergii (2003), *Religioznyi filosofskii put'*, Moscow: Mysl'.

Oliver Smith and Elizabeth Theokritoff

Vladimir Soloviev (1853-1900) – The Ultimate Spiritualisation of All Created Matter

Introduction

Often regarded as the father of the Russian philosophical tradition, Vladimir Soloviev's influence on theological thought in that country was immense. The son of Russia's most prominent historian and the inspiration behind at least one of Dostoevsky's *Brothers Karamazov*, Soloviev was revered and reviled in equal measure. Possessed of a poetic gift almost the equal of his philosophical talent, symbolist poets such as Alexander Blok would look back to him as the wellspring of their literary imaginings, while his pretensions to construct a new, "universal" Christianity, as well as his reputed leanings toward Roman Catholicism, would earn him the suspicion of many in the Orthodox world. When the 24-year-old Soloviev began delivering his "Lectures on Theanthropy" (1877-1881, published in 1995 as *Lectures in Divine Humanity*), the impression it left on Russian intellectual life was immediate and long-lasting. In these lectures, Soloviev attempted to apply the Chalcedonian definition (of the union of divine and human natures in Christ) to the entire history of the universe, constructing a theology of creation rooted in both the historical incarnation and a temporalised process leading to the ultimate spiritualisation of all created matter. The lectures were the first mature explication of Soloviev's system, which never received complete articulation, and came on the back of a period of theological and literary experimentation that followed a series of mystical experiences he had undergone in the preceding years. It is here that Sophia – the three visions of whom Soloviev was later to describe as the most significant events of his life – for the first time receives explicit definition as "God's body, the matter of Divinity", borne by Christ who is "both Logos and Sophia".[2] Much of Soloviev's thought can be understood as an attempt to explicate his vision of a redeemed creation: what is the nature of a world transfigured in the form of Wisdom? What is the role of humanity in the salvific work of God, and what status does the material world enjoy in this perspective?

Soloviev's theology is complex and multifaceted. A visionary and mystic, he was at the same time a consummate theoretical philosopher. From his early *Kritika otvlechennykh nachal* ("Critique of Abstract Principles", 2000; Russian original 1880) to his late masterpiece on ethics, *Justification of the Good* (2005; Russian original 1894), he displayed an uncommon fascination with first principles, constructing the foundations of his ethical system in the latter work from the primary data of human consciousness and empirical reality. Yet his primary impulse was not in examining the *a priori* laws of the human mind or spirit, but in reading the divine in creation and consciously aligning human endeavour with the salvific economy he observed occurring unconsciously in nature. In his advocacy for human involvement in God's work in creation, he wrote of an art form involving the closest interaction between humanity and world, in which the latter is not worked *upon* but emulated and extended into consciousness both of itself and of its derivation from God. The aesthetic link between art and nature, he wrote, "consists not in a repetition, but in an extension of the artistic act that is begun by nature – in an impending and more complete resolution of the same aesthetic problem".[3] It was to the explication of this task, and its eventual goal, that he was to dedicate the greater part of his short life.

Creation and its Materiality

Having experimented with different forms of spiritualism and Gnosticism in his early years, inheriting from them a distaste for matter and a desire to restore the world of pure spirits, from the late 1870s onward Soloviev sought to incorporate the full integrity of creation within a soteriological framework that was permeated by his overriding

---

2 Soloviev (1995), 108.

3 Soloviev (2003c), 68.

concern for All-Unity: the idea that God, while remaining one, must encapsulate everything in order to realise God's self as the one and all. Although often labelled a pantheist, Soloviev's resolute condemnation of absolute dualism did not equate to a merging of the divine and creaturely realms. All-Unity in his treatment exists in the creaturely realm only *in potentia*. There is a fissure between creation in its temporal separation from the divine and the eternal kingdom of God that lies on the other side of the eschaton, which is reparable only through a historical process involving the communication by God of the fullness of absolute life to the created order. This process is consistently described by Soloviev in soteriological terms, the goal being to heal humanity and the entire world through the restoration of its unity with God so that all creation may become a faithful image of the divine. The ultimate destiny of all created matter, including the flesh which exists in bondage to decay, is spiritualisation, through which it is to become both the "foundation and uttermost expression of the absolute idea".[4] This ideal is derived by Soloviev from a dual foundation: firstly, what the philosopher calls his "organic logic" of the absolute, which draws heavily on elements from Hegel and Schelling; and secondly, the ethical mandate given in the experiential data of what he called "religious feeling".

Developing Hegelian thinking on the absolute (*Geist*) as organism, as well as Plato's dialectics of the one and many, in his early work Soloviev attempts to articulate the place that belongs to the principle of the "many" (material being proper) in God as the "all-one substance": how can material separation and non-unity exist within the divine, which, if we are to avoid dualism, can have nothing absolutely outside itself?

> The many … cannot exist absolutely since that would be a contradiction. … Thus, alongside the absolute substance as such, which is all-one *in actu*, we must posit another being, which is also absolute but not identical with the absolute as such[.] This second all-one … has a divine element, All-Unity as its eternal potential, which gradually transitions into actuality; on the other hand, it has in itself that non-divine, particular, non-all, natural, or material element, by virtue of which it is not all-one, but only becomes so.[5]

The historical and transhistorical unfolding of this "other", "All-Unity in the process of becoming", is the single most dominant theme in Soloviev's sophiology, in which the "other" is associated in different accounts with the church, the body of Christ, creation, matter and humanity, which are in their turn all held under the unifying matrix of Sophia herself. The sheer number of terms introduced here by Soloviev can often lead to a confusion of different spheres – anthropology with ecclesiology, Christology with pneumatology – and certainly results in a diminution of philosophical clarity when looking at his work as a whole. From a theological perspective, however, Soloviev's propensity to use multiple terms to anchor a single reality or concept has the effect, no doubt intended, of destabilising monological understandings of his central themes, whereby all things strive to exceed themselves in movement toward the other. This is pre-eminently true of God, whose love for creation is such that even the creaturely may be incorporated into God's kingdom.

---

4 Soloviev (2001), 169.

5 Soloviev (2001), 284.

Yet the ideal of creation as the "other" of God, and the object of the latter's transfigurative energies, should not be regarded as a logical construct alone. Soloviev argued that there inhered in religious consciousness a certain gravitational pull toward the good, according to which ideal activity in and on the world arose not deductively but intuitively. "The reality of the Deity is not a deduction from religious experience but the content of it – that which is experienced."[6] Such a view allowed him to make broad statements based on the experiential data of religious feeling and the spiritual life:

> The energy or activity of the human spirit can not be satisfied with the abstract content of an idea and ideals – it requires their actual embodiment, requires that the spiritual principle ultimately take command of material reality, and this assumes the capability of such spiritualization in matter itself – assumes a spiritual and holy corporeality.[7]

It was this "holy corporeality" that Soloviev saw as the defining characteristic of the "religious materialism" of the Jewish people. The inherent perfectibility of matter, believed in instinctively by Israel, was an area he believed to have been neglected by much Christian theology, as well as post-Cartesian philosophers who promoted the false viewpoint that nature was merely lifeless matter and a soulless machine. Soloviev was one of the first 19th-century thinkers to discuss anthropogenic climate change, describing phenomena such as the desertification of the Russian steppe in the context of a "general elemental process, which no doubt was speeded up by the population's careless and predatory attitude toward nature".[8] For him, the unsustainable exploitation of earth's resources was wrong not only for the effects it had on human and animal communities and ecosystems. Indeed, in *Justification of the Good*, Soloviev develops a basis in legal and ethical philosophy for the "rights of matter" itself: "matter", he wrote, "has a right to be spiritualized".[9] This radical step toward the recognition of the rights even of inanimate nature can be seen as the correlative of Soloviev's conviction in the "redemption and union [of matter] with the divinity, its transformation into God-matter", whose mediator is the "true, perfect human being – the God-man".[10]

Theanthropy and the Role of Humanity in Salvation

Soloviev reserved some of his strongest criticism for what he called "homely Christianity", where the concern was only for individual life and private deeds. He looked toward a universal Christianity, in which all people regardless of creed would unite in one common task of universal rebirth. Toward the end of his life, he lost a measure of his hope in the external union of religions and nations, yet he continued to assert that salvation belongs to the individual only insofar as it belongs to universal humanity, from which the former cannot be separated.

Given the emphasis he placed on the universality of salvation, one of the most strik-

---

6 Soloviev (2005), 144.

7 Soloviev (2008), 56.

8 Soloviev (1990), 47

9 Soloviev (2005), 288.

10 Soloviev (2003), 23.

ing aspects of Soloviev's thought is the extent to which he allocates a role to individual human endeavour in the work of salvation. In a typical transcription of Kantian ethics into lived experience, he wrote: "[R]eligious feeling expressed in the form of the categorical imperative commands us … to make all our fellow-beings morally perfect and free from pain, deathless, and incorruptible in their bodies."[11] This work of salvation was not, however, conceived solely as a practical, pseudo-scientific task to be conducted by the isolated individual. For Soloviev, it represented the recapitulation of the path of Christ at the individual and cosmic levels, and was fundamentally a theanthropic, that is to say a divine-human, endeavour. Centred in the incarnation, humanity's own participation in salvation necessarily involved as its first stage the repetition of Christ's conforming of his humanity to God through kenotic self-giving, thereby achieving the perfect union of the divine and human natures. "It is clear", wrote Soloviev, "that humanity can truly spiritualize nature, that is, call forth and develop its inner life, only by his own overflowing spirituality."[12] Through the turning inwards toward God in Christ which enables the renunciation of individual limitation, human beings become channels of the divine energies to the world, mediators between the divine and creaturely spheres. Incorporated into Christ's resurrected body, the flesh of the human being is vivified by the Spirit that had raised the God-man, now ascended in corporeal form, to receive a share in its divine corporeality. Salvation for Soloviev is therefore quite literally the abolition of death through participation (on the model of Platonic metaxy, a concept later developed by Bulgakov) in the eternal life of God. Yet the economy of salvation he promotes is not restricted to humanity.

> As instruments of divine grace we must bring its action to bear upon animal nature and the whole of our world in general, for theandric power has no bounds. The incarnation of God brings about the salvation of mankind; in the same way the union of mankind with God must bring about the salvation of the whole of earthly creation: as mankind is, in the form of the Church, the living body of Christ, so the natural world must become the living body of redeemed mankind.[13]

Soloviev's eschatology thus actualises the interdependency he posits between humanity and creation as an analogue of Christ's hypostatic union: humanity and creation become symbiotic members in the universal spiritual organism of the realised kingdom of God.

Eschatology and Aesthetics

The connection between Soloviev's eschatology and aesthetics can be observed throughout his writings. He regularly wrote about the spiritual-corporeal transfiguration of creation as a kind of art form, necessitating the advent of a new kind of artist. "Universal resurrection means the creation of a perfect form for all that exists. It is the ultimate expression and realisation of the good meaning of the universe, and is therefore the end of history."[14] Humanity's co-activity with God, then, consists not in the new creation of creaturely life, but in the gathering of such content into formal perfec-

---

[11] Soloviev (2005), 146.

[12] Soloviev (2005), 399-400.

[13] Soloviev (1938), 81.

[14] Soloviev (2005), lxv.

tion, a form that Soloviev associates with the incarnation of "absolute beauty". "Material objective reality can be introduced into moral order only through its illumination, its inspiration, i.e., only in the form of beauty."[15] The problem of beauty can be summarised in the question Soloviev poses to his readers in a late piece on the poet Aleksei Tolstoy: "Is the full, final expression of highest perfection as the real, palpable incarnation of the absolute in definite forms possible?"[16] The Christian church, in Soloviev's view, had, through its doctrinal victory over iconoclasm, answered a resounding "yes", but this "yes" must transition into act: it must not remain "simply a passive reverence for God or an act of worship, but must be activity in and with him (theurgy)".[17]

The aestheticisation of reality in an eschatological landscape did not, however, equate to the elimination of the dark, the chaotic and the formless, and the triumph of the purely elegant or sublime over "lower" forms of creaturely being. Soloviev's model is one not of exclusion but of incorporation within an ever-expanding horizon of divine wholeness. Indeed, there is a strong sense in his work that the saving purposes of God are revealed in the evolutionary processes of the cosmos precisely through the medium of beauty, which transfigures without abolishing, and incorporates without merging. This is what Soloviev meant when he reformulated Dostoevsky's famous maxim in the present tense: "beauty *is* saving the world". Beauty itself is the trace of God's eternal presence in time, but it is also the goal of creation's strivings toward the ideal future, namely to preserve through beauty the fullness of creaturely being in historical time. This is illustrated by a peculiar yet important example from *Justification of the Good*, when Soloviev describes, with the help of an intricate play on words, the fate of less complex life forms in the emergence of "higher" ones. "The lower form – that of the worm (*cherv'*)," he writes, "was not excluded as intrinsically unworthy, but received a new and more fitting position. It ceased to be the sole and obvious foundation of life, but decently clothed still exists within the body in the form of the alimentary canal (*chrevo*) – a subservient part of the organism, hidden for the sake of beauty."[18] Likewise, as beauty acquires an inner dimension in the moral virtues and spiritual life of humanity, human sin is not, in Soloviev's conception, so much extinguished as transformed in service of the good through beauty. The saint for him is someone who has "conquered the power of evil by subordinating it to its higher principle", thereby transforming it into the "foundation and carrier of good".[19] This example is mirrored in the natural world by the diamond, whose "dark matter of carbon" is the "bearer of the principle of light".[20]

Creation in its perfected form, as absolute beauty, is in Soloviev's handling the embodiment of divine Wisdom, in which the "contradiction between the ideal and sensual, spirit and matter, is overcome … and God appears as the unity of himself and his

15 Soloviev (2003), 69.
16 Soloviev (1991), 490.
17 Soloviev (1938), 131.
18 Soloviev (2005), 224.
19 Soloviev (1995), 153.
20 Soloviev (2003), 35.

other".[21] Although the contradiction is removed, however, the full integrity of the material creation is preserved and continues, even in the darker aspects of its materiality, to act as the bearer of the good.

References and Recommended Reading

Kornblatt, Judith (2009), "Who is Solovyov and What is Sophia?", in: *The Wisdom Writings of Vladimir Solovyov*, Ithaca / London: Cornell University Press, 3-97.

Rosenthal, Bernice and Martha Bonachevsky-Chomiak (eds.) (1990), *A Revolution of Spirit: Crisis of Value in Russia 1890-1924*, New York: Fordham University Press.

Smith, Oliver (2011), *Vladimir Soloviev and the Spiritualization of Matter*, Boston: Academic Studies Press.

Soloviev, Vladimir (1938), *God, Man and the Church: the Spiritual Foundations of Life*, London: James Clarke.

--- (1990), "The Enemy from the East", in: Rosenthal and Bonachevsky-Chomiak (eds.), 43-52.

--- (1991), "Poezia gr. A. K. Tolstogo", in: R. Galtseva and I. Rodnianskaia (eds.), *Filosofiia iskusstva i literaturnaia kritika*, Moscow: Iskusstvo, 483-505.

--- (1995), *Lectures in Divine Humanity*, Hudson: Lindisfarne.

--- (2001), "Kritika otvlechennykh nachal", in: N. V. Kotrelev (ed.), *Polnoe sobranie sochinenii, Tom 3*, Moscow: Nauka, 7-360.

--- (2003), *Heart of Reality: Essays on Beauty, Love and Ethics*, Notre Dame: University of Notre Dame Press.

--- (2005), *Justification of the Good: An Essay on Moral Philosophy*, Grand Rapids: Eerdmans.

--- (2008), "The Jews and the Christian Question", in: *Freedom, Faith, and Dogma: Essays on Christianity and Judaism*, Albany: State University of New York Press, 43-88.

Valliere, Paul (2007), "Vladimir Solov'ev (1853-1900): Commentary", in: J. Witte Jr. and F. S. Alexander (eds.), *The Teachings of Modern Orthodox Christianity: On Law, Politics, and Human Nature*, New York: Columbia University Press, 33-68.

Oliver Smith

Pavel Florensky (1882-1937) – An Aesthetics of Holiness

Introduction

The life and work of Pavel Florensky bear witness to the tragedy of the Soviet experiment and the endurance of the human spirit. A polymath and Orthodox priest, with extraordinary talent in disparate disciplines ranging from the theoretical sciences and mathematics to philosophy and theology, Florensky was exiled to various labour camps from 1933 onward, and shot on the orders of the KGB in 1937. He had, from the time of his childhood in the Caucasus mountains, always displayed what Aleksandr Men' would describe as a "passionate love for matter", which drew him close to figures such as Teilhard de Chardin, as well as the venerated Russian saint Seraphim of Sarov. His conviction in the God-given unity of the created order accessible through mystical experience, where the "eyes are opened and we see the forest as a single creature, humanity as a single *Grand Être*",[22] shares much with Soloviev, from whom he inherits, and expands on, the concepts of All-Unity, theanthropy and Sophia. Yet Florensky's sophiology is much more self-consciously churched than that of other

[21] Soloviev (1991), 492-493.

[22] Florensky (2000b), 108.

thinkers, not in the sense that it proceeds from Orthodox tradition (there is still broad disagreement on this point) but in that it grounds itself in the concrete realia of liturgical life. "There has been enough philosophizing on religion and about religion", he said before the defence of his Master's dissertation (later to become his major work of 1914; published in English as *The Pillar and Ground of the Truth*, 2004). "One must philosophize *in* religion, immersing oneself in its environment."[23] Faithful to this agenda, Florensky unfolds before his reader a sort of sacral phenomenology. If sophiology affirmed the inseparability of spiritual and physical realities, Florensky's version of it, which he named "concrete metaphysics", sought to uncover the noumenal foundation of each, individual thing, not in its separation from its accidental properties, but in its very phenomenality: to discover the point at which the ascending smoke of the thurible becomes the real body of communal prayer, or – to take the example from one of his most widely read works, *Iconostasis* (2000; Russian original 1922) – to explicate how the icon manifests in actuality that toward which it points. His vision of salvation is no less concrete, centring on the figure of the Christian ascetic (*podvizhnik*) in whom can be traced the perceptible signs of the acquisition of the Holy Spirit. Florensky develops these examples not to build an ethics of salvation as the path of holiness, since holiness for him is not so much a matter of ethical as of ontological superiority. The intense scrutiny his work gives to cultic objects and religious persons, evident at its strongest in the posthumously published fragments of *Filosofiia kul'ta* ("Philosophy of Cult", Russian originals 1908-1922) amounts therefore to an aesthetics of holiness – the study of elevated ontological space and time, where the dynamics of the ascent of the creaturely to God can be sought, emulated and directed.

For Florensky, the goal of creation was the sanctification of reality, which he envisaged along the lines of the liturgical transformation of the mundane in the form of divine beauty. "To perceive all of creation in its original triumphant beauty ... Always to see beauty in everything would be 'to be resurrected before the universal resurrection', to have a foretaste of the last Revelation, that of the Comforter."[24] Yet one of the most interesting things about his understanding of this sanctification through beauty was that it was not indifferent to the varying status of the objects undergoing the process. "Nothing ascends Mount Tabor in exactly the same way," he wrote.[25] The higher the ascent of the creature, the lower God's grace descends to meet it, and the more complete the transfiguration of the phenomenon. Indeed, Florensky's "Philosophy of Cult" is a strikingly bold, though incomplete, attempt at a hierarchisation of the levels of sanctification, from water through to the space-time continuum itself, as what he calls "the organization of our salvation".[26] Since, as Florensky puts it, "God thinks through things", the result of such a project is not so much a blueprint for salvation as the charting of the ways and modes in which the historical in the creature ascends toward the suprahistorical, in the process revealing the movement of God's grace and the potential of human beings to become its ever more conscious channels.

[23] Florensky (1914), 95.

[24] Florensky (2004a), 226.

[25] Florensky (2004b), 221.

[26] Florensky (2004b), 221.

Naming and Symbolism

Florensky was one of the most prominent figures in *Imeslavie* (Name-Glorifying), a dogmatic movement within the Orthodox Church originally begun on Mount Athos, whose central claim was that the "Name of God is God Himself". Yet his development of this idea is not only restricted to God but encompasses the entire realm of the word and, in particular, the name: "the name of a thing is the substance of a thing".[27] To understand how he comes to make this statement we need to understand that cognition for Florensky, as for other sophiologists, involves the "real going of the knower out of himself or (what is the same thing) a real going of what is known into the knower, a real unification of the knower and what is known".[28] Yet what is different about Florensky (and to a certain extent Bulgakov) is his consistent emphasis on the word as the child of a "cognitive marriage" between the energies of two separate beings. The word here is understood as a revelation, a kind of lightning that makes of two isolated points an ontological isotrope, bridging the space between the I and the other. In the sphere of the word, the individual posits its actual essence, creatively weaving its own inner content into the fabric of language. Yet at the same time this creativity occurs on a supra-individual plane: the individual here joins with the common heritage of an entire people (and more widely, through the connection between all languages, all humanity), facilitating the syncretisation of individual life with time – through the historical memory the word bears in itself – and space, through its literal egress into a communal hermeneutic realm. This is the "magic" of the word, the syncretic conjoining of perceiver and perceived.

Our relation to creation, therefore, is enjoyed through the word. Yet this relation, for Florensky, can be of different types and hues. When one perceives the world scientifically (subject to object; ego to other), the relation is one of concept to concept; both are schematic, lacking life, dynamism and energy. But when one looks at the world magically, the relationship that emerges is of a living human being to a living world. The magus is "a part of nature and she is a part of him. He enters a marriage with nature [and] his thoughts pour into his words, which are already nascent actions".[29] The use of the words "magic" and "magus", with their clear link to pre-Christian paganism, created controversy at the time, but Florensky picks them not incidentally. "The thing is created by the name," he wrote.[30] The word is constitutive of the very essence of the object. This act of creation, however, does not derive from the human being, although it requires our cooperation. "The name itself blesses or curses, and we are just the instrument of its activity and of that benevolent environment in which it operates … The name is given to us but not created by us."[31] All names, whether those borne by animate life or inanimate matter, are expressions of the Word of God, the Logos through whom all creation came into being. In a mirroring of the movement whereby the divine Logos, the principle of creation, descends to receive a personal name in Jesus Christ, so each creaturely name is called to gravitate toward its divine

[27] Florensky (1909), 413.

[28] Florensky (2004a), 55.

[29] Florensky (1909), 296.

[30] Florensky (1909), 413.

[31] Florensky (2008), 307.

prototype. There is thus a teleological thrust to all names in Florensky ("to live according to the name"), according to which their holders not only imitate the essence of the name, but the name itself participates in them, enabling their ascent to the mystical foundation of their being in God.

Yet, along with receiving, and living into, a name, humanity is also endowed with the power to name, and here is where the crux of its interaction with creation lies. It can choose to exercise this power from its own centre, the word thus emergent determining the thing at which it is directed. Or, through an act of kenotic obedience, it can renounce the potential command over matter it enjoys through the word, allowing the name of the thing to arise organically (or, Florensky might say, "magically") in the space between "the I" and "the other". In the first case, the natural world loses its link to divine creativity, and becomes the instrument of human rationality and innovation. In the second, the human being becomes a channel for the grace of God, and we already have the seeds of a new creation since the name in this case does not stultify but moves with the creative power of the divine Logos for the purposes of salvation. It is this second understanding of creaturely reality that Florensky has in mind when he talks about the symbol, which not only "designates something other, but itself becomes the real bearer of this other, the living interpenetration of two beings". The symbol is therefore being which is "larger than itself", and names are the energies through which this being, in whatever aspect, reveals itself to the human perceiver. The ultimate goal, for Florensky, is not only the ascent of humanity to God but the descent of God onto humanity and all of created matter. This process he understood in aesthetic terms as a new kind of symbolism, an art form "born of the descent", where experience of the highest realm is incarnated in real images which subsequently attain a super-reality. All things are called to ascend to their source in God in accordance with their name-essence in a process of rebirth enabled by the historical descent of God in Christ and His continuing descent in the sacramental life of the church.

Sophia and the Countenance of Nature

The different emphases Florensky puts on the relationship between humanity and creation are captured in the trichotomy of terms he develops in his work *Iconostasis*: "mask", "face" and "countenance". The "face" is the repository of phenomenal experience, the appearance of things and persons to daylight consciousness. There is thus an equivocity to the face, which stands at the border between subjectivity and objectivity, never giving itself to be known as absolutely real yet at the same time calling out to be grounded in a concrete ontology, arousing its perceiver to a further process of knowing. The "countenance" (in Russian: *lik*, the word used for the iconic face) is the manifestation of this ontological reality, the conformation of the face as bearer of the image of God into actual likeness with God. Its opposite, meanwhile, is the "mask", which presumes to create ontological reality by uncovering the essence of things, but in reality points to nothing, an empty semblance of reality. Florensky equates the eschatological realisation of the kingdom of God with the final unveiling of the countenance of nature, its sacralisation in the form of Sophia, "the Great Root by which creation goes into the intra-Trinitarian life".[32]

---

[32] Florensky (2004a), 237.

There is a dual aspect to the incarnation of Sophia for Florensky: the first enjoyed through the revelation of the momentary overcoming of the forces of death and separation; and the second the fruit of the path of ascesis, the conscious work of the human person on herself and the world. The revelation of Sophia as the true creation is enjoyed "in the personal, sincere love of two, in friendship, when to the loving one is given – in a preliminary way, without ascesis – the power to overcome his self-identity, to remove the boundaries of his I, to transcend himself, and to acquire his own I in the I of another, a Friend".[33] The metaphors of friendship and marriage that pepper Florensky's work operate more substantially, therefore, than at the level of mere analogy: friendship, as the creation in love of a personal "you" – whether that of another human individual or a natural landscape – is the environment in which the countenance comes to inhabit the face of both perceiver and perceived. Yet, this revelation is only a partaking of the joys of a redeemed world *ex ante*, and constitutes a call for humanity, through spiritual effort (*podvig*), to work toward the final salvation of the entire created order. This task would not culminate, as it would for Soloviev, in a kind of erotic sublimation of the union between God and creation, but in the persistent fostering of friendship between the world and God, with humanity as their mediator.

Unlike Soloviev, and more consistently than Bulgakov, Florensky refuses to engage in speculation on the derivation of the creature from God. The creation does not exist by necessity but as the free gift of a loving God. He focuses much more on the path of ascent, which involves the central elements of Orthodox ascesis, than of descent. When he talks, therefore, about the "organization of our salvation", he does not mean the forcing of the divine energies into particular vessels picked by humanity for their most efficient passage, but the identification of the workings of God in creation through the discernment of those symbols through which the divine has seen fit to move. The architecture of the church, and particularly the liturgy, are the central paradigms of such organisation, but the organisation of matter in them, its symbolic hierarchy, has at its centre not human innovation but the mysterious economy of the divine in the Eucharist and other sacraments. The descent of God, then, is neither effected nor merited by humanity, but merely prepared for: it is always the revelation of mystery and its acceptance as pure gift. The ultimate resting place of the sacramental descent is, for Florensky, the furthermost bounds of the cosmos:

> In the sacraments the very roots of our nature acquire the highest measure of sanctification ... There are no defined limits to ritual: beginning as sacrament, it descends, branching and dividing, into church life, from here to the life around the church, then into everyday life, into the fabric of culture and further, like tiny hairs and tendrils – often almost or completely invisible – is absorbed into the bowels of the earth, into cosmic life, no longer merely a human ritual confined by the limits of human society but encompassing the entire creation, all being, the elements themselves.[34]

Such is the cosmic significance Florensky places on church ritual, whose central concern is not so much thanksgiving and remembrance as the creation of an efficacious environment for the purposes of salvation of humanity and world.

---

[33] Florensky (2004a), 283.

[34] Florensky (2004b), 213.

References and Recommended Reading

Bychkov, Victor (1993), *The Aesthetic Face of Being: Art in the Theology of Pavel Florensky*, Crestwood: St Vladimir's Seminary Press.

Cassedy, Stephen (1996), "P. A. Florensky and the Celebration of Matter", in: Judith Kornblatt and Richard F. Gustafson (eds.), *Russian Religious Thought*, Madison: University of Wisconsin Press, 95-111.

Florensky, Pavel (1909), "Obshchie korni idealizma", *Bogoslovskii vestnik*, Vol. 1, 2, 284-297; Vol. 1, 3, 409-423.

--- (1914), "Razum i dialektika (Vstupitel'noe slovo pered zashchitoiu na stepen' magistra knigi «O Dukhovnoi Istine»)", *Bogoslovskii vestnik*, Vol. 3, 9, 86-98.

--- (2000a), *Iconostasis*, Crestwood; St Vladimir's Seminary Press.

--- (2000b), "Smysl idealizma", in: A. S. Trubachev (ed.), *Sochineniia v 4-i tomakh*, Vol. 3, 2, 66-144, Moscow: Mysl'.

--- (2004a), *The Pillar and Ground of the Truth: An Essay in Orthodox Theodicy in Twelve Letters*, Princeton: Princeton University Press.

--- (2004b), *Filosofiia kul'ta (opyt pravoslavnoi antropoditsei)*, Moscow: Mysl'.

--- (2008), "U vodorazdelov Mysli", in: *Imena: Sochineniia*, Moscow: Eksmo, 5-322.

Hutchings, Stephen (1999), "Making Sense of the Sensual in Pavel Florenskii's Aesthetics: The Dialectics of Finite Being", *Slavic Review*, Vol. 58, 1, 96-116.

Oliver Smith

Sergii Bulgakov (1871-1944) – Conformity with the Divine Sophia

Introduction

Sergii Bulgakov was a Russian Orthodox theologian and priest whose works, while controversial from an Eastern Orthodox perspective, demonstrate his deep immersion in Western modern thought, including politics and economics. His early career in political economy was followed by a period of disillusionment with the Marxist view of humanity and his eventual turn to Russian Orthodoxy in 1909. The death of his four-year-old son triggered an experience of the resurrection that led him to the work of Soloviev, from whom he inherits the concept of divine Wisdom, which he first develops in his 1912 work *Filosophiia khozyaistva* ("Philosophy of Economy"). He was elected to the Russian Church Council in 1917, but its activities were sharply suppressed following the October Revolution. After his ordination in 1918 he fled to the Crimea, and was forced to move to Paris in 1922. He spent much of his life (1925-1944) living as an exile in Paris at the Russian Theological Institute, Saint-Serge. Among his most famous works are the "little trilogy" of *The Friend of the Bridegroom* (2003; Russian original 1927), *The Burning Bush* (2009; Russian original 1927) and *Jacob's Ladder* (2010; Russian original 1929), which explore the relation between Sophia and John the Baptist, the Virgin Mary, and the angels respectively. He controversially used Schelling in interpreting the doctrine of the Trinity in "The Tragedy of Philosophy", published in German in 1927. It was largely this work that triggered in 1935 charges of heresy from two of the Russian jurisdictions, the Church in Exile based in Yugoslavia, and the Moscow Patriarchate. The main charge against him – that he taught that Wisdom is a fourth hypostasis – was strenuously denied by Bulgakov, and the third Russian jurisdiction, the Exarchate of the Ecumenical Patriarchate for Western Europe, continued to support him. In the midst of these controversies he penned arguably his greatest trilogy, *The Lamb of God* (2008; Russian original 1933); *The Comforter* (2004; Russian original 1936) and *The Bride of the Lamb* (2002; Russian original 1945), under the general title of *Theanthropy*. He produced an important summary of his work in *Sophia, The Wisdom of God* (1993), first translated into English in 1937 from an unpublished Russian manuscript. He contracted cancer of the throat in 1939, but despite this managed to write his last significant work, *Apokalipsis Ioanna* ("The Apocalypse of John", 1948) in the year of his death, 1944.

Divine Sophia as Ousia

The perspective that Bulgakov brings to the relationship between creation and salvation takes its premise from his understanding of Sophia, or divine Wisdom. His provocative view from an Eastern Orthodox perspective is that Sophia or Wisdom is not simply one of the divine energies of God but reflects God's very being and eternal divine life, so that she is "the sum and unity of all his attributes".[35] This is crucially important for Bulgakov, since he believes that without *ousia* (being) the divine hypostases become too abstract, resulting in Spirit without nature. Resisting the charge that Sophia is a fourth hypostasis, his sophiology seeks to show that divine Wisdom informs all three hypostases as their ground, or essential being. The antinomy that follows is that God both *has* Sophia as part of God's identity, but also that Sophia exists *in* God as the ground of God's being.

Ousia and Sophia are used interchangeably, although Sophia only has existence as the three hypostases. In order to clarify his meaning, Bulgakov compares God's ontological life, expressed in the Bible as Sophia or Glory, with our knowledge of the human body. Just as the human body expresses something of the spirit of human beings, so the *ousia* of God acts like a "spiritual prototype in the fullness of divine life".[36] It is important to note that Bulgakov is not suggesting that God has "flesh", but rather that "spiritual body" in the human sphere has a parallel counterpart in God. He goes further still in suggesting that, just as the rational soul and sensible body are distinct in the human being, so it is with the Godhead where the Logos as wisdom is analogous to the rational soul, and Holy Spirit as glory to the human body. The personal life of the Deity is therefore expressive of fullness, a "unity of all with all and in all" that provides "the ground of the energy of love within the Godhead".[37]

Creaturely Sophia

For Bulgakov, the creaturely world comes from nothing, therefore God is the only source of all that is. God remains the source of creaturely being, while creaturely being is distinct from divine being. God establishes "nothing" and this "nothing" expresses the idea of incompleteness within creaturely becoming. Here we see the influence of Platonic ideas on Bulgakov's thought. Every form of being has an origin outside itself, and its emergence fills a void. He envisages, then, two poles – the positive source of being and the void of nothing. But while the positive form truly exists, the "nothing" is the counterpart to the fullness and remains deficient. Creatureliness is therefore tied

[35] Bulgakov (1993), 54.

[36] Bulgakov (1993), 8.

[37] Bulgakov (1993), 59.

into a pattern of becoming that is dependent on the divine bestowal of power. Bulgakov resists the idea that the world is self-enclosed; rather, it is predestined for communion and union with God.[38]

Bulgakov insists that creation is not necessary for God's being but comes into being through Divine Sophia. Bulgakov clearly means much more here than simply that the world is created in a wise manner, as articulated in Psalm 104:24. Rather, Wisdom is the power through which creation comes to be. Nor is it enough for Bulgakov to identify Wisdom solely with the Logos, as some interpretations of Proverbs 8:22-31, in the light of John 1:3, imply, since this makes the Logos the creator of the world. Instead, the "beginning" of creation is not so much an expression of temporality, but an expression of the principle of creaturely life rooted in the divine life, the "essential Wisdom of God" that is common to all three persons of the Trinity.[39] More explicitly, God calls the world into existence by his creative fiat through his Word. Drawing on the Genesis narrative, Bulgakov distinguishes the specific role of each trinitarian hypostasis: God the Father is initiator and maker of the world; the Word contains "every word of God concerning creation"; and the Spirit brings creation to fulfilment. For Bulgakov, the Father acts hypostatically in the work of creation, while the Son and Spirit "abandon themselves to the will of the Father as his word and action".[40] The participation of the Son and Spirit in the work of creation is therefore through and in the divine Sophia, and their hypostases are "concealed" kenotically.

The gift of God the Creator to the creature is therefore an imprint of the divine prototypes, as well as a capacity to maintain its own existence, as derived through the work of the Holy Spirit, representing the power of beauty or divine glory. This quickening activity of the Holy Spirit is prior even to the emergence of specific forms, drawing on Genesis 1:2, where the Spirit of God is described as moving on the face of the waters. Here we find wisdom in creation described as "ontologically identical with its prototype, the same Wisdom that exists in God".[41] This is not pantheism, since the source and origin of wisdom is in the Godhead, and the world exists in God, meaning by the power of the Godhead. Rather, it is a sophianic *panentheism* where the world is in God, rather than God being equated with the material world. The created world is therefore creaturely Sophia, in that the principle on which it is based belongs to the being of God, even though the world remains God's creature, rather than being the creator. For Bulgakov the overriding motivation for creating the world is not necessity in the sense of ontological requirement, but the result of a free expression of overflowing love. Here he parts company with pantheist philosophies that suggest a natural necessity for creation, seeing it instead as a voluntary, personal act of self-abandonment.

Bulgakov diverges also from the patristic tradition in his rejection of the sufficiency of the Logos in providing a unifying principle between God and the world. For him, such reliance on the hypostasis of the Logos can easily slip into Arian subordianism. By grounding the link between God and the world in ontology, considered first in the

---

38 Bulgakov (2008), 163.

39 Bulgakov (1993), 67.

40 Bulgakov (1993), 68.

41 Bulgakov (1993), 71-72.

self-revelation of God's nature, and then in God's revelation in the world, we find, through the language of Sophia, a way of describing the reality of God's presence, divine and creaturely, eternal and temporal.

Creaturely Sophia in a State of Becoming

For Bulgakov creation and salvation are built into the world's being in the sense that creaturely Sophia is in a continuous state of potentiality or *dynamis*. The world was created in its fullness as God originally intended, but its present state does not necessarily correspond to this original status. The creaturely likeness of divine Sophia only approximates the way in which the world process has developed, the world in many respects being flawed and fallen. Bulgakov tries to clarify this tension by speaking of two different forms of Sophia, one in God and one in the creature. This amounts to a contrast between the perfection of divine eternity versus temporal becoming. He also draws an analogy between the antinomy expressed in the distinction between God and the Absolute, on the one hand, and that between creaturely and divine Sophia, on the other.

As for other writers from the Eastern Orthodox tradition, for Bulgakov humanity plays a crucial role in understanding the relationship between God and world. Humanity represents the entirety of creation in microcosm, and God's image in creation is expressed in human form. The theological anthropology found in *The Bride of the Lamb* presents humanity as grounded in creation within the community of the church and orientated towards the reception of grace leading to deification. The image of God is significant as an expression both of the divine image in humanity and of "humanity" in God. The incarnation is therefore an expression of an eternal "humanity" in God, by which Bulgakov means that our whole humanity, rather than one particular characteristic, is expressive of the image of God.[42] This view differs from scholastic writers, for example, who identified the divine image in humanity with human reason. There is a sense, however, in which this image-bearing is incomplete, since although it is "a constant tendency at the heart of our being", it is at the same time still to come, yet to be revealed. Bulgakov expresses this in sophianic language: divine Sophia as a principle in humanity is not yet identical with the present being of humanity. Human nature exists as persons, as hypostases, which Bulgakov believes are given by God at the time of their creation. But in the divine Logos human nature is eternally hypostatised: he is the everlasting human being, the divine prototype. This allows Bulgakov to distinguish between the theanthropy expressed in the Logos and that expressed in the Holy Spirit. Only the former constitutes the hypostatic centre for heavenly humankind, while both embody theanthropy. He draws an analogy here with the relation between masculinity and femininity in humanity, such that God's image-bearing in humanity is reflected in the interrelationship between the genders. The image of God for Bulgakov also represents a task for humanity, even if through sin that task is never properly fulfilled. Like many other Orthodox writers, Bulgakov believes that the whole of created nature fell into disorder as a result of the sinfulness of humanity.

[42] The fullest account of his doctrine of the incarnation is in Bulgakov (2008), 157-211. Here he goes as far as saying that the world was created in order that God might become incarnate in it as an expression of profound love. See Bulgakov (2008), 169.

Salvation and the Restoration of Creation

As in the fall of Adam all creation becomes bound to sin, so in the incarnation there is a reinstatement of theanthropy and the prospect of a wider restoration of the created world. The incarnation is therefore for Bulgakov an atoning act, one whose "purpose extends beyond this to the complete divinization of the creation".[43] The human reception of the Logos does not vitiate humanity since this latter is written into the divine, and vice versa. The union of two natures in one person in Christ is expressed as the union of creaturely and divine wisdom. While in humans creaturely wisdom is obscured by sin, in Christ human nature is free of sin. Bulgakov envisages the incarnation as a kenotic act where the Logos is expressed in the person of the man Jesus without ceasing to be God.[44] The seeds of soteriology are therefore planted firmly in the incarnation, since the purpose of the self-limitation of divine Wisdom in creaturely existence in humans was to raise up the creaturely to the heavenly glorified state. In becoming human, the Word incarnate as divine Wisdom is divested of glory in order to take up the mantle of creaturely wisdom that is in the state of becoming. Bulgakov can therefore claim that "He remains in the nature of God, but devoid of his glory".[45] The kenosis in this sense is supplemented by Bulgakov's understanding of the passion as a human kenosis, an act of obedience even unto death. His understanding of the atonement is one that acknowledges the offence imparted to God's justice by human sin whereby Christ, as representative of humanity, feels the full force of the world's sin despite being sinless. Bulgakov, therefore, views the passion narrative as operational on various levels. In a metaphysical sense, Christ represents Adam. In a spiritual sense, Christ shows the outpouring of compassionate love as one who was willing to face the darkness and weight of sin and the wrath of God against that sin. Bulgakov believes that the dreadful bodily sufferings of Christ were somehow required in order to redeem the "animal-bodily being of humankind".[46]

The glorification of Christ emerges, therefore, from his obedience and through the gift of the Father. The result – the immortality given to the glorified body of Christ – Bulgakov believes to be a new creative act of God. But such a gift has a precedent in human nature as such, which now becomes worthy of receiving this gift by the obedience of Christ's free offering on the cross. Rather oddly, perhaps, the kenosis of the Son for Bulgakov is prolonged after Christ's death until the Spirit is sent at Pentecost. Bulgakov envisages the relation between creaturely and divine wisdom in Christ as engaged in a struggle and gradual conformity. He thus posits the substantial unity of created and divine wisdom in Christ, who also displays the ontological distinction between divine and created natures. These distinctions are carried through to eternity, but are now fully interpenetrated through *perichoresis*. This allows Bulgakov to claim that not only has Christ raised humanity to the state before the fall, but also to a state of full divinisation, or *theosis*. In Christ, "for the first time the true idea of theanthropy

---

[43] Bulgakov (1993), 82.

[44] Bulgakov believes that Protestantism makes this mistake in envisaging forms of kenosis where Jesus seems to lose his authority. For a more detailed treatment of Bulgakov's understanding of Christ as incarnate Wisdom, see Deane-Drummond, 111-127.

[45] Bulgakov (1993), 90.

[46] Bulgakov (1993), 91.

according to the conception of the Creator, is realised in its integrity, in the unshadowed clarity of its form".[47] It is therefore the union of the two natures in Christ that grounds the redemption of humanity, and thence the whole world.

The ministry of Christ in salvation is continued in the work of the ecclesial community, marked by eucharistic practice that echoes the participation of the elements of this world in that of the glorified body of Christ. The purpose is to bring the whole world into conformity with the divine intention, that is, creaturely wisdom. The incarnation grounds this future expectation, so that the whole world of "flesh" forms a potential extension of Christ's body. For Bulgakov, the glorification of creation is mediated through the work of the Holy Spirit that is yet to be fully manifest; the Spirit therefore in some sense exercises a parallel kenosis to that found in the case of the Logos.

References and Recommended Reading

Bulgakov, Sergii (1912), *Filosophiia khozyaistva*, Moscow.
--- (1927), *Die Tragödie de Philosophie*, Darmstadt.
--- (1948), *Apokalipsis Ioanna: Opyt dogmaticheskogo istolkovaniia*, Paris: YMCA Press.
--- (1993), *Sophia, The Wisdom of God: An Outline of Sophiology*, Hudson: Lindisfarne.
--- (2002), *The Bride of the Lamb*, Grand Rapids: Eerdmans.
--- (2003), *The Friend of the Bridegroom: On the Orthodox Veneration of the Forerunner*, Grand Rapids: Eerdmans.
--- (2004), *The Comforter*, Grand Rapids: Eerdmans.
--- (2008), *The Lamb of God*, Grand Rapids: Eerdmans.
--- (2009) *The Burning Bush*, Grand Rapids: Eerdmans.
--- (2010), *Jacob's Ladder*, Grand Rapids: Eerdmans.
Deane-Drummond, Celia E. (2009), *Christ and Evolution: Wonder and Wisdom*, London: SCM.
Nichols, Aidan (2005), *Wisdom from Above: A Primer in the Theology of Father Sergei Bulgakov*, Leominster: Gracewing.

Celia E. Deane-Drummond

Georges Florovsky (1893-1979) – *Agon* of Divine and Human Freedom

Protopresbyter Georges Vasilievich Florovsky (1893-1979) was a leading Russian émigré scholar who taught in France and the United States. He was the chief originator of the neo-patristic movement in 20th-century Orthodox theology. Preferring to write incisive essays, he published in his lifetime three book-length studies: *Eastern Fathers of the 4th Century* (1987; Russian original 1931, reprint 1990), *Vizantiskie Ottsy V-VIII vekov*[48] (Russian original 1933, reprint 1972) and his masterwork, *Ways of Russian Theology* (1979, 1987; Russian original 1937).

Florovsky gave considerable energy to ecumenical involvement, being a founding member of the World Council of Churches in which, until his last decade, he was a leading voice. His key contributions concerning ecclesiology and tradition achieved

---

[47] Bulgakov (1993), 95.

[48] This work was published, after Florovsky's death, in an English version of two volumes which also included other extensive lecture materials not found in the published Russian original. See Florovsky (1987c, 1987d).

mature form in this context. Florovsky's influence in Orthodox circles has been seminal. Yet distinct contours of his thought remain understudied, and important dimensions still await appropriation.

Florovsky's diverse creative offerings were closely tied to insights set forth in his essays on creation and redemption, essays he considered his own best work.[49] No less than for the neo-patristic turn which he helped to effect, Florovsky's importance lies in his exploration of created contingency and the historic singularity of Christ's saving deeds as the foundation of free and significant human action in history.

Creation, Contingency and Freedom

Florovsky's university studies in logic had been influenced by Marburg neo-Kantianism and the mathematical philosophy of Georg Cantor. It was against their attempt to arrive at the ideal structures of cognition on a calculus-based model, through deduction, that Florovsky in his philosophical essays of the early 1920s first emphasised creation *ex nihilo*. According to Florovsky's "logical relativism", judgements function within a system dependent on axioms which cannot be validated within the terms of that system, being neither deducible *a priori* nor unrelated to experience, which is always limited. To claim an absolute foundation requires proving the necessity of a particular world-order. Yet such necessity, whether of the empirical world or the *logoi* which form its basis, eludes demonstration. One must choose between two beliefs: either the world is necessary, or else it is dependent on some free will outside itself for existence.

Florovsky touches on a central problem of post-Kantian metaphysics: how are synthetic *a priori* judgements possible? The existence of synthetic objects demands the world itself be such an object, i.e. non-necessary, incapable of closed definition, and limited by another. To speak meaningfully of "possibilities" requires an extramundane, free contingent causality (here he invokes Duns Scotus). The structure of judgement can thus be reduced to "the fundamental metaphysical *a priori* of necessity and freedom".[50]

Florovsky explored this interest in contingency and freedom in his philosophy of history, attacking Romanticism, utopianism and idealism as forms of monism which reduced free acts to deterministic laws. Vladimir Soloviev's synthesis of "All-Unity" he criticised for justifying evil as necessary to historical process. For Florovsky, history – the order of creation unique to acting persons – is neither theogony nor evolution,[51] but an *agon* marked by divine interventions, sinful rebellions and graced creative leaps, the last of which he equated with ascetic activity (*podvig*) as such.

These concerns Florovsky brought to his correspondence with Sergii Bulgakov, his

---

[49] The key essays appear in several variants. See Florovsky (1928), (1930), (1949), (1951), (1953), and the essays "Creation and Creaturehood" in Florovsky (1976), 43-80 and "Redemption" in Florovsky (1976), 95-162.

[50] See Florovsky (1989), 73.

[51] In distinguishing his theory of history from that of preformationist evolutionary development, Florovsky employed another analogy borrowed from biology, epigenesis, to express the idea that persons become what they are in history through free interaction with others and with their environment. See Florovsky (1930).

respected elder colleague and sometime father confessor, whom he met in 1923. At the heart of their *Auseinandersetzung* was the legacy of Soloviev, whose sophiology Florovsky rejected as gnostic (Bulgakov later partially concurred). Against Bulgakov's attempt to find sophiological precedents in Gregory Palamas, Florovsky argued that true Sophia is uncreated *energeia*: not created nature or the substrate of created becoming, but grace – radically other than the world.[52]

In a dense tapestry of patristic documentation, Florovsky's creation essays offer an implicit critique of Bulgakov's sophiology. Where Bulgakov sees in creation a divine "necessity of love", Florovsky insists that the world might have not existed at all. Both relate the doctrine of creation to the "two natures" of the Chalcedonian definition. Yet where Bulgakov posits a correlation between God and creation in Sophia, attributing "eternal divine-humanity" to the Logos, Florovsky finds an absolute hiatus: the "union" – "unconfused" – is achieved only in the historic God-man.

In Soloviev and especially Florensky, Florovsky detected a return to pre-Nicene issues – "the religion of the Logos and not that of Christ".[53] The continuum between God and the world represented by Sophia was in fact supertemporal, realised from the beginning in the "eternal world", of which the incarnation was only a certain manifestation in time.[54] Florovsky underlined repeatedly the Origenist dilemma which lay behind the Arian controversy: how to affirm both the Son's full divinity and the contingency of creation. This challenge, he emphasised, was answered by Athanasius with his distinction between generation according to essence and creation as a work of will.

Further clarification was given in Maximus the Confessor's concept of divine *logoi*. Neither essence nor hypostasis, the *logoi* are "designs and calls", the "transcendental entelechy" of creatures, God's "volitional thoughts" regarding the world. In this sense, there exists a double contingency – both the world in its actual existence, and the "ideas" or "preordinations" of God's will. Yet while the *logoi* of creation are eternal, the world itself is created *ex nihilo* in both form and being, and so constitutes an ontological novelty.

Novelty is crucial to the theology of history that constitutes Florovsky's deepest interest. Whereas for Greek thought, only the "necessary" could claim permanence and truth, revelation shows the possibility of free contingent acts becoming permanent – "singular events" becoming truth. Christ's actions were not simply instances of general law, but "unique and 'ultimate' ... wrought once forever, *eph hapax*".[55] In the "absolute novelty" of the incarnation, an eschatological element is inserted into the historical process, revealing the overarching design, the alpha and omega, of creation. The purpose of the Creator's original fiat is disclosed in the creative fiat of the Virgin, whose obedience in faith, love and grace is the paradigm for human freedom. Our understanding of creation must therefore begin from Christology and not from sophiology or triadology. As Florovsky wrote to Bulgakov in 1926: "Only in history, in the

52 Pentkovskii (1993), 205-206. In his published works, Florovsky, following the apostle Paul and the Nicene fathers, more often tended to give a Christological (rather than "energetic") interpretation of Sophia: the Wisdom of God is the incarnate and crucified Word, Jesus Christ.

53 Florovsky (1989), 126.

54 See Florovsky (1987e), 87.

55 See Florovsky's essay "The Predicament of the Christian Historian", in Florovsky (1974), 58.

realm of historical experience, are we capable of understanding the creaturehood of creation."[56]

Atonement and New Creation

The controversy occasioning the first version of Florovsky's essay on redemption, "On the Death on the Cross" (published in Russian in 1930), was not sophiological, but concerned Metropolitan Antony Khrapovitsky's book *The Dogma of Redemption* (1979; Russian original 1917). Antony held that Christ's moral suffering for the sins of the world in Gethsemane constituted redemption. In response, Florovsky stresses that the predicament from which Christ came to save humanity concerns not simply morality, but mortality. Redemption is accomplished not only by Christ's suffering, but by his death. Christ's whole life is redemptive, a recapitulation of Adam; yet its climax is the cross. This is the death of God incarnate: the penetration of immortal life into death and Hades. The cross is the "life-giving tree", the power of resurrection.

Florovsky's redemption essays should be read together with his treatment of Antony in *Ways of Russian Theology*. Florovsky likened Antony's interpretation of the "moral idea" of redemption to Kant's second *Critique*. Here the "metaphysical realism" of the Fathers, their dogmatic concern for the objective character of events in space and time, is abandoned in favour of psychologism and moralism, and the sacramental dimension eclipsed entirely by the pastorate.

All Florovsky's essays on redemption conclude, fittingly, with liturgy and sacraments. Christ's death was a baptism of blood, a cleansing of human nature and the cosmos, effecting universal resurrection. The sacrifice on the cross is a liturgy consummated in heaven, where Christ is still presenting us to God, as advocate and high priest. Atonement includes resurrection and ascension, a sacrifice offered not only for remission of sins, but also for our glorification – *theosis*.

In the sacraments, the same high priest both recapitulates creation and redemption and builds up his body, the *totus Christus*, in history. The church is a eucharistic body, "constituted" in the sacraments. Florovsky's ecclesiology is Chalcedonian, the crucial point being Christ's human nature, "his own and yet universal". However, he notes, neither "nature" nor "incarnation" alone is here sufficient. Ecclesiology must be developed "only within the comprehensive scheme of the divine *oikonomia* of salvation."[57] As the body of Christ, the *pleroma* of salvation, the church is a "living summary of Christ's redemptive work". The shape of the body corresponds to the *forma servi* and *forma gloriae* of her head. Yet the distinction between the two states, militant and triumphant, should not be overstressed: even now, the "glory" is hidden within the historic church, and the Lord does not put off the form which he assumed. As Florovsky wrote to Archimandrite Sophrony in 1958, "Christ in his ascension is no less man than 'in his days with us', and perhaps more".[58]

Florovsky approaches the saving events from Christ's birth to Pentecost as temporally distinct moments of one redemptive deed: "The Spirit is the Spirit of Christ …

[56] Pentkovski (1993), 207.

[57] See Florovsky (1955).

[58] Sakharov, 78.

The Pentecost is the mystery of the Crucified Lord."[59] Between Pentecost and *parousia* is a time of human decision, free response to the decision God has already made in Christ. "God initiates, accompanies, and completes everything in the process of salvation."[60] Yet the "ancient law of freedom" requires that the universal *apokatastasis* of human nature effected by Christ's resurrection be expressed in a personal resurrection of the will and synergistic love, a martyric struggle which Florovsky understands as *imitatio Christi* (here contrast Lossky). Hell remains a terrible possibility, which people may inexplicably choose. Florovsky's rejection of universalism is at the service of a positive eschatology. What human beings become in time is of ultimate significance: it is "the human personality with all of its concrete aspects, and consequently, with all the personal relations, such as friendship and love" – and "in this sense, also culture" – that "shall pass from history into eternity".[61]

In the late 1930s, and again in the 1950s, Florovsky worked on a book entitled "*In Ligno Crucis*: The Patristic Doctrine of the Atonement".[62] The unpublished preface and original manuscript reveal the ecumenical breadth of Florovsky's soteriology: Latin Fathers and liturgy appear alongside Greek as witnesses to a common Catholic doctrine.

Influenced (like Khrapovitsky) by the "moral expiation" theory of Kazan Academy professor Victor Nesmelov (1863-1937), Florovsky in the 1920s and 1930s was ambivalent in acknowledging a substitutionary dimension to atonement. Study of his library and unpublished papers, however, suggests some reassessment during the 1950s. In one essay from this period, entitled "Eschatology in the Patristic Age", he does not hesitate to invoke the *Book of Common Prayer* to describe Christ's death as "a full, perfect, and sufficient sacrifice, oblation and satisfaction".[63]

In any case, Florovsky placed all such soteriological motifs within a broader cosmological scope. While emphasising that theology must build not on probabilities but actual events – we know the incarnate Lord as saviour of a fallen world – he nevertheless suggests that the incarnation might be regarded as "an integral part of the original plan of Creation".[64]

With a provocative echo of Anselm in its title, Florovsky's "*Cur Deus Homo?*"[65] (1957) – an essay originally intended as an excursus to "*In Ligno Crucis*" – cautiously advances this thesis with reference to both Fathers and scholastics, addressing, as Pelikan noted, a problem "fundamental to the Augustinian heritage of Western theology: how to affirm simultaneously the goodness of the Creation and the necessity of the Incarnation".[66] Florovsky finds in Maximus the Confessor support for the Scotist

---

59 Letter of Florovsky to Arthur Dobbie Bateman (12 December 1963), published in Gallaher, citation on page 61.

60 Florovsky (1987a), 21.

61 Public lecture of Florovsky, quoted in Sviridov, 73.

62 The book was never completed or published. The essay published as "Redemption" (in Florovsky 1976), however, contains the core material from the late 1930s.

63 Florovsky (1975), 65.

64 Florovsky (1951), 20.

65 Florovsky (1976), 310-314.

66 Pelikan, 12.

view of the incarnation as the first object of God's creative will – an absolute predestination, independent of Adam's fall. Like Bulgakov (whom he cites here), Florovsky holds that the world was created so that creatures might be deified through inclusion in the body of the incarnate Son. The question of the ultimate motive of the incarnation must be approached within the perspective of the doctrine of creation.

Conclusion

Florovsky's theology is characterised by the unity of creation and salvation, while also preserving the difference between grace and nature and the significance of both evil and heroic virtue in history. An adequate conception of creation is crucial to the whole of Christian belief, yet can be apprehended only through Christology (and thus eschatology). Salvation is the "whole Christ, head and body", and culminates in the "new creation".

Comparison of Florovsky with the better-known thought of his student, John Zizioulas, is enlightening. Zizioulas both repeats and creatively extends Florovsky at crucial points. Behind their common accent on freedom and the transcendence of "nature", however, are significant divergences. Though lacking the kind of robust treatment of natural capacity found in Dumitru Stăniloae, Florovsky nevertheless rejected (in his critique of Lossky's ecclesiology) the crude schematic opposition between person and nature. Whereas Zizioulas tends to characterise freedom as the person's escape from nature and nature's *telos*, Florovsky clarified that grace "does not destroy what is 'natural': *hyper physin* does not mean *para physin*".[67] Not liberation from the bonds of creatureliness, but rather ascetic self-determination and historical creativity – the freedom of the "deed": such is Florovsky's interest in exploring the freedom proper to the human person. Zizioulas's communion ontology, identified with the trinitarian mode of being and *eschata* of human persons, gives scant attention to historical act. In contrast, agency is crucial to Florovsky's treatment of person and freedom: history is never swamped by eschatology.

Certain readers, enthusiastic for Bulgakov, have mistakenly cast Florovsky's theology as nominalist. Recourse to Maximian *logoi* aside, Florovsky himself anticipated this criticism in a 1925 essay on historical interpretation, where he strictly differentiated his historical "singularism" from nominalism.[68] Stronger affinities are to be found with Duns Scotus, whom Florovsky cited positively at every stage of his career. Comparative study of Florovsky and Scotus on the themes of creation and salvation could be fruitful – an offering to the dialogue with Latin scholasticism which Florovsky himself called for in conclusion to *Ways of Russian Theology*.

References and Recommended Reading

Blane, Andrew (1993), *Georges Florovsky: Russian Intellectual and Orthodox Churchman*, Crestwood: St Vladimir's Seminary Press.

Florovsky, Georges (1928), "L'idée de la création dans la philosophie chrétienne", *Logos: Revue Internationale de la Synthèse Orthodoxe*, No. 1, 3-30.

--- (1930a), "Evolution und Epigenesis (Zur Problematik der Geschichte)", *Der Russische Gedanke*,

[67] Florovsky (1972), 27.

[68] See Florovsky (1977).

Vol. 1, 240-252.
--- (1930b), "O Smerti Krestnoi" ("On the Death on the Cross"), *Pravoslavnaya Mysl'*, No. 2, 148-187.
--- (1949), "The Idea of Creation in Christian Philosophy", *Eastern Churches Quarterly*, Vol. 8, 2, 53-77.
--- (1951), "The Lamb of God", *Scottish Journal of Theology*, Vol. 4, 1, 13-28.
--- (1953), "On the Tree of the Cross", *St Vladimir's Seminary Quarterly*, Vol. 1, 3-4, 11-34.
--- (1955), "Christ and His Church: Suggestions and Comments" in: Olivier Rousseau (ed.), *L'Église et les Églises, 1054-1954, Volume 2: Neuf siècles de douloureuse Séparation entre l'Orient et l'Occident: Etudes et travaux sur l'unité chrétienne, offerts à Dom Lambert Beauduin*, Chevtogne: Éditions Chevtogne, 179-190.
--- (1972), *Bible, Church, Tradition: An Eastern Orthodox View*, Belmont: Nordland.
--- (1972b), *Vizantiiskie ottsy V-VIII vekov: Iz chtenii v Pravoslavnom Bogoslovskom Institute v Parizhe*, Surrey: Gregg International.
--- (1974), *Christianity and Culture*, Belmont: Nordland.
--- (1975), *Aspects of Church History*, Belmont: Nordland.
--- (1976), *Creation and Redemption*, Belmont: Nordland.
--- (1977), "Types of Historical Interpretation", in: Louis J. Shein (ed.), *Readings in Russian Philosophical Thought: Philosophy of History*, Waterloo: Wilfred Laurier University Press, 89-108.
--- (1979), *Ways of Russian Theology, Volume 1*, Belmont, MA: Nordland.
--- (1987a), *Byzantine Ascetic and Spiritual Fathers*, Vaduz: Büchervertriebsanstalt.
--- (1987b), *Eastern Fathers of the 4th Century*, Vaduz: Büchervertriebsanstalt.
--- (1987c), *The Byzantine Fathers of the 5th Century*, Vaduz: Büchervertriebsanstalt.
--- (1987d), *The Byzantine Fathers of the 6th to the 8th Century*, Vaduz: Büchervertriebsanstalt.
--- (1987e), *Ways of Russian Theology, Volume 2*, Vaduz: Büchervertriebsanstalt.
--- (1989), *Philosophy: Philosophical Problems and Movements*, Vaduz: Büchervertriebsanstalt.
--- (1990), *Vostochnye Ottsy IV veka*, Paris: YMCA Press. English translation = 1987b.
Gallaher, Anastassy Brandon (2005), "Georges Florovsky on Reading the Life of St. Seraphim", *Sobornost*, Vol. 27, 1, 58-70.
Khrapovitsky, Antony (1979), *The Dogma of Redemption*, Montreal: Monastery Press.
Klimoff, Alexis (2005), "Georges Florovsky and the Sophiological Controversy", *St Vladimir's Theological Quarterly*, Vol. 49, 1-2, 67-100.
Pelikan, Jaroslav (1973), "*Puti Russkogo Bogoslova:* When Orthodoxy Comes West", in: *The Heritage of the Eastern Church: Essays in Honor of the Very Reverend Georges Vasilievich Florovsky, Orientalia Christiana Analecta*, Vol. 195, Rome: Pontifical Oriental Institute, 11-16.
Pentkovski, A. M. (ed.) (1993), "Pis'ma G. Florovskogo S. Bulgakovu i S. Tyshkevichu", *Simvol*, Vol. 29, 199-216.
Sakharov, Sofronii (2008), *Perepiska s protoiereem Georgiem Florovskim*, Essex: Svyato-Ioanno-Predetechenskii Monast'ir' / Moscow: Svyato-Troitskaya Sergieva Lavra.
Sviridov, Ioann (1989), "Certain Aspects of the Theology of Archpriest George Florovsky (for the Tenth Anniversary of His Demise)", *The Journal of the Moscow Patriarchate*, Vol. 4, 67-74.

Matthew Baker

Vladimir Lossky (1903-1958) – A Metaphysics of Love

Creation as Dynamic Intentionality: Vladimir Lossky's Metaphysics of Love

Vladimir Lossky (1903-1958) is arguably one of the most influential Orthodox theologians of the past century. Son of the famous Russian philosopher Nicholas Lossky, he was one of many Russian émigrés to Paris, where he lived and taught after the Bolshevik Revolution until his tragically sudden death. His major works include *The Mystical Theology of the Eastern Church* (1976; French original 1944), and *The Vision of God* (1983; French original 1962), which explores the patristic background to the teaching of St Gregory Palamas.

In God's relation to the created order, one discerns in Vladimir Lossky's thought a type of metaphysics of love. The primacy of love flows naturally from the distinction between uncreated and created; only the love of God can create an "other" outside Godself namely created being. This love, as the metaphysical principle of creation, also represents the soteriological principle of union with the divine, revealed in the person of Christ. Insofar as God's love is ecstatic in going forth from Godself to create an other, it is this same ecstatic love that allows creation to transcend its own limits in order to unite with the uncreated. This ecstatic love of God is thus the very life source of all creation, and the gift which grants to creation the capacity for its own ecstatic love toward God.

Divine Ideas

Lossky posits a creation based not on necessity but on God's free, loving will. The logical consequence of this is the identification of the "divine ideas" with the energies rather than the essence of God.

Of all the Greek fathers, the most extensive passage in Lossky's treatment of the divine ideas comes from John of Damascus:

> God, he says, contemplated all things before their existence, formulating them in His mind; and each being received its existence at a particular moment, according to His eternal thought and will (*kata ten theletiken autou achronon ennoian*), which is a predestination (*proorismos*), an image (*eikon*) and a model (*paradeigma*).[69]

According to Lossky, the term *theletike ennoia*, which he translates as "thought-will" – or, more accurately, "volitional thought" – is very important.[70] For one, it indicates that the divine ideas are identified with God's will and not with God's essence. Thus, they are neither necessary nor determinative of God's being. Moreover, the "volitional thought" of God gives to the ideas a dynamic and intentional character. The ideas themselves, rather than serving as models for replication, intend creation toward a particular end. "The divine ideas are inseparable from the creative intention",[71] an intention which, for Lossky, is communion in God's love. Thus, "they no longer constitute a 'hinterworld', but the very depth of the creature, its method of participation in divine energy, *its vocation to the highest love*".[72] Their purpose is to "determine the different modes according to which created beings participate in the creative energies".[73]

The different "modes of participation" are what account for the diversity of created existence. As image, the more faithfully created existence corresponds to its divine ideas, that is, the greater its level of participation in the uncreated energies according

[69] Lossky (1976), 94.

[70] Lossky (1976), 94.

[71] Lossky, (1978), 58.

[72] Lossky, (1978), 58 (emphasis – AP).

[73] Lossky (1976), 95.

to the "mode" intended by the divine ideas, the more truly it reflects the uncreated light of the energies. Thus, "if the divine ideas are not the essence of God itself, if they are thus, as it were, separated from the essence by the will", then three important conclusions can be drawn: (a) "not only the act of creation but also the very thoughts of God Himself can no longer be considered as a necessary determination of His nature and part of the intelligible content of the divine Being"; (b) "the created universe is not seen, as in platonic or platonizing thought, under the pale and attenuated aspect of a poor replica of the Godhead; rather it appears as an entirely new being"; (c) creation itself is "willed by God and the joy of His Wisdom".[74] The "joy" of God is indicative of the dynamic character of creation, which is not satisfied simply to be an image, but wills to be in the image, ever gravitating toward "its vocation to the highest love", toward the degree of participation in the divine energies intended by God through "Wisdom" in the divine ideas.

The *logoi*, or reasons, of created things are for Lossky synonymous with the divine ideas. *Logoi* are the "reasons" or intentions for created existence. Each created thing has a particular *logos* insofar as it has a particular destiny in terms of participation in the uncreated energies. There are *logoi* inasmuch as there exists a diversity of participations in the uncreated energies. These predeterminations or participations are constituted by the will of God, the "thought-wills", i.e. the divine ideas.

> [The will of God] is the point of contact between the infinite and the creative ideas of things, the *logoi*, the "words" ... Every created thing has its point of contact with the Godhead; and this point of contact is the idea, reason or *logos* which is at the same time the end towards which it tends.[75]

Insofar as the *logos* – the divine idea, the intention, the will of God for creation – is loving communion with God, then all *logoi* express this one *logos*. Yet, while the degree of participation in the energies in the case of a cow may be the same as for all other animals, this is not necessarily the case for rational human beings. All the *logoi* are "contained in the Logos, the second person of the Trinity who is the first principle and the last end of all created things".[76]

Why is the second person of the Trinity the *Logos*? As Lossky explains it, in relation to the world, i.e. in the economic realm, the Son manifests the divine will.[77] The *Logos* is "the threshold from which flow the creative outpourings, the particular *logoi* of creatures, and the centre towards which in their turn all created beings tend, as to their final end".[78] This discussion further reveals how the incarnation, understood as the union between the divine and the human, forms the basis for Lossky's creation theology. The *Logos* as beginning and end is revealed to us in Christ, in that the Trinity itself constitutes "the summit of cataphatic theology". If our "end and final fulfillment lies in union with Him, or deification",[79] then we know this only through Christ. More than this, Christ accomplishes this end for us. Thus, Christ is the *Logos* not

74 Lossky (1976), 95.
75 Lossky (1976), 98.
76 Lossky (1976), 98.
77 Lossky (1976), 99.
78 Lossky (1976), 98.
79 Lossky (1976), 98.

simply by manifesting the end, but by being the end, the union of the divine and the human. In tending toward their end, created things also tend toward their beginning, since "all things were created by the Logos".[80]

Analogy

Lossky calls the capacity of created beings to participate in the uncreated energies the "analogy" of the created thing. For this concept of analogy, he draws mostly from Dionysius the Areopagite. As with the divine ideas, the notion of union with God influences his treatment of the theme. Analogy indicates, above all, a certain similarity-in-difference between the Creator and the created. If the divine ideas determine the degree of participation on the part of the created being, then the analogy signifies the capacity of the created being to participate in God. The analogy of the created being is not simply a passive reflection indicating a particular perfection of the divine being: "The analogy according to pseudo-Dionysius signifies the capacity proportional to the creature to participate in the energies ... of God."[81] The analogous relationship is thus not passive, according to Lossky, but active. The analogy is "a desire of the creature to conform to the uncreated energies of God, which appear to him as the Good and the Beautiful".[82] Lossky's treatment of analogy makes even clearer his metaphysics of love, as the analogy of the created being is the desire for the Good and the Beautiful. This capacity to desire the Good is given by God's love.[83] The greater the degree of participation, the greater the analogy and, accordingly, the greater the capacity to love. Insofar as the analogy is the capacity to love, namely to participate in God, then the analogy determines the end of this love, or the degree of participation. There is an analogy proper to each created thing, and the degree of participation is not the same for all. Thus, there is a hierarchy of created being based on the analogies, which should not be interpreted as some deserving more love than others, but as an interdependency oriented toward the fulfilment of God's loving intent for creation.[84] The capacity for creation to manifest the love of God ultimately depends on those who can freely respond to the call of God's love.

Lossky concludes that for Dionysius analogy signifies both the capacity to love God and the limit of this love by which each being attains union. As ends or limits of the created being's capacity to love, the analogies are the divine ideas, the predetermination of participation in the uncreated energies of God.[85] There are thus the divine analogies, i.e. the ideas, and created analogies, i.e. the capacity to love God. Union with God consists in the meeting of the two analogies, in which the capacity to love reaches the limit predetermined by the divine ideas. As Lossky explains in an article written more than twenty years after "La notion des 'Analogies' chez Denys le Pseudo-Aréopagite": "in the analogy of each created nature, there is an encounter and a synergy of two wills: the liberty of the creature and predetermination (*proorismos*) – the idea

[80] Lossky (1976), 100.
[81] Lossky (1931), 292.
[82] Lossky (1931), 294.
[83] Lossky (1931), 295.
[84] Lossky (1931), 292-293, 298.
[85] Lossky (1931), 229-300.

(*paradeigma*) or divine will addressed to each being".[86] Union occurs when the will or "the liberty of the creature" is one with the "divine will addressed to each being". Created existence cannot accomplish the union of these two will-analogies by its own power. This union occurs in, and is made possible by, Christ alone.[87] Union with God is accomplished in and through Christ, who unites the human and the divine and fulfils the divine intention. Christ thus stands at the beginning and the end of creation: the *Logos* through whom all things are created and from whom pour forth the *logoi* of created beings is also the God-man in which the human will and the divine "thought-wills" become one.[88]

Created Through and For Love

Love is that which begins and ends the circle of the created order. Creation itself owes its existence to the love of God. The very fact of creation *ex nihilo* requires that God go outside of Godself to create an other. This going outside of Godself is the ecstatic love of God. Thus, creation *ex nihilo* means creation out of the ecstatic love of God whose effect is created existence. God creates not because God's goodness or wisdom necessitates the existence of creation, but because of God's freedom-as-love. The source of creation is not a God bound by necessity, but a personal God, which for Lossky equates to an ecstatic love. Such an ecstatic love is a freedom to go beyond oneself toward another and, in God's case, toward creating an other. A personal God is one not bound by necessity, but one who relates to the "other" in freedom and love.

The fact that creation is based on love constitutes it as a divine risk. Moreover, only a personal God, for Lossky, can take a risk in creating.

> This category of divine risk, which is proper to a personal God freely creating personal beings endowed with freedom, is foreign to all abstract conceptions of the divine dominion ... *he who takes no risks does not love*: the God of the theology manuals can love only himself, and it is his own perfection which he loves even in his creatures. He does not love any *person*: for personal love is love for another than oneself.[89]

What God risks, is "creating a universe whose perfection is continually jeopardized by the freedom of those in whom that perfection ought to reach its highest level".[90] The perfection which Lossky speaks of is a free love for the Creator according to one's capacity.

The love of God does not end with the divine risk. God created so that creation might enjoy perfection, which is free loving communion with God. God does not simply intend this end but works toward the completion of the circle of love. It is this loving activity of God in creation that inspires in created being a love for the Creator.[91] Love is "an uncreated gift – 'a divine energy' – which continually inflames the soul

[86] Lossky (1974), 41.
[87] Lossky (1931), 307.
[88] Lossky (1931), 305.
[89] Lossky (1974), 214 (emphasis – AP).
[90] Lossky (1974), 214.
[91] Lossky (1931), 295.

and unites it to God by the power of the Holy Spirit".[92] Love in the created order is more than an intention to create on God's part; it is the very divine energy which creates, and which stirs creation toward its final end which is love. It forms the foundation for the apophatic and cataphatic ways, which are nothing other than the flow of love to and from the Creator. As Lossky poignantly summarises his vision early in his career:

> The two ways in theology correspond to the way of divine love through which God proceeds outside of Godself, creating all in order to be manifest in all, and returning all created beings to the divine union by the love that God inspires in them. In this "eternal circle" of divine Love, God appears both as Lover (*Amour*), proceeding outside of God's essence and creating all things by the divine energies, and as Beloved (*Aimé*), remaining united in himself in his procession, and imparticipable even in participation. As Lover (*Amour*), God gives his infinity to creatures proportionally by defining their "analogies" (ideas); as Beloved (*Aimé*), he produces in created being the love that is the analogy of the will of beings, making them desire union in the divine energies, according to the pre-established mode of each.[93]

References and Recommended Reading

Lossky, Vladimir (1931), "La notion des 'Analogies' chez Denys le Pseudo-Aréopagite", *Archives d'Histoire Doctrinale et Littéraire du Moyen-Age*, Vol. 5, 279-309.
--- (1974), *In the Image and Likeness of God*, Crestwood: St Vladimir's Seminary Press.
--- (1976), *The Mystical Theology of the Eastern Church*, Crestwood: St Vladimir's Seminary Press.
--- (1978), *Orthodox Theology: An Introduction*, Crestwood: St Vladimir's Seminary Press.
--- (1983), *The Vision of God*, Crestwood: St Vladimir's Seminary Press.
Papanikolaou, Aristotle (2006), *Being with God: Trinity, Apophaticism and Divine-Human Communion*, Notre Dame: University of Notre Dame Press.
Williams, Rowan (1975), "The Theology of Vladimir Nikolaievich Lossky: An Exposition and Critique", Ph.D. dissertation, Oxford University.

Aristotle Papanikolaou

Dumitru Stăniloae (1903-1993) – The Dynamism of the Cosmos

Introduction

Dumitru Stăniloae (1903-1993) was one of the most creative and influential figures of 20th-century Orthodox theology. He studied in Athens, Munich and Paris before returning to his native Romania to become professor at the Theological Institutes of Sibiu and, later, Bucharest. His work engages extensively with the church fathers and with modern Orthodox, Catholic and Protestant theologians. Despite a spell in prison camp (1958-1964), he continued writing almost to his death. His principal works include *Iisus Hristos sau restaurarea omului* ("Jesus Christ or the Restoration of the Human Being", 1993; first edition 1943), *Teologia Dogmatică Ortodoxă pentru Institutele Teologice* ("Orthodox Dogmatic Theology for Theological Institutes", originally pub-

[92] Lossky (1978), 212.
[93] Lossky (1931), 304-305.

lished in Romanian in three volumes, 1978),[94] *Theology and the Church* (1980), *Prière de Jesus et expérience du Saint-Esprit* (1981), *Prayer and Holiness: The Icon of Man Renewed in God* (1982), and *Spiritualitate şi comuniune în liturghia ortodoxă* ("Spirituality and Communion in the Orthodox Liturgy", 1986).

Pneumatological Theology of Creation and Salvation

Stăniloae's overarching vision sees salvation as the original purpose of creation. He believes that by the act of creation, God introduced a cosmic dynamism into the world so that the whole universe could return to him as the source of its existence and fulfilment of its life. The original aim of the creation was to proceed from mere existence to an eternal well-being, to communion with the Creator (note the echo of St Maximus the Confessor, with his triad of being – eternal being – eternal well-being). The human being, however, perverted the positive dynamic of creation by its fall, leading to an ever-greater distance from God, which ultimately culminated in death. Against this background, Stăniloae understands the incarnation of the Logos as a restoration of the dynamism of the world perverted by the fall. The incarnation of the Logos reveals, on the one hand, that God is the source of all created existence, the origin and aim of the world. On the other hand, the Son of God by his incarnation opens to creation an infinite perspective, becoming the subject of the human dynamism of reason and love. By his death and resurrection, Christ renewed human nature and with it returned the dynamism of the cosmos to its original condition, at the same time opening up the world to true communion with God. Stăniloae calls this restoration of the world "pneumatisation" or "spiritualisation". Spiritualisation here means the indwelling of the Holy Spirit in human nature, so that the latter becomes clear, transparent and receptive to the uncreated energies of God. By this process of spiritualisation and dynamic participation in communion with God, every human being receives the status of god by grace and is transformed into a bearer of the uncreated energy of God. The spiritualisation of human nature has cosmic resonances, since the human being, as a "sort of natural bond", actively integrates him- or herself and the entire world into communion with God. Through this process, human being and world are transfigured by the uncreated energies of God.

Stăniloae's theology of creation is combined with a cosmic ecclesiology and based on a trinitarian pneumatology. For him, the mystery of the church is actually the mystery of the union between the Trinity and the creature, a union effected by Christ in the Holy Spirit: "The Spirit of the resurrected Christ leads us from inside towards an eschatological Pentecost where he will irradiate entirely from the transparent body of Christ, as well as from our hearts which will become more and more transparent through the union with Christ".[95]

---

[94] These three volumes were translated into English as *Orthodox Dogmatic Theology: The Experience of God, Volume 1: Revelation and Knowledge of the Triune God* (2005); *The Experience of God: Orthodox Dogmatic Theology, Volume 2: The World, Creation and Deification* (2005); *The Experience of God: Orthodox Dogmatic Theology, Volume 3: The Person of Jesus Christ as God and Savior* (2011). All these volumes were published by Holy Cross Orthodox Press (in Brookline Massachusetts). Unless otherwise stated, this essay draws principally on the German translations of the original Romanian volumes that I have access to. See Stăniloae (1985), (1990), (1995).

[95] Stăniloae (1974), 248 (translation – DM).

Ecclesiological and Cosmic Soteriology: The Church as a Continuation of the Redemptive Work of Christ

Stăniloae describes the redemptive work of the Son as the restoration, healing and deification (*theosis*) of the human nature assumed by him. The Son of God took on human nature not only to deify it, but also in order to initiate the transformation of the world. He filled his human nature "with his divinity" and released it "from the effects, suffering and death resulting from original sin", thus fulfilling the aim of his incarnation as the *theosis* of all humanity. He accepted a human body in order to allow all human beings to participate in his deified human nature, to clothe themselves "in divine radiance" and beauty. Stăniloae understands this participation not only as the restoration, sanctification and *theosis* of human nature, but also as the glorification of God. When human beings are sanctified, God is glorified.

In this context, Stăniloae defines the church as the continuation of the salvific work of Christ, while the divinised human nature of Christ spreads out upon the whole of humanity. This ever-expansive indwelling of Christ constitutes the basis of the church.

The pneumatological dimension of this soteriological restoration of communion with God consists in the fact that it occurs only by the work of the Holy Spirit. Because the Holy Spirit dwells as divine hypostasis in the Son from eternity, and shines forth from him, this same Spirit gains through the incarnation a centre from which to radiate outwards in the human nature of Christ. By his death for us, Christ made his human nature completely transparent to God. His human nature became spiritualised, transforming itself into "the most receptive place of the Spirit".[96] Therefore Stăniloae interprets the transfiguration of the body of Christ by the resurrection as "pneumatisation", effecting the intensive presence of the Holy Spirit who enables the body of Christ to radiate the light of divine glory. The Holy Spirit transforms the human body of Christ into a sanctified and ecclesiological body (*soma pneumatikon*); he penetrates the matter of Christ's body and thereby institutes a "new, pneumatological order" for the world. Stăniloae calls this spiritual order "the stage of eschatological, everlasting life". The resurrection of Christ as a revelation of everlasting life, therefore, has a radical pneumatological meaning for the history of the world.

The "new, pneumatological causality" introduced into history by the resurrection of Christ also opens up access to a new way of existence. The Holy Spirit shines forth from the completely spiritualised body of Christ in the world and continues the redemptive work of Christ. This work of the Holy Spirit Stăniloae calls "church".

Stăniloae describes the church as an "eschatological community" and the "coming of the new creation" because it arises "from the body of the risen Christ". The new life of the church is realised in Christ and the Holy Spirit as participation in the infinity of divine love. However, the Holy Spirit, as the Spirit of Christ, has the special work of uniting all believers with Christ and leading them to resurrection. Stăniloae therefore defines the church as a "place" in which the resurrection is anticipated. He even goes so far as to call the church a "laboratory of resurrection". The church offers the way to the eschatological resurrection since the Holy Spirit transforms human beings through incorporation into the resurrected body / life of Christ.

---

96 See Stăniloae (1985), 53.

The Church as Sacrament

Stăniloae understands sacrament as the union of God with his creatures and, finally, with the whole creation. This union, begun already with the act of creation, will end with the perfect indwelling of God in creation. At this point, Stăniloae makes a distinction between three sacraments. The first sacrament is the creation, the second the sacrament of Christ and the third the church.

For Stăniloae, Jesus Christ is the second sacrament because the Creator established in him the most intimate union with creation by accepting human nature in the person of the Son. In him the Creator becomes at the same time a human being and the human becomes at the same time creator. Jesus Christ is therefore the perfect "link" between God and God's creatures. He opened for all human beings the way and possibility of union with God in himself. He bridged in his own person the "ontological gap" between God and creation.

Alongside the sacrament of creation and the sacrament of Christ, Stăniloae describes the church as the "third sacrament" which implements the unity between Creator and creation realised in Christ. The church embodies "nothing other than the continuation ... of the sacrament of Christ".[97] Stăniloae interprets this continuation pneumatologically, namely as the sanctification and spiritualisation of creation by the indwelling of the Holy Spirit, by which the church exists in history as a force field of the Holy Spirit. In the church, the union of the first sacrament (creation) with the second sacrament (Christ) takes place. The union of God with God's creation brings with it the increase of the church, because the restored creation is one with the transfigured body of Christ. However, the sacrament of the church and that of Christ cannot be separated from one another because Christ constitutes the church and keeps it alive by the Holy Spirit. As an extension of his incarnation and of his body, the church constitutes that particular space in which the uncreated energy of the Holy Spirit divinises the world.

Stăniloae describes the liturgy of the church as an "event of resurrection",[98] an epiklesis of the Holy Spirit. By the action of the Holy Spirit we can anticipate the resurrection in the church, namely everlasting life, the eschatological future of the world.

The church is thus "the liturgical centre of creation", a new way of existence and doxological communion with the Holy Trinity. Not only human beings but the whole universe is called to become church, that is, a transparent medium of divine holiness and God's indwelling beauty.

The Holy Spirit in Creation: Anthropocentrism and Mystical Materialism

According to Stăniloae, the Holy Spirit moved above the waters and gave form to all things called into existence by the Logos, and was "always in harmony with the will of the Logos and in cooperation with him". The Son "initiates" and the Spirit completes the act of creation. Stăniloae therefore describes the Holy Spirit as the "last factor in the creation of matter", and the "constant force that lends form to different existences

[97] Stăniloae (1995), 17 (translation – DM).

[98] Stăniloae (1986).

at all levels".[99] The intra-trinitarian love of God spreads out to human subjects who are capable of being God's partners in dialogue through the ecstatic power of the Holy Spirit. The Holy Spirit works the transformation of creation while bringing human beings into communion with God.

How does Stăniloae justify his anthropocentric theology? Stăniloae describes the human being as a "link" that unifies, on the one hand, all elements of creation in himself and, on the other, the world with God. The human being is able to transcend and transform the material world through the energies of the Holy Spirit. Stăniloae bases the intermediary function of the human being on his conviction that each human being hypostasises the whole of cosmic nature. On account of this ontological continuity between humanity and nature, which allows nature to participate in the deification of the person, Stăniloae defines the human being as the "sense of the world", especially emphasising the human soul as facilitator of an unmediated relationship with God.

Stăniloae offers another argument for the special position of the human being in the universe. The self-awareness of the human being and the incarnation of God's Son give him reason to suppose that the world was created for the consciousness of the human being, so that humanity could come of age in it, attaining ever-deeper communion with God.

This anthropocentric worldview in Stăniloae's theology of creation is combined with a synergetic understanding of salvation. In his opinion, humans in cooperation with the Holy Spirit make the world transparent to God. The human being as "priest of the whole universe" is able to transform the universe and endow nature with the Spirit of God through his own spirit, which transcends the world. This work of transfiguration and pneumatisation is crucial for Stăniloae's synergetic view of salvation. The divine Spirit works through the human spirit, a process Stăniloae describes as "free cooperation" between the human being and the Holy Spirit. This cooperation demonstrates the special dignity and vocation of humans, who are endowed with free will and rationality by God.

How does Stăniloae understand the relation between God and his creation before and after the fall of humankind? An answer to this question can be found in the first volume of his dogmatics, in which he describes the initial creation as having been filled with the divine Spirit. According to Stăniloae, death in humans and in nature is due solely to the fall of mankind, which separated creation from the divine energies. Sin led to a "loss of the divine Spirit" of life and with it an impairment of creation in its vital resources. Only the resurrection of Christ could effect the destruction of death and the restoration of the fullness of the Holy Spirit. For Stăniloae, the resurrection of Christ marks not only the beginning of the new creation and the restoration of communion between human beings and God, but also the advent of a certain "pneumatic causality", which in its turn leads to the sanctification and divinisation of the whole universe. "From the risen and exalted Christ the Holy Spirit shines forth immediately and superabundantly, exactly as heat radiates from an incandescent body".[100]

[99] Stăniloae (1995), 34 (translation – DM).

[100] Stăniloae (1980), 199.

Conclusion

One of Stăniloae's greatest contributions to contemporary thinking on creation and salvation is to show how the process of "spiritualisation" is not a denial but an affirmation of material creation. The Holy Spirit introduces into creation the uncreated energies and the fullness of divine communion. The world thus becomes a "medium" and "transparent organ of the divinity" which radiates the perfect beauty of God. This beauty of the new creation is founded on "the intimate connection between the Spirit and the reality" of the world.[101] Spiritualised matter shares in the new, imperishable life. Spiritualisation does not mean for Stăniloae the dissolution of the material world, since transfigured matter remains matter "even in the state of resurrection". Stăniloae calls this "the mystery of spiritualised matter", of the restored universe and the resurrected body.[102] Based on this transfiguration of creation by the Holy Spirit, Stăniloae assents to a "mystical materialism" which presumes the "eternity of matter", a sanctified matter renewed by the infinite complexity, light and beauty of the Holy Spirit.[103]

References and Recommended Reading

Bartos, Emil and Ware, Kallistos (2002), *Deification in Eastern Orthodox Theology: An Evaluation and Critique of the Theology of Dumitru Stăniloae*, Milton Keynes: Paternoster.

Munteanu, Daniel (2003), *Der tröstende Geist der Liebe: Zu einer ökumenischen Lehre vom Heiligen Geist über die trinitarischen Theologien J. Moltmanns und D. Stăniloaes*, Neukirchen-Vluyn: Neukirchener Verlag.

Stăniloae, Dumitru (1969a), "Orthodoxy, Life in the Resurrection", *Eastern Churches Review*, Vols. 2-4, 371-375.

--- (1969b), "The World as Gift and Sacrament of God's Love", *Sobornost*, Vol. 9, 662-673.

--- (1973), "L'homme, image de Dieu dans le monde", *Contacts*, Vol. 25, 287-309.

--- (1974), "Le Saint-Esprit dans la théologie et la vie de l'eglise orthodoxe", *Contacts*, Vol. 26, 227-256.

--- (1978), *Teologia Dogmatică Ortodoxă pentru Institutele Teologice*, Bucharest: Ed. Institutului Biblic si de Misiune al Bisericii Ortodoxe Romane.

--- (1980), *Theology and the Church*, Crestwood: St Vladimir's Seminary Press.

--- (1981), *Prière de Jesus et expérience du Saint-Esprit*, Paris: Desclée de Brouwer.

--- (1982), *Prayer and Holiness: The Icon of Man Renewed in God*, Fairacres Publication 82, Oxford: SLG.

--- (1985), *Orthodoxe Dogmatik I*, Gütersloh: Gütersloher Verlagshaus.

--- (1986), *Spiritualitate şi comuniune în liturghia ortodoxă*, Craiova: Mitropoliei Olteniei.

--- (1990), *Orthodoxe Dogmatik II*, Gütersloh: Gütersloher Verlagshaus.

--- (1993), *Iisus Hristos sau restaurarea omului* (second edition), Craiova: Omniscop.

--- (1995), *Orthodoxe Dogmatik III*, Gütersloh: Gütersloher Verlagshaus.

Daniel Munteanu

---

[101] See Stăniloae (1995), 326.

[102] Stăniloae (1995), 336.

[103] Stăniloae (1995), 338.

John Zizioulas (1931-) – Being as Communion

Introduction

Among modern Orthodox theologians, John Zizioulas is probably the best known in the West. He was a lay theologian before becoming titular Metropolitan of Pergamon, teaching for many years at Glasgow and London universities. Inspired mainly by the Greek Fathers but also by modern existentialist trends, his thought (often described as personalistic ontology and eucharistic theology) has sparked animated debate in ecumenical theology and has had enormous influence in inter-church dialogue.

In seeking Zizioulas's view of creation and salvation, it becomes clear that the ontological perspective (*creatio ex nihilo*; the dialectic between created and uncreated) and the existential hermeneutical dimension (personhood; freedom; communion and otherness; the human being as priest of creation) are the pivotal themes of his thought. Zizioulas emphasises the central role of humanity in liberating creation from its natural boundaries and mortality in order to let it truly and eternally be. In so doing, he promotes a new ecological ethos which reassesses the sacredness of creaturehood on the basis of its dialectical relationship with God, providing humanity with an important means of confronting the contemporary ecological crisis.

The Ontological Perspective: Creatio ex Nihilo and the Dialectical Relationship between the Created and the Uncreated

According to Zizioulas, the central challenge of Greek thought faced by the Fathers of the church was the issue of the self-referentiality of being (being = being). The church was here confronted by two dominant perspectives on creation. On the one side was Gnosticism, which believed that the world is "penetrated by evil". In this case, escape from the "evil" world was considered necessary for salvation. On the other side was the Platonic view. According to this latter, the created world is penetrated by divine presence. While the concept of the created world is here highlighted for the first time, Plato's Demiurge is in fact a decorator and not a creator *ex nihilo* in an absolute sense.

The whole question ultimately revolves around one's understanding of the concept of creation, which must be examined dialectically, along with the notion of the beginning (*arche*). For Zizioulas, the fact that the world had a beginning, especially in an absolute sense, seemed to be utter nonsense to the Greek mind. Nevertheless, forming a Christian view of creation requires a literal understanding of the beginning of created existence, as well as the unoriginate existence of the Creator.

Christian theology was thus forced to innovate. "Creation as *ktisis* is a notion encountered for the first time ... with the Apostle Paul, and it clearly presupposes an absolutely ontological beginning".[104] Zizioulas therefore speaks of the need to introduce the term "ktisiology" into the Christian vocabulary. By using the term *ktisis* rather than *demiourgia* (the latter being the activity of Plato's Demiurge, who was shaping an existing substrate), Zizioulas emphasises that the concept of the beginning of creation is ontologically absolute, and that the Fathers ascribed this ontological meaning to the axiom of creation "from (absolute) nothing".

---

[104] Zizioulas (2006), 253.

From the time of Athanasius and Nicaea, an awareness began to develop that between God and the world "there exists an absolute, 'abysmal' otherness". If it were possible for something to arise from nothing, then it was also possible that a totally other being could exist vis-á-vis God's being. As Zizioulas notes, "the doctrine of creation out of nothing was about otherness and freedom in ontology."[105] This view of creatio *ex nihilo* established the parameters for the dialectic between the created and the uncreated, which required an understanding of the relationship between God and creation as one of reciprocal poles in a relationship of absolute, ecstatic otherness, and the existence of a third pole of absolute nothingness toward which the other two should look. In this context, absolute nothingness signifies the lack of any kind of metaphysical kinship between God and creation at the level of existence.

Existential Implications of the Theology of Creation

The basic conclusion that follows from creation *ex nihilo* is that the world is not eternal. Because otherwise if the world were eternal it would not need to be created and if it was not created from nothing then the world was created from something that has some other existence. This is clearly a reversal of classical approaches and leads to the conclusion that "existence is the fruit of freedom" since the closed ontology of the ancients, as well as the self-referentiality of being, are now abolished.

The fact that the world was created from nothing and is not eternal means that there is also the possibility that it would return to nothing and could not live eternally. Zizioulas stresses that one negative prospect is the ultimate activation of "the limitations and potential dangers inherent in creaturehood, if creation is left to itself", inasmuch as nothingness continuously permeates and penetrates the world. Zizioulas's emphasis on "nothing" indicates the abysmal chasm between God and creation and necessarily signifies that creation's very being constitutes a gift from God.

The Salvation of Creation and the Role of the First Adam

The crux of the question regarding creation and salvation is this: "How did God want the world to survive?"[106] In the history of ideas, various solutions have been proposed. Zizioulas emphasises the danger of falling into a view of "natural affinity" between God and the world if we accept that the world was endowed with a natural capacity for survival.

This leads, for one thing, to the notion of the "immortality of the soul", which Zizioulas regards as problematic. If there is anything that gives to the created the possibility of existing in a natural way, it inevitably leads to an obligatory immortality. Equally unacceptable is a related proposition based on moral or juridical foundations, which supposes that the created being could improve itself by practising natural or divine law. For Zizioulas, a proposal such as this cannot offer transcendence from death inasmuch as this latter is an ontological problem.

Zizioulas here highlights the role of humanity. According to Genesis, human beings first appeared at the end of creation, yet were placed in the centre of creation. Thus,

---

105 Zizioulas (2006), 18.

106 Zizioulas (1989), 44.

the doctrine of creation concerns not only the world but also the issue of freedom, and primarily the role that man could play within it.

Imago Dei and the Fall

Zizioulas develops his anthropology in correspondence with his ktisiology (and ecclesiology). He repeatedly invokes the name of Darwin in order to demonstrate that the difference between humanity and the rest of creation is a difference of degree not of kind, which is wholly unrelated to human rationality; the association of human uniqueness and rationality is a view he regards as partially responsible for the ecological crisis.[107]

Zizioulas's anthropological approach directly correlates the concept of freedom with the idea of humanity as created in the image of God. He adopts Gregory of Nyssa's interpretation of freedom, pointing out that in speaking of an image of God, it is necessary to refer to an exclusive characteristic of God's being. Yet, since humans are creatures, we cannot escape the fact of our existence, and therefore we cannot say that we are absolutely free. Herein lies the significance of the relationship between human freedom and the fall. Zizioulas notes that it was human freedom that made the fall possible.[108] The fall is perceived as "idolatry", i.e. turning created existence into an absolute point of self-referentiality.

Zizioulas emphasises the importance of freedom in this perspective, noting that "*man*" came to believe that he could rule creation as though it was his creature, thereby opening up a gulf between humanity and nature with all the attendant consequences for the environment.

Salvation: Christ as Priest of Creation

How then can creation be saved in Zizioulas's view? Focussing his answer to this question on the person of Christ, Zizioulas examines the Christology of Chalcedon from two perspectives: the cosmological and the ecclesiological. We must also, however, keep in mind the patristic idea of "hypostatic union" which, according to Zizioulas, gives priority to the person of Christ rather than to the two natures. Interpreting Maximus, he notes that, in order for death to be overcome, a relationship is necessary between the created and the uncreated, and that it is the human being who is to undertake this role. However, the fall foiled this divinely ordained task, necessitating a change in the divine plan. What was required was for the human to become human.

The fall changed the natural condition of "difference" (*diaphora*) between created and uncreated into one of "division" (*diairese*) (Maximus),[109] leading again to the nonexistence that preceded creation. In this context, Zizioulas proposes an existential interpretation of the Chalcedonian phrase "without confusion" (*asynchytos*) and "indivisibly" (*adiairetos*), which describe the relationship between God and humanity in the person of Christ. The word "indivisibly" highlights the necessity that there be no separation between created and uncreated; on the contrary, there must be real communion

[107] Zizioulas (1989), 4.
[108] Zizioulas (2008), 98.
[109] Zizioulas (2006), 22.

at the ontological level in order to avoid both the self-referentiality of the creation and death. The words "without confusion" guarantee the freedom and otherness of the two realities; otherwise, the relationship would not be free. The two terms are mediated in the person of Christ, in whom communion and otherness coincide. His resurrection offers the whole of creation victory over death and salvation.

It is therefore clear that without the incarnation of the Logos, the ontological distance between God and world cannot be overcome. Christ can thus be understood as the human being *par excellence*, who brings God and the world into relationship.

Zizioulas proposes the idea of the human being as the "priest of creation", which has clear ecotheological implications. The starting point for this conception is the person of Christ, while the framework is ecclesiological. Beginning with the conviction that humans constitute the ecclesial community which offers the gifts of Creation, this view recognises that creation in all its expressions borrows its being from God the Creator. Communion between the created and the uncreated is achieved through the act of offering which is the eucharistic Anaphora, and every believer as a member of this Body is called to act like Christ as a "priest of creation",[110] allowing creation to exist authentically in a personal and catholic way that transcends its natural limitations.

Conclusion

In conclusion, I offer some critical observations concerning Zizioulas's understanding of the type of relation that exists between God and creation and the means that God uses to save the world. Although his ontological and existential interpretation of the issue is indeed original and creative some hermeneutical-methodological questions remain open.

a) When Zizioulas speaks about *creatio ex nihilo*, he frequently refers to nothingness as the beginning of creation (at the level of nature), but he does not place a corresponding emphasis on the love of God as the cause of creation (at the level of grace). In his writings, his primary concern seems to be on safeguarding the absolute dialectic that preserves the otherness and chasm between the uncreated and the created; he is only secondarily concerned with the bridging of this gap. Perhaps Zizioulas avoids emphasising *creatio ex amore* in Christ for fear of bringing the created and the uncreated too close, even from a soteriological perspective.

b) Zizioulas sees the fall as "revealing and actualizing the limitations and potential dangers inherent in creaturehood, if creation is left to itself".[111] This formulation has aroused suspicion about the possible conflation of creation with the fall. He believes that the priority of nature over the person which characterises the created order because of its existence *ex nihilo* constitutes the main problem of the creation as a whole. There is thus a latent distinction and antithesis, clearly of an ontological and existential character, between created limits and absolute personal freedom, and it is not clear whether this is caused by creaturehood itself or by the fall.

c) If this is the case, what is the position and role of Jesus Christ? Is the person of

[110] Zizioulas (1990), 5.

[111] Zizioulas (1985), 102.

Christ the vantage point from which every aspect of Creation is to be considered (the act of creation and the salvation of the *ktisis*)? A study of Zizioulas's early work reveals an attempt to connect the Logos of God with the beginning of creation in an ontological perspective. Christ "is the 'beginning [*arche*]' of the world (ontological, cosmological Christology) because he is going to be the beginning [*arche*] of the world [to come] (eschatological Christology)".[112]

In Zizioulas's treatment of the Nicene Creed in his later work, God the Father appears as the cause (*aitia*) not only of the personal mode of existence of the Trinity, but also of creation.[113] Zizioulas bases his approach on that of the Cappadocians, but he focuses his attention primarily on Maximus in the framework of a relational ontology, which highlights the importance of communion-in-otherness between God and creation through the agency of the human being (as "microcosmos").

The crucial question concerns the role of the incarnate Logos, firstly in the protology of creation – as, according to John (John 1:3) and the Creed, "all things were made" through the Logos – and secondly in the history and eschatology of creation. In his emphasis on ontological Christology and on humanity as the link between God and creation, Zizioulas at times seems to overlook the fact that Christ is the sole mediator of creation and its salvation, recapitulating it in himself and bringing it to the Father, with humanity playing a corresponding role only in our dependence on him. If this is the case, the only way in which we can approach creation is from a soteriological point of view, through the resurrected and ascended Christ.

In the final reckoning, it seems that, for Zizioulas, the integrity of being (the ontological rather than the soteriological horizon) forms the foundation on which a discourse on God's action in creating and saving can be constructed.

References and Recommended Reading

Ables, Travis (2009), "Being Church: A Critique of Zizioulas' Communion Ecclesiology", in: Gesa Elsbeth Thiessen (ed.), *Ecumenical Ecclesiology: Unity, Diversity and Otherness in a Fragmented World*, Edinburgh: T & T Clark, 115-127.

McPartlan, Paul (1993), *The Eucharist Makes the Church: Henri de Lubac and John Zizioulas in Dialogue*, Edinburgh: T & T Clark.

Papanikolaou, Aristotle (2006), *Being with God: Trinity, Apophaticism, and Divine-Human Communion*, Notre Dame: University of Notre Dame Press.

Zizioulas, John (1985), *Being as Communion*, Crestwood: St Vladimir's Seminary Press.

--- (1989, 1990), "Preserving God's Creation: Three Lectures on Theology and Ecology", *King's Theological Review*, Vol. 12, 1-5, 41-45; Vol. 13, 1-5.

--- (2003), *Ellinismos kai Christianismos: I synantisi dyo kosmon*, Athens: Apostoliki Diakonia.

--- (2006), *Communion and Otherness*, Edinburgh: T & T Clark.

--- (2008), *Lectures in Christian Dogmatics*, Edinburgh: T & T Clark.

Nikolaos Asproulis

[112] Zizioulas (2003), 115.

[113] Zizioulas (2006), 113-118; (2008), 106.

Christos Yannaras (1935-) and Panayiotis Nellas (1936-1986) – Transcending Created Finitude

Introduction

Christos Yannaras and Panayiotis Nellas, friends from their student days, were both members of the Greek Zoe movement, an influential movement of spiritual renewal stamped by pietism. Both left Zoe in their mid twenties, under the influence of the neo-patristic current of thought flowing from the Paris-based theologians of the Russian emigration, to pursue postgraduate studies in France and Germany. Subsequently they returned to Greece to become leading figures in the Greek renewal of theology in the 1960s.

Nellas's influence was limited by his premature death. He nevertheless published important work based principally on his intensive study of the 14th-century theologian and mystic, Nicolas Kavasilas. These are "Prolegomena to the Study of Nicolas Kavasilas" (see 1968) and "The Teaching of Nicolas Kavasilas on Justification" (see 1975), both available only in Greek; and *Zoon theoumenon* (1979), translated into English as *Deification in Christ: The Nature of the Human Person* (1987). He also launched a series of publications, *Epi tas Pigas* (To the Sources) along the lines of Sources Chrétiennes, and in 1982 started the journal *Synaxi* – still the most influential theological journal in Greece – with the aim of promoting theological discussion beyond professional academic circles.

Like Nellas, Yannaras has sought to bring patristic theology to bear on the problems of the modern world. For many years he was professor of philosophy at the Panteion University in Athens, where he engaged with vital contemporary issues from a profoundly Christian point of view. His output has been immense. Among his books published in English are *The Freedom of Morality* (1984), *Elements of Faith* (1991), *Postmodern Metaphysics* (2004), *Orthodoxy and the West* (2004), *On the Absence and Unknowability of God* (2005), *Variations on the Song of Songs* (2005), *Person and Eros* (2007) and *Relational Ontology* (2011). He has been justly described (by Yannis Spiteris) as "the theologian most read in Greece today",[114] and (by Andrew Louth) as "without doubt one of the most important living Orthodox thinkers".[115] He continues in his eighth decade to be innovative and challenging on a wide variety of topics. Indeed, in the last few years he has developed his thinking on creation and salvation in important new ways.

The Recovery of the Patristic Approach to Creation

Less speculative than Yannaras, Nellas is a careful patristic exegete rather than a systematic theologian. With regard to the human condition after the fall, he builds on the exegetical insights of the church fathers to present us with a series of very suggestive interpretations of the symbolic language of the Genesis account of creation.

The main lines of this account are as follows. The whole of the visible world was created for humankind, and it is through humankind – created "in the image of God" –

---

[114] Spiteris, 298.

[115] Louth, 329.

that it is to be offered back to God. To grow fully into the image was the purpose for which Adam was created but which he failed to fulfil. Adam's failure constitutes the fall. Nellas is attracted by Kavasilas's statement that human nature at the fall sank into materiality – not in the Origenist sense of acquiring a material body, but in the sense of becoming opaque to the rays of divine light and therefore invisible to God. (This is the symbolic meaning of God's inability to see Adam in the garden in Genesis 3:9.) After the fall, the deiform person falls away and becomes imprisoned in its biological condition. Sin becomes second nature. The whole cosmos is drawn into humanity's disordered state, which is why the whole of creation groans in travail (Rom. 8:22). Humanity has deliberately set up the "dividing wall of enmity" (Eph. 2:14), refusing to accept a conscious relationship with God. As a result we have the illusion of life, but all the time sin is destroying our life like a disease.

The pain suffered by humankind after the fall is self-inflicted, a loss of receptivity to God, not a punishment meted out as a result of divine wrath. Nellas is quite clear on this. To attribute the cause of pain and death to God as Augustine and Anselm do, he says, is an error tantamount to heresy. God's justice is not something that needs to be "satisfied". But humanity was not left without help. First came the "garments of skin" that God made for Adam and his wife (Gen. 3:21). This clothing represents a change in the characteristics of being in God's image. The "in the image" is an orientation towards eternity, towards humanity's theocentric fulfilment and completion. The "garments of skin", made as they are of material from dead animals, represent mortality, the physiological effect of the fall. But as protection from the elements they also represent God's gift of a new relationship with nature, a new form of dominion over a nature now serving human need.

A New Hermeneutic Proposal

Nellas's purpose in constructing his symbolic picture was to establish a basis for Orthodox theology to be able to offer something to the modern world. The fathers, he was convinced, offer us insights into the origin, structure and destiny of humanity. Yannaras takes this a step further, especially in *Relational Ontology* (2011) and *The Enigma of Evil* (2012). In these two books he interprets Genesis in a way that tries as much as possible to take cognisance of the world as we know it. Two things trouble him in traditional exegesis. The first is its tendency to historicise the fall. It is still necessary in an Orthodox context to insist that denying the historicity of the Genesis story is not inconsistent with Christian faith – it is not outside the boundaries of the church's experience, as Yannaras puts it. Indeed, our modern scientific knowledge of the cosmogenic process makes a symbolic reading of Genesis imperative. Most symbolic readings, however, even one as rich as that of Nellas, still historicise the fall. But there never has been a time when nature was not "red in tooth and claw". The biocycle and the food chain have been operative since the first appearance of animate beings. A convincing symbolic reading has to take account of this. It has to refer not to an imaginary past but to the human situation as it really is.

The second thing that troubles Yannaras is the prevalence of a legal / juridical understanding of the fall that makes the historicity of the incarnation depend on the historicity of the fall. Paul's First Adam / Second Adam scheme is central to much Christian thinking. From it has developed the idea of the sacrifice of the cross as an expiation, a form of "satisfaction" for an original historical act of disobedience. Such an idea of divine "justice" is offensive today. The historicity of the incarnation, following an important strand of the Greek patristic tradition, needs to be freed from any idea that it was a response on God's part to human transgression.

Yannaras' solution to these problems is to posit that the world as we find it is the world as God created it. It has not been "corrupted" by some human sin so as to become inimical to humankind. What we call "natural evil" is simply existential finitude, the essential characteristic of the mode of createdness. Genesis teaches us to look beyond these existential limitations (which we experience in negative terms as decay, pain and death) and see creation as the result of a personal act. Either we can accept nature, says Yannaras, as irrevocably subject to the limitations of the created, to the irrationality of pain and death, or we can see it as the created result of an uncreated personal energy summoning us to the immediacy of a vital relation with the uncreated. In other words, either we can simply see nature as subject to laws that are oblivious to human well-being, or we can take seriously the implications of the statement in Genesis that the created world is "very good".

The symbolism of Genesis prompts us to choose the latter approach. The tree of the knowledge of good and evil stands for our potential to transcend the limitations of createdness. It is highly significant that it is only after Adam has eaten of the tree that God perceives a likeness to the divine in him: "Behold, the man has become like one of us" (Gen. 3:22). By ignoring the command not to eat of the tree, Adam refused the blessing of a transcendent relationship with God and chose self-contained autonomy instead. He aspired to likeness with God, but only by the mode by which God *is not*. Evil is a mode of existence, not a separate essence or nature. This is why Yannaras challenges Florovsky's interpretation of the fall, which seems to him to make of evil another causality hostile to the causality of creation. In other words, Florovsky appears to ontologise what in reality is only a mode of existence. Moreover, he speaks of evil as bringing down an irreparable disaster on created rational existences. But if that were so, God's creation would have been a failure, which cannot be. Nor can there be a polarised ontology of good and evil. What appears to be evil is simply the mode of the created, which is not evil because it is created, but only in a relative sense as the denial of the mode of fullness. The story of the fall is therefore a symbolic representation of our choice of self-contained autonomy, of non-relationship with God. It does not refer to a historical point at which creation became subject to corruption and decay.

Salvation as Deification

Modern Orthodox theology, says Nellas, rightly understands salvation not only negatively as redemption from the evils of slavery and death, but also positively as rebirth and deification, or *theosis*. Nellas follows the Fathers in seeing a fundamentally unbroken trajectory from humankind's deiform beginning to its theocentric end. The fall inflicted a wound on humanity but did not destroy the "in the image", nor did it frustrate the purpose for which humanity was created. The Logos became human, as intended from eternity, encountering humanity in its deiform core in order to raise it up to a new theandric mode of being. Before their hypostatic union in Christ, the two natures, human and divine, had a separate existence. After it, the human nature, while remaining fully human, was deified through its assumption by the divine. Human beings can participate in this, their *theosis* – the path to their completion and fulfilment in union with the Father – being accomplished through their Christification, which is initiated by baptism and continued actively through growth in the blessed flesh of Christ, the eucharistic body of the church. We do not grow merely as passive recipients of grace. Our work and that of God are closely interwoven factors of salvation which Nellas insists cannot be separated as they have been in the Western tradition since Augustine.

Nellas presents a therapeutic model of salvation, the healing by Christ of humanity's wounded nature through his incarnation and sacrifice on the cross. He also sees salvation as the outcome of Christ's triumphant struggle with the devil. For Yannaras, the latter point is a mythical element in the gospels that does not need to be accommodated in a modern interpretation of salvation. For him, as already noted, the fall is a symbolic representation of our choice of self-contained autonomy, of non-relationship with God. It is not a historical point at which creation became subject to decay and death, or at which it succumbed to demonic attack. The existential limitations of the created cosmos belong to its created character as such. If this then is the nature of evil, what is salvation? Salvation is to transcend the mortality of nature by realising the personal mode of existence which is God's. Accomplished historically by Christ through his self-surrender to the Father on the cross, salvation is appropriated by us through Christ in the eucharistic synaxis, the taking of food with thanksgiving being an experience of life as relation. This has implications for the whole cosmos. We are not redeemed from the world; we are the rational part of creation that brings it freely to fulfilment in God. Salvation therefore has an ontological dimension. It is not just a matter of the will, though of course the will plays a vital role, for a progressive *metanoia* is required from us, a putting to death of the "old man" of individualistic self-centredness and a rising in the "new man" of total personal self-offering. The fragmented state of human nature was restored in the theandric person of Christ, which raised what was in the *image* to the hypostatic reality of the *likeness*. Only creation's ultimate hypostatic union with God gives it meaning. The salvation of humanity in and through Christ means that our participation in the "new creation" is recapitulated in the person of Christ and has been raised by him through the cross to union with the Father.

Is Yannaras, then, a universalist? No, there are those for whom eternity will be experienced only as a ceaseless annihilation of relation. Yet the human person is no longer condemned to remain within the existential limits of natural individuality. To avail ourselves of this, however, we must become that which we were created to be – partakers in the freedom of love, which is true life – in the personal mode of existence which is the existence of God. It is only in the degree we can realise the personal mode of existence that belongs properly to God that we can transcend the mortality of our nature.

Conclusion

Both Nellas and Yannaras present rich symbolic readings of Genesis that seek to address modern concerns about the meaning of human existence and our relationship with the physical world around us. By putting on Christ, we are able to grow towards our fulfilment as human beings so that we come to participate in the divine mode of being. Yannaras goes further than Nellas in boldly asserting that the limitations of our "fallen" humanity are to be identified with the mode of createdness itself. In suggesting how the transcending of created finitude is the fulfilment of the purpose of our existence – not as isolated individuals but as the conscious rational tip of creation – he offers a credible alternative to the Barthian insistence that we find our fulfilment in our very finitude. None of this is the product of pure intellectualism but is the fruit of wrestling with the reality of human suffering.

References and Recommended Reading

Louth, Andrew (2009), "Some Recent Works by Christos Yannaras in English Translation", *Modern Theology*, Vol. 25, 329-340.
Nellas, Panayiotis (1968), *Prolegomena eis tin meletin Nikolaou tou Kavasila*, Athens: Panayiotis Nellas.
--- (1975), *I peri dikaioseos didaskalia Nikolaou tou Kavasila*, Athens: Karamperopoulos.
--- (1979), *Zoon theoumenon: Prooptikes yia mia orthodoxi katanoisi tou anthropou*, Athens: Armos. English translation (1987), *Deification in Christ: The Nature of the Human Person*, Crestwood: St Vladimir's Seminary Press.
Nichols, Aidan (1995), *Light from the East*, London: Sheed and Ward.
Russell, Norman (2006), "Modern Greek Theologians and the Greek Fathers", *Philosophy and Theology*, Vol. 18, 77-92.
Spiteris, Yannis (1992). *La teologia ortodossa neo-greca*, Bologna: Dehoniane.
Yannaras, Christos (1984), *The Freedom of Morality*, Crestwood: St Vladimir's Seminary Press.
--- (1991), *Elements of Faith*, Edinburgh: T & T Clark.
--- (2004a), *Postmodern Metaphysics*, Brookline: Holy Cross Orthodox Press.
--- (2004b), *Orthodoxy and the West*, Brookline: Holy Cross Orthodox Press.
--- (2005a), *On the Absence and Unknowability of God*, London / New York: T & T Clark International.
--- (2005b), *Variations on the Song of Songs*, Brookline: Holy Cross Orthodox Press.
--- (2007), *Person and Eros*, Brookline: Holy Cross Orthodox Press.
--- (2011), *Relational Ontology*, Brookline: Holy Cross Orthodox Press.
--- (2012), *The Enigma of Evil*, Brookline: Holy Cross Orthodox Press.

Norman Russell

Further Developments

In contemporary Orthodox writing, the unity of creation and salvation is generally taken for granted and rarely explored systematically. Numerous writers who have articulated a theology of creation in an "ecotheological" context, such as Patriarchs Bartholomew of Constantinople and Ignatius IV of Antioch, Metropolitan Kallistos (Ware) and John Chryssavgis, offer a sacramental vision of the cosmos and a cosmic vision of salvation. They draw on patristic theology and develop the thought of many of the writers discussed above, as well as other heirs to the Paris renewal in Russian theology. These include the liturgical theologian Alexander Schmemann, for whom human thanksgiving and offering restore the world to its original meaning, which is at the same time its ultimate meaning and goal; and Olivier Clément, for whom cosmology is a "gnosis" given in Christ, revealing a world created to become Eucharist. Importantly, this is a vision emerging just as strongly from liturgical and spiritual life as from theological study, as can also be observed in Metropolitan Anthony (Bloom) of Sourozh or pioneers of the modern Athonite revival such as archimandrites Vasileios of Iviron and Aimilianos of Simonopetra.

Those who explore the unity of creation and salvation more systematically generally do so in dialogue with the Church Fathers – usually Maximus, but also Palamas and Irenaeus. In Russia, many of the pre-eminent theologians of recent decades received their spiritual formation in the underground "catacomb church" of the Soviet era, in which Soloviev and his successors, including representatives of the Paris School, were read and re-appropriated. The remarkable influence of Aleksandr Men', whose insistence that the salvific work of the gospel, hitherto operative in various conditions of cultural domesticity and specificity, was still in its infancy, offered to a globalised and globalising world a vision of creation and salvation that was at once universal, in the sense of encompassing the entire cosmos, and ecumenical, in that it necessarily involved all humanity. More recently, as a counterpart of Men', Sergei Khoruzhii has developed a new school of thinking under the name of "synergetic anthropology", which aims to introduce a qualitatively new understanding of the human being as an "energetic phenomenon" drawing on the essence-energy distinction in Palamism and the ascetic practices of Athonite hesychasm while paying due attention to post-Heideggerian Western thought. The Russian synergetic school recapitulates much of the emphasis of previous Eastern thought on creation and salvation – the resolution of the divine-creaturely dynamic into the ontological relation between humanity, as the focus of creation, and God; the envisioning of a historical movement of creaturely being toward deification through human agency – yet what is new is its singular focus on the energetic nexus of creaturely transformation. The "catching of the divine energies" that move in creation, or the acquisition (*stiazhanie*) of divine grace, is understood as the prerogative of ascesis, the final goal being the synergy (*synergia*) of divine and human energies. In such a way, Khoruzhii develops the patristic concept of synergy into the basis for a new anthropological conception of the human constitution directed toward the "unlocking" of this human constitution in a newly constellated realm of personal being of the kind shared by the hypostases of the Holy Trinity.

Modern writers frequently revisit the idea, developed most fully by Maximus, of a "word" or "essential principle" belonging to each entity and embracing its creation, becoming and ultimate rest in God. This is explored in detail, and in dialogue with contemporary theological thinking, in Nikolaos Loudovikos's recent *A Eucharistic Ontology* (2010). It is also worked out, rather more accessibly, by Basil Osborne in his book *The Healing Word* (2008), with its insistence on a world inherently "God-friendly", created for the coming of the Saviour. His conclusion – of obvious ecological relevance – is that for humans to live according to their own essential principle requires being in tune with the "deep structure" of the universe.

A rather different but no less Christocentric understanding of creation and salvation is suggested by John Behr. Taking Irenaeus as his starting point, he argues that creation and salvation cannot be seen as distinct entities at all, but rather as the continuous activity of God in his handiwork, bringing the creature to the stature of the Saviour for whom it came into being. It is not clear how non-human creation fits into the picture; but this illustrates again the degree to which the unity of creation and salvation is embedded in contemporary Orthodox thought, and continues to inspire new exploration.

References and Recommended Reading

Behr, John (2006), *The Mystery of Christ: Life in Death*, Crestwood: St Vladimir's Seminary Press.

Chryssavgis, John (2004), *Light through Darkness: The Orthodox Tradition*, London: Darton, Longman and Todd.

Clément, Olivier (2000), *On Human Being: A Spiritual Anthropology*, London: New City.

Khoruzhii, Sergei (1998), *K fenomenologii askezy*, Moscow: Izd-vo gumanitarnoi literatury.

Loudovikos, Nikolaos (2010), *A Eucharistic Ontology: Maximus the Confessor's Eschatological Ontology of Being as Dialogical Reciprocity*, Brookline: Holy Cross Orthodox Press.

Men', Alexander (1996), *Christianity for the 21st Century: The Prophetic Writings of Alexander Men'* (edited by E. Roberts and A. Shukman), New York: Continuum.

Osborne, Basil (2008), *The Healing Word*, London: Darton, Longman and Todd.

Schmemann, Alexander (2003), *Introduction to Liturgical Theology*, Crestwood: St Vladimir's Seminary Press.

Theokritoff, Elizabeth (2009), *Living in God's Creation: Orthodox Perspectives on Ecology*, Crestwood: St Vladimir's Seminary Press.

Ware, Kallistos (1995), *The Orthodox Way*, Crestwood: St Vladimir's Seminary Press.

Elizabeth Theokritoff and Oliver Smith

2. Roman Catholic Theologies

Edited by Denis Edwards

Introduction

The Roman Catholic theological tradition has been incarnational and sacramental in character. It has tended to embrace the natural world as God's good creation. Theology is usually thought of as involving the whole of reality, in the pre-Reformation and pre-Enlightenment threefold pattern of interrelationships between human beings, the rest of the natural world and God. The whole created world, and every entity in it, has been seen as the place of divine presence. Every creature is understood as held in being by the transcendent triune God, who is profoundly immanent to each as the source of its existence and actions. The natural world is seen as revelatory of the Creator, and theologians from Augustine to Bonaventure speak of the "Book of Nature" that is to be read alongside of, and illuminated by, the "Book of the Bible".

For the great medieval theologians, the God who brings us salvation in Jesus Christ is the God of creation. Hildegard of Bingen (1098-1179), for example, combines a rich theology of the saving love of Jesus Christ with a theology of the Holy Spirit present in the whole natural world as the ever-present source of life. She uses the word "greenness" (*veriditas*) to speak of the fruitfulness of the Spirit in the green abundance of nature and in the abundance of grace in our spiritual journeys. For Bonaventure (1221-1274) the whole of creation springs from the "Fountain of Fullness" (*fontalis plenitudo*) and is created through the Word, the divine exemplar for all creatures, as the free expression of the ecstatic fecundity of the divine life of the Trinity. The natural world is the work of art produced by divine Wisdom, the Wisdom made flesh for our salvation in Jesus of Nazareth. Thomas Aquinas (1225-1274) combines a positive view of God's creation with a classical theology of redemption in Christ. He too sees the abundance and the diversity of creation as the self-expression of the Creator:

> The distinction and variety of things comes from the intention of the first agent. God brought many things into being in order that the divine goodness might be communicated to creatures and be represented in them. Because this divine goodness could not be adequately represented by one creature alone, God produced many diverse creatures so that what was lacking in one in the representation of divine goodness might by supplied by another. For goodness, which in God is simple and uniform, is manifold and divided in creatures. Thus the whole universe together participates in divine goodness more perfectly and represents it better than any single creature whatsoever (*Summa Theologiae*, 1.47.1).

Aquinas sees God, the primary cause, as acting in creation through all the interconnected world of created (secondary) causes, which have their own dignity and integrity. His legacy is one of respect for the natural world and thus for the role of the natural sciences. While he sees our humanity as distorted by sin and in radical need of redemption, he does not see it as totally corrupt, but as open to grace, so that the saving grace of Jesus Christ builds on nature.

This positive assessment of the place of creation in Roman Catholic theology needs qualification. Neo-Platonism left its mark in hierarchical patterns of thought and tendencies towards dualism. Catholic piety was too often individualistic and escapist in its attitude to creation. Catholic leadership failed drastically in its response to emerging science in the Galileo affair, in part because of an inadequate biblical hermeneutic. In the 19th century the Catholic Church strenuously resisted the positive gains of modernity, but did not altogether escape its narrowing of vision to the individual subject. It failed to come to terms with Darwin's evolutionary insights until the 1950s, by which time a flourishing of biblical scholarship had cleared the way for Roman Catholics to embrace both the new insights of evolutionary science and the theological insights of the Bible. Teilhard de Chardin (1881-1955), the most original and creative 20th-century Catholic thinker on the relationship between science and theology, was not allowed to publish his theological work during his lifetime.

The modernist crisis in the Catholic Church of the early 20th century had meant that instead of continuing in the tradition set by great creative 19th-century thinkers, like Johann Adam Möhler (1796-1838) and John Henry Newman (1801-1890), Catholic intellectual life was dominated by lifeless neo-scholastic "manual theology". From the 1930s some theologians in Belgium, Germany and France began to break free of "manual theology" and to return to the great sources of Christian tradition, understood as the Scriptures, the liturgical tradition, the Fathers of the Church and the great medieval thinkers like Aquinas and Bonaventure, seen now in their own historical context.

In spite of the fact that this *ressourcement* theology had led in some instances to disciplinary action by church authority against particular views, it flourished and provided the theological foundation for the renewal of church life by the Second Vatican Council (1962-1965). Key figures in this movement of theology include Dom Odo Casel, Romano Guardini, Karl Adam, Marie-Dominique Chenu, Yves Congar, Henri de Lubac, Jean Danielou and Joseph Ratzinger. By and large this theology was characterised by evident respect and love for the great biblical, liturgical and theological tradition of Christianity combined with an openness to the modern world and a dialogical approach to it.

In the context of the *ressourcement* and the renewal of theology before, in and after the Council, four major theological figures emerged who have shaped Catholic theology over the last generation, and who shape it still. The German theologian Karl Rahner (1904-1984) built on Aquinas to develop a transcendental theology of the human person as a subject radically open in knowing and loving to absolute Mystery and as finding in Christ the Word of God that reveals and saves. Rahner's theology treats explicitly of the interrelationship between creation and salvation and of the interrelationship between science and theology. Canadian theologian Bernard Lonergan (1904-1984) was a transcendental Thomist whose approach has some parallels with Rahner's, but who was far more focussed on dealing creatively with fundamental methodological issues in philosophy and theology. He made major contributions to systematic theology in the areas of the theology of the incarnation and of the Trinity, and opened up a dialogue between theology and economics.

Swiss theologian Hans Urs von Balthasar (1905-1988) opposed what he saw as Rahner's accommodation to modernity and sought to develop a Christ-centred theology that challenged post-Enlightenment culture. Von Balthasar united theology and mysticism in a broad synthesis, understood as a theological aesthetics that opens to a theological dramatics of the glory of God incarnate in Jesus Christ. Belgian theologian Edward Schillebeeckx (1914-2009) began his work with some of the more philosophical issues that concerned Rahner and Lonergan, but moved decisively to an exegetical approach to the New Testament in his later theological works on Jesus, salvation and the church. For Schillebeeckx, salvation is a central theme, above all in the light of the excess of human suffering, but salvation is always seen in the context of a strongly positive theology of creation.

Denis Edwards

Karl Rahner (1904-1984) – The Divine Self-Bestowal

Introduction

Karl Rahner's theology is astonishing in its range as well as its depth. Most of his publications are in the form of short essays, some exploring the theological meaning of an immense variety of everyday experiences, others rethinking the central truths of Christian faith. Throughout his career he was concerned to engage with the evolutionary worldview of contemporary science. One of the keys to his theology is the way he sees creation and salvation in Christ as united in the divine act of self-bestowing love.

Born in Freiburg-im-Breisgau on 5 March 1904, Rahner entered the Society of Jesus in 1922. His theology was deeply influenced by the mysticism of Ignatius, with its basis in the experience of God and its commitment to the radical following of Jesus and to finding God in all things. In 1934 Rahner returned to Freiburg where he attended the seminars of Martin Heidegger and began his doctoral work which involved a rereading of Aquinas in the light of questions raided by Kant, with the aid of the transcendental Thomism of Joseph Maréchal. In his early work Rahner contributed to the "turn to the subject" in Roman Catholic theology. He proposed that in all human acts of knowledge and love of a specific other in the world, there is always an implicit transcendental openness to the infinite, to mystery. The "whither" of this experience of transcendence is revealed in Christ to be the God of grace, ever-present in self-offering love. Rahner became an influential figure at the Second Vatican Council and a leading contributor to post-conciliar theology.

A good overview of Rahner's theology is found in his *Foundations of Christian Faith: An Introduction to the Idea of Christianity* (1978). Key essays on the theme of this book can be found in the twenty-three volumes of his *Theological Investigations* (1961-1992):[1] "The Eternal Significance of the Humanity of Jesus for our Salvation" (*TI 3*, 35-46); "Dogmatic Questions on Easter" (*TI 4*, 121-133); "The Hermeneutics of Eschatological Assertions" (*TI 4*, 323-346); "Christology within an Evolutionary View of the World" (*TI 5*, 157-192); "Christology in the Setting of Modern Man's Understanding of Himself and his World" (*TI 11*, 215-229); "Natural Science and Christian Faith" (*TI 21*, 16-55); and "The Specific Character of the Christian Concept of God" (*TI 21*, 185-195). Also relevant arc his *Hominization: The Evolutionary Origin of Man as a Theological Problem* (1965) and his essay "Evolution" in the *Encylopedia of Theology: A Concise Sacramentum Mundi* (1975), which he edited.

---

1 References in parentheses in this section are to Rahner's *Theological Investigations* (*TI*).

Creation and Salvation as Divine Self-Bestowal

What is central to Rahner's understanding of Christian revelation is that God gives God's self to us in the Word made flesh and in the Spirit poured out in grace. God is revealed as a God who bestows God's very self on creatures. Based on the nature of the self-bestowal revealed in the Christ-event, Rahner sees this same self-bestowal as defining every aspect of God's action in creation, salvation and final fulfilment. He sees the creation of the universe of creatures as an element in the radical decision of God to give God's self in love to that which in not divine. The story of the universe, and everything that science can tell us about its evolution, is part of a larger story, the story of divine self-bestowal. When God wills to bestow God's self in love, creation comes to be as the addressee of this self-bestowal. The history of the evolution of the universe, and of life on our planet, exists within this larger vision of the divine purpose.

In *The Cambridge Companion to Karl Rahner*, Harvey Egan suggests that the shortest possible summary of Rahner's theological enterprise is "his creative appropriation of Scotus's view that God creates in order to communicate *self* and that creation exists to be the recipient of God's free gift of self".[2] The incarnation is not simply the result of sin, but always God's intention and the very meaning of the creation of a universe of creatures. Given that sin exists, God's self-giving in the incarnation brings forgiveness, healing, transformation and deification.

God freely chooses, from the beginning, to create a world in which the Word would be made flesh and the Spirit poured out. As Rahner puts it in his *Foundations of Christian Faith*, creation and incarnation are "two moments and two phases of the *one* process of God's self-giving and self-expression, although it is an intrinsically differentiated process".[3]

In the relationship of grace, God does not simply act on us in the way a creaturely efficient cause might act on another created reality. Rahner sees God's action in grace as more like that of a formal cause, in that God, while remaining completely the transcendent One, freely gives God's self to the human creature and so transforms the creature. On the basis that creation is one and that the one history of creation is directed to divine self-bestowal, Rahner proposes that the divine indwelling characteristic of grace is an appropriate analogy for characterising the fundamental relationship that God has with the world in general. This means that Rahner can say that while pantheism is rejected and God remains ever-transcendent, the creative immanence of God to the world is of such a kind that the reality of God is imparted to the world as its supreme specification. It is not simply that God creates something different over against God's self, but that God freely communicates God's own reality to the created other. The universe emerges in the process of God's self-bestowal. The transcendent God is immanent to the world of creatures in self-giving love.

---

[2] Marmion and Hines, 16.

[3] Rahner (1978), 197.

The Self-Transcendence of Creation

Alongside the concept of divine self-bestowal, a second fundamental concept in Rahner's thought unites creation, incarnation and final fulfilment, the idea of the self-transcendence of creation. This concept is worked out in Rahner's anthropology and in his evolutionary Christology, but it functions in many aspects of his theology, including his eschatology. The two concepts are deeply interrelated. It is God's self-bestowal in creation and incarnation that enables the self-transcendence of creaturely reality.

Traditional theology understood God's ongoing creative act as both sustaining creatures in being (*conservatio*) and enabling them to act (*concursus*). Rahner embraces this theology but transforms it into a theology of becoming, a theology of active self-transcendence. He reflects on the transitions to the new in the history of the universe, particularly when matter becomes life, and when life becomes self-conscious spirit. He sees that the emergence of the new is in need of explanation, not only at the level of science, which has its own integrity, but also at the level of theology. God's creative act needs to be understood not only as enabling the universe to exist, but also as enabling it to become what is radically new. He sees self-transcendence as a dynamism that is truly intrinsic to creation but which occurs through the creative presence and power of the immanent God. In a late article he writes of the "constant pressure" of the divine being that enables creation to become more than it is in itself (*TI 21*, 37).

The "self" in self-transcendence indicates that the evolutionary capacity is truly intrinsic to the created universe. The capacity for emergence comes from within and, at the empirical level, the emergence of the new is completely open to scientific explanation. There are no gaps at the empirical level that theology should fill. God's creative presence and action operates at another level. Just as God's creative act enables creatures to exist and to interact, so this same creative presence of God enables the new to emerge. Emergence is a creaturely reality, but it exists because of God's creative act. God's presence in self-bestowing love enables creatures to exist, to interact and to emerge into the new.

To use an image from process theology, the divine "lure" towards emergence, along with its divine enabling and empowering, comes from the Creator Spirit. It does not belong to the essence of the creature and, as God's creative act, cannot be discerned by the natural sciences. It is understood in terms of the interior, dynamic relationship of all things in the evolving universe to their Creator. What can be discerned by the sciences is the result of this divine act, a world of creatures that exist and interact in dynamic patterns of emergence.

Rahner proposes a theology of self-transcendence that embraces creation and incarnation and the final transformation of creaturely reality in God. He sees the material universe as transcending itself in the emergence of life, and life transcending itself in the human. In human beings, the universe becomes open to self-consciousness and freedom, and to a fully personal response to God's self-bestowal in grace. Within this context of an emergent and self-transcending universe, the Christ-event is the radical self-transcendence of the created universe into God. From the side of creatures, Jesus is a human being of flesh and blood, made of elements formed in the stars, part of evolutionary history here on earth. From the side of God, Jesus Christ is the irreversible culmination of God's self-bestowal, the eternal Word of God made flesh in our history. Jesus is both God's radical self-bestowal to creation and, in his life and death, the radical "yes!" of creation to God.

It can be concluded that for Rahner, there are two fundamental characteristics of divine action in creation and salvation. On the one hand, divine action is an act of divine self-bestowal. On the other hand, this divine action works dynamically through the self-transcendence of creatures. These two aspects are mutually interrelated: It is God present in self-bestowing love who enables creaturely self-transcendence. As Rahner constantly insists, divine action and creaturely action are not in competition. God's action enables creaturely emergence in and through the processes and laws of nature studied by the sciences. For Karl Rahner, divine self-bestowal and creaturely self-transcendence both characterise not only creation, grace and incarnation, but also the final consummation of all things in Christ.

Resurrection as the Beginning of the Transformation of the Universe

In an article written in the 1950s, and found in the fourth volume of his *Theological Investigations*, Rahner explores doctrinal questions concerning the resurrection. He notes that much Western theology has tended to give central place to Christ's death, while the resurrection has been marginalised. Rahner finds that when compared with its New Testament origins, the theology of resurrection has suffered an "astonishing process of shrinkage". A central reason for this shrinkage, he suggests, is that Western theology has tended to adopt a purely juridical interpretation of the redemption. Jesus Christ, as both fully divine and fully human, has been seen as able to make satisfaction for the insult offered to God by human sin. In this kind of theology there is little place for the resurrection, except in terms of the personal bliss of Jesus in his glorified humanity.

This Western focus is in stark contrast to the theology of the East, where the resurrection plays a fundamental role in the theology of salvation. In this Eastern view, redemption is seen as a real ontological process which began in the incarnation and ends in the divinisation of the world. There are three themes in this kind of theology that play an important role in Rahner's thought: salvation as ontological rather than juridical, the idea of the divinisation of the world rather than the salvation of humans in isolation from the rest of creation, and the resurrection of Christ as the beginning of this divinising transfiguration of creation.

The death of Jesus remains central for Rahner, but always in close interconnection with the resurrection. He sees death as the final act of a human being by which the whole of a person's life is gathered up in a free decision. The death of Christ is the definitive act of freedom that encompasses his whole life. The resurrection is not simply an event that occurs after Jesus' death, but a manifestation of what happens in the death, as Jesus freely hands his whole bodily existence into the mystery of a loving God. Part of this world is handed over freely into God, in complete obedience and love, and is fully taken up into God. This event is salvific for the whole of reality. The resurrection is the event in which God irrevocably adopts creaturely reality as God's own reality. This adoption occurs by God's primordial act, which has "already" found expression in the incarnation of the Word. It is this that culminates in the resurrection, when God divinises and transfigures the creature.

Because of the unity of the world that springs from the Creator, this is an event for the whole of creation. What occurs in Jesus, as part of the physical, biological and human world, is ontologically, and not simply juridically, "the embryonically final beginning of the glorification and divinisation of the whole of reality" (*TI 4*, 129). It is, as Rahner states in his *Encyclopedia of Theology*, "the beginning of the transformation of the world as an ontologically interconnected occurrence".[4] In the resurrection of Jesus, the final destiny of the world is decided and already begun. In his risen state Jesus is freed from the limiting individuality of his unglorified body and is present to all of creation. Jesus risen is both the divine promise and the real beginning of the fulfilment of the whole creation.

The history of Jesus that reaches its completion in death abides in the resurrection life and possesses a saving function. The saving significance of his life is fully accepted by God and set free to work in the transformation of the world. The transfigured reality of Christ remains the mediator to the immediacy of God. Rahner holds to the theological principle that the humanity of Jesus has enduring significance for the salvation of the world. Jesus Christ is forever the openness of created reality to God.

Conclusion

For Karl Rahner, creation and salvation are deeply united in the one act of divine self-bestowal to creation. It is God present in self-bestowing love who enables a universe of creatures to evolve in an emergent way through self-transcendence. Jesus Christ is God's radical self-bestowal to a world of creatures and, in his life and death, he is at the same time the culmination of the self-transcendence of the world of creatures to God. The resurrection of Christ is the divine promise, and the real beginning, of the deifying transformation and fulfilment of the whole universe of creatures.

References and Recommended Reading

Edwards, Denis (2006), "Resurrection of the Body and Transformation of the Universe in the Theology of Karl Rahner", *Philosophy and Theology*, Vol. 18, 357-383.

Marmion, D. and Hines, M. E. (eds.) (2005), *The Cambridge Companion to Karl Rahner*, Cambridge: Cambridge University Press.

O'Donovan, L. (1980), *A World of Grace: An Introduction to the Themes and Foundations of Karl Rahner's Theology*, New York: Seabury.

O'Meara, T. F. (2007), *God in the World: A Guide to Karl Rahner's Theology*, Collegeville: Liturgical Press.

Rahner, Karl (1961-1992), *Theological Investigations* (23 volumes), London, Baltimore and New York.

--- (1965), *Hominization: The Evolutionary Origin of Man as a Theological Problem*, London: Burns and Oats.

--- (1975), "Evolution", in: Karl Rahner(ed.), *Encylopedia of Theology: A Concise Sacramentum Mundi*, London: Burns and Oats.

--- (1978), *Foundations of Christian Faith: An Introduction to the Idea of Christianity* (translated by William Dych), New York: Seabury.

Denis Edwards

[4] Rahner (1975), 1142.

Bernard Lonergan (1904-1984) – God Operates Always and Everywhere

Introduction

Bernard Lonergan was a Jesuit priest, a philosopher and theologian. He was also educated in mathematics and economics. In his short biography, *Lonergan*, Frederick Crowe, SJ observes that Lonergan's formation in the tradition of Ignatius of Loyola contributed a key idea of his later theology: God operates always and everywhere.[5] This pervasive and unrelenting presence of God throughout time and space is the remote context of his theology of creation and salvation.

Lonergan is best known for his works on methodology and the reclaiming of the human subject. The aim of his life work was to address the major problems of his time within the context of Catholic theology, which he regarded as being seriously behind in addressing modernity. He did so by demonstrating (a) the underlying intelligibility of the world (including creation) and (b) the ability of the human subject to grasp this intelligibility, to make judgements about truth and falsehood and to decide authentically about value and praxis. His two major and best-known works are *Insight: A Study of Human Understanding* (1957) and *Method in Theology* (1972). While these works are foundational in understanding the entire corpus of his thought, Lonergan addressed the theology of salvation more specifically in *On the Incarnate Word* (1964); in "Mission and Spirit" and "Christology Today: Methodological Reflections";[6] and in *The Way to Nicea: The Dialectical Development of Trinitarian Theology* (1976). *Insight* is also valuable in understanding his view of creation within the modern scientific context.

For Lonergan there is no division between creation and salvation. Neither was seen as necessity – God was not bound to create or to redeem. So the intelligibility of the universe as created and redeemed rests on the contingent nature of both. The facts are that the universe exists and is experienced in a certain way, and that humans have been redeemed according to New Testament revelation. The intelligibility that inheres in both is due to the order that belongs to the creative act of God. It is important to note that Lonergan does not understand intelligibility to mean that the full reality of God is graspable by human intelligence. Rather, God is also the subject of religious experience and, hence, "an orientation to transcendent mystery" lies at the heart of systematic theology. In *Insight*, Lonergan defines the term "mystery".[7] Mystery relates to two aspects of humanness: the unrestricted questioning at the heart of human knowing and a corresponding orientation to personal transformation in human life. The continuing emergence of the physical universe, the history of the world and the daily joys and struggles of the human community within a created and redeemed world all constitute a richly diverse but unified process originating in the love of the same God.

Making Sense of Creation in Modernity

Lonergan's articulation of the theology of creation addresses, first of all, the modern scientific understanding of the functioning of the physical universe. So, his account of

---

5 Crowe (1992), 2.

6 See Crowe (1985), 23-34, 74-99.

7 Lonergan (1957), 554-572.

creation is not concerned primarily with how the Creator creates. Nor is his theology an apologetic which would counter scientific discoveries and theories, correlate them to Christian tradition, or fall back to an assertion that all is unknowable about God's role in creation. For Lonergan, the world is intelligible. As creations of God, humans possess a capacity for grasping intelligibility that inheres in the entire universe, all of which is the product of an intelligent God.

The physical universe is subject to laws and it is emergent, according to Lonergan. In *Insight*, he lays out an account of the intelligibility of the universe. By this account, he addresses two modern misperceptions of the physical universe: (a) that the universe is a determined, mechanical process governed by either known or discoverable laws and (b) that the nature of the universe is not governed by any discernable laws but is merely a chaos, composed of discrete events. How could such a universe be the creation of a God as Christians have traditionally understood God – omnipotent, omniscient and all-caring? Lonergan calls his account of the intelligibility of the universe "emergent probability".

Emergent probability consists of the order inherent in both statistical and classical laws, both operating in the emergence and survival of cyclic relationships which Lonergan calls "schemes of recurrence". Classical laws and laws of probability both result from the human acts of knowing – paying attention to data, understanding the data, validating through judgement the insight into data and affirming a virtually unconditioned truth. Such a truth is by definition what one can make of the available data at any particular time; a virtually unconditioned truth remains always open to new insights and judgements. What differs between classical and statistical laws is merely the kind of data one is processing. Classical laws refer to what is observed to be the ideal, "everything else being equal", while statistical laws relate to the concrete circumstances in which "everything else" is hardly ever equal. Both kinds of laws indicate order.

The universe is also emergent. By this Lonergan means that whole new realities come into being over time. They come into being within schemes of relationships, all of which are mutually interactive. The occurrence and survival of events are probable and the likelihood is also mutually conditioned and dependent. So if there are events A, B and C, their interdependent likelihood of occurrence and survival might be related as follows: If A occurs, then B will occur and then C, but if C occurs, then A will continue to occur, initiating the cycle again. Schemes interact themselves similarly and thus affect whole patterns of emergence in world process. Thus emergent probability offers a heuristic of which physical and historical occurrences are instances. As noted above, what Lonergan accomplishes in his heuristic account is an account of the universe as intelligible.

The emergent world process also exhibits a vertical finality. For Lonergan the process is at the same time hierarchal and dynamic. He explains these qualities of the universe within his notion of vertical finality. Just as the divinely given and divinely oriented human desire to know heads towards a fuller grasp of the intelligibility inherent in all, so too the universe is so structured that it heads towards fuller being. In Lonergan's words, finality means "an upwardly but indeterminately directed dynamism towards ever fuller realization of being". The universe "is not at rest, not static, not fixed in the present, but in process, in tension, in fluid".[8] In such a hierarchy, finality can be of several kinds, depending on the end of the process. What we observe, however, is the relationship of the emergent universe to the end, not the end itself. Hierarchy in evolution portrays a vertical finality in which each higher stage is not of higher value than the former, but rather each successive stage sublates the former. The lower remains necessary and the stages are usually mutually beneficial as well as beneficial to the entire process. Sublation confronts the modern mistakes of reductionism, on the one hand, and instrumentalisation, on the other. Whole realities are not understood as mere composites of former, lower parts; a new dimension is added. While the former levels are instrumental in the emergence of the present, they retain their own intrinsic wholeness and identity that is not fully explainable in terms of that utility.

In his account of world process, Lonergan is also concerned to show the integral place of humankind within the whole created order. "The advent of man [*sic*] does not abrogate that rule of emergent probability", he wrote in *Insight*.[9] God did not make a mistake in creating as God did. Humans form an integral part of emergent probability. Whereas human activity is intelligible in terms of classical and statistical laws, and thus subject to such laws, humans also can take initiative in influencing probabilities. In other words, while human history is intelligible, humans are also intelligent. In authentically following the human quest for fuller being, exercising authentic knowing, deciding and acting, humans enact intelligent schemes or exert corrective influence on existing schemes also toward a finality, the absolute of which is fullness of being in God. While Lonergan gives his initial account of world process and the integral human role within it, he understands such process within a world already subject to divine redemption. In terms of sublation, natural processes are sublated within the power of God's unlimited and unceasing love, but God's love also precedes the authentic operation of world process, sustains world process and is its very source.

Creation, Sin and Redemption

Lonergan begins with the contingency of sin and redemption on the basis of revelation. There is sin and there is redemption. The question for him is what sense can one make of these realities; what is their immanent intelligibility? Lonergan addressed this question in a course on Christology which was later published as *On the Incarnate Word* (1964). In this course, he explores the many images and symbols that the New Testament and the Christian tradition have invoked in order to understand and explain the meaning of salvation by Jesus Christ. The images and symbols all give us clues, he concludes, to the intelligibility of redemption. "It is the victory of suffering, of accepting the consequences of sin, the evils of this world, in the spirit that animated Christ. It is the transformation of the world that arises when evil is transformed into good by the Christian spirit."[10] The understanding of this conclusion is explicated further throughout the rest of Lonergan's works. Most importantly, the intelligibility of redemption by the life, death and resurrection of Christ rests on his understanding of sin. Lonergan works this out within his account of world process, that is, emergent probability.

---

[8] Lonergan (1957), 452, 445.

[9] Lonergan (1957), 235.

[10] Lonergan (1988), 28.

Lonergan recognised the varieties and degrees of what has been traditionally labelled sin: individual egotism, group biases and what he called "the longer cycle of decline". It is the latter which consumes most of Lonergan's attention and which most clearly arises from his conception of the unity of creation and redemption.

First of all, it should be noted that Lonergan sees all sin as a surd, that which is non-intelligible. Since being coincides with that which is intelligible, the fullness of being with the sum total of all that is known and can be known, sin is non-being. Thus the longer cycle of decline wreaks havoc on the intelligibility of a world created and loved by God. The longer cycle of decline results from an ambiguity in the common-sense world of practicality and ordinary human life. In the experience of everyday, the decisions by which we live, one can observe an ambiguity. Common sense is defined by its attention to the immediate and to the practical solution. While this is necessary to building a viable human life, it may also lead to a dysfunction. The dysfunction occurs where practicality reigns unchecked by higher viewpoints and more long-term perspectives. What might be detrimental in the long run is over time systematically excluded from ordinary life. Such long-term views are the purview of theory and of culture. As this process of exclusion intensifies, theory and culture are devalued and eventually isolated from society. If left unchecked, eventually the longer viewpoints and such insights as those of the arts, the academy and religion, become no longer available to the proceeding generations. Seeking solutions becomes increasingly difficult. Society has become largely unintelligible and the data required to change it have become largely unavailable. This situation is what Lonergan calls "the social surd".

From an existential perspective, the social surd is a condition of alienation in which humans become the victims of their own creation. In building on Lonergan's theology of sin and redemption, William Loewe suggests that the category of original sin in contemporary terms "designates the dynamics of alienation and dehumanization in so far as they inform the situation into which we are born and into which we are socialized".[11] The longer cycle of decline is Lonergan's heuristic explanation of such sinful situations. How then is redemption a solution to sin? Lonergan addresses this question from two viewpoints: (a) from the objective reality of Christ's life, death and resurrection and (b) from the perspective of human, especially Christian, activity in the world.

Despite original sin, however articulated, humans still share the created capacity to love family and friends, to build community and to fight evil. There is a natural capacity to love God, Lonergan claims in an essay entitled "Mission and Spirit".[12] However, humans live under the reign of sin and "redemption lies not in what is possible to nature but in what is effected by the grace of God".[13] The sending of the Son into the world was (like the creation) a self-communication of God, a gift of divine love. Loewe has identified Lonergan's "law of the cross" to be a succinct summary of his theology of redemption. The law of the cross moves from the biblical expressions of death as the penalty for sin, through transformation of death through love to the blessing of

[11] Loewe, 162.

[12] See Crowe (1985), 23-34.

[13] Crowe (1985), 30.

new life.[14] Dying here means more than physical death. Primarily it refers to the dying of dehumanisation and victimhood which are the result of sin. The longer cycle of decline results in such dying. In choosing death, Jesus confronted the cycle of decline that existed during his lifetime in a specific society. Jesus' life portrays a subversion of the society of his day – the inequalities of his society, the false expectations of a messiah with power, the oppression of a people. His death was a continuation; any choice but death in his circumstances would have indicated a capitulation to a sinful condition. Through his life and death, dying was transformed in his love for his Father and for the world. His dying then was not as a victim of a vengeful or punitive God. Rather, Jesus transformed the inevitable outcome of his refusal to be subjugated to a sinful world into an act of love and into the blessing of new life.

From the perspective of human activity in the world, Lonergan painstakingly lays out in *Method in Theology* the structure of transformation within a series of conversions. These conversions are the path to authentic new life, the transformed dying that confronts the reality of sin. They are the solution to evil. On the one hand, they originate in the nature of humans from their creation – the orientation to mystery. On the other hand, they are the fruit of an experience that humans did not bring about but "underwent", the experience of grace. Grace, the infusion of the Holy Spirit, sublates (does not replace) the human experience for self-transcendence and the human experience of frustration with "a world distorted by sin" as well as one's own incapacity "to break with evil ways". One's heart is touched at the personal level so that new circumstances and new encounters occur; the reality of the sin of the world becomes clearer; and one experiences a new community in which faith, hope and love can overcome the dying that is the penalty of sin.[15]

Conclusion

In Lonergan's theology, the unity of creation and salvation rests on the unity of a loving, revealing and acting God. Salvation does not abrogate creation, just as the emergence of humans does not abrogate the rest of creation. His heuristic account of emergent probability uncovers an intelligibility in the plan of God for the world. This intelligibility itself is grounded in the mystery of a divine presence, an absolute finality that is operative in the free and dynamic orientation of all things to that love that both creates and transforms all.

References and Recommended Reading

Crowe, Frederick E. (1992), *Lonergan*, Collegeville, Minnesota: Liturgical Press.

Crowe, Frederick E. (ed.) (1985), *A Third Collection: Papers by Bernard J. F. Lonergan SJ*, Mahwah: Paulist Press.

Dalton, Anne Marie (1999), *A Theology for the Earth: The Contributions of Thomas Berry and Bernard Lonergan*, Ottawa: University of Ottawa Press.

Loewe, William P. (1996), *A College Student's Introduction to Christology*, Collegeville: Liturgical Press.

Lonergan, Bernard (1957), *Insight: A Study of Human Understanding*, London: Longman, Green and Co.

[14] Loewe, 163-173.

[15] See Crowe (1985), 32-33.

--- (1964), *On the Incarnate Word*, Rome: Pontifical Gregorian University.
--- (1972), *Method in Theology*, New York: Herder and Herder.
--- (1976), *The Way to Nicea: The Dialectical Development of Trinitarian Theology*, London: Darton, Longman and Todd.
--- (1988), *Philosophical and Theological Papers* (edited by Robert C. Croker and Frederick E. Crowe), Toronto: University of Toronto Press.

Anne Marie Dalton

Hans Urs von Balthasar (1905-1988) – A Theo-Drama

Introduction[16]

Hans Urs von Balthasar was born in Lucerne, Switzerland, on 12 August 1905 and initially studied German literature and philosophy at the universities of Vienna, Berlin and Zurich. As a boy he was educated in Benedictine and Jesuit schools, and the influence of the Jesuit tradition of Ignatius of Loyola remained highly significant to his thought. *The Spiritual Exercises* were formative in his decision to become a priest while a doctoral student in Zurich and had a significant influence on the subsequent development of his theology. The latter shows up both his background in literary studies and an enduring influence of Thomas Aquinas, especially Aquinas's metaphysics, interpreted through the mysticism of Thomas Przywara. Following his posting to Basle as university chaplain, he encountered the Protestant theologian Karl Barth and the mystic Adrienne von Speyr, both of whom had a decisive influence on his thought. He was a prolific author, writer and editor of quite staggering proportions, as well as a founder of a publishing house, Johannes Verlag. He was author of some eighty books and five hundred articles and translated a hundred works, edited ten essay collections and brought sixty volumes of Speyr's writing to completion.

Perhaps best known of all his works is his multi-volume trilogy, *The Glory of the Lord* (*Herrlichkeit*), *Theological Dramatics* (*Theodramatik*) and *Theo-logic* (*Theologik*). While Balthasar was certainly influenced by theologians from other traditions, his intention, at least, was to write a distinctively Catholic approach to theology, rather than to find the lowest common denominator. In particular, he was hostile to influences of Enlightenment thought that seemed to undercut the distinctive approach of the church in its mission. Balthasar did, however, allow for the truths that were present in the church to be also present in society, including ideas such as human rights. He was suspicious of varieties of Catholicism that put so much emphasis on the social and political context that it lost its distinctively Christian message. He was also critical of what he saw as implicit uncritical acceptance of the assumptions of modernity and the ideal of progress. A notable aspect of his biography was his exclusion from the deliberations of Vatican II, though this left him freer to criticise the subsequent texts. Nonetheless, subsequent pontiffs, including the present Pope Benedict XVI, have drawn decisively on Balthasar's corpus for their own work. Balthasar's contribution was eventually formally recognised in 1984 by his being offered the first International Paul VI Prize for contributions to Catholic thought, just four years before his death in 1988.

[16] For this essay I am drawing on Aidan Nichols's helpful book *Divine Fruitfulness* since it raises the social and political context of Balthasar's life particularly clearly. See Nichols, 1-19.

Influence of Irenaeus and Maximus the Confessor

Hans Urs von Balthasar has not been appreciated sufficiently for his work on the doctrine of creation, given the paucity of discussion of this topic in secondary literature. This probably reflects his own attention to other areas of significance, including most specifically the development of his great trilogy on theological aesthetics, theological drama and theo-logic mentioned above. However, my suggestion is that this lacuna is somewhat unfortunate, since the forenamed trilogy and most of the rest of his work presuppose a strong doctrine of creation that is heavily influenced by the early Church Fathers, more especially Irenaeus of Lyons and Maximus the Confessor.

Irenaeus is particularly significant, as his writing was directed against those who wanted to deny the value and importance of the material world, the Gnostics, whose views were echoed in modern systems of thought that tend to devalue the natural world, or oppose body and spirit. The Gnostics, therefore, denied the value and goodness of the material world that Christianity affirms. For Balthasar, the reply of Irenaeus to Gnosticism was the Incarnation of God, so that God becoming flesh means that the possibility of the "redemption and resurrection of the entire earthly world is not just a possibility but a reality".[17]

Maximus the Confessor is also employed against Gnostic forms of theology. Balthasar postulates that when Wisdom, as the focal point of divine involvement in the world, "finally shone forth for Christian faith as the personal Word, the human Christ, all doubts about the possibility of a reconciliation between God and the world disappeared".[18] Balthasar recognises in Maximus the unity of the presence of God in the world, in earth and heaven, sense and intellect, so that the unity of the Transcendent is stressed. The theology that emerges is, therefore, one that is cosmic in scope and oriented to praising God in cosmic liturgy. Creation therefore tells us *that* the divine is, rather than *what* God is like, so we find a negative theology here, where affirmative statements about creation relate to what "this Being is not".[19] Maximus affirms the idea of divine mystery as being in motion, endowing those creaturely beings capable of longing and love with an inner share in divine life. This dialectical idea of motion and rest means that the creaturely difference from and similarity to God are inseparable from each other.[20]

We arrive at a highly affirming doctrine of creation where the "fecundity of this divine unity" becomes reflected in "the unity of all things and their respective differences" so that all created things are "an image of the divine unity and uniqueness". Furthermore, the divine unity becomes the source of the deepest identity of individuals, as well as their loving communion with each other. The paradox which "unites creatures by distinguishing them, and distinguishes them by uniting them", found throughout the universe, takes its origin in their relation to God.[21] More specifically, like Irenaeus, it is the Christological, incarnational relation that grounds such a theo-

---

17 Balthasar (1990), 9.

18 Balthasar (1988), 82.

19 Balthasar (1988), 87.

20 Balthasar (1988), 90.

21 Balthasar (1988), 69-70.

logy. His interpretation of Maximus is therefore not unexpected, where the creaturely world cannot reach its goal towards the divine by its own natural powers. However, his theology is significant for Balthasar in providing a bridge between the natural and the supernatural, in that "it conceives our fulfilment in grace as the goal of all the striving of our nature as it really is".[22]

Balthasar on Word and Creation

Given this close reading of creation through a Christological lens that Balthasar finds in Irenaeus and Maximus the Confessor, his *Explorations in Theology* (1989) begin with a discussion of "The Word Made Flesh", but this is done in order to affirm the theological significance of creation, rather than to deny its importance. For Balthasar, therefore, the creation cannot be understood apart from an acknowledgement of the involvement of the Word of God for the creation of all things and their salvation.[23] Creation has within it a rational character informed by the Logos, it is a Word "lying deeply hidden in the nature of things" in a manner that is permanent.[24] This discussion of creation beginning with the Word of God is particularly important for Balthasar in the sense that it tries to counter other alternatives.[25] These alternatives are German idealism, where creation is identified with revelation and manifestation of divine Being, or a reaction against that idealism, in a naïve dualism between a revelation derived from creation and one coming from the Word of God in Christ. The third possible position is one that starts from principles drawn from natural revelation and then views revelation in the Word as the crown and summit of the former revelation. Against all these alternatives Balthasar insists on the primary revelation in the Word, and it is only through that Word that revelation in creation can be understood. It means, therefore, that when God created the world, something began which was to be perfected in the order of Christ's redemption, but without giving any impression that grace was simply an epiphenomenon of nature. The true essence of creatureliness is a kind of active readiness to receive God's will without anticipating it.[26]

Here we find a further pillar in Balthasar's theology that is important in relation to creation and salvation, and that is the development of the notion of the analogy of being. The analogy only really makes sense in the light of his discussion on the Word of God as present in all created things. It allows him to state that the spiritual speech of human beings presupposes the speech of nature, and the speech of revelation presupposes the speech of God's creation. Here human beings and the natural world are in analogous relationship to God and all creaturely being.[27] Human beings are definitively superior to the rest of nature with respect to their freedom, in Balthasar's view, but this is in order to show humanity that God acts in freedom over the creaturely world.[28]

---

22 Balthasar (1988), 151.

23 Balthasar (1989), 11.

24 Balthasar (1989), 23.

25 Balthasar (1989), 47-48.

26 Balthasar (1989), 60.

27 Balthasar (1989), 84.

28 The greater comparative freedom of human beings to make decisions compared with other creatures, including higher primates, would not be in dispute among cognitive scientists today. The

The first book of Balthasar's trilogy, *The Glory of the Lord* (1982), is, as one might expect, a reading of creation as a manifestation of God.[29] The difference between God and creaturely being does not preclude the glory of God being seen radiating in and through the form of the world. This idea also provides the basis for Balthasar's retrieval of the philosophical principles of truth, goodness and beauty. Of course, such affirmations are challenged by the presence of sinfulness in the world, expressed in a Nietzschean will to power, and by the "ugly" reality that we find ourselves in. Against this, Balthasar argues that if creation has been redeemed, then grace, not the will to power, must dominate the world. Even if the world seems unredeemed, that is because of the failure to recognise the sacramental presence of the Word in the world.

Yet the theological aesthetics that Balthasar seeks to promote assumes the dynamism of living systems that tells us something important about the relationship between God and the world. It is worth quoting this in full, as it shows the way Balthasar perceives the natural world in a way that is mystical, yet qualified:

> In a flower, a certain interior reality opens its eye and reveals something beyond and more profound than a form which delights us by its proportion and colour. In the rhythm of the form of plants, from seed to full growth, from bud to fruit, there is manifested an essence ... And in the totality of beings, as they ascend and maintain their equilibrium, there is revealed a mystery of Being which it would be even more blasphemous and blind to interpret by reducing it to a neutral "existence".[30]

Here he is clearly influenced by the Romantics, finding in the natural world a law of "nature" that "surpasses and contains" both social and individual human activity. Balthasar is not giving priority to the natural world so much as finding throughout the universe a law of reality, or of Being, as such, such that providence governs the basis for human conduct. Indeed, for Balthasar it amounts to a form of "violence" to base knowledge purely on a rationalist construction that brackets out what is unknowable.[31] How far and to what extent the splendour found in creation corresponds to revelation that Christian theology names as "supernatural" is impossible to fathom, so for him we should not pass over reflection on creaturely existence too quickly.[32] But there is still a tension here in Balthasar's thought, where he invites the creaturely spirit to "move away from and beyond itself and entrust and surrender itself to that mystery".[33]

Salvation Through Theo-Drama

But Balthasar does not intend such ideas about the natural world to leave the impression that he fails to take sin and suffering seriously. Indeed it is probably because Bal-

---

language of "superiority" is perhaps unfortunate, but Balthasar wants to insist that the freedom of humans is to show humanity that, by analogy, God exercises absolute freedom, rather than to suggest that it entitles human beings to exercise their superior freedom over creation in a manipulative way. See Balthasar (1989), 85.

[29] Balthasar (1982), 430.

[30] Balthasar (1982), 444.

[31] Balthasar (1982), 447.

[32] Balthasar (1982), 449.

[33] Balthasar (1982), 450. In this case, Balthasar is referring to his metaphysical concept of the mystery of Being.

thasar takes the suffering of the world so seriously that the development of his understanding of salvation takes the form that it does, namely, one that perceives the processes of the world through the historical lens of theo-drama.[34] The mode of expression of the Word in the natural world discussed above had to become explicit as an external Word because of sin, so that he can say that "the Incarnation of the Word means the most extreme manifestness within the deepest concealment".[35] Manifestness in as much as now God becomes human and thus explains who God is through the human sphere; concealment in that now God as absolute and infinite Being becomes identified with just one individual human person, a strategy that "appears to be an undertaking condemned to failure".[36] Revelation is therefore within creation, rather than alongside it. The concealment of glory also goes deeper than this, however, in that the revelation of God is found in the passion of Christ, including his descent into hell.[37] Quash appreciates the significance of this move, namely that, through this, Christ comes to the limit of everything that might be possible within the creaturely realm. Christ sinks into this state as an act of loving obedience and as a way of total identification with humans in all their suffering and sinfulness, yet being without sin.

Balthasar's understanding of salvation therefore takes its cues from his interpretation of the cross of Christ and his entry into hell. The alienation between God and creatures is bridged through Christ crossing the abyss for the sake of humanity. By being united with Christ, the possibility that human beings can share in the relational character of God's trinitarian life becomes a reality. Of course, this begs the question whether the punitive language of the atonement that Balthasar seems to rely on, at least in places, is consistent with the portrait of a loving God open to such participation. Another question relates to the extent to which other creatures might share in this eschatological trajectory.[38] Yet it is in the light of his earlier Christological interpretation of creation that theo-drama makes sense, for God's entire world drama is concentrated on the action of Christ on Good Friday, Holy Saturday and Easter Day. The absolute freedom of God becomes expressed as creaturely freedom in Christ, so that Balthasar can say, "This is the climax and turning point of the theo-drama."[39] Yet, since the Word is also there from the beginning of the act of God in creation, it therefore makes sense to see creation and salvation in the thought of Balthasar as being to some extent woven together, one does not make sense without the other. It is, as it were, a whisper in the natural world that becomes expressed eventually as an explicit act of theo-drama (and less through a process of emergence) as an anticipation echoed from the beginning of Gods' creative Word and that acts in bringing forth the universe and all its creatures.

[34] Space does not permit a detailed discussion of this topic, but an excellent secondary source on this aspect of Balthasar's work may be found in Quash (2005).

[35] Balthasar (1982), 451.

[36] Balthasar (1982), 451.

[37] Arguably, Balthasar's discussion of the significance of Holy Saturday, Christ's descent into hell, is one of the most original aspects of his thought. See, for example, Quash (2004), 152-153.

[38] I have discussed difficulties with Balthasar's doctrine of atonement and the limits of his eschatology in relation to other creatures elsewhere. See Deane-Drummond.

[39] Balthasar (1994), 318.

References and Recommended Reading

Balthasar, Hans Urs von (1982), *The Glory of the Lord, Volume 1: Seeing the Form* (translated by Erasmo Leivà-Merikakis), Edinburgh: T & T Clark / San Francisco: Ignatius Press.

--- (1988), *Cosmic Liturgy: The Universe according to Maximus the Confessor* (translated by Brian E. Daley), San Francisco: Ignatius Press.

--- (1989), *Explorations in Theology, Volume 1: The Word Made Flesh* (translated by A. V. Littledale and Alexander Dru), San Francisco: Ignatius Press.

--- (1990), *The Scandal of the Incarnation: Irenaeus Against the Heresies* (translated by John Saward), San Francisco: Ignatius Press.

--- (1994), *Theodrama: Theological Dramatic Theory, Volume 4: The Action* (translated by Graham Harrison), San Francisco: Ignatius Press.

Deane-Drummond, Celia E. (2010), "The Breadth of Glory: A Trinitarian Eschatology for the Earth through Critical Engagement with Hans Urs von Balthasar", *International Journal of Systematic Theology*, Vol. 12, 1, 46-64.

Nichols, Aidan (2007), *Divine Fruitfulness: A Guide Through Balthasar's Theology Beyond the Trilogy*, London: T & T Clark / Continuum.

Oakes, Edward and Moss, David (eds.) (2004), *The Cambridge Companion to Hans Urs von Balthasar*, Cambridge: Cambridge University Press.

Quash, Ben (2004), "The Theo-Drama", in: Oakes and Moss (eds.), 143-157.

--- (2005), *Theology and the Drama of History*, Cambridge: Cambridge University Press.

Celia E. Deane-Drummond

Edward Schillebeeckx (1914-2009) – In Search of a Better Tomorrow

Introduction

Edward Schillebeeckx is considered one of the most important Catholic theologians of the post-war period. His theological writings cover a wide range of religious topics, including eschatology, ecclesiology, soteriology and, above all, Christology. Although his perspective underwent various stages of development in the course of a long career, it was consistently characterised by a profound and developing interest in two primary relationships, namely the one between men and women and the world in which they live and between the church and secular society. This becomes evident by studying the content and evolution of his thought, which became increasingly focused on Christology, especially as it pertains to society, social issues and the human community. Throughout his career Schillebeeckx was deeply involved in the church (as priest and Dominican monk), the academy (as scholar and professor) and society at large (as social critic and cultural commentator). In all his varied publications, a common theme can be discerned: confidence in the permanent process of creation as well as in salvation, especially as it relates to the elimination of human suffering – a theme that was especially prevalent and well articulated in his later Christology, the most important and influential aspect of his theology.

Born in Antwerp, Belgium, on 12 November 1914, Schillebeeckx was raised in Kortenberg during his formative years. Although he had attended a Jesuit high school as a youth, at the age of nineteen he became a formal member of the Dominican Order, to which he belonged for the remainder of his life. From 1947 to 1957 he held a professorship in Louvain, after which he moved to Nijmegen, where he resided until his death in 2009. It was in Nijmegen, as professor at the local Catholic university, that he developed his theology and produced the writings that would bring him to international notoriety and repute.[40]

Although Schillebeeckx's writings were written in his native Dutch, as his reputation became established, most of these were translated into English. His literary output is considerable, consisting of numerous articles and books. Here is a brief delineation of his major monographs:

- *De Sacramentele Heilseconomie: Theologische Bezinning op S. Thomas' Sacramenteleer in het Licht van de Traditie en van de Hedendaagse Sacramentsproblematiek* (Bilthoven: Nelissen, 1952): An important Dutch work presenting Schillebeeckx's view of salvation.
- *Christ the Sacrament of the Encounter with God* (New York: Sheed and Ward, 1963; Dutch original 1959): A presentation of Schillebeeckx's early Christology.
- *Marriage, Secular Reality and Saving Mystery* (London: Sheed and Ward, 1965, 1968; Dutch original 1963-1964): A discussion and presentation of the Catholic discussion on marriage and sexuality, and on marriage as a saving mystery.
- *Revelation and Theology* (London, New York: Sheed and Ward, 1967; Dutch original 1964): A book of essays on the topic of revelation in which concepts of creation and salvation are discussed.
- *God the Future of Man* (New York: Sheed and Ward, 1968; Dutch original 1967-1968): A work discussing various eschatological perspectives, especially as they relate to social, cultural and earthly concerns.
- *The Eucharist* (1968; Dutch original 1967), *God and Men* (1969; Dutch original 1965) and *World and Church* (1971; Dutch original 1966): Works dealing with the two relationships that were of paramount concern to Schillebeeckx throughout his career (all three published in London by Sheed and Ward).
- *The Understanding of Faith: Interpretation and Criticism* (New York, London: Sheed and Ward, 1974; Dutch original 1972): A work, primarily influenced by Jürgen Habermas's early philosophy, presenting the critical hermeneutic method that Schillebeeckx applied in his later Christology.
- *Jesus: An Experiment in Christology* (London: Collins, 1979; Dutch edition 1974), *Christ: The Christian Experience in the Modern World* (London: SCM, 1980; Dutch original 1977) and *Church: The Human Story of God* (London: SCM, 1990; Dutch original 1989): Three volumes presenting Schillebeeckx's later Christology.

The Suffering and Salvation of Human Beings: A Primary Theological Theme

Schillebeeckx undertook a critical examination of the Christian faith and its implications for the world at large, from which a particular conception of society gradually emerged. In this conception, men and women are viewed as agents embedded in a particular historical, cultural and societal context, acting to oppose those forces that would undermine their earthly as well as their divine hopes. Here human beings are con-

[40] See Kennedy, 24-28.

ceived as being rooted in earthly history, with its dual sides of suffering and salvation, but also as being situated in the creation of God, which holds the promise of charity and future fulfilment. According to Schillebeeckx, there exists within each of us an inherent faith in the goodness, divinity and everlasting nature of God's creation, but this can be overshadowed by destructive tendencies that threaten this faith and the hopeful promise of God. Once we embrace the life exemplified and offered by Jesus, however, we can experience the communion and joy that follows from his invitation. Through his manner of living, Jesus reveals the means by which to resist the destructive forces of history and society.[41] Central to this perspective is the notion of solidarity with the world's voiceless "non-persons": the destitute, the marginalised, the disenfranchised and the weak: "The option for the poor and the outcasts is an intrinsic consequence of the specific and Christian universal love for humankind."[42]

A Catholic Theology of Culture

Schillebeeckx's theological writings from 1945 onward reflect his increasing concern with the relationship of God's creation to societal and cultural issues, as well as his attempt to reach beyond the strict confines of the church to a consideration of humanity as a whole. It was during this period that he appeared in public forums, wrote newspaper articles and became widely known as a Catholic theologian who was broadly concerned with humanity's daily existential struggle. Of importance here is the acknowledgement of earthly suffering and the possibility of liberation in the here-and-now.[43] In this regard, Schillebeeckx viewed theology as a function of culture and thus as a potential cultural agent. This early phase of his theology therefore constitutes an important background for the concept of praxis in his later Christology. At its core is a concern not so much with concepts and dogmas, but more with the articulation and improvement of fundamental human relationships. Over the next four decades, in pursuit of this aim, Schillebeeckx became increasingly interested in examining how the experience of God can transform individuals into socially conscious beings who express their faith in terms of concrete actions for the betterment of humanity.

All of us, he concludes, are necessarily situated in a given historical reality, and thus our relationship with God is necessarily expressed within the context of concrete life circumstances. And because those circumstances necessarily contain existential threats that we must strive to overcome, our religious expressions can be understood as envisionings of a better tomorrow: the righteous human community (*humanum*) and ultimate the kingdom of God, as manifest in the life of Jesus – i.e. the ordained original community, made possible by our living relationship with the living God. These expressions can be further conceived as ways of interpreting our lives, our circumstances and our history that enable us to transcend present limiting conditions and envision new possibilities for living. The believer comprehends these visions of the good human community (*humanum*) in terms of his or her experience of the kingdom of God. The concrete meaning of this emerges in the New Testament descriptions of Jesus' way of living, which invites all persons to communion and joy. Indeed it is the appli-

---

41 See McManus, 162-173.

42 Schillebeeckx (1990), 169.

43 See Borgman.

cation of his example in our daily lives that instils faith and enables us to improve our relation to each other and the world. In Schillebeeckx's view, religious faith calls upon us to oppose those forces that threaten our lives and cause suffering and marginalisation. In other words, God's promised world of justice for all categories of persons is concretely manifest through acts of faith that oppose present injustices, imbalances and oppressions. This approach is perfectly exemplified by Jesus' way of living, which can be understood as praxis according to the rules of the kingdom of God. Schillebeeckx calls this "orthopraxis", or praxis that engenders a feeling of solidarity with the impoverished and subjugated non-persons of the world. Orthopraxis is indicative of a broader view of society, the world and history, in which hope for the future and faith in the goodness and divinity of creation becomes a motivating factor in our lives.

Experience, Faith and Praxis: Rooted in Relations between Men and Women

The concept of experience has a foundational function in Schillebeeckx's theology. He had an early interest in phenomenology, and his later theology is rooted in its concepts, which he especially applied to his theological anthropology: a method by which biblical narratives are interpreted in such a way that they become relevant and applicable to contemporary circumstances. Important to this understanding is the notion that men and women are always interpreting, and that experience is always interpreted experience.[44] In Schillebeeckx's theological development it is possible to discern three stages of thought, all of which are founded upon the concept of experience: (a) the construction of a theological anthropology informed by phenomenological concepts; (b) the extension of this theological anthropology from the narrow framework of the church to a critical evaluation of society at large; and (c) the development of a hermeneutical view of the relationship between experience and interpretation, which finds expression in his later Christology. Here Jesus is seen as someone who said "no" to the destructive forces that were responsible for his rejection and demise, and who thus left an enduring impression that gave birth to the early Jesus movement and the founding of the church. In this way, Jesus becomes a symbol of contrast to the evil and destructiveness of the world. Of vital importance in this regard are the encounters that Jesus had with the men and women of his time. The experience of contrast between the reality of our daily lives and God's ordained community, highlighted by the narrative of Jesus' life, becomes a force for societal change by pointing towards an alternative to humankind's destructive tendencies. According to Schillebeeckx, opposition to that which destroys community and hope for the future is most ardently expressed in relation to (and by) the poor, oppressed and suffering non-persons of the world; from the plight of the world's non-persons (and from feelings of solidarity with them) arises the real force for societal change, the orthopraxis or praxis in faith for a better future.

The Christological Project: The Christian Experience in a World of Suffering Reveals Salvation

Schillebeeckx's lifelong concern with societal issues is reflected throughout his theological development and is most clearly articulated in his later Christological project, in which he calls for the emergence of culturally integrated, socially conscious human

44 Schillebeeckx (1980), 31.

beings that are hopeful of the future. Within persons of faith, situated in a cultural context, a concept of society is said to arise. Focusing on men and women with faith in the ultimate triumph of what is right, Schillebeeckx examines and clarifies their relation to a wider social and environmental sphere. It is the calculating human being that creates narrowness and limits living relationships. As such, Schillebeeckx aims to formulate a theology that instils faith in others, causing them to transform, rise up and actively engage in the betterment of their world.

Central to this project is his attempt to interpret biblical texts such that they become relevant and applicable to contemporary societal realities. Having been influenced by the views of prominent critical and hermeneutical thinkers, Schillebeeckx enunciates a critical hermeneutical theology, with the perceptive, interpretive and expressive human being at its core. This critical theology is employed in his Christological project within a societal context and used as a focus in his interpretation of New Testament narratives. The immediate experience of those that actually met Jesus, whose praxis was always in accordance with the rules of the kingdom of God, inspired a faith that was stronger than Jesus' apparent death. From this faith, an interpretative language emerged that was connected to a concrete social reality. At its centre were the experiences of the men and women Jesus encountered. According to Schillebeeckx, these can be understood as unique experiences of goodness that are in contrast to the common condition of human suffering. The experience of this contrast is of fundamental importance because it highlights the possibility of counteracting human suffering and alienation with charity and an invitation to communion: "Liberation or 'salvation', then, is the conquest of all human, personal and social forms of alienation; salvation is the being in the wholeness of man, of his life and his history."[45]

Liberation Forces in the Relationships between Men and Women

The social dimension pervades Schillebeeckx's theology. Humanity is characterised by relationships between men and women, seen "in the light of the dogma of creation and salvation".[46] Salvation is viewed as something that is attained within creation, i.e. here on earth. In his Christological project, Schillebeeckx develops the conception of a mediated, indirect relationship between the individual and God, meaning that it is through humankind that God acts. The significance of this lies in the understanding that God's presence can be found in the conception of what can, but has not yet become, a social reality, i.e. the righteous human community as ordained by God (*humanum*). In this view, all persons are seen as having the latent potential to commit themselves to the realisation of this *humanum*, which is "... grounded in the absolute saving and creative presence of God".[47] The goal and meaning of creation lies in humanity's participation in the future of God's kingdom, expressed in human terms as a commitment to charity and solidarity, which rests upon the mystery of love and the personal experience of contrast between destructive and productive human relationships. God is thus immanent in his creation, and precisely in this way reveals his transcendence and eternity.[48]

---

45 Schillebeeckx (1979), 624.

46 Cooper, 8.

47 See Hilkert, 134-135.

48 See Dolphin, 266.

One may therefore conclude that "For Schillebeeckx, today's Christian identity is granted significance when the contrasting secular experience is brought into relationship with the basic Christian experience of salvation. In our human struggle for justice and liberation, the God of love and grace is articulated and expressed."[49]

A Theology with Contemporary Relevance

Schillebeeckx's focus on the embeddedness of men and women in a given sociocultural context endows his theology with contemporary relevance. In his view, all theology must be a reflection on the praxis of faith and must contain an analysis of this praxis. The social awareness and communal commitment of the believer, as elaborated in Schillebeeckx's later Christology, is said to be essential to the sustenance of human societies, with their inherent tension between bondage and freedom. A relevant analysis of praxis is impossible without a systematic understanding of human beings in the context of society, where faithful men and women remain true to their lives, their neighbours and their communities. Understanding this is viewed as being necessary to the theologian's task, and in this respect Schillebeeckx appears to lead the way. Through the development of his theology over several decades, Schillebeeckx came to understand the importance of each historical and societal context, thus sensing the need for an interdisciplinary, dialogical approach to theology.[50] His theological reflections entail a view of the human being as belonging to God and God's future, on the one hand, and as being embedded in concrete, earthly living situations, on the other.

References and Recommended Reading

Boeve, Lieven, Depoortere, Frederiek and Van Erp, Stephan (eds.) (2010), *Edward Schillebeeckx and Contemporary Theology*, London: T & T Clark.

Borgman, Erik (2003), *Edward Schillebeeckx: A Theologian in his History, Volume 1: A Catholic Theology of Culture (1914-1965)*, London: Continuum.

Cooper, Jennifer (2011), *Humanity in the Mystery of God: The Theological Anthropology of Edward Schillebeeckx*, London: T & T Clark.

Dolphin, Kathleen (2010), "Theology for the 21st Century: A Commentary on the Symposium", in: Boeve, Depoortere and Van Erp (eds.), 265-272.

Hilkert, Mary Catherine (2010), "The Threatened *Humanum* as *Imago Dei*: Anthropology and Christian Ethics", in: Boeve, Depoortere and Van Erp (eds.), 127-141.

Kennedy, Philip (1993), *Schillebeeckx*, London: Geoffrey Chapman.

McManus, Kathleen Anne (2003), *Unbroken Communion: The Place and Suffering in the Theology of Edward Schillebeeckx*, Oxford: Rowman and Littlefield.

Rego, Aloysius (2006), *Suffering and Salvation: The Salvific Meaning of Suffering in the Later Theology of Edward Schillebeeckx*, Louvain: Peeters.

Schillebeeckx, Edward (1979), *Jesus: An Experiment in Christology*, New York: Crossroad.

--- (1980), *Christ: The Christian Experiences in the Modern World*, London: SCM.

--- (1990), *Church: The Human Story of God*, London: Crossroad.

Schoof, Ted and Van de Westelaken, Jan (1997), *Bibliography 1936-1996 of Edward Schillebeeckx OP*, Nijmegen: Nelissen.

Bo Claesson

[49] See Boeve, Depoortere and Van Erp, xii.

[50] See Rego, 18-32.

Further Developments

The vitality of Roman Catholic theological tradition today is found not so much in great figures like the four discussed above, but in a range of global theological movements. These include the liberation theology pioneered by theologians like Gustavo Gutiérrez and John Sobrino and two other writers discussed in chapter 10 of this volume, Leonardo Boff and Ivone Gabara. A second vital movement is feminist theology, which very often embraces an ecofeminist approach, exemplified in the different approaches of Rosemary Radford Ruether, Elizabeth Johnson and Catherina Halkes, discussed in chapter 8 of this volume. Others committed to both ecological and feminist theology include contributors to this volume Mary Grey, Heather Eaton, Anne Marie Dalton and Susan Rakoczy. While much Roman Catholic theology now springs from North America, its future will surely come from the vigorous ecclesial communities of Africa, Asia and Latin America.

Many of those who have focussed directly on ecological theology in the Roman Catholic tradition look back to the inspiration provided by the vision of Teilhard de Chardin. Over the last generation it was Thomas Berry who pioneered Christian commitment to Earth and promoted engagement with the scientific story of the universe as the new story of creation. Teilhard and Berry are discussed in chapter 6 of this volume. Other influential figures have included Matthew Fox with his creation theology and spirituality and the missionary prophet of ecological praxis Sean McDonagh. Berry and Fox have been critical of some aspects of Christianity – including the central tradition of sin and redemption. They have tended to focus on creation rather than on salvation in Christ.

Other Roman Catholic theologians believe that a truly Christian ecological theology will need to be a theology of both creation and salvation, understood together as united in the one divine economy. It will be a theology where salvation is understood not in an individualistic sense but as the transformation and fulfilment of human beings and, with them, of the whole creation, through the Word made flesh and in life-giving Spirit. Some recent contributions to the beginnings of this project of Christian ecological theology from Roman Catholic scholars include the following:

- Celia Deane-Drummond has written widely on ecological theology and on the science-theology interface, including *The Ethics of Nature* (Oxford: Blackwell, 2004), *Eco-Theology* (London: Darton, Longman and Todd, 2008) and *Christ and Evolution: Wonder and Wisdom* (Minneapolis: Fortress, 2009).

- Ilia Delio brings a Franciscan approach to ecological theology and to evolutionary theology, as co-author of *Care for Creation: A Franciscan Spirituality of the Earth* (Cincinnati: Franciscan Messenger Press, 2008) and author of *Christ in Evolution* (Maryknoll: Orbis, 2008) and *The Emergent Christ: Exploring the Meaning of Catholic in an Evolutionary Universe* (Maryknoll: Orbis, 2011).

- Denis Edwards contributes to ecological theology in *Breath of Life: A Theology of the Creator Spirit* (Maryknoll: Orbis, 2004), *Ecology at the Heart of Faith* (Maryknoll: Orbis, 2006) and *How God Acts: Creation, Redemption and Special Divine Action* (Minneapolis: Fortress, 2010).

- John F. Haught has been prominent in the engagement with science. Some of his contributions are *God after Darwin: A Theology of Evolution* (Boulder: Westview, 2000), *Christianity and Science: Towards a Theology of Nature* (Maryknoll: Orbis, 2007) and *Making Sense of Evolution: Darwin, God and the Drama of Life* (Louisville: Westminster John Knox, 2010).

- Elizabeth Johnson has consistently integrated ecological concerns in her theology as is evident in her *Women, Earth, and Creator Spirit* (New York: Paulist Press, 1993) and *Quest for the Living God: Mapping Frontiers in the Theology of God* (New York: Continuum, 2007).
- Jame Schaefer is author of *Theological Foundations for Environmental Ethics: Reconstructing Patristic and Medieval Concepts* (Washington: Georgetown University Press, 2009). She has led a research programme through the Catholic Theological Society of America from 2008 until 2011, with results to be published as *Confronting the Climate Crisis: Catholic Theological Perspectives* by Marquette University Press. See also *God, Creation, and Climate Change: A Catholic Response to the Environmental Crisis* (Maryknoll: Orbis, 2010), edited by Richard W. Miller.
- Helpful collections include *All Creation is Groaning: An Interdisciplinary Vision for Life in a Sacred Universe* (Collegeville: Liturgical Press, 1999), edited by Carol Dempsey and Russel A. Butkus, and *Environmental Science and Theology in Dialogue* (Maryknoll: Orbis, 2011), edited by Russel A. Butkus and Steven A. Kolmes; *Green Discipleship: Catholic Theological Ethics and the Environment*, edited by Tobias Winright (Winona: Anselm Academic, 2011).
- Roman Catholic theology is usually in dialogue with teachings of the Catholic magisterium. The foundational document in Catholic teaching on ecological issues is Pope John Paul II's text for the World Day of Peace, 1 January 1990, entitled *Peace with God the Creator; Peace with All of Creation.*[51]
- Many further papal statements culminated in an integration of Christian ecological concerns into Benedict XVI's 2009 social encyclical *Caritas in Veritate.*[52]

Ecological theology that engages fully with the Christian tradition is still at its beginning among Roman Catholic theologians. It is worth noting that much work in this field is done in a collegial and ecumenical fashion.

Denis Edwards

[51] See <www.vatican.va/holy_father/john_paul_ii/messages/peace/documents/hf_jp-ii_mes_19891208_xxiii-world-day-for-peace_en.html>, retrieved 14 August 2011.

[52] See <www.vatican.va/holy_father/benedict_xvi/encyclicals/documents/hf_ben-xvi_enc_ 20090629 caritas-in-veritate_en.html>, retrieved 14 August 2011.

3. North Atlantic Lutheran Theologies

Edited by Svein Rise

Introduction

Martin Luther (1483-1545) and the Lutheran Confessions make a clear-cut distinction between the creation benefits of God and the redemption in Christ. *The Apology* (XVI. 2), one of the central Lutheran Confessions from the Reformation period, distinguishes, for example, between *regnum civile* (the secular realm) and *regnum Christi* (the kingdom of Jesus Christ), two spheres of God's work, concepts which in medieval times were often mixed up; the former becomes subordinate to the latter, both realms thus losing their identity. This is typified by Thomas Aquinas's work *Summa Theologica*, claiming that the Creator is recognised through his creation (Rom. 1:20). Accordingly, salvation is on a higher level than creation, the latter being natural whereas the former is supernatural. Therefore reason does not have access to salvation as salvation requires revelation, understood as the transmission of supernatural knowledge.

According to the *Confessio Augustana* the structures of creation are liberated from the guardianship of the church and restored to their God-given unique reality. Rather than an escape from the world, a stewardship of the world was required. During the Lutheran orthodoxy J. A. Quenstedt (1617-1688) emphasised not only creation out of nothing, but also God's providence, which includes both continuing creation and divine miracles. This aspect receded in the Enlightenment period, which characteristically underlined the idea that this world is the best possible one, for example in the philosophy of Leibniz (1768-1834), well-known for his thesis on *harmonia praestabilita* (pre-established world harmony). With Friedrich Schleiermacher (1768-1834) a movement towards pantheism may be detected: God and the world are considered inseparable correlatives, while faith's general sense of dependence is interwoven with natural surroundings. Similar ideas are found in the work of the philosopher G. W. F. Hegel (1770-1831): the human reason in his works is imagined to correlate with the divine reason and the human spirit with the Spirit of God.

With Albrecht Ritschl (1822-1889) and his disciples one finds, however, a strong reaction to traditional natural theology. Here the starting point for theological reflection is God's love as expressed in the revelation of Jesus Christ. Creation and salvation are not related through a theoretical understanding of the world, but rather through an ethical-religious recognition of the purpose of humanity. The belief in God's work of creation becomes a practical conviction that human existence promotes the ethical purpose, established by the revealed love in Jesus Christ. This corresponds with ideas found in Thomas where creation and nature are related in such a way that redemption (the supranatural) supersedes creation (the natural). Revealed theology and soteriology are thus isolated from creation. Redemption understood as the very content of revealed theology is lifted up as something higher than the ordinary created existence. In opposition to Thomas and the scholastic tradition, Lutheran systematic theologies stressed that it is the fall of humanity (and not just the inferiority of nature) that rendered the natural perception of God as inadequate and necessitated salvation.

Moving forward to 20th-century theology, we see that the theme of creation and salvation, also in a Lutheran context, is by and large neglected. Admittedly, prominent theologians in the so-called Lutheran renaissance (from 1918 onwards) tried to raise the issue. Their agenda was to distance themselves from liberal Ritschlianism and the religious history school and to strengthen the theological focus on the young Luther's experience of justification. Central theologians in this renewal of Lutheranism were Karl Holl, Carl Stange, Emmanuel Hirsch, Paul Althaus, Gustav Wehrung and Heinrich Bornkamm, together with Scandinavian theologians such as Gustav Aulén, Anders Nygren and Torstein Bohlin. The Lutheran renaissance is characterised by its emphasis on the fundamental importance of eschatology in theology. However, because of its one-sided focus on an individualised perspective, as for instance in the resurrection of the body, it did not come to grips in a more comprehensive way with the relationship between the eschatological work of the Spirit and God's work in creation. One example is Paul Althaus's famous book *The Last Things* (first edition 1926) in which eschatology is reduced to an appendix to the created world.

The Lutheran dogmatists of the inter- and post-war period were also not able to connect the themes of creation and salvation in an appropriate manner. Two reasons for this may be mentioned. On the one hand, there is the political confusion resulting from the inter- and post-war tendency to justify the national-socialist ideology of blood (race) and soil through creation theology – which rendered the theme of creation and salvation difficult to deal with. On the other hand, there was an apologetic impulse: faced with the mechanistic natural sciences of the turn of the century, Wilhelm Herrmann prescribed a dualistic theology particularly reflected in Rudolf Bultmann's (1884-1976) exegesis and systematics. In his works eschatology is reduced to existential experiences, to the presence and not the future, God lost his sovereignty in the created world. Salvation brought about by God is realised here and now. Redemption is made complete in the spiritual processing of existing miseries. This, in fact, implies a surrendering to the secular sciences, particularly the natural sciences. It is owing to Karl Heim's opposition to Bultmann that a spiritualisation of eschatology was avoided, Heim related eschatology to the restoration of creation on the basis of the resurrection of Jesus Christ. This prevented a spiritualising break with the created order. However, Heim and the other Lutheran systematic theologians of that time lacked a thorough trinitarian approach to Christian dogmatics.

The central Lutheran figures presented in this chapter vary in their ability to relate creation and salvation in such a trinitarian way. These include a group of German and North American theologians, namely Paul Tillich (1886-1965), Joseph Sittler (1904-1987), Dietrich Bonhoeffer (1906-1945), Wolfhart Pannenberg (1928-) and Robert Jenson (1930-).

The theological positions of especially Pannenberg and Jenson have to be understood in the light of the retrieval of trinitarian theology during the last few decades, which was at least partly influenced by ecumenical contact with the Eastern church. It is therefore not surprising that there are nowadays clear connections between Lutheran and Orthodox theologies with regard to both practical theology (spirituality) and theoretical theology (dogmatics).

Svein Rise

Paul Tillich (1886-1965) – The New Being in Christ

Introduction

Being a son of a Lutheran minister, receiving education as well as ordination in Germany, and teaching theology and / or philosophy at various universities in his fatherland before his emigration to the USA at the age of 47, Tillich aptly characterised his thought as "on the boundary", which was also the title of his autobiography published as a book in 1967. In addition to his *Systematic Theology* (published in three volumes in 1951, 1957 and 1963),[1] Tillich published many popular yet relatively small books, including *The Courage to Be* (1952), *Love, Power, and Justice* (1954) and *The Dynamics of Faith* (1957), and a few sermon collections, including *The Shaking of the Foundations* (1949), *The New Being* (1956), *The Eternal Now* (1963), which offer useful introductions to his theology.

In Tillich's theology, the centrality of the concept of New Being, which is derived from the biblical expression of "new creation" (Gal. 6:15, 2 Cor. 5:17), clearly indicates the strong connection between his doctrines of creation and salvation. As Tillich puts it:

> Salvation does not destroy creation; but it transforms the Old Creation into a New one. Therefore we can speak of the New in terms of a *re*-newal: The threefold "*re*", namely, *re*-conciliation, *re*-union, *re*-surrection.[2]

As we will see, Tillich's more systematic exposition of the doctrines of creation and salvation, which was shaped by his method of correlation as well as his attitude towards nature, offers a distinctive approach for integrating the two doctrines, with significant implications for ecological theology.

Romantic Attitude towards Nature

Tillich had lifelong interests in a theology of nature, which was the conceptual expression of his predominantly aesthetic-meditative, rather than scientific-analytical or technological-controlling attitude towards nature. He identified several factors contributing to his "Romantic" attitude towards nature: his mystical experience of communication with and participation in nature; the impact of German poetic literature, especially the Romantic school; and his Lutheran theological background, which affirms the presence of the infinite in everything finite. Partially owing to this attitude towards nature, Tillich was, on the one hand, attracted to Schelling's philosophy, which exercised tremendous impact on Tillich's own theology, and on the other hand, critical towards Ritschlian theology as well as Calvinism and Puritanism in America.[3]

In his sermon "Nature, also, Mourns for a Lost Good?", Tillich uses Psalm 19:2-5, Romans 8:19-22 and Revelation 21:1 and 22:1-2 to elaborate the main theme that humankind and nature belong together in their created glory, in their tragedy and in their salvation. Tillich highlights that "The Bible speaks again and again of the salva-

---

[1] References in parenthesis in the text below are to the 1978 edition of Tillich's *Systematic Theology*, abbreviated as *ST*.

[2] Tillich (1956), 20.

[3] Tillich (1961), 4-5.

tion of the *world*, as it speaks of the creation of the *world* and the subjection of the *world* to anti-Divine forces. And *world* means nature as well as man [and woman]."[4] Tillich's emphasis on the participation of nature in the process of fall and salvation is very much in line with an ecological understanding of the interdependence of humankind and nature, as well as his own understanding of the basic ontological structure of the interdependence between ego-self and world (*ST 1*, 170-171).

Method of Correlation and Existentialist Interpretation

In his *Systematic Theology*, Tillich attempts to interpret the Christian doctrines according to his theological method of correlation (*ST 1*, 3-68; *ST 2*, 3-16). The method, with its apologetic intention, attempts to interpret the Christian doctrines as the answers to the questions implied in human existence. Though Tillich employs some ontological concepts associated with existentialism, including essence, existence and being, the way the method is actually used is to take the analysis of human existence furnished by existentialism to formulate the existential question(s) for theology to answer, rather than to adopt existentialism as a metaphysical framework taking existence preceding essence to be imposed on Christian faith.

Following this method, Tillich's *Systematic Theology* is structured into five major parts, and each part starts with a question of human existence followed by a theological answer based on exposition of corresponding doctrine(s). Owing to this organising principle, the structure of Tillich's theological system highlights the correlation between the existential question and the theological answer, rather than the connection or coherence among different doctrines. Given this primary aim of answering the question concerning human existence, Tillich's exposition of the doctrines of creation and salvation neglects neither the divine action nor the participation of non-human creatures.

Doctrine of Creation

In the second part of his *Systematic Theology*, Tillich offers his understanding of "God as Creating" under the doctrine of God, which actually refers to God the Father. Tillich suggests that the doctrine of creation is "the basic description of the relation between God and the world", rather than a story of an event taking place "once upon a time". In line with his method of correlation, the doctrine of creation, which correlates with the analysis of human finitude, offers an answer to the existential question of finitude by discovering the meaning of finitude in creatureliness (*ST 1*, 252-253).

According to Tillich, the meaning of finitude in creatureliness is based on the divine creativity, which is not different from the divine life. In his own words, "God is creative because he is God" (*ST 1*, 252). Since the divine life is essentially creative, the divine creativity includes not only the "originating creativity" (of the past), but also the "sustaining creativity" (of the present) and the "directing creativity" (of the future). In other words, "God *has* created the world, he is creative in the present moment, and he will creatively fulfil his *telos*" (*ST 1*, 252).

Tillich's interpretation of "originating creativity" is focused on the traditional doc-

---

[4] Tillich (1962), 83, 89 (emphasis original).

trine of *creatio ex nihilo*, which implies that an element of non-being is to be found not only in human life, but also in the divine life. "God is infinite because he has the finite (and with it that element of non-being which belongs to finitude) within himself united with his infinity" (*ST 1*, 252). Similarly, creatureliness necessarily implies finitude, which refers to the natural necessity of death and the element of non-being in creatureliness. Finitude is not tragic, but gives rise to tragedy if one denies one's finitude and attempts to transcend or overcome it. In other words, the Creator is not to be blamed for the tragic character of existence, which does not belong to the essential nature of things and is not rooted in the creative ground of being (*ST 1*, 253-254).

According to Tillich, God's "sustaining creativity" implies not only "the continuity of the structure of reality as the basis for being and acting", but also that "God is immanent in the world as its permanent creative ground and is transcendent to the world through freedom"(*ST 1*, 262-263). Tillich further elaborates that God's "directing creativity" implies the purposefulness of creation.

> From the standpoint of the creature, the purpose of creation is the creature itself and the actualization of its potentialities. From the standpoint of the creator, the purpose of creation is the exercise of his creativity, which has no purpose beyond itself because the divine life is essentially creative (*ST 1*, 263-264).

God's directing creativity, which "creatively directing everything toward its fulfillment" without interference, "always creates through the freedom of man [and woman] and through the spontaneity and structural wholeness of all creatures" (*ST 1*, 266-267). The divine creation allows the freedom of the creatures, which makes possible the existence of evil (*ST 1*, 269). The fall, according to Tillich's ontological interpretation, refers to the transition or estrangement from essence to existence, an ontological process taking place in both nature and humankind (*ST 2*, 31-33). As the trans-historical quality of all events in time and space, the fall is a cosmic event, rather than a particular event taking place in history (*ST 2*, 37, 40).

With regard to the significance of the doctrine of divine creativity for the understanding of the creatures, Tillich summarises:

> Creation into time produces the possibility of self-realization, estrangement and reconciliation of the creature, which in eschatological terminology, is the way from essence through existence to essentialization (*ST 3*, 422).

Doctrine of Salvation

Tillich takes Christology as a function of soteriology (*ST 2*, 150), and uses the distinction of "new aeon" and "old aeon" to explain the universal impact of Christ. The old aeon means the predicament of human beings and the state of estrangement of their world. Christ means the one who is supposed to bring the new aeon, the universal regeneration, or the new reality (*ST 2*, 27, 118). Being consistent with the doctrine of creation, Tillich suggests, "The conquest of existential estrangement in the New Being, which is the being of the Christ, does not remove finitude and anxiety, ambiguity and tragedy; but it does have the character of taking the negativities of existence into unbroken unity with God" (*ST 2*, 134). Jesus as the Christ is recognised as the "Saviour" or "Mediator" because "In Christ the eternal God-Man [human] Unity has appeared under the conditions of existence" (*ST 2*, 169).

For Tillich, "atonement is always both a divine act and a human action" (*ST 2*, 170), though most of the prevalent theories of atonement tend to focus one-sidedly on either the human-subjective side or the divine-objective side. In order to have a better balance between the two sides of atonement, Tillich proposes to replace the concept of substitution with the concept of participation (*ST 2*, 173). Together with the concept of New Being, Tillich articulates a theory concerning the threefold character of salvation: salvation as participation in the New Being (regeneration); salvation as acceptance of the New Being (justification) and salvation as transformation by the New Being (sanctification) (*ST 2*, 176-180). This understanding of salvation is much broader than the doctrine of justification by faith emphasised in traditional Lutheran theology, and places greater emphasis on the human role in salvation.

In fact, Tillich's exposition of the role of Christ in salvation implies the pivotal role that the human being plays in the process of salvation. As Tillich explains, the appearing of the New Being in Jesus as the Christ "gives cosmic significance to the person and confirms the insight that only in a personal life can the New Being manifest itself" (*ST 2*, 121). This is not to deny the role of nature in salvation. Human beings, Tillich explains, belong to various realms, including the physical, biological and psychological realms. Therefore, what happens to the human being happens implicitly to all realms of life (*ST 2*, 120). Inversely, nature also participates in every act of human freedom. As the biological, psychological and sociological powers are effective in every individual decision, nature participates inwardly in the good and evil that human beings do. Outwardly, nature also shows analogies to humankind's doing good and evil. In short, humanity and nature reach into each other, and cannot be separated from each other (*ST 2*, 42-43). As both nature and humanity participate in the fall, they are so interdependent that the salvation of the one without the other is unthinkable. Accordingly, as the bearer of the New Being, the function of Christ is not only to save individuals or to transform the historical existence of human being, but to renew the whole universe (*ST 2*, 95).

In Tillich's theology, nature is a bearer and an object of salvation, rather than an enemy of salvation to be controlled in scientific, technical and moral terms or to be deprived of any inherent power.[5] His doctrine of the participation of nature in the process of fall and salvation is further highlighted in his understanding of salvation as multidimensional healing. According to his understanding of life as a multidimensional unity (*ST 3*, 11-30), Tillich suggests that salvation should also be holistic and related to all the dimensions of human life, including the inorganic dimension. Tillich explains that salvation, according to its original meaning, should be understood as healing (*salvus*) (*ST 2*, 166), which should include every act of healing such as the healing of sickness, of demonic possession and of servitude to sin and death (*ST 1*, 146). Salvation is thus not a matter of none or all, total or non-existent, because "In some degree all men participate in the healing power of the New Being. Otherwise, they would have no being" (*ST 2*, 167).

This understanding of the universality of salvation is supported by Tillich's pneumatology, which suggests that "Since humankind is never left alone by God, since it is continuously under the impact of the Spiritual Presence, there is *always* New Being in

[5] Tillich (1957b), 103.

history" (*ST 3*, 140). For Tillich, the divine Spirit is "the actuality of New Being" (*ST 2*, 180), the one "who has made the man Jesus of Nazareth into the Messiah" and "the power which creates the New Being, in the Christ, in individuals, in the church" (*ST 2*, 178). The prominent role of the Holy Spirit in salvation is a rather distinctive feature of Tillich's soteriology and indicates the trinitarian character of Tillich's theology as a whole.[6]

Conclusion

The characteristics of Tillich's understanding of salvation, including universally present, multidimensional and involving, rather than at the expense of, human participation, are based on and echo his doctrine of creation. Furthermore, his expositions of the doctrines of creation and of salvation emphasise the divine love and relatedness, rather than the divine sovereignty or intelligence. Approaching the end of his *Systematic Theology*, Tillich indicates:

> In this view the world process means something for God. He is not a separated self-sufficient entity who, driven by a whim, creates what he wants and saves whom he wants. Rather, the eternal act of creation is driven by a love which finds fulfillment only through the other who has the freedom to accept and to reject love. God, so to speak, drives toward the actualization and essentialization of everything that has being (*ST 3*, 422).

Admittedly, Tillich's interpretation of the doctrines of creation and salvation remains largely ontological rather than ecological. However, the ecological implications of his doctrines of creation and salvation, including his relational, organic or immanent model of God-World relationship as well as his doctrine of the participation of nature in the process of fall and salvation, have been explored by some contemporary scholars.[7] His theology remains a valuable source of insights for ecological theology, including inter-religious dialogue on ecological issues.

References and Recommended Reading

Drummy, Michael F. (2000), *Being and Earth: Paul Tillich's Theology of Nature*, Lanham: University Press of America.

Gilkey, Langdon (1990), *Gilkey on Tillich*, New York: Crossroad.

Lai, Pan-chiu (1991), *Towards a Trinitarian Theology of Religions: A Study of Paul Tillich's Thought*, Kampen: Kok Pharos.

--- (1999), "Paul Tillich and Ecological Theology", *The Journal of Religion*, Vol. 79, 2, 233-249.

O'Neill, Andrew (2008), *Tillich: A Guide for the Perplexed*, London: T & T Clark.

Re Manning, Russell (ed.) (2009), *The Cambridge Companion to Paul Tillich*, Cambridge: Cambridge University Press.

Santmire, H. Paul (1985), *The Travail of Nature: The Ambiguous Ecological Promise of Christian Theology*, Philadelphia: Fortress.

Thomas, J. Heywood (2000), *Tillich*, London: Continuum.

Tillich, Paul (1949), *The Shaking of the Foundations*, London: SCM. Also published (1962) by Harmondsworth: Penguin.

--- (1952), *The Courage to Be*, London: Nisbet.

--- (1954), *Love, Power, and Justice*, Oxford: Oxford University Press.

[6] Lai Pan-chiu (1991), chapters 7-9.

[7] Santmire, 141, 252; Lai Pan-chiu (1999); Drummy.

--- (1956), *The New Being*, London: SCM.
--- (1957a), *The Dynamics of Faith*, New York: Harper and Row.
--- (1957b), *The Protestant Era*, Chicago: University of Chicago Press.
--- (1961), "Autobiographical Reflections of Paul Tillich", in: C. W. Kegley and R. W. Bretall (eds.), *Theology of Paul Tillich*, New York: Macmillan, 3-21.
--- (1963), *The Eternal Now*, New York: Charles Scribner's Sons.
--- (1978), *Systematic Theology* (3 volumes), London: SCM.

Lai Pan-chiu

Dietrich Bonhoeffer (1906-1945) – Jesus Christ and the Restoration, Preservation and Reconciliation of Creation

Context and Influences

Given Bonhoeffer's popularity it is surprising that his distinctive understanding of the interconnectedness of creation and redemption is relatively unexplored. In response to attempts by theologians sympathetic to Nazism to commandeer Luther's theology of creation, Bonhoeffer took a serious interest in creation from 1932. Like many in the Lutheran tradition, initially he prioritised "salvation history" above the doctrine of creation, but in the mature theology of his *Ethics*, he attempted – arguably with mixed results – to correct the neglect of the category of the natural in Protestant thought. In his *Ethics* Bonhoeffer uses several strikingly original tropes to describe the relation of salvation in Christ to creation.

Bonhoeffer grew up in Berlin where his father was professor of psychiatry and neurology from 1912. Aged 21, Bonhoeffer completed a doctoral dissertation on the church, entitled *Sanctorum Communio*, at Berlin University (1998; German original 1930). This was followed by a habilitation thesis, *Act and Being* (1996; German original 1931), on the doctrine of revelation. *Act and Being* established that true knowledge of one's creaturehood is possible only by participation in Christ: "As those living in Christ, the new human beings know themselves in identity with the old human beings that have passed through death – as God's creatures."[8] In preparation for ordination Bonhoeffer was an assistant minister in Barcelona (1928-1929) and from 1930 to 1931 he was a visiting scholar at Union Seminary, New York. These experiences gave his formation an international dimension many contemporaries lacked. Though his regional church incorporated reformed and Lutheran traditions, Bonhoeffer always leaned strongly towards Luther's theology. However, from the mid 1920s, to the consternation of his liberal theological teachers, he embraced – though never uncritically – the theology of Karl Barth. From 1932 Bonhoeffer was increasingly engaged in a struggle against state interference in church life – as a lecturer in Berlin, as a pastor in London (1933-1935) and as director of an illegal seminary for the Confessing Church (from 1935) until his arrest by the Gestapo in April 1943. *Life Together* (1996, written in 1937) is a reflection on Christian community from this period and *Discipleship* (2001; German original 1937) an exploration, in dialogue with the Sermon on the Mount, of what it means to follow Jesus. After evidence emerged of Bonhoeffer's complicity in

---

[8] Bonhoeffer (1996a), 151.

the July 1944 attempt on Hitler's life, he was executed at the Flossenburg concentration camp on 9 April 1945. The political context of Bonhoeffer's life shaped his writing to an unusual degree and his life story, ending on a Nazi gallows, has for better and for worse shaped his posthumous reception.

Creation and Fall

Though Bonhoeffer deals often with creation and salvation in his writings, we may usefully focus on two books where his thinking is particularly well developed. During the winter semester of 1932 / 1933 Bonhoeffer lectured on creation and sin, subsequently published as *Creation and Fall* (1997; German original 1933). The decision of a "dogmatic" theologian to offer a "theological exposition" of Genesis chapters 1-3 was unusual enough, but the decision to "take the Bible", including Hebrew Scripture, "as the book of the church" was boldly controversial in a semester that coincided with Hitler's appointment as Reich Chancellor on 30 January 1933. Bonhoeffer's biblical hermeneutic led him to the axiom that: "Only the church, which knows of the end, knows also of the beginning ... In the church, therefore, the story of creation must be read in a way that begins with Christ and only then moves on toward him as its goal" (p. 22). Knowledge of creation is, therefore, only possible for Bonhoeffer on the basis of God's own testimony to creation through his word. In a striking claim Bonhoeffer asserts, for example, that we may know that God's act of creation was *ex nihilo* because the God of "the utter beginning, is the God of the resurrection", suggesting that God's act of salvation "witnesses" to his act of creation. In developing this idea, Bonhoeffer maintained, with Barth, the importance of God's freedom in relation to creation. But he also echoed Luther in conceiving creation in terms of a "speech-act". In a dense passage that neatly illustrates both influences, he writes that: "God is never the creation but always the Creator ... there is no continuum that ties God to, or unites God with, God's work – except God's word" (p. 40). We do not, that is, recognise God as Creator from what he has made, as if one can move backwards from effect to cause: uniquely with God, God's spoken command "let there be" is in a single moment also God's creative act. Creation, for Bonhoeffer, was once-for-all, a genuine beginning.

Within the created cosmos humanity has a special role since there is a "peculiar relation between humankind and God" (p. 62) that is based on a particular kind of likeness of human beings to God: "The likeness, the analogia, of humankind to God is not analogia entis but *analogia relationis*" (p. 65). This view protects God's aseity (God is not ontologically like us) but also attests that God, in Christ, is free *for* relationship with human beings rather than free *from* them.

In a consciously Augustinian / Lutheran turn, Bonhoeffer gives the fall a central place in his theology of creation. Acknowledging the "scientific naïveté" (p. 50) of the writers of Genesis, Bonhoeffer claims that the story of the fall of Adam confronts, disturbs and criticises us (p. 92), describing imaginatively the true state of fallen creation in relation to God. Prior to the fall God and humanity lived in a unity based on Adam's simple obedience to God. At the fall Adam / Eve are separated from God because humankind "is now sicut deus [like God]. It now lives out of its own resources, creates its own life, is its own creator; it no longer needs the Creator, it has itself become creator, inasmuch as it creates its own life. Thereby its creatureliness is eliminated, destroyed" (p. 115).

The final stage of Bonhoeffer's theological exposition is to explore God's changed relationship with creation following the fall: "the Creator is now the preserver; the created world is now the fallen but preserved world" (p. 139). As the Creator wrested the cosmos from nothing, after the fall it will return to nothing without God's continual upholding (*Erhaltung*) of it in being. The vocabulary of creation and preservation derives from Luther, but there is already a suggestion here that Bonhoeffer is prepared to think independently where creation is concerned, and in *Creation and Fall* several features of Bonhoeffer's mature theology of creation and salvation are already in place. These include: his Christocentric approach to creation and his methodological preference for theology that works from Scripture. Though never explicit, the political context is throughout present between the lines.

Ethics

From 1933 until the outbreak of war, Bonhoeffer worked to resist Nazism within and without the church. Theologians sympathetic to the social and political transformation effected by the Nazis made use of the orders of creation theologically to underpin the claim that the German people is established by God, who also appoints a *Führer* to lead it towards its national destiny. Serious theologians, including the Swiss reformed theologian Emil Brunner, continued to make extensive use of the "orders of creation"; but by 1940 Bonhoeffer had reached the view that the dependence of creation upon the command of God needed to be thoroughly overhauled in order to reclaim it from the Nazis. Bonhoeffer's *Ethics*, published posthumously in 1949 and subsequently twice significantly reordered in new editions (the latest in English in 2005), is a collection of fragments – some more finished than others – dating from the summer of 1940 to the early period of Bonhoeffer's imprisonment in 1943. The fragments use several different "motifs". For example, one fragment explores ethics as a conformation to the form or character of Jesus Christ, while another describes ethics in terms of obedience to divine command. In spite of such differences, Bonhoeffer's approach in the fragments is essentially consistent in its Christology, its biblical hermeneutic, its conceptualisation of theological ethics and, most importantly for our purposes here, in its understanding of the relation between creation and salvation. Here I identify briefly three key elements.

a) Christ and the Reconciliation of Disintegrated Creation

After the fall, as Bonhoeffer established in *Creation and Fall*, the world fragments, splits or disintegrates. Creation is no longer one with God, and creation itself becomes impossibly disintegrated. One result is thinking "in terms of two realms" pitted against each other, "worldly-Christian, natural-supernatural, profane-sacred, rational-revelational". Opposites that were one at creation result from the split effected by sin. In Christ, God enters the reality of the world to reconcile and to reunite disintegrated reality. Christians participate in this unification through faith in Christ. This is the first trope used by Bonhoeffer, linking creation and Christ's work of redemption.

b) Natural Life

One example, though Bonhoeffer does not explicitly say so, of "thinking in two realms" is the way in which "[t]he concept of the natural has fallen into disrepute in Protestant ethics" (p. 171), which can tend to see Christian faith as aimed towards the supernatural and away from the natural. Life lived in a reality reunited in Christ is one in which "[t]he natural is that form of life preserved by God for the fallen world that is directed toward justification, salvation and renewal through Christ" (p. 174). Bonhoeffer characterises this relation – of natural life to saved and renewed life in Christ – variously as a "preparing of the way", or as a relation between "the penultimate and the ultimate" (p. 146-170), in which the ultimate holds open a space for the penultimate. On this basis, in the most obvious form of "applied" ethics in the fragments, Bonhoeffer discusses a number of concrete moral issues through the lens of the category of the natural, including euthanasia, suicide and marriage.

c) Divine Orders and the Divine Mandates

In the final substantial section to be written, the influence of Barth's *Church Dogmatics* II.2, of which Bonhoeffer had obtained galley proofs, is evident. It concerns "The Concrete Commandment and the Divine Mandates". The mandates are Bonhoeffer's attempt concretely to describe the penultimate spheres of preservation kept open in creation by Christ. The new term is intended to distance his account from the morally compromised "orders of creation", but also to base them in living relationships (including relationships of authority) rather than in static structures. In English, the etymological link between divine com*mand* and the divine *mand*ate helpfully links them to the speech act on which the mandates depend: "By 'mandate' we understand the concrete divine commission grounded in the revelation of Christ and the testimony of scripture; it is the authorization and legitimization to declare a particular divine commandment, the conferring of divine authority on an earthly institution" (p. 389). The *Ethics* gives more than one list of examples of such "mandates", and there is some variance, but in this best-developed account they include church, family, culture and government. Barth judged that Bonhoeffer's concept of the mandates had a whiff of "north-German patriarchalism" about them, meaning that the emphasis on the authority of office holders (fathers, pastors, magistrates, etc.) within the mandates underwrote a social and political conservatism. This section is, in any case, incomplete. But the attempt to link the ultimate gospel of Christ to penultimate social structures within creation signals a commendable – and original attempt, especially from within the Lutheran tradition, to link creation and salvation.

Conclusion: A World Come of Age?

Bonhoeffer's final theological writings were in the form of letters to his friend Eberhard Bethge, smuggled from his prison cell. For a time, in the 1960s, the prison theology was interpreted as a radical new phase – a move, as one commentator put it, from church to world. More recent scholarship has been keener to see underlying continuities between the prison letters and what preceded them. But the last word belongs to his *Letters and Papers from Prison* (see 2010) nonetheless. Prophetically aware of signs of secularisation, Bonhoeffer is conscious of men and women living, in a term adapted from Hugo Grotius, "*etsi deus non daretur* – 'as if there were no God'" (p. 476). Bonhoeffer aims to embrace a "World Come of Age" not simply because religion can no longer be taken for granted but also because he advocates a "profound this-worldliness that shows discipline and includes the ever present knowledge of death and resurrection" (p. 541). This is not, to be sure, a developed constructive theology of creation, or anywhere close to it: but it is, perhaps, a more welcoming standpoint from which such a theology could be developed than many theologians in the Lutheran tradition had achieved.

References and Recommended Reading

Bonhoeffer, Dietrich (1998), *Sanctorum Communio*, Dietrich Bonhoeffer Works in English 1, Minneapolis: Fortress.

--- (1996a), *Act and Being*, Dietrich Bonhoeffer Works in English 2, Minneapolis: Fortress.

--- (1996b), *Life Together / Prayerbook of the Bible*, Dietrich Bonhoeffer Works in English 5, Minneapolis: Fortress.

--- (1997), *Creation and Fall: A Theological Exposition of Genesis 1-3*, Dietrich Bonhoeffer Works in English 3, Minneapolis: Fortress.

--- (2001) *Discipleship*, Dietrich Bonhoeffer Works in English 4, Minneapolis: Fortress.

--- (2005), *Ethics*, Dietrich Bonhoeffer Works in English 6, Minneapolis: Fortress.

--- (2008), *Dietrich Bonhoeffer: Barcelona, Berlin, New York: 1928-1931*, Dietrich Bonhoeffer Works in English 10, Minneapolis: Fortress.

--- (2010), *Letters and Papers from Prison*, Dietrich Bonhoeffer Works in English 8, Minneapolis: Fortress.

Green, Clifford J. (1999), *Bonhoeffer: A Theology of Sociality* (revised edition), Grand Rapids: Eerdmans.

Nielsen, Kirsten Busch (2010), *Der gebrochene Macht der Sünde: Der Beitrag Dietrich Bonhoeffers zur Hamartiologie*, Leipzig: Evangelische Verlagsanstalt.

Plant, Stephen (2004), *Bonhoeffer*, Outstanding Christian Thinkers Series, London: Continuum.

Stephen J. Plant

Joseph Sittler (1904-1987) – The Cosmic Christ

Unless you have a crucified God, you don't have a big enough God.[9]

Introduction

Joseph Sittler was an important theologian. One indication of his significance can be found in his influence within and on the ecumenical movement. For example, in his chronicle of the Christology of the Faith and Order Movement of the World Council of Churches, Conrad Simonson points to the pivotal role of Sittler, especially his New Delhi speech of 1961, "Called to Unity", in challenging the church to expand the scope of its Christological vision to include nothing less than all of reality. As Simonson says:

> *Time* magazine ventured the opinion that the most original and challenging address to the Assembly was given by Dr. Joseph Sittler, Lutheran professor at the University of Chicago Divinity School. ... What is needed, he [Sittler] concluded, is an all-encompassing Christian vision ... with a core of spirituality illuminating "economics, politics, and all other areas of human affairs.[10]

---

[9] Sittler (1981), 119.

[10] Simonson, 94.

Sittler's unique and lasting contribution, according to Simonson, is his "Christology of nature" – a Christology "as large as the nature and destiny of man" and "expanded to its cosmic dimensions".[11]

Peter Bakken likewise remarks that because of "his early attention to the environment as a theological issue", Joseph Sittler "has been called 'the most original American theologian of his time'".[12] Bakken asserts that "Sittler's main concern was to expand Christians' understanding of grace to include *more* than the individual's relationship to Jesus".[13] Finally, Paul Santmire includes Sittler in his short list of Christian theologians who have offered the most creative and fruitful reflections on a Christian ecological theology. According to Santmire:

> The inner-theological challenge that Sittler presents to Western theology must be perceived as both radical and revolutionary. His challenge is in fact a call for a kind of paradigm shift in Christian thought, away from an exclusively the-anthropological soteriology, to what can be called an inclusive or universal soteriology, which envisions the final salvation of all things as the *telos* of creation, not just the salvation of a kingdom of rational spirits, in the fashion of most post-Kantian Protestant theology.[14]

Though Joseph Sittler died in December of 1987, his legacy lives on, especially with respect to the development of an expansive view of creation and salvation.

The Scope of Grace

So what exactly is Sittler's universal soteriology? We begin with the topic of grace, since Sittler himself again and again points to this theme as being of central importance to his theological project and, in his view, to the future of Christian theology. For example, Sittler states that:

> I am interested in the reality or the presence of the grace of God in the creation, because only the doctrine of grace will be adequate to change the spirit of our minds whereby we deal with timber and oil, fish and animals, and the structure of cities, urban design, homes for people, places to work – all these mundane, concrete things that yet constitute the anchorage of our hearts, the home of our daily lives.[15]

Sittler elaborates on this claim when, in referring to the ecological character of reality as the necessary context for doing theology, he asserts: "If we are to ask which of the comprehensive Christian doctrines is the one large enough and ready enough and interiorly most capable of articulating a theological relationship between theology and ecology, I would suggest that the doctrine of grace is the one."[16]

Sittler argues, however, that no traditional doctrine of grace will be adequate. The doctrine of grace must be reformulated to meet both the demands of Scripture and the needs of the modern world. For example, in his magnum opus, *Essays on Nature and*

---

[11] Simonson, vii, 94.

[12] Bakken, 35.

[13] Bakken, 390.

[14] Santmire (1982), 199.

[15] Sittler (1986), 14.

[16] Sittler (1970), 180.

Grace (1972),[17] Sittler clearly states both the problem and his own understanding of its solution:

> In virtue of what gift, love, understanding, and appropriate behavior can man live with the world-as-nature so as rightly to enjoy and use it? That is the problem. It is the thesis of these chapters that nothing short of a radical relocation and reconceptualization of the reality and the doctrine of grace is an adequate answer to that problem (p. 6).

Sittler's entire life project could fairly be described as an attempt to reconceive the doctrine of grace in such a way that its full cosmic scope is visible.

In various places Sittler traces the history of the narrowing of the scope of grace.[18] His main conclusion is that "the doctrine of grace has been almost exclusively administered in relation to man as sinner" (p. 14). That is, grace has been "completely identified with the work of God according to the Second Article, the grace of God in Jesus Christ".[19] In yet other words, "Christology is reduced to soteriology".[20] Sittler insists that this "almost exclusive elaboration of Christology under the article of redemption is reductive of biblical scope and of the richness of theological tradition" (p. 11). Viewing grace exclusively in terms of sin and redemption fails to do justice both to the riches of the biblical testimony to grace and to the expansive scope of grace articulated within the Christian tradition.

The most serious consequence of this reduction of grace is that "the realms of history and the moral" are identified "as the sole realm of grace" so as "to shrink to no effect the biblical Christology of nature".[21] In other words, because grace has often been reduced to human history, the cosmic scope of Christ's work has gone unrecognised. In short, Sittler refers to "the necessity to speak of the Triune God and his grace in a way that breaks out of a Protestant disposition to confine the reality of grace to the second article".[22] While "grace came by Jesus Christ" and "has in him its absolute embodiment", grace "was not created by Jesus Christ".[23]

If then it is clear what Sittler sees as problematic, what precisely is Sittler's own view? Sittler describes grace as the energy and essence of God. For example, Sittler acknowledges that "grace is indeed commonly postulated as the elemental character of God in his relation to all that is not God" and goes on to affirm that "grace is that God-as-communicating nothing less or other than himself as Presence" (p. 75). In the economy of God, grace is basic and pervasive: "The reality of grace is the fundamental reality of God the Creator in his creation, God the Redeemer in his redemption, and God the Sanctifier and Illuminator in all occasions of the common life where sanctifying grace is beheld, bestowed, and lived by" (p. 88). Employing the distinction between divine essence and energy, *ousia* and *energeia*, Sittler affirms that grace is "a

[17] Subsequent references in parenthesis in this section are to Sittler's *Essays on Nature and Grace*.

[18] For example, Sittler (1978), 42-43; (1964), 255-256; (1972a), 76ff.

[19] Sittler (1978), 42.

[20] Sittler (1964), 255.

[21] Sittler (1962), 10.

[22] Sittler (1971), 125.

[23] Sittler (1971), 125.

proper divine energy of the Trinity as such".[24] Put simply, grace is "the energy of love" (p. 87).

One important consequence of the above affirmation, according to Sittler, is that we must see grace as pervasive in all God does. In contrast to a delimitation of grace to only certain divine acts, Sittler argues that "in the great catholic tradition grace comes in creation, in redemption, in sanctification or the unfolding and maturation of the Christian life".[25] And since "the God of grace *is* a God of grace in the fullness of his being as Creator, Redeemer, and Sanctifier ... the region of grace is all that is, has been, and will be" (p. 86). Grace is not characteristic of only certain divine actions, nor is grace limited to only certain regions or spheres of existence. In typical trinitarian fashion Sittler affirms that "if grace is postulated of God the Creator, God the Redeemer, and God the Sanctifier, then the presence and power and availability of grace must be postulated with equivalent scope" (p. 83).

Creation as the Theatre of Grace

Like many others, Sittler points to the eclipse of the Christian doctrine of creation as a significant factor in the loss of a vision of the natural world as graced.[26] Because of "this virtual demise of a vigorous doctrine of the Creation", argues Sittler,

> ... it is difficult but possible to get men to understand that pollution is biologically disastrous, aesthetically offensive, equally obviously economically self-destructive and socially reductive of the quality of human life. But it is a very difficult job to get even Christians to see that so to deal with the Creation is *Christianly* blasphemous. A proper doctrine of creation and redemption would make it perfectly clear that from a Christian point of view the ecological crisis presents us not simply with moral tasks but requires of us a freshly renovated and fundamental theology of the first article.[27]

Only renewed attention to the doctrine of creation will provide the necessary theological and ethical resources to think and act responsibly.

The challenge, as Sittler sees it, is to develop a "holy naturalism" that creatively steers a course between utilitarian anthropocentrism and reductionistic naturalism. In his attempt to develop a naturalism shaped by Christian categories, Sittler makes one central claim: "The world is not God, but it is God's. Or to put the issue another way, nature and grace belong together."[28] The world is neither divine nor autonomous – to be neither worshipped nor viewed as empty of divine presence.

This may be summarised in what is perhaps Sittler's most pervasive theme with respect to his attempt to fashion a holy naturalism. In a variety of ways Sittler affirms that creation is the locus of grace. He argues, for example, that because "God creates his creation in grace" therefore "the creation itself is a realm of grace".[29] Sittler insists

---

[24] Sittler (1971), 127.

[25] Sittler (1978), 11.

[26] Others who note this *Schöpfungsvergessenheit* are Lønning, 5; Barbour, 217; and Wingren, 353ff.

[27] Sittler (1970), 179.

[28] Sittler (1970), 178.

[29] Sittler (1986), 13.

that "despite human rapacity and despoliation" the natural world is still "a field of grace".[30] Elsewhere, sounding a familiar theme, Sittler affirms that "the grace of God must find the theatre of its acknowledgement not just in the forgiveness of sins and the sacrament and the sermon, etc., but in the very giftedness of the natural world as itself a theatre of grace".[31]

The Cosmic Christ in Creation and Redemption

Sittler's views on grace and creation provide important background for his Christology. Sittler begins by arguing that we must expand the scope of Christology to encompass all that has being. In other words, a necessary dimension in the development of a "Christology for nature" is the articulation of a cosmic Christology. The pressure to enlarge the scope of Christology arises, Sittler insists, from the Bible.

More exactly, Sittler claims that "it is possible and legitimate to see a growing magnitude in the Christological utterances of the New Testament" – "an ever-widening orbit of christological meaning, scope, and force" (p. 11). There are not only differences in the biblical testimony to Christ, argues Sittler, but "differences-in-motion" such that talk of a "christological momentum may be the most accurate term for what the literature of the New Testament discloses" (p. 29). In short, while Sittler acknowledges that there is a genuine plurality in the New Testament witness to Christ that cannot be systematised, he also insists that "there clearly is a momentum and a directionality at work in the scope and variety of the New Testament witness to Jesus as the Christ" – a momentum characterised by "widening circles of reference" until in Colossians and Ephesians "all things" are enfolded within the work of Christ.[32]

Sittler thus speaks of a "rhetoric of cosmic extension" in the Bible (p. 36ff.). There is "an undilutable momentum, a 'blooming' of the language of Christ-testimony, in the New Testament" that has its roots in Israel's faith and finds its fullest expression in Colossians 1, Ephesians 1 and Romans 8 (p. 30). As Sittler states in his famous New Delhi address, which is an extended meditation on Colossians 1:15-20, "the sweep of God's restorative action in Christ is no smaller than the six-times repeated *ta panta*".[33] Indeed, says Sittler, "all things are permeable to his [Christ's] cosmic redemption because all things subsist in him. He comes to all things, not as a stranger, for he is first-born of all creation, and in him all things were created."[34]

Sittler finds in the early church, especially Irenaeus, resources for "a Christology of the total cosmos" (p. 55). What attracts Sittler to "the cosmic Christology of Irenaeus" is "the idea that the Incarnate Word is in himself the unity and harmony not only of men, but also of the entire material universe", which Irenaeus works out using the language of recapitulation (p. 63). In other words, "the God who is man's Redeemer dare not be acknowledged as other or less than the Creator of the world" and thus "the scope of Lordship dare not be specified as less than the scope of all that is" (p. 116). Our Redeemer is our Creator, and our Creator is the Creator of everything.

---

30 Sittler (1981), 86.

31 Sittler (1972b), 82; cf. 81.

32 Sittler (1972c), 334.

33 Sittler (1962), 6.

34 Sittler (1962), 6.

In his Christology Sittler describes Christ as "the personal concentration of the grace of God".[35] All creation is grace, but there is an "absolute concentration of the reality of grace at the point of Christ" (p. 77). Therefore the scope of grace must be understood "both in its Christ-concentration and its extent" (p. 25). While Christ is the incarnation of grace, grace is evident in all creation.

Our Redeemer is Our Creator

In summary, Joseph Sittler's theology attempts to do justice to God's work both of creation and of salvation. Sittler neither compartmentalises creation and salvation, as if the orders of creation are somehow separate from the work of Jesus Christ, nor fuses creation and salvation, as if creation is itself an act of salvation. They are distinct acts, but both originate in the grace of a triune God. Christology is not reduced to soteriology, nor is grace reduced to the work of Christ on earth. In response to Mercy Amba Oduyoye's pressing question: "Is the God of our redemption the same as the God of our creation?" Sittler answers with a resounding "yes". Our Redeemer is our Creator. And our Creator is a God of grace. Because of that, we can live with hope.

References and Recommended Reading

Bakken, Peter (1991), "The Ecology of Grace: Ultimacy and Environmental Ethics in Aldo Leopold and Joseph Sittler", Ph.D. dissertation, University of Chicago.

Barbour, Ian G. (1990), *Religion in an Age of Science*, San Francisco: Harper and Row.

Lønning, Per (1989), *Creation – An Ecumenical Challenge? Reflections Issuing from a Study by the Institute for Ecumenical Research Strasbourg France*, Macon: Mercer.

Santmire, H. Paul (1982), "Studying the Doctrine of Creation", *Dialog*, Vol. 21, 195-200.

Simonson, Conrad (1972), *The Christology of the Faith and Order Movement*, Leiden: Brill.

Sittler, Joseph (1954), "A Theology for Earth", *The Christian Scholar*, Vol. 37, 367-374.

--- (1962), "Called to Unity", *Southeast Asia Journal of Theology*, Vol. 3, 6-15.

--- (1964), "Nature and Grace: Reflections on an Old Rubric", *Dialog*, Vol. 3, 252-256.

--- (1966), *The Anguish of Preaching*, Philadelphia: Fortress.

--- (1970), "Ecological Commitment as Theological Responsibility", *Zygon: Journal of Religion and Science*, Vol. 5, 172-181.

--- (1971), "The Presence and Acts of the Triune God in Creation and History", in: Vilmos Vajta (ed.), *The Gospel and Human Destiny*, Minneapolis: Augsburg, 90-135.

--- (1972a) *Essays on Nature and Grace*, Philadelphia: Fortress.

--- (1972b), "The Perils of Futurist Thinking", in: John Roslansky (ed.), *Shaping the Future*, Amsterdam: North Holland, 66-82.

--- (1972c), "The Scope of Christological Reflection", *Interpretation*, Vol. 26, 328-337.

--- (1978), "The Sittler Speeches", in: Phil Schroeder(ed.), *Center for the Study of Campus Ministry Yearbook 1977-1978*, Valparaiso: Valparaiso University, 8-61.

--- (1981), *Grace Notes and Other Fragments* (selected and edited by Robert Herhold and Linda Marie Delloff), Minneapolis: Augsburg.

--- (1986), *Gravity and Grace: Reflections and Provocations* (edited by Linda Marie Delloff), Minneapolis: Augsburg.

Wingren, Gustaf (1984), "The Doctrine of Creation: Not an Appendix but the First Article", *Word and World*, Vol. 4, 353-371.

Steven Bouma-Prediger

[35] Sittler (1966), 59. See also Sittler (1986), 106, where Sittler refers to Jesus as "the incomparable and incandescent concreteness" of God.

Wolfhart Pannenberg (1928-) – The Creative Power of Love Revealed

Introduction

According to Wolfhart Pannenberg, God's divinity is dependent on God being the all-decisive power and on his sovereignty over creation. However, God's omnipotence is not fully demonstrated until the final restoration of creation. It is at the closure of history that God's reality and might is definitively established. Therefore all historical processes, reaching their consummation in redemption, will have to be interpreted as a self-demonstration of God's presence. Thus, in Pannenberg's theology, the relation between creation and salvation is integrated in his fundamental understanding of who God is. Likewise, a discussion of creation and salvation will need to address the central themes of revelation and Christology.

Wolfhart Pannenberg was born on 2 October 1928 in Stettin on the Oder, in northeast Germany, now part of Poland. In 1942 his family moved to Berlin, where Pannenberg developed his interests in music and philosophy. As a student at Humboldt University in East Berlin, he was later so fascinated by the study of Christianity that he decided to build his academic career on theology, while still continuing his studies in philosophy. After one year in Göttingen, Pannenberg left for Basel, where Karl Barth's lectures were important stimuli for his theology of revelation. Later Hans von Campenhausen, Gerhard von Rad and Edmund Schlink became his mentors. It was Schlink who awoke his interest in ecumenical theology, also showing him the significance of interdisciplinary dialogue, especially with the natural sciences. It is therefore characteristic that Pannenberg as professor at the theological faculty of the University of Munich, from 1968 to 1994, over a period of several years also functioned as head of the newly established institute for ecumenics at the university. He was, furthermore, an active participant in a number of interdisciplinary forums focusing on theological and philosophical dialogue. Thus he expressed his concern for the centrality of theological universality, also implying that theology can only regain its credibility through its interdisciplinary character.

In 1961 Wolfhart Pannenberg published a programmatic book translated as *Revelation as History* (1968), establishing him as a public theologian of revelation and creation. This book was the result of discussions in the so-called Heidelberg Circle, formed by a group of theologians who intended to probe the systematic-theological implications of von Rad's exegetical views. Pannenberg elaborated on his revelation theology in the Christological work *Jesus: God and Man* (1968; German original 1964), developing the implications for anthropology and creation theology in the books *What Is Man?* (1970; German original 1962), and *Anthropology in Theological Perspective* (1985; German original 1983). Other publications relevant for the theme of creation and salvation include *Theology and the Philosophy of Science* (1976; German original 1973), *Metaphysics and the Idea of God* (1990; German original 1988), *Systematic Theology, Volume 1* (1991; German original 1988), *Volume 2* (1994; German original 1991), *Volume 3* (1998; German original 1993). In the discussion below I will commence with his understanding of creation as expressed in *Revelation as History* as well as in *Jesus: God and Man*.

View of Revelation

Pannenberg's view of revelation is closely linked to that of Karl Barth. He claims that revelation can only take place where God discloses himself to human beings. He implies that revelation is always self-revelation and that God uses means appropriate for that. Moreover, the consequence is that revelation is not related to mysterious phenomena of a supernatural nature, but always to specific realities in the created world. Theological differences do surface in terms of the emphasis on the *place* where revelation happens. The programmatic features of *Revelation as History* are seen in the change of focus from the proclamation of the Word (Barth) to history and creation. This provides for the possibility of indirect revelation and for a recognition by all who can see. In addition, an indirect revelation makes it possible to imagine that all of history – the universal history – is the setting where God manifests Godself. This, furthermore, implies that God's ultimate appearance can only take place at the end of history.

The connection between *Jesus: God and Man* and *Revelation as History* is easily detectable, as Pannenberg in his work on Christology consistently emphasises the unity of Jesus with God through the category of revelation. The key to grasping this is the significance of the person of Jesus (Christology) as well as the created world in general (creation theology) for revelation. Pannenberg's point of departure is that the judgement and salvation teaching of Jesus is an anticipation of God's future, ultimate rule. The context for Pannenberg's perspective on resurrection is apocalyptic eschatology, a point which is important to bear in mind when working with this issue. The proleptic character of Jesus' presence and work is closely connected with an understanding of apocalypse in post-exilic Judaism. On this Pannenberg bases his thesis that the end of history and the restoration of creation are proleptically present in Christology, that is, revealed in the life and fate of Jesus.

Creation

God's omnipotent sovereignty over creation does not mean that God *faces* the created as someone passively "watching over it". On the contrary, God is actively involved in creation, upholding it through his creative power. Pannenberg's approach here is to hold together the life of nature with the biblical stories of life on earth. He claims that every living being is dependent on a transcendent reality in order to transcend itself, corresponding with the biblical worldview on life as dependent on the Spirit's creative energy. The truth in the simple biblical picture is that life on earth comes into being and continues to exist by God's ability to breathe life into it, that is, through the "movement" God himself is, his "breath", his spirit (Hebrew: *ruah*). Pannenberg's argument must be understood as part of his view on reality as a totality: Just as every phenomenon in life depends on its environment, these surroundings again depend on their transcending context, finally demonstrating that all life processes are created and sustained by the energy of the Spirit.

Pannenberg's view may be described as a "phenomenology of the spirit". It is of vital importance for grasping his creation theology. According to him, the phenomena of life are not reduced to functions of secular sciences. The biblical texts also contain insights which can inform biology: according to modern biology living organisms are open, not closed, systems. All organisms feed on their surroundings, from the least complex biological organisms to the most advanced species, including humans.

It is evident that Pannenberg seeks to overcome the dualism between spirit and matter, spirit and nature. Like Teilhard de Chardin, Pannenberg binds spirit and energy so closely together that energy has to be seen as self-manifestations of the Spirit. Just as the Spirit participates in and creates nature, nature may be regarded as an expression of the Spirit without their becoming identical. Pannenberg, in this way, seems to have overcome a mechanical worldview in which God ends up having no function at all.

Finally: Pannenberg reinforces his argument for the unity of existence by referring to the field theory of modern physics, in which totality has an ontological priority over individual entities. It facilitates his belief that God – and no one else – is the unifying power of everything that exists. Furthermore, it enables us to imagine that God is the creator and redeemer of all reality, also claiming that the Spirit is not to be divided by being restricted to two unrelated spheres of existence: creation and redemption. This is nothing but an attempt to articulate the meaning of the notion of *Spiritus Creator* anew: If the Spirit does not create life, creation is nothing.

Salvation as Restoration of Creation / the Created Order

Pannenberg's arguments for the connection between creation and salvation are built upon trinitarian theology. He claims that God is sovereign over the created order, while emphasising nonetheless that God has relinquished the work of redemption to the Son and the Spirit. This becomes fully comprehensible only when considering the personal relationships between Father, Son and Spirit as expressed in Scripture: According to Pannenberg it is not sufficient to proclaim that the Father gives birth to the Son, as the Father also entrusts his sovereignty to the Son by sending him forth and by sharing in his suffering. The resurrection of the Son is not merely a confirmation of the life of the Son, but also a confirmation of the Father who sent him. Correspondingly, the Spirit does not only go forth from the Father, as the Spirit is also received by the Son and given to all those who believe in him. Moreover, in this the Spirit glorifies the Father and the Son. This element of mutuality in the personal relations in the Trinity does not suspend the sovereignty of the Father – Pannenberg uses the word "monarchy" here – as the sovereignty cannot be abstracted from the work of the Son and the Spirit. That Jesus proclaims the arrival of God's kingdom is, in fact, realised by the obedience of the Son and by the glorifying activity of the Spirit. This motivates the created order to participate in this obedience and to spread the knowledge of the Father's kingdom.

Pannenberg's views on creation and salvation clearly suggest both discontinuity and continuity with the tradition. The discontinuity is expressed through the Son serving the Father in obedience to the Father's will, but still having his own independent realm of service. Such service is expressed in the Son's saving actions, by allowing human beings to enter by faith into God's salvation, and by faith becoming visible in the community of the worship service, in prayer, in liturgy, in praise. However, in this very setting there is also continuity: when the believers in the worship fellowship praise the Saviour, the Father and his sovereignty is also glorified. Consequently, we may gather that salvation is not something being added to creation, as in a mathematical addition, for in salvation the work of the Creator is made visible and becomes completed.

The Creative Power of Love

How can the Creator's work reach completion in a sinful world? Pannenberg maintains that the autonomy characteristic of the persons in the Godhead is reflected in the freedom human beings are given to separate themselves from the lordship of the Creator. According to Pannenberg, this equals removing oneself from the very source of life itself: the life-giving power of the Spirit, referred to above as the *Spiritus Creator*.

This power, however, is also the source of *love*, for when we say that "God is spirit", we also say that "God is love" since these are two sides of the same coin. The "power" of the Spirit rests in its ability to call creation out of nothing by giving existence to the created order. This is the life-giving aspect of the Spirit. The corresponding life-giving aspect of love – the "power" of love – is not forceful power and the commandments of the law, but obedience, for through obedience – that of Christ – love conquered sin, death, hatred, envy and injustice. According to Pannenberg, it is only through love that one can contribute to making the world new.

One of the best illustrations of how love is unfolded in human activity is evident from his distinction between love and law. The merits of love, he says, are that it can create new forms of relationships and new ways of encountering specific situations. In this context he discusses the creative imagination of love, able to adapt to the unexpected, unforeseen situations, as for example that given in the New Testament parable of the man who fell among robbers (Luke 10:25-37). The Samaritan who did not know the victim previously becomes his neighbour. In this way love is seen as liberty, and only liberty can do justice when faced with actual destitution and injustice. The old order of things constantly demands casuistic extensions and elaborations in new situations, while love in its creativity appeals to immediate human choices and actions. Today this is relevant not least in people's interaction with the environment and vulnerable nature. More than ever, it is imperative through the creativity of love to find new and unfettered ways of conserving the bio-physical environment. Even if Jesus summed up the Old Testament's notion of divine justice in the commandment of loving God and one's neighbour, love is, according to Pannenberg, still not primarily a commandment but a living reality. It is an impulse emanating from God's inner being towards the world, seizing humanity, drawing us into God's own movement. That is the abiding insight in Augustine's polemics with Pelagius: love as motivational power is of a different character compared to obedience regarding a commandment. This corresponds, furthermore, to Paul's theology which claims that love is a charisma, enabling us to relate to God's created gifts and to God's redeeming love. When Paul in this context uses the word "charisma", corresponding to the outpouring of God's love in the heart of people through the Spirit of God, he demonstrates that this is more than human actions; rather, this is a sphere in which humanity may move, a domain of power emanating from God and connecting humans with God. Thus it is shown that when we presuppose love, as discussed by Søren Kierkegaard in *Works of Love*, we presuppose a power surpassing ourselves and driving us toward our neighbour like the Samaritan in the parable was moved to exert love towards the man fallen among robbers.

Conclusion

Pannenberg is undoubtedly one of the most high-profile and influential apologists of the 20th century. His theology includes an energetic attempt to respond to the atheist accusation that religion is only a function of human wishes and needs. Pannenberg's strategy is not to promote the idea that the message of Christianity is adaptable, but rather to give plausible reasons for its truth, which is possible only where the universal and rational implications of theology are presented. Because faith lives in the hope of the full attainment of God's kingdom in the world, in the realm of reason and the rational, Christians are not given a mandate to withdraw to the subjective interiors, isolated from worldly experiences. This provides motivation also for faith's involvement on behalf of creation.

References and Recommended Reading

Braaten, Carl E. and Clayton, Philip (eds.) (1988), *The Theology of Wolfhart Pannenberg: Twelve American Critiques, with an Autobiographical Essay and Response*, Minneapolis: Augsburg.
Grenz, Stanley J. (2004), *Rediscovering the Triune God: The Trinity in Contemporary Theology*, Minneapolis: Fortress.
Pannenberg, Wolfhart (1968a), *Revelation as History*, New York: Macmillan.
--- (1968b), *Jesus: God and Man*, Philadelphia: Westminster.
--- (1970), *What is Man?* Philadelphia: Fortress.
--- (1976), *Theology and the Philosophy of Science*, Philadelphia: Westminster
--- (1985), *Anthropology in Theological Perspective*, Philadelphia: Westminster.
--- (1990), *Metaphysics and the Idea of God*, Edinburgh: T & T Clark.
--- (1991), *Systematic Theology, Volume 1*, Grand Rapids: Eerdmans.
--- (1994), *Systematic Theology, Volume 2*, Grand Rapids: Eerdmans.
--- (1998), *Systematic Theology, Volume 3*, Grand Rapids: Eerdmans.
Rise, Svein (1997), *The Christology of Wolfhart Pannenberg: Identity and Relevance*, New York: Mellen University Press.

Svein Rise

Robert W. Jenson (1930-) – A Dramatic Teleology of Creation

Introduction

Robert W. Jenson was born on 2 August 1930 in Eau Claire, Wisconsin, in the USA. He retired in 2005 as senior scholar for research at the Center of Theological Inquiry in Princeton, New Jersey. Before that he taught at Luther College in Decorah (1961-1966), at the Lutheran Theological Seminary in Gettysburg (1968-1988), and also at St. Olaf College in Northfield (1988-1998). He was also the Lutheran World Federation Lecturer in Theology at Oxford in the UK (1966-1968; 1972-1973). Jenson did his doctoral studies under Peter Brunner in Heidelberg on the theology of Karl Barth and Barth's influence on his theology is apparent. Jenson is one of several seminal theologians of our time who have pointed to the importance of the Cappadocian Fathers as sources for the re-appropriation of trinitarian insights.

Jenson's theology can be described as trinitarian, narrative, eschatological, ecumenical and ecclesiological. His main dogmatic works include the following: *Systematic Theology, Volume 1: The Triune God* (1997) and *Systematic Theology, Volume 2: The*

Works of God (1999) – his magnum opus,[36] *God after God: The God of the Past and the God of the Future, Seen in the Work of Karl Barth* (1969), *Alpha and Omega: A Study in the Theology of Karl Barth* (1963, 1969), *Triune Identity* (1982), *Christian Dogmatics* (1984, edited with Braaten), and *Story and Promise: A Brief Theology of the Gospel about Jesus* (1973).

Jenson's more ecumenically focused books include: *Visible Words: The Interpretation and Practice of the Christian Sacraments* (1978), *Unbaptized God: The Basic Flaw in Ecumenical Theology* (1992), *The Catholicity of the Reformation* (1996), *Jews and Christians* (2003), *In One Body through the Cross: The Princeton Proposal for Christian Unity* (2003) and *The Ecumenical Future* (2004). The last five books were co-edited with Carl Braaten. Although Jenson comes from the Lutheran tradition, he will not have his systematic theology labelled as Lutheran theology, because he works out his theology in the context and in the "anticipation of the one church" (*ST 1*, viii).

Theology as Story and Promise

Jenson developed his theology as a story of hope in reaction to the postmodern loss of story and promise. When Jenson tells God's story, he begins with the notion that the immanent Trinity is the economic Trinity. This leads to a very specific understanding about the relationship between God and time in which Jenson regards the definition of God's eternity as timeless as unbiblical and incompatible with the story of creation and redemption. God is not timeless, but God is lively, active, an event. The triune God is an event and the biblical narrative is the final truth of God's own reality in the mutual relations of the Father, Son and the Spirit. God's story thus takes on an ontological status and time becomes something God is not immune to, but something within the Trinity. This "timefulness" of God (his temporal infinity) is central to the relations within the Trinity and "the Father is the 'whence' of God's life; the Spirit is the 'whither' of God's life; and ... the Son is that life's specious present" (*ST 1*, 218-219).

Creation, salvation and fulfilment are thus all included within the life of the Trinity, in the event or story of God. From the accounts of creation onwards, the grand narrative is not a mythic account, with purely ontological, a-temporal claims, but rather a purposive entity with a history. It is thus within the triune God that creation (and us) finds its story (meaning) and promise (hope).

Creation

According to Jenson, it is within the trinitarian relations that creation takes place, because "Father, Son and Spirit can make room in himself for others, and the room he makes is our created time. The opening of that room is the act of creation" (*ST 1*, 226). This opening of room (space and time as creation) within God is possible because "the Spirit is *Spiritus Creator* as he frees the Father from retaining all being with himself and so frees what the Father initiates from being the mere emanation it would have been were the Father God by himself" (*ST 2*, 26). The work of the Son in this is that "he mediates between the Father's originating and the Spirit's liberating" (*ST 2*, 26-27), "thereby to hold open the creatures' space in being" (*ST 2*, 27). Creation is thus

[36] References in parenthesis in the text below are to these two volumes of Jenson's *Systematic Theology* (*ST 1* and *ST 2*).

not only taking place within God, but also "externally". However, Jenson does not move away from the notion of creation as the opening up of space for creatures within the divine being, but he takes care to qualify this "withinness". To be a creature in specific relation to the Father is to be a "motif in the orchestration that occurs when God's musicality opens *ad extra*" (*ST* 2, 39). Jenson balances this internality and otherness of creation by saying "insofar as to be a creature is to be other than God, we may say that the Father's love of the Son as other than himself is the possibility of creation's otherness from God" (*ST* 2, 48).

Can creation be "within" God, but fail to be part of God? Firstly, "roominess" is a metaphor in terms of which the continuing relatedness of the creation to God is being constructed. Secondly, Jenson says that God "must have his own place within creation if he is not simply to absorb the creature within himself" (*ST* 2, 120) and according to him this "own place" of God is heaven. Heaven is "the space between the man Jesus and the Father, insofar as this space is at once the space between a creature and God and the inner-triune difference between the Son and the Father. The latter difference is the possibility of space and creatures in it; its identity with the former is the possibility of God's spatial location over against them" (*ST* 2, 123). Jenson remains thus well short of committing to panentheism although he has sometimes been accused of "pan-en-trinitarianism".

Creation, as space and time "within God's being", is in coherence with Jenson's narrative and trinitarian theology. For him, God does not "create spatial objects that thereupon move through time; he creates … histories" (*ST* 2, 46). The story of God, which includes the story of creation, is that God creates precisely a history. The universe is an intelligible whole, a history, because it has an intended end – a story with a promise.

Salvation

Jenson defines sin as that which God does not want done. He follows Aquinas's exposition and says that sin is "original" in that none of us has an origin prior to it and in that humanity as a whole somehow sins as one. For Jenson, we are therefore compelled to posit a "fall" of humankind occurring within created time, and the story in the third chapter of Genesis is a description of the historical first happening of what thereafter always happens – of the first community of our biological ancestors who disobeyed God's command.

Jenson rejects the view that reconciliation is only God's reaction to human sin and says it must be part of God's eternal will to rescue us in Christ. However, the coming of Jesus to sinful man is not to be understood as a mere stratagem on God's part, but as part of a real historical encounter – the fall and redemption happen in created time. The whole history is not something with a solution given in advance, because creation and reconciliation will then collapse into each other. If this happens, then nothing essential happens in our time, and this would not fit into Jenson's description of God's story as one of dramatic coherence. For Jenson, the unity of creation and reconciliation lies in Jesus Christ, and thus it cannot be determined in advance. It occurs in the life history of Jesus.

In Jesus' crucifixion we thus see not merely God's accommodation to an unfortunate situation, but the opening of a depth in God in which he loves and sacrifices himself for sinners. The cross exposes us as rebels seeking to eliminate God from our lives, despite the fact that we, and our world, are God's good creation. In the cross God saves, in that he condemns and rejects our rebellion, and thereby claims us as his own. On the one hand, it is God's eternal will to create us as creatures destined to participate in his life. On the other hand, God's will and the direction of history are hidden by human rebellion and God's judgement. Jenson says that the gospel does not explain the rule of history's hidden Lord and that one does not see through history in advance by means of a series "in order thats". The unity of God's one eternal will is for Jenson an event that occurred in time at the cross.

What implication does this have for creation? Creation as a whole has not itself willed its condition and awaits its great deliverance, but creation is until then subjected to pointlessness. This subjection is decreed by God as a hopeful act. Jenson says that the "presumption must be that a creation that simply continued on the way of its own teleology while humanity went on the way of sin could not suffer the birth pangs of that humanity's redemption, while an adoption of human children into glory that occurred independently of the rest of creation would not be a 'redemption of the body'" (*ST 2*, 151). Creation (as *creatura*) must thus be included in salvation – it longs for redemption from the curse of humanity's sin, its subjection to pointlessness.

There is, however, the mystery of evil that is not sin, of "arbitrary disaster to the garden ... and of undeserved ... disaster to us from that garden" (*ST 2*, 151). This is all part of the actual creation that God has made with the teleology with which he made it. Therefore Jenson says that "if the whole creation has a goal, and if that goal is the adoption into God of the *totus Christus*, of Jesus ... then sin and Crucifixion must be the crises of *all* creation's teleology, as this is actually worked out within God's will. It is vital to remember that creation's teleology is a dramatic teleology, so that such crises cannot be strange to it" (*ST 2*, 151). The goal of creation is thus affected by sin and that is why the cosmos itself has a curse of pointlessness in which all events seem to lead into empty infinity. The sin of humans, of denying our goal in God, is thus also true for creation in that it denies its goal in God and so loses its meaning.

This "dramatic teleology of creation" fits in with Jenson's soteriology as being rooted in the eternal will of God, but also as something that must be described as an event in our history. The actual event of the cross and resurrection, its historical nature, is very important "as the necessary conclusion and bearer of the meaning, so to speak, of the narrative".[37] The unity of the crucifixion and the resurrection is a narrative unity – a dramatic unity. So the gospel tells a "powerful and biblically integrated story of the crucifixion; this story *is* just so the story of God's act to bring us back to himself at his own cost, and of our being brought back. ... that is the real story of what God does to reconcile us ... The Gospel's passion narrative is the authentic and entire account of God's reconciling action and our reconciliation, as events in his life and ours" (*ST 1*, 189).

Justification is thus a triune event: "It is the underived event of communal faithfulness in God, as this is set free by the Spirit and is actual in the reality of the incarnate Son. That we are justified means that this history is not only God's but is made to be

[37] Forde, 135.

ours also" (*ST* 2, 301). Jenson explains this whole doctrine in terms of a trinitarian ontology: "... we come before God the Father to receive God the Spirit just and only as we are one with God the Son. Thus *we* are first *within* God, and only thereby opened to him so that he can also, by the infinite *perichoresis* of his life and our participation in it, be within us."[38] So to be justified means that we, as the body and spouse of the Son, are included in the event of communal faithfulness in God. We are reconciled to God to become part of his *perichoresis*, his community. Salvation is thus entry into the life of the triune God, but Jenson adds that fulfilment would be entry into "God's specific infinity" (*ST* 2, 318), and this will take place with the final judgement. The last judgement is in all its ways a closure of the human narrative, but also for creation. The story of God, his creation and us, has a very specific promise.

Promise of Deification

The specific promise of the gospel is deification, but Jenson specifies this by saying that we will not cease to be creatures; that we will "receive and bear God"; and that "the redeemed do not become additional God-humans. Rather they become ... members of the *totus Christus*" (*ST* 2, 341). Jenson describes this deification with a musical image: "as the harmony of the divine consciousness is finally musical, so the harmony of creation, sheerly as such, is musical. And since the very being of creation is this harmony, to be a creature is, in this respect, to be harmonized, to fit in an endlessly complicated web of mutually appropriate relations" (*ST* 2, 41).

How will creation be part of this "music"? Creation is first of all a stage where God's drama with his people takes place, but Jenson qualifies this by saying "it does not follow, when galaxy clusters ... are once there, that they do not have their own meaning for the Creator" (*ST* 2, 115). The teleology that creation has also within itself, arises from the fact that "Creatures who are neither human nor angelic ... the earth ... exist in that God wills there to be a stage for the story of the Son; and their coherence and regularities are partial orders established and unified in a teleology constituted by their bending to this eschatological plot" (*ST* 2, 127). Creation will finally also be included in the event that is God, because "the triune God is too intimately involved with his creation for its final transformation to be founded in anything less than an event of his own life" (*ST* 2, 338). The teleology of the universe will be restored and the "devil and his angels will have been finally expelled from the world ... there will be no teleological gaps or disruptions to give purchase to ateleological explanation" (*ST* 2, 351).

Our, and creation's, fulfilment will be in God. The story's promise is deification (as Jenson qualifies it with the emphasis on our being harmonised with God), to be part of the great "fugue" whom God is. This understanding of creation's true teleology brings a responsibility: "When we acknowledge our place in God ... we may after all expand the second 'great commandment' to include not only our human neighbours but all our fellow creatures ... 'You shall delight in each creature as in yourself'" (*ST* 2, 130).

References and Recommended Reading

Braaten, Carl E. and Jenson, Robert W. (eds.) (1984), *Christian Dogmatics*, Philadelphia: Fortress.

[38] Jenson (1995), 426.

--- (1996), *The Catholicity of the Reformation*, Grand Rapids: Eerdmans.
--- (2003a), *Jews and Christians*, Grand Rapids: Eerdmans.
--- (2003b), *In One Body through the Cross: The Princeton Proposal for Christian Unity*, Grand Rapids: Eerdmans.
--- (2004), *The Ecumenical Future*, Grand Rapids: Eerdmans.
Forde, Gerhard O. (2000), "Robert Jenson's Soteriology", in: Gunton (ed.), 126-138.
Gunton, Colin E. (ed.) (2000), *Trinity, Time, and Church. A Response to the Theology of Robert W. Jenson*, Grand Rapids: Eerdmans.
Jenson, Robert W. (1963), *Alpha and Omega: A Study in the Theology of Karl Barth*, New York: Thomas Nelson.
--- (1969), *God after God: The God of the Past and the God of the Future, Seen in the Work of Karl Barth*, Indianapolis: Bobs-Merrill.
--- (1973), *Story and Promise: A Brief Theology of the Gospel about Jesus*, Philadelphia: Fortress.
--- (1978), *Visible Words: The Interpretation and Practice of the Christian Sacraments*, Philadelphia: Fortress.
--- (1982), *Triune Identity*, Philadelphia: Fortress.
--- (1992), *Unbaptized God: The Basic Flaw in Ecumenical Theology*, Minneapolis: Fortress.
--- (1995), "Justification as a Triune Event", *Modern Theology*, Vol. 11, 4, 421-427.
--- (1997), *Systematic Theology, Volume 1: The Triune God*, Oxford: Oxford University Press.
--- (1999), *Systematic Theology Volume 2: The Works of God*, Oxford: Oxford University Press.
Verhoef, Anné H. (2008), "How is Robert Jenson Telling the Story?", *Scriptura*, Vol. 98, 2, 231-243.

Anné H. Verhoef

Further Developments

Based on the discussion of these North Atlantic Lutheran theologies, we may in this concluding sequence ask where this tradition is heading towards. It seems clear that in the contributions in question, there is a will to sustain the Lutheran distinction between *regnum civile* (the secular realm) and *regnum Christi* (the kingdom of Jesus Christ), even if we see varying degrees of success in the theological justification of the connection between the two realms of God's work. Analyses have shown that only through the relations in the persons of the Godhead, the doctrine of the Trinity, it is possible to give reasons for both continuity and discontinuity, creation and salvation. Pannenberg and Jenson are both theologians who have in our time renewed a trinitarian understanding of the Christian faith as the best way to relate the various doctrinal themes. There are also other Lutheran theologians following a similar model in order to renew the Lutheran tradition. Some of them do that with specific reference to debates in ecotheology. Examples of such theologians include Niels Henrik Gregersen (Denmark), Christoph Schwöbel (Germany), Ted Peters, Larry Rasmussen and Paul Santmire (the USA), Klaus Nürnberger (South Africa) and finally Lambert Schuurman (Latin America).

As one of the most distinctive representatives of newer forms of Lutheranism, I want to single out Niels Henrik Gregersen, who expands upon central elements found in both Pannenberg and Jenson. In his later works he has founded his thinking especially on what he calls "Depth Incarnation". This idea means that the Logos of God has not only taken on a human form, but has also united itself with the world of materiality. According to Gregersen, by becoming flesh in Jesus Christ, God's eternal Logos enters into all dimensions of existence. In classical Greek thinking, the connotations of *sarx* (flesh) include everything that exists in the immanent world, like wind, water, earth and fire. Translated into modern concepts, this means that *sarx* comprises the whole material universe from quarks to atoms in their manifold combinations and transformations through chemical and biological evolution.

Furthermore, Gregersen is concerned with the Stoic background for the idea of Depth Incarnation. Research has shown that the texts of both Paul and John presuppose a synthesis of Stoic and Jewish ideas. If this is correct, early Christian thinking has more similarities with today's scientific cosmology than what is expressed in modern existential interpretations of Christianity. In this cosmology the world is not divided into two separate spheres: heaven and earth, flesh and spirit, soul and body. Gregersen refers to the creation story, which claims that Logos from the beginning was active as Creator and Redeemer, also stating that Logos became "flesh" in the life history of Jesus. It is thus no accident that two concepts of universal importance – Logos and *sarx* – are united in John 1:14. Based on the strong emphasis of the connection between God's Logos and the material world, one must, according to Gregersen, be open to salvation meaning the transformation of the biological and physical texture of the world, as what is imprinted by Christ does not remain unmoved and unchanged. In this manner we can imagine that the incarnation is a dynamic process, not just an event.

Through Gregersen, I have given a glimpse of a theological thinking which may be fruitful for further reflection on Christian ecotheology, which, for instance, takes dialogue with other sciences seriously.

References and Recommended Reading

Gregersen, Niels Henrik (ed.) (2003), *From Complexity to Life: On the Emergence of Life and Meaning*, New York: Oxford University Press.

--- (ed.) (2008), *Wolfhart Pannenberg: The Historicity of Nature, Essays on Science and Theology*, Philadelphia: Templeton Foundation Press.

Nürnberger, Klaus (1999), *Prosperity, Poverty and Pollution: Managing the Approaching Crisis*, Pietermaritzburg: Cluster.

--- (2011), *Regaining Sanity for the Earth*, Pietermaritzburg: Cluster.

Peters, Ted (1993), *Toward a Theology of Nature: Essays on Science and Faith* (with Wolfhart Pannenberg), Louisville: Westminster John Knox.

Peters, Ted (ed.) (1989), *Cosmos as Creation: Theology and Science in Consonance*, Nashville: Abingdon.

Santmire, H. Paul (1985), *The Travail of Nature: The Ambiguous Ecological Promise of Christian Theology*, Philadelphia: Fortress.

--- (2000), *Nature Reborn: The Ecological and Cosmic Promise of Christian Theology*, Minneapolis: Fortress.

Schuurman, Lambert (1970), "Some Observations on the Relevance of Luther's Theory of the Two Realms for the Theological Task in Latin America", *Lutheran Quarterly*, Vol. 22, 3, 78-90.

Schwöbel, Christoph (1997), "God, Creation and the Christian Community: The Dogmatic Basis of a Christian Ethic of Createdness", in: Gunton, Colin E. (ed.), *The Doctrine of Creation*, Edinburgh: T & T Clark, 149-176.

Svein Rise

4. West-European Reformed Theologies

Edited by Ernst M. Conradie

Introduction

The reformed tradition may be understood as an ongoing conversation within itself and with others about what constitutes the tradition. Its core intuition is expressed in the motto *semper reformanda* ("always reforming"). In this light, current ecological threats provide the latest stimulus for continued reformation. That ongoing reformation is necessary is evident from the sustained suspicion, since Max Weber's famous thesis on Protestantism and the spirit of capitalism, that the current neo-liberal economic order with its destructive ecological impact is deeply intertwined with the legacy of John Calvin. This suspicion is strengthened by the broad correlation between countries with historically high greenhouse emissions and countries where the reformed tradition has had a major influence – including western Europe, the UK, the USA, South Africa and now South Korea.

H. Richard Niebuhr's famous typology on the relationship between "Christ and culture" may provide a helpful point of entry into the reformed approach to the closely related problem of the relationship between creation and salvation. The reformed impulse is one calling for the transformation of culture instead of the models of "Christ against culture" (Anabaptist?), "the Christ of culture" (*corpus Christianum*), "Christ above culture" (Roman Catholic?), or "Christ and culture in paradox" (Lutheran?). This emphasis on social transformation is related to typically reformed tenets such as the third use of the law (as a guide for gratitude), the emphasis on sanctification and not just justification, the historic interest, since the Genevan reformation, in societal problems (political, economic, medical, educational) and the sustained emphasis on the work of the Holy Spirit in church and society. It therefore comes as no surprise that reformed theologians have been at the forefront of current ecumenical discourse on justice, peace and ecological sustainability. In short, the emphasis on social transformation may well be destructive, but it may also incite a call for the conversion of the global economy towards sustainable alternatives.

At the heart of this ecological reformation of the reformed tradition lies the need for a renewed understanding of the relationship between creation and salvation. Can the destruction elicited by the reformed tradition be inverted towards a salvific impulse for the whole household of God? Ironically, in-depth theological reflection on this problem may be regarded as one of the strengths of the tradition, albeit that the main exponents of the tradition as discussed in this chapter have widely diverging positions in this regard.

This chapter focuses on significant figures standing in the reformed tradition in western Europe, more specifically in Switzerland, Germany and the Netherlands, in the 20th century. All these figures have grappled intensely with the relationship between nature and grace. This has to be understood in the context of the disastrous impact of natural theology (a theology of blood and soil) in Nazi Germany and apartheid South Africa. All of them would agree with the reformed notion that the actual contrast is between sin and grace, not nature and grace. Both sin and grace have to do with that which is natural, bodily and earthly. Sin destroys body and earth alike. Grace brings salvation also for nature. "Nature" is here used as shorthand for God's creation understood as *creatura*.

This common intuition, nevertheless, allows for very different positions on creation and salvation. These differences typically emerge when creation is understood as *creatio*, as God's work. The question is then: how does God's work of creation relate to God's work of salvation? Where does the priority lie, also in terms of the eternal divine counsel? Teleologically, is creation for the sake of salvation (or covenant) or is salvation for the sake of creation? Noetically, have we come to know God first as Creator or first as Saviour? How are the first and the second articles of the creed related to each other? Does the key perhaps lie in the third article?

The differences between the figures discussed in this chapter are indicated by the following brief formulations: Herman Bavinck (1854-1921) retrieved Calvin's vision by insisting that grace does not abolish nature, but may be understood as a "restoration" of nature, allowing God's world to flourish again. He introduced the term "re-creation" to emphasise the continuity between God's work of creation and of salvation. Karl Barth (1886-1968) regarded this position as too naïve, allowing for elaborate constructions of what is natural (creation ordinances), and insisted that the focus should remain on God's revelation in Jesus Christ. Creation was necessary for the sake of incarnation. Accordingly, creation is seen as the external basis for God's covenant with humanity in Jesus Christ. Oepke Noordmans (1871-1956) radicalised Barth's critique by arguing that creation is not to be understood as formation but as separation, as God's gracious judgement for forgiven sinners. Noordmans focused on the cross instead of the incarnation to develop a "critical concept of creation" and famously described creation as "a spot of light around the cross". In response, Arnold van Ruler (1908-1970) developed an equally radical affirmation of God's sustained loyalty to creation. Salvation is for the sake of creation. Christ is God's "emergency measure" to ensure that creation can flourish once again in God's presence. Van Ruler affirmed Bavinck's notion of re-creation but understood it also eschatologically. Jürgen Moltmann (1926-) has learned from both Barth and Van Ruler, but emphasises the need for a far more radical transformation of God's creation in the light of the history of suffering, including natural suffering. Theology thus becomes a response to the theodicy problem. He understands salvation as God's liberating victory over evil and not primarily as forgiveness of sin. He departs from Van Ruler by using the term "new creation" instead of "re-creation" to describe the eschatological consummation of all things as radically "new".

It should be noted that this is only one strand within the larger reformed tradition. In continental Europe there are many other figures that could also be considered, including, for example, Abraham Kuyper (1837-1920) and the very different approach followed by Emil Brunner (1889-1966). More recently, scholars like Bram van de Beek (1946-) and Michael Welker (1947-) have contributed to a reformed understanding of creation and salvation. Then one must also mention Arminian and liberal tendencies which allow for a more cultured form of Christianity and thus for more continuity between creation and salvation. Often salvation is understood here as "moral formation", "education", "development" or the "reconstruction" of societal structures.

In the UK there has been considerable interest in the theme of creation and salvation through the work of Thomas Torrance (1913-2007), Colin Gunton (1941-2003), Alister McGrath (1953-) and John Webster (1955-). The influence of Karl Barth on each of these theologians is more than evident, albeit in quite different ways. All affirmed Barth's Christological reorientation of theology and sought to develop it in a more consistently trinitarian way. Most of them became involved in dialogue on theology and science and expressed more interest in that which is natural than Barth's critique of natural theology may appear to allow.

The reformed tradition in the USA is as diverse as anywhere else. One particular strand is worth mentioning for its distinctness, namely Princeton fundamentalism (a form of reformed orthodoxy) and its historic influence on later forms of fundamentalism and creationism, prompting a very different understanding of the relationship between creation and salvation. The neo-Calvinist theology continued at Westminster Theological Seminary understands salvation in terms of the restoration of the orders of creation. Christian reconstructionism is an extreme right-wing radicalisation of such a theology. By contrast, the reformed theological centres associated with Princeton and Grand Rapids currently focus on the interpretation of figures discussed in this chapter, such as Kuyper, Bavinck and, especially, Barth.

In South Africa, apartheid theology may be understood as a form of creation theology based on God's ordinances, while salvation may be understood as the restoration of the separation of different ethnic groups created by God (*sic*!) and affirmed after the attempts to impose unity symbolised by the tower of Babel. By contrast, the critical voices against apartheid theology within the reformed tradition in South Africa have emphasised a Barthian theology of reconciliation, arguing that apartheid assumed the fundamental irreconcilability of people on the basis that they are "too different" and therefore have to be kept apart. This vision is expressed in the famous Confession of Belhar (1982 / 1986). This critique of natural theology coincided with an emphasis on the eschatological uniqueness of the (unity of the) church and prompted an ecclesiocentric shift, but (with some exceptions) did not allow much interest in creation theology or in dialogue on theology and the natural science. This merely illustrates the need and the difficulty of doing justice both to God's work of creation and God's work of salvation.

Branches of the reformed / Presbyterian tradition have taken root in many other parts of the world, including Africa and South East Asia. It is difficult to generalise in this regard. Typically, one may find the full spectrum of reformed theologies mixed with contextual considerations. This emphasis on context (and contextual hermeneutics) is itself a typically reformed impulse and another area in which theological discourse on the relationship between creation and salvation, between gospel and culture, or between church and society, is situated. The figures that are discussed in this chapter provide some indication of the diverse ways in which these relationships are addressed in all these different contexts. More recent contributions within this strand of the reformed tradition will be mentioned in the conclusion to this chapter.

References and Recommended Reading

Brunner, H. Emil (1949), *The Christian Doctrine of Creation and Redemption*, London: Lutterworth.
Conradie, Ernst M. (ed.) (2011), *Creation and Salvation: Dialogue on Abraham Kuyper's Legacy for*

Contemporary Ecotheology, Leiden: Brill.
Gunton, Colin E. (1992), *Christ and Creation*, Carlisle: Paternoster.
--- (1998), *The Triune Creator: A Historical and Systematic Study*, Grand Rapids: Eerdmans.
McGrath, Alister E. (2002), *The Re-enchantment of Nature: Science, Religion and the Human Sense of Wonder*, London: Hodder and Stoughton.
Thomas, Günter (2009), *Neue Schöpfung: Systematisch-theologische Untersuchungen zur Hoffnung auf das "Lebem in der zukünftigen Welt"*, Neukirchen-Vluyn: Neukirchener Verlag.
Van de Beek, A. (1996), *Schepping: De Wereld als Voorspel voor de Eeuwigheid*, Nijkerk: Callenbach.
Welker, Michael (1999), *Creation and Reality*, Minneapolis: Fortress.

Ernst M. Conradie

Herman Bavinck (1854-1921) – Grace Restores Nature

Introduction

In the year 1892 the Reformed Churches in The Netherlands (Gereformeerde Kerken in Nederland) came into being as a union of two groups that had split up from the Dutch Reformed Church (Nederlandse Hervormde Kerk), namely the Secession (*Afscheiding*, 1834) and the *Doleantie* (1886). During the first decades of the existence of the Reformed Churches, Abraham Kuyper (1834-1921) and Herman Bavinck (1854-1921) were their undisputed theological leaders. While Abraham Kuyper was the former leader of the *Doleantie*, Herman Bavinck belonged to the tradition of the Secession. From 1883-1902 Bavinck taught dogmatics at the theological school of the Secession churches at Kampen; from 1902 until his death he worked as professor in dogmatics at the Free University, Amsterdam. Bavinck's main work is his four-volume *Gereformeerde Dogmatiek* (Dutch originals first published between 1895 and 1901), which was recently translated into English as *Reformed Dogmatics*.

From the very beginning of his career Herman Bavinck was deeply interested in the relationship between creation and salvation. He develops his views in discussion with other Christian traditions, especially Roman Catholicism. This can be seen, for instance, in public lectures at the Theological School at Kampen entitled "The Catholicity of Christianity and Church" (1992; Dutch original 1888) and "Common Grace" (1989; Dutch original 1894), in the section on the relationship between revelation and grace in his *Reformed Dogmatics* (*RD 1*, 356ff.), and in the section on the order of salvation (*RD 3*, 512ff.).[1]

Bavinck's Polemics with Roman Catholicism

According to Bavinck, the Roman Catholic view (whose roots can already be found in the second and the third century) is characterised by the distinction and the contrast between "natural and supernatural religion" (CG, 45). On this distinction Rome has built its whole theological system (CCC, 229).

According to Rome (Bavinck argues), in the divine mind two conceptions of hu-

[1] References in parentheses in this section are to volumes of Bavinck's *Reformed Dogmatics* (*RD*), or to the essays on "The Catholicity of Christianity and Church" (CCC) and "Common Grace" (GC).

manity exist. Firstly, God created the human as "an earthly, sensuous, rational and moral being" in a purely natural state (*in puris naturalibus*) (CG, 45). To this natural state God added a "superadded gift" (*donum superadditum*), which consists in humanity being created after God's own image. This *donum superadditum* was lost through sin. Because of that, original sin consists, in Rome's view, almost completely in the loss of the *donum superadditum* and the reversion to the natural state. "Apart from the harmful influence of his social environment", Bavinck writes, a human being, according to Rome, is still born in a condition like that of Adam before the fall; however, lacking the *donum superadditum*. In this natural state man can be "a true, good, and complete human being" (CG, 45f.). This implies that one "can possess a good and complete ethic, and can practice genuine virtues" (CG, 46). Thus, one "is capable of an earthly life that is in all respects sinless" (CG, 46). Owing to the power of sin, however, most people are far away from such a natural, sinless life. But conceived in the abstract, the ideal does not seem impossible. If one succeeded in living such a virtuous, natural life and fulfilled one's natural religious obligations, one's state after death would be equal to that of children who die unbaptised: one would not be punished, but only lack supernatural blessedness (CG, 46).

But, Bavinck writes, according to Rome, God also has a second and higher idea of human destiny. Distinct from the natural order, there is "another order of things that are supernatural in the strict, absolute sense of the term" (CG, 46). This supernatural order transcends the knowledge of fallen humanity (and the sinless natural human being). Therefore, it can only be known by supernatural revelation. In his sovereign freedom, God determined this supernatural order to be the destiny of humanity: "God appointed for man not just an earthly but a heavenly, supernatural blessedness" (CG, 46). For reaching this end, one's natural gifts are not sufficient. Because the *donum superadditum* has been lost for two reasons (still according to Rome) a supernatural grace is necessary: "First of all it was necessary in an accidental way, to support the natural gifts of man that had been more or less weakened by the fall. Second, it was necessary in an absolute sense to make man capable of attaining his supernatural destination" (CG, 47). According to Rome, the preservation and distribution of this supernatural grace is entrusted to the church: "Through the priest and the sacrament working *ex opera operato*, the church causes supernatural grace infused into a man, thus making him capable of good works flowing forth from the supernatural fountain of love" (CG, 47).

According to Bavinck, this Roman Catholic view must be rejected completely. In his works again and again one finds a polite but incisive criticism of Rome's viewpoints. At its roots, Bavinck states, it is "Pelagian" (*RD 3*, 512f, CG, 47, CCC, 229). It is "an 'add-on' or supplementary system": the image of God supplements our humanity and grace is added onto nature (CCC, 229). Such a supplementary system affects the nature of Christian faith: "the pope supplements Christ, the Mass supplements Christ's sacrifice, tradition supplements Holy Scripture" (CCC, 229). It also affects Christian ethics: "human ordinances supplement divine commands" (CCC, 229f.). Or, as he elsewhere writes: "evangelical councils are supplementary to ethical precepts" (CCC, 229). Therefore, in his doctrine of sanctification (*RD 4*, 237ff.) as well in his "Reformed Ethics" (which was recently discovered in the Bavinck Archives), Bavinck rejects the Roman Catholic distinction between precepts and commands.

Rome's supplementary system, according to Bavinck, also implies a depreciation of creation and nature. In itself Rome considers the natural order as good, but "of a lower order" (CCC, 230). In other words: nature in itself "is good, not corrupt; it is only missing that which in its own strength it could never reach" (CCC, 229). According to Bavinck, Rome does not abolish nature, but suppresses it. Although Rome leaves – even more than Protestantism tends to do – space and freedom for science and art, the state, earthly vocations, marriage, family, possessions, etc., "it downgrades the natural by stamping it as profane and unhallowed" (see *RD* 1, 360).

Bavinck also severely criticises Rome's view of God's grace. He acknowledges that in Rome's view grace does have a dual role: to elevate and to make well (*RD 3*, 576f.). However, in Rome's thinking, most of all grace is "a supernatural quality added to human beings by which they are in principle taken up into a supernatural order" (*RD 3*, 577). The second role of grace – to make well – is almost completely forced into the shadows. As a consequence, Bavinck argues, in Rome's supplementary system creation and re-creation remain two realities independent of each other: "Nothing remains but a compromise between the natural and the supernatural" (CCC, 229). In Bavinck's view, Rome does not do justice to the devastating power of sin nor to God's grace. Grace "does not reform and renew that which exists, it only completes and perfects creation" (CCC, 229).

Nature, Sin and Grace

According to Bavinck, Christianity is an *Erlösungsreligion* – a religion of salvation (CG, 59). This means that it "should govern all people and sanctify all creatures irrespective of geography, nationality, place, and time" (CCC, 221). This, however, is only possible if the core of thinking is not the contrast between natural and supernatural religion, but the antithesis between sin and grace.

If this is true, it is very important to define what the character of sin and grace is. Again, Bavinck develops his view in discussion with Roman Catholicism. He writes: "Sin is certainly not a substance but a quality, not *materia* [matter] but *forma* [form]. Sin is not the essence of things but rather cleaves to the essence; it is a *privatio* [privation], albeit *actuosa* [active], and to that extent accidental" (see *RD* 3, 136-146, CG, 60f.). Thus, sin has inserted itself into the world as an alien element.

Although sin is accidental in nature, we may not lose sight of the devastating power of sin. Therefore Bavinck emphasises that sin has deeply penetrated into all forms of created life and has affected the entire organism of the world: "left to itself, sin would have made desolate and destroyed all things" (CG, 61).

However, because sin is accidental in nature, it also can be separated and removed from created reality: "The world is and remains susceptible of purification and redemption" (CG, 61). The world's essence can be rescued, and its original state can return; that is, it can be redirected towards the original goal that God had for creation. It is exactly this that God brings about through grace. Grace is not opposed to nature, but only to sin: "It restores what was corrupted by sin" (*RD 3*, 573-579). Because of this, re-creation is a keyword in Bavinck's theology. Grace does not create a new cosmos, but rather makes the cosmos new. Therefore Bavinck can summarise the relationship between creation and salvation, as well as the relationship between nature and grace in one (Thomistic!) formula: "gratia non tollit naturam, sed perficit" – grace does not abolish nature, but restores it (see *RD* 1, 322, 443). With his view that the essence of the Christian religion consists in the re-creation of the cosmos into the kingdom of God, Bavinck claims to stand firmly within the tradition of the Reformation, especially of Calvinism.

According to Bavinck, it was Calvin who "traced the operation of sin to a greater extent than Luther did" (CCC, 237). In Luther's theology, Roman Catholic dualism has not completely been overcome, because he limits the grace of God; the gospel only changes humanity inwardly: one's heart and one's conscience (CCC, 237). Calvin also traced the operation of sin to a greater depth than Zwingli, because although the latter tried to realise the reforming and renewing power of the gospel in all areas of life, he failed in giving a theoretical account of it (CCC, 237).

Bavinck therefore argues that it was Calvin "whose labours completed the Reformation and saved Protestantism" (CCC, 237). In summary: "In the powerful mind of the French Reformer, re-creation is not a system that supplements creation, as in Catholicism, not a religious reformation that leaves creation intact, as in Luther, much less a radically new creation as in Anabaptism, but a joyful tiding of the renewal of all creatures" (CCC, 238).

Because God in God's grace re-creates the cosmos, Bavinck emphasises that Christian faith is not – as Rome states – "a quantitative reality that spreads itself in a transcendent fashion over the natural" (CCC, 236). Instead, it is "a religious and ethical power that enters the natural in an immanent fashion and eliminates only that which is unholy" (CCC, 236).

In accordance with this immanent fashion, Bavinck often states (e.g. *RD* 4, 396, 684) that Christian faith not only is a treasure hidden in a field, or a pearl of great price for which a man sells everything he has in order to buy it (Matt. 13:44-46). It also is a yeast that a woman takes and hides in three measures of flour until it is all leavened (Matt. 13:33).

This metaphor of Christian faith as a leaven indicates that a Christian, according to Bavinck, may not withdraw from the world, but rather has a task in the world. At this point Bavinck opposes his own ecclesiastical tradition. Members of the Secession churches were inclined to separate themselves from the world. According to Bavinck, such an attitude is wrong. Every kind of separatism and asceticism must be cut off at the root (CCC, 242f.). Therefore he writes: "Faith appears to be great, indeed, when a person renounces all and shuts himself up in isolation. But even greater, it seems to me, is the faith of a person who, while keeping the kingdom of heaven as a treasure, at the same time brings it out into the world as a leaven, certain that He who is for us is greater than he who is against us and that He is able to preserve us from evil even in the midst of the world" (CCC, 248).

References and Recommended Reading

Bavinck, Herman (1989), "Common Grace" (translated by R. C. van Leeuwen), *Calvin Theological Journal*, Vol. 24, 38-65.

--- (1992), "The Catholicity of Christianity and Church" (translated by John Bolt), *Calvin Theological Journal*, Vol. 27, 220-251.

--- (2003), *Reformed Dogmatics, Volume 1: Prolegomena*, Grand Rapids: Baker Academic.

--- (2004), *Reformed Dogmatics, Volume 2: God and Creation*, Grand Rapids: Baker Academic.
--- (2006), *Reformed Dogmatics, Volume 3: Sin and Salvation in Christ*, Grand Rapids: Baker Academic.
--- (2008), *Reformed Dogmatics, Volume 4: Holy Spirit, Church, and New Creation*, Grand Rapids: Baker Academic.
Keulen, Dirk van (2010), "Herman Bavinck's Reformed Ethics: Some Remarks about Unpublished Manuscripts in the Libraries of Kampen and Amsterdam", *The Bavinck Review*, Vol. 1, 25-56, <bavinck.calvinseminary.edu>, retrieved 31 August 2011.
Veenhof, Jan (2006), *Nature and Grace in Herman Bavinck* (translated by Albert M. Wolters), Sioux Center: Dordt College Press.
--- (2011), "Revelation and Grace in Herman Bavinck", in: John Bowlin (ed.), *The Kuyper Center Review, Volume 2: Revelation and Common Grace*, Grand Rapids: Eerdmans, 3-13.

Dirk van Keulen

Oepke Noordmans (1871-1956) – Creation as God's Judgement

Introduction: Re-creation as the Transformative Power of the Spirit

By the year 1900 one could observe in Dutch Protestantism three main streams which characterised the theological scene at that time: the so-called neo-Calvinists, the liberals and the "ethical direction". What connected them was the conviction that in changing times a reorientation regarding the Christian confession was required. The neo-Calvinists, coming from the so-called Reformed Churches in the Netherlands (Gereformeerde Kerken in Nederland), were led by two strong leaders, Abraham Kuyper (1834-1921) and Herman Bavinck (1854-1921). Their neo-Calvinism showed theologically a strong orientation to pre-given structures in creation, developed in a cosmic-scholastic dogmatics in which the Holy Scripture is an all-determining principle. The liberals (*vrijzinnigen*), represented by theologians like Karel Hendrik Roessingh (1886-1925), combined a fresh interest in the ecclesial confessions with reception of new insights in biblical science. The third group, the ethical direction, belonging to the Dutch Reformed Church (Nederlandse Hervormde Kerk), is the one with which Oepke Noordmans (1871-1956) originally aligned himself. One finds him there with other prominent representatives of this theological position such as Gerhardus van der Leeuw (1890-1950) and Kornelis Heiko Miskotte (1894-1976). Theologically, the ethical direction may be associated with German *Kulturprotestantismus*. On the basis of their ethical position they criticised the intellectualism of the neo-Calvinist belief in revelation as well as the subjectivism of the liberal approach. "Ethical" meant for them an interplay between doctrine and life, Word and Spirit.

Throughout his life Noordmans moved away from his original "ethical" background. After World War I he understood that a threatened humanity asked for a more adequate theological approach than ethical theology could provide with its interest in the shape of human life as a "religious personality". One had to develop a stronger biblically oriented view on the divine truth that critically interrupts human affairs. That is the reason why Noordmans, already in writings in 1921, demonstrated a familiarity with Karl Barth's intentions, before anyone else in the Netherlands had heard about Barth and his *Römerbrief*. Noordmans never became a Barthian; he had already found his own profile, when reading Barth. Whereas Barth was looking for theological renewal through a Christological approach, Noordmans turned to pneumatology. With this concentration on the work of the Holy Spirit as a central theological theme, Noordmans did not stand alone in the Dutch context. One may say that Dutch reformed theology had always already inherited a pneumatological orientation, in the sense that the work of the Holy Spirit was seen as the appropriation of salvation. Noordmans went a step further. His original contribution to 20th-century theology is that he asked for attention to the work of the Spirit as *Spiritus Creator*. That brings us to the theme of this volume: the relationship between creation and salvation, seen as acts of God. What Noordmans argued for is this: that the doctrine of creation, the doctrine of Christ and salvation as re-creation should be founded upon the activity of the Spirit. In this way, he introduced a new way of theological thinking. I will explore the main aspects of this undertaking below and demonstrate its significance for an understanding of the relationship of creation and salvation.

This has to be understood in the light of his suggestion that a "critical concept of creation" is required. This is explained in Noordmans' famous motto: "Creation is separation". The word "concept" may be misleading here: what Noordmans has in his mind is a critical perspective or a judgement (*oordeel*). Concepts suppose a philosophical framework and are often static. Throughout his life Noordmans studied the work of great philosophers, such as Descartes, Pascal, Bergson and Heidegger intensively, in relation to his own methodological reflection. However, according to him, both disciplines should be distinguished sharply (expressed in his distinction between "church" and "school"). According to Noordmans, theology has to operate with biblically oriented perspectives, perspectives that cannot be merely borrowed from nature or culture. One of Noordmans' volumes of reflections bears the title *Geestelijke Perspectieven* ("Spiritual Perspectives", Dutch original 1930). This suggests that, according to Noordmans, theological thinking should be guided by the perspectives of creation and salvation which God reveals in history. These are God-given perspectives, not intellectual themes. One can speak about them intellectually, but then in such a way that the character of such a perspective is affirmed. Noordmans rejects a theological method – which he finds in neo-Calvinism – in which these divine realities are forced into preconceived conceptual schemes. To use an expression of Jan T. Bakker's: "the story contains the concept and not the other way round". Noordmans' renewal of the conception of creation was sharply expressed in the following phrase from his main dogmatic work, namely *Herschepping* ("Re-creation", first published in 1934): "Creation is a spot of light around the cross" (*VW* 2, 45, translation – EMC).[2] I will explore this famous statement in more detail in the discussion below.

Although nominated several times, Noordmans never obtained a teaching position at a faculty of theology. He remained a minister in a Dutch village. As such his undoubted authority was widely recognised and he was often asked for advice on theological questions. Many theologians saw him as a leading figure, as is evident from the two volumes of letters in the *Verzamelde Werken van Dr. O. Noordmans* ("Collected

[2] In the text below I will refer to different volumes of Noordmans's *Collected Works*, but mostly to the second volume which includes the main dogmatic works. His collected works were published in ten volumes between 1978 and 2004. References in parenthesis in the text refer to these volumes (*VW*), which are unfortunately only available in Dutch.

Works of Dr O. Noordmans", 1978-2004). In 1935 Noordmans received an honorary doctorate from the University of Groningen.

A Theological Concept of Religion

In order to understand Noordmans' view on the relationship between creation and salvation (as divine acts) and the innovation he brought about through his "critical concept of creation", we need to investigate his understanding of Christian religion. The young Noordmans, in a critical discussion with his own theological roots in so-called ethical theology, developed a distinction which can be regarded as the key to understanding his views on creation and salvation. Here Lutheran (Kohlbrugge) and reformed (Barth) accents are connected. Noordmans speaks of "great and small religion" or of "divine and human ethics".

"Great religion" is the expression he uses for the ethos of God. It is God's graceful power that redeems human beings from a deadly legality. Here one may consider the so-called adulterous woman in John 8. Or the murderer on the cross, saved by Jesus to join him in paradise (Luke 23:42f.). Great religion affirms divine realities, expressed in traditional doctrine through terms such as "predestination" and "kenosis". On the basis of his renewed study of Calvin and Lutheran and reformed theologies of that time, Noordmans discovered the eschatological nature of such concepts. Great religion as an eschatological reality indicates that God keeps the demonic and the humane apart (which tends to be blurred in human ethics) and directs humans towards and protects them for God's future – the kingdom. It implies further that one may serve God with one's shortcomings, not with one's acquired knowledge or morality.

The other pole of the distinction, "small religion", is Noordmans' expression for human religiosity and ethics. It is expressed through belief in creation in which God is seen as a guarantor for a rational-moral world order and through Christian piety or moral consciousness. In small religion the focus is on categories emphasised in "ethical theology, such as personality, character, conscience – ideas which stood helpless amidst the storm of destructive events in the first half of the 20th century in western Europe. In 1925 Noordmans wrote: "European cultural life endured a severe crisis and in the trenches the personal was pushed back upon its natural basis" (*VW 3*, 525, translation – EMC). In this situation Noordmans realised that dynamic concepts may become dated in history, including the "ethical-theological" idea of the "personality". Noordmans saw that the Christian creed may be more modern than any other dominant idea in world history. Its formulations, as a summary of the gospel, are God-given perspectives, "windows" (*VW 1*, 307), by which human beings can discover the destination of their lives, for which they are looking in vain in themselves. For Noordmans, the creed reveals a movement, which he describes with the expression "great religion". This movement is due to the power of the Spirit. According to Noordmans, *credo* (I believe) presupposes the presence of the Spirit. This pneumatological approach as articulation of God's ethos has one significant implication. The salvific truths of the creed, with its centre in the salvation in Jesus Christ, are not understood as complete, well-circumscribed propositional truths, but as a dynamic truth only coming into being through the work of the Spirit. As the work of the Spirit, salvation is a lived reality, directed towards liberation from anxiety and futility and a life lived in God's future.[3]

What is the significance of this distinction between great religion and small religion, embedded in the dynamics of the activity of the Spirit, for Noordmans' understanding of the relationship between creation and salvation? According to Noordmans, in great religion, salvation does not follow upon creation; the one stands in opposition to the other. Noordmans suggests that in salvation, understood as a divine judgement, God's creation is called into being. Creation (as that which comes from God and has its own existence from God's hand), is separated from evil through God's grace and taken into "God's heart" (*VW 3*, 517). Salvation is therefore not a process within creation, focussing on the restoration of creation; that is exactly what is meant by small religion. Noordmans says: "Creation *is* good and does not need to be made good. The only question is whether it can offer a point of departure for salvation. And that Kohlbrugge and also Luther deny. Here God serves again as the point of departure … In the great religion God acts, in salvation, quite freely upon his creation. He does not repeat or improve on his work, because it was good" (*VW 3*, 517, translation – EMC). Great religion implies that God takes human beings out of a life of sin. From creation to re-creation there is no straight line – something Noordmans finds in the theology of Abraham Kuyper and Klaas Schilder (cf. *VW 4*).

Noordmans' Understanding of Creation in Herschepping (Re-creation)

The most formative years for Noordmans' renewal of the concept of creation were in the 1930s. In these years of crisis and new paganism he writes his dogmatic main work *Herschepping* ("Re-creation", first published in1934) in which he offers his own exposition of Christian doctrine. He probably took the word "re-creation" from Herman Bavinck, this "excellent church teacher" as he writes, although he also criticised Bavinck's use of Thomas Aquinas on the relationship between nature and grace (*VW 2*, 205f.). According to Noordmans, re-creation does not entail, as Bavinck maintains, the restoration of creation. It is a completely new work of God in the Spirit. As we heard him saying before: we do not need to be redeemed of creation, we have to be taught in order to see in a better way what creation is.

In order to explain this, Noordmans proposes a deep methodical intervention. He carries through a reversal of the first and the second article of faith. Speaking about God the Creator is only possible on the basis of speaking about the cross of Jesus Christ. We hear: "The gospels proclaim a new trinitarian work and from the cross we see creation better than from paradise" (*VW 2*, 412, translation – EMC). And: "Creation, in the way science is treating it, is not the real creation. It is an abstraction. In the *real* creation we meet sin and suffering, which fits with the Jesus of the Twelve Articles … When we do not take creation as a self-enclosed whole, but connect it closely with Christ, as we connect the gospel with the Holy Spirit, then it becomes no dark chaos or self-glorifying Greek cosmos, but a spot of light around the cross. And in that spot sin is revealed … That creation is a critical concept, the Bible teaches us. It starts

[3] Noordmans agrees with Bavinck on this point. Bavinck maintained that for reformed theology the *satisfactio vicaria* is no ready-made entity, but an active principle that includes God's work of re-creation. For both Noordmans and Bavinck salvation is not a generalised principle but a power at work in a person at a given time that transforms the world. See Noordmans, *VW* 1, 293.

with creation, without telling us much more about it. It only states that everything was good. With that statement we have a criterion in our hands, to see that everything is fallen" (*VW 2*, 245f., translation – EMC). The good creation (*creatura*) as derived from God is only known by God. That implies that the good creation does exist, but only as a hidden reality. We only learn to see it in proximity to the crucified Christ. This vision of the hidden reality of creation that is only revealed through God's work of salvation forms the basis for Noordmans' view that creation is separation.

With this methodological intervention Noordmans resists an (in his view) unfruitful fixation on a beginning that has to be restored – something he finds in Kuyper's doctrine of creation. One may summarise the main elements of Noordmans' position in this way:

(1) The Bible does not approach creation in terms of a physical beginning or of a historical process. The Bible speaks about creation in terms of revelation, that is, as a world around the cross (*VW 2*, 265).

(2) The belief in the Creator is, according to the Twelve Articles, additional to the belief in the Father (*VW 2*, 249). That is fundamental for a theological epistemology and thus for rethinking the relationship between creation and salvation.

(3) We cannot know the Father from a romanticised consideration of nature or from a cultivation of human life, but only from the cross of his Son (*VW 2*, 251).

(4) The Father / Creator creates by separation because creation is based on a judgement. This is already the case in the beginning, when darkness is separated from light (*VW 2*, 252).

(5) To say that the Father can be known from the cross is to affirm the biblical truth that the Father has followed his creation in its fallenness.

(6) The Son has to be "in his Father's house" (Luke 2:49; see *VW 2*, 247, 267). According to Noordmans' explanation of this text, we encounter creation in the Bible (as the Father's house) as a reality of sickness, misery and death. And in this reality the Son does his salvific work. This is expressed in *Herschepping* in the phrase: "In the incarnation God as Sufferer stands against God as Creator" (*VW 2*, 282, translation – EMC). This tension constitutes the heart of the gospel. The new creation comes only because God through his Son participates in the suffering of the world. This implies that the Creator can be no demiurge. Salvation is not suspended to a fulfilment in another world, but by changing the appearance of this world.

(7) From this follows that salvation is, for Noordmans, a multidimensional concept which can only be understood in a trinitarian way. Salvation is an affirmation of the world (affirming the goodness of creation), a subjection of the world to critique (the judgement upon death and violence) and the transformation of the world (by opening a new future for human beings).

(8) The cross constitutes a revelation of love and justice; therefore one has to understand the vicarious suffering not legally but prophetically (*VW 2*, 508): it reveals a new world, new relations, a new way of being human. Jesus' words on the cross are, according to Noordmans, creative words. They separate human lives from the destruction and despair in which they are imprisoned.

(9) To see creation from the perspective of the cross is according to Noordmans not an episode, it is "a cosmic principle" (*VW 2*, 282). Something eternal (*VW 2*, 386) is created here between God and humanity. This eternal reality is the reconciliation that cannot be derived from something in our reality. It suggests that God acts completely freely upon the world through a vulnerable human being with no honour, in order to free God's creatures from circumstances that appear to be completely intractable.

(10) This reconciliation is understood as re-creation when taken up in the dynamic activity of the Spirit (John 16:14). It is nothing less than re-creation, since through such work of the Spirit human beings are enabled through the power of the Spirit to act creatively towards reconciliation in the world. God's true work of creation is the re-creation through the Spirit – if one participates in that creative movement from God. In this way God's work returns to God so that God is glorified and justified (*VW 2*, 305).

The Spirit of Re-creation and the Earth: Asceticism as a Keyword for a Christian form of Life in the World

What are the implications of Noordmans' view on re-creation as the activity of the Spirit for the earth in which we live, ecologically, politically, culturally? I note three elements for further reflection:

(1) Re-creation as separation means to save (separate) human beings from "the evil of closedness and being locked up" in culture (*VW 6*, 613), from the lack of openness in political and economic systems. As such, it implies a criterion for knowledge. The Spirit of re-creation offers resistance against the spirit of all kinds of totalitarian thinking in which the concrete subject with a name, an identity, a thought and a dream is thrashed.

(2) Re-creation as act of the Spirit unlocks human destiny so that determinism (by the laws of nature) and fatalism (predetermined historical events) do not have the last word. Re-creation remains a new gift from God in which the creature receives a destiny (being predestined to be a citizen in God's kingdom of love and justice) and a freedom that unravels one from the fatalities of one's existence (*VW 2*, 238v.) As such, re-creation forms the basis for a theological anthropology.

(3) Re-creation forms the point of departure for a life in the Spirit. Christian ethics becomes possible within the space of the divine ethos. Christian ethics is understood by Noordmans in terms of teaching ascesis. Noordmans does not understand ascesis as the denial of life or abandoning one's cultural responsibilities, but as a searching for an appropriate measure and limits, a life of vigilance and attention in order to guard against the perversion of that which is material, bodily and earthly. Such an ascesis seeks to recognise in every sphere of society (science, culture, politics, religion, sexuality) what may contribute to our well-being and what may destroy it. This is no Kuyperian cultural programme but suggests an attitude of "spiritual independence (*VW 6*, 464) in which the power of Word and Spirit is sought within every sphere of society in order to separate the demonic and the humane from each other.

References and Recommended Reading

Kooi, Akke van der (1992), *Het Heilige en de Heilige Geest bij Noordmans*, Kampen: Kok.
Neven, Gerrit W. (2002), "About the Hermeneutical Function of the Dogma in Vattimo and Noordmans", in: Onno Zijlstra (ed.), *Letting Go: Rethinking Kenosis*, Bern: Peter Lang, 213-239.
Noordmans, Oepke (1930), *Geestelijke Perspectieven,* Amsterdam.
--- (1934), *Herschepping*, Utrecht: Boekhoven.
--- (1978-2004), *Verzamelde Werken van Dr. O. Noordmans* (10 volumes), Kampen: Kok.
--- (1960), *Das Evangelium des Geistes* (partial translation of *Gestalte en Geest, VW 8*, translated by H. W. de Knijff and H. Stoevesandt), Zurich: TVZ.

Akke van der Kooi

Karl Barth (1886-1968) – Creation as the External Basis of the Covenant

Karl Barth was the most influential Protestant theologian of the 20th century. Shaped in the European crisis of two wars, this Swiss pastor's theology attacked religious assumptions that had permitted cultures to so disastrously associate their ambitions with God's interests. Its first word was articulated in his *The Epistle to the Romans* (1933; first German edition 1919), which exploded the liberal synthesis of theology and culture that had held sway in European theology up until World War I. Rejecting methods of doing theology that began by reasoning from experience and nature, Barth insisted anew on the sovereignty of God, on God's transcendence from a finite creation, on the sinfulness of humanity and on the self-revealed Word as the only possibility for Christian thought.

Barth's thirteen-volume *Church Dogmatics* (1956-1975) restated theology in respect of God's infinite difference from the world and yet in response to God's "nevertheless" – God's free decision for the world in Jesus Christ. Barth's preoccupying theme is the priority of God's action to created being, and therefore the priority of grace to human experience and reasoning. Humans may know something of God only from God's action for their sake, and therefore, for Barth, only in the election of Jesus Christ. Every major topic in theology and ethics, from the Trinity to the commandment not to kill, is treated in direct relation to God's self-revelation in Christ. It is thirteen volumes of therapy for attempts to appropriate God for human power.

Barth's legacy for ecotheology, however, is ambiguous if not hostile. A major initiative of his project was the defeat of nature as a source of theological knowledge. He was never more polemical than when rejecting the natural theology of Emil Brunner or the analogical reasoning from creation that characterised Thomist Catholic theology. If modern theology had reconstructed grace in its image of nature, Barth needed to suppress and discipline nature in order to restore the priority of grace. So his doctrine of creation describes the material world as "the external basis of the covenant" and interprets the covenant "as the internal basis of creation" (*CD III.1*).[4] The reality of nature must be thoroughly determined and circumscribed by God's act towards humanity in Christ.

Ecotheologians usually invoke Barth as foil rather than friend. If an environmental ethic needs to overcome anthropocentric preoccupations with salvation and to establish

4 References in parenthesis are to volumes of *Church Dogmatics* (*CD*).

intrinsic value for nature, Barth seems to only present the obstacles. Even if an environmental ethic could do without those criteria, perhaps in a stewardship ethic, Barth makes it difficult. His sections on ethics are devoted to establishing the priority of God's command and refusing norms that could arise from creation. He teases the biocentrism of Albert Schweitzer on this score, and refuses to consider whether or how God's grace might extend beyond humanity. While not impossible that God should save other creatures in other ways, Barth says, it is not given humanity to know. This seems to him to be the sort of religious question humans are likely to use for the ends of divinising their own powers (*CD III.2*, 93).

Nevertheless – there is always a "nevertheless" with Barth – within the arena made by God's redemptive grace, the natural world does appear with its own integrity. Within the election of humanity in Jesus Christ the created world in all its variety and beauty may be rightly seen, freed of its bondage to humans who would rule it and interpret it in terms of their religious mandate. Barth's theological therapy for the perverted political powers of Europe, stripping them of any pretence to divine mandate, may work a kind of freedom for other-than-human creation as well. And at points Barth shows evidence of personal concern about the destructive rise of industrial powers.

For a theological ethic of stewardship, making sense of Barth is crucial, for he presents most starkly the problems that a stewardship theology must overcome, and he develops the resources for cultural criticism and environmental responsibility that a stewardship ethic needs. Reading Barth ecologically thus tests the ecological implications of a high Protestant doctrine of salvation focused on the immediacy of God's saving Word to the individual.[5]

Creation as the Place of Salvation

Understanding Barth requires tracking the movement of his dialectical method. For Barth, creation appears in the dialectic made by the Word's summoning address to humanity and humanity's response. The immediacy of that event, it turns out, includes creation. It does not happen in empty space, as if humans were disembodied spirits; God addresses creatures in specific createdness and in the special habitat of their createdness. Theology, therefore, has a mandate to investigate how humans rightly relate to their habitat as creatures, for the event of grace includes their createdness

Barth begins to narrate the human place in the earth from the two creation sagas of Genesis. Genesis 1 seems characterised by rule based on dominion, while Genesis 2 seems characterised by humble service. Which worldview does Barth prefer? Rather than vindicate one over the other, Barth puts the two in dialectical relation in order to show how God's act of salvation opens creation as a place of encounter with God. This is typical of his approach to the whole question.

In the first creation saga Barth's exegesis offers an account of theocentric dominion that excludes from the doctrine of creation any fascist political ecologies. Making creation "the external basis of the covenant" cuts two ways. It makes creation subject to humanity only as humans are subject to the covenant of God's restoration. For Barth, writing in the shadow of World War II, that lets God's redemptive claim on

[5] See chapters 8 and 9 of Jenkins (2008), from which the remainder of this essay draws.

humanity regulate what social sense humans may make of their natural environments.

Barth sees the first saga specifically denying any natural claim to dominion, for it shows humans "complete" creation not by natural fit, but by standing in sixth-day anticipation of the Creator's special regard for creation. This sort of dominion undoes any notion of a general fact about humanity's earthly prerogative; instead it signifies God's promise to act for creation. The focus thus shifts from humanity's place to God's invitation, from the world as human stage to creation as the arena of encounter with the commanding God. Dominion does not name human status, then, but the elective manner of God's association with creation.

With respect to some contemporary stewardship theologies, Barth does not envision stewards operating as delegated vice-regents in the management of the earth. Instead, Barth reads the stewardship relation in Genesis 1 as witness to God's act of making creation into an arena for creatures to come into God's relationship. In other words, Barth uses the strong dominion imagery of Genesis 1 to critically confront perverse human grasping for domination. Dominion is not about human control or partnership or status; it is not about humanity at all. The dominion is God's, to which humanity is permitted to stands as mere witness.

Barth thus reads dominion in Genesis 1 in a way that resists Nazi political ecologies that narrated the natural dominion of an Aryan race over their homeland. He intensifies the resistance by insisting that non-human nature does not share any creative partnership with God, but rather responds to divine fiat. Because God possesses all creaturely existence, humans may not fear any natural spirit or cosmic principle, nor venerate or demonise any mystical race. Barth intentionally takes up the homeland and habitat vocabulary of National Socialism, divests it of its religious powers, and opens it to the freedom opened for humanity in God's dominion (*CD III.1*, 94-227).

Genesis 2 compels Barth to consider creation from the opposite angle, in which the earth itself appears most important to God, and humanity is "introduced only as the being who had to be created for the sake of the earth and to serve it" (*CD III.1*, 235). In this saga, says Barth, readers find humanity in more intimate connection with the earth, belonging to it and dedicated to its care. Here, integrated into the created order, humans perform an ecological service: "to make that which has been planted thrive, God needs the farmer or gardener" (*CD III.1*, 235).

For readers tempted to find in Genesis 2 the cosmology for which they were looking, Barth's dialectic interrupts again. The story here is the same one as in the first, only told from a different angle. Neither is this saga about humanity's status in creation; it is about how God's summons to humanity makes them at home in creation. Grace makes place. Humans know themselves at home on earth not from any cosmology, high or low, but only in the event that addresses them as ones summoned to obedience by the Word (*CD III.1*, 251-254).

What then does that obedience concretely entail in regard to ecological problems? When Barth returns to the question three volumes later in his chapter on "The Command of God the Creator" (*CD III.4*), God's act seems to make for a bluntly anthropocentric ethic of creation. Where the garden stewardship was an exercise bringing forth the earth's greenery, now the object of God's fecund benefit is human life itself. Humans are asked of their own lives questions that previously would have been asked of the orchard: will they appreciate this gift and make it fruitful? It seems as if earth and garden have disappeared into moral metaphors for the human life.

Throughout the volume on the ethics of creation, God's command seems to overwhelm and displace concern for the earth, silencing any claims of nature. Even when Barth seems flushed with sympathy for animals, he limits how much respect for them he will allow. In his remarkable commentary on killing animals for food, Barth does begin to invent ways of allowing himself to hear animals voice moral claims. Still, it is only in the dialectical command of God to desist from killing and the extraordinary permission to take and eat (*CD III.4*, 352-355). Barth's ethic of creation seems finally a silencing of creatures.

Reconciliation

Nevertheless, that silencing is not the last word. The pattern of the *Dogmatics*, sometimes against Barth's own concrete judgements, is to let God's action open creation as an arena of encounter with the reconciling Christ. In his unfinished volume IV, Barth explicates how Jesus acts redemptively for humanity, and so sustains the whole cosmos in the affirmation of God (*CD IV.2*, 30). Here the salvation of humanity sustains the cosmos, because as the very creature whose fall permits chaos to menace creation, humans are recuperated into God's fellowship by being given the task of enacting God's ongoing "yes" to creation.

The doctrine of reconciliation thus consummates the creation stories of Sabbath and Garden, at once abrogating and re-establishing them in the act of Christ. Christ's work becomes the relational context, the ecology, that sets the pattern for human creatures.

In the habitat of the elected community, says Barth, humans therefore learn how to enact the Creator's "Yes" from within encounter with Christ, "as members of his territory" (*CD IV.3*, 41). Barth's exegesis consistently shies away from finding any cosmic soteriology in the likely New Testament passages, but his doctrine of reconciliation mediates a cosmic affirmation through redeemed humans. Christ saves all creation from menacing destruction by bringing the blighted creature into the special place of his fellowship. In that grove, prodigal creatures are saved by being granted caretaking service of that which they would destroy.

That salvation takes this form shows Barth's keen awareness of humanity's propensity to destroy creation. In Christ, God shows true dominion by becoming a servant; however, "the human for whom God is God in this way in Jesus Christ is the very opposite – the servant who wants to be lord" (*CD IV.1*, 432). Hungry for power and grasping for religious mandate, would-be stewards claim the honour of dominion for themselves without honouring the Creator's will for a peaceful, verdant earth. Claiming the work for themselves, on account of their own supposed glories, human pseudo-lordship betrays the promised land into barren alienation.

The root of ecological problems, in this view, does not lie in faulty cosmology or inadequate metaphors for God. It is more basic and irresolvable: humans destroy and alienate the earth in their attempts to grasp divinity, in their rebellion against God's sovereignty. Too proud for the faithful service that is actual lordship, humans attempt "to pass from the decision of obedience to God to that of their own choice, from service in the garden to rule". They act as if lordship were "that one can penetrate and master and control all things" (*CD IV.1*, 434-435). Arrogating to themselves administrative responsibility for ecological order, yet incapable on their own of saying "Yes" to creation, humans release their powers over all earth. Exploiting the earth in the name of stewardship, humans thus reverse the order of grace: they refuse the sustaining habitat made for them by the Creator in order to establish their own regime, an unavoidably destructive empire.

There is only one hope: that God overcomes this sinfulness and summons these sinful would-be lords into real lordship, as part of the way that God reconciles sinners. Hope for a besieged earth lies in God's reconciling action towards the rebellious destroyers.

Within that saving act, after volumes of "No" to human rebellion and grasping in natural theology, Barth can say surprisingly affirmative things about nature. In the environment of Christ, creation's witness no longer speaks abstractly and mysteriously, but concretely as the "sphere and place of the reconciliation". By the coming of the Reconciler the "self-witness of creation can also speak and tell of what God says, and *therefore speaks as from God*" (emphasis added). Nature's witnesses "are taken, lifted, assumed and integrated into the action of God's self-giving and self-declaring" (*CD IV.3*, 163-164). Prised away from the competency of natural reason to say so on its own, Barth finds it safe even to say that "nature does objectively offer a proof of God".[6]

From within the event of salvation, then, creation makes its claims. Theologically received, natural sciences illuminate the place in which humans encounter and respond to the Word. The regular phenomena of nature, its laws and orders, its rhythms and dynamism, its contrariety and diversity, serve the work of God, and so become ethically relevant for stewardship (*CD IV.1*, 141-147). "What they say can so harmonize with what God says that to hear God is to hear them, and to hear them is to hear God, so that listening to the polyphony of creation … is listening to the symphony for which it was elected and determined" (*CD IV.3*, 159).

Conclusion

In Barth's dialectics of grace and nature the stewardship and creation care theologies being developed by evangelical Protestant communities may find support for accounts of environmental destruction rooted in sin and resolvable by redemption. They also face similar problems to Barth. Barth is notorious for replacing nature-based social violence with revelation-based hierarchies, as in his account of male-female relations. An analogous question faces a theological ethic so accepting of human priority: can a theological strategy make its object human obedience and confidently avoid sanctioning the structure of continued human domination?

References and Recommended Reading

Barth, Karl (1933), *The Epistle to the Romans* (translated from the sixth edition by Edwyn C. Hoskins), Oxford: Oxford University Press.

(1956-1975), *Church Dogmatics* (14 volumes), (translated by G. W. Bromiley and T. F. Torrance), Edinburgh: T & T Clark.

6 See Zuckmayer, Barth and Stoevesandt, 42.

Jenkins, Willis (2008), *Ecologies of Grace: Environmental Ethics and Christian Theology*, Oxford: Oxford University Press.
Zuckmayer, Carl, Barth, Karl and Stoevesandt, Hinrich (1982), *A Late Friendship: The Letters of Karl Barth and Carl Zuckmayer*, Grand Rapids: Eerdmans.

Willis Jenkins

Arnold van Ruler (1908-1970) – God's Joy in Re-creation

Very few theologians have grappled as intensively with the relationship between creation and salvation, the natural and the spiritual, the goodness of God's original creation and the need for God's emergency interventions on behalf of sinful *'adam*, as the Dutch theologian Arnold Albert van Ruler (1908-1970). Van Ruler consistently shunned all hints of dualism in thinking about the human condition – from creation, through salvation and onwards, right through to the eschaton.

The translation of eight key texts from Van Ruler's oeuvre by John Bolt, entitled *Calvinist Trinitarianism and Theocentric Politics* (1989), provides English readers access to the imaginative approach of this original Christian thinker, also on this theme.[7] For the purpose of this essay, we follow Van Ruler's argument by means of one particular text, written in his typical idiomatic Dutch, shortly before his death in 1970.[8] Here he is in serious conversation with the "ultra-reformed", a conservative church grouping in the Netherlands, from which he himself came and that remained close to his heart, in spite of his severe critique of their appropriation of salvation.

Ultra-Reformed and Liberal

In this treatise – which became his final statement on this issue – he strongly challenged the "ultra-reformed" views on the relationship between creation and salvation. In the process he also addressed other versions of Christian thinking that equally fall short of his *re-creatio* view of sanctification, which formed the core focus of his theology: how God's grace is "mixed into" our existence in such a way that, while retaining our being and identity as creatures, we are re-created, renewed, transformed, to become what God, our Creator, intended us to be. Right through his extensive oeuvre, Van Ruler applied his typology of a handful of possible definitions of this crucial aspect of Christian doctrine: how our being saved relates to our being human. He exposes inter alia the Barthian, Roman Catholic and Anabaptist models as at heart being dualist, and in some cases even docetic or gnostic.[9] Following his argument, addressed

[7] Key texts in this volume (Van Ruler, 1989) that are relevant to the theme of creation and salvation include the essays "The Necessity of a Trinitarian Theology" (1-25), "Grammar of a Pneumatology" (47-87) and "Christ Taking Form in the World" (105-148). A number of other important essays have not been translated into English. See especially the notes entitled "De Verhouding van Schepping en Verlossing" (Dutch original 1958) in Van Ruler (2009), 97-101; the early essay "Natuur en Genade" (Dutch original 1938) in Van Ruler (1969), 121-133 and the essay "De Verhouding van het Kosmologische en het Eschatologische Element in de Christologie" (Dutch original 1961) in Van Ruler (1969), 156-174.

[8] See Van Ruler (1971). Subsequent page references in parenthesis in this section are to this extended essay (translations – CL).

[9] See Van Ruler (1989), 106-108, 128-132.

to his own ultra-reformed friends, we can simultaneously observe how he links their "heretical tendencies" to these contrary visions of the human condition:

> Our natural state is that which we have received, what was given to us at birth. But when a person is not only born, but also reborn – what is his state then? Then he has received something additionally. He knows of more than merely the natural life he shares with all other people. He also knows of spiritual life. This he has entered through being born again. This was infused into him. Now he has, as it were, two lives: natural life given by birth (which he only gives up in death) and spiritual life by his rebirth (which continues through death into life eternal).
>
> What now, in ultra-reformed thinking, is the relationship of the one to the other? The natural is the general. All people have that. The spiritual is the special. This only some people have. The natural was always there, with a certain matter-of-factness. No one is amazed by it anymore. The spiritual, however, has been added. That is a big mystery, a miracle of God's grace. The natural is the visible, the ordinary, the common. The spiritual is in principle the invisible, the extraordinary, the particular. The natural is the earthly. The spiritual is the heavenly. The natural is the lower. The spiritual is the higher. An ultra-reformed Christian will not easily say: the natural is per se evil, "non-being", and the spiritual alone is good, the only "true being" … As a Christian, and a reformed one at that, one simply has to respect creation and cannot deny that the earthly, visible, material, natural reality is part of God's work. Whoever denied that would take a big step outside of Christianity itself. The ultra-reformed constantly, however, have a tendency to take this step, but are prevented, at the last moment, by the doctrine of the church to actually do so. Essentially, however, they constantly remain on this slippery road. This tendency, this reaching out towards full heresy, must be recognised as heretical itself and addressed as such (p. 137-138).

Against this background, Van Ruler proceeds to tease out some consequences of such a dualist stand in the real world for ultra-reformed Christians.[10] Does such a Christian experience his (or her) daily work as "service to God" or is God actually only served in the inner spiritual life and in the "conventicle", the true inner church? How much space is there in the life and world of such a Christian for science, art, culture? What about amusement, games, sport, television? Maybe there is one exception on this reserved attitude: interest and involvement in politics, based on the realisation that God's kingdom is a political concept with political consequences. However, aside from this one possible exception, "the ultra-reformed dualism of natural life, coming from birth, and spiritual life, coming out of being born again, can only be judged as heretical" (p. 139).

In a humorous "test case", Van Ruler asks penetrating questions about sexual issues: "Can a truly born-again child of God truly enjoy coitus, including the passion, sensuality, and lust accompanying it? Obviously, ultra-reformed men and women also live together as husband and wife in marriage. It seems as though, quite frequently, natural children are born from spiritual people. Do they only have a spiritual marriage,

---

[10] What makes this analysis so relevant for our day is that the majority of contemporary Christians may be living with such a split view of reality, in one form or another.

living together as brother and sister …? Do they only have sexual intercourse because it is God's calling, for the sake of procreation, without any bodily pleasure?" (p. 139). For him, these questions, only answered by embarrassed silence, are not frivolous or irrelevant. Sexuality is indeed one of the most fundamental elements of all that has been given to us at birth. How this element is dealt with from the perspective of being born again is therefore essential for the relationship between "the natural" and the "spiritual", "nature" and "grace", "creation" and "salvation" (p. 139-140).

Two Realities

For Van Ruler, these questions are essential for a correct understanding of the purpose of God's "special" revelation and God's saving work through Israel and Christ. In dealing with these fundamentals of a Christian understanding of the world, and life itself, he distinguishes between "means" and "ends":[11]

> On the one hand we have the fact of the reality of the world, in nature and history. There is something and not nothing. At least, that is what we believe. It is an aspect of what we believe, of our Judaeo-Christian faith and, from that, also our European worldview, that reality is not a veil of appearance, which treacherously covers the precipice of nothingness. Reality is really there and is real. This reality principle is formulated, underlined and consolidated in the Christian dogma of creation. Moreover, this dogma not only holds that the world is real, but also that this reality is good, having been willed and posited by God.
>
> On the other hand, we have the fact of the election of Israel, set apart from all the nations of the earth. Israel is taken up in the covenant of grace. It receives the law of God. In this history it is comprehensively led out of the servanthood of heathenism and demons. Prophecy and psalms rise up from these experiences. But all of this is not sufficient. Eventually God sends God's Son. In him and his work the goal is reached. Is this the goal of creation; or only the goal of the election of Israel and the covenant with them? Is it properly the goal of the covenant? Is it not a means – an emergency measure – to reach the goal of the latter (viz. the world as kingdom of God)? Be that as it may, the Christ event is – in the context of the history of Israel – an enormous reality. It is a separate reality; also an entirely new one. God becomes human. God's rule becomes tangible. Guilt is being atoned. Death is conquered. Life eternal is brought to light. The Spirit is poured out. People are called and born again. They are gathered in the church. There salvation is preached. Human beings receive their share of redemption: outside of the church, that is: outside of the communion with Christ, there is no salvation. This is also celebrated. Liturgy moves from creaturely praise to worship of the Saviour" (p. 140-141).

For Van Ruler the crucial question, which needs to be answered by all Christian doctrinal approaches, is how these two realities relate to one another: on the one hand, the reality of the world, in nature and history, and on the other hand, salvation given through Israel, Christ and the church. These realities, in Christian perspective, need to be balanced: the moment we only have eyes for salvation or redemption, we end up in Gnosticism; the moment we only focus on creation, we end up in ultra-liberalism. Both of these extreme possibilities fall outside of the ambit of Christian faith; they are

[11] See also Van Ruler (1989), 53-87.

even beyond heresy. Merely stating that we need to hold fast to both will also not do. We need to define their mutual relationship. At this point van Ruler then discusses several main answers provided in Christian dogmatic history – as he has done in several other analyses.[12]

Has salvation come to replace creation, and if so, why? The gnostic answer is, yes, indeed, creation has been replaced by salvation because creation as such was far from good. Or, creation has been corrupted by sin to such an extent that it could not be fixed again and thus had to make way for a totally new creation, a *nova creatio*. This is the Anabaptist answer of the 16th century, which could easily, also in the revolutionary spirit of our own day, lead to revolutionary violence. Van Ruler was concerned that Moltmann's eschatology tended in this direction.

Another possibility is to say, like proponents of the Dutch "ethical direction", that God only partially expressed God's intentions in creation; the Word of creation was a *verbum abbreviatum*, a shorthand version, which needs the Word of incarnation, in which God gave full expression of God's divinity in humanity, thus drawing humanity towards divinity. Incarnation becomes the fulfilment of creation.

This perspective is taken to its full consequences along a different route by Karl Barth. In his view, God chooses to be God of and for human beings; in this choice God becomes who God is; God's essence is constituted by the covenant; God's grace is really all that exists. God, as a matter of fact, called forth creation on account of the covenant and grace. Creation is the external ground, the sacramental prefiguration, of the covenant. The covenant is nothing less than the internal base on which creation rests, the purpose and goal of creation. The covenant, as realised in the person and history of Jesus Christ, is the true reality, preceding and carrying everything that exists, even sin. Salvation, grace and communion of God with us and us with God are the all-embracing reality. This approach, according to Van Ruler, leads to soteriological answers being given to ontological questions.

Rome deals with the relationship of creation, sin and salvation by means of yet another theological logic. Catholics believe that through sin humanity has lost its focus on and communion with God and the supernatural world. In this world "above", in the quest for "divinity", lies the human destiny. In Christ the way towards this goal is opened again, and grace supplements "fallen" nature to regain what has been lost. For Van Ruler this road leads to divinisation, which cannot be the goal of the creation or the re-creation of the human being.

Over against these "solutions" Van Ruler posits that in reformed thinking humanity did not so much lose something, but rather had something added: sin (the guilt of sin, but also the power of sin) and perdition. Creation is to be redeemed from what we have brought upon ourselves by "adding" sin. At its core this salvation is atonement of guilt and justification of the sinner. Per definition the saved human being is then placed back, through redemption, into creation, even into its fallen state.

For the question how we should view the relation between birth and rebirth, the natural and the spiritual, it makes a big difference which of the answers, as sketched above, we choose. Van Ruler urges his ultra-reformed friends to choose, against the

---

[12] See again Van Ruler (1989), 106-108, 128-132.

dualisms of their own making and those of the Anabaptists (a totally new creation, the old being discarded like a pair of old shoes), the Catholics (grace supplementing, elevating nature), and even Barth's (the "soteriologising" of creation), for the following version of the reformed rendering:

> God the Creator had (and still has!) a different goal in mind from the one realised through salvation. The intention with creation is that creation itself and all creatures rejoice in their existence before God, finding their being in the praise and service of God. Through salvation God had to follow a detour towards this goal. That was because of sin. For this purpose (only) the Mediator had to come into the picture and atonement had to be brought about. The sinner must learn to live from grace, something which cannot happen without the work of God's Spirit. The pouring out and dwelling in of the Spirit thus also had to happen. All of this, constituting what we call "salvation", is an enormous process of "shattering": of God on the cross and in the sacrifice, of the human being in the acknowledgement and confession of sin and the letting go of guilt. For this detour of salvation the whole apparatus of Israel, its messiah and the church, is needed. But the goal does not lie (only) in bringing the sinner to his or her knees and receiving God's grace. That is indeed necessary, there is no other way – it belongs to spiritual life; it forms the deepest core of it. But that is not the purpose of it; the goal is that creation is saved from the precipice of lostness to be what it is supposed to be: creation "in front of" God. Salvation is more important than the Saviour. That which is saved is more important than its salvation. The original goal is also the eventual goal, which is exclusively this: that creation finds its being again in rejoicing in itself before its Creator as a liturgy of service.

Conclusion

Van Ruler concludes that the very concept of salvation suggests that the purpose of salvation is not salvation itself or about "being saved" or even about the Saviour but about the being of the saved. He explains that the relationship between salvation and being is governed by four factors, namely (a) Jesus Christ as the Saviour, (b) salvation as the work of the Mediator, (c) salvation as the outcome of such work (analogous to the distinction between *creatio* and *creatura*) and (d) that which is saved, namely the being of the saved. He then asks how these are related. What is the means and what is the end? He responds:

> So what is the ultimate aim? Is the aim the first, the Saviour? Is Christ the aim, the meaning of history? Or does the aim lie in the second, in salvation? Is salvation the original and finally the only aim, around which everything not only hinges but is directed towards? Then we are pure supralapsarians. Supralapsarianism maintains that salvation is the highest point of view in the eternal counsel of God, that God is finally a God of grace. Or is the real aim the third, the saved being, the savedness of being? Then we are still supralapsarians. The only thing that we should then be joyful about is salvation. In my view, the Christian-Jewish focus is on the fourth, the being that is saved, not only in its savedness but in its being. Through the salvation such being can be again and can find joy in itself together with the triune God.[13]

[13] Van Ruler (1978), 55 (translation – EMC).

References and Recommended Reading

Keulen, Dirk van, Harinck, George and Brink, Gijsbert van den (eds.) (2009), *Men Moet Telkens Opnieuw de Reuzenzwaai aan de Rekstok Maken: Verder met Van Ruler*, Zoetermeer: Boekencentrum.

Ruler, A. A. van (1969), *Theologisch Werk, Deel I*, Nijkerk: Callenbach.

--- (1971), "Ultra-Gereformeerd en Vrijzinnig", in: *Theologisch Werk, Deel III*, Nijkerk: Callenbach, 98-163.

--- (1978), *Verwachting en Voltooiing: Een Bundel Theologische Opstellen en Voordrachten*, Nijkerk: Callenbach.

--- (1989), *Calvinist Trinitarianism and Theocentric Politics: Essays towards a Public Theology* (edited and translated by John Bolt), Lewiston: Edwin Mellen.

--- (2009), *Verzameld Werk, Deel III: God, Schepping, Mens, Zonde* (edited by Dirk van Keulen), Zoetermeer: Boekencentrum.

Christo Lombard

Jürgen Moltmann (1926-) – The Justification of God

Introduction

Where can one find a theology that can do justice to both God's work of creation and of salvation? Jürgen Moltmann's sizable oeuvre has been highly influential and promising in this regard. He consistently stresses the redemptive thrust of God's acts of creation and the creative thrust of God's acts of redemption on the basis of a consistently eschatological approach. Moltmann has addressed nuclear and ecological threats explicitly and is indeed a key figure in current ecotheology.

Moltmann was born on 8 April 1926 near Hamburg in Germany. He became an unwilling conscript in Hitler's war effort and landed up as a prisoner of war in Scotland where he became a Christian through reading the book of Psalms. He then studied theology and eventually became professor of systematic theology in Tübingen. He was deeply influenced by Karl Barth, Dietrich Bonhoeffer and Arnold van Ruler, whose positions have been discussed earlier in this volume. The latter's theology of the apostolate, he later commented, liberated him from the presumption that there could be no theology after Barth. While Barth's early theology emphasises the radical transcendence of God, Moltmann seeks to affirm God's presence in (human) history in terms of categories such as the Sabbath, God's *Shekinah*, the Messianic Way and the notion of *adventus* (the coming of Christ). Moltmann's conversation partners also include the neo-Marxist philosophy of Ernst Bloch and several Jewish scholars.

Moltmann's work became widely recognised upon the publication of *Theology of Hope* (1967). This was followed by *The Crucified God* (1974) and *The Church in the Power of the Spirit* (1977). He then commenced with a series of "systematic contributions to theology" which included *The Trinity and the Kingdom of God* (1981), *God in Creation: An Ecological Doctrine of Creation* (1985), *The Way of Jesus Christ: Christology in Messianic Dimensions* (1990), *The Spirit of Life: A Universal Affirmation* (1993), *The Coming of God: Christian Eschatology* (1996) and *Experiences in Theology: Ways and Forms of Christian Theology* (2000). Other contributions important for the theme of creation and salvation include *The Future of Creation* (1979), *God for a Secular Society: The Public Relevance of Theology* (1999), *Science and Wisdom*

(2003), his autobiography *A Broad Place* (2008) and finally *Sun of Righteousness, Arise: God's Future for Humanity and the Earth* (2010).[14]

Theology as Theodicy

Moltmann's entire oeuvre may be construed as a theological response to the suffering that defined the 20th century. Here theodicy becomes the primary theological task. His political theology is anti-bourgeois, standing in solidarity with the victims of modernity, not a progressive theology of the established middle classes.

Political theology was born after the war from the horror over the failure of the German church and theology to address the crimes against humanity associated most notably with Auschwitz. In *The Crucified God* Moltmann wrote, "I experienced a very 'dark night' in my soul, for the pictures of Bergen-Belsen concentration camp and horror over the crimes of Auschwitz, had weighed on me and many other people of my generation since 1945. Much time passed before we could emerge from the silence that stops the mouths of people over whom the cloud of the victims hangs heavy" (p. xi).

Moltmann argues that theodicy does not require an explanation for suffering – since that would somehow render it acceptable. He insists that his theology of the cross should not be understood as an answer to the theodicy problem. Instead, it requires the willingness to live with the open wound of the unanswerable but unavoidable question: "My God, why have you forsaken me?" What is required is a protest against suffering – God's own protest. Only in this way can God be justified (theodicy). Following Bonhoeffer, Moltmann insists that only a suffering God can be credible to humankind today.

Given an acute sense of the difference between the suffering of victims and the very different forms of suffering experienced by oppressors, Moltmann consistently refrains from universalising discourse on sin and guilt. The gospel can only be made cheap (Bonhoeffer) where a generalised message of God's forgiveness is proclaimed. His intuition is that it would be obscene to universalise human guilt in the cases of Auschwitz, Hiroshima, the Gulag, the victims of racism and genocide, the poverty of those marginalised by the global economy, the plight of women in patriarchal societies and the non human victims of ecological destruction. Moltmann's theological response to such suffering includes the key themes of creation, salvation and eschatological consummation.

Creation

Like other recent theologians, Moltmann avoids a portrayal of the triune God as apathetic and distant from the world. God is open to time, influenced by historical changes and therefore affected by suffering. He speaks of creation as not so much *ex nihilo* but *ex amore Dei*. God freely limits Godself by that which is not God, by creation, the object of God's love.

The key to Moltmann's position is his controversial use of the kabbalistic notion of God's primordial self-restriction (*zimsum*). This suggests that God allowed room with-

14 All these English translations were done by Margaret Kohl and were published within a few years following the German originals by Fortress and SCM Press.

in Godself for the emergence of something that is different from Godself. God created the world in Godself, giving it time in God's eternity, finitude within God's infinity, space within God's omnipresence, freedom within God's love. God becomes vulnerable by being in a reciprocal relationship, since the response of the beloved cannot be taken for granted. The act of creation may, therefore, already be understood as kenosis. God's pain in giving birth to the world anticipates the pain of incarnation and cross as well as the groaning of the Spirit for a new creation. Such reciprocity leads to God's compassion, solidarity, self-surrender and infinite sorrow.

The self-withdrawal of God also implies that creation is devoid of divine characteristics and therefore finite and imperfect. However, there is more at stake here. This self-withdrawal of God creates empty space to be filled by the emergence of creatures. Moltmann describes this in terms of the emergence of a *nihil*, which is a partial negation of divine being, but not the negation of creaturely being. Nothingness does not form part of God's being from all eternity, but the emergence of nothingness forms the reverse side of God's withdrawing. It is this void, being threatened by a primordial *nihil*, which accounts for much of the suffering in the world. It was out of chaos, darkness and flood that God created the world. The only response available to God is to reoccupy this vacated space.

Salvation as the Justification of God

Moltmann portrays the history of creation as a history of suffering and death in God's good creation. If suffering is rooted in creaturely reality (not only the result of human sin), then sin itself may be understood as the result of human fear of death – and not only the fear of God. Dying, Moltmann maintains, is already implied in the command to be fruitful and multiply. Sin and death are therefore dialectically related to one another. Sin enters human existence through fear of death and death follows on sin as the consequence of violence.

This implies that salvation has to include redemption from the suffering embedded in creation itself. It cannot be understood merely in terms of overcoming human alienation from God resulting from sin. The history of creation is the story of God's passionate and compassionate love through which God seeks to overcome the alienation between Creator and creation without abolishing the distinction between the two. This is possible through God's re-entering the godforsaken world through the *Shekinah* of God's Spirit and the coming of the Messiah. The ontological gap between Creator and creation is thus overcome through God's reoccupation of creation, but then in a perichoretic way so that creation is not overwhelmed by God's presence.

For Moltmann, the cross of Jesus Christ constitutes the turning point in the dialectic narrative of God's work. The cross demonstrates God's solidarity with a suffering creation, God's vicarious love for the godforsaken world threatened by annihilation, and the protest of divine love against the suffering of creation. God enters the nothingness (which resulted from God's self-withdrawal) by drawing it into God's own being. God is not dead; death is taken up within God. The alienating otherness of creation is overcome when such otherness is taken up in God's own being. Being abandoned by God becomes something that took place within Godself. This is the paradox of God's own godforsakenness. The crucified God, the justification of God, not of sinners, is for

Moltmann the only response available to the reproach that God created suffering, death and evil together with the world and humanity.

On this basis Moltmann's theology of salvation moves away from an Anselmian notion of expiatory suffering for human sins towards what Gustaf Aulén described as the *Christus Victor* tradition: victory over the forces of death, liberation from oppression and an end to suffering. Moltmann resists a generalised notion of the forgiveness of sinners – which tends to mystify it, making people blind to specific manifestations of injustice so that it becomes innocuous to confess one's sins. Accordingly, justification is not understood primarily as forgiveness offered to sinners (perpetrators, those who are guilty). Instead, Moltmann understands justification as a response to the "cry for justice" of the victims of injustice. In *The Spirit of Life* he uses the category of an affirmation of life with respect to social outcasts, the marginalised, the victims of injustice. Such affirmation recognises human dignity and the integrity of all life. It offers liberation to victims deprived of justice and the liberation of unjust perpetrators. For Moltmann the only way in which God can be declared just in the face of global suffering is to proclaim universal salvation. In the final judgement God redeems Godself in the eyes of the whole suffering creation.

Although Moltmann therefore refuses to universalise human guilt, he views human sin as a manifestation of the suffering embedded in God's creation. He resists the temptation to generalise human accountability, but does not hesitate to universalise suffering. If the victims are not responsible for their suffering, then no human being can ultimately be responsible. The only way is to hold God responsible. Theology thus becomes theodicy.

Consummation

Moltmann describes the consummation of all things in terms of the mutual indwelling of God in the world (theo-en-pan-ism) and of the world in God (panentheism). In the beginning the Creator is a God who can be inhabited, but in the end creation is made into God's habitat. What comes into being through God's contraction is now gathered up again as God's own. God not only comes to dwell in creation (*adventus* and *Shekinah*); the whole creation is called to participate (*perichoresis*) in the life of the triune God. For Moltmann, creaturely reality is opened up for God's indwelling. Through this perichoretic indwelling of God in the world every wrong in history is redressed, every form of suffering is healed. This allows for the participation of God and creation in the celebration of an eternal Sabbath – characterised by festivities, joy, laughter, dancing and play. Christian hope, Moltmann maintains, expects eternal joy in the dance of fellowship with all created being and with the triune God. Indeed, the laughter of the universe is God's delight.

Moltmann describes the eschatological consummation as a new creation. The eschaton implies more than reparation or restoration. This is the necessary consequence of his recognition that suffering and death are embedded in creation itself. Such suffering requires a new creation. The "new" in "new creation" is new compared to sin and to creation. God cannot be content only to overcome sin; the conditions that made sin possible should be overcome. The radically new breaks the power of a closed future and crushes disabling despair by opening new possibilities.

If the eschaton entails a new creation, how is this *novum* possible? Is reality itself structured in such a way as to allow new things to emerge, perhaps following Bloch's materialist ontology of not-yet being? Such a materialist view of the emergence of the *novum* would neither address the finitude of creation nor human mortality. An alternative would be to relate the possibility of a *novum* to God's transcendence, the God who "calls into being the things that are not" (Rom. 4:17) through God's promises. In *The Coming of God* Moltmann balances God's primordial self-withdrawal (*zimzum*) with the eschatological notion of *aevum* (relative eternity) so that the Creator is distinguished from creation also in the eschaton.

This emphasis on the radically new threatens the continuity between this earth and the new earth. Without that, Christian hope will be less consoling. Moltmann has been criticised (especially among reformed scholars) for this emphasis on the discontinuity between creation and eschaton. The argument is that Moltmann is unable, against his own intentions, to consistently affirm God's faithfulness to this creation. He tends to conflate two sources of suffering, namely natural suffering and suffering resulting from human sin. Thus the created order itself is faulted because of its inherent finitude. If the self-limitation of God assumes a primordial *nihil*, the eschaton constitutes an annihilation of the created order. This results in an inability to maintain the continuity between God's good creation and the eschaton.

Conclusion

Douglas Farrow suggests that there is a "neo-Platonist" circular movement in Moltmann's version of the story of God's work. However, this is more of a dialectical spiral movement which is Hegelian in structure if not in content. The Trinity provides the clue to the meaning of history. Moltmann's theology commences with the triune God (not the One) and concludes with the participation of the whole of creation in God's own being or, more precisely, the mutual *perichoresis* of God in creation and creation in God. The turning point of the story is the cross where it becomes evident that creation is godforsaken and where Godself becomes godforsaken. This turning point itself is balanced through the resurrection which Moltmann interprets as God's promise to renew the whole creation. The resurrection of Jesus Christ elicits hope for the resurrection of nature. This is indeed the dominant motif in Moltmann's theological vision, from a *Theology of Hope* (1967) to *Sun of Righteousness, Arise* (2010).

References and Recommended Reading

Bauckham, Richard (ed.) (1999), *God Will Be All In All: The Eschatology of Jürgen Moltmann*, Edinburgh: T & T Clark.

Bouma-Prediger, Steven (1995), *The Greening of Theology: The Ecological Models of Rosemary Radford Ruether, Joseph Sittler, and Jürgen Moltmann*, Atlanta: Scholars Press.

Conradie, Ernst M. (2008), "The Justification of God? The Story of God's Work according to Jürgen Moltmann" (parts 1 and 2), *Scriptura*, Vol. 97, 76-105.

Farrow, Douglas (1998), "In the End is the Beginning: A Review of Jürgen Moltmann's Systematic Contributions", *Modern Theology*, Vol. 14, 3, 425-447.

Müller-Fahrenholz, Geiko (2000), *The Kingdom and the Power: The Theology of Jürgen Moltmann*, London: SCM.

Ernst M. Conradie

Further Developments in a Reforming Tradition

Reformed theology, following John Calvin's example, typically seeks to maintain a fruitful tension between faith in God as Creator and God as Saviour. It also seeks to occupy the middle ground between salvation as elevation (the polemics with Roman Catholicism) and as new creation (the polemics with the radical reformation). The key here is the concept "re-creation", introduced into Dutch Protestantism by Abraham Kuyper and, especially, Herman Bavinck, which suggests that the eschatological completion of God's acts of salvation is indeed creative and aimed at healing God's own creation.

However, as this chapter indicates, this term, "re-creation", did not preclude diverging interpretations of the relation between creation and salvation. One way of framing the point of divergence is whether the "re" in "*re-creatio*" should be understood as a "repairing" (of this creation, with the focus on *creatura*) or as "again" (with the focus on *creatio* as act), which would indicate an act in which God would create anew – and where the continuity between this creation (*creatura*) in which we live, infected by sin as it is, and the outcome of God's act of re-creation is not foregrounded.

If the focus is on creaturely continuity, then the question is whether re-creation is to be understood merely as repristination? If so, how could one guard against apartheid theology, where the message of salvation was portrayed in terms of the restoration (through law and order) of the diversity of races that was supposedly embedded in the "orders of creation"? Or should one consider Kuyper's own version, namely that God's redemptive work restored (reinvigorated) the developmental potential of creation (thus allowing for historical progression). The alternative to re-creation as restoration is to allow for a far more elaborate notion of re-creation, where there is indeed room for completion and fulfilment, if not elevation, that would also address the problem of natural suffering, if not natural evil. Between repristination and elevation one finds a whole series of possible theological concepts where a sense of both continuity and discontinuity is acknowledged, but with diverging connotations: reanimation, rebirth, rebuilding, recapitulation, recollection, reconciliation, reconstruction, recovering, redemption, reflection, reformation, refreshment, regeneration, reinvigoration, remembering, remuneration, renewal, reparation, representation, reproduction, respect, restitution, restoration, resurrection, revolution, but in short, re-creation.

Several reformed theologians have recognised the significance of such theological reflection for a wide variety of social issues where the meaning of the message of salvation for the world is at stake. This is framed in different ways, for example on the relationship between God and the world, gospel and culture, church and state, church and civil society, grace and nature, and so forth. Often the rhetoric of dialectic rather than analogy is employed to emphasise a prophetic contrast. This allows the gospel to challenge reigning constellations of power. The reformed tradition is often at its weakest where it becomes all too well established in a particular cultural context.

It is not difficult to see the significance of such debates for Christian reflection on environmental destruction. Reformed theologians have indeed been deeply involved in current discourse on Christian ecotheology. Their interests range across the many themes addressed in ecotheology, certainly including the pertinent issues of economic injustices, the ideology of consumerism and consumerist culture, the environmental destruction resulting from that, climate change, animal issues, biotechnology, the many faces of poverty, various forms on conflict and violence and work on peace and reconciliation. An important example of such a critique of economic injustices and ecological destruction is found in the document *Covenanting for Justice in the Economy and the Earth: "The Accra Confession"*, adopted by the 24th General Council of the former World Alliance of Reformed Churches in Accra, Ghana, 30 July to 13 August 2004. Positions on the relationship between creation and salvation are typically assumed, but remain implicit in such work.

In this concluding section a number of recent monographs published after 1990 in English from within the reformed tradition will be mentioned in chronological order in the form of a brief literature survey. The focus will be on contributions that are influenced by the strand of reformed theology discussed in this chapter, that address the themes of creation and salvation in one way or another and that are overtly addressing environmental concerns. These contributions come from all over the world, given the now global spread of reformed Christianity.

- In *Creation, Eschaton, and Ethics: The Ethical Significance of the Creation – Eschaton Relation in the Thought of Emil Brunner and Jürgen Moltmann* (New York: Peter Lang, 1991), Doug Schuurman explores the crucial problem of the continuity and the discontinuity between creation and eschaton with overt reference to environmental issues.
- In *Animal Theology* (London: SCM Press, 1994), Andrew Linzey addresses a range of issues in animal ethics from the conviction that creation, incarnation and reconciliation are three sides of the one mystery of God's work accomplished in Christ.
- In his doctoral thesis entitled "Reformed Theology, Modernity and the Environmental Crisis" (University of Cape Town, 1996), David Field explores the suspicion that the roots of the environmental crisis are associated with the roots of the reformed tradition.
- In *Caring for Creation* (Grand Rapids: Baker, 1998), Calvin DeWitt defends a reformed / evangelical notion of environmental stewardship as opposed to a logic of domination.
- In *The Triune Creator* (Grand Rapids: Eerdmans, 1998), Colin Gunton engages in a historical and systematic survey of Christian discourse on creation (and redemption) and offers conclusions on an "ethic of createdness".
- In *Creation and Reality* (Minneapolis: Fortress, 1999), Michael Welker shows how the Genesis creation narratives challenge our reigning but sterile notions of nature, transcendence, revelation and of life itself.
- In *For the Beauty of the Earth* (Grand Rapids: Baker Academic, 2000, revised edition 2009), Steven Bouma-Prediger explores the relationship between Christianity and the natural world and offers an evangelical vision of creation care.
- In *Hope for the Earth* (Eugene: Wipf and Stock, 2000 / 2005), Ernst Conradie explores an eschatological approach to environmental praxis, ethos and spirituality on the basis of an analysis of the three predicaments of the impact of sin, finitude and the limitations of human knowledge and power.

- In his doctoral thesis *Environmental Ethics and Ecological Theology* (VU University Amsterdam, 2005), Robert Borrong offers reformed perspectives on ecological concerns in the Indonesian context.
- In *Ecologies of Grace* (Oxford University Press, 2008), Willis Jenkins investigates the ways in which various forms of Christian environmental ethics are shaped by underlying notions of salvation.
- In the edited volume *Creation and Salvation: Dialogue on Abraham Kuyper's Legacy for Contemporary Ecotheology* (Leiden: Brill, 2011), Ernst Conradie and seven respondents explore the theme addressed in this chapter with specific reference to Kuyper's vision.
- In *Salvation means Creation Healed: The Ecology of Sin and Grace* (Eugene: Cascade, 2011), Howard Snyder seeks to overcome the divorce between earth and heaven through a notion of salvation as "creation healed". He spells out the implications of that for an evangelical ethos of stewardship.

The diverse contributions included in this chapter indicate that discourse on creation and salvation lie very much at the heart of reformed contributions to ecotheology, that the tradition is vibrant and that much further work needs to be done in this regard.

Ernst M. Conradie

5. Nordic Theologies

Edited by Mika Vähäkangas

Introduction

Christianity and theology in the Nordic region may be sketched by means of various contrasts, including the northern versus the southern context, which partly correlates with the cultural-linguistic divide between Scandinavians and Fenno-Ugrians. Another divide is between Lutheran state religiosity and Pietistic revivalism that have existed, and still exist, side by side and overlapping each other. Yet another tension relates to the way in which modernity is addressed, which correlates both with the context and the theological-ecclesiastic position of particular theologians.

Nordic countries consist of two cultural-linguistically diverse areas: Scandinavia, covering the Swedish, Danish, Norwegian and Icelandic cultures and languages, and the Finnish and Sami languages and cultures that differ considerably from the first group. The national boundaries do not follow the cultural ones – the Sami, for example, have no state of their own. Even though the population of this northern corner of Europe is small, the natural environment of this geographically large area varies from the harsh arctic fells through vast forests to the central European type of agriculture-dominated landscape of Denmark and southern Sweden.

All theology takes place in a context. The most visible Nordic theology has mostly been done in universities in the very south of the area: many of the internationally known theologians have studied at Lund (southern Sweden) or in Denmark. This may be partly related to their cultural and contextual proximity to central Europe, whereby the resulting theology becomes more palatable to a West European and North American audience. This chapter also concentrates on the better-known southern Scandinavian theology but highlights two examples coming from a lesser-known linguistic and cultural sphere offering a different northern perspective.

The place and role of human beings vis-à-vis the natural environment in the different Nordic contexts used to vary considerably between the scarcely populated and climatically demanding north, on the one hand, and the densely populated and climatically moderate south, on the other. In the north, no person can claim mastery of nature – how could (s)he, in the middle of endless forests, swamps and fells? Rather than being one of subduing nature, the task of the human inhabitants has been one of adjusting and eking out one's living. In such contexts, one lives in and with the natural environment. Owing to the Sami's nature religion and the relatively late process of modernisation, the disenchantment of the world is still in progress among some of the people of the north. At the other end of Scandinavia, almost all land has been rendered "useful" from the point of view of human economic activities. Nature has been subdued and moulded according to human needs. Alienation from nature has eventually become a central issue, leading to calls for a re-enchantment of one's view of the world through new types of spiritualities.

Nordic Christianity has been characterised for centuries by the Lutheran understanding of the relation between the state and the church – which left little space for teachings and power structures of the Reformation, except for Eastern Orthodoxy in the eastern parts of Finland. Lutheran orthodoxy consolidated the Reformation teachings and power structures and carried out an extensive programme of popular education concentrating on literacy and Lutheran doctrines. Lutheran orthodoxy laid the foundation for the rigidly formalistic "state churchism" and a wide array of Pietistic revival movements. Folk religion remained strong, especially among the nomadic Sami people – this in spite of the oftentimes harsh governmental and ecclesiastic persecution of the Sami's forms of nature religion.

A strong characteristic of Nordic Lutheranism is the (formerly) ubiquitous revival movements of a Pietistic type. In general, they tended to stick to the teachings of Lutheran orthodoxy on grace, while emphasising the need of conversion. These movements were, and many of them still are, typically lay led and founded, even if they would eventually groom pastors from their own ranks. The hierarchies of state churches were often very critically disposed towards revivals, which were considered extreme or banal. Some of them eventually drifted outside the structures of the state church leading to free churches, while the majority remained within the state churches in spite of tensions with the ecclesiastic hierarchy. The contribution to academic theology of such movements tends to be very limited, but since many of the Nordic academic theologians have had revivalist influences in their personal background, the impact of such movements has filtered through to academic discussions.

The advent of the Enlightenment in the Nordic countries was largely a state-initiated and state-controlled enterprise. As local congregations in the state churches were typically the strongest governmental organisation at the local level, the role of pastors in spreading Enlightenment ideals was central. The pastors were supposed to be the beacons of development and education. This Enlightenment project was actually in direct continuity with Lutheran orthodoxy with the latter's emphasis on national education. University-educated pastors were the conveyors of new rational and scientific ideas, whereas in many cases the reaction against these ideas, in the form of revivals, came from the laity. The dividing lines were naturally not very clear, with some pastors preferring traditional teachings, for example concerning the inerrancy of the Scriptures, while many laypersons later adopted secular values.

The difference between modern state church Christianity and a revivalist Pietistic form of faith is most visible in views on Christian mission. While the state churches considered education and civilisation as their mission, the revival movements were geared towards conversion. The approach of state churches to people reminds one of the attitude of the colonialists towards the colonised: The colonised need to be subdued, transformed through civilisation and uplifted to the right standard of human living. And part of this was indeed a form of colonialism, for example in northern Sweden, which was Sami- and Finnish-speaking in most areas only a century ago. In due course, these languages and cultures were suffocated, partly even through the use of force, so that the Swedish language and "higher" culture replaced the "lower" forms, especially during the 20th century. The attitude of the Finnish and Norwegian governments towards the Sami was likewise colonial.

On the other side of the divide, the Pietistic fixation on conversion may be regarded as a modern reaction against modernity. It is modern in its individualism and anti-modern in much of the ideological content. It is relatively problematic for the status quo because of the way in which the ruling ecclesiastic hierarchies are countered by taking the Lutheran principle of the common priesthood of all believers seriously. The Nordic free churches (i.e. churches free from state control), including Pentecostalism, have to be seen as a continuation and extension of such revival movements. In an increasingly secularised and pluralistic situation, practically all of the churches, be it former state churches or the revival movements or the free churches, are continuously losing ground in terms of membership and their public role. The former state churches still have some ceremonial functions and thereby a degree of visibility.

From an outside perspective, the Danish philosopher-theologian Søren Kierkegaard (1813-1855) is often considered to be the most notable Nordic theologian. His passionate plea for radical conversion can be considered as a form of Pietistic thought with a strong existentialist twist. His programme was probably too far ahead of its time, and it did not find much resonance in Nordic ecclesiastic life or theology. Even later Kierkegaard's thought has not played a very crucial role in Nordic theology. However, Kierkegaard's thought was largely received in existential philosophy, and existentially oriented theologies made his influence felt in the Nordic countries too, albeit pretty much through a detour abroad.[1]

Kierkegaard's fellow Dane and contemporary, N. F. S. Grundtvig (1783-1872), even if hardly known outside the Nordic region, can be counted as one of the foundational Nordic theologians. His thought, which may be regarded as a Pietistic type of critique of Enlightenment rationalism, draws heavily on the centrality of education and civilisation. Unlike the blatantly individualistic Kierkegaard, Grundtvig always emphasised the role of community. In his theological thought, Grundtvig balances the typically redemption-centred theology with a very strong sense of createdness, or the doctrine of creation. As such, his theology serves as a via media which provides room both for renewed ecclesiastic practices and for university theology. Especially through his educational programme and the psalms he composed, his influence reached all of the Nordic countries.[2]

Another notable contemporary to Kierkegaard was the Swedish theologian and natural scientist Lars Levi Læstadius. His life, thought and theology have gone virtually unnoticed in the English-speaking world in spite of his deep, wide and still-continuing influence on northern Nordic ecclesiastic life. We first turn to this thinker in order to start with a northern dimension. Læstadius jokingly called himself the "highest priest" in Sweden when he was commissioned to the very northernmost parish of the country at Karesuando.

References and Recommended Reading

Allchin, A. M. (1998), *N. F. S. Grundtvig: An Introduction to his Life and Work*, London: Darton, Longman and Todd.

Carlisle, Claire (2006), *Kierkegaard: A Guide for the Perplexed*, London: Continuum.

Hannay, Alastair and Marino, Gordon (eds.) (1997), *The Cambridge Companion to Kierkegaard*, Cambridge: Cambridge University Press.

Mika Vähäkangas

---

[1] For an introduction to Kierkegaard, see for example Carlisle; Hannay and Marino.

[2] For an introduction to Grundtvig, see Allchin.

Lars Levi Læstadius (1800-1861) – A Hybrid of Enchantment and Disenchantment

Lars Levi Læstadius was a pastor of the Swedish state church in the northernmost parts of Sweden inhabited mostly by nomadic Sami and partly also by agriculturalist-pastoralist Finns. He was a notable natural scientist and an ethnologist on Sami traditions as well as the creator of the Western Sami written language. As a university-educated Swede (though of Sami origin from mother's side), a scientist and a pastor, he represented Western civilisation and the Enlightenment among the despised native populations. However, coming himself from the northern parts of the country, he was no foreigner to the land in terms of wandering in the endless wildernesses or speaking the languages of the people besides Swedish, the state language.[3]

In 1844, on one of his inspection tours, he met a young woman called Maria, a revivalist Christian Sami, who told him how she had been saved. The seasoned pastor went through a strong experience of spiritual renewal that ended his search for the graceful God.[4] Thereafter, he would preach revival and temperance – liquor was one of the powerful tools for the colonial economic domination of the Sami population – leading many herders to lose their reindeer flocks to the liquor sellers. Læstadius became the leader of the nascent revival movement, which is up to this day probably the strongest in the whole of the Nordic region. This revival was not built on a void, but can be considered a continuation, redirection and renewal of the already existing but fading Sami folk revival, the "shouters", who had incorporated Christian revivalist thought into the Sami traditional worldview. Another root of Læstadius's revival movement was derived from his mother's background in the Pietistic "reader" movement. As Læstadius's spirited proclamation began to attract publicity, it soon became a target for especially ecclesiastic-theological attacks. His colourful, sometimes even almost obscene, language and aggressive critique of the state church's spiritual laxity did not make him popular in theological circles.

Having primarily been trained as a scientist, Læstadius excelled especially in botany, collecting and analyzing thousands of specimens for himself and for French researchers whose several expeditions he assisted. He thus joined the Linné project of classifying and thereby rationally explaining nature[5] even though his philosophical conviction differed from Linnean rationalism. Læstadius's first publication was an exhortation and plan to pioneer farming in Lapland whereby he joined in the Enlightenment tradition of taming and subduing nature. Farming formed a part of his livelihood too. A pastor with a big family in one of the poorest areas of Sweden had to complement his income through farming in order to make ends meet.

At the same time, however, Læstadius never ceased to marvel at the wonders of God's creation. For him, nature was not demystified, because it provided vivid evidence of the loving care of the heavenly parent (*taivaallinen vanhin*). In his preaching, Læstadius had problems calling the loving God "Father" since he was the son of an

---

3 See Franzén, 260; Outakoski, 53-54; Østtveit Elgvin (2010), 106-108.

4 See Larsson, 56-57. However, Laestadius's theological views were strongly revivalist and Pietistic even before this event described by Laestadius (1843).

5 See Franzén.

alcoholic. Instead, God's fatherhood referred to his anger.[6] The loving God was quite feminine to him, giving birth to the believers and breastfeeding them. However, this did not make Læstadius a proto-feminist – he strongly supported the traditional gender roles of his time.

His view of nature followed the romantic and vitalistic philosophical traditions, most probably due to their closeness to the Sami worldview – which is sometimes described in terms of animistic or nature religion.[7] In his posthumously published magnum opus, *Dårhushjonet* ("Madhouse Patient", 1997), he departs from psychology to defend his teaching on salvation. In his psychology, he sees a human being as a tripartite spirit-soul-body entity that has to be approached in a holistic manner. Such tripartite holism reflects the Holy Trinity. In spite of this strongly romantic and holistic starting point, Læstadius does not jump on the bandwagon of pantheistic romantic philosophers, but emphasises the thorough depravity of human nature after the fall vis-à-vis natural knowledge of God or an ability to fulfil the divine law. Yet, for him, this does not point to any gap between the natural sciences and theology or between creation and salvation. Instead, their relationship needs to be seen in the right light in order that any of these would be correctly understood. Læstadius's position could therefore be described as holistic and yet not pantheistic or monistic – he strongly acknowledged the reality of sin and evil. His starting point was also scientific without being rationalistic. Instead, he used romantic natural theories to fight rationalism.

At the same time he waged war on the opposite front, namely with respect to the Church of Sweden's conservative side, which rejected rationalism but made Lutheran dogmatism its bunker. According to Læstadius, the result is that one tends to lose sight of a living faith and a personal relation to God. This true faith is preceded by repentance and deep remorse when a human sees how far from God's demands of righteousness s/he falls. Even the seemingly good deeds of a non-believer appear in the light of the non-believer's egoistic and twisted motives as basically evil. From a psychological point of view, a human being is misled by his or her fallen nature in the form of passions. Only when the Holy Spirit takes the lead and comes in place of passions in the believer's spirit, s/he becomes acceptable to God and thereby redeemed.

Living in and of nature, like his congregants, Læstadius's preaching was impregnated with vivid nature images, most of his examples and metaphors for spiritual life were gleaned from natural events.[8] To display the sinner's position between the devil and God, he told his congregation of his hunting experience: His dog was chasing a wild rabbit that, as its last resort, jumped into the lap of the hunter. Likewise, the sinner, terrified of God's wrath, seeks after solace in the forgiveness of God.[9] We may guess that the pastor's family missed rabbit stew for dinner that night!

---

6 See Østtveit Elgvin (2010), 44, 70, 241-245, 263-264; Østtveit Elgvin (2000), 250. Laestadius's view of God actually had mother-like features, like the image of God breastfeeding (Østtveit Elgvin, 2010, 243, 244) or giving birth to the believers (Østtveit Elgvin, 2010, 245, 257). On his deathbed he even saw a vision of a bare-breasted woman coming to fetch him – obviously referring to the Heavenly Parent. See Østtveit Elgvin (2010), 267-268.

7 See Haetta, 2.

8 See Østtveit Elgvin (2008), 2, 6-10; (2000).

9 See Laestadius (1997), 1372-1373; see also Østtveit Elgvin (2008), 6.

Another prime example of Læstadius's use of nature in his preaching is his "bird sermon" – a sermon built solely on metaphors fetched from bird life. This sermon portrays another dimension of his view on nature, namely his viewing of it through Sami traditions. The way he describes in detail the character and qualities of each bird leans very strongly on Sami mythology – where various birds play their roles in the cosmos and represent certain qualities.

Læstadius's view of nature, in spite of his scientific education and career, was not demystified and not void of Sami mythical creatures. His ethnological work shows a profound knowledge of Sami traditions, gleaned from his childhood.[10] Even though he did not believe in Sami divination, condemned as witchcraft by the Swedish state and church,[11] the subterranean Sami and Finnish semi-divinities (Finnish: *maahinen*; Sami: *kadniha*; the closest English equivalent of which is perhaps "goblins") often feature in his sermons. Nowhere does he deny the existence of these creatures, in the way he denied "witchcraft". In his ethnological work he describes them neutrally, whereas he attacks them strongly in his sermons as sinful opponents of Christ. However, Christians have to pray for them to repent and convert, because even they have the chance of forgiveness and thereby humanisation. Læstadius presents a theory of their origin as those children of Eve that she had not managed to wash before God came to see them. Eve hid them, therefore, and as a result they remain (spiritually) dirty and hidden under the ground by an edict of God.[12] Here the preacher uses Sami tradition that weds local and Judeo-Christian mythology together.

In Sami traditions, the subterranean people are comforting nature divinities that seek a positive relation to humans. They are among the last of the Sami divinities, believed in by some even today.[13] In spite of preaching against their sinfulness, Læstadius actually contributed to their survival in folk belief among the Sami and the Finnish-speaking ethnic groups in Lapland. Since Læstadius, as the greatest spiritual authority of the region, never denied their existence, many people saw no reason to question their existence either. When experiencing their presence in nature, people could reconcile their traditional beliefs with Christianity. Læstadius thus served in an ambiguous way as a bridge between Christianity and Sami nature religion.[14]

The Pietist revival launched by Læstadius was initially a strongly Sami movement. When it expanded, it turned, ethnically speaking, primarily into a Finnish movement. After Læstadius's death, his heritage was soon sanitised from Sami mythological dimensions, for example by editing some of it out of his published sermons. His image also became increasingly Swedish, diminishing the Sami dimension, the Sami being considered of a lower race during a time when categories of race were influential. The movement's relationship to the Sami culture also attained a more condemning tone than its founder had used, for example by describing traditional singing (*jojk*; *juoigan*) as sinful, something Læstadius never did.

---

[10] See Laestadius (2002).

[11] See Outakoski, 40

[12] See Laestadius's sermon on New Year's Day 1853, in Outakoski, 62-67, 92, 95, 97, 154; Østtveit Elgvin (2010), 130.

[13] See Outakoski, 81, 152-153.

[14] See Outakoski, 155.

In terms of the Enlightenment project of classifying and subduing nature, Læstadius was a very ambivalent person. On the one hand, he participated in the Linné-initiated project of creating taxonomies of nature and favoured pioneer farming, both being cases of taming and subduing. At the same time, however, he maintained his partial Sami background, which was geared towards a mystical symbiosis with nature. In the sparsely populated Lapland of the 19th century, environmental degradation was no issue – the poor nomad, pastoralist and agriculturalist population had to manage in the harsh arctic environment. In this context, new scientific methods of farming could be seen as a means of survival that could hardly affect the seemingly limitless natural environment.

To conclude, Læstadius could be described as a hybrid of two worlds in many ways: of Swedish and Sami, of the traditional worldview's enchantment of nature and a scientific disenchantment, of pre-Christian Sami traditions and Lutheran Pietism, of ecclesial hierarchy and folk religion, of the colonisers and the colonised. In Nordic theology, his person is among the most controversial and multifaceted, open to various interpretations and giving rise to a myriad of bitterly rivalling Laestadian revivalist factions. At any rate, there are clear indications that his theological work was deeply and consciously contextual. He took the northern natural, cultural and linguistic realities into account in his preaching and popular writings. In his more academically oriented literary writings his approach was to address the intellectual currents of the educated elite.

References and Recommended Reading

Franzén, Olle (1973), *Naturhistorikern Lars Levi Læstadius*, Tornedalica 15, Umeå.

Haetta, Odd Mathis (2011), "Den gamle samiske religion som folketro i dagens samiske kristne miljøer", Paper presented at the Kyrkohistoriska dagen, Uppsala University, 14 April 2011.

Læstadius, Lars Levi (1843), *Crapula Mundi*, Hernoesandi: Jonas Svedbom.

--- (1997), *Dårhushjonet: En blick i nådens ordning*, Skellefteå: Artos.

--- (2002), *Fragments of Lappish Mythology*, Beaverton: Aspasia.

Larsson, Bengt (1999), *Lars Levi Læstadius: Hans liv och verk och den laestadianska väckelsen*, Skellefteå: Artos.

Østtveit Elgvin, Lily-Anne (2000), "Lars Levi Læstadius' natursyn og naturbilder i hans forkynnelse", *Prismet: Pedagogisk tidskrift*, Vol. 51, 6, 247-254.

--- (2008), "Lars Levi Læstadius og naturen", *Eureka Digital*, 13-2008.

--- (2010), *Lars Levi Læstadius' spiritualitet*, Bibliotheca Theologiae Practicae 88, Skellefteå: Artos.

Outakoski, Nilla (1991), *Lars Levi Laestadiuksen saarnojen maahiskuva*, Scripta Historica 17, Oulu: Oulun Historiaseura.

Mika Vähäkangas

Gustaf Aulén (1879-1977) – A Theologian Drawing from History

Gustaf Aulén is among the best-known Swedish theologians. He is also one of the prime examples of the so-called Lund theologians, a theological school of thought at its height in the early and mid 20th century, based at the University of Lund. He is best known for his work on the historical-theological interpretation of atonement. Thus, his theology emphasised redemption rather than creation even if, in the light of his mature theology, redemption opens towards creation.

Aulén served first as professor of dogmatics and thereafter as the bishop of Strängnäs to return to Lund as an active pensioner involved in both theology and church matters for several more decades. Aulén made a lasting impression on theology internationally and on the Church of Sweden locally through his extraordinarily long period of activity and his extremely large corpus of publications. History played a significant role in Aulén's understanding of Christian faith. It is helpful to see how he situated himself in the specific historic context of the Swedish church. This is visible in his book *Hundra års svensk kyrkodebatt* ("A Swedish Church Debate of a Hundred Years") that was published in 1953 towards the end of his service as a bishop.

In this book, Aulén introduces and interprets the changes in the Swedish church and theology since the mid 19th century. He sketches the history of the Church of Sweden in a play of three acts. The prologue is the time of misery marked by liberal Enlightenment theology that severely weakened the church. This pitiful state was completed by the separatist and congregationalist views of liberal theologians on the church. The first act is characterised by the emergency action that was formed in Lund and Uppsala towards the end of the 19th century through a critique of congregationalism and separatist ecclesiologies.

The second act is the reconstruction period that was spearheaded by the leading figures of the so-called young-church movement. This movement started among the students. Its vision was to turn the Church of Sweden into a real folk church from a government-backed state-church. The idea of a folk church was not directed against the state-church system as such but sought to make the church into a living organism within the Swedish nation. From here on, Aulén is on the stage, participating as a side character in the role of professor in Lund while the ecumenical giant, professor and archbishop, Nathan Söderblom, and the folk-church theologian, professor and bishop, Einar Billing, play the main roles.

The third act is played when Aulén serves as the bishop of Strängnäs. The leaders of the young-church movement have left the stage and even a later proponent of the movement, Bishop J. A. Eklund, is left in the shadows in Aulén's plot. This third act is predominantly played by two parties, the first has a renewed interest in the Bible and the second is the high-church movement. The latter drew its inspiration from the Anglican Communion and concentrated on liturgical renewal. This drama sketched by Aulén ends at his retirement just before the Church of Sweden accepted women's ordination.

Aulén's interpretation of the phases that the Church of Sweden lived through represents, in general, the church's understanding of itself. Aulén saw his personal role more as an ecclesiastic reconstruction worker rather than a partisan for any individual group. This distancing from the church political battles facilitated his simultaneous support for the low-church biblicist movement and the high-church liturgical movement. He hoped for a revived interest in the Bible as well as for a new aesthetic passion for the liturgy, which did not oppose each other in his view.

Locating himself in this ecclesiastic and historical context reveals the two significant starting points of his theology: The epochs of the history of theology and the understanding of symbols as the mother tongue of faith. Thus, Aulén's theology characteristically combines hermeneutics with the sketching of theological epochs. Sketching these epochs constitutes an attempt to save the Christian faith and the history of theology from sinking into endless details. In this way, Aulén sets out to lift up the essential and the central in order to create meaning and to provide a plot in history. This fruitful theory on the function of epochs labels Aulén's view on the history of the Church of Sweden, his studies in history of theology, like *Christus Victor* (1931; Swedish original 1930), as well as his later works in the 1960s and the 1970s.

Aulén already formulated his understanding of the three dominating models of Christian theology faith quite early on. He builds on this basic understanding in practically all of his books, a position that found international acclaim through the publication of *Christus Victor* in 1931. The organising principle of this analysis was based on the motif research which was typical for Lund theology at that time. In this research, one lifts up a specific theological motif and uses it as a lens through which the field and history of theology are viewed. The prime example of this approach was Anders Nygren's *Agape and Eros* (1932; Swedish original 1930) which formed the flag bearer of this theological programme. Aulén's contribution to the Lundensian motif research in *Christus Victor* is that he combines the motifs with a chronological plot that creates dramatic clarity and structures the book. In his approach, Aulén attacks the juridical, medieval, Latin and scholastic understanding of redemption, which he (wrongly) attributes to Anselm. Aulén wants to go back to the early Christian "dramatic" understanding of redemption, which resurfaces in the history of theology in a renewed and deeper form in Luther's theology. This shows clearly his loyalty to the evangelical Lutheran tradition in the Church of Sweden. However, he was ecumenically open to other traditions, and the resemblance of his programme to *la nouvelle théologie* creates several points of contact with the Catholic tradition, especially after the Second Vatican Council.

Aulén's version of the Lundensian motif research developed later in 20th-century hermeneutics into the study of conceptual metaphors or cultural-specific symbols. This suggests that theology is regulated by one basic motif. It is usually latent but it plays a crucial role in organising the relationship between details and thereby forming the structure of theology. For Aulén, the basic motif for Christianity is the early church's so-called Christ-drama in which God engages in Christ in a fight against the devil. This basic motif is complemented by another basic motif, namely agape. According to the Lund theologians' approach, strongly moulded by Lutheran traditions, the task of theology is to clarify the role and nature of agape understood as God's love. The opposite of that would then be a juridical understanding of salvation. Aulén called his approach "classical" just as the Anglican high-church movement called its views "classical".

In his study *The Drama and the Symbols* (1970; Swedish original 1965) and in the book *Kristen gudstro i förändringens värld* ("Christian Faith in God in a World of Change", 1967), Aulén deals with his basic idea of symbols as the mother tongue of faith. He calls his approach here a "hermeneutically conscious analysis". With it he is able to offer a number of fruitful analyses of Christian faith in contemporary literature. The dramatic basic motif as the founding idea for Christianity is visible in Aulén's analysis of Dag Hammarskjöld in the book *Dag Hammarskjöld's White Book: An Analysis of Markings* (1969). Here he offers a deepened picture of the UN general secretary's worldview.

Aulén's thesis about symbols as the mother tongue of faith seems to have resulted from his openness to language and his understanding of God's unfathomability. He did not delve deeper into the methodological discussions like his younger contemporaries such as Rudolf Bultmann, Karl Rahner or Paul Ricoeur.

Aulén's idea of the centrality of symbols for faith met with critique and opposition both in Swedish theology and in the church. This critique motivated him into a renewed study of the historical Jesus in *Jesus in Contemporary Historical Research* (1976, Swedish original 1973). The ecclesiastic opposition against Aulén's Lundensian mythical-poetic understanding of the Bible and dogma was strong. In this opposition, the low-church, revivalist, Lutheranism-oriented biblicists and high-church, Anglican-oriented liturgists found each other. A specific bone of contention was the question of women's ordination, which Aulén had supported from early on.

Aulén was attacked by two parties that he had been supporting. His support for the Anglican-oriented liturgical movement was based on the aesthetical values that the movement was working for. However, he was strongly opposed to the high-church type of emphasis on Episcopal hierarchies. Perhaps the reason for this was that the emphasis on hierarchy in the church went hand in hand with the Latin juridical understanding of salvation during the medieval investiture controversy. He was personally involved in the aesthetical dimension of the movement, at any rate, especially through church music as a composer of hymn music and a writer of lyrics. He was also involved in the practical work of renewing the liturgy in the Church of Sweden, especially by creating the order of children's Sunday services.

Aulén's theological work concentrated heavily on redemption. At the very end of his last autobiographical book *Från mina nittiosex år* ("From My Ninety-Six Years", 1975), Aulén closes his written theological work with a quotation from Anders Frostenson's hymn (no. 289 in the Church of Sweden hymnal) to which he composed a new tune in his last summer at his summer place on Öland island. He describes how he received a strong vision of what the poem is all about: "the coast, the beaches, water, grass, flowers, wind and the open landscape … and as the last emphasis of all of it, that which collects all these pictures gleaned from the world of creation and gives them a new, rich, content, the wonderful words: 'and the endless home'" (translation – MV). The hymn expresses a new way in which God's love can be described in Aulén's theology. At the end of his theological career Aulén himself pointed out how his theology could open towards ecological considerations: symbols in combination with aesthetics in exploring God's love can serve as the starting point.

References and Recommended Reading

Aulén, Gustaf (1930), *Den kristna försoningstanken: Huvudtyper och Brytningar, Olaus-Petri-Föreläsningar hållna vid Uppsala Universitet*, Stockholm: Diakonistyrelsen. English translation (1931), *Christus Victor: An Historical Study of the Three Main Types of the Idea of the Atonement*, London: SPCK.

--- (1953), *Hundra års svensk kyrkodebatt: En drama i tre akter*, Stockholm: Diakonistyrelsen.

--- (1965), *Dramat och symbolerna: En bok om gudsbildens problematic*, Stockholm: Diakonistyrelsen. English translation (1970), *The Drama and the Symbols: A Book on Images of God and the Problems They Raise*, London.

--- (1967), *Kristen gudstro i förändringens värld*, SPI:s kyrkopedagogiska serie 1, Stockholm: SPI.

--- (1969), *Dag Hammarskjöld's White Book: An Analysis of Markings*, Philadelphia: Fortress.

--- (1973), *Jesus i nutida historisk forskning*, Stockholm: Verbum. English translation (1976), *Jesus in Contemporary Historical Research*, Philadelphia: Fortress.
--- (1975), *Från mina nittiosex år: Hänt och tänkt*, Stockholm: Verbum.
Nygren, Anders (1930, 1936), *Den kristna kärlekstanken genom tiderna: Eros och agape* (2 volumes), Stockholm: Diakonistyrelsen. English translation (1932, 1939), *Agape and Eros: The History of the Christian Idea of Love* (2 volumes), London: SPCK.

Henry Cöster

K. E. Løgstrup (1905-1981) – An Ethics of Nature

While Aulén's thought can be seen as orientated towards creation through beauty, Knud Ejler Christian (K. E.) Løgstrup would set out on this journey through ethics, or goodness. Løgstrup can be considered the most original and important Danish thinker since Søren Kierkegaard – whom he leaned on in many respects even as he was also highly critical of him. Løgstrup was a theologian and spent most of his professional career as a professor of philosophy of religion at the University of Aarhus in Denmark. His thought has inspired many Nordic theologians.

Løgstrup was strongly involved in societal matters all through his life. He joined the resistance movement during the Nazi occupation of Denmark in the Second World War and had to spend the last part of the war in hiding. From the late 1960s onwards and in tune with the growing awareness of the ecological crisis following Rachel Carson's *Silent Spring* (1962), Løgstrup became increasingly interested in the relation between humans and nature and worked with it both in his ethical and metaphysical writings.

In general, Løgstrup's ethics can be described as a way of presenting a description of reality (the universe) that is very close to our everyday experiences. Ethics is what meets us in our encounters with other people (and nature). It faces us partly as a spontaneous reaction to their needs, partly in a demand to take care of those needs and partly as a formulation of norms and principles to help us fulfil (or escape from) those needs. Ethics can therefore be characterised as descriptive in the sense that we should find the answers we are looking for in the situations that give rise to such questions.

Ethics should thus be understood as ontologically founded in the sense that the answers are something we find in the situations, not something we decide upon. In other words, we do not invent ethics, we explore it. Ethics is absolute in the sense that it has its source in a power that has made the universe a possibility, and ethics is relative in the sense that it is only in an interpretation of the genuine ethical phenomenon that we can formulate the ethical as it shows itself to us.

To Løgstrup the universe as it presents itself to us in our perception carries the possibility of being interpreted as created. Certain characteristics of the universe lend themselves to this interpretation. First and foremost, the sheer existence of the universe itself is a mystery. As Løgstrup sees it, everything that exists did not exist at some point and will stop existing at some point. Existence is thus something that takes place between creation and annihilation –which is also the title of one of Løgstrup's most acclaimed metaphysical works, *Skabelse og tilintetgørelse* ("Creation and Annihilation", 1978). The fact that things do exist for a while indicates to Løgstrup that there is some power that keeps things in existence for this while.

Løgstrup labels this power "the power to be in all there is". He describes this in a dialogue with Kant's critique of the cosmological proof of God's existence:

> The idea of God as the power to exist in everything that exists does not consist of our endeavors in cognition, neither of cognition's endeavors to come to know its own possibilities nor of cognition's endeavors to come to know how something existing is possible. Certainly it is concerned with the existing, but it is not concerned with coming to know how its conditions make its existence possible. The idea of the omnipresent, divine power, on the other hand consists of an immediate confidentiality with the existing thing. The confidentiality is a confidentiality with the fact that what exists exists at all. Since everything that exists sooner or later meets with its annihilation, the idea arises that, as long as it exists, its existence is due to a power to exist which the existing thing does not itself have.[15]

Another characteristic that lends itself to what Løgstrup calls a "religious interpretation" is the epistemological observation that our understanding of the universe is something that unfolds in a silent dialogue with the universe itself. In discussion with Kant and Heidegger, Løgstrup suggests that it is not only the human condition that decides how we understand the universe. The universe puts forth its own understanding and meaning to our perception and Løgstrup thus describes our understanding of the universe as a "countered transcendence".

When we understand what a tree is, it is not just we who decide what it is through our scientific perspective and our need of the tree as a resource. The tree itself is active in shaping our understanding. We can neglect what the tree is in itself and just examine it as a phenomenon and use it as a resource – but to Løgstrup we also have the opportunity to recognise that the tree is something more and that this more should play a part in our understanding.

Løgstrup's ethical thinking was developed as a pure human-centred ethics in the 1950s and 1960s. Only in the 1970s, through his metaphysical and epistemological thoughts on nature and the universe, did he look into the ethics of nature. His thoughts in this area need to be explored further, although thinkers such as Ole Jensen[16] and Jakob Wolf[17] have already taken the first steps.

The notion of nature as continuously being created by "the power to be in all that is" in a universe existing in the space between creation and annihilation places humans in a situation where they have to take responsibility for their use of nature. Løgstrup distinguishes between the use and misuse of nature. But as the main interest in his writings is to use metaphysical and epistemological thoughts to establish a religious interpretation of the universe as a meaningful although not unavoidable opportunity, the more practical ethical implications of this distinction remain vague. In general, though, it can be said that an ethics of nature, developed along Løgstrupian lines, will be characterised by an emphasis on the importance of nature to humans on not just a physical but also a psychological level, just as there is a shift from looking at nature

---

15 Løgstrup (1995a), 97-98.

16 For Jensen's views on his teacher Løgstrup, see Jensen (2007); and on ecology and theology, see Jensen (1980).

17 Wolf (2009); Wolf (2010); Gjerris and Wolf (2009).

primarily as a resource to a more appreciative kind of recognition of the intrinsic ethical importance of nature.

A keyword in a Løgstrupian ethics of nature thus becomes "humbleness". This humbleness is directed not only at the power that keeps the universe, nature and us around, but also humbleness towards the nature that sustains our lives mentally and physically and shares with us the basic conditions of existence. It is humbleness toward nature that appears to us as more than simply matter.

References and Recommended Reading

Bjerg, Svend (1994), *Århusteologerne: P. G. Lindhardt, K. E. Løgstrup, Regin Prenter og Johannes Sløk: Den store generation i det 20. århundredes danske teologi*, Viborg: Lindhart og Ringhof.

Carson, Rachel (1962), *The Silent Spring*, Greenwich: Fawcett.

Gjerris, Mickey and Wolf, Jakob (2009), "A Religious Perspective on Climate Change", *Studia Theologica*, Vol. 63, 2, 119-139.

Jensen, Ole (1980), *Frem til naturen og andre essays*, Copenhagen: Fremad.

--- (2007), *Historien om K. E. Løgstrup*, Copenhagen: Anis.

Løgstrup, K. E. (1978), *Skabelse og tilintetgørelse: Religionsfilosofiske betragtninger, Metafysik 4*, Copenhagen: Gyldendal.

--- (1995a), *Metaphysics* (2 volumes), Milwaukee: Marquette University Press.

--- (1995b), *The Ethical Demand*, Notre Dame: University of Notre Dame Press.

--- (2007), *Beyond the Ethical Demand*, Notre Dame: University of Notre Dame Press.

Niekerk, K. v. K. and Andersen, S. (2007), *Concern for the Other: Perspectives on the Ethics of K. E. Løgstrup*, Notre Dame: University of Notre Dame Press.

Wolf, Jakob (2009), "Et religiøst perspektiv på klimaforandringerne", in: Jakob Wolf, Mickey Gjerris, J. E. Olesen and C. Gamborg (eds.), *Jorden brænder: Klimaforandringerne i videnskabsteoretisk og etisk perspektiv*, Fredriksberg: Alfa, 107-127.

--- (2010), "Theology and Climate Change", *Ecumenical Review*, Vol. 62, 2, 131-136.

Mickey Gjerris

Regin Prenter (1907-1990) – In Search of the Sacramental Dimension of Creation

Løgstrup's contemporary Dane and Aarhus University colleague Regin Prenter's way of approaching creation was through constructive systematic theological thinking. The relationship between creation and redemption played a central role in his thought. Prenter influenced the Nordic theological discourse from the early 1930s to the late 1980s through his many books and numerous articles. His best-known book, *Creation and Redemption* (1967, Danish original 1955) has been a textbook at many Lutheran colleges. Prenter studied theology in Copenhagen and made trips for his classical education to Strasbourg, Bonn and Lincoln, where he became familiar with ecumenical theology, Karl Barth's late theology and Anglicanism (in particular with F. D. Maurice and Michael Ramsey). That fostered what Prenter himself called an "evangelical Catholicism".

Prenter was ordained in 1935 and became a minister in Hvilsager-Lime and later at the cathedral of Aarhus. In that period he participated actively in the resistance against the Nazi-ideology and was a zealous defender of the Jews. One year after the publication of his doctoral dissertation, *Spiritus Creator* (1944), Prenter was employed as a professor of dogmatics at the newly established faculty of theology in Aarhus. He resigned from his position at the University of Aarhus in 1972, protesting against the dominating Marxist influence at the time. He then became minister in Branderup and continued authoring theological books and articles until his death in 1990.

Prenter grew up in a family influenced by Grundtvig, in Frederikssund in Denmark, where both classical cultural education and church attendance were natural parts of life. The duality between a rich creation theology and an equally rich sacramental theology, which is typical to N. S. F. Grundtvig's theology, would influence Prenter's entire life and thinking. His theology, in its entirety, can be regarded as a "Grundtvigian theology of the covenant".

He was attentive to nature as an element of creation theology, so that there are reasons to believe that he would have made numerous "ecotheological" contributions if he had been alive today when nature appears more vulnerable and damaged than ever. In his autobiographical book *Erindringer* (1985), he highlights his great passion for yearly walks in the Norwegian mountains and describes theological work as a mountain hike, being in a constantly changing landscape and seeing new horizons.

Indeed, his theology is characterised by a constant assimilation of new elements and insights. Even though his asserting style could suggest that his theories were static, a closer examination reveals that they actually present a dynamic theology of change. This is true not only for the different material-dogmatic loci, but also for his fundamental theology.

Prenter's theology can be divided into three phases: a Barthian-Grundtvigian phase, a Lutheran-Grundtvigian phase and lastly a more purely Grundtvigian phase. I will offer a brief introduction to Prenter's views on the relationship between creation and salvation in the different phases, with an emphasis on his understanding of nature and creation.

In his first theological phase, Karl Barth, and partly also F. D. Maurice, set out the basic paradigm. In his first academic article, "Die sogennante 'kirchliche Anschauung' N. S. F. Grundtvigs als Frage an die evangelische Theologie von heute" ("The So-Called Ecclesiastical Approach of N. S. F. Grundtvig as a Question to Today's Protestant Theology", 1934), Prenter distinguishes between the gospel as "the actual theology" and creation theology as "the secondary theology". In line with his Barthian paradigm, he saw a concentric relationship between these. First, the gospel constitutes the centre. Then, secondly, creation theology comes to make up the surroundings – noetically as well as ontologically. Here, Barth's "gospel and law" applies, not Luther's "law and gospel". In this paradigm the church is not the *place* for particular grace, but, rather the *sign* of universal grace.

His article "Sakramentalt livssyn" ("A Sacramental View of Life", 1941) in the anthology *Ordets Herredømme* ("The Kingdom of the Word") is typical for his creation theology during this phase. Based on St Augustine's sign-theory, Prenter distinguishes between "natural" and "given" sacraments. The natural sacraments refer to everything in nature that can reflect God's reality, while the given sacraments refer to the specific sacraments that were instituted by the historical Jesus. According to Prenter, in order that creation be rightly included and resettled in theological reflection after urbanisation and industrialization, such a broad notion of the sacrament is needed. Such a sacramental view of life may well be called "natural theology", but not in the traditional sense of the word, as if it would be possible to acknowledge theological knowledge outside of the gospel. To the contrary, according to Prenter, it is only in the light of the gospel that the signs of God's grace can be acknowledged in nature. Prenter thus recognises God's acts of grace in creation, but rejects any natural metaphysics in the classical sense. Yet, he acknowledges the need to recognise the sacramental nature of creation.

After his dissertation *Spiritus Creator* (1944), Luther, and not Barth, became the authoritative theological mentor. Prenter's *Creation and Redemption* (1967), is typical of this phase. In his doctoral dissertation the challenge to Barth's thinking is implicit, but shortly thereafter Prenter forcefully attacks various parts of Barth's *Church Dogmatics*. In his article "Die Einheit von Schöpfung und Erlösung: Zur Schöpfungslehre Karl Barths" ("The Unity of Creation and Redemption: On Karl Barth's Doctrine of Creation", 1946), Prenter criticises Barth for representing what he calls a Platonising "creation-docetism". Here, the focus for Prenter is not creation in the light of Christ but rather the distinction between creation and redemption as different acts of God. According to Prenter, Barth's Christomonism is not in accordance with a Lutheran realistic understanding of the independence of the act of creation.

In line with this fundamental theological change, Prenter maintains a rich creation theology, opposed to Friedrich Gogarten and supported by K. E. Løgstrup. However, he rejects that this would be soteriologically relevant for anyone other than believers. He no longer maintains that the goodness in creation may be sacramental signs, but rather that death and judgement paradoxically form a part of redemption for believers. The judgement under the law in creation is for believers "the gospel of creation". The church is no longer a *sign* of God's universal grace, but a *place* for the believers to receive the particular grace given concretely by virtue of the sacraments. Anthropologically, this correlates with sin as a perversion of the human person (image of God) and not of its nature, which remains uncorrupted after the fall. By faith the personal relation to God (the image of God) is restored.

Prenter's last phase starts in the 1960s and is characterised by a greater emphasis than previously on Grundtvig's view on theological interdependency (reciprocity). He now highlights the interdependency between the persons in the immanent Trinity.[18] By giving more importance to the goodness of creation, he emphasises the synergy between a human being's own righteousness (*justitia activa*) and the foreign righteousness of Christ (*justitia aliena*).[19] Likewise, he highlights the synergy between non-ecclesiological and ecclesiological Christology, between liturgy and Scripture,[20] and between ordained leaders and laypersons.[21]

Anthropologically this Grundtvigian turn appears when Prenter now argues that not only the human "nature", but also the *imago Dei* remains uncorrupted after the fall. Thus, he contends that there is a soteriological continuity between creation and redemption, and he even describes the God-image present in every human being as a

[18] See Prenter (1977).

[19] See Prenter (1964).

[20] See Prenter (1966).

[21] See Prenter (1965).

"motivation" for God's act of redemption. In *Kirkens lutherske bekendelse* ("The Lutheran Confession of the Church", 1978), a modification of his theological anthropology emerges when Prenter supplements his earlier particular theory of redemption with a universal theory. In this universal theory, the godlike human being, together with the entire creation, is saved from the power of sin and death. Prenter also suggests that the redemptive act of the Holy Spirit can be effective outside the church. He no longer says that the Word *creates* the church, but rather that it *calls* upon the already chosen believers. In this latter phase, the church is considered not only the concrete place of rebirth, but simultaneously also a sign of God's universal grace.

Throughout his career, Prenter maintained a rich theology of creation together with a strong sense of nature and culture. Already early on, he identified urbanisation as one of the most crucial elements of alienation for the modern human being. To Prenter, the human being as created in the image of God is a creature of nature, integrated into the entirety of creation. Adam is created from earth – *adamah*. Even though sin and faith are exclusively human categories, Prenter cannot speak of the human being as independent of the other parts of creation. Thus, "human being" is to Prenter not only a personal term concerning sin and atonement, but also a cosmic term concerning creation and redemption (salvation).

His last Grundtvigian phase portrays the most complex part of his thinking. Nature not only has an inherent value but also a hermeneutical value as the present creation, an idea he also supports during his Lutheran phase. Additionally, by his acknowledging the action of the Holy Spirit outside of the church and by his recognising the existence of the image of God after the fall, nature also obtains a sacramental value in relation to the redemption. On this basis, not only death and judgement would have soteriological meaning for believers, as in *Creation and Redemption*, but also the goodness and beauty of creation – as universal signs of God's grace. This is the late Prenter's Grundtvigian correlate of his early Barthian notion of a sacramental view of life. Nature has to be protected in order to preserve its inherent value, but also to avoid sacramental sacrilege. In nature, human beings live in the grace of God – a grace that starts and ends in the sacramental life of the church.

References and Recommended Reading

Njå, Ådne (2008), *Det ånder himmelske over støvet: Faser i Regin Prenters grundtvigske paktsteologi*, Dissertation, Det teologiske fakultet, Universitetet i Oslo, Oslo: UniPub.

Prenter, Regin (1934), "Die sogenannte 'Kirchliche Anschauung' N. S. F. Grundtvigs als Frage an die evangelische Theologie von heute", *Evangelische Teologie*, Vol. 1, 278-288.

--- (1941), "Sakramentalt livssyn", in: *Ordets Herredømme*, Copenhagen: Det Tredje Standpunkts Forlag, 30-53.

--- (1944), *Spiritus Creator: Studier i Luthers Theologi*, Copenhagen: Universitetsforlaget i Aarhus.

--- (1946), "Die Einheit von Schöpfung und Erlösung: Zur Schöpfungslehre Karl Barths", in: Regin Prenter (ed.) (1977), *Theologie und Gottesdienst, Gesammelte Aufsätze*, Aarhus / Göttingen: Aros, 9-27.

--- (1955), *Skabelse og Genløsning*, Copenhagen: Gads. English translation (1967), *Creation and Redemption*, Philadelphia: Fortress.

--- (1964), "Luthers 'Synergismus'?", in: Regin Prenter (ed.) (1977), *Theologie und Gottesdienst: Gesammelte Aufsätze*, Göttingen: Aros, 222-246.

--- (1965), *Kirkens embede: Udkast til en det kirkelige embedes dogmatikk med luthersk udgangspunkt*, Copenhagen: Universitetsforlaget i Aarhus.

--- (1966), *Connaître Christ*, Neuchâtel: Delachaux et Niestlé.
--- (1977), "Der Gott der Liebe ist: Das Verhältnis der Gotteslehre zur Christologie", in: Regin Prenter (ed.), *Theologie und Gottesdienst: Gesammelte Aufsätze*, Aarhus / Göttingen: Aros, 275-291. First published in 1971, *Theologische Literaturzeitung*, Vol. 96, 401-413.
--- (1978), *Kirkens lutherske bekendelse*, Fredericia: Lohses.
--- (1985), *Erindringer*, Aarhus: Aros.

Ådne Njå

Gustaf Wingren (1910-2000) – Creation and Redemption as *Recapitulatio*

Gustaf Wingren, a Swedish theologian based at Lund University a generation after Aulén, is known for tirelessly stressing the themes of creation, law, vocation and so forth, but his theology also explores the very rich relationship between creation and salvation. His profound theological insights stem from more than fifteen years as a young scholar studying Irenaeus and Martin Luther.

In Wingren's articulation of the relationship between creation and salvation, *recapitulatio* plays a crucial role. We will look at his theology in six consecutive steps. The first three are foundational, as this is where he gets his insights and inspiration from; Marcion serves as a warning, while Irenaeus and Luther become role models. Then there are two scholars who influence him heavily, namely Lund professor Anders Nygren, who in many ways had become his mentor and Karl Barth, with whom he disagrees on fundamental points, yet who is the one, in my estimation, who provides him with kerygmatic inspiration. Finally there is K. E. Løgstrup, who had an increasing impact on Wingren. This relationship may be seen as a kind of recapitulation of what he already found in Irenaeus, albeit in more secular terms.

Wingren was educated theologically within what by then had become the influential Lund school of theology represented by Aulén, Nygren and the internationally lesser-known Ragnar Bring. This school was closely linked to the emerging Luther research, which was also characterised by thorough historical investigation, which was descriptive in nature but nevertheless quite confessional in orientation. Wingren started early with studies on Irenaeus and Marcion and would probably have ended up as an early-church scholar had the Second World War not come in between. In the middle of 1938 he spent a few months in Berlin, where he could find material regarding these early-church fathers, and not least Harnack's material on Marcion. But further studies along that line were not to be. Back in Lund he was advised to change his research topic to Luther.

Wingren wanted to show that Harnack was unjustified in trying to rehabilitate Marcion from Gnostic influence, so as to give some credence to Marcion's theology: "It was just the notion of salvation, of *agape*, which Marcion wanted to safeguard. And this notion he thought he could best serve through severing creation as well as law from God … what carries weight is the statement that one ought to preserve the Old Testament in order to save the New from distortion," he writes in an essay on Marcion's interpretation of the Christian faith.[22] To Marcion God was a very distant God, the unknown island; only one, namely Jesus, could say anything about this God's

[22] Wingren (1936), 332 (translation – HE).

existence. The demiurge had created the world and the body, not the real God. Instead of having creation as the common ground, Marcion and the Gnostics talk about God's revelation in Christ. With Marcion and the Gnostics, God's existence becomes a problem, just as is the case in our time.[23]

When observed from Irenaeus' point of view, the contrast between Marcion and mainline Christian theology remains equally stark. Wingren takes the relationship between sin and death as the theological locus of discussion. According to Irenaeus, there is a clear link between these two, which is demonstrated by Jesus when he says to the paralytic, while healing him, "your sins are forgiven" (Matt. 9:1-8). For Irenaeus, sin is the cause of death, which differs strongly from Harnack's views. Wingren concludes in his book *Man and the Incarnation: A Study in the Biblical Theology of Irenaeus*:[24] "Harnack's approach is bound up with the almost complete lack of a belief in Creation in modern Protestant theology and what we might call its 'inwardness'. The statements which Irenaeus makes about death can be understood only in relation to his belief in the Creator ..." (p. 56).

In his *Adversus Haeresis* Irenaeus seems to refer to Justin Martyr who argued for the recapitulation of creation by the only-begotten Son. So, what most likely stems from Justin is taken over by Irenaeus and used to the full. Wingren concurs. The term *recapitulatio* captures God's whole salvific work from the perspective of creation. It recurs in the chapter titles of Wingren's Irenaeus book four times: Christ as the incarnate, Christ's conflict and victory (suffering, death and resurrection), life in the church, and the consummation. We can here only comment on the first aspect. In the incarnation "it is God who reveals Himself, but ... it is also revealed what man ought to be" (p. 95).

Adam, as the name of humanity, plays an important role in Irenaeus' thought. He "is very emphatic that in the Incarnation Christ assumes the form of Adam, thereby recapitulating His image and creation. Had he not done so, the man whom God at the beginning had destined for life would still be subject to death, in complete contradiction to the purpose of God" (p. 95). Individualism is avoided when he continues: "The Verbum has assumed the old creation of Adam, infused it with God's undefeated life, and thereby renewed it" (p. 96). This was "His renewal of Adam, His *recapitulatio* of the old Creation" (p. 98). Indeed, the human being "is destined to be like God, but he was never destined to be God" (p. 99).

Wingren had two main sources upon which he built his theological thought, namely Irenaeus and Luther. For his doctorate (completed in 1942) he concentrated on Luther's understanding of vocation and related issues like law and creation. He dealt with things like the strict dualism between faith and works, the two kingdoms, and the different uses of the law. According to Wingren, in his attempt to safeguard the purity of the gospel Luther works out a strict dualism. There is a movement downwards and another upwards. In his dissertation[25] he observes that "God does not need our good

---

[23] Wingren (1972), 89f.

[24] See Wingren (2004). Subsequent references in parenthesis are to this English translation of the original work in Swedish.

[25] See Wingren (1942). Subsequent references in parenthesis are to the English translation of this work (1958).

works, but our neighbour does. It is faith that God wants. Faith ascends to heaven" (p. 10). The work of Christ is also victory over law:

> The conscience alone, through faith in the work of Christ, is freed from a false faith. Christ frees neither the hand from its work, nor the body from its office. The hand, the body, and their vocation belong to earth. There is no redemption in that, but that is not the idea. The purpose is that one's neighbor be served (p. 11).

In this way, Wingren interprets the traditional Lutheran doctrine of the two kingdoms in such a way that these two are strictly separated.

For Wingren, the strength of Luther's doctrine of vocation "is the relation between stability and mobility, between freedom and constraint … The duality of stability and mobility gives its peculiar color to Luther's view of creation" (p. xii). With this view of creation Wingren differs markedly from any kind of status quo theology based on the orders of creation. In his Luther studies, sanctification or imitation are not at the forefront but one's neighbour is; this makes his theology dynamic.[26] The creative impulse in the creation concept is an expression of Luther's radicalism: "Creare est semper novum facere" (to create is always to make something new). In this sense, as Bengt Kristensson Uggla analyses Wingren's thought, "law is neither a fixed entity, nor codified in the Bible or in tradition, but stands out as something in constant flux awaiting the unexpected … From this perspective law does not stand out as something conserving, in line with order theology, but must instead be understood in terms of process and steady change."[27]

The first and the second use of the law (Luther used expressions like "civil" or "political" for designing the first use and "spiritual" or "theological" for the second use) suggests, however, that the downward movement is also linked up with God, even with God's salvific acts. In his book *Creation and Law* (2003; Swedish original 1958),[28] Wingren points out that "God's demand that men should continue to 'have dominion' over Creation is part of His continuing Creation of the world" (p. 150). But God uses his continued engagement in an ongoing creation also to bring humans to the gospel. The law "burdens men's consciences with guilt which the man sees in his own heart *coram Deo* …" (p. 174).

Nygren was Wingren's predecessor and the latter owed a lot to the former. However Wingren also distanced himself from Nygren, trying to pave the way for a new era, as soon as he was installed as professor in Lund in 1951. In his two major works, on Luther and Irenaeus, Wingren follows Nygren's history-of-ideas approach. Wingren also adopted Nygren's "baffling homogeneity" when dealing with historical material and it will eventually show in his dealing with Barth.

However, Wingren tried to undo two of his predecessor Nygren's major achievements. Firstly, in response to Nygren's towering work *Agape and Eros* with its isolation of the agape motif, Wingren contends that agape is not enough. Nygren uses Irenaeus and Luther as examples of pure agape. Wingren does not deny this but says that more is needed. In the everyday world the Christian vocation is paramount, and

---

26 See Lévinas (1972) on "humanism of the other".

27 Kristensson Uggla, 73.

28 See Wingren (2003). Subsequent references in parenthesis are to this work.

love of one's neighbour is the core of this vocation, taking many different shapes that are not necessarily inspired by the gospel or the church. All humans are involved in the act of love by being created by God. Agape love is not as pure or exclusive as Nygren thought.[29]

Secondly, Wingren denounced Nygren's attempt to build theology upon a philosophical foundation.[30] In his inaugural lecture he compared the two main types of systematic theology at the time, dialectic theology and Lundensian motif research (represented by Nygren). He opts for a dialectic approach with its emphasis on biblical exegesis as the way forward. Theology is ultimately not about unearthing particular "motifs" but about taking the kerygmatic function of the biblical material seriously. He expresses a profound scepticism regarding Nygren's attempt to lay a philosophical foundation for theology. There is only one way forward: "Calling this systematic theology may possibly be motivated by Nygren's philosophy – but that is to be cut out".[31] With Nygren present at the lecture this was indeed not an invitation to dialogue but to a feud where it was frankly declared that the old was defunct and a new route was pursued. In a dramatic way Wingren thus indicated that he was coming closer to kerygmatic theology in general, and more specifically to Karl Barth. While this is true in some ways, it is not accurate in all respects.

Wingren's book *Predikan* ("Preaching", 1949) provides a clear signal of the new direction that he took. He left behind a history of ideas approach and its descriptive method in favour of what he now called a "dual anthropological and hermeneutical approach". It was a matter of tying together two dominating interests of his, an exegetical analysis of the biblical texts and the homiletic need to address people concretely. He gained some insights in this regard during a short spell as an acting professor replacing Karl Barth in Basel in the early summer of 1947. Wingren observed that *Predikan* was the most important book that he ever produced.[32] His main hypothesis is that the word of God is made manifest only in proclamation and that the human is created by the same word at the beginning and destined to live by the same word from the mouth of God.[33] It has been a matter of debate in how far Wingren was influenced by Barth. Wingren has even called himself a "half-Barthian", which has not been very helpful in the attempt to understand his theological relationship to Barth. In *Predikan* he asserts that the Barthian way of linking kerygma and theology is a strength, not a weakness.[34]

But Wingren felt a continuous need to build a front against Barth. Firstly, Wingren accused Barth of creating an unbridgeable divide between God and humans, whereas the real divide is to be found between God and evil, manifested in the devil. The implication was that Barth intellectualised evil in a reductionist way, an interpretation which clearly angered Barth.[35] Secondly, Wingren regarded the way in which Barth

---

[29] Sigurdson, 74.

[30] See Nygren (1921), (1922), (1923).

[31] Kristensson Uggla, 42.

[32] Kristensson Uggla, 93.

[33] Wingren (1949), 1.

[34] Sigurdson, 110.

[35] Sigurdson, 45; see also Engdahl, 177-195, 179.

put the gospel before the law as a major issue. He claims that: "Since the Law is revealed and its meaning fully perceived only when the Gospel is revealed, Gospel has priority over Law" (p. 13). Thirdly, Barth's denial of any form of value objectivity is apparent. Here he certainly was influenced by "Religionskritik" already articulated in the previous century, notably by scholars like Feuerbach. Theoretically speaking, there is no possibility to establish "what is good" in general, no rule of nature to follow. Even the common good has to be recognised at one point only. For theology that is the sole, exclusive revelation in Christ.[36]

This brings us to Wingren's appreciation of Løgstrup, who developed a philosophy on the factuality of creation. Wingren, at least from the 1960s onwards, uses Løgstrup as a way of reconnecting himself with Irenaeus and his notion of *recapitulation*. In this process he pays much less attention to Luther and his dualistic theology. Instead of Luther, he makes use of Løgstrup's phenomenology in his theology and he is thereby accepting a more secular terminology. For example, in his book *Växling och kontinuitet* ("Change and Continuity", 1972), he maintains: "'Creation' can be described as a 'spontaneous life manifestation', i.e. a continuous outgiving movement. 'Destruction' can be described as a 'circulating life manifestation', i.e. a movement that is not able to leave the individual. The Christian faith deals with God's struggle against destruction through new creation."[37] Wingren here in a way replaces Old Testament creation faith with Løgstrup and pays less attention to the law as a coercive factor in human life than previously. There is an affinity to Irenaeus and *recapitulatio*. The emphasis is no longer on Lutheran and reformed notions such as sin, guilt and forgiveness but on creation, destruction and re-creation.[38] The return to Irenaeus is irrevocable as seen in his book *Credo*: "The whole of Jesus' life could from one angle be said to be a recapturing of that which is created, a disruption of destruction. This goes for his birth as well as his life's work among people."[39]

There are a number of issues relating to Wingren's theology that remain open here. With such an approach to creation theology, what are the criteria for the good life, a good society, even a human rights culture? The struggle motif is prevalent in his theology. With hindsight one may ask why he allowed the Second World War to shut him up in Sweden in Luther research, with the result that this research could not relate to the struggle going on in Germany (cf. Barth, Bonhoeffer). Ireneaus remains a companion through Wingren's life, later on also thanks to Løgstrup, who introduced a secular terminology for interpreting Irenaeus. Does Wingren appreciate the significance of this terminological shift? Long after the theological foundation is laid, already nearing retirement, Wingren goes through a period of contextualisation and radicalisation; Wingren's theology certainly allows for an ecological dimension. Only late in life, he was influenced in this regard by people like the Danish theologian Ole Jensen of a younger generation, who were tackling environmental issues directly.[40]

---

[36] Wingren (1972), 114.

[37] Wingren (1972), 109 (translation – HE).

[38] Sigurdson, 109.

[39] Wingren (1974), 79 (translation – HE).

[40] See, for example, Jensen.

References and Recommended Reading

Engdahl, Hans (2011), "Abraham Kuyper and F. J. M. Potgieter: Some Swedish-Lutheran Perspectives", in: Ernst M. Conradie (ed.), *Creation and Salvation: Dialogue on Abraham Kuyper's Legacy for Contemporary Ecotheology*, Leiden: Brill, 177-195.
Jensen, Ole (1979), *I tillväxtens våld: Ekologi och religion*, Stockholm: Skeab / Verbum.
Kristensson Uggla, Bengt (2010), *Gustaf Wingren: Människan och teologin*, Stockholm: Symposion.
Lévinas, Emmanuel (1972), *Humanisme de l'autre homme*, Montpellier: Fata Morgana.
Nygren, Anders (1921), *Religiöst apriori: Dess filosofiska förutsättningar och teologiska konsekvenser*, Lund: Gleerupska Universitets-Bokhandeln. English translation (2000), *Religious Apriori*, Linköping: Linköping University Electronic Press.
--- (1922), *Dogmatikens vetenskapliga grundläggning med särskild hänsyn till den Kant-Schleiermacherska problemställningen*, Lund: Gleerup.
--- (1923), *Filosofisk och kristen etik*, Lund: Gleerup.
--- (1930, 1936), *Den kristna kärlekstanken genom tiderna: Eros och agape* (2 volumes), Stockholm: Diakonistyrelsen. English translation (1932, 1939), *Agape and Eros: The History of the Christian Idea of Love* (2 volumes), London: SPCK.
Sigurdson, Ola (1996), *Karl Barth som den andre*, Stockholm: Symposion.
Wingren, Gustaf (1936), "Marcions kristendomstolkning", *Svensk Teologisk Kvartalskrift*, Vol. 12, 4, 318-338.
--- (1942), *Luthers lära om kallelsen*, Lund: Gleerup. English translation (1958), *Luther on Vocation*, Edinburgh / London: Oliver and Boyd.
--- (1949), *Predikan: En principiell studie*, Lund: Gleerup. English translation (1960), *The Living Word: A Theological Study of Preaching and the Church*, London: SCM.
--- (1958), *Skapelsen och lagen*, Lund: Gleerup. English translation (2003), *Creation and Law*, Eugene: Wipf and Stock.
--- (1972), *Växling och kontinuitet*, Lund: Gleerup.
--- (1974), *Credo*, Skellefteå: Artos. English translation (1981), *Credo*, Minneapolis: Augsburg.
--- (2004), *Man and the Incarnation: A Study in the Biblical Theology of Irenaeus*, Eugene: Wipf and Stock.

Hans S. A. Engdahl

Seppo A. Teinonen (1924-1995) – In Search of the Aesthetics of Creation

If one finds a path from soteriology towards a re-evaluation of the value of creation via aesthetics in Aulén, the same applies to Seppo A. Teinonen too. However, while Aulén found his anchoring point in history and was drawn to an Anglican-style liturgical aesthetics, Teinonen's starting point was Catholic spirituality, especially an Ignatian one. This professor of ecumenical studies and later of dogmatics in the Faculty of Theology at the University of Helsinki was a living bridge between the Finnish Lutheran religiosity and southern European Roman Catholicism.

In the foreword to his doctoral thesis *Economic Growth and the Quality of Life* (1975), Martti Lindqvist, a leading Finnish ethicist, expressed his gratitude to Teinonen, saying that his *Doktorvater* was "a living example of what purposeful and unflagging effort can achieve".[41] Teinonen was not merely a Protestant workaholic. In the medieval sense, he was an ascetic who devoted his life to translating a considerable amount of classical mystical texts into Finnish, including for instance Bonaventure's *The Soul's Journey into God*, Ignatius Loyola's *Spiritual Exercises*, Teresa of Ávila's

[41] Lindqvist, 3.

The Interior Castle and John of the Cross's *The Dark Night of the Soul*.

By distinguishing between immanent and transcendent asceticism Max Weber tried to illustrate the relation that prevailed between a Protestant ethic and the rise of capitalism. Whereas a medieval mystic would live a life of faith in the belief of receiving a reward in afterlife (Weber's transcendent asceticism), a Protestant would see the ultimate goal of life in terms of daily work and would interpret professional success in his or her career as a sign of God's grace (immanent asceticism). By directing his energies to the translation of medieval mystical literature Teinonen turned, so to say, the Weberian thesis upside down. He was actually a person who with a Protestant determination promulgated the transcendent ideals of medieval asceticism in the context that was becoming more and more inner-worldly and secular. Like a salmon he swam upstream. It goes without saying that a lifestyle based on medieval ascetic ideals is ecologically less consuming than a way of life in which success in the working life turns out to be an indicator of God's blessing.

In his soteriology Teinonen departed considerably from the Pietism-impregnated Lutheranism of Finland by drawing his inspiration from Ignatius Loyola. The very opening of the Ignatian exercises expresses concisely the soteriological point that Teinonen subscribed to and often quoted: "Man is created to praise, reverence, and serve God our Lord and by this means to save his soul."[42] The context in which this praise, reverence and service to God takes place is the Mass where salvation is actualised. However, such salvation and service to God does not mean isolation from the world or from creation. On the contrary, since the eucharistic elements, bread and wine, are "fruit of the earth" and "work of human hands", these opening words of the eucharistic liturgy tell us clearly what kind of relation there prevails between creation and salvation: they belong intimately together.

In the Finnish theological context Teinonen was a pioneer in introducing the theme of creation into Christ-centred Lutheran theology. In 1967 he published a book entitled *Luominen ja lunastus* ("Creation and Redemption") which included the Finnish translation of two ecumenical addresses, "God in Nature and History"[43] and "Creation, New Creation, and the Unity of the Church".[44] Teinonen's foreword illustrates the motives for making the two ecumenical documents available to Finnish readers: "It has been typical for secular thinking to discard transcendent and religious interpretations of human existence; on the contrary, the secular mind has tried to observe the world and humankind in terms of its own, that is, without any reference to their transcendent ground. … In such a situation the churches have much to comment on the secular way of thinking."[45]

In the beginning of the 1970s Teinonen touched repeatedly on the themes of creation and salvation and the fervency with which he spoke especially of Joseph Sittler's

---

42 This is the opening sentence of the "Principle and Foundation" section of the first week of *Exercitia Spiritualia* in the very opening of the Ignatian exercises, a widely available Christian classic.

43 The original was written by Hendrikus Berkhof (1965).

44 Teinonen (1967, 15) describes the background of the paper that was drafted by Anglicans David E. Jenkins and G. W. H. Lampe as well as Lutherans K. E. Løgstrup and Gustaf Wingren in 1966. The document was adopted at a Faith and Order meeting in Bristol (30 July – 8 August 1967).

45 Teinonen (1967), 10 (translation – PA)

study *The Ecology and Faith* (1970) made an indelible impression on young students. By underlining the connection between the doctrine of creation and salvation Teinonen paved the way for a theology that was more sensitive to environmental issues.

Teinonen was a prolific scholar and in his literary production one finds several references to Harvey Cox's famous book *The Secular City* (1965). At first sight one may think that this radical manifesto has nothing to do with ecotheology. In Teinonen's case, however, this is not true. Stimulated by Cox's book and as a counterbalance to the paper-flavoured university life, he retired to the countryside whenever it was possible. Because he had been born on the western coast of Finland, the sea was to play an important role in his spiritual life. The sea became a symbol of the pilgrim's progress, the end where all rivers ultimately flow. Like the Galilean fishermen, Teinonen wanted to be a fisherman too. But more than this religious motive, the striving for a self-sustaining lifestyle guided his everyday life. The striving for the self-sustaining way of life was for Teinonen a conscious choice. It was an apparent protest against the increasing consumerism, a new ideology (idolatry) that was a great challenge for the generation that had passed through the horrors of the Second World War.

In the beginning of the 1980s Teinonen took to the corpus of St. Francis's writings. Along with the translation work, he acquainted himself with the saint's poem *The Canticle of Brother Sun*. As a literary artist Teinonen took great pains to give the poem a literal form that could mediate the delicate tone in which it had originally been composed. By focusing his concentration on this work he became gradually aware of the ecological horizons that were concealed in this hymn. "Beauty will save the world", and aesthetic and religious experiences were the two sides of the same coin. If one lost the former, one lost the latter. Accordingly, there cannot be any sincere ecotheology apart from a sensitive aesthetic experience or, more emphatically, all ecotheology must be aesthetically sensitive. According to Teinonen there is a strong ecotheological manifesto in the sixth doxology of the *Canticle*, in the verse that reads as follows:

> Be praised, my Lord,
> through our Sister Mother Earth,
> who sustains and guides us,
> and produces diverse fruits with coloured flowers and herbs.

References and Recommended Reading

Berkhof, Hendrikus (1965), "God in Nature and History", *Study Encounter*, Vol. 1, 3, 142-160.

Cox, Harvey (1965), *The Secular City: Secularization and Urbanization in Theological Perspective*, New York: Macmillan.

Lindqvist, Martti (1975), *Economic Growth and the Quality of Life: An Analysis of the Debate within the World Council of Churches 1966-1974*, Helsinki: Missiologian ja Ekumeniikan Seura.

Loyola, Ignatius (2011), *Spiritual Exercises of St. Ignatius 21 Through 31*, Society of Jesus, Oregon Province, <www.nwjesuits.org/JesuitSpirituality/Exercises/SpEx021_031.html>, retrieved 18 September 2011.

Sittler, Joseph (1970), *The Ecology of Faith*, Philadelphia: Fortress.

Teinonen, Seppo A. (1961), *Missio Politica Oecumenica: A Contribution to the Study of the Theology of Ecumenical Work in International Politics*, Helsinki: Lähetystieteellinen Seura.

Teinonen, Seppo A. (ed.) (1967), *Luominen ja lunastus: Kaksi teologista puheenvuoroa*, Pieksämäki: Suomen Kirkon Sisälähetysseura.

Pauli Annala

Further Developments

Churches of the Nordic region have lost much of their social, cultural and political importance. The deconstruction of the Lutheran state church system is not the reason for this change but rather a symptom. In the rapidly changing world of increasing secularism and consumerist materialism, the churches, and often even theologians, have not been able to read the signs of the times early enough, thereby rendering Christian faith irrelevant and unintelligible. Theological discussions have become nonsensical to the majority of people because it does not address their life realities. In this challenging situation, most of the churches seem to concentrate on themselves, reflecting on how best to survive as organisations. Theology is adapting to the situation by converting itself into religious studies and / or the historical study of Christianity.

This situation calls for a renewed effort to make the Christian faith intelligible today. It also challenges the churches and theologians to search for new theological and ecclesiastic programmes. One of the great challenges is to reinvent a sense of communality and communion, also beyond the human sphere, including the rest of creation. The era of nationalistic state and folk churches is over. It was based on the already existing fictitious national-ethnic unities whereby the church could simply make use of national and ethnic notions of community. The vision of Aulén and of other proponents of the folk-church model has come to the end of the road, at least in the traditional form. In pluralistic societies that are receiving an increasing number of immigrants, it is no longer possible to muse around myths of monolithic national entities when even the dominating ethnic groups are so pluralistic. This provides a lease of life to traditionally marginalised groups that can become visible and heard, like the Sami, for example.

Læstadius's harsh critique of the state church targeted the problem of the Christianisation of the status quo, resulting in less than appropriate forms of faith, where the powers that be used Christianity as a fig leaf for their greed and lust for power. On the folk level, Christianity did not bring about a renewal of life. Læstadius and other revivalist thinkers provided conversion as the solution. During the period of Lutheran orthodoxy, Pietisms of different types could build on the education carried out by state churches in their civilising function. Pietistic revivals were thus more a form of renewal of the old structures than a complete novelty. Today a revivalist programme envisioned by Læstadius would not function as a programme for renewing church and society. This is due to a situation wherein the Lutheran religious hegemony is quickly eroding, thereby rendering Lutheran Pietism marginal as a renewal movement.

Later theologians like Wingren and Løgstrup paved the way for theological thought that would take the changing context seriously. What is typical for today's Nordic theologians working on ecological themes is that they usually not only address environmental degradation but also the larger Nordic context. This is illustrated by the work of the contemporary Nordic ecotheologian Sigurd Bergmann, based at Trondheim University in Norway, who has studied in Göttingen and Uppsala but also in Lund. Like Lund theologians before him, he started from the study of an early theologian, namely Gregory of Nazianz.[46] Unlike his Lund predecessors, Bergmann poses

---

[46] See Bergmann (1995).

ecologically relevant questions to the Church Father's cosmology and treats the issue from a liberation theological perspective. Like Aulén, Bergmann also explores the link between the natural environment and aesthetics.[47] He builds a strong link between aesthetics and contextuality, thereby binding together these three dimensions of his theology.[48] His approach is at the same time strongly constructive since he is not content with merely describing and analyzing the positions of others.[49]

Finnish Seppo Kjellberg approaches the contextual ecological issues from the urban context, with a practically oriented approach that emphasises the need of communality.[50] His thought is at the same time political and activist,[51] distancing him from the Nordic tradition of strongly distinguishing between the theological and the political, in line with Lutheran teaching on the two kingdoms.

Such leaning towards politics and activism is especially evident in Nordic ecotheology in feminist contributions. Pauliina Kainulainen, attached to the University of Eastern Finland, draws her inspiration from Latin American women's liberation theology, especially from Ivone Gebara.[52] Kainulainen's approach is strongly Finnish in the sense of building on Finnish traditional rural notions of a relationship with nature, still very alive among much of the population. She modifies these views by updating them through the use of feminist views. Swedish Maria Jansdotter from Karlstad University uses Luce Irigaray as the theoretical point of departure in her ecotheological analysis of the Swedish Lutheran hymnal. According to her, in spite of the seemingly feminist approach of the newest hymnal supplement, the deep level of symbolism still reflects the old patriarchy.[53] She also points out that although the Lutheran tradition (as interpreted by Wingren) does not represent disembodied views but maintains the unity of the bodily and the spiritual spheres, a patriarchal concept of God still prevails, even though there are also openings for Lutheran feminist ecotheology. The Swedish secularised context may be taken into account by acknowledging that God is perceived in nature rather than in a transcendent realm.[54] Pauliina Kainulainen sails partly in the same waters and proposes a panentheistic solution to the perceived loss of God from the sight of the modern human being.[55] Kerstin Andersson, who submitted her doctoral dissertation at Uppsala University in Sweden, approaches ecofeministic theology from an ethical point of view, proposing a movement from anthropocentrism to biocentrism in theology.[56] Ethics seems to be never far from an ecofeminist approach.

Danish pastor and doctor in environmental ethics Martin Ishøj addresses climate change from an ethical point of view, leading to theological considerations. Central to his ethical argumentation is the imbalance between Western consumerism and the

---

[47] See Bergmann (2007).

[48] See Bergmann (2003).

[49] See, for example, Bergmann (1997).

[50] See Kjellberg (2000).

[51] See, for example, Kjellberg (1975), (2008).

[52] See Kainulainen (2005).

[53] See Jansdotter (2007), (2009).

[54] See Jansdotter (2006), also Kainulainen (2008).

[55] See Kainulainen (2008), also Kainulainen (2007).

[56] See Andersson.

plight of the poor. Consumerism contributes to climate change, which pauperises huge segments of the global population. The issue is not only that the affluent are not sharing resources with the poor, but also that they are destroying the livelihood of the poor. Ishøj proposes a theological solution where the concept of cosmic Christ plays a central role.[57] This is not very far from the ecofeminist ideas of God's presence in nature.

Recent years have also witnessed the beginnings of two additional Nordic approaches to ecologically sensitive theological reflection: that of the Sami and of the Orthodox tradition. Reflection on the significance of the Sami worldview for ecotheology is especially found in Norway. The Reverend Tore Johnsen, who leads the Sami Church Council, has constructed an ecotheology by taking into account several dimensions of Sami worldview and culture.[58] Roald Kristiansen from Tromsø University has written on ecotheology[59] and on the Sami's history of religion in relation to nature.[60]

Nordic Orthodox ecotheological work has begun to germinate in Finland, where the position of the Orthodox Church is long established and there is thus a more secure ground for opening up to issues wider than the immediate ecclesiastic and ecumenical context. In other Nordic countries the Orthodox churches are immigrant churches faced with the challenge of adjusting to a new environment. Teuvo Laitila, who teaches at the University of Eastern Finland, currently researches the views of Christian and Muslim mystics on nature and especially on animals. In his work, Laitila as a cultural anthropologist and theologian combines cultural and theological analysis. His analysis of the Carelian orthodox tradition of spiritual struggle for sanctification indicates the ways in which this tradition contributes to a holistic relationship with nature.[61] Fr. Heikki Huttunen, the general secretary of the Finnish Ecumenical Council, is currently working on a doctoral dissertation on ecotheology. This work will undoubtedly build bridges between the Orthodox traditions and the West.

One can conclude that Nordic ecotheology is very contextual and ethical. It has a strong urge to be relevant and to contribute to public discourse. In this respect, it differs significantly from the present theological and religious climate of the region where theology and churches either tend to become marginalised or attempt to ride on the past glories and the power of tradition. Ecotheology is one of the few directions from where one may expect a renewal and revitalization of Nordic theology.

References and Recommended Reading

Andersson, Kerstin (2007), *Människan, naturen och Gud: En studie av miljöetiken i nutida kristen teologi*, Uppsala Studies in Social Ethics 35, Uppsala: Acta Universitatis Upsaliensis.

Bergmann, Sigurd (1995), *Geist, der Natur befreit: Die trinitarische Kosmologie Gregors von Nazianz im Horizont einer ökologischen Theologie der Befreiung*, Mainz: Grünewald.

--- (1997), *Geist, der lebendig macht: Lavierungen zur ökologischen Befreiungstheologie*, Frankfurt am Main: Verlag für Interkulturelle Kommunikation.

--- (2003), *God in Context: A Survey on Contextual Theology*, Aldershot: Ashgate.

57 See Ishøj, also Sørensen, Arler and Ishøj.

58 See Johnsen (2005), (2007a), (2007b).

59 See Kristiansen (1985), (1989), (1993a), (2007).

60 See Kristiansen (1993b), (1994). On northern Norwegian Lofot islanders' relation to nature and religion, see Kristiansen (1995).

61 Laitila (1995); Laitila (2002).

--- (2005), *Creation Set Free: The Spirit as Liberator of Nature*, Grand Rapids: Eerdmans.
--- (2007), "Andens ekologi: I teologisk och est / etisk belysning", in: Mæland and Tomren (eds.), 67-85.
Ishøy, Martin (2009), *Klimaklar kristendom: Miljøteologiske begrundelser*, Fredriksberg: Anis.
Jansdotter, Maria (2006), "Ecofeminist Theology in a Swedish Context: Existing Potentials and Possible Contributions", *Ecotheology*, Vol. 11, 4, 481-493.
--- (2007), "Förlossning från Moder natur och frälsning till Fader Gud? En ekofeministisk analys av psalmtexter i Svenska kyrkans Psalmer i 2000-talet med utgångspunkt i Luce Irigarays kultur – och teologikritik", in: Mæland and Tomren (eds.), 189-208.
--- (2009), "Redemption from Mother Nature to Our Father the Lord? An Ecofeminist Analysis of Hymns in the Swedish Church Edition of Psalmer i 2000-talet", *Feminist Theology*, Vol. 18, 1, 74-91.
Johnsen, Tore (2005), *Sámi luondduteologiija: Samisk naturteologi på grunnlag av nålevende tradisjonsstoff og nedtegnede myter*, Institutt for religionsvitenskap, Det samfunnsvitenskapelige fakultet, Universitetet i Tromsø.
--- (2007a), *Jordens barn, solens barn, vindens barn: Kristen tro i et samisk landskap*, Oslo: Verbum.
--- (2007b), "Teologi fra Livets Sirkel: Økoteologiske refleksjoner med utgangspunkt i samisk joikepoesi og indiansk filosofi", in: Mæland and Tomren (eds.), 211-227.
Kainulainen, Pauliina (2005), *Maan viisaus: Ivone Gebaran ekofeministinen käsitys tietämisestä ja teologiasta*, University of Joensuu Publications in Theology 13, Joensuu: University of Joensuu.
--- (2008), "Panenteistinen jumalakäsitys ekoteologisena löytönä", *Teologinen Aikakauskirja*, Vol. 5, 113, 425-435.
Kainulainen, Pauliina (ed.) (2007), *Pyhän kosketus luonnossa: Johdatus kristilliseen ekoteologiaan*, Helsinki: Kirjapaja.
Kjellberg, Seppo (1975), *Kirkon poliittinen tehtävä eräiden teologien mukaan*, Tampere: Kirkon tutkimuskeskus.
--- (2000), *Urban Ecotheology*, Utrecht: International Books.
--- (2008), *Punavihreitä pakinoita*, Huittinen: Minunkirjani.
Kristiansen, Roald (1985), "Økologisk teologi som frigjøringsteologi", *Kirke og Kultur*, Vol. 90, 6, 368-375.
--- (1989), *Creation and Emptiness: Transforming the Doctrine of Creation in Dialogue with the Kyoto School of Philosophy*, Ann Arbor: UMI.
--- (1993a), *Økoteologi: Religiøsitet og Naturforståelse*, Frederiksberg: Anis.
--- (1993b), "Samisk religion og læstadianismen", *Prismet: Pedagogisk tidskrift*, Vol. 44, 1, 18-20.
--- (1994), "Samisk religion i en økologisk sammenheng", *Kirke og Kultur*, Vol. 99, 2, 145-160.
--- (1995), "Om å være from og framsynt: Nordnorsk natur og religiøsitet", in: Marit A. Hauan and Ann Helene Bolstad Skjelbred (eds.), *Mellom sagn og virkelighet i nordnorsk tradisjon*, Oslo: Vett og Viten, 73-83.
--- (2007), "Økoteologi anno 2007: Tilbakeblikk og perspektiver på veien fremover", in: Mæland and Tomren (eds.), 11-27.
Laitila, Teuvo (1995), "Kilvoittelu ja vaihto ihmisen eettisinä suhteina luontoon karjalaisen perinteen valossa", *Ortodoksia*, Vol. 44, 85-98.
--- (2002), "Pyhyys ihmisen ja luonnon eettisenä suhteena karjalaisen ortodoksisuuden näkökulmasta", in: Laaksonen, Pekka and Mettomäki Sirkka-Liisa (eds.), *Pyhän perintö: Kirjoituksia suomalaisesta pyhästä Kalevalassa, kansanperinteessä, luonnossa ja taiteessa*, Helsinki: Suomalaisen Kirjallisuuden Seura, 173-180.
Mæland, Bård and Tomren, Tom Sverre (eds.) (2007), *Økoteologi: Kontekstuelle perspektiver på miljø og teologi*, Oslo: Tapir.
Sørensen, Merete, Arler, F.and Ishøj, Martin (eds.) (1998), *Miljø og etik*, Aarhus: NSU.

Mika Vähäkangas

6. Science and Theology Discourse

Edited by Ernst M. Conradie

Introduction

This chapter is concerned with theological thinkers whose work is shaped by their interaction with various aspects of science. Within the field of theology and science, there are dozens of different conversations and many distinct voices. Each has a particular set of questions, concerns, approaches and commitments.

The chapter falls into two halves. In the first, Christopher Southgate discusses the work of Ian Barbour, Arthur Peacocke and John Polkinghorne. These three "scientist-theologians" are usually thought of as the pre-eminent exponents of the science-religion debate – at least as viewed from within the Christian world and the Anglo-American scene.

In the second half of the chapter Heather Eaton discusses the work of Pierre Teilhard de Chardin, Thomas Berry and Anne Primavesi. These authors share a deep influence from Roman Catholic Christian traditions as well as a comprehensive engagement with science, and in particular evolutionary sciences. Teilhard and Berry are known for their focus on evolutionary cosmology. Primavesi brings forward a feminist analysis. All have contributed to a stream of thought at the headwaters of theology and science, with notable similarities and yet fundamental differences.

So the two halves of the chapter will offer contrasts, but we hope also a helpful complementarity.

Ernst M. Conradie

Ian Barbour – Arthur Peacocke – John Polkinghorne

In this first part of the chapter the positions of three scientist-theologians writing in English who have made major contributions to the science-theology conversation since the 1970s, namely Ian Barbour, Arthur Peacocke and John Polkinghorne, will be discussed. None of the three, to my knowledge, has reflected specifically on the interaction of the motifs of creation and salvation. I therefore propose to illustrate their approaches, and so to illuminate key fault-lines with regard to this interaction, by comparing their positions on some of the key areas that concern us in this volume – their theologies of creation, their understandings of providence and their approach to redemption and eschatology. Such a comparison has, in fact, been made by Polkinghorne[1] and recently formed part of a very helpful survey of the field by Barbour.[2] Some of the comparisons between these three draw also on my own published work.[3] Before proceeding to this theological comparison, I offer brief sketches of each of the three, which themselves will shed light on the various positions they adopt. As all

[1] See Polkinghorne (1996b).

[2] See Barbour (2010).

[3] See Southgate (2004), (2011b).

three have done their theology in conversation with the natural sciences, I also indicate a crucial question arising for the theme of creation and salvation out of the conversation with science.

Ian Barbour (1923-) – On the Need for Critical Realism

Ian Barbour is the senior figure, and many accounts of the modern debate trace its origin to Barbour's *Issues in Science and Religion* (1966).[4] His own scientific background was in physics, and he has been based for most of his career at Carleton College in Minnesota. He won the Templeton Prize in 1999 and was honoured in 2003 with a festschrift edited by Robert John Russell.

In the introduction to *Issues in Science and Religion* Barbour lists three types of question: methods of inquiry in science and religion, man's [*sic*] relation to nature and God's relation to nature.[5] Much of the driving force for the book, one senses, came from a desire to show that scientific and religious thought are not two radically different types of practice that must necessarily be in conflict, but rather that they share common methods and concerns. So Barbour undertakes a historical survey designed to show why some of the classic conflicts between the two disciplines came about and then examines the parallels and contrasts between the two in 20th-century thought.

This work led him both to a consideration of the use of models in both types of discipline (see *Myths, Models and Paradigms*, 1974) and to his now-famous taxonomy of different relations between science and religion, published in his Gifford Lectures of 1991 and later refined in his *Religion and Science* (1998).[6] In contributing to his festschrift, I wrote that Barbour "lays out possibilities, and invites his hearers and his readers to share his thinking; he empowers them to evaluate it ... For that gift of mapping the terrain, for his philosophical skill which did so much both to ground the science-religion conversation and to give it a wider audience, and for his breadth of interest, which has kept ecological concern alongside debates with metaphysics and with quantum theory, for all this we owe Ian Barbour a great debt."[7]

One of Barbour's great contributions has been to highlight the possibility that both science and theology are critical-realist disciplines. This continues to be a fiercely contested position both in the philosophy of science and in the science-theology debate.[8] It suffers from the huge problem that science does not simply refine and refine its positions in a progressively greater and greater correspondence with the truth; every science undergoes periodic transformations in which a confidently-held theory is abandoned, or suffers major modification, in the light of a new one being proposed, or

---

4 Peacocke, in particular, used to contest this attribution. For all his great and oft-expressed respect for Barbour, he would point to a tradition in English scholarship going back through Charles Raven (1885-1964) to the authors of the collection *Lux Mundi* (Gore, 1889). It was that tradition to which Peacocke felt himself to be heir.

5 Barbour (1966), 1.

6 It is sometimes forgotten that the second half of Barbour's Gifford lectures was a consideration of the ethics of technology – this was an important contribution to the developing debate about environmentalism.

7 Southgate (2004), 246.

8 For a helpful review and discussion, see Losch.

acquiring greater support. So it is impossible to be sure that the critical element of critical realism is leading to a progressively greater correspondence between theory and reality. Nevertheless, Barbour has been right to point to the realist instincts of almost all working scientists and most theologians.

What is striking is the way Barbour has been a central commentator and shaper of the debate although his own theological position is (to most European eyes) at the edge of it. Barbour espouses a theology based on A. N. Whitehead's process metaphysics – we shall see as we compare the selected thinkers that this process-based theology at times draws him close to Peacocke and Polkinghorne (as on the temporality of God's experience) but at other junctures places him at a distance (as on kenosis in creation).

Arthur Peacocke (1924-2006) – God as Composer

Arthur Peacocke's scientific work had been in physical biochemistry (I remember encountering him first in biochemistry seminars in Cambridge). He was ordained as an Anglican priest in 1971 and became Dean of Clare College, Cambridge, before moving to direct the Ian Ramsey Centre in Oxford. He began writing on the science-religion debate in the early 1970s. Peacocke was instrumental in the formation of both the UK Science and Religion Forum and the Society of Ordained Scientists. He was a constant encourager of the explorations of others, encouragement for which I personally am very grateful. In 1996 he published *From DNA to Dean*, which begins with a short summary of his career. In 2001 he was awarded the Templeton Prize.

Peacocke's key theological motifs were naturalism: we should take with the utmost seriousness the way that science describes the world, as indicative of the way God endowed and continues to endow that world with both being and becoming;[9] and panentheism: God is the one "in whom we live and move and have our being" (Acts 17:22);[10] God is best understood as "the circumambient Reality in which the world persists and exists".[11] Peacocke had a very strong sense of God as immanent in the processes of the world and proposed a series of intriguing poetic images for this relationship. For example, he writes of a possible image for God as creator being "a composer who, beginning with an arrangement of notes in an apparently simple subject, elaborates and expands it into a fugue",[12] and yet as we 'listen' to the 'work' we can find the composer only as immanent in the 'music' itself".[13]

A motif strong in Peacocke, as distinct from the other two thinkers, reflecting his more "catholic" sensibilities, is a sense of the sacramental character of the creation and

9 Emphases particularly evident in the expanded form of his Gifford Lectures, published as *Theology for a Scientific Age* (1993). Peacocke's last published work was a defence of his theological naturalism in the collection *All That Is* (2007).

10 This is the title of an important collection of essays Peacocke edited with Philip Clayton (2004). Here Polkinghorne's view differs sharply from Peacocke's. Polkinghorne rejects panentheism in this age, but holds to eschatological panentheism – only "[t]he new creation will be wholly sacramental, totally suffused with the divine presence" (2011), 107.

11 Peacocke (1993), 158, see also 371-372.

12 Peacocke (1993), 174.

13 See Peacocke (1993), 176. Peacocke's continuing fascination with music as a metaphor for creation finds expression in Peacocke and Pederson.

indeed of the human being as the priest of creation. He explored the sacramentality of creation in his *Paths from Science towards God* (2001) and *The Palace of Glory* (2005). In the latter book he writes very movingly of the stuff of the universe becoming manifest as the vehicle, presence and means of the Creator's self-offering, the suffering and outpouring of the divine life. "The cruciform eucharist makes explicit the cruciform nature of the created order."[14] Also of our eucharistic self-offering as participation in the reformation and new creation of humanity. The valuation of creation and incarnation here are inspiring indeed (though the theodicy problems of an evolutionary creation – implicit in that phrase from Holmes Rolston about cruciform creation[15] – are only briefly touched on). For Peacocke this sacramental understanding draws on "the old unitary view of creation and salvation"[16] – creation, even as it is, can be eloquent of God's glory and the instrument of the divine purpose. Peacocke was already writing of humans as priests of creation in his Bampton Lectures, *Creation and the World of Science*;[17] there was within those lectures the seed of a more extensive ecotheology that Peacocke did not in the end develop – the subject is the poorer for this.

John Polkinghorne (1930-) – God's Kenotic Work of Love

John Polkinghorne was professor of mathematical physics at Cambridge from 1968 to 1979 before seeking ordination as an Anglican priest. He began writing about the science-religion debate with his book *One World* (1986). As we shall see, Polkinghorne is both the boldest of the three in his theological proposals and (paradoxically) the most conservative in his approach to traditional Christian doctrine. He published an autobiography, *From Physicist to Priest* (2007), along with over twenty books on the science-religion debate.[18] He won the Templeton Prize in 2002 and in the same year became the first President of the International Society for Science and Religion.

Polkinghorne's key themes are evident in the titles of his early books. *One World* expressed his conviction that there must be a unity to truth – science and theology must therefore, at their best, point to this single reality. *Science and Creation* (1988) tackled the exploration of that unity in relation to the doctrine of creation. This is the most appealing element of Christian doctrine for a natural scientist, especially a physicist, to explore. How things originated is a subject of endless curiosity to the scientist – how and why things that seem to connote meaning and purpose came to be as they are is a major issue for the theologian. Moreover, there is a sense in which origins are safer to investigate than present-day issues, such as why so much natural disaster and

14 Peacocke (2005), 83.

15 Rolston, 144.

16 Peacocke (1993), 296.

17 Peacocke (1979), see especially 295-297, 314-315.

18 Polkinghorne has a passion for communicating these vitally important ideas at all levels of engagement with the debate. Thus he has written popular accounts of the issues under discussion in *Quarks, Chaos and Christianity* (1994), for example, and of quantum physics in *The Quantum World* (1984), but he has also tackled the issues in depth and in innovative ways in, for example, his Gifford Lectures of 1993-1994, published in the UK as *Science and Christian Belief* (1994) and his Terry Lectures at Yale in 1996, published as *Belief in God in an Age of Science* (1998).

creaturely suffering continues to pervade the world and why humans continue to act in such improvident and selfish ways. So Polkinghorne's *Science and Providence* (1989) was a striking example of the theological daring mentioned above. In tackling the thorny question of God's providential action in the world, he sided with Peacocke in rejecting the quantum level as the distinctive locus of this providential activity. But Polkinghorne then advanced the (much misunderstood) notion that the unpredictability of non-linear systems in the macroscopic world is an index of their openness to the future, and it is within that openness that there is space for God to act undetectably. As he sometimes proclaimed on a sweatshirt given him by his wife, his position has been that "Epistemology Models Ontology". However this proposal was often misunderstood to be a claim about the indeterminacy of chaotic systems as science characterises them, and a number of scholars hastened to point out to Polkinghorne that the equations governing such systems were deterministic.[19] In fact, he was pursuing a subtler and again a more radical claim – that the equations we currently suppose to characterise these systems are only approximations to a more profound reality.[20] I will return to this theme below in comparing his position with that of Peacocke.

Polkinghorne would sign up, like the other two scholars, to the umbrella position on epistemology known as critical realism.[21] We noted above a key problem with this position. Moreover, postmodern philosophy has constantly stressed how the way we approach problems, and the way in which we express our solutions, is particular and limiting. It is affected by all sorts of factors that may or may not promote closeness to the ways things really are. Polkinghorne has made certain gestures towards recognising the force of these criticisms, but ultimately one senses that his heart is still in the modern project of science, and that he regards these critiques as peripheral to epistemology rather than central.[22] First and foremost, as he makes clear in *Theology in the Context of Science* (2008), science now forms a leading part in the store of "general human knowledge" that has always been part of the context of theological reflection about the world.[23] On this the three selected thinkers would all be agreed.

Science and Theology

The million-dollar question, of course, is to what extent science is allowed preeminence as a system of knowledge, such that Christian theology must allow its classic doctrinal positions to be altered by reflection on this "context". This would be in Barbour's terms a kind of "dialogue", but one that only ran one way. Interestingly, Neil Messer, in devising a taxonomy of his own to describe a range of ways in which scien-

[19] See, for example, Murphy, 327-328.

[20] See Polkinghorne (1995). For a sympathetic analysis, see Saunders, chapter 7.

[21] For a criticism of Polkinghorne's critical realism in relation to his postulates on divine action, see Drees (1995), 227-228.

[22] See Murray and also Van Huyssteen for judicious recognitions of the force of postmodern understandings of epistemology. Peacocke too has claimed explicitly that "science withstands the postmodernist critique" (2001a, 22-24) For another thinker who – though from a very different theological stable than Polkinghorne – has recently made a passionate plea for theologians to take the enterprise of science, and its purchase on reality, with the utmost seriousness, see Drees (2010).

[23] See Polkinghorne (2008), 4.

tific theory and Christian doctrine might be related to one another,[24] identifies Polkinghorne as an example of a thinker in whose work "both science and Christian doctrine contribute, neither having sole control over its shape".[25] Messer contrasts this with Peacocke, whose method he identifies as one in which "both science and Christian doctrine contribute to the account; its shape is determined by the scientific contribution, and the input from Christian doctrine must be adjusted to fit the outlines determined by the natural sciences".[26]

The approach Messer himself advocates is one that gives doctrine priority over the conclusions of science, an approach he finds at its most characteristic in Karl Barth. Barbour does not feature among Messer's examples; I suggest that he would regard Barbour as someone who had already allowed doctrinal convictions to be subject to the conclusions of process metaphysics. This metaphysics then functions as "the other", which is accorded priority over doctrine.

Messer's interesting analysis oversimplifies in three ways. First, in his unwillingness to recognise the profound difference between the approaches of Barbour, Peacocke and Polkinghorne, on the one hand, and creationists and hard-naturalistic atheists, on the other. Peacocke's position appears in Messer's taxonomy next to that of scientific atheists. But all three of the selected theologians stand first and foremost committed to the Christian faith (just as Barth was). They all want to do, in Barbour's terms, "theology of nature" based on a prior commitment to a religious tradition, not develop a "natural theology" that uses science as data for God without reference to revelation or tradition.[27] Second, (and in contrast to Barth) the three thinkers all stand committed to some form of conversation with the methods and findings of the natural sciences. They would therefore – Polkinghorne as much as Peacocke – resist the temptation to restate classic Christian doctrines in ways that close down the conversation with science. An unwillingness to hold to positions that close down that conversation lies, I believe, behind Peacocke and Polkinghorne's rejections of a literal-historical interpretation of the doctrine of the fall (see below). Third, and most importantly for the theme of this volume, the question is not so much whether "doctrine" as a whole is to be accorded priority over scientific insights, as *which* doctrine(s) are to be taken as prior. In Messer's Barthian approach, God's salvation of the world in Christ is the centre of his position, his "doctrinal key",[28] the "lens" through which he reads the conversation between doctrine and science.[29] That is not the case with Peacocke, whose core doctrinal convictions lie more in the area of seeing the processes by which matter, complexity and consciousness arise as solely resulting from the gracious (and kenotic) continuous-creative action of a God transcendent and immanent[30] (see below),

[24] Messer (2007), 49-62.

[25] Messer (2007), 58.

[26] Messer (2007), 54.

[27] See Barbour (1998), 98-101.

[28] See Conradie (2006), (2009), (2010).

[29] See, for example, Horrell, Hunt and Southgate. This is why, in an area of debate, namely evolutionary theodicy, in which it might seem necessary to abandon the absoluteness of either God's goodness or God's sovereignty in creation, Messer unhesitatingly defends the goodness of the God he knows in the work of Christ, despite the theological cost. See Messer (2009); Southgate (2011a).

[30] See Peacocke (1991).

or Barbour's process-informed conviction that God is best understood as "the source of novelty and order", the one who "elicits the self-creation of individual entities".[31] It is perhaps harder to locate the doctrinal key to Polkinghorne's work. It is noteworthy, however, that his 1993-1994 Gifford Lectures were based on a commitment to the Nicene Creed – a doctrinal formulation which is (arguably) overwhelmingly concerned with the doctrine of salvation.[32]

The Fall

This essay has already moved into the territory of comparison, and I develop the comparison between Barbour, Peacocke and Polkinghorne further, first by contrasting their approaches to the fall. The doctrine of the fall has a number of variants, but they are all based on the notion that the cosmos is not as God intended it, because of the choices and actions of freely choosing creatures. In classical Christian thought, therefore, the doctrine stands at the hinge connecting the themes of creation and salvation. God created the world *ex nihilo* and sustains it and endows it with processes by which it unfolds (*creatio continua*). The activity of freely-choosing creatures has damaged and continues to damage that divine economy of creation – hence the need for the initiative of salvation. The damage to the cosmos has typically been blamed on human disobedience through the great story of Eden (Gen. 3), though it is noteworthy that this is not a common motif in the rest of the Hebrew Bible.

The traditional Christian conviction, then, is that the fall that damaged both human relations with God and the character of the creation more generally was a particular moment in time, depicted in the Genesis 3 narrative. An alternative view, only glancingly referred to in Scripture at Luke 10:18, but gathering force in the tradition, is that the fall is primordial – it was a single event, but it was the fall of Lucifer (and his partner angels). The activity of the serpent in the garden of Eden is then taken (without explicit biblical support) to reflect this primordial angelic fall. The third option is to read the Eden story as a mythic account of a perennial truth about being human: we always – for reasons more or less mysterious – tend to disobey our Creator and then to hide from him.

How then do the three selected scholars place themselves in relation to these options? Barbour plumps unhesitatingly for the third. He writes:

> In historic Christianity creation, the fall, and redemption were understood as separate and successive events which provided the narrative framework of a cosmic story. Today we can see them as three ongoing features of a single process of continuing creation, continuing fallenness, and continuing redemption.[33]

Peacocke writes:

> There is *no* past period for which there is reason to affirm that human beings pos-

---

[31] Barbour (1998), 104.

[32] One clause deals with God's creation of heaven and earth, and one with the Holy Spirit as "the Lord, the giver of life". The majority of the creed is concerned with Christology – how God could become man "for us men and for our salvation" – and with the saving work of Christ in dying and rising again, and the remainder with the resultant work of the Spirit and the church.

[33] Barbour (2002), 50.

> sessed moral perfection existing in a paradisiacal situation from which there has only been a subsequent decline. All the evidence points to a creature slowly emerging into awareness ... So there is no sense in which we can talk of a "fall" from a past perfection. There was no golden age, no perfect past, no individuals, "Adam" or "Eve" from whom all human beings have now descended and declined and who were perfect in their relationships and behaviour.[34]

For Peacocke the fall is the classic case of where traditional theology "urgently needs recasting".[35] For Polkinghorne, too, it is the doctrine "most difficult to reconcile with scientific thought". He writes,

> ... a world exploring and realizing its own potentiality through the shifting operations of happenstance. That world must contain impermanence as the ground of change, death as the prerequisite of new life. Its blind alleys and malfunctions will produce what humans perceive as the physical evil of disease and disaster. In that sense the universe is everywhere "fallen" and it has always been so.[36]

But also:

> Once such a world evolves to the point of containing self-conscious freely-choosing beings, it faces the possibility of a further "fall" into moral evil, exemplified by lives of selfishness and rebellion. This, when it occurs, is then a new development in cosmic history, consequent on the new emergent of self-consciousness.[37]

Whence do the differences of nuance lying behind these quotations arise? First, I believe, from the fact that Peacocke, of the three, is the most deeply engaged with the science in question – that of evolution by natural selection. He is therefore able to see the extent to which evolution can be a "disguised friend" of theology (a quotation from Aubrey Moore's essay in *Lux Mundi*[38]) – helping us to see that a God immanent in all things might uphold a process that simultaneously generates value and disvalue. Second, Barbour has less need than the other two to assert the ways in which contemporary Christian thought must learn from the sciences, and to be ready to forsake literal readings of its ancient narratives, because he himself has embraced the metanarrative of process thought, which at once leads to different starting-points on certain doctrinal issues.

Third, I detect in these responses a greater instinct in Polkinghorne to try and retrieve a reading of the classic Christian narrative that accords it some literal force, as compared with Barbour and Peacocke who are happy to regard the Eden story as a reflection of the perennial human condition. Note that the latter view does not accord fallenness less force or importance within the overall Christian worldview. Polkinghorne wants (rightly in my view) to insist both that there can have been no unfallen state and also that the emergence of human consciousness must have been accompanied by the human rejection of personal relationship with God such as had not up to

---

[34] Peacocke (1993), 222-223.

[35] Peacocke (1991), 45.

[36] Polkinghorne (1991), 98.

[37] Polkinghorne (1991), 99.

[38] See Peacocke (2001a), 136.

then been feasible.[39] Barbour and Peacocke probe this question further. They are not so interested in a possible "moment of disobedience" as in the thought that our evolutionary inheritance (both biological and cultural) would necessarily lead us to be creatures who assert their own autonomy and self-interest at the expense of other individuals and obedience to God.[40]

Creation

Let us now return to the questions of origins, of creation *ab initio*, and ask ourselves how these three theologians would tackle it. The classic Christian position that emerged from the early centuries was that of *creatio ex nihilo* (hereafter CEN) – God created every entity out of absolutely nothing. This is a position that has come under some attack recently (e.g. May), but has also had its defenders (e.g. Copan and Lane Craig). It is as Keith Ward (a theologian who perhaps deserves his own place in this survey of major Anglo-American figures writing on science and theology[41]) has put it, "implicit in the Biblical doctrine that God is the creator of heaven and earth, that he can do all things, that nothing is beyond his power".[42]

This is an area of the subject where one might expect a significant difference between Barbour and the other two thinkers. Because it is so important in process schemes that God has experiences that are like the experiences of other entities, many process thinkers are willing to abandon *creatio ex nihilo*, preferring to regard God and the universe as co-eternal.[43] Nevertheless, Barbour seems willing to consider a number of options for theological engagement with cosmology and notes that: "Whitehead himself said that God's primordial nature transcends our cosmic epoch",[44] though also that a unique big bang would require "a more extensive revision of Whitehead's thought" than some other theories.[45] Barbour's agnosticism about origins holds him at some distance from the debate that has arisen over CEN since the scientific "context" changed around 1980.

It was in 1981 that Stephen Hawking, attending a conference at the Vatican on contemporary cosmology, commented that:

> the participants were granted an audience with the Pope [John Paul II]. He told us that it was all right to study the evolution of the universe after the big bang, but we should not inquire into the big bang itself because that was the moment of Creation and therefore the work of God. I was glad then that he did not know the subject of the talk I had just given at the conference – the possibility that space-time was finite

---

[39] In doing so, Polkinghorne would not want to go as far as R. J. Berry, who in order to retrieve a literal reading of the Eden story, develops an account of the emergence of "Homo divinus", two humans who were called out for special relationship with God and federal headship of the creation, only to disobey.

[40] See Barbour (2002), 51-53; Peacocke (1993), chapter 12.

[41] See in particular his *Divine Action* (1990); *Religion and Creation* (1996); *Ten Big Questions in Science and Religion* (2008).

[42] Ward (1990), 6.

[43] For exceptions see Pailin; Bracken.

[44] Barbour (2002), 115.

[45] See Barbour (2002), 116.

> but had no boundary, which means that it had no beginning, no moment of Creation.[46]

The physicist continues, ironically, "I had no wish to share the fate of Galileo ...". However, Hawking has ventured various theological comments much more extreme than any uttered by Galileo, most famously that:

> So long as the universe had a beginning, we could suppose that it had a creator. But if the universe is really completely self-contained, having no boundary or edge, it would have neither beginning nor end: it would simply be. What place, then, for a creator?[47]

In other words, the apparent consonance (a term all three theologians have embraced) between CEN and big bang cosmology had shifted, because of a speculative theoretical proposal that suggested that the universe we know might not have needed a beginning. Robert John Russell has investigated this debate in detail.[48] He lists a range of theological responses, including that of Barbour and Peacocke. Russell criticises Peacocke for his insistence that whatever science might discover about origin, "the central characteristic core of the doctrine of creation itself would not be affected" because that core is about the cosmos "owing its existence to God".[49] Russell's own proposal, in which a temporal beginning is not determinative of the truth of CEN, but would serve as a character witness to its truth, is deserving of close attention.

Polkinghorne, for whom the subject is much closer to his scientific expertise,[50] is curiously unwilling to explore this area. He is happy to say with Peacocke that CEN is answering the question "Why is there something not nothing?" – rather than the question of temporal origin.[51] This may be because his scientific instincts tell him to be very cautious about the various theories that are unfolding about the very early universe, such as string theory.[52]

Whatever may be the precise interaction between *creatio ex nihilo* and the physics of the day, there is a profound fault-line between the theology of creation propounded by Barbour and by the other two thinkers. This concerns the need to posit kenosis – divine self-emptying – as part of the dynamic of creation. This motif was explored in a fine collection of essays edited by Polkinghorne under the title *The Work of Love* (2001). Barbour contributes the first essay in the book. While affirming all the benefits that the theologians of kenotic creation hope to gain from their position, in particular the critique of patriarchy, the affirmation of the integrity of nature and the reality of human freedom and a conviction that God suffers with the suffering of creatures, Barbour attributes limitations of divine knowledge and power to "metaphysical necessity"

---

46 Hawking, 116.

47 Hawking, 140-141.

48 For a technical exposition of the possibilities under discussion up to 2008, see his *Cosmology: From Alpha to Omega* (2008), especially chapter 3.

49 See Peacocke (1979), 79. This in itself calls into question Messer's characterisation of Peacocke's views.

50 Polkinghorne has spent much time at the particle accelerator at CERN, which seeks to generate particles at energies not present since very early in the history of the universe.

51 See Polkinghorne (2008), 68.

52 See Polkinghorne (2011), 51.

rather than to "voluntary self-limitation".[53] It is of the nature of entities – including God – in the process scheme that "[n]o being can have a monopoly of power or effect unilateral control".[54] Whereas Peacocke and Polkinghorne, approaching the theme of creation from a more classical theism, are attracted to the motif of kenotic creation as a way of conveying how God allows creaturely entities the freedom to flourish.

Here again there are interesting differences between the two. Both are heirs of Jürgen Moltmann's invocation of Luria's concept of *zimsum* – God "withdraws" to make space for the created order. But Peacocke, the biochemist, is most engaged with the suffering intrinsic to an evolutionary process,[55] and is convinced that a loving Creator God – the God we glimpse in Jesus – must suffer all the natural evils of the world. Divine kenosis, then, is expressed first and foremost in this willingness to suffer. Polkinghorne is aware of these considerations, which he includes under his "free-process" approach to natural evil (see below). But his interests in kenosis go broader and include: kenosis of omnipotence, of simple eternity (in allowing temporal experience to be part of the divine life), of omniscience and of causal status. By this last consideration he means that in acting providentially God allows himself to be a cause among causes, not determining events but allowing "an interweaving of providential and creaturely causalities".[56] This is one of those occasions when a classical Christian theist draws close to a process account, but the crucial difference is that this divine restraint is a divine decision, not a metaphysical necessity as in Barbour.

It is worth noting before leaving this topic that the whole notion of God's self-emptying to make space for the other has been challenged, especially tellingly by Ted Peters and Martinez Hewlett, who allege that to invoke the need for divine kenosis in creation is to misunderstand the nature of God's relation to the world. Power, for example, is not a zero-sum game, a "fixed amount of pie",[57] and nor is freedom. Created entities acquire their power and their freedom not because God has *limited* God's power and freedom, but because the divine power and freedom makes the creation what it is. Colin Gunton has also criticised the use of the concept of kenosis in creation, especially with respect to Moltmann's image of God withdrawing Godself to make space for what is not-God. Gunton asks,

> If God as creator is the one who gives reality to the other, must he do it by making space within rather than without himself? ... (Kenosis) is a concept designed to deal with God's bearing in relation to a fallen world, not to be applied promiscuously to any of God's relations to the world ... there is no suggestion in the Bible that the act of creation is anything but the joyful giving of reality to the other.[58]

These considerations, however, leave intact the notion that in choosing to suffer with the suffering of creatures, God forsakes at least the attribute of impassibility.

---

[53] Barbour (2001), 12.

[54] Barbour (2001), 13.

[55] For an extended analysis of the theological implications of this suffering, see Southgate (2008).

[56] Polkinghorne (2001), 102-105, quotation on 105.

[57] Peters and Hewlett, 143.

[58] Gunton, 141.

Providential Divine Action

The third area of comparison concerns the debate about providential divine action already touched on above. God's particular engagement with particular situations and persons as a manifestation of God's character as Creator, lover of his creatures and Saviour is as axiomatic to traditional theology as is a historical understanding of the fall. However, as with the fall, there have been some recent voices strongly critical of the tradition. An especially lucid example is the work of Maurice Wiles.

The theology of providence occupies a particularly fascinating and central place in the discussion of creation and salvation. Is it best to regard providence as an aspect of God's continuing creative activity or as the way in which, within this world which is gradually passing away, God's redeeming hand can be seen? Even as one poses such a question one must realise that it is a human-scale question, part of our wholly inadequate effort to gain some sort of purchase on the divine activity, which no doubt is all of piece and unified by God's unwavering pattern of faithfulness and love (what Whitehead would have called the "primordial nature of God"). The other human-scale question that eats away at any conviction as to God's special providential action is the ubiquity and seeming arbitrariness of suffering within creation.

Just as with the fall, one can identify three general categories of approach to providential divine action. The first type of approach is to take seriously the biblical picture of a God active in all sorts of situation, answering prayer in evident ways, including making very unusual events happen, healing the sick and of course raising the body of Jesus from the dead. A second approach concedes that something very remarkable happened at the resurrection and perhaps can happen in the personal relationships between human persons and God, but resists the notion of a God who, having set up laws and processes in the universe, would then require to tinker with them. A third approach would say that it is God's creative activity in designing and upholding the laws of the universe that *constitutes* God's action in the world.[59]

This is an area of theology in which the metaphysical scheme of process thinkers is particularly attractive. Because Whitehead projected experience from that of complex organisms onto much simpler entities so that centres of experience seeking harmony and intensity occur at every level, it is possible to posit a self-interested resistance on the part of creatures all the way down the ladder of complexity. As Paul Fiddes has written:

> Process thinkers argue that something akin to the basic features of human experience – feeling and enjoyment – must be present everywhere. However hard it is to express the term of the analogy at the lower levels of creation … nevertheless I believe that process thought is on to something here. Some overall vision of the "responsiveness" and "resistance" of creation to the Spirit of God is needed for a doctrine of creative evolution, (and) for a proper theodicy …[60]

A "proper theodicy" emerges because the God of process theology only ever acts to

[59] A fourth approach is the neo-Thomist model of primary and secondary causality by which God's primary causality underpins all other causation. For a recent exploration of this position, see Edwards (2010).

[60] Fiddes, 228.

seek to persuade entities of the paths that will lead to states of truer fulfilment for all the entities in the system. Whether a God who only ever seeks to persuade is an adequate divine response to human evil is another matter.[61] But the process scheme offers a uniform model of divine activity at every level of complexity in the created world, though "persuasion" of an electron will of course be a much less sophisticated process than persuasion of a person along the paths of love.[62]

Although a proper theodicy of natural evil and a consistent model of divine action are highly desirable theological prizes, most scholars outside the community of process thinkers would consider that they are bought at too high a price in terms of metaphysical commitment to a process view of reality, in particular to panexperientialism.[63]

Of the two other thinkers, Polkinghorne is the more attracted to the first approach to providence, to a belief that God's providential action is manifested in the world in all sorts of ways, in healing and in response to prayer. So he would by no means rule out praying for rain, and it would be reasonable, on his view, to expect that prayer to make a difference.[64] As indicated above, his suggested mechanism for God to act in the world undetectably and without breaching physical law is via the sensitivity of non-linear systems in the macroscopic world.

Peacocke's instinct is very different, much closer to the second of the positions on divine action sketched above.[65] He is at pains to stress that the physical laws that science discovers should be our best guide to God's activity in the world. So providence is largely subsumed, for Peacocke, under *creatio continua*. However, he believes something very special happened at the resurrection (not involving the bones of Jesus).[66] Moreover, Peacocke considers that God's "whole-part influence", affecting "holistically the state of the World-System",[67] can have particular effects, expressing the particular purposes of God in particular situations, including the experience of God by human persons in the course of worship.[68]

Although neither thinker would concede that he agreed with the other, the positions of Peacocke and Polkinghorne on the mechanism of God's providential action are not as dissimilar as has sometimes appeared. Polkinghorne writes:

> It is important to recognise that, in this scheme, the significance of the sensitivity of chaotic systems to the effects of small triggers is diagnostic of their requiring to be treated in holistic terms and of their being open to top-down causality through the input of active information. It is not proposed that this is the localized mechanism by which agency is exercised. *I do not suppose that either we or God interact with the world by the carefully calculated adjustment of the infinitesimal details of initial conditions so as to bring about a desired result. The whole thrust of the proposal is*

---

61 For a critical analysis, see Surin, 86-92.

62 For his own summary of this type of position, see Barbour (2002), 31-36.

63 For a defence of panexperientialism see Barbour (2002), 36-37.

64 Polkinghorne (1989), 32, see also chapter 6.

65 Wiles's work, cited above, and that of Gordon Kaufman, which underpinned it, would be examples of the third, as would the rather different position of Christopher Knight.

66 See Peacocke (1993), 279-288.

67 Peacocke (2008), 220.

68 For a summary of his last position on divine action, see Peacocke (2008).

> *expressed in terms of the complete holistic situation, not in terms of the clever manipulation of bits and pieces* [emphasis – CS]. It is, therefore, a proposal for realizing a true kind of top-down causality. It may fittingly be called contextualism, for it supposes the behavior of parts to be influenced by their overall context.[69]

And:

> It seems entirely conceivable that God also interacts with the creation through the input of active information into its open physical process. We glimpse, in a rudimentary way, what might lie behind theology's language of God's "guiding" and "drawing on" creation, language often associated with talk of the Spirit working immanently on the inside of creation.[70]

This is close to Peacocke's emphases on divine immanence, whole-part influence and God as the ultimate boundary condition. It is the difference in emphasis between these two careful and committed thinkers that remains fascinating. Polkinghorne's stress is still on the question "Why do certain things happen and not others?" Hence his interest in God choosing the paths of systems through chaotic attractors. Peacocke still wants to stress God's respect for the freedom of the systems God has created. However, Polkinghorne's system-open-to-God-as-overall-context is very similar to Peacocke's whole-part-influence-on-the-world-as-a-whole, given that they both agree that (a) the future is not known to God – God is working with at least a genuine epistemic openness – and (b) divine action can have *particular* effects.

Both thinkers are very sensitive to the problem of theodicy, especially in relation to natural evil. Both see the pain and suffering intrinsic to the evolutionary process as the necessary cost of the values that emerge within it. Polkinghorne relies on a "free-process defence" – "God allows the physical world to be itself … in that independence which is Love's gift of freedom to the one beloved."[71] Peacocke's preference is to insist that God suffers "in, with and under" every element of the evolutionary process. He writes: "God suffers in and with the sufferings of created humanity and so, by a natural extension, with those of all creation, since humanity is an evolved part of it. The suffering of God, which we could glimpse only tentatively in the processes of creation, is in Jesus the Christ concentrated to a point of intensity and transparency which reveals itself to all who focus on him."[72] Fascinatingly, a slightly later essay alters this to "… intensity and transparency that reveals it as expressive of the perennial relation of God to the creation".[73] His thinking was clearly moving at the end of his career towards a focus on the significance of the sufferings of the non-human creation.

Salvation

At the heart of any Christian theodicy, whatever other moves are made in relation to soul-making, or freedom of will or process, must be God's commitment to the creation in Jesus and Jesus' willingness to suffer in and for a sinful world. This is also the

---

69 Polkinghorne (1995), 154.

70 Polkinghorne (1996), 248.

71 Polkinghorne (1989), 66.

72 Peacocke (1998), 372.

73 Peacocke (2001b), 42.

Christian's core confession about God's saving initiative. So we must now ask: what view of the passion and cross of Jesus lies at the core of the soteriology of each of these three thinkers? Barbour affirms the kenosis involved not only in the self-limitation of Christ's power, but also the self-limitation of God's power in allowing Christ's death.[74] However, like many process thinkers he takes with great seriousness feminist critiques of theologies of self-sacrifice, and this makes it harder for him to embrace any of the traditional models of atonement.

Polkinghorne affirms a traditional belief in the centrality of the incarnation, cross and resurrection,[75] though he is content to note the church's historic reluctance to affirm one model of atonement at the expense of the others.[76] Peacocke offers a more developed theology of atonement, with a strong preference for the Abelardian model of Christ as the exemplar of love. Peacocke regards the "objective" theories of the transformation of the state of humanity as all of a piece with the traditional beliefs in the fall that he has rejected (see above), and insists with Fiddes that "human response must actually be part of the act of salvation, not merely a reaction to it afterwards".[77] This is consistent with Peacocke's theology of God's companioning of the long process of emergence of consciousness and personhood – it might be said that, for Peacocke, not only providence but even atonement is being caught up in *creatio continua*.

After exploring in some detail various divergences between the three selected thinkers, I want to note a very striking convergence of view. All three have insisted that the future is not known to God in its every detail – that the world of creaturely becoming does not exist until it happens and is in a measure open to the interaction of law and chance. For Barbour, this follows directly from his process views – God is a contributor to every event, but not a determiner of events; therefore God cannot know the future. For Peacocke, this issue was important in his defence of the significance of chance – in particular within the evolutionary process. In his *God and the New Biology* (1986), he analysed the nature of chance and was at pains to affirm – against Jacques Monod in *Chance and Necessity* (1972) – that the existence of real indeterminacy did not imply meaninglessness in the universe, but rather was wholly compatible with the character of the God, immanent within the world's explorations, that was presumed by Peacocke's theology. Polkinghorne too is committed to the openness and indeterminacy of macroscopic systems – this, as we saw above, is a bold metaphysical guess, based on his sense that "science's account of the causal structure of the world" is "patchy in its character".[78] This consensus among these scientist-theologians that the future is not known in detail to God is striking, particularly as it is at variance with the mainstream of theological tradition.[79]

---

74 Barbour (2002), 108.

75 Polkinghorne (1994a), chapters 5-7.

76 See Polkinghorne (2008), 97-98.

77 Quoted in Peacocke (1993), 327.

78 Polkinghorne (2008), 79.

79 Divine responsiveness to time is at variance with the classical stance of Christian theology (in, for example, Thomas Aquinas). Polkinghorne's assertion of divine temporality has been criticised on scientific grounds, for instance by Willem B. Drees who asks, "What time is God's time?" (1996), 261-266.

The Future of the Cosmos

Lastly, I compare the views of the three selected thinkers on the final fate of the cosmos and what might constitute the redeemed state of creatures. This is an area in which Polkinghorne has taken a strong lead, especially with his monograph *The God of Hope and the End of the World* (2002). His emphases include:

- A sense that here theology must diverge from science, because it must insist on hope and the persistence of meaning, neither of which the scientific narrative of the fate of the universe can offer;
- An insistence that for the Christian the new creation must emerge *ex vetere*, not as something entirely new. Likewise, human persons will be re-embodied, but they will be selves in continuity with the selves of their first life;[80]
- Therefore the eschatological state of matter is in some continuity with the protological creation, but also in discontinuity, freed from "the thermodynamic drift to disorder which is the course of mortality in the present age".[81]

Much of Polkinghorne's reflection on these issues is fuelled by his consideration of the resurrection body of Jesus, which he sees as a prolepsis of the state of redeemed matter in general. Here we can see a profound parting of the ways from Peacocke, who for equally robust theological reasons does not believe that Jesus' tomb was empty.[82] So Peacocke lacks that starting-point for eschatological speculation that has been so important to Polkinghorne. Indeed he has devoted little attention to this theme, though there is a chapter in his Bampton Lectures that surveys the options.[83] His stress there is on the "*unveiling* of God's *meaning* and purpose".[84] He quotes Traherne, "The WORLD is unknown, till the Value and Glory of it is seen."[85] Because of Peacocke's strong sense of the long evolutionary narrative as productive of the values we see come to fruition in humanity and in the incarnation, because of his view of the immanence of God in creation, and therefore of creation's sacramentality, and because his theology of atonement is exemplarist rather than objective, his sense of the shape of the Christian narrative is very different from Polkinghorne's. It is a narrative of gradual disclosure, rather than of the resurrection as inaugurating an era characterised by radical discontinuity. That is not to say that Peacocke has no eschatology. But he is not concerned to speculate in physical terms as Polkinghorne is – rather he is attracted to an existential eschatology such as is implied by the thought of Wolfhart Pannenberg. Peacocke writes: "there is the possibility or, rather, the opportunity for man to be open to this transcendent element in his immediate present and so commit himself to the open future".[86] So Peacocke's narrative is one of the gradual emergence of conscious-

---

80 Polkinghorne guesses that non-human creatures might be represented as types, though pets might have individual redeemed existence. For a critique of this view, see Southgate (2008), chapter 5.

81 Polkinghorne (2011), 106.

82 Peacocke (1993), 279-288.

83 Peacocke (1979), chapter 8.

84 Peacocke (1979), 330.

85 Quoted in Peacocke (1979), 331.

86 Peacocke (1979), 336. One imagines Peacocke would have warmed to the thought of Kathryn Tanner on de-temporalised eschatology. See Tanner (2000), (2007).

ness and progressive divine disclosure to this consciousness. As such, it resembles more that of a process thinker, with a long path towards progressively greater fulfilment, than the more traditional sense that humanity is rescued from the rebellion of sin by a great objective act of God and then lives within the eschatological phase of God's plan within the growing shape of the "new creation".

Barbour is clearly attracted to a process eschatology such as that of David Ray Griffin. Barbour notes Griffin's point that eschatology can be thought of as classical Christianity's way of reconciling the omnipotence of God and the continuing existence of evil. Since process theology foregoes a sense of God's omnipotence, it does not have to take this line and can therefore develop a different approach to the future. In a theology in which divine power is reconceived "as empowerment rather than overpowering control",[87] it is easier to embrace a realised eschatology in which "God empowers us to resist evil now rather than to expect God's unilateral action in the future. [Such a view] provides grounds for hope of God's victory over evil, but it offers no risk-free guarantee."[88]

Clearly there are hints of a realised eschatology in the gospels, especially in John. However, the very strongly eschatological flavour of the New Testament (which Peacocke also recognises[89]) stemmed not from a desire to reconcile two positions in philosophical theology, but from a very strong conviction that God in Christ inaugurated a new age in which the proper human response was one of prayerful expectation of further transformative works of divine power (cf. 1 Thess. 5). If anything, when the early Christians became aware that a world full of evil was persisting longer than anticipated, that awareness diluted, rather than intensified, the eschatological emphasis of early Christianity. Moreover, neither Barbour's nor Peacocke's position addresses the ultimate fate of the material universe. The Christian confession here – at least that derived from Pauline thought, such as that of Romans 8 and Colossians 1, and from Revelation – is that God's power and love will transform the creation into a state full of blessing, a state which indeed, as Polkinghorne says, will be "totally suffused with the divine presence".[90] This is an area of theology where indeed – to return to the categories Messer proposes – doctrine must be given priority over what science can currently know.

Peacocke and Barbour are right to stress that God's saving initiative requires a response in the here and now, a response which it is open to humans to make, but Polkinghorne is surely right to address the question of the final state of matter and to insist that it is finally completely dependent on the operation of God's sovereign power. The sort of eschatology to which Barbour is attracted, based on human empowerment, is a very interesting one, one that perhaps contains seeds of an old-fashioned American optimism about what humans might be capable of. However, it is not, I venture to suggest, congruent with the age-old Christian conviction that our hope resides, can

---

87 Barbour (2002), 118.

88 Barbour, (2002), 117. Barbour notes the various process views on whether human life beyond death will be solely objective (in the mind of God), or subjective, or "in a new kind of community transcending individuality" (2002, 117), though without making clear his own preference.

89 Peacocke (1979), 335.

90 Polkinghorne (2011), 107.

only reside, in God alone and that that hope rests secure in God's ultimate, and assured, victory over evil.

Conclusion

As I mentioned at the beginning of this chapter, I am not aware of Barbour, Peacocke or Polkinghorne offering an explicit treatment of the interplay between the motifs of creation and salvation. Nevertheless, the comparison between their approaches is revealing. Peacocke is the most naturalistic of the three, the most convinced that "the Church must rethink its message in today's language for a society deeply impressed by and indebted to science".[91]

It is therefore unsurprising that he concerns himself with the narrative of creation's long unfolding and writes of God using the processes he has created to explore the possibilities for creation, with little sense that God would put pressure on those processes. Rather, he inclines to the view that the processes have within them a bias towards complexification, greater than most scientists have realised.[92] Barbour, as we have seen, is drawn to a process-theological version of a similar focus – God as the origin of entities' self-creation, to which must be added the Whiteheadian conviction that all that is of value is retained in the divine memory. God is therefore continually redeeming the experience of entities in the sense that nothing important will be lost. Polkinghorne lays more emphasis on God's mighty transforming act in bringing in the new creation. Of this great transformation the resurrection is the prolepsis. So the theology of providence remains the key fault-line in the distinction between the three selected thinkers. While God's providential action is for Barbour and Peacocke a way of understanding *creatio continua*, Polkinghorne's focus on providence is best seen as part of his theology of eschatological salvation, as part of God's desire for creaturely healing, still inadequately realised while we remain within the existing order of things.

Further Developments

The key foci of the discussion of Barbour, Peacocke and Polkinghorne above continue to be vigorously debated. I draw out here some elements that bear particularly on the central theme of the relation of the motifs of creation and salvation, giving special consideration to debates of relevance to ecotheology.

a) *Creation out of nothing*: The doctrine of creation out of nothing has acquired an interesting eco-ethical dimension, stemming out of the work of Catherine Keller (see chapter 7). Her affirmation of the *tehom* of Genesis 1:2 as neither an absolute *nihil* nor a negative chaos, but rather as the wellspring of possibilities, is accompanied by a rejection of *creatio ex nihilo* as both unscriptural and liable to promote oppressive colonisation. The theological ethics of this is explored by Whitney Bauman. An alternative suggestion, more hospitable to the traditional doctrine, has recently come from Andrew Robinson (through personal communication). He points out that if God is taken to have created everything that exists out of absolutely nothing, that this was the

---

[91] Peacocke (1991), 52.

[92] That is no doubt why Peacocke was an early enthusiast for the work of Simon Conway Morris. See Peacocke (2001a), 82; Conway Morris (1998, 2003).

one act of making that did not consume any materials. Our own creaturely making, indeed our whole existence, requires consumption. As Wendell Berry has tellingly written:

> To live, we must daily break the body and shed the blood of Creation. When we do this knowingly, lovingly, skilfully, reverently, it is a sacrament. When we do it ignorantly, greedily, clumsily, destructively, it is a desecration. In such a desecration we condemn ourselves to spiritual and moral loneliness, and others to want.[93]

In other words, as creatures we can never truly originate anything as the divine Creator does. However, there is encouragement in Berry's words that, though we can only seek to conduct our own "making" as redeemed creatures, we can do so reverently and meaningfully in our "breaking". This is a profound notion for ecotheology.

b) *Divine action*: Two important recent contributions are those of Denis Edwards[94] and Philip Clayton and Steven Knapp.[95] It is noteworthy that Clayton and Knapp's work, and that of Wesley Wildman cited there, tends to shift the ground of the discussion of providence away from mechanism and towards moral considerations.[96] Clayton and Knapp's conviction that God could, morally, offer only axiological comfort moves divine action away from the language of healing (from the time of the gospels closely associated with salvation) in the direction of the process-theological emphasis on divine lure. That, in turn, bears on the question of whether God might be expected to rescue "the human project" from the destructive effects of its ways with the planet, or whether all God will continue to offer is encouragement to virtue.

c) *The fall*: Whether a fall at a moment of time is necessary to Christian theology (in particular in relation to theodicy in respect of evolution) continues to be keenly debated, for example by Messer and by Southgate.[97] The issue, as Messer identifies it, is one central to theological ethics – whether divine creation, as per the divine intention, contains violence. Messer is apprehensive that such an attribution would license violence among creatures. Yet Southgate shows that the alternatives suffer from severe problems in terms of coherence with science and in relation to divine sovereignty. His strong insistence that we live in the eschatological phase of our journey with God, distances him from the (to him necessary) ambiguities of the protological creation.

d) Another issue that is opened up (or perhaps reopened with new clarity) by this debate is the *overall shape of the Christian narrative*. Classically this has been depicted as a U-shape involving creation, fall and redemption. Fiddes, however, has cast doubt on whether this is the only narrative shape that the Christian Scriptures can sustain. There are two questions that are particularly relevant for further reflection on the relationship between creation and salvation:

- Is the incarnation the divine response to human sin, or is it part of the divine plan

---

93 Wendell Berry, 281.

94 Edwards (2010).

95 Clayton and Knapp.

96 For a survey see Southgate (2011b), chapter 10.

97 See Messer; Southgate (2011a; 2012).

from the foundation of the world (cf. Rev. 13:8) and therefore the culmination instead of the Creator's long engagement with creaturely life, suffering, in Peacocke's phrase, "in, with and under" the life of creatures?[98]

- Is the cross and the resurrection the decisive moment in history, the moment that initiates the eschaton (which would be the classic understanding emerging from the conciliar creeds and the one espoused by Polkinghorne), or is the Christ-event the perfect exemplar of the divine love, to which creatures are invited to respond within a creation that continues to evolve (the approach that the work of Peacocke and Barbour suggests).

The inclusion in these debates of the descriptions of the cosmos offered by the natural sciences has interesting effects. The discussions of the fall offered by Peacocke and Barbour, reinforced by the failure of the sciences to point to any primordial perfection, move the debate on the first question away from the Christ-event as divine response required because of non-necessary human rebellion. It might be thought that such a science-influenced theological shift would also move the second question above in the direction of an exemplarist model and away from the "hinge-of-history" approach. It is important to note that this needs not necessarily be the case. The Christ-event can still inaugurate the transformation of the material world (as hinted at in Col. 1:20 and Eph. 1:10) without being a direct response to human sin. Moreover the predictions of cosmological physics – that this universe will eventually fade away to a state lacking all structure or meaning – tend to stand against models based solely on God's long-patient offering to creatures of examples of the divine love. They remind us that physics cannot give an account of the hope that for the Christian lies firmly in Christ Jesus.

e) *Eschatology*: At the time of writing the most recent study is that of Wilkinson, which is interestingly critical of some major science-influenced theologians of the eschaton, such as Moltmann and Pannenberg. A contrary approach is that of Kathryn Tanner in her "de-temporalised eschatology".[99] Tanner insists that Christian thought should part company with concerns over the scientific predictions of the fate of the universe and concentrate instead on eschatological action in the present – whatever draws the believer closer into relationship with God and into the Kingdom. Ingenious move though this is, it seems to do insufficient justice either to the resurrection as prolepsis of redeemed existence, or indeed to the redemption of non-human creatures.[100] There is a widespread insistence that Christian ethics must be eschatological and that eschatology must attend to ethics.[101] The need for such an eschatological approach, of an inspiring vision of "hope for the earth", is recognised in diverging contributions to ecotheology, including those of Jürgen Moltmann, John Haught and Ernst Conradie.[102]

---

[98] Peacocke (2001a), 86.

[99] Tanner (2000; 2007). For critical discussion of Tanner's work, see also Barton.

[100] See Southgate (2008), chapter 5.

[101] For an exegetical study confirming this close correlation, see Horrell, Hunt and Southgate.

[102] See the discussion on Moltmann in chapter 4, on Haught in chapter 7 and Conradie (2005).

References and Recommended Reading

Barbour, Ian G. (1966), *Issues in Science and Religion*, London: SCM.

--- (1974), *Myths, Models and Paradigms: The Nature of Scientific and Religious Knowledge*, London: SCM.

--- (1998), *Religion and Science: Historical and Contemporary Issues*, London: SCM.

--- (2001), "God's Power: A Process View", in: Polkinghorne (ed.), 1-20.

--- (2002), *Nature, Human Nature and God*, Minneapolis: Fortress.

--- (2010), "John Polkinghorne on Three Scientist-Theologians", *Theology and Science*, Vol. 8, 3, 247-264.

Bauman, Whitney (2009), *Theology, Creation and Environmental Ethics*, London: Routledge.

Berry, R. J. (2011), "Adam or Adamah?", *Science and Christian Belief*, Vol. 23, 23-48.

Berry, Wendell (1981), *The Gift of Good Land: Further Essays Cultural and Agricultural*, San Francisco: North Point.

Bracken, Joseph P. (2006), *Christianity and Process Thought: Spirituality for a Changing World*, West Conshohocken: Templeton Foundation Press.

Clayton, Philip and Knapp, Steven (2011), *The Predicament of Belief: Science, Philosophy and Faith*, New York: Oxford University Press.

Clayton, Philip and Peacocke, Arthur (eds.) (2004), *In Whom We Live and Move and Have our Being: Panentheistic Reflections on God's Presence in a Scientific World*, Grand Rapids: Eerdmans.

Conradie, Ernst M. (2005), *Hope for the Earth: Vistas on a New Century*, Eugene: Wipf and Stock.

--- (2006), "The Road towards an Ecological Biblical and Theological Hermeneutics", *Scriptura*, Vol. 93, 305-314.

--- (2009), "Interpreting the Bible amidst Ecological Degradation", *Theology*, Vol. 112, 199-207.

--- (2010), "What on Earth is an Ecological Hermeneutics? Some Broad Parameters", in: D. G. Horrell et al. (eds.), *Ecological Hermeneutics: Biblical, Historical and Theological Perspectives*, London: T & T Clark / New York: Continuum, 295-314.

Conway Morris, S. (1998), *The Crucible of Creation*, Oxford: Oxford University Press.

--- (2003), *Life's Solution: Inevitable Humans in a Lonely Universe*, Cambridge: Cambridge University Press.

Copan, Paul and Lane Craig, William (2004), *Creation Out of Nothing: A Biblical, Philosophical, and Scientific Exploration*, Grand Rapids: Baker.

Drees, Willem B. (1995), "Gaps for God?", in: Robert J. Russell, Nancey Murphy and Arthur R. Peacocke (eds.), *Chaos and Complexity: Scientific Perspectives on Divine Action*, Vatican City: Vatican Observatory / Berkeley: Center for Theology and the Natural Sciences, 223-237.

--- (1996), *Religion, Science and Naturalism*, Cambridge: Cambridge University Press.

--- (2010), *Religion and Science in Context: A Guide to the Debates*, London: Routledge.

Edwards, Denis (2010), *How God Acts: Creation, Redemption, and Special Divine Action*, Minneapolis: Fortress.

Fiddes, Paul S. (1988), *The Creative Suffering of God*, Oxford: Clarendon.

Gore, Charles (ed.) (1889), *Lux Mundi: A Series of Studies in the Religion of the Incarnation*, London: John Murray.

Gunton, Colin E. (1998), *The Triune Creator: A Historical and Systematic Study*, Edinburgh: Edinburgh University Press.

Hawking, Stephen W. (1988), *A Brief History of Time*, London: Bantam.

Horrell, David G., Hunt, Cherryl and Southgate, Christopher (2010), *Greening Paul: Re-reading the Apostle in a Time of Ecological Crisis*, Waco: Baylor University Press.

Kaufman, Gordon (1972), *God the Problem*, Cambridge: Harvard University Press.

Knight, Christopher (2007), *The God of Nature: Incarnation and Contemporary Science*, Minneapolis: Fortress.

Losch, Andreas (2011), "Critical Realism: A Sustainable Bridge between Science and Religion", *Theology and Science*, Vol. 8, 4, 393-416.

May, Gerhard (1994), *Creatio ex Nihilo: The Doctrine of "Creation out of Nothing" in Early Christian Thought* (translated by A. S. Worrall), Edinburgh: T & T Clark.

Messer, Neil (2007), *Selfish Genes and Christian Ethics: Theological and Ethical Reflections on*

Evolutionary Biology, London: SCM.
--- (2009), "Natural Evil after Darwin", in: Michael Northcott and R. J. Berry (eds.), *Theology after Darwin*, Milton Keynes: Paternoster, 139-154.
Monod, Jacques (1972), *Chance and Necessity*, London: Collins.
Murphy, Nancey (1995), "Divine Action in the Natural Order: Buridan's Ass and Schrödinger's Cat", in: Robert J. Russell, Nancey Murphy and Arthur R. Peacocke (eds.), *Chaos and Complexity: Scientific Perspectives on Divine Action*, Vatican City: Vatican Observatory / Berkeley: Center for Theology and the Natural Sciences, 325-357.
Murray, Paul D. (2011), "Truth and Reason in Science and Theology: Points of Tension, Correlation and Compatibility", in: Southgate (ed.), 89-124.
Pailin, David (1989), *God and the Processes of Reality*, London: Routledge.
Peacocke, Arthur R. (1979), *Creation and the World of Science: The Bampton Lectures 1978*, Oxford: Clarendon.
--- (1986), *God and the New Biology*, London: Dent.
--- (1991), "The Challenge of Science to Theology and the Church", in: D. W. Hardy and P. Sedgwick (eds.), *The Weight of Glory: A Vision and Practice for Christian Faith: The Future of Liberal Theology*, Edinburgh: T & T Clark, 37-53.
--- (1993), *Theology for a Scientific Age: Being and Becoming – Natural, Divine, and Human*, London: SCM.
--- (1996), *From DNA to Dean: Reflections and Explorations of a Priest-Scientist*, Norwich: Canterbury.
--- (1998), "Biological Evolution: A Positive Theological Appraisal", in: Robert J. Russell, William R. Stoeger and Francisco J. Ayala (eds.), *Evolutionary and Molecular Biology: Scientific Perspectives on Divine Action*, Vatican City: Vatican Observatory / Berkeley: Center for Theology and the Natural Sciences, 357-376.
--- (2001a), *Paths from Science towards God: The End of All Our Exploring*, Oxford: Westview.
--- (2001b), "The Cost of New Life", in: John Polkinghorne (ed.), *The Work of Love: Creation as Kenosis*, London: SPCK / Grand Rapids: Eerdmans, 21-42.
--- (2005), *The Palace of Glory: God's World and Science*, Adelaide: ATF.
--- (2007), *All That Is: A Naturalistic Faith for the 21st Century* (edited by Philip Clayton), Minneapolis: Fortress.
--- (2008), "Reflections on 'Scientific Perspectives on Divine Action'", in: Robert J. Russell, Nancey Murphy and William R. Stoeger (eds.), *Scientific Perspectives on Divine Action: Twenty Years of Challenge and Progress*, Vatican City / Berkeley: Vatican Observatory / Center for Theology and the Natural Sciences, 201-223
Peacocke, Arthur and Pederson, Ann (2006), *The Music of Creation*, Minneapolis: Fortress.
Peters, Ted and Hewlett, Martinez (2003), *Evolution from Creation to New Creation: Conflict, Conversation and Convergence*, Nashville: Abingdon.
Polkinghorne, John C. (1984), *The Quantum World*, London: Longman.
--- (1986), *One World: The Interaction of Science and Theology*, London: SPCK.
--- (1988), *Science and Creation: The Search for Understanding*, London: SPCK.
--- (1989), *Science and Providence: God's Interaction with the World*, London: SPCK.
--- (1991), *Reason and Reality: The Relationship between Science and Theology*, London: SPCK.
--- (1994a), *Science and Christian Belief: Theological Reflections of a Bottom-Up Thinker*, London: SPCK.
--- (1994b), *Quarks, Chaos and Christianity: Questions to Science and Religion*, London: Triangle.
--- (1995), "The Metaphysics of Divine Action", in: Robert J. Russell, Nancey Murphy and Arthur R. Peacocke (eds.), *Chaos and Complexity: Scientific Perspectives on Divine Action*, Vatican City: Vatican Observatory / Berkeley: Center for Theology and the Natural Sciences, 243-252.
--- (1996a), "Chaos Theory and Divine Action", in: W. M. Richardson and W. J. Wildman (eds.), *Religion and Science: History, Method and Dialogue*, London: Routledge, 243-252.
--- (1996b), *Scientists as Theologians: A Comparison of the Writings of Ian Barbour, Arthur Peacocke and John Polkinghorne*, London: SPCK.
--- (1998), *Belief in God in an Age of Science*, New Haven / London: Yale University Press.
--- (2001), "Kenotic Creation and Divine Action", in: Polkinghorne (ed.), 90-106.

--- (2002), *The God of Hope and the End of the World*, London: SPCK.
--- (2007), *From Physicist to Priest: An Autobiography*, London: SPCK.
--- (2008), *Theology in the Context of Science*, London: SPCK.
--- (2011), *Science and Religion in the Quest for Truth*, London: SPCK.
Polkinghorne, John (ed.) (2001), *The Work of Love: Creation as Kenosis*, London: SPCK / Grand Rapids: Eerdmans.
Rolston, Holmes, III (2006), *Science and Religion: A Critical Survey*, Philadelphia: Templeton Foundation Press.
Russell, Robert John (2008), *Cosmology: From Alpha to Omega*, Minneapolis: Fortress.
Russell, Robert John (ed.) (2004), *Fifty Years in Science and Religion: Ian G. Barbour and his Legacy*, Aldershot / Burlington: Ashgate.
Saunders, Nicholas (2002), *Divine Action and Modern Science*, Cambridge: Cambridge University Press.
Southgate, Christopher (2004), "Environmental Ethics and the Science-Religion Debate: A British Perspective on Barbour", in: Robert J. Russell (ed.), 239-248.
--- (2008), *The Groaning of Creation: God, Evolution and the Problem of Evil*, Louisville: Westminster John Knox.
--- (2011a) "Re-reading Genesis, John and Job: A Christian's Response to Darwinism", *Zygon: Journal of Religion and Science*, Vol. 46, 2, 370-395.
--- (2012), "Natural Theology and Ecology", in: Fraser Watts and Russell Re Manning (eds.), *The Oxford Handbook of Natural Theology*, Oxford: Oxford University Press (forthcoming).
Southgate, Christopher (ed.) (2011b), *God, Humanity and the Cosmos: A Textbook in Science and Religion* (third edition), London: T & T Clark / New York: Continuum.
Surin, Kenneth (1986), *Theology and the Problem of Evil*, Oxford: Blackwell.
Tanner, Kathryn (2000), "Eschatology without a Future?", in: John Polkinghorne and Michael Welker (eds.), *The End of the World and the Ends of God*, Harrisburg: Trinity Press International, 222-237.
--- (2007), "Eschatology and Ethics", in: G. Meilaender and W. Werpehowski (eds.), *The Oxford Companion to Theological Ethics*, Oxford: Oxford University Press, 41-56.
Tracy, Thomas F. (1995), "Particular Providence and the God of the Gaps", in: Robert J. Russell, Nancey Murphy and Arthur R. Peacocke (eds.), *Chaos and Complexity: Scientific Perspectives on Divine Action*, Vatican City: Vatican Observatory / Berkeley: Center for Theology and the Natural Sciences, 289-324.
Van Huyssteen, J. Wentzel (1998), *Duet or Duel? Theology and Science in a Postmodern World*, London: SCM.
Ward, Keith (1990), *Divine Action*, London: Collins.
--- (1996), *Religion and Creation*, Oxford: Clarendon.
--- (2008), *The Big Questions in Science and Religion*, Philadelphia: Templeton Foundation Press.
Wiles, Maurice (1986), *God's Action in the World: The Bampton Lectures for 1986*, London: SCM.
Wilkinson, David (2010), *Christian Eschatology and the Physical Universe*, London: T & T Clark / New York: Continuum.

Christopher Southgate

Pierre Teilhard de Chardin (1881-1955) – The Divine Milieu

> Evolution is a general condition to which all theories, all hypotheses, all systems must bow and which they must satisfy henceforward if they are to be thinkable and true. Evolution is a light illuminating all facts.[103]

Pierre Teilhard de Chardin, born within an aristocratic French family and the fourth of eleven children, lived his childhood within the Auvergne region of France. The land-

[103] Teilhard de Chardin (1959), 219.

scape, with its fertile basins, breath-taking mountain ranges and rocky craters, influenced the intellectual, psychic and spiritual inner landscape of Teilhard's world.

Teilhard was a quiet, exceptionally attentive, inquiring and sensitive youth. He observed in great detail the natural world, encouraged by his father's keen interest in the same. At a young age, Teilhard sought the nature and structures of realities that surrounded him, meaning that he scrutinised the stability of rocks, the power of fire, the decay of life and the change, impermanence and even fragility of life and the earth. This fuelled his desire to understand and to find what unifies, is essential and incorruptible in the structure and nature of reality.

A second influence was the Catholic intellectual, spiritual and pious aspects of Teilhard's formative years. Raised in a devout family and educated in Catholic institutions, Teilhard was steeped in a culture of spirituality, devotion and prayer. At the age of seventeen Teilhard entered the Jesuit novitiate and remained a Jesuit throughout his life as a priest, World War I stretcher-bearer, university lecturer, scientist and writer.

Teilhard's commitment to a religious life and to a scientific understanding of earth processes was nurtured within the Jesuit communities. He studied theology and geology and obtained a doctorate in palaeontology. Much of his professional life was as a research scientist. Teilhard was often involved in archaeological fieldwork and excavations – at times for years – where he unearthed and studied fossils, geological formations and early humans such as the Peking Man. At various times Teilhard lived in France, Egypt, England, China and the United States and travelled widely.

Before discussing theological details it is important to know that Teilhard"s life and thought are infused with strong emotions and experiences of familial love, friendships, suffering, joy and intense passions. He wrote extensively: research papers, books, letters, poems and prayers. Teilhard's deepest desire was to see and to make others see. His quest was to see the essence of things and to see the origins, goals and core of reality related to the most comprehensive horizon. Teilhard's sense that all dimensions of reality are interconnected and have a divine origin, centre and *telos* were only strengthened over his lifetime. His theological language is rich, expansive and full of unique expressions. He often used metaphors of sight, building, energy, fire, music, luminosity and the essence or heart of the matter.

Teilhard's journey to these insights is an adventure worth studying and is well documented in numerous biographies on his life and thought. Relevant influences included the notions of a "biosphere" from Eduard Suess and later enlarged by Vladimir Vernadsky, and a noosphere", also from Vernadsky, Henri Bergson's concept of creative evolution and élan vital, cosmogenesis coined by Helena Blavatsky, and the works of Charles Darwin and Maurice Blondel among others. Teilhard revised and integrated these together in an innovative and unprecedented manner. He also oriented them towards a comprehensive synthesis, not only of science and theology, but also of cosmic origins to the present – from the Alpha to the Omega point of all reality.

To understand anything about Teilhard's views of creation and salvation, one needs to grasp how deeply he immersed himself in evolutionary sciences. Evolution, for him, is not a speculative theory among other theories of creation, or a dialogue partner with theology, or something to be debated with the Bible as a different or parallel mode of revelation. Evolution is the primary context out of which everything, including theology, emerges and to which it needs to refer. Evolution is the process and dynamic of reality and of all dimensions of reality. This focus on a comprehensive context and developmental processes is later broadened to his notion of cosmogenesis, but it is initially rooted in his evolutionary expertise. Furthermore, science and theology address one phenomenon, for Teilhard, as there is a fundamental unity to reality. Reality is an integral psychic, spiritual and material phenomenon. Thus science and theology are not two knowledge systems about the same phenomenon. To understand anything about larger contexts and processes requires a comprehensive integration of science and theology. Therefore creation, revelation, salvation are processes, embedded and integrated into the evolutionary processes.

Against theological and ecclesial climates that emphasised a static cosmos as the background to the human drama, Teilhard knew that evolutionary processes governed the universe, the earth, the biosphere and human emergence and development. Theology needed to be unified with the new cosmology and evolutionary sciences. Religious experiences and knowledge, including theological doctrines, needed to be revised within an evolutionary framework. And theology needed to move beyond a predominantly moral sphere. These are some of the reasons why Teilhard is arduous to understand and became theologically controversial. It is also his genius and utterly unique contribution to 20th-century theology.

The Phenomenon of Man (1959; French original 1955) is Teilhard's most comprehensive and foundational treatise. Like much of Teilhard's works, it is scientific and spiritual, factual and interpretative, philosophical, theological and metaphysical, logical and visionary, and defying designation. For Teilhard, it was a scientific work about the human phenomenon, but, as he claimed, the whole phenomenon, from the beginning of the stuff of the universe to an ultimate destiny.

Teilhard distinguished what he called the "without" from the "within" of things. The without is the observable. This includes the structures and changes from the establishment and bonding arrangements of atomic structures to the formation of molecules and mega molecules out of which arose and evolved all matter. The starting point for understanding the without is the discernable atomic structures and behaviours. To understand in any depth the movement and activities of atoms and molecules there must be a commensurate and consistent theory of energy. Further, for Teilhard, we needed a theory that connects the structure and activity with the processes and purposes of the developmental transformations. Teilhard pondered these as a whole, meaning he would not separate anything from its structures, activities, developments and directionality. The inquiries into what, how, going where and why are fundamentally one question for Teilhard.

Teilhard studied bacteria cultures in the same manner, and then plants. He explained that for plants, the without and observable cannot explain the life dynamics of plants. With insects it is more difficult, with vertebrates futile, and then it breaks down completely with humans. As life evolved, the without of things – the observable – becomes increasingly incapable of explaining the behaviour, development, increasing complexity and evolutionary directionality. Some form of interiority, *élan vital*, *Geist*, spirit or *telos* is increasingly present, active, effective and indeed successful.

The within of things is a subtle, nuanced union of matter, energy, spirit and *telos* that unites the interior dynamics with the transformations to increasing levels of complexity. The within of things is manifested in the overall orientation of cosmic and evolutionary processes that compels atoms to transform to molecules … to form planets, earth, an atmosphere and biosphere, to life, consciousness and self-consciousness.

Teilhard used the term "consciousness" with many qualifications. Consciousness itself is differentiated and evolves from nascent traces to that of life and mind. Inert matter does not have consciousness per se, although through his lengthy discussions of the within of things, Teilhard maintained that something interior, not observable yet clearly present, moves the process of evolution. Overall, in *The Phenomenon of Man*, he wanted to write the natural history from the without and the within of things, which combined spirituality and science. Only in this manner could he later speak of creation being a "Divine Milieu".

There are laws, patterns and dynamics of plurality, and tangential, radial and unifying energies that govern matter, and these are relatively observable. From matter comes life, for Teilhard. Although this process is not observable, it is reasonable and consistent; that is, life emerged from the foundational atomic and molecular processes that formed matter. Matter and life are on a continuum, as are matter, energy, spirit and *telos*. Life, at any stage of complexity, was neither added in nor required a particular divine intervention. Life emerged from the within of things.

Yet, life assumes a pre-life. Atoms are the nascent – pre-life – form of life, as are molecules, mega-molecules, composite matter and so forth. Life comes from the within of things. And life, like matter, emerged and complexified in a development process. Life moved from micro-organisms to cellular revolution and then to the multifaceted emergence and evolution of an intricate biosphere, which cultivated consciousness because each development stage was extant in the previous one.

There is one more step in Teilhard's thought that is important to appreciate in his elegant blend of science and theology. Each stage of evolution is nascent in the previous, but not in a simple embryonic or potential form. There are critical changes that alter the very ontology of reality. For example, in the transformation from the atomic to the molecular structures, the new arrangements of the parts required the acquisition of another dimension – a further degree of interiority – that allowed reality to complexify and advance to another level. Every evolutionary development required a richer and intensified organised structure that corresponds to a richer and more concentrated interiority and consciousness. Scientifically, creation thickens, intensifies and crosses new ontological thresholds. Theologically, creation is revelatory of profound, expansive and manifested dimensions of divine activities.

Evolution is one event for Teilhard. He was interested in what he called the "grand orthogenesis" of everything – and that moves towards higher degrees of immanent spontaneity and consciousness. Teilhard's focus on the impetus and processes of life led him to formulate his thought within descriptions of genesis: cosmogenesis, geogenesis, biogenesis, anthropogenesis, psychogenesis. These are stages of development and spheres of reality, each more multidimensional and dense with interiority and consciousness, surpassing the previous. Teilhard is well known for his notion that with the arrival of humans and the emergence of self-consciousness, the earth has now created and is wrapped in a "noosphere": a realm of mind that envelops the biosphere.

This noosphere is a threshold of conscious reflection, activity and spiritual advancement that most interested Teilhard. This sphere represented a metamorphosis – a new threshold – and opened up genuinely new possibilities of reality on a cosmic scale. This realm of thought and mind allows for a personal and conscious appropriation of the depths and breadth of reality: this "Divine Milieu" in which we are all immersed and from which we come. It is the personal dimension of the universe rising up into human consciousness – "noogenesis". This noosphere is intensifying and is the evolutionary edge of the earth's and eventually the universe's activity.

These are difficult notions within Teilhard's work. He seems less focused on the lives of humans than he is on *homo sapiens*, a form of consciousness that emerged from within these evolutionary processes. It interested him greatly that the universe has become personalised in this evolutionary development. Impersonal matter has become intensified and personalised in a self-conscious subject. For Teilhard that meant that the universe is, and has always been, a deeply personal reality, animated by a personal, creative and loving energy. This is a classic form of panentheism: God within and beyond all reality.

For Teilhard, "creation" is a verb, as is "revelation" and "salvation". These are intertwined processes of increasing concentration and intensity, imbedded in evolutionary progressions of increasing complexity that thicken the nature of all reality. Once Teilhard established the mutually intertwined nature of matter, spirit, evolution, interiority, consciousness and a personal self-consciousness, he then addressed Christology. Teilhard had an understanding of Christology that is difficult to render clear. It is full of unique, poetic, prayerful and metaphoric language condensed from his ingenious, fluid and mystic depths. No current Christological theology is adequate for comparison, as they are too narrow, unsophisticated and intellectually ill-equipped to fathom Teilhard's meaning.

For Teilhard, as the universe evolves, the noosphere will become saturated with a personalised consciousness – which represents the personal dimensions of the divine. This is a form of a universalised Christ, or Christ-sphere of the universe. It will be most present at the Omega (or end – as completion and fulfilment) point. This is best understood as energy. This Christic dimension of reality is an intensified personal or subjective consciousness and is described as love. As love is always personal, the universe will be saturated with the presence of love – a Christic presence: a universe saturated with personal love, or Christogenesis. This is the ultimate creation, revelation and salvation. Teilhard wrote in *How I Believe* (1969):

> I believe that the Universe is an Evolution. I believe that Evolution proceeds towards Spirit. I believe that the Spirit is fully realized in a form of Personality. I believe that the supremely Personal is the Universal Christ.[104]

Conclusion

It is crucial to realise that Teilhard took a lifetime and dozens of publications to try to clarify his expansive scientific knowledge and comprehensive approach together with his mystic depth and spiritual perceptions. He took extraordinary pains to elucidate the

[104] See the preface of Teilhard de Chardin (1969a).

nuances. Yet many, including the ecclesial authorities, were unable to comprehend him. Few had anywhere near Teilhard's acumen, intellectual skills and piercing attentive spirit. They did not share his concerns and were not asking his questions. Theology was mostly addressing morality and had framed creation, revelation and redemption in response to sin. Most theologians were not preoccupied with cosmology or evolution or had a desire to grapple with the challenges facing theology from cosmic and evolutionary sciences. Many would say Teilhard was ahead of his time.

Teilhard used the best science of his day. His knowledge and intuitions about evolution have been corroborated with scientific concepts such as punctuated equilibrium, directional groping, the anthropic principle and the emergence of complexity consciousness. Current science is more advanced than what Teilhard understood, as it should be.

There are certainly theological critiques of Teilhard's work: his notion of evolutionary advancement, anthropocentrism, human progress and optimism, Christology and more. These are readily found. However, even among the critics, few have dared to walk the path he did, or understand what he was attempting to understand, let alone wrestle with his proposals. Yet, over the past few decades theology has begun a conversation in earnest with evolutionary sciences, and Teilhard's work is now of considerable interest. The rethinking of theology in light of cosmology and evolution is still in the early stages and is extremely challenging. While Teilhard's responses to these challenges may not hold, the contributions he offered, and offers, are breath-taking and still not fully grasped by most theologians.

Teilhard was one of the first scientists and still one of only a few theologians to realise that the human and the universe are part of one reality; immersed in the same process, the same creative energies, the same evolutionary dynamics and orientation. The immersion into the deep creative powers of the universe is the most direct contact a human can have with the divine, as suggests Thomas Berry, scholar of Teilhard and previous president of the American Teilhard Association from 1975 to 1987. It is to his contribution that we now turn.

References and Recommended Reading

Teilhard de Chardin, P. (1959), *The Phenomenon of Man*, New York: Harper.
--- (1960), *The Divine Milieu: An Essay on the Interior Life*, New York: Harper.
--- 1964), *The Future of Man*, New York: Harper and Row.
--- (1965a), *Building the Earth*, Wilkes-Barre: Dimension.
--- (1965b), *Hymn of the Universe*, New York: Harper and Row.
--- (1968), *Science and Christ*, London: Collins.
--- (1969a), *How I Believe*, New York: Harper and Row.
--- (1969b), *Human Energy*, London: Collins.
--- (1970a), *Activation of Energy*, London: Collins.
--- (1970b), *Let Me Explain*, London: Collins.
--- (1971), *Christianity and Evolution*, New York: Harcourt Brace Jovanovich.
--- (1974), *On Suffering*, New York: Harper and Row.
--- (1975), *Toward the Future*, London: Collins.
--- (1979), *The Heart of Matter*, New York: Harcourt Brace Jovanovich.
--- (1980), *Early Man in China*, New York: AMS Press.

Heather Eaton

Thomas Berry (1914-2009) – The Universe Story

Thomas Berry, born William Nathan, was the third of thirteen children in a prominent Catholic family from the Appalachians and later Greensboro, North Carolina. Raised in a vibrant and well-educated family, Berry was a pensive, introspective and intellectually gifted child. Berry often described himself as a brooder, saying that there are two ideal locations for those who brood: prisons or monasteries. He chose the latter. He entered the Passionist Order at the age of 20 and was ordained at 28, when he took the name Thomas after Thomas Aquinas.

Berry's early formation was deeply Catholic, meaning that he was immersed in the vast intellectual themes of classical theology, as well as having an intimate knowledge of the tomes of Thomas Aquinas and later Pierre Teilhard de Chardin. During these years he also studied European intellectual and cultural history, as well as being attentive to interiority and spiritual practices. He completed a Ph.D. at the Catholic University of America with a focus on Giambattista Vico's philosophy of history. He lived in China in 1948 during the rise of Mao Zedong and keenly observed the mechanisms of the vast cultural shifts taking place.

Berry was a remarkably educated person and a product of the intellectual climate. From Western thinkers, he was influenced by Pierre Teilhard de Chardin, Rudolf Otto, Mircea Eliade and Christopher Dawson, as well as by the discussions of religion by Clifford Geertz, Wilfred Cantwell Smith, Paul Tillich and Emile Durkheim. From Eastern thought, the works of Aurobindo Ghose and Mohammed Iqbal, among others, were persuasive. He learned Latin, Italian, Spanish, German, Chinese and Sanskrit. Berry was known as a Christian thinker and a scholar of the two centres of Asian cultures, India and China, knowledgeable of Hindu, Buddhist, Confucian, Daoist and Zen traditions. Berry studied and collaborated with several indigenous peoples in North America and with the T'boli tribal peoples of the Philippines.

Berry became a cultural historian of religions, with facets of phenomenology and anthropology of religions. But these categories do not encompass his expertise. Further, over his lifetime Berry acquired extensive knowledge of politics, economics, natural sciences and cosmology. He wrote countless essays on a vast array of topics, which became "The Riverdale Papers", and published a dozen books, including early works on Asian religions, namely *Buddhism* (1968) and *Religions of India* (1972), and well-known publications such as *The Dream of the Earth* (1988), *The Great Work* (2000) and *The Sacred Universe* (2009). Between 1970 and 1995 he founded and directed the Riverdale Center of Religious Research. He developed and chaired the history of religions programme at Fordham University (1966-1979) and from 1975 to 1987 he was president of the American Teilhard Association.

The richness and genius of Berry's thought are not rendered immediately evident in his published works. The breadth and depth of his comprehension of numerous fields of knowledge are astounding. His appreciation for many modes of knowing is characteristic of his thought and writings. Influenced by Vico, Carl Jung and others, Berry probed beneath a hyper-rationalised knowing to the realm of dreams, myths imagination, *poesis* and symbolic consciousness. He understood that this myth-making aspect of human functioning, which includes religious processes, is the most potent, creative, fertile and profound realm of human activity. It is through this capacity that humans not only make meaning, but also develop narratives saturated with symbols, values, ethics and priorities within which communities navigate all dimensions of existence.

What is important here is that the ecological crisis, in all its manifestations, came to dominate Berry's concerns. The latter part of his life, some thirty years, was dedicated to responding to the socio-ecological crisis. Berry is still one of a few who have grasped the magnitude of this crisis comprising the end of the Cenozoic era. To fathom the causes and to have any viable future, all aspects of human activities need to be addressed, at the point that is most profound.

For Berry, this point is the recognition that all human communities function within salvation narratives. Life itself has no meaning, no contours or parameters outside of a story. Further, this kind of story renders the account of how the world came to be and how we fit into the grand scheme of things. It provides, guides and shapes our personal and collective life purposes, actions and interactions, and it offers ethical orientations. Outside the story, there is no context in which human life can function in meaningful ways.

Berry perceived that the greatest need, in light of the ecological crisis, was to foster a sense of a new story, that of the universe and of earth, to allow for a macrophase period of cultural development. Humanity, especially Euro-Western societies, must end their assault on the biosphere, and to do so they need a new overall orientation: a new story. Over many decades, with intensive and extensive intellectual acumen, Berry began to put together his insights about a "new story" for the industrialised world – if humanity is to respond to the ecological devastation by taking over much of the biosphere and the planetary processes.

This "functional cosmology", as he called it, began its public journey with an essay entitled "The New Story" (1978) included in *The Dream of the Earth* (1988). This "story of the universe" is a proposal for religious, cultural and ecological recovery. Woven throughout, in an implicit form, are Berry's notions of creation and salvation. Four aspects of Berry's work will indicate the meaning he gave to these terms.

The first is that Berry developed a deep appreciation for the penetrating and specific experiences that gave rise to distinct religious insights and traditions. This includes those based on an awareness of divine being (Hinduism), of the changing and sorrowful nature of reality (Buddhism), of an all-embracing harmony in the cosmic and human orders (Confucianism), of dynamic forces immanent in the universe (Daoism) and of a divine presence within the history of the monotheistic traditions. Furthermore, although the originating experiences and subsequent interpretations are dissimilar, religions address experiences and themes within human existence such as trans-human awareness, revelations, salvation, sacrifice, rebirth, virtues, sacredness and rituals. Unlike for Mircea Eliade, for Berry these are descriptive not normative forms. They are neither within all religions, nor equivalent in content. Berry claimed: "Religion takes its origin here in the deep mysteries of what we see, hear, touch, taste and savor."[105] Religions provide the interpretative patterns to existence, in narrative form. They are creative in form and salvific in purpose.

Scattered throughout Berry's writings are references to "the human condition": the

[105] Berry (2009b), 147.

inner tensions and restlessness with which humanity must inevitably wrestle. Of these tensions the most prevalent are disquiet, sorrow and angst, and wonder, joy and celebration. These tensions vary according to the individual and specific cultural context, as well as to how they are conceptualised, symbolised, accepted or repulsed, resolved or transcended, and within what horizons of meaning or worldview. Religions, however, are central to dealing with such tensions.

The omnipresent existential restlessness is often interpreted as unacceptable. In an early essay Berry wrote: "Religion, as well as the entire spiritual, cultural, moral and intellectual life of man [*sic*] rests on a simple awareness that the human condition is an undesirable condition, that man [*sic*] must rebel against this condition."[106] Salvation is thus interpreted as deliverance from one's existential limits.

Familiar interpretations of Christian salvation would emphasise a deliverance of one kind or another: from error, from the detrimental aspects of decay, finitude, suffering or death, from various evils and from injustices. Yet none of these were central to Berry's thought. Although early in his work he discussed existential angst, he did not accentuate an escape from it, but rather an appreciation of the diverse ways religions sought to manage them creatively. Later he shifted his explanation of this restlessness to notions of inner spontaneities and creative dynamics. Salvation herein becomes an alignment with the larger contexts of creative dynamics within the evolutionary and cosmological processes. Berry overtly stressed that whatever salvation is or would be, it can only be rooted in the dynamics and developments of the cosmological and evolutionary processes. These are fundamentally creative, which means that salvation is an activity within creation, imbedded within the creative dynamics of reality. There is no salvation as a deliverance from the created and creative order or from the conditions of life as existential restlessness and death. This is not a moral (or any other) form of fatalism or despondency. Nor is it a lack of concern for injustices. Rather, it is that humans, in contemporary Euro-Western cultures in particular, seem incapable of thriving within the limits of life as given, and this is acutely problematic.

A second aspect is Berry's critiques of most contemporary Christian theology. For Berry, the cultural repercussions of the Christian tradition on Western civilisation(s) are pervasive, yet rarely acknowledged. Theology is inattentive to the dominant mode of Christian religious consciousness and the ensuing cultural practices, promises and consequences. The lack of knowledge about religions scandalised him. Theology has no adequate theory of religion or a suitable intellectual grasp on the experiential bases, symbolic and mythic nature and cultural scope of religion(s). Berry contested the shrinking horizons and narrow intellectual sources of existing Christian theologies. He critiqued the fixation on the normative meanings of doctrines, revelations and beliefs, which has led to a fundamentalism ubiquitous across Christian theologies. He confronted the persistent, yet intellectually feeble, promise of a better world here or elsewhere. He lamented that the realms of the numinous, trans-rational, aesthetic, emotional or imaginative are suspect or too difficult to investigate. He found unacceptable the apologetic, defensive or insular stance most Christian traditions take in the face of the massive social and global upheavals of the present. Berry was exasperated by the inability of Christian traditions to address the ecological crisis in any satis-

[106] Berry, "The Christian Process", in "The Riverdale Papers", Vol. 7 (unpublished).

factory manner. He saw this as a consequence of theology's neglect of contemporary sciences and ecological decline correlated with ideas that salvation is either an escape from this world / the earth or limited to morality.

These critiques are double edged, because within Euro-Western Christian cultural processes there is a type of religious consciousness, interiority and psychic orientation that limits the capacity to respond to the current situation. And Christian theology is barricaded from realising this in any depth. The problem is not "Christianity", but that the Christian processes and promises permeate the psychic orientation and cultural expectations. As Euro-Western Christianity ebbs from cultural power, the commitments to a different, better world do not diminish. For Berry, Euro-Western civilisation has fostered a refusal to accept the conditions and limits of life, and thus is blind to seeing the detrimental effects of its praxis to "improve the world". Most of Christian theology is submerged in the same waters.

A third aspect is that for Berry the world's religions, as they are functioning contextually and intellectually, are not capable of dealing with the ecological crisis in the larger biological, narrative and spiritual dimensions. The established religions themselves are at the end of their mandate and have realised most of their potential in their current orientations. Moreover, some religions are either embedded in the expanding socio-ecological problems or have causal connections. In *The Dream of the Earth* he wrote, "... any effective response to these issues requires a religious context. ... We cannot do without the traditional religions, but they cannot presently do what needs to be done. We need a new type of religious orientation."[107]

Berry, similar to Teilhard de Chardin, considered the discoveries of cosmological and evolutionary sciences to be of the order of a revelatory experience. Berry immersed himself in these sciences. He studied carefully what can be known of the processes and dynamics of the macro-dimensions out of which the human species emerged. For Berry, whatever capacities developed within the human, or within any species, they must first be a capacity of the universe and earth. Thus any religious or spiritual tradition or sensibility reflects a pre-existent aspect of the realities out of which the human species arose. Thus spirituality, and religious consciousness, is foremost a dimension of the universe, developed within the earth's evolutionary processes.

It was the macro-phase parameters of reality – insofar as humans can know them – that became paramount, and for Berry, infinitely practical. The universe, from the big bang to the present, is the ultimate reference point that will guide us through this era. The universe is the text without a context, as he would claim. Everything else is universe referenced. He would often assert that the universe is the primary reference, primary sacred community and primary bearer of revelation. Human life, in all its complexity and diversity, is best understood in continuity with the processes and dynamics of the universe and within the evolutionary activities of the earth. Religions need to situate and reinterpret themselves within this larger context or reference point.

The fourth aspect is to what degree Berry appreciated the sacred dimension of the universe. Perhaps as a Catholic, a Thomistic and Teilhardian scholar, he had an appreciation of sacramentality related to the universe. Yet is was from science that Berry

[107] Berry (1988), 87.

perceived the astounding creativity of the universe – that something so extraordinary, complex, with sequences of transformations, intricacies and interrelatedness, and so much more could emerge (i.e. cosmogenesis) was incredible. This was revelatory beyond anything else throughout all of time, because it was being revealed to a consciousness that emerged from within. Berry described humans as the universe reflecting on itself, or the self-consciousness of the universe. No humans had ever known this with such assurance. The universe, meaning all aspects of reality as far as we can know them, was not only being understood with greater clarity. It is that everything is so much *more* than ever assumed or imagined previously. And this new knowledge changes everything. To understand anything, we need to consider the universe to be the primary point of reference. To understand anything about humans we need to consider the earth as primary and humans as secondary. The reference points for understanding ourselves, our role within the scheme of things, and the parameters and dynamics of the scheme of things, all change with this new knowledge. Our reference points, including those for religion, are too small. Berry maintained that we need to situate religious consciousness within the processes of the universe and earth, not the reverse.

In many respects Berry agreed with Thomas Aquinas in that errors of reasoning about the natural world led directly to errors concerning the divine world. Both sought a synthesis between faith and reason, religion and science, and modes of knowing and reality. Berry also followed Teilhard de Chardin's work that tried to shift the central focus of Western Christian theology from redemption to creation. For all three, creation meant knowing the relevant sciences. Berry did not share with Teilhard the supremacy of humanity, the sacrifice of the biosphere for human advancement or the principal interpretation of the cosmological realm as Christian symbolism. Further, Berry was interested in the integral functioning and creativity of the universe and earth as a whole process, more so than in the overall destiny.

For Berry, the creative and salvific activities are intertwined, enmeshed and embedded in the atomic, molecular and biotic forms, with a further entanglement among the material, psychic and spiritual dynamisms. Also, they are processes and are ongoing. Thus, as the earth's creativity diminishes, so does any relevant meaning of salvation. It is the earth, in all its complexity, majesty, diversity and exigencies that educates and orients the spiritual sensitivities of the human species. It is too simple to say that the thriving of the earth, in its integrity and creativity, is salvation, but it is not overall incorrect.

By the end of Berry's life he focused on the power of creativity, wonder and awe as the most potent aspects of the human psyche and spirit. For him these are primarily an activity of the universe and secondarily a human activity. Once this is grasped in depth, a portion of the immense powers of creation and salvation within the universe and earth dynamics are made available to the human realm.

References and Recommended Reading

Berry, Thomas (1967), *Buddhism*, New York: Hawthorn. Also published (1989) by New York: Columbia University Press.

--- (1972), *Religions of India*, New York: Bruce-Macmillan, 1971. Also published (1992) by New York: Columbia University Press.

--- (1978), "The New Story", *Teilhard Studies, Volume 1* (published by the American Teilhard Association), Chambersburg: Anima.
--- (1982), "Teilhard in the Ecological Age", *Teilhard Studies, Volume 7* (published by the American Teilhard Association), Chambersburg: Anima.
--- (1988), *The Dream of the Earth*, San Francisco: Sierra Club Books.
--- (2000), *The Great Work: Our Way Into the Future*, New York: Harmony / Bell Tower.
--- (2006), *Evening Thoughts: Reflecting on Earth as Sacred Community* (edited by Mary Evelyn Tucker), San Francisco: Sierra Club Books / Berkeley: The University of California Press.
--- (2009a), *The Christian Future and the Fate of Earth* (edited by Mary Evelyn Tucker and John Grim), Maryknoll: Orbis.
--- (2009b), *The Sacred Universe: Earth, Spirituality, and Religion in the 21st Century* (edited with a foreword by Mary Evelyn Tucker), New York: Columbia University Press.

Heather Eaton

Anne Primavesi (1934-) – The Gift of Gaia

Anne Primavesi hails from Ireland. She received her Ph.D. in systematic theology from the University of London and lived most of her professional life in England. She has been a Research Fellow at the Centre for Interdisciplinary Study of Religion at Birkbeck College, the Westar Institute, and in Environmental Theology at the University of Bristol, as well as teaching and presenting in numerous institutions around the English-speaking world.

Primavesi has published several significant books and dozens of articles probing into what the Gaia theory brings to theology in light of the current ecological challenges. Each book builds on the previous one, expanding the initial creative amalgam not only of theology and science but that of evolution and ecological theology.

None of her work deals directly, or even indirectly, with creation and salvation. Occasionally, Primavesi will critique narrow understandings of either, but her work has not been focused specifically on these topics. Her emphasis has been on the necessity to situate theology within an evolutionary paradigm, but not in a one-dimensional manner. Her purpose is to reinterpret and enliven theology to be intellectually relevant, spiritually insightful and culturally resourceful in the contemporary era. This means scientifically literate, justice oriented, in dialogue with a host of "others" and concerned about the health and future of the earth's life communities.

Although intellectually rigorous, Primavesi explores rather than systematises her themes. She blends different disciplines and methods: historical research, classical and contemporary theologies, earth sciences deliberated with analysis and critique, systematic de- or reconstructions, lamentation, poetry and prayer. She draws upon dozens of thinkers, writers and poets per book. She manoeuvres her topics with a kind of *poesis* that opens up imaginative and creative spaces. This does not lend itself to a methodical analysis of her work. In terms of style, any contribution she makes is from a fluid exchange of linguistic, poetic, intellectual, creative and imaginative expressions. Everything has multiple meanings. However, it may be accurate to say that Primavesi's work is about retrieving, reclaiming and reconstructing theology in such a way that it can be a creative and salvific force in the Western world. Salvific in this sense means to support the flourishing of the biosphere. As Primavesi deals with a different aspect in every book, the best way to appreciate her contributions is to address each in turn. In this manner the various themes and insights will be recognised.

Primavesi came on to the theological scene with an incisive critique of Christian patriarchy and hierarchy in *From Apocalypse to Genesis: Ecology, Feminism and Christianity* (1991). She offers an in-depth ecofeminist argument, with ecofeminism defined in general terms as the study of and resistance to the associated exploitation and subjugation of women and the natural world. It is evident that Primavesi is someone who is deeply distressed by the oppression of women, ecological crises, militarism and the global patterns of social injustice, and she hears the urgency of the cries. Most responding to this confluence of issues turn to social and political sciences to advance a form of liberation theology. Primavesi uses an involved set of tools and themes, with an intricate combination of ecological sciences, feminist systematic theology and historical and biblical scholarship.

One theme throughout is that together patriarchy and hierarchy have caused layers of distortions of thought and action. The core argument is that the connections between overemphasis on human salvation from sin, the destructive effects of Western cultures on the natural world, and the subordination of women have shaped much the cultural norms and practices. Within this argument is the topic of the many forms of power: power over, power with and power from within. Primavesi confronts the destructive forms of power over that have dominated Christian theological interpretations and influenced ecclesial and cultural practices. There is a subtle relationship between power from within, drawn from an ecological model of the world, and creation and salvation, although it is not explicitly developed. *From Apocalypse to Genesis* was a cutting-edge book at that time and indicated the detailed level of scholarship that is characteristic of Primavesi's writings.

Throughout her work, Primavesi searches the Christian tradition not only for the roots of alienation from women and the natural world, but also for new options. Her main interest is in the strands of the tradition that can offer fresh interpretative readings and possibilities that will allow for humanity to cultivate life-sustaining relationships with the larger earth communities.

From an ecological viewpoint, Primavesi is known for her long-standing engagement with James Lovelock and Lynn Margulis's work on the Gaia theory. Although only briefly alluded to in *From Apocalypse to Genesis*, in all subsequent works Primavesi assumes the validity of an evolutionary, ecosystems or whole-earth approach. The earth is described as an innovative system of interacting living and non-living components: a symbio-genesis, understood from within a deep ecology paradigm.

Primavesi's next important contribution is that of *Sacred Gaia: Holistic Theology and Earth System Science* (2000). Here she lays down her theology and science foundation, from an evolutionary stance, taking considerable pains to expose features of evolutionary science which are then brought to bear on aspects of theology. One of the goals is to take seriously theology as an earth science. While she offers many meanings to this, one is to reconsider what is meant by God's relationship to the world. How this question is answered, in any era, permeates the underpinnings of all theological interpretations. What is ludicrous to Primavesi is that this relationship could be limited to some humans, or even just human history, within a fraction of evolutionary history.

Primavesi picks up again the problem with hierarchical thinking and structures, and indicates how these are restrictive both in theology and in a narrow comprehension of Darwin. She reinforces the Gaian and evolutionary insights of the profound interconnectedness among living entities, including humanity.

Perhaps one of the most salient and impressive aspects of this and subsequent works is the richness of the image "Sacred Gaia". Again, in her nuanced and detailed style, Primavesi stresses the connection, diversity and sacredness of all beings as discrete forms within an interconnected whole. Her emphasis is on the intricate unity of the whole; in other words, the interrelationality of diversity that combines to make other entities. This process is manifest from multicellular organisms to the planetary systems. Primavesi points out constantly the fallacy of separating out parts as if they function without other aspects of the whole. This is a form of conceptualising that she confronts with force.

Primavesi delves into the meaning of the sacred, historically and with various examples. She concludes that this word only yields its meaning at a symbolic level. As with all theological symbols, they are composites, or combinations of insights that remain ambivalent at the core. The sacred, for example, contains opposites and tensions, representing something enchanting and terrible, desirable and frightening, immanent and transcendent, and so on. For Primavesi, theology must root itself in a worldview of a sacred earth and its extraordinary processes in order to appreciate what she calls "discerning the gift". The richness of life, in its development and diversity, is always functioning as a gift. The gift of Gaia is an omnipresent reality, and Primavesi concludes her exploration with a profound linkage between gift and grace.

It is important to note that Primavesi is not aiming for any kind of orderly treatise or for a conceptual or abstract coherence as in previous formulations of systematic theology. She sees that the natural sciences are rendering an understanding of the world that is so different from the presuppositions entrenched within theology that one must start with the natural sciences. Theology is a second step. Theology needs to attend to the world as science is discovering it and not make anything smaller in order to fit within narrow theological assumptions. For Primavesi, we cannot make the world, or God, smaller than the whole within which we exist, and this whole can only be glimpsed with awe.

With *Gaia's Gift: Earth, Ourselves and God After Copernicus* (2003), Primavesi continues her exploration of theology as an earth science and strengthens her argument for a revolution in theology. She restates the need to understand the earth as a system and a whole, noting various interpretations of the earth, such as human entitlement, homocentrism, heliocentrism and a multitude of issues that swirl around epistemology.

Primavesi's main interest is shedding light on the Copernican revolution. Several chapters are devoted to Copernicus, the debates and issues with Galileo, Kepler and others, and the discoveries that the earth is not the centre of the universe. She describes in depth this historical moment and reveals the story of the shift from an earth-centred to a heliocentric worldview. Not only are the facts presented, they are discussed using a variety of postmodern epistemological and critical theories. This allows one to comprehend a blend of what occurred, the parameters of interpretation, the reference points and the underlying worldviews.

Primavesi starkly presents the androcentrism and anthropocentrism and, indeed, arogance embedded in most Western thought systems. She exposes the extreme difficulty that science and theology have in recognising these homocentric patterns of perception. Theology is saturated with human-centred reference points. Throughout the book, Primavesi reveals the reference points hidden within both scientific and religious theories about the world. The third insight is that once one steps outside these traditional theological paradigms, it is plainly obvious that God is fashioned in the image of a rational, linear and conceptual human consciousness. From here Primavesi draws from the wells of earth sciences to reveal the existential themes of interrelationality, interdependence and diversity that are the earth's processes. She shows in poetry and prose the unique and awesome gift-exchange that is endemic to the earth-life systems to which we belong. It is the existential reality of Gaia's gift of life that should, and could, orient theology to see a sacred dimension hidden within these processes: a Sacred Gaia.

The theological ramifications are daunting and pointed to frequently. Primavesi is working out some of the details of doing theology from the earth sciences. This orientation has little in common with conventional theology or even ecotheology, or other discourses on religion and science. One can sense similarities with Pierre Teilhard de Chardin and Thomas Berry in the overall orientation. Yet theirs were more of a comprehensive proposal, whereas Primavesi's work is akin to historical excavation and the explorations of possibilities.

Gaia's Gift, also using philosophy, science and theology, is primarily based in the existential reality of evolution and the complexity of Gaia. If we want to grasp what a revolution of reference points means, this is where we must begin. And that is why the Copernican revolution matters; because Primavesi asserts that we need to do it again, and on a much larger scale. We are not the centre of the universe, nor is the earth in our solar system, and nor are we on this planet. This radical shift of reference point is decisive if we want to address the urgent problems now facing life on earth.

In 2004 the book *Making God Laugh: Human Arrogance and Ecological Humility* appeared and continued the same trajectory, although with distinct emphases. Overall, Primavesi challenges the claim that we can know what God knows or that we can know God's plans for us and for the world. Such arrogance must surely make God laugh! Primavesi shows how this thinking is erroneous and further that the consequences are immeasurably destructive.

Through multiple avenues Primavesi shows how Christians have assumed their centrality to all things and that this is connected to, even legitimised, the exploitation of the earth's communities of life. She suggests that it is time to replace human arrogance with ecological humility through a scientific understanding of ourselves as interdependent members of the whole earth community.

Primavesi has a brief yet explicit foray into views of salvation. Much of this is critique. She is especially interested in the image of God at the base of notions of salvation. God as ruler, judge or omnipotent is problematic. She wants to highlight an image of God who laid the foundations of the earth in geological (deep) time, brought forth living creatures – all of whom are blessed – who does not deal with us according to our sins and who does not have favourites. Salvation must be rethought in terms of well-being, wholeness and within what is known of evolutionary history. Primavesi argues eloquently for Christianity to evolve, mutate and adapt, as do genes. This she considers to be a shift from historical to ecological consciousness. Furthermore, Primavesi draws on biblical themes and historical Christian thinkers to support her claim. It is this unique blend that makes her insights evocative, provocative and compelling.

In *Gaia and Climate Change: A Theology of Gift Events* (2009), Primavesi pursues the same themes in the light of data on climate change and a more theological orientation. Sporadically, she uses the terms "salvation" and "creation". Most of this is an appeal for new ways of thinking, which she suggests is highly inconvenient for theologians. Primavesi is against what she calls the "time specific, separate and sectarian theological narratives of a personal salvation history".[108] Her goal is an ecocentric rather than an anthropocentric approach that will transform the utilitarian theological worldview into one concerned with the welfare of all beings and an attentiveness to their suffering. This means eradicating the violent images of God and opposing oppressive relationships and exploitative attitudes.

In terms of creation, Primavesi links the vitality and creativity of earth life directly with God's vitality. Because the earth possesses the capacity of beginning something new, this vitality and nascent potential between God and the earth is intertwined. Primavesi does not assume that any language is literal; she does not consider pantheism or panentheism. Creation is an event that recurs and releases God's vitality. Furthermore, creation occurs between earth and sky and keeps our attention fixed on what is available to the sense perceptions. In this book Primavesi deals with what she terms as "events", which are scientific, historical, within human perception and with various philosophical and epistemological categories. Most of these are "creation" events.

This book has deep theological undertones and overtures that take the themes of previous works such as those of power, gift, unconditional giving, non-possession, inter-rationality. While often drawn from science, she applies them to theological images of God, of Jesus, of divine presence.

Primavesi's most recent book is *Cultivating Unity within the Biodiversity of God* (2011). She builds on her previous distinction between Christendom and Christianity. The former is the hierarchical, patriarchal political-religious system of exploitation. The latter, Christianity, is always what can be imagined, inspired or envisaged in every age. In this book Primavesi deals specifically with texts, stories and interpretations of Jesus. She is seeking compatibility between an ecological consciousness, a just and peaceful world and a version of Christianity that connects these. The specific topics of creation and salvation are not developed but certainly implied.

Conclusion

Primavesi offers a very sophisticated rethinking of theology from an earth-centred, evolutionary stance. She exposes, explains and critiques the obstacles. She builds bridges with countless examples from history, science, theology, poetry, spirituality and art. One of which I am particularly fond is the bridge between the scientific existence of ecological niches and the epistemological preference for situated knowledge.

[108] Primavesi (2008), 15.

Primavesi desires a deeply intelligent, relevant and potent Christianity for the contemporary world; one that combines the best of scientific knowledge and which is responsive to the worst of human injustices, exploitation and ecological degradation. The terms "creation" and "salvation" appear rarely, and usually disparagingly. Yet the work of Primavesi yields an extraordinarily creative rethinking of theological foundations that potentially have salvific consequences: the thriving of earth communities.

References and Recommended Reading

Primavesi, Anne (1991), *From Apocalypse to Genesis: Ecology, Feminism and Christianity*, Tunbridge Wells: Burns and Oates.
--- (2000), *Sacred Gaia: Holistic Theology and Earth System Science*, London / New York: Routledge.
--- (2003), *Gaia's Gift: Earth, Ourselves, and God After Copernicus*, London / New York: Routledge.
--- (2004), *Making God Laugh: Human Arrogance and Ecological Humility*, Salem: Polebridge.
--- (2008), *Gaia and Climate Change: A Theology of Gift Events*, London / New York: Routledge.
--- (2011), *Cultivating Unity within the Biodiversity of God*, Salem: Polebridge.

Heather Eaton

Further Developments

Conversations between science and religion have been burgeoning over the past few decades, especially but not only, in an Anglo-Saxon context. This chapter has explored only a few of the strands that are relevant to a reflection on the relationship between creation and salvation from the various intersections of religion and science. Elsewhere in this volume the contributions of Lutheran scholars like Wolfhart Pannenberg and Niels-Hendrik Gregersen, of Catholic ecotheologians like Rosemary Radford Ruether and Ivone Gebara, and of process theologians like John Haught and Catherine Keller are specifically highlighted. The purpose of this concluding section is to comment on the ways in which such insights have been made relevant in the context of ecotheology.

The significance of the exchanges between science and theology for Christian ecotheology has been recognised, albeit in distinct ways. Typically the distinctions reflect the different approaches, models and typologies employed to relate science with theology. Such differences are central to understanding both the variety of conversations between theology and science, and why only a small part of this exchange is pertinent to ecotheology. For example, in some discussions the predominant rubric is a dialectic between faith and reason. For others the quest is for a compatibility with or coherence between science and theology pertaining to epistemology, horizons of meaning, driving questions, kinds of data and so forth. Some defend or reject the plausibility of theological assertions in the light of contemporary science. Others offer a theological reinterpretation of scientific data (following the example of Pierre Teilhard de Chardin). Many discern an ecological or spiritual vision, a life-affirming narrative or a moral tone in the work of Thomas Berry. Others merely use scientific data to offer ethical and theological perspectives on particular ecological concerns (such as climate change, access to potable water, biodiversity and biotechnology).

In the realm of ecotheology, there is a plethora of exchanges between theology and science – too many to indicate here. It is important, in all cases, to discern the driving or leading questions. In simple terms, for some the primary interest, and ultimate priority, is theological: finding resources within the texts and traditions, suggesting foundational meanings of doctrines and dogmas, expanding metaphors, exploring new imagery or rituals, or generating ecclesial statements – all using various blends of science and theology. For others, the primary emphasis is a broad or particular focus with respect to the ecological crises, often based within an ecological worldview, because their priority is to address ecological ruin. The interaction with the theological tradition may then be less doctrinal and more thematic, invoking the prophetic, wisdom, liberation, creation, justice, spirituality, vision, religious imagination and inspiration.

The differences in leading questions may explain why some classical topics appear in certain streams of ecotheology, such as Christology, redemption, the Trinity, resurrection, sin or even God, while in others, topics such as the Spirit, creation, the sacred / holy and cosmic or earth teleology have prominence. There can be tensions between a fidelity to theological claims – beliefs, truths, revelation, Scriptural authority – and an ecological worldview based on evolution, earth or nature-based "revelations" or spiritualities. Although these distinctions are exceedingly simplistic, they point to genuine differences in questions, assumptions, methods, content and conclusions that are worth considering.

Below is a sketch of various contributions where discourse on science and theology have been related to ecological concerns explicitly (whether in connection with reflection on creation and salvation or not), without seeking to systematise such contributions or to offer a comprehensive survey.

In most of his contributions, Denis Edwards sketches insights emerging from contemporary science in order to explore the plausibility of Christian views of God's action in the world. This is the case in his recent *How God Acts: Creation, Redemption, and Special Divine Action* (Minneapolis: Fortress, 2010). He usually highlights the ecological significance of a Christian understanding of the world, for example in *Ecology at the Heart of Faith* (Maryknoll: Orbis, 2006).

The topic of theodicy in terms of divine, natural, planetary, human and animal suffering is widely discussed. Several scholars have extended contemporary debates on the theodicy problem that focus on the issue of natural suffering towards ecological concerns on the "groaning of creation". Authors contributing to this field include Christopher Southgate in *The Groaning of Creation: God, Evolution and the Problem of Evil* (Louisville: Westminster John Knox, 2008): David Bentley Hart, a Greek Orthodox patristic scholar, in *The Doors of the Sea: Where was God in the Tsunami?* (Grand Rapids: Eerdmans, 2005) and Lisa Sideris in *Environmental Ethics, Ecological Theology and Natural Selection* (New York: Columbia University Press, 2003).

Those inspired by Teilhard's expansive proposals have taken it into many directions. The intersection between evolution and the emergence of spirituality is highly attractive to those concerned about religious responses to the ecological crisis. For example, in *Spirit of One Earth: Reflections on Teilhard De Chardin and Global Spirituality* (St Paul: Paragon House, 1998), Ursula King reflects on the new awareness of the oneness of the earth in an era of an emerging global civilisation. The volume *Teil-*

hard in the 21st Century: The Emerging Spirit of Earth edited by Arthur Fabel and Donald St. John (Maryknoll: Orbis, 2003) also indicates the versatility and the ecological significance of Teilhard's insights.

Thomas Berry's views on the ecological significance of the new understandings of the processes of the universe and of Earth have been the most fertile source for ecotheology, by far, as well as for the larger field of religion and ecology. Hundreds of books, articles, conferences, websites, educational programmes – in retreat centres, educational farms and even a monastery – have developed to grapple with his thought. Countless publications in ecotheology reference his work. This is not to say that all agree with his premises or conclusions. Rather, it is that either in whole or part, Berry's work is considered by many to be foundational to the field of ecotheology.

It is difficult to extrapolate the themes of creation and redemption from Berry's work in any conventional manner, since he redefines them and also the context out of which they should be interpreted. As much of theology is preoccupied with doctrine or social justice issues, it took time for Berry's work to be understood since it cannot be contained in these preoccupations. His notions of deep time, process, emergent complexity, earth dynamics and interrelatedness are only beginning to have an impact in theological circles. Berry offers a new sensibility to theology. He interprets a sacred or holy dimension within the dynamics and structures of the universe and the earth, which provide a context out of which to reflect theologically. He was very clear that he was not doing constructive theology, but that his work had theological implications.

Over time, influential theologians engaged with Berry, including liberation theologians such as Charles Birch, Leonardo Boff and Ivone Gebara; systematic theologians such as John Haught, Elizabeth Johnson, Jay McDaniel, Sallie McFague, Paul Santmire and Mark Wallace; ethicists such as John Cobb, Barbara Holmes and Larry Rasmussen, biblical scholars such as Norman Habel; feminists such as Heather Eaton, Ursula King and Rosemary Radford Ruether; and many more. These works may differ from Berry in some aspects, but they have interacted with central ideas or insights, and developed more so than critiqued them.

Berry's influence is also evident in hundreds of ecotheology authors working in popular media or publications, including Diarmuid Ó Murchú, Cletus Wessel, Michael Dowd, Miriam McGillis, to name a few. Again, this does not imply agreement with all aspects, but rather that Berry's work has significant impacts since it is wrestled with more than any other author's, at least in North Atlantic ecotheology. Berry is also the source of inspiration of much work in the Forum on Religion and Ecology, coordinated by Mary Evelyn Tucker and John Grim, both students of Berry's.[109]

A quite different take on the ecological significance of discourse on science and theology is found in the work of Celia Deane-Drummond. In her many contributions to environmental ethics she employs her background in the field of biology to address particular issues, for example in the field of biotechnology. See, for example, her *Creation through Wisdom: Theology and the New Biology* (Edinburgh: T & T Clark, 2000) and *The Ethics of Nature*. (Oxford: Blackwell, 2004). She has also widened such engagements to reflect on the significance of the scientific enterprise as such. In *Wis-*

[109] See <http://fore.research.yale.edu/>, retrieved 15 December 2012.

dom and Wonder: Conversations in Science, Spirituality, and Theology (Philadelphia: Templeton Foundation Press, 2006), she develops a theology of wisdom that is clearly geared towards ecological concerns.

Ernst M. Conradie and Heather Eaton

7. Process and Relational Theisms

Edited by John Culp

Introduction

Relational theisms emphasise the importance and mutuality of the relationship between God and the world and include both historical movements such as Arminianism and contemporary theologies such as process theology and open theology. Contemporary process theology in some ways resembles earlier thinkers such as Heraclitus and Hegel and has developed in a variety of ways since mid 20th century. However, process theology usually refers to the theological appropriation of the thought of Alfred North Whitehead (1861-1947) and Charles Hartshorne (1897-2000). The phrase "the openness of God" was first used by Richard Rice as the title of his 1980 book and was later used as the title of a 1994 book with essays by Rice, Clark Pinnock (1937-2010), William Hasker, David Basinger and John Sanders. Some open theists such as Gregory Boyd and Tom Oord have drawn on Hartshorne and Whitehead, while others such as Pinnock and Sanders primarily utilise biblical resources in developing the concept of God as mutually related to creation.

Process theology and open theism share a firm commitment to understanding the relationship between God and the world as a relationship of mutual influence. The importance of mutual relationship becomes clear in the divine activity of creating and redeeming. In both creation and salvation, divine activity occurs in relationship to the activity of created reality, especially human existence. Thus the world has value for God. At the same time the world does not exist without divine activity. Salvation involves a human response to divine action as well as the divine action providing for salvation. The crucial nature of created existence for God provides theological motivation for concern and action in relation to the environment. Process theology and open theism do differ in their understanding of the nature of divine action and the priority of divine nature in relation to divine will. Process theists understand divine action as always in conjunction with the action of non-divine actualities, while open theists hold that God's self-limitation makes room for non-divine action. Open theists hold that finally God can act independently of non-divine realities. Also, process theists give priority to God's divine nature as love over the divine will, while open theists hold that the divine will to love directs the expression of the divine nature.

The four thinkers considered in this section exemplify both the historical development of process and relational theisms' understandings of God's creative and saving activities and the range of options for understanding those doctrines in the context of the environment. John B. Cobb, Jr. initiated lengthy consideration of the environment in process theology. Cobb's emphasis upon event and relatedness leads to God working with and through creation both to create and to save. Salvation is necessary, owing both to the nature of reality, which requires loss in order to initiate novel actualities, and to the possibility of the rejection of divine possibilities for actualisation. John Haught's concern for the relationship between science and religion brings the Roman Catholic tradition to process theology. Drawing on Lonergan, Rahner and Teilhard de Chardin, Haught emphasises evolutionary development to an ultimate redemption that affirms both universal and personal fulfilment. Haught moves beyond Whitehead's identification of redemption with God's preservation of value that has been actualised to develop more fully the recognition of salvation as including personal meaning. Catherine Keller, a student of John Cobb's, pushes process theology to emphasise more thoroughly the importance of created existence for God by rejecting any apocalyptic conclusion to history. Creation occurs through God's luring of the deep into a new and developing order without any specific goal or conclusion. The complexity of creation due to the interrelatedness of the divine and the multiplicity of possibilities makes any final end impossible to imagine or hope for. Every possible outcome is present within the ongoing process of creation. Keller's rejection of the desire for an absolute power that determines the outcome leads to salvation as participation in creative activities responding to the universal presence of the divine Spirit. Although open theism agrees with process theism that the future is open for both God and created reality, open theism draws more directly from biblical resources and retains a stronger sense of the ultimate role of God. Only God can choose to take the risk of limiting God's actions to responding to the creation in a loving manner. However, God can and will intervene directly within the creation in order to bring about salvation.

The positions on creation from nothing and the ultimate redemption of reality illustrate the range of these essays. Keller undertakes to deconstruct the doctrine of creation from nothing. Creation is out of chaos. Cobb also rejects creation from nothing as implying too great a control by God over creation, a control that inconsistently limits the contribution that creation makes to God. Haught does not directly address the issue of creation from nothing, and open theism strongly affirms creation from nothing. In different ways, Haught and open theism describe a greater role for divine direction in the becoming creation although this control is not a control that unilaterally determines what will become. For Haught the fulfilment of creation draws current events into what they can most fully become. For open theism, divine interaction with creation is limited by God's decision rather than by the existence of chaos. The ultimate redemption of reality reflects a similar range of positions in relation to divine activity. Open theists tend to affirm a more definite end, ultimately brought about by divine action. Among open theists, Gregory Boyd anticipates a more traditional conclusion to history, while Sanders thinks the content of the eschaton is significantly undefined because it involves the actions of both God and the creatures.[1] Haught also affirms a definite conclusion or fulfilment to history although this fulfilment grows out of the present state of creation. Cobb affirms the importance of a source of hope for the future, but does not understand the future to be an already divinely established goal or outcome other than the actualisation of value as beauty. Keller goes even further in the indeterminacy and uncertainty of the future. Keller refuses to allow any determination of the nature of final redemption.

John Culp

---

1 John Sanders pointed out this distinction to me. See also Sanders *The God Who Risks: A Theology of Divine Providence* (Downers Grove: InterVarsity Press, 2007), 246.

John B. Cobb, Jr. (1925-) – The Relational Nature of Reality

Introduction

A Christian Natural Theology in 1965 established John B. Cobb, Jr. as a significant process theologian. In 1969, Cobb began working on responses to the impending ecological crises. In the 1980s, recognising the importance of economic theory for public policy about environment, Cobb began challenging dominant economic concepts. Cobb has continued developing theological resources that call Christians to act on behalf of the environment. His theological understanding of God's creating and saving activities is directly applied to ecological concerns. He utilises Alfred North Whitehead's philosophy to provide an understanding of Christian faith that values the biosphere and is consistent with the insights and resources of the Hebrew Bible, the New Testament and Christian theology.

Cobb's major publications dealing with theology and ecology develop his foundational process theology, his treatments of the doctrines of divine creating and saving, and his application of those resources to ecology. His early statement of process theology in *A Christian Natural Theology* was followed by the more specific *God and the World* (1969) and then by *Process Theology: An Introductory Exposition* (1976), written with David Ray Griffin, his student and colleague (all three published by Westminster, Philadelphia). Cobb treated the topics of creation and salvation in *Can Christ Become Good News Again?* (St Louis: Chalice, 1991) and *Grace and Responsibility* (Nashville: Abingdon, 1995), expressing a Wesleyan theological perspective. Cobb's first major publication dealing with ecology was *Is It Too Late? A Theology of Ecology* (Beverly Hills: Bruce, 1972). He then collaborated with Charles Birch on *The Liberation of Life: From the Cell to the Community* (Cambridge University Press, 1981) and with Herman Daly and his son Cliff Cobb on *For the Common Good: Redirecting the Economy Toward Community, the Environment, and a Sustainable Future* (Boston: Beacon, 1989). Continuing to advocate for Christian action on behalf of the environment, Cobb published *Sustainability: Economics, Ecology, and Justice* (Maryknoll: Orbis, 1992) and *Sustaining the Common Good: A Christian Perspective on the Global Economy* (Cleveland: Pilgrim, 1994). His most recent publication is an edited book with extensive interaction with the other contributors, *Back to Darwin: A Richer Account of Evolution* (Grand Rapids: Eerdmans, 2008).

Two Crucial Concepts

Two concepts provide the conceptual basis for Cobb's challenge to theological tendencies to ignore ecological concerns. The first concept identifies reality as composed of events. This challenges the traditional intuition that what is real is stable and unchanging. The doctrine of substance crystallised this way of thinking by holding that everything that exists does so as a specific manifestation of an underlying unchanging substance. Drawing on Whitehead's cosmology, Cobb describes an event as the result of the interaction between the influence of past events and possibilities. Relationships with past events in part compose the new event and are internal to the identity of the new event. Each event decides how to integrate past events into a unity that actualises one of the possible relationships to the past events. Understanding reality as based upon events has important implications for the nature of the world and how God acts in creating and saving the world. The identity and value of the world does not derive from a substantial basis that is unchanging. Change makes it possible for new realities to come into existence and no longer only indicates loss and destruction. Each new event possesses value that is unique to each actuality. This means that an event has value even if it is not a human event and even if it is not identical to God. The resulting diversity of value has both immediate and everlasting value to God. In God's continuing creating, God makes possible multiple values. Through God's saving grace, value is preserved.

The relational nature of reality provides the second foundational concept. Thinking of reality as events rather than substances implies the interconnected nature of reality. This relational nature of reality occurs at all levels of reality and in the relationship among those levels. At the individual level, every event exists in relation with all prior events and may be significantly shaped by those prior events. The whole of reality also exists as an interconnected system in which all of the parts depend upon each other either directly or indirectly. Affirming the relation between the whole and the individual does not reject the validity and importance of individual identity but does challenge thinking of a person as existing prior to relationships. Individual identity does not exist independently from relationships. Instead, the set of relationships that constitute an individual are unique. Additionally, God and the world are constituted by their relationships with each other. The interrelated events composing the complex unity of the world depend upon God's presentation of the possibility for transcending the determination of the past in order to come into existence. God receives from the world the actuality accomplished by events in the world. This relational worldview has significant implications for understanding God, human and natural existence and ecology. In a relational worldview, God is present in both the natural and the human realms, but is not the sole cause of what happens due to the influence of other events. The relational nature of reality also challenges the dualism of the natural and the human that has often led to ecological crisis. Further, a relational understanding shifts the focus from understanding bodies as machines to understanding bodies as communities of interrelated events. Thinking of bodies as communities supports the development of new events rather than seeking to control objects. Finally, a relational view opposes any separation between justice and ecology by overcoming both the modern separation between history and nature and the metaphysical separation of God from the world.

God's Creating and Saving Activities

Cobb's theology distinguishes God's creating action from God's saving actions although these two divine activities are closely related. God's creating initiates novel value through the presentation of possibilities that have not been actualised in the past. But this initiation does not determine the identity of the created reality, because the new actualisations of value also involve the decisions of the becoming events. God's dependence upon the decision of the new event appears to reduce the significance of God's creating activity. However, without God's presentation of possible new values, new events could do nothing more than repeat the past. Thus God's creative activity makes new events possible in a way that allows for the value of every form of existence. This understanding of God's creative action supports the value of the complexity of the biosphere that emerges through the process of evolution. Recognising the complexity and value of the evolutionary process again guards against limiting value to a specific species. The intrinsic value of all existence and especially life and its self-enjoyment in all forms affirms the goodness of creation. The goodness of creation comes from the interaction between God and creation rather than from God's arbitrary declaration that the creation has value. The goal of God's creative activity is a just, participatory and sustainable world in which the value of all creation is upheld. In this type of a world, humans play a vital role in the achievement of new values.

God's saving activity both preserves value that has been accomplished and redeems loss due to the rejection of possibilities. The completion of the creative unification of influences in an event results in the loss of the value of the immediacy of that event. God responds to the loss due to this perpetual perishing by retaining the intrinsic value of each event in God. This cosmic aspect of salvation retains the intrinsic value of each event instead of reducing the event's value to its usefulness for later events. Cosmic salvation provides a basis for other forms of hope for salvation by preserving actualised value. In addition to loss due to perpetual perishing, loss may also occur through the rejection of possibilities. The loss of a particular moment of joy due to the rejection of that possibility can never be replaced. Salvation as redemption brings forgiveness for decisions that destroy potential values. Forgiveness for rejection of possibilities brings healing and liberation. Accepting the divine saving action enables a sensitive responsiveness to new possibilities for responding to the ecological crisis. This responsiveness, however, must be more than mere hope. Hope in God enables people to participate in God's saving of individuals and the earth in spite of repeated failures to accept the possibilities for salvation of the earth that God has offered. Belief in the Spirit as the giver of life and love provides the ground for hope that makes it possible to do something about the disastrous situation the planet confronts. A Christian response to the ecological crisis requires belief in God as a basis for hope, acceptance of the call to sacrifice and freedom from traditional morality concerned only with self-expression and personal freedom.

While God's creating activity differs from God's saving activity, creating and saving interact in Cobb's theology. In creating, God acts in love to present novel possibilities that result in personal and specific values. God's saving activity provides for the preservation of those values from loss, through the occurrence of new values or the rejection of possible actualisations. God's creating and saving activities can also be distinguished in terms of types of priority. God's creative activity takes temporal and ontological priority by making value actual. But God's saving activity takes theological priority because of the divine relationship to created reality that seeks the fulfilment of creative activity. Although such distinctions avoid confusing or collapsing God's activities, the interaction between God's creating and saving indicates mutual dependence. Without God's creative action there could be no preservation. But without God's saving action actuality would have no lasting value. God's creating and saving activities are similar in that each involves both divine and created activity. Both human and non-human creation plays a part in the created activity by cooperating with divine activity. This interrelationship of God and the world avoids an overemphasis upon divine sovereignty that would make salvation simply a continuation of divine power in creation. God's saving activity preserves the cooperative creation of value and demonstrates the importance of human action in relation to God's creation.

Application Seeking Sustainability

Cobb has utilised his basic understanding of reality and God's creating and saving action to address responsibility for the environment, the welfare of animals and economic theories that hinder care for the environment. Salvation for the environment should be a central element of every theology of salvation rather than an occasional concern due to a particular crisis. God's creating and saving activity applies to the earth as well as its human inhabitants. Concern for the environment begins by overcoming the series of dualisms that characterise much of contemporary thought and deny the significance of the environment for theology. The dualisms between God and the world, between the human and the non-human and between nature and history have contributed to the neglect of nature and the growing ecological crisis. Further, diversity must be recognised as possessing both immediate and everlasting value to God because of the intrinsic value of all existence. Affirming the value of specific creatures and the value of the whole brings an awareness of the community of the biosphere. The awareness of community leads to accepting the obligation to be creative and thus to contribute to the community, which includes God. Supporting the existence of different types of realities – rather than controlling all other realities – acknowledges and contributes to the preservation of accomplished values and opens possibilities for new values. A sensitive response to new possibilities and the needs of the present can contribute to the well-being of the environment through human cooperation with divine action. Cobb's concern for the environment leads him to call for care for animals as part of the environment. He argues for considering animals as having more than instrumental value. The intrinsic value of animal experience finds support in biblical materials and foundational Christian doctrines. God's creating and saving all of reality means God values the experience of animals. However, the value of animal experience is not identical to the value of human experience. While deep ecology may affirm the equality of all values, Cobb holds a deep ecology that recognises a hierarchy of value. Rather than either a dualism of intrinsic and instrumental value or a monism of equality of value, different types of existence make different types of contributions to others, the whole and to God. Seeking changes that care for the environment and respect for the value of animal experience led Cobb to address the economic structures in contemporary culture. The emphasis on the individual in economic theory has led to the loss of cultural and biological diversity, of community and of the richness of the natural environment, because of a primary concern with economic growth. Cobb does not deny the importance of the individual to the global economy but calls for recognition of the value of both the specific and the whole. Also, Christians are called to worship God not wealth. God's care for the earth calls for placing the long-term well-being of the earth above individual enrichment. Sustainability becomes the goal rather than enrichment.

Conclusion

Cobb challenges Christians to accept their responsibility for all of reality. His theology of God's creating and saving activity affirms that new values would not be possible without divine creative activity, that God preserves all value and that humans are responsible for responding to God's activities of creating and saving.

References and Recommended Reading

Cobb, John B. Jr. (1970), "The Meaning of Salvation", *Mid-Stream*, Vol. 9, 4, 127-163.
--- (1971), "Christian Theism and the Ecological Crisis", *Religious Education*, Vol. 66, 1, 31-35.
--- (1980), "Process Theology and Environmental Issues", *The Journal of Religion*, Vol. 60, 4, 440-458.
--- (1984), "Process Theology and an Ecological Model", in: Philip N. Joranson and Ken Butigan (eds.), *Cry of the Environment: Rebuilding the Christian Creation Tradition*, Santa Fe: Bear and Company, 329-336.
--- (1987), "The Resurrection of the Soul", *Harvard Theological Review*, Vol. 80, 2, 213-227.
--- (1988a), "Ecology, Science, and Religion: Toward a Postmodern Worldview", in: David Ray Griffin (ed.), *The Reenchantment of Science: Postmodern Proposals*, Albany: State University of New York Press, 99-113.
--- (1988b), "Befriending an Amoral Nature", *Zygon: Journal of Religion and Science*, Vol. 23, 4, 431-436.
--- (1992), "Postmodern Christianity in Quest of Eco-Justice", in: Dieter T. Hessel (ed.), *After Nature's Revolt: Eco-Justice and Theology*, Philadelphia: Fortress, 21-39.

John Culp

John Haught (1942-) – Unfolding God's Gift

Introduction

John F. Haught received his Ph.D. in Theology from the Catholic University of America in 1970. He taught at Georgetown University from 1970-2005 as a professor specialising in systematic theology. His theology focuses on questions regarding cosmology, biological evolution, cosmic purpose, ecology and the relationship between science and religion. He has gained particular notoriety for his work dealing with the relationship between theology and evolutionary biology. In 2005, Haught was called as an expert witness arguing against the inclusion of Intelligent Design in high school biology textbooks by the Dover Area School District in Pennsylvania. While the majority of Haught's writing, teaching and lecturing has produced a theology that takes biological and cosmic evolution seriously, his first published book *Religion and Self-Acceptance* (1976) focused on the epistemology of Bernard Lonergan. Haught continues to draw upon Lonerganian notions in dealing with the scientific enterprise. To be sure, Haught's work draws upon Whitehead and process thought, but his use of Lonergan, Rahner and to a lesser extent Teilhard highlights both his Roman Catholicism and the fact that Haught is not a doctrinaire process theologian. Haught's theology of nature is enriched by process thought as well as by the work of theologians and philosophers such as Lonergan, Rahner, Michael Polanyi, Hans Jonas and Paul Tillich. In this sense, Haught's work invites one to consider the future of process thought.

Most of Haught's corpus deals with questions closely linked to creation and salvation. *Nature and Purpose* (1980) introduced many of the key themes found in his later works. *The Cosmic Adventure: Science, Religion and the Quest for Purpose* (1984) expanded upon these themes and, along with *God after Darwin* (2000), represents one of the most complete surveys of Haught's thought. *The Promise of Nature: Ecology and Cosmic Purpose* (1993) widens Haught's cosmology by considering ecological questions. *Christianity and Science: Toward a Theology of Nature* (2007) expresses

Haught's views on creation, the presence of mind in the universe, and resurrection. Haught's many works directly dealing with evolutionary biology include *God after Darwin: A Theology of Evolution* (2000), *Responses to 101 Questions on God and Evolution* (2001), *Deeper than Darwin: The Prospect for Religion in the Age of Evolution* (2003) and *Making Sense of Evolution: Darwin, God and the Drama of Life* (2010). Each book presents a narrative reading of cosmic history that takes scientific data seriously while offering an optimistic view of the ultimate future of the universe. Notably, *Deeper than Darwin* contends that the cosmos is open to multiple levels of non-competing explanations. Finally, *Is Nature Enough? Meaning and Truth in the Age of Science* (2006) and *God and the New Atheism: A Critical Response to Dawkins, Harris and Hitchens* (2008) argue against the explanatory hegemony of rigid naturalism and materialistic reductionism. This push by Haught helps make space for theologians to discuss topics such as creation and salvation in wider circles.

Relationship of Creation to Salvation

Haught has engaged the questions of creation and salvation with great frequency and care. He portrays creation and salvation as deeply related. God creates by unfolding God's gift aimed toward manifesting beauty by harmonising contrasts. God's redeeming action graciously offers an absolute future to creation. Haught argues that evolution demands that we view divine action not as pushing creation forward from the past *a retro*, but as God "drawing the world from up ahead (ab ante) toward the future".[2] In two of his major works, Haught uses the following quote from Teilhard when discussing creation to illustrate this point, "The fact is that creation has never stopped. The creative act is one huge continual gesture, drawn out over the totality of time. It is still going on; and incessantly even if imperceptibly, the world is constantly emerging a little farther above nothingness."[3] Whitehead's notion of objective immortality makes creation and salvation intimately related for Haught. He sees the novel events of an adventurous cosmos responding to God's luring call toward beauty also being simultaneously taken into God's memory. Haught's theology goes so far as to argue that creation and salvation are distinguishable but not separable from one another.

Creation

For Haught, creation is pregnant with promise and part of the work of salvation is God luring creation toward the fulfilment of this promise. Haught's image of God luring or attracting the cosmos toward greater beauty, freedom and consciousness is important, as it is linked with his deep commitment to the idea that God allows for the universe to "be itself" by non-coercively attracting it to something greater than nothingness. This kenotic or self-emptying gift of letting the universe have its own identity allows for the cosmos to be distinct from God and prevents creation from being a mere puppet.[4] For Haught, God being distinct from creation does not entail God being inert, impersonal or absent. Haught explains that hope in the future tends to impact events in the present. Therefore, God's gift of an unfinished universe exerts persuasive influence on the

---

2 Haught (2000), 81.

3 Haught (1995), 117 and Haught (2000), 37.

4 Haught (2000), 56.

cosmos without coercively impacting the unfolding of history.[5] Haught goes so far as to describe God's revelation as being the gift of an unwritten future rather than the transmission of information.[6]

To understand Haught's views on creation and salvation one must engage his notion of "deep time", because it is in the long recesses of cosmic history that both the creative act and the redemptive work take place. In this deep time, the divine is actively luring the cosmos toward greater beauty and complexity in a non-coercive manner. This is accomplished through God's gracious offer of an open-ended future. In *Deeper than Darwin* Haught describes deep time as "an almost unimaginably extensive amount of time".[7] In Haught's frequent presentations on science and religion, he uses a thirty-volume set of encyclopaedias as an analogy for cosmic history. Haught's analogy has changed over time as physicists continue to refine their views on the length of cosmic history. In its current incarnation, each encyclopaedia is depicted as being 450 pages in length with each page representing one million years of cosmic history. The encyclopaedias in total roughly represent the 13.7 billion years of cosmic history. Haught notes that the first twenty volumes are devoid of life or mind, that complex life does not emerge until volume 29 and that homo sapiens does not emerge until the bottom fifth of page 450 of volume 30.[8]

Rather than infer that large periods of cosmic history being devoid of life and mind are a cause for pessimism, Haught explains that theists should anticipate a slow and meandering process in the quest to know God. Haught presents God as an infinite love graciously self-emptying that love to the world. He echoes Karl Rahner in contending that an extended cosmic history is to be expected because infinite love cannot be received in a moment, but rather the cosmos would need time to respond and be open to such an outpouring of divine love. He goes on to state that the cosmos' reception of God's self-emptying also may be reasonably expected to be strenuous and frustrating for large periods of time.[9]

During the deep time of cosmic history, Haught says, one can narrate developments of novel structures that are not fully explained by reductive analysis. For instance, the existence of DNA depends upon deterministic laws of physics and chemistry, but the sequence of the DNA is something Haught argues to be extraneous from the chemistry of the DNA molecule. Haught makes use of Michael Polanyi's work to argue that an added layer of information is present in the alphabetic sequence of DNA structures one finds among living creatures on earth.[10] This and many other instances of ordered novelty entering the cosmic story allows for one to assuredly say that things at present are different from what they were in the past and to also hope that the future will be significantly different from the present.[11]

---

[5] Haught (2000), 41-42, 100-102.

[6] Haught (1990), 66.

[7] Haught (2003), 59-61, 70.

[8] Haught (2008), "Science, Death, and Resurrection", Paper presented at Christ Church Cathedral, Cincinnati, Ohio, 11 June 2008.

[9] Haught (2003), 82-83.

[10] Haught (1984), 56-58.

[11] Haught (1993), 111-112.

Finally, Haught asserts that the narrative of cosmic history invites multiple levels of explanation for various phenomena. While the scientific method produces many good explanations, the category of the future is forever removed from scientific analysis, yet it is open to theological explanations. Haught sees Teilhard's reading of a gradual increase in consciousness in cosmic history as being theologically reasonable while simply offering an optimistic interpretation of the pessimistic interpretations of the cosmos's deep time. This optimism is partially grounded in Teilhard's recognition that evolutionary biology forces a recognition that life and mind are part of the universe story and not dualistically cut off from matter. Haught finds this to be optimistic in nature and calls for a wider empiricism that investigates the presence of mind in the universe.[12]

Redemption

Haught's views on salvation can be summarised as a synthesis of Whitehead's concept of objective immortality, Rahner's views on death and Teilhard's vision of an incarnational cosmos moving toward Christ-Omega. As noted, Haught describes creation as a long movement carried out over the vast epoch of time. He argues that God's redemptive work goes beyond creation to include cosmic events existing eternally within the divine memory. This allows humans to enter into a deeper relationship with creation at death and for a culmination to cosmic history. For Haught, salvation is partially accomplished because the cosmic events taken into God's loving memory attain permanence as they cannot be lost or erased. This permanence of events adds a level of value to the existence of all things.[13]

Haught's concept of sin further develops his concept of salvation. Haught does not speak a great deal about personal sin in his writings. He does subscribe to a view traditional to process theology that both monotony and chaos detract from cosmic beauty. Haught links ecological abuses to undermining the inherent beauty and value in nature.[14] This could offer a location for developing the idea of societal sin further. Beyond Haught's use of Whiteheadian aesthetics, a close reading of his work does offer a nuanced view of original sin. He describes original sin as not being a "defilement", but rather as "the aggregation in human history and culture of all the effects of our habitual refusal to take our appropriate place in the ongoing creation of the universe".[15] Haught's notion of sin is deeply imbedded in the idea of human refusal to move toward unity and to cling to the provincial. The seeds for future work on the relationship between creation, sin and salvation as related to cosmic purpose are present within Haught's work, even if sin itself is not a recurrent theme in his writing. In looking at personal salvation, Haught moves beyond Whitehead by recourse to Karl Rahner's views on the subject of death. Haught sees death as a moment of deepening one's connection to the cosmos rather than a gnostic liberation from physical matter. He states that creedal beliefs in the incarnation and resurrection of the body invite Christians to think of death as an ending of a limited relationship with creation while also

---

[12] Haught (2007), 74-75.

[13] Haught (1993), 130-132.

[14] Haught (1993), 27-28.

[15] Haught (2003), 175.

being an invitation to a deeper relationship with the cosmos.[16]

Finally, Haught asserts that final redemption is to be found in the forthcoming apex of cosmic history. As noted, Haught sees God as attracting cosmic events from the future rather than pushing history forward from the past. In Haught's system, Teilhard's Christ-Omega is the ultimate future that lures all cosmic groping toward greater beauty and consciousness. This God acts on the cosmos transcendentally in a non-coercive manner by inviting the distinct universe into communion with the divine. Haught does not allow for Christ-Omega to be a Platonic form that only occupies a transcendent future. He urges readers to consider the implications of the incarnation meaning that Christ-Omega is also eminently present, offering existing creation the invitation to deeper unity. This deeper unity with God offers creation more intense modes of existence and therefore also adds to his notions of salvation.[17] It is important to note that Haught's frequent use of Teilhard's vision sets him apart from other Roman Catholic scholars who make use of Whitehead, such as Joseph Bracken.

Conclusion

Haught's theology of creation and salvation is a combination of Alfred North Whitehead's aesthetics, Pierre Teilhard de Chardin's eschatology and Karl Rahner's awareness of an extended cosmic history, or of what Haught calls "deep time". Fittingly, Haught's focus on the unfinished quality of the cosmos invites thinkers to consider where his project may lead. It is fruitful to consider Haught's own words regarding process theology when categorising his work, "In fact, I think that, like all theologies, it is still unfinished and in need of much development."[18] Haught's emphasis on novelty and beauty as well as his use of concepts such as "objective immortality" are in concert with many other process theologians. Still, Haught has made use of a variegated set of sources in producing his theology. His use of Teilhard is not abnormal for process theologians, but Haught's work does offer a rich invitation for further research on the "family resemblance" that exists between process thought and the work of Karl Rahner, Bernard Lonergan, Paul Tillich, Michael Polanyi and Hans Jonas. Philosopher Nicholas Rescher stresses that "the unity in process thought is not doctrinal but thematic".[19] In this sense, Haught allows for the work of many thinkers who are not typically viewed as process philosophers or theologians to be recast as at least possessing a thematic resonance with process thought.

References and Recommended Reading

Haught, John F. (1976), *Religion and Self-Acceptance*, New York: Paulist Press.
--- (1980), *Nature and Purpose*, Lanham: University Press of America.
--- (1984), *The Cosmic Adventure: Science, Religion and the Quest for Purpose*, Mahwah: Paulist Press.
--- (1990), *What is Religion? An Introduction*, Mahwah: Paulist Press.
--- (1993), *The Promise of Nature: Ecology and Cosmic Purpose*, Mahwah: Paulist Press.
--- (1995), *Science and Religion: From Conflict to Conversation*, Mahwah: Paulist Press.

16 Haught (2000), 162.
17 Haught (2003), 162-164, 175.
18 Haught (1993), 32.
19 Rescher, 45.

--- (2000), *God after Darwin: A Theology of Evolution*, Boulder: Westview.
--- (2001), *Responses to 101 Questions on God and Evolution*, Mahwah: Paulist Press
--- (2003), *Deeper than Darwin: The Prospect for Religion in the Age of Evolution*, Boulder: Westview.
--- (2006), *Is Nature Enough? Meaning and Truth in the Age of Science*, Cambridge: Cambridge University Press.
--- (2007), *Christianity and Science: Toward a Theology of Nature*, Maryknoll: Orbis.
--- (2008), *God and the New Atheism: A Critical Response to Dawkins, Harris and Hitchens*, Louisville: Westminster John Knox.
--- (2010), *Making Sense of Evolution: Darwin, God and the Drama of Life*, Louisville: Westminster John Knox.
Rescher, Nicholas (2000), *Process Philosophy: A Survey of Basic Issues*, Pittsburgh: The University of Pittsburgh Press.

Dan Martin

Catherine Keller (1953-) – A Creative and Responsive Love from the Deep

Introduction

Contemporary feminist and constructive theologian Catherine Keller has been a leading and influential voice in ecotheology for two decades. Her most important contribution to creation theology thus far is her masterpiece, *Face of the Deep* (2003), a compellingly multifaceted engagement with the opening verses of Genesis that opens up into a rich and critical conversation with the history of the doctrine of creation in Christian, and to a lesser extent Jewish, traditions.

A professor of constructive theology at Drew Theological Seminary in Madison, New Jersey, since 1986, Keller pursued her doctoral work at Claremont Graduate University under the tutelage of John B. Cobb, Jr. Her Claremont dissertation was published in 1986 under the title *From a Broken Web: Separation, Sexism and Self*; this initial Keller offering remains a classic feminist exploration of human selfhood and relations. While this text in theological and philosophical anthropology is not without some consideration of the more-than-human world, it is in subsequent publications that her passionate interest in ecotheology becomes most pronounced.

Encountering Apocalyptic

For example, in her work *Apocalypse Now and Then: A Feminist Guide to the End of the World* (1996),[20] Keller gently but persistently probes the world-denying, even world-destroying, themes pulsating in the texts of the New Testament book of Revelation and its interpreters through the centuries of the Christian era. Particularly enlightening is her engagement with the journals and other writings of Christopher Columbus who understood himself to be Christ's herald of "the New Heaven and Earth which our Lord made, as St. John writes in the Apocalypse", confident that Christ "showed [him] where to go" in his apocalyptically tinged journeys to the *otro mundo*. Columbus's favoured, recurring image for this other world is a woman's breast, such that, in Keller's words, "the continent looms as forbidden fruit, the virgin body ripe for the pluck-

[20] References in parentheses in the text below are to this work.

ing, the mother breast ready to suckle death-ridden, depressed Europe into its rebirth" (p. 157). Dreams of a paradisiacal new world too easily become transmuted into violent lust for land, gold and bodies, "mass enslavement of natives and nature" (p. 156). Columbus, influenced by the prophecies of Joachim de Fiore, believed the world would come to its end in 1650; his apocalypses (literally, "uncoverings") of the new world would be instrumental, he believed, in this eschatological orchestration. Keller ironically indicates that half of the island of Hispaniola's 250 000 native inhabitants died within two years of Columbus's arrival through murder, maltreatment or suicide; in subsequent generations slave labour gradually erased the native people on Hispaniola such that by 1650 – the year Columbus had seen from afar as marking the present world's demise – there were none left at all. A robust illustration! "The end of the world proved, as ever, more local, less equal than predicted" (p. 156).

Keller suspects, then, that Christian eschatologies have all too often fuelled world destruction instead of world salvation. Even theologies of hope such as Moltmann's come under careful scrutiny: "One must ask whether the terms of [Moltmann's] confidence in the new creation do not once again fatally, indeed fatalistically, undermine the 'struggle for creation.' … How would the end of the temporal evanescence of life, growth, and mortality mean anything but the end of nature?" (p. 18). For Keller, "the end of the temporal evanescence of life, growth, and mortality" – the end of the world as we know it – is finally a destructive, (un-)self-fulfilling fantasy whose roots lie in the belief in an omnipotent Creator who calls forth our vast universe *ex nihilo*. Only a power able to create all things out of nothing is able to guarantee a radically new world whose conditions are entirely independent of the old one. It is just such a power that she, in company with others who more readily and happily lay claim to the self-designation of "process theologian", questions.

Creatio ex Profundis

Such considerations lead naturally to Keller's next major work, the book that appropriately demands the most careful attention of those who attempt to discern the relations between doctrines of creation and salvation. *Face of the Deep: A Theology of Becoming* (2003)[21] winds its serpentine way through the opening of Genesis via witty and wise engagements with a plethora of texts, including *Enuma Elish*, Augustine's *Confessions*, deconstructive theories, Barth's infamous struggles with *das Nichtige*, Melville's *Moby Dick*, feminist thought, Whitehead, Jewish mysticism and chaos theory – and so many more – to embody the very pluriform and "messy" cosmos Keller endeavours to describe.

Keller's fundamental point vis-à-vis Genesis 1:1-2 is that the passage does not imply, let alone explicitly teach, the notion of *creatio ex nihilo*. This point of course has been argued by many others, but Keller teases out a massive web of questions and implications from Genesis' *tohu va-bohu* and its mysterious "darkness upon the face of the deep" – chaotic waters that are never explicitly narrated as having been created. Instead of a clean-cut, sheared and sheer beginning of creation out of nothing by the irresistible command of an omnipotent Creator, Keller suggests that we read in Genesis' opening a bottomless process – a "churning, complicating darkness" (p. 9) – spin-

[21] References in parentheses in the text below are to this work.

ning out an infinity of possibilities. The trick for us, Keller suggests, is to embrace this churning, complicating darkness rather than to deny, demonise or flee it. This appreciative love for the watery depths with no beginning or end she calls "tehomophilia" – and it raises critical theological questions, to be sure.

Questions

First, what sort of image does Keller present, or assume, as appropriate to the deity narrated in Genesis 1? She explores the Hebrew designation *Elohim* and its pluralistic possibilities, which from the very beginning raise questions about a sole power or simple origin of everything. Such a messy lack of uniformity, even in the Creator, can be troubling. But Keller relentlessly explores the variety of possible paths of interpretation. The Trinity? God and his angels? Gods, somehow? She appeals to the Jewish mystical tradition and its *sefirot* – "a bi-gendered plurality" pulsating within the infinitely complex divine life – as an intriguing deconstruction of the simple "propositionality" that "God creates" (p. 179). At most, this deity is a co-creating power whose "Let there be" is less a command and more an alluring invitation; in Keller's words, "divinity *lures* but does not pre*determine*" (p. 195, emphasis added).

Creation, then, does not proceed cleanly *ex nihilo*. It is always already in process as *creatio continua*. Our world is processive though not at all necessarily progressive; there is no single, straight line heading for a happily guaranteed *telos*. Instead, reality always is an emergent web of possibilities, *tohu va-bohu*. Thus, no final end can be imagined or hoped for, and Keller would question such a hope, anyway, as both unrealistic and potentially violent: too often human beings who wield political, economic or military power seek to bring about such a desired end, no matter the cost, through coercive (and generally destructive) measures. The cure for this spiritual and emotional illness is, most simply, learning to live creatively, even hopefully, with the ambiguities and unpredictabilities of chaos. "To love is to bear with the chaos. Not to like it or to foster it but to recognize there the unformed future" (p. 29).

This point leads, then, to a question regarding the way(s) in which Keller understands soteriology, given her interpretation of *creatio ex profundis* – creation ever-emerging from the depths of infinitely complex layers of the world's times and places. Her "theology of becoming finds grace within, not outside, that very flow, that ...passion and flux" (p. 79). This is crucial to understanding Keller's interpretation of the relation between creation and salvation; indeed, it seems fair to suggest that for her, whatever is entailed in "salvation" is essentially collapsed into the theological category of "creation". Salvation, understood as a life of creative and responsive love, cannot even begin to occur as long as we erect intellectual and spiritual barriers against the chaotic depths symbolically narrated to us in Genesis 1. We must, in a sense, find our place – our place to love – in those watery depths.

Perhaps it is not illegitimate to ask whether Keller's soteriology is recognisably or particularly Christian. There is good reason to suspect that she may not find such a question overly bothersome. It is certainly the case that she betrays little interest in or sympathy with traditional Christological or soteriological categories. "Creation is always incarnation – and would have been so without the birth of the Nazarene" (p. 226). Thus, at most Jesus is *representative* of the universal processes of God and world co-creating, rather than being somehow a causal or definitive factor in the world's salvation. Nonetheless, even at this point – where divine incarnation is the rule rather than the exception in the bustling life of the world – Keller seeks support in early Christian fathers like Augustine and Athanasius, particularly in the latter's noticeably strong teaching of the universal presence of the Logos in all creatures and in the universe as a whole. So, for Keller, "[I]t matters whether an imprint of the materiality within God and the God within materiality can still faintly be read from the Nicene origin. And surprisingly it can. Even at the hardening heart of orthodoxy, a classical panentheism still modulates the ontotheology" (p. 63). Granted, there is nothing in and of itself salvific about either the universal presence of a divine Logos, or about our belief in such a presence. Salvation, if it is found anywhere, is found in the nature of our decisions in response to the loving allurements of this Logos / Sophia. The flowing relationality of the world can be for good, but it certainly can also be for ill – depending upon our deeds in relation to that relationality. "If incarnation is always going on, so is the carnage" (p. 220).

Will there come an end to the carnage? Given her theology of becoming, what can Keller coherently envision, or at least hope for, with regard to planet Earth? That is not up to God, at least not God alone. Keller, commenting on Job: "It is not up to God to right our moral wrongs, to fix our injustices and correct our oppressions. That doesn't happen. To depend on God to intervene, to justify 'himself,' to operate as the just patriarch is to abdicate our own moral responsibility for the earth" (p. 140). It should be noted that just as the doctrine of *creatio ex nihilo* can insure hope for a completed and fulfilled creation (for such a God possesses all the power necessary to bring about such an end), so a doctrine of *creatio ex profundis* can really only promise (not more of the same, but) an unending plethora of possibilities swirling forth from the chaotic depths. Those possibilities include the possible futures for the world our choices will conspire to create.

References and Recommended Reading

Adams, Carol J. (ed.) (1993), *Ecofeminism and the Sacred*, New York: Continuum.
Keller, Catherine (1986), *From a Broken Web: Separation, Sexism, and Self*, Boston: Beacon.
--- (1996), *Apocalypse Now and Then: A Feminist Guide to the End of the World*, Boston: Beacon.
--- (2003), *Face of the Deep: A Theology of Becoming*, New York: Routledge.
--- (2005), *God and Power: Counter-Apocalyptic Journeys*, Minneapolis: Fortress.

Michael Lodahl

Open Theistic Perspectives – The Freedom of Creation

Introduction

Open theism affirms that the omnipotent God, in an act of self-limitation, created beings *ex nihilo* with the intention that creatures would come to experience the love inherent in the Trinity.[22] God is "open" in two important senses.[23] First, God is open to

[22] An earlier version of this material appeared in the *Wesleyan Theological Journal*. Used with permission.

and affected by what creatures bring about, and second, God is open to the future in that, even for God, there is more than one possible future. God has "dynamic omniscience", meaning that God knows all the past and present as definite and God knows the future as possibilities.[24] Also, God has chosen to rely upon creatures for a great many aspects of life and history. Consequently, God takes risks because not everything in creation goes the way God specifically wants it to go. God has often had to adjust divine plans and implement flexible strategies in light of what creatures have done with their freedom.[25]

Creation

With this basic understanding in mind we can now proceed to a discussion of the nature of creation. Creation is more than simply the production of matter. In fact, creation should not be understood as a non-recurring event in the past which God preserves, but as a beginning with a dynamic structure that enables the creation itself to produce new beings, events and relations. In the Genesis accounts the original creation contained some structure and was reliable, but it was not static or complete, because God did not desire that it remain as it was.[26] That creation is ongoing is seen in the divine call for plants and animals to multiply, which would render the earth different from what it was at the beginning. God empowers creatures to bring about new states of affairs. When humans, for instance, begin to occupy the land (Gen. 1:28), it will take on characteristics it did not have on the seventh day. God chooses to bring about a world in which God is not the only one who makes things new and different. In this respect creation is "open" because God instantiated a reliable but dynamic and open-ended rather than static world.

The empowerment of creatures implies that God is a "power-sharing" deity. God calls upon the waters, land, plants and animals to bring about new realities such that the creatures become creators, imitating God. Humans are given a vocation to be God's regents on earth in God's stead. In this respect, human vocation is necessary for the continuance of at least some aspects of creation. God thus enters upon a journey with creatures in which the outcome is neither predetermined nor foreknown.

Also, it needs to be noted that the Bible depicts God as Creator in the sense that God works to produce new social, religious, political and economic realities. That God is Creator in these important areas of life is significant in order to connect the doctrines of creation and salvation.

Salvation

God took a risk in empowering creatures and the risk has transpired: creation has mis-

---

23 For an exposition of open theism see Sanders and also Pinnock et al.

24 The openness model appears in this chapter because it bears some affinities with process theology, such as dynamic omniscience and divine temporality. However, it is important to note two crucial differences between open theism and process thought. Openness affirms divine omnipotence and that God's relation to and dependence upon creation is voluntary.

25 The openness model is somewhat similar to the views of Jürgen Moltmann and John Polkinghorne (discussed elsewhere in this volume).

26 This section is heavily indebted to Fretheim (2005).

carried. Sin mars all the spheres of divine creativity just mentioned: our relationship with God, with the physical world as well as our relations with other humans. Each of the areas harmed by sin requires reconciliation and healing, which is why the New Testament contains a plethora of images regarding atonement and salvation. Jesus' life, death and resurrection are the touchstones by which Christians align their life stories with that of Jesus. Jesus models loving ways of relating to others, overcomes hate with forgiveness and is the ground of hope that destruction and death can be overcome. The incarnation and resurrection are creative acts of God by which new possibilities for the world arise. The resurrection of Jesus and the sending of the Holy Spirit are indications of an inaugurated eschatology in which the "new creation" has already begun but is not yet completed. The renewal of the heavens and the earth and the various relationships therein are granted the possibility of redemption.

This redemption involves four elements. First, it involves a reconciliation of sinful creatures to God (not God to creatures) as well as the reconciliation of creatures with one another. Second, redemption is addressed to whole persons – bodies and minds, not just souls. The New Testament writers did not concentrate on getting immaterial substances to heaven after death. Rather, they were concerned with the welfare of embodied persons as seen by their discussions of such things as food, clothing and employment. Third, sin has infected all of the relationships in which we find ourselves, but God is working to heal the diseased relations by creating communities who work to overcome sinful racial, socio-economic and gendered structures (Gal. 3:28). Fourth, the renewal which began in the resurrection of Jesus continues to spread and will culminate one day in a renewed heaven and earth in which there is no sin to fracture our relationships. The new creation has been inaugurated and God calls us to participate in the divine mission in order to complete it.

If salvation involves bodies then it involves the physical order. However, many Christians believe that although the "new" creation involves resurrected human bodies, it means the destruction of the present physical world. Such a view can lead to a lack of concern for the environment and so some responses are needed. First, redemption is not the annihilation of creation but rather its renewal. Just as human bodies are not annihilated when they experience salvation in Jesus, so the present heaven and earth will not be annihilated but renewed. It is common for biblical scholars to point out that in the passages about the new creation, "new" means new in quality and is contrasted with the old. Evangelicals in North America typically believe that "the earth and the works that are upon it will be burned up" (2 Pet. 3:10). That is, God is going to annihilate the present physical creation. However, this understanding is based on a mistranslation because the text should read: "the earth and everything that is done on it will be disclosed".[27] The Greek word for what is translated "burned up" or "disclosed" is *heureskein*, which means "to find out". God is going to reveal the truth about what has happened by refining creation, not by destroying it.

Another response is that even if one remains convinced that the present world is going to be destroyed by God, there are reasons why Christians should not contribute to the destruction of the environment now. To begin with, even if God is going to destroy it, there is no biblical warrant for anyone but God to do so – there is no biblical call to

[27] See Bouma-Prediger, 68-69.

destroy the planet. Also, wanton contamination of the environment conflicts with the mission of Jesus. If Jesus is the model for the Christian life and Jesus cared for the broken bodies of people, then we do not follow Jesus when we make others sick by contaminating the environment. If, for example, our discarded electronic devices end up in areas where poor people live and the heavy metals seep into the water supply, poisoning the people who live there, then we are helping to make them sick. In the United States cases of asthma are sharply increasing, owing to high levels of particles in the air. Slowly making our neighbours sick is in opposition to the mission of Jesus.

Issues

With this summary of an openness understanding of creation and salvation in hand, several issues arise. First, how should we understand the relationship between creation and salvation? To begin with, creation is not a one-time event but an ongoing process. The history of evolution manifests the ongoing and unfinished nature of divine creation. As mentioned above, God's original creation included a dynamic infrastructure with its own autonomy, which allows for the creation of new beings and types of relations. Next, the freedom of the creation entailed divine risk-taking and God's creation has become deeply defaced by sin. Creation is the framework within which sin arises, and it is also the framework in which salvation is carried out. Furthermore, God is Creator, not just of original matter, but also in the social, religious and other areas of human existence. Since sin has distorted these aspects of creation, salvation is understood as God's creative work to renew the physical and social dimensions of life. Also, according to Paul, the Son of God, the Redeemer, is also the one through whom God created the universe (Col. 2:16). The spoiled creation is the subject of God's redemptive work, so creation and salvation cannot be isolated from one another. But neither can they be collapsed into each other, because God did not create in order to redeem creation: sin was not part of God's original design. God has had to adjust the divine plan to include redemption as a means to a new creation.

A second issue is how to avoid an escapist eschatology which obliterates hope for this earth. Openness theology affirms the majority of traditional Christian teachings, including the resurrection of bodies to new life. Salvation is understood to include both the redemption of all spheres of life on earth and the continued life with God after death in the new heavens and earth. Many proponents of open theism are evangelicals and many evangelicals believe that God is going to destroy the earth. Some interpret this to mean that if God is going to destroy the earth, then it is not within our power to destroy it. Hence, they believe we can pollute and use up the natural resources because God will not allow the planet to be destroyed before the time set for its destruction. Calvinist theologian Calvin Beisner claims we can rest assured that God will not let us run out of natural resources since God miraculously created more oil for a widow in order to pay off her debts (2 Kings 4:1-7).[28]

Open theism seeks to avoid two polarities in this regard: the evangelical belief that God will take care of everything and the process theology belief that God cannot guarantee salvation. Against the notion that God will resolve all of the problems unilaterally, openness affirms that God has granted a great deal of independence to creatures.

[28] See Beisner, 25-26.

Above, it was said that God decided to rely on humans by giving us a vocation that is necessary for the continuance of creation. Just as God elected to rely on creatures to continue the work of creation, God has decided to rely on us in many aspects of salvation (e.g. to evangelise and feed the hungry). Does this mean that we could contaminate the environment to such an extent as to make life untenable? Given that God has not prevented us from wreaking horrible wars, droughts and the like, this seems a reasonable conclusion. It seems that God has chosen to solicit our cooperation in the divine work of salvation rather than simply to do it by God's own self. Since God decided to make some important features of the continuance of creation dependent upon human vocation, the view that God is in control and what humans do is irrelevant must be rejected.

The second polarity is process theology's lack of eschatological hope that God will bring about the new heavens and new earth. The God of process theology cannot unilaterally cause an electron to move, so the preservation of the planet is decidedly on our shoulders, not God's. The openness-of-God model affirms divine omnipotence and that God can work unilaterally within creation. The biblical record testifies that God historically brought about that which did not exist on a number of occasions. Proponents of open theism live in the tension between the two polarities of escapist theologies and the lack of hope in process theology.

A third issue is how to understand salvation in the context of environmental threats. For open theism, salvation entails both our incorporation into the divine life and our relations with other creatures. Again, two polarities need to be avoided: that salvation is only about getting to heaven and that it is only about healing the planet. The Evangelical Declaration on the Care of Creation says: "We resist both ideologies which would presume the Gospel has nothing to do with the care of non-human creation and also ideologies which would reduce the Gospel to nothing more than the care of that creation".[29] Open theists believe that salvation is about both this life and the next because the salvation already begun will not be complete until God resurrects us to a renewed bodily life in the new heavens and earth. Open theists go beyond the process ideas of "objective immortality" (God has eternal memories of what we were) or "subjective immortality" (the survival of a disembodied soul). Jesus was raised bodily from the dead, confirming both that death has not the final word and that God continues to value physical existence.

In addition to this eschatological embodiment, open theists affirm that salvation requires the transformation of embodied existence, not just the salvation of "souls". Salvation engages every sphere of life affected by sin: economic, political and environmental. James says that true religion is caring for widows and orphans (1:27) as well as feeding and clothing the poor (2:15). Paraphrasing James, we might ask how one could claim to love one's neighbour while at the same time acting in ways that unnecessarily pollute the air and water supplies of our neighbours. The redemption of creation includes both salvation of individuals and healing of the environment because God wants to redeem every sphere of life affected by sin. God works to redeem whole persons and the way we treat the environment affects our embodied neighbours. The renewed heaven and earth means the continuation of God's physical creation, but in a

[29] Cited in Bouma-Prediger, 128.

transformed state in which we, as embodied beings, live appropriately with all other embodied beings. If God cares for embodied existence on this planet and God will not give up on it, then neither should we. If divine dominion does not exploit the land but cares for it, then human dominion, which should image God's dominion, should also care for it.[30]

References and Recommended Reading

Beisner, Calvin (1997), *Where Garden Meets Wilderness: Evangelical Entry into the Environmental Debate*, Grand Rapids: Acton Institute / Eerdmans.

Bouma-Prediger, Steven (2010), *For the Beauty of the Earth: A Christian Vision of Creation Care* (revised edition), Grand Rapids: Baker.

Fretheim, Terence (2005), *God and Creation in the Old Testament: A Relational Theology of Creation*, Nashville: Abingdon.

Pinnock, Clark et al. (1994), *The Openness of God*, Downers Grove: InterVarsity Press.

Sanders, John (2007), *The God Who Risks: A Theology of Divine Providence*, Downers Grove: InterVarsity Press.

Verhey, Allen (2010), *Nature and Altering It*, Grand Rapids: Eerdmans.

John Sanders

Further Developments

Process / relational theisms provide a conceptual basis for ecotheology and the applications of that conceptual basis to efforts to develop an adequate response to ecological problems. The conceptual basis both distinguishes between God's creative and saving activities and closely relates those divine activities. God's presentation of possible values to possible existence results in actualised value in ongoing creative activity. God's saving activity, again working through the responses of created reality, preserves accomplished value and calls for new values. This interrelated understanding of divine and created activity, both in bringing value into existence and in fulfilling value, supports the intrinsic value of all created reality. No pre-established identity limits this value. No external determination of value frustrates the accomplishment of unique value. This conceptual structure supports action on behalf of the whole biosphere because of its emphasis upon the importance of existence. God's creative activity calls for action on God's part and on the part of what has come to exist in order to preserve and fulfil what God has made possible. Sanders adds biblical support for this understanding of the importance of the biosphere. Both God's risky creation that was not created in order to redeem and God's call to care for every aspect of those around us affirm the value of existence.

A number of thinkers have contributed to the concern of process / relational theisms for the biosphere. Prior to the work of John B. Cobb, Jr., Bernard Meland expresses concern for the environment. Jay McDaniel considers the well-being of the biosphere and has continued to deal with ecological concerns in his writings. Nancy Howell brings a feminist concern for the well-being of animals. Michael Lodahl provides an open theism approach to ecotheology. Roland Faber utilises both process philosophy and continental philosophy in his consideration of the environment.

---

[30] See Verhey, 84-85.

The tension between the more thorough-going process position of thinkers such as Keller and the more traditional relational theism of open theism calls for further development of the process / relational understanding of creation and salvation. The affirmation of the value of existence without any pre-established definition of that value challenges the possibility of hope for the fulfilment of God's creative intent. If God is limited by either the existence of reality other than God, such as Keller's chaosmos, or God's will to accept limitation by what God has created, hope for such fulfilment becomes tenuous. The difficulty in having hope is not simply due to powers competing with God, but it is more profoundly the issue of what is to be hoped for. Without clarity in order to recognise the actualisation of the hoped for redemption, such redemption cannot be identified.

Cobb affirms the importance of hope and bases that hope upon God's activity in ongoing creation and in the preservation and luring of the present. Thomas Jay Oord responds to the issue of the possibility of hope by basing hope on the reliability of God rather than the ultimate fulfilment of God's creative activity. Oord does this by giving precedence to the divine nature over the divine will. This does not deny the importance of God's will to create and to redeem. Instead, God's will manifests the reliability of the diverse expressions of the divine nature. As an alternative to basing hope on God's nature, John Sanders in *The God Who Risks* (2007) bases hope on God's active love as demonstrated in history, rather than on God's immutability. This divine nature of love leads to the self-emptying of God making possible the actualisation of value that is not pre-established by divine action or by the anticipation of specific forms of existence. Oord describes God's nature as "essential kenosis". Likewise, Jürgen Moltmann and John Polkinghorne utilise a concept of kenosis to understand God's creative activity.

References and Recommended Reading

Faber, Roland (2008), "Ecotheology, Ecoprocess, and *Ecotheosis*: A Theopoetical Intervention", *Salzburger Theologische Zeitschrift*, Vol. 12, 1, 75-115.

Howell, Nancy (2000), *A Feminist Cosmology: Ecology, Solidarity, and Metaphysics*, Amherst: Humanity Books.

Lodahl, Michael (2003), *God of Nature and of Grace: Reading the World in a Wesleyan Way*, Nashville: Abingdon.

McDaniel, Jay B. (1989), *Of God and Pelicans: A Theology of Reverence for Life*, Louisville: Westminster John Knox.

Oord, Thomas J. (2010), "The Work of Love: Creation as Kenosis", *Wesleyan Theological Journal*, Vol. 45, 1, 81-107.

Polkinghorne, John (ed.) (2001), *The Work of Love: Creation as Kenosis*, London: SPCK / Grand Rapids: Eerdmans.

Sanders, John (2007), *The God Who Risks: A Theology of Divine Providence*, Downers Grove: Inter-Varsity Press.

John Culp

8. Western Ecofeminist Theologies

Edited by Susan Rakoczy

Introduction

The first Earth Day was held in 1970 in the United States. Although few events were organised, they attracted a good deal of both curiosity and derision. A few years earlier Rachel Carson (1907-1964) in her book *Silent Spring* (1962) had called attention to the widespread use of pesticides, which she argued was destroying the environment. She warned that soon there might be springs without the joyous songs of birds. Many people scoffed at her conclusions. It was a woman who had raised the alarm about an ecological crisis.

Carson, who was a biologist, would have found ecofeminism a congenial dialogue partner. The word comes from the French *ecofeminisme* which was first used in 1974 by Francoise d'Eaubonne. Ecofeminism joins feminism and ecology and exposes both the oppression of men by women and the domination of the natural world by humanity. Since the earth is our only home (unless and until humanity travels to other parts of the universe), it must be a hospitable and flourishing home for all.

The ecological degradation of the early 21st century especially affects poor women in Africa, Asia and Latin America. They must walk long distances for water and firewood. Climate change affects food production, which at the subsistence level is generally the responsibility of women. Families are at risk from all types of industrial pollution and pesticides. The process of climate change will impact the poor, especially in Africa, in very dramatic ways as food production becomes ever more precarious.

Ecofeminism: A New Consciousness

The goal of ecofeminism is a radical transformation of human consciousness from a person-centred perspective to one in which humanity is seen as connected to all of creation. This will demand a conversion to the needs of others, human and non-human, with whom we share this one earth.

The ways that the relationship between women and nature have been articulated provide evidence of the pervasive power of patriarchy to shape human thought and action. Terms such as "Mother Earth" identify women with the natural world and both have been objects of male exploitation and oppression. A phrase such as "the rape of the earth" demonstrates that the violent exploitation of the land is connected to the violence which too many women experience from both family members and strangers. The oppressions of patriarchy and kyriarchy daily impact upon women's lives and the earth.

Ecofeminism has profound implications for the way the global economy is structured, types of social and political movements and theology and religious practices. The current global economic system is premised on the axiom that financial profit is all that matters. Wealth demonstrates how successfully a person can manipulate the system for the benefit of their own bank account. The needs of the poor and the earth are of no account; greed is the only creed.

Ecofeminist Theologies

Linked to the larger body of feminist theologies around the world, which includes the voices and experiences of all women in all religions, ecofeminist theologies demand that talk be translated into action. Its goal is liberative praxis for the sake of all of creation.

Because it is a theological movement, and not only linked with the various ecological movements such as deep ecology, ecofeminist theologies challenge the received traditions of the world religions, especially Christianity, whose dualism of mind and matter has had such negative effects both on women and on the natural world.

The five sections of this chapter present the voices and insights of women in Europe, the United Kingdom and the United States who have written about the relationship of creation and salvation from an ecofeminist perspective. In other chapters the contributions of feminist theologians to liberation theology, African theology, Asian theologies, Nordic theologies, North American theologies from the margins, process theology and discourse on science and theology will also be explored.

Mary Grey of the United Kingdom presents the work of Catherina Halkes (1920-2011) of the Netherlands who "made the path by walking" as she helped develop feminist theology in the Catholic Church after Vatican II (1962-1965). This included her reflections on the meaning of creation.

Sallie McFague (1933-) of the United States is known especially for her work on new images of God. In her article on McFague, Annalet van Schalkwyk of South Africa argues that McFague's use of the new cosmology challenges us to realise that it is in all of creation that salvation occurs.

Anne Marie Dalton from Canada analyses the work of Rosemary Radford Ruether (1936-) of the United States who made some of the first major contributions to ecofeminist theology. Ruether's ecofeminism focuses on relationality: earth-human relationships and human-human relationships in the pervasive presence of God. She also has a special emphasis on ecofeminism and liberation.

Susan Rakoczy of South Africa demonstrates that the ecofeminist theology of Elizabeth Johnson (1941-) of the United States is rooted in her pneumatology, a perspective which embraces wholeness, not division. The Spirit who is Life is the bond of unity between creation and salvation. Johnson insists that ecofeminism has profound ethical implications that call for change by humanity in order that all creation may flourish.

In her analysis of Grace Jantzen's (1948-2006) work, Janet Trisk also of South Africa focuses on Jantzen's questions about violence and sin and their opposite – salvation as flourishing for all of creation.

These five essays present the foundational insights of ecofeminism and demonstrate the theological creativity of these women, which is at the service of humanity and all of creation. Other voices, for example that of Dorothee Sölle, could have been added to this chapter, but the voices included here are sufficient to indicate the rich diversity of ecofeminist theology.

Susan Rakoczy

Catharina Halkes (1920-2011) – The Renewal of the Earth

Introduction

Catherina Halkes is a key figure for women's role in theology in the Roman Catholic Church, as well as for all women in feminist theology in Europe in its key developing stages. She even embodied the hopes and dreams of countless women beyond the boundaries of her small country. In addition she has influenced the development of Women Studies as an academic subject in the universities of the Netherlands and wider. She has also been an immense personal inspiration to me.[1]

Her influence cannot be restricted to ecological theology alone, and the understanding of creation and redemption: she has had a much wider role. Rooted in the progressive theology of the Second Vatican Council, she developed a wide-ranging pastoral theological influence on theology. It could be said that her legacy will be seen as opening up different areas of theology and related disciplines to the feminist lens, and being at the forefront of developments in many fields, always with the critical eyes of a Christian faith that has never wavered, despite continuing disappointment and personal suffering at the unflinchingly repressive attitudes of the Roman Catholic Church, to which she remained consistently loyal.[2]

Early Theological Developments

Catharina J. M. Halkes was born in 1920 in the Netherlands and grew up in the village of Vlaardingen, near the city of Rotterdam. From 1945 she studied linguistics and literature at the University of Leiden. Involvement in theology came with Dutch Catholic women's groups, where she began to focus on lay empowerment and the cooperation of men and women in pastoral work. From 1964 she studied pastoral theology, joining the faculty of the Catholic University of Nijmegen in 1967. She became pastoral supervisor in the Department of Practical Theology in 1970.

It was the Second Vatican Council (1962-1965) that was the catalyst for her deeper theological involvement and thinking and she became part of a working group advising the Dutch bishops: this group sought to incorporate women and married men into ordained ministry in a declericalised model of church. Her book *Storm na de Stilte* ("Storm after the Silence", 1964), called for an inclusive model of ministry. The Dutch Pastoral Council (1969-1971), which brought together bishops, priests, nuns, laymen and laywomen in a national synod, seemed to be on the verge of church reform that would incorporate these changes.

But, sadly, Catholicism in the Netherlands began to suffer from increasing intervention from the Vatican to stifle these progressive trends. Dramatically, at the very time when dioceses were split, conservative bishops appointed and progressive Dutch Catholics excluded from official circles, feminist theology began to blossom in theological faculties. Women and Faith ("Vrouw en Geloof") groups also sprang up at

---

[1] After being present at my Ph.D. defence at the University of Leuven, Belgium, she invited me to apply to be her successor as Chair of Feminism and Christendom at the University of Nijmegen, the Netherlands, a chair that had been set up in her honour. I occupied this position from 1988 to 1992.

[2] She died at the age of 90 on 21 April 2011 in Nijmegen, the Netherlands.

parish and diocesan levels. In 1985 when Pope John Paul II visited the Netherlands, Catherina Halkes was forbidden to give an address. This was the catalyst for the formation of the Eighth of May Movement, where progressive Dutch Catholic feminist, peace and justice groups began to network independently of the bishops.[3]

It can be said that it was through Catherina Halkes's reading of American feminist theology, especially with the writings of Mary Daly, Rosemary Radford Ruether and Elisabeth Schüssler Fiorenza, and her introduction of it to the Netherlands' audiences, (on both academic and pastoral levels) that a significant movement began. In 1983 the first European chair in feminist theology was established at the University of Nijmegen and she was appointed to it. The rest, as they say, is history.

Yet, in the subsequent 28 years, what had seemed like a tremendous success story was weakened by a rigid clamping down from the hierarchy, the loss of a younger generation to the church and the subsequent loss of young feminist theologians to the church, as they pursued different trends of gender studies in the academy which were less church-related. As she herself commented:

> In Feminist Theology Church and tradition have disappeared from view: A younger generation is now influential, which has gone through the secularization process and is influenced by (post) modern currents in philosophy and literary criticism.[4]

Creation and Salvation in the Works of Catherina Halkes

Halkes's work is permeated by her belief in the goal of transformation for all human beings, men and women in a transformed society, which is the kingdom of God. All the required transformations are interlinked. Male domination over women has distorted not only personal relations and social structures, but also relations with nature. Nature has been imaged as like the female in patriarchal ideology. The transformation of power relations from male domination to man-woman mutuality thus must govern transformation on all three levels: personal, social and ecological.

Her views are more fully expressed in the later writings, especially in "Humanity Re-imaged: New Directions in Feminist Theological Anthropology".[5] Rooted in the basic Christian theological symbols of creation – incarnation – resurrection – eschaton, Halkes sees the Christian story calling us into a process of renewal and transformation whose goal is the reign of God on earth where all creatures live in just relations in community:

> I want to draw the conclusion that creation – incarnation – resurrection – eschaton belong together in one grand process, and they must not be separated from each other. We have been given the promise of the Kingdom of God; already we are living in the last days, if we believe in that promise and live accordingly.[6]

At the heart of the redemptive mystery is the divine incarnation in Christ – but Halkes

---

[3] Sadly, this movement and similar groups, like the Marienburg Group, have become, to all intents and purposes defunct, owing to the deliberately enforced conservatism of the Roman Catholic Church.

[4] Halkes (1993b), 34.

[5] Halkes (1993a).

[6] Halkes (1993a), 85.

refuses to limit Jesus to a male person in such a way that women would be excluded from sacramental priesthood.

But it is in her last book, *New Creation: Christian Feminism and the Renewal of the Earth* (1991), where Halkes develops her transformative vision as a full-blown ecological feminist theology. Two factors are key in her approach. The first is the summons of the World Council of Churches' conciliar process for justice, peace and the integrity of creation:

> The phrase "justice, peace and the integrity of creation" (JPIC) is shorthand for a fuller statement: "To engage member churches in a conciliar process of mutual commitment (covenant) to justice, peace and the integrity of creation should be a priority for World Council programmes." Originally intended as a programme priority for the WCC by its Vancouver assembly (1983) and addressed to its member churches, it was subsequently expanded to include churches that are not members of the WCC, regional and national ecumenical organizations and all other movements committed to these issues.[7]

This process, inaugurated in Basle in 1989 with much celebration and high hopes, was taken very seriously in the Netherlands. For Halkes it was the spur for developing her creation / redemption emancipatory theology into a new dimension, the connection between women, nature and justice. All the foundation stones had been laid in her pastoral leadership role, her background in sacramental Catholic theology and her keen interest in theological anthropology. The other factor is her ability to take the best of what is offered from many quarters and to create a synthesis available to many-levelled audiences. So she is able to grasp the significance of the many published works of ecofeminists authors at an interdisciplinary level and, in terms of theological contributions, especially the works of Rosemary Radford Ruether and Sallie McFague, but neither had yet published books that would later be of greater ecotheological significance, like *Gaia and God* (Ruether) and *The Body of God* (McFague).[8]

Responding to the WCC appeal, Halkes begins a dialogue between these themes by reflecting on images of "woman" and "nature" in Western culture, images that have contributed to the domination of both. Aiming to help contemplation of the more deep-seated causes of the inequality of power between women and men and the division between nature and culture, her book discusses some of the roots of the ecological crisis and points to changes that are necessary not only for survival but also for living both humanly and creatively and for leaving our children prospects for the future.

Part I of *New Creation* focuses, in an interdisciplinary way, on images in the history of Western thought that have depicted nature as a lifeless object to be dominated, women as passive and closer to nature than men, and men as creators of culture – specifically the "male is to female as culture is to nature" opposition. Halkes flags the use of these images in natural science and philosophy – the scientist Francis Bacon is a particularly disastrous figure – and points out connections between the domination of women and the oppression of indigenous peoples in European imperialist history. Addressing theological themes, Halkes again engages with the Genesis creation sto-

7 Niles (2003).

8 Both of these were published in 1993.

ries, especially the interpretation that human beings are to dominate nature through technology. She asks: What can hinder and what can serve the development of an adequate creation theology? She criticises theologians who have separated nature and history, presenting a transcendent God disconnected from nature, and overemphasising God's redemptive activity while ignoring God's continuous act of blessing expressed in nature's fertility. Jürgen Moltmann is valued in his interpretation of the Sabbath as the "feast of creation" and his trinitarian theology which connects the God who transcends the world with the God whose living presence is in the world.[9]

Halkes's own theological anthropology sees female and male, created in God's image and called to be "God's representatives" who "preserve and keep watch over the garden" and who "see to it that justice is done to everything and everyone".[10] She believes that Christ sets in motion a new life in the Spirit which strives for "equal relationships between men and women, between whites and nonwhites, between rich and poor"[11] and denounces forms of domination promoted by our "culture of violence". Her final chapter is a kind of dream, with humanity and nature re-imagined, giving an image of the world as God's body.

Rather than focusing on some of the book's shortcomings, (as some of its reviewers do – regarding some of its themes as underdeveloped), this work should be considered as an introductory, groundbreaking work, which has set the scene in Roman Catholic ecofeminist and ecological theology for the next two decades. Further, Halkes was quick to see the implications for spirituality and, in fact, spelled this out in her final valedictory address at the University of Nijmegen in 1988.[12]

Here she understands an intense experience of the earth and the whole of nature as God's good creation as a positive aspect of a Christian feminist spirituality. Realising how we belong to and participate in the cosmos as a whole does not mean returning to nature religion, but rather living and thinking so as to include nature. So creation is not deified, as in nature religions, nor is it rendered godless. Traces of God are found in creation, and human beings are called to be co-creators. Women protest against a strong anthropocentric doctrine of creation extolling *man* as "lord of creation" – which means domination over women, children and slaves, and a ruthless subjection of nature – and are called to be witnesses for a redirection towards the proper use of nature.

Halkes was adamant in holding together creation and salvation: a dominant theology of redemption tends to neglect creation theology, she says, advocating the inclusion of images and symbols of Mother Earth, Sister Moon and Brother Sun in liturgies, incorporating the celebration of heaven, earth and the world in dance and play.[13]

---

9 Halkes (1991), 91.

10 Halkes (1991), 132.

11 Halkes (1991), 141.

12 Halkes (1988).

13 On the one hand, Catholic liturgy has of old incorporated many natural elements, such as fire, water and oil; prayer-times of monasteries and convents were adapted to the rhythm of day and night, light and darkness. The liturgical year still has its seasons and their changes. But from the feminist point of view, she poses the question as to whether the Roman liturgy after Vatican II does not bear the stamp of purely male rationality? On the one hand we have a spirituality of the symbolic, on the other the efforts of renewal in the "social-critical" climate of the 1960s. What remains to be celebrated has been buried under a heavy layer of socio-ethical warnings. Halkes wants to

Conclusion

Sin, in Halkes's understanding of salvation / redemption, is the refusal to turn away from wrong and oppressive relations, on personal, societal and ecological levels. So the process of *metanoia*, of conversion, must also mean a conversion from distorted relations to the rest of creation into a sustaining and caretaking relation that allows all other creatures to flourish equally with humanity. To be engaged in this transformative conversion is our human calling, which is to grow ever more fully into our potential as image of God, becoming the "likeness of God", a redeemed humanity with the entire creation that is God's kingdom realised, the face of the earth renewed and God's glory manifest. This is the rich vision of Catherina Halkes.

References and Recommended Reading

Halkes, Catherina (1964), *Storm na de Stilte*, Utrecht: Ambo.
--- (1988), "Feminism and Spirituality", *Spirituality Today*, Vol. 40, 3, 220-236.
--- (1989), *En Alles Zal Worden Herschapen*, Baarn: Ten Have.
--- (1991), *New Creation: Christian Feminism and the Renewal of the Earth*, London: SPCK.
--- (1993a), "Humanity Re-imaged: New Directions in Feminist Theological Anthropology", in: Ursula King (ed.), *Liberating Women: New Theological Directions*, Bristol: University of Bristol, 75-93.
--- (1993b), "Towards a History of Feminist Theology in Europe", in: *Feminist Theology in a European Context*, Yearbook of the European Society of Women in Theological Research, Vol. 1, Kampen: Kok Pharos, 11-37.
Niles, D. Preman (2003), "Justice, Peace and Integrity of Creation", *World Council of Churches*, Article of the month November 2003, <www-coe.org/wcc/who/dictionary-article11.html>, retrieved 22 October 2011.

Mary C. Grey

Sallie McFague (1933-) – Healing God's Body

Introduction: The Body of God

Sallie McFague's theology needs to be understood in relation to the new cosmology, or the re-mythologisation of the understanding of the evolution of the universe, the earth and life on earth in postmodern science. This emerges in her own work and in that of other ecological theologians and thinkers such as Thomas Berry (1990), Brian Swimme (1992), Larry Rasmussen (1996) and Anne Primavesi (2000). She boldly reinterprets and re-mythologises this unfolding ecological and scientific understanding of the earth and cosmos as the "Body of God", and discerns the need for doing so in the light of the ecological crisis which threatens the future of humanity and nature. Her theology therefore entails an ecological revision and reformulation of traditional theology.[14]

---

give the deeper levels of human experience a new opportunity in the liturgy, to retrieve for a moment old symbols and rituals which direct us beyond ourselves and our daily activities, not to escape reality, but to derive motivation from such moments of transcendence in order to act critically.

14 McFague (1993), 84.

Salvation and Christ in the Body of God

As such, one has to regard her understanding of salvation as a further revision of traditional theology. McFague regards the salvation story of Christ's sacrificial, substitutionary atonement and complete redemption by Jesus in place of and for all humankind as inappropriate in the context of the search for a sustainable world. Apart from the situation that this salvation story is no longer credible within the postmodern scientific understanding of reality; it entails individualistic, anthropocentric salvation. In the traditional view, the incarnation of God occurs at one point in time only – in the man Jesus sent to earth by God the Father. It takes place outside and apart from humanity and the whole natural world. It is dualistic and disengaged from nature. God is not present everywhere, all the time, in the whole of the cosmos and the earth. This does not fit well with McFague's sacramental and immanent interpretation of the cosmos and the earth as the body of God, as contained in and infused by God. If Christ saves all of this from the outside, then salvation has no significance at all for the members of the body of God. It then does not make sense that Christ saves without the participation of the members of her body, to help to heal other creatures and to let all creatures flourish. She says: "If God is present only in Jesus and if Jesus 'does it all', then we do not have to meet God in the face of a starving person or in the remains of a clear-cut forest, nor do we have to help that starving person or that devastated forest."[15]

In order to understand McFague's sense of salvation as for the whole of creation and not only for humanity, one needs insight into her particular Christology. The cosmos and the earth, understood as the body of God, is read through the story of Jesus.

From the paradigmatic story of Jesus the direction of creation is towards inclusive love for all, especially the oppressed, the outcast, the vulnerable. This paradigm suggests a trajectory for creation, one that we cannot read off evolutionary history, but from our wager of faith in the destabilising, non-hierarchical, inclusive life, teachings and death of Jesus of Nazareth.[16] Creation is the space and the scope in which salvation needs to be understood. The paradigmatic story of Christ is contextually and concretely important for every member of the cosmic body of Christ. The historical, particular body of Christ is reflected in each member of the body of the earth and the cosmos.[17] The story of Jesus suggests that the shape of God's body includes all, especially the needy and outcast. The distinctive characteristic of a Christic theology of embodiment in an era of ecological disaster is a focus on oppressed, vulnerable, suffering *bodies*, those who are in pain because of the indifference or greed of the more powerful. In an ecological age, this includes the oppressed non-human living beings and the earth itself. It becomes a contextual ecological theology with a focus on the suffering of the earth as the "new poor". In an ecological perspective on salvation as liberation, God's love is unlimited and oriented especially to the bodies of the most oppressed. God has a preferential option for those bodies who are the most disadvantaged by patriarchal and anthropocentric systems of power which oppress and destroy the bodies of the poor and vulnerable, be they human or other-than-human. During a time of ecological crisis, the focus is especially on other-than-human bodies and sys-

---

15 McFague (2001), 157-159.

16 McFague (1993), 160.

17 McFague (1993), 163.

tems of life which are threatened by humans.[18] The destabilising, non-hierarchical, inclusive life, teachings and death of Jesus of Nazareth therefore overturn another dualistic hierarchy, namely that of humanity over nature. This duality persists even in liberation theology.[19] God's love now reaches out and enfolds the whole suffering body of the earth with its human and other-than-human members. In this sense, God does not distinguish between human suffering and ecological devastation.

From this point of view, I think that Sigurd Bergmann may misunderstand McFague when he implies that McFague's model of the body of God suspends the uniqueness of Christ's own historical acts of salvation and the salvific meaning of Christ's suffering.[20] As I read McFague, she does the opposite: she directly relates the historicity and the contextuality of the life and death of the body of the man Jesus with the life, death and regeneration of life in the larger body of the cosmos.[21]

When McFague says that nature is the "new poor", she does not mean that nature is intrinsically poor and less valuable than humanity. Rather, nature, in its vibrant diversity and complexity, has intrinsic value. A statement of the World Council of Churches on the meaning of the "integrity of creation" is valuable here: "The value of all creatures in and for themselves, for one another, and for God, and their interconnectedness in a diverse whole that has unique value for God, together constitute the integrity of creation."[22] This also means that humanity is poor when we do not recognise that we need, and are enriched by, the integrity of creation. Humanity is poor without nature. However, McFague terms nature as the "new poor" because *we* have made nature poor by our anthropocentric worldview, our assumption of having power over nature and our ravaging and destruction of nature. It is a comment not about the workings of nature but of human sin. The love of God for nature which speaks through Jesus' destabilising parables does not imply a sentimental divine love for every living organism. Rather, it brings to mind the righteous judgement of the Creator whose body, composed of so many diverse forms, is being diminished and damaged by humans – that greedy, albeit conscious and hence responsible, part of the body of God.[23]

Judgement?

Although McFague herself does not develop this theme of the righteous judgement of God over humanity's greed and destruction, it is taken forward by William French[24] in a provocative manner: he appreciates how McFague's panentheistic understanding of the world as God's body can radicalise our sense of God's immanence and love, but he remarks that the world as body of God also has a powerful, terrifying dimension: "To be balanced, however, panentheism needs also to be more explicit about how God is

---

[18] McFague (1993), 162-165.

[19] McFague (2001), 161.

[20] Bergman (2005), 239.

[21] McFague (1993), 179.

[22] Quoted in McFague (1993), 165. The original reference is an appendix in Birch, Eakin and McDaniel (1990), entitled "Liberating Life: A Report to the World Council of Churches", 273-290, quotation on 277, also 290.

[23] McFague (1993), 165-166.

[24] French, 142.

also present to us in the judgement and sometimes anger, in eco-demise. In pumping out CFC's we deplete the ozone shield – God's skin? – and thus damage God, the ecosystem and ourselves. Is it too crude to see in rising skin cancer rates, global warming fears, in species extinctions, in human diseases borne from pollution, in soil-erosion, the negative judgement of God against our activities?"

Is McFague perhaps too careful, in the greater part of her oeuvre, to relate the wrath of God to punishment, redemption and salvation? Perhaps she under-uses and underestimates the meaning of redemption as deliverance from sin because she finds traditional atonement theology to be unsatisfactory, and rather chooses to use the word "salvation" because she interprets it in a more positive way as healing and as preservation from destruction.[25] But is a mother's wrath not followed by redemption in the sense of saving a child from its own wrongdoing, and of bringing justice and order to a household?[26]

Salvation and Healing

McFague further argues that the salvific story of the destabilising, non-hierarchal, inclusive life, teachings, death (and resurrection) of Jesus as it is relevant for the whole natural life, the earth and the cosmos, is continued in the parables that suggest a subversion of the status quo and in the stories on salvation through healing and the stories on salvation and food, as told in the gospels.[27]

The central claim and theme of the gospel, namely, that the Word became flesh – also in the body of nature – is developed more deeply in the healing ministry of Jesus. Salvation comes through Jesus' healing of bodies. McFague suggests that in the organic model of doing theology, the body is the main attraction, and the healing stories seem to agree. They focus attention on bodily pain and bodily relief. The centrality of the healing stories stands over and against any minimising of the body. Bodies count, the healing ministry of Jesus claims. This fits in very well with an ecological sensibility. If the parables are the deconstructive phase of Jesus' ministry of salvation, overturning oppressive, dualistic hierarchies, then the healing stories are the reconstructive phase, not promising the kingdom but working for the kingdom through what in ecological terms may be called practices of sustainability – working, healing and caring so that all the members of the earth-body can function, and so that the earth can continue to sustain future generations. Bodily health and well-being is a priority of the gospel, not only for vulnerable human bodies but also for vulnerable bodies in the threatened ecosystems of the earth. It is a priority for salvation.[28]

Salvation and Food

A third characteristic aspect of Jesus' ministry to the body is his practice of eating with sinners and outcasts. This might be called the prospective phase, in contrast to the deconstructive phase (the parables) and the reconstructive phase (the healing stories). "This practice was as much a scandal to Jesus' contemporaries as were the destabilis-

[25] McFague (1993), 168.
[26] McFague (1987), 114, 117.
[27] McFague (1993), 168.
[28] McFague (1993), 167-168.

ing parables and the miraculous healings. It is also, although for different reasons, scandalous in an ecological era."[29] It suggests that all are invited to the banquet of life.

Two motives come to the fore: First, whatever food there is, be it only a few loaves, should be shared. Here is an exhortation that the basic needs of all creatures, including the most needy, be met with what available resources there are. Second, is the hope for abundance, for a feast that satisfies the deepest hungers of all creatures, of all creation. By focussing on food, which, along with breath, is the most immediate and necessary component of bodily health, the motif of God's love for all and especially the most vulnerable, which runs through McFague's ecological theology, is deepened and radicalised. Food is basic to all life and is, increasingly, a symbol of the planet's crisis: the lifestyle of greedy consumerism which is at the expense of the basic needs of all other living things.

So, this one metaphor of food includes not only what is most basic but also what is deepest and widest. The eating practices and feeding stories of Jesus not only suggest a survival strategy for the diversity of all life forms, but also project a vision when all shall gather at one table – the lion, the lamb and human beings – and eat their fill. It is a vision of salvation as wholeness, characterised by the overcoming of the differences between people and other living beings, and their inclusion in one feast of life. It is not merely a metaphor of fulfilment – it is physical – all creatures need food for survival and bodily health. The body of God must be fed. Salvation is as basic as this.[30]

Human Agency

In order to fully understand McFague's notion of salvation, it is necessary to explore her notion of human sin. While, on the one hand, the new creation story gives us a new sense of our responsibility as well as our limitations in relation to the rest of the community of living beings, it also gives us an earthly notion of sin. Sin is to live disproportionately, falsely, inappropriately within this space, refusing to accept the limitations and responsibilities of our place in creation, and thereby destroying and displacing species, biodiversity, ecosystems and habitats for the survival of millions of organisms and living systems, let alone the survival of millions of people.[31] This lifestyle has devastating and tragic consequences for humanity and the whole earth.

How do Christians respond to this devastation and radically change their sinful lifestyle? The only way is to participate in the subversive ministry of salvation of Jesus. McFague proposes that we do this by fighting "... with all our intelligence, power and imagination for the inclusion of all, especially those presently excluded in our time and place"[32] by the "displacement" caused by human injustice. In our time of ecological disaster, "the inclusion of all" means working for sustainable communities in which both humans and other-than-humans can be at home.

---

[29] McFague (1993), 169.

[30] McFague (1993), 169-170.

[31] McFague (2001), 76.

[32] McFague (1993), 178.

In Conclusion: The Eschaton

In the Christian tradition, eschatology has often involved a concern with death and the afterlife, with the "last things" such as judgement, hell and heaven, and with the second coming. McFague, however, interprets it as the breaking of new possibilities, of hope for a new creation. It means living with a vision to a different present based upon a new future. Salvation, or the good life for all in a new world, means first and foremost that the basic physical needs of the earth's creatures have to be met. We are all bodies who need the basics of food, clean air and water, shelter and space, support and community, and so forth, to live. Salvation, in an organic model, can never again be a-temporal, otherworldly and non-spatial. Viewing the new creation from the point of view of the body gives us a new way of seeing salvation and sin: as honouring and fulfilling or as degrading and destroying the body.[33]

In the Christic reading of the new creation, the vulnerable and the marginalised are now included in a community of abundant life. While, in the old paradigm, humanity's greed has made nature the "new poor", human beings now need to actively redress this. Human beings have a special responsibility to create a sustainable, wholesome future for the rich variety of living beings of our planet.[34] Life abundant means abundance for all living beings – and not only for a minority of rich and middle class people. It implies re-imagining the good life in just and sustainable ways so that the greater community of life can live in abundance.[35]

References and Recommended Reading

Bergmann, Sigurd (2005), *Creation Set Free: The Spirit as Liberator of Nature* (translated by Douglas Stott), Grand Rapids: Eerdmans.

Berry, Thomas (1988, 1990), *The Dream of the Earth*, San Francisco: Sierra Book Club.

Birch, Charles, Eakin, William and McDaniel, Jay B. (1990), *Liberating Life: Contemporary Approaches to Ecological Theology*, Maryknoll: Orbis.

French, William C. (1995), "The World as God's Body: Theological Ethics and Panentheism", in: Maureen A. Tilley and Susan A. Ross (eds.), *Broken and Whole: Essays on Religion and the Body*, Lanham: University Press of America, 135-144.

McFague, Sallie (1987), *Models of God: Theology for an Ecological, Nuclear Age*, Philadelphia: Fortress.

--- (1993), *The Body of God: An Ecological Theology*, Minneapolis: Fortress.

--- (2001), *Life Abundant: Rethinking Theology and Economy for a Planet in Peril*, Minneapolis: Fortress.

--- (2008), *A New Climate for Theology*, Minneapolis: Fortress.

Primavesi, Anne (2000), *Sacred Gaia: Holistic Theology and Earth System Science*, London / New York: Routledge.

Rasmussen, Larry (1996), *Earth Community, Earth Ethics*, Maryknoll: Orbis.

Swimme, Brian and Berry, Thomas (1992), *The Universe Story: From the Primordial Flashing Forth to the Ecozoic Era*, New York: Penguin.

Annalet van Schalkwyk

---

[33] McFague (1993), 198-200.

[34] McFague (1993), 201.

[35] McFague (2001), xii.

Rosemary Radford Ruether (1936-) – Life-Giving Relationships Restored

Rosemary Radford Ruether has been one of the most prolific thinkers and writers engaging the Christian tradition in addressing contemporary issues. Her works cover a wide range of topics, but the focus is social justice, bringing together ecology and gender issues. While Ruether rarely engages in systematic theology, her work implicitly reveals a theology of creation and salvation, one that challenges as well as appreciates traditional understandings of both.

Rosemary Radford was born in 1936 to a Roman Catholic mother and Episcopalian father and spent her early childhood in Georgetown, Texas, and in Athens, Greece. After her father's death in 1948, she moved first to Washington and then to California. In *Religious Feminism and the Future of the Planet* (New York: Continuum, 2001), authored with Rita Gross, Ruether attributes her ease of ecumenism to her early formation in an ecumenical family which included Jewish relatives as well as mixed Christian denominations. The name Ruether is that of her husband, Herman Ruether. Ruether's formal educational background includes a B.A. in philosophy and history from Scripps College, an M.A. in ancient history and a Ph.D. in classics and patristics from Claremont Graduate School (1965). Ruether was an activist in the civil rights and peace movements as well as the feminist movement and interreligious groups. She remained throughout her career a firm supporter of liberation theology, especially as formulated by women in minority groups because of race, ethnicity or class.

Theological reflection on the relationship between creation and salvation arises with Ruether from a feminist perspective on the history of the Christian tradition. The concern with this relationship runs through all her works. Christian feminists have attempted to reconstruct Christian teachings to combat the patriarchal readings they have inherited. Dualities, especially those which led to a devaluing of the body and the earth and the association of material being with women, stem from and reinforce systems of oppression for women, the earth and the poor. Ruether treats these themes throughout her many works, but there are a few works which give a more focussed overview of her theology: *The Church against Itself* (London: Sheed and Ward, 1967); *Liberation Theology: Human Hope Confronts Christian History and American Power* (New York: Paulist Press, 1972); *Sexism and God-Talk : Toward a Feminist Theology* (Boston: Beacon, 1993; first edition, 1983); *Gaia and God: An Ecofeminist Theology of Earth Healing* (San Francisco: HarperCollins, 1992); and *Women and Redemption: A Theological History* (Minneapolis: Augsburg Fortress, 1998). Sections of *The Radical Kingdom: The Western Experience of Messianic Hope* (New York: Harper and Row, 1970) and *Religious Feminism and the Future of the Planet* (see above) are also helpful in clarifying Ruether's position.

The Context of Ruether's Theology

Ruether is first and foremost a historian in that she views theology out of an historic perspective but always under a horizon of its present mediation. How does theology mediate justice and liberation, for women, for the earth, for the poor and oppressed? At the conclusion of her early work, *The Church against Itself*, Ruether claims that theological doctrines are always framed out of particular sociopolitical contexts and that as these contexts change, so too the theological understandings of the church do and ought to change. Sometimes this is for better, often it has been for worse. Furthermore, according to Ruether, the church tends to understand the development of theological doctrine as an organic process, each new interpretation improving and adapting that which went before. There is no room, she claims, for the acknowledgement of distortions and mistakes. In her view, the fact of the living presence of the Spirit of God "not only as a past event mediated by memory" means that reform has a radical structure. Even Scripture contains human words about God's Word. God's Word rests in the primal encounter of humankind with God.

Of course, all theology is the result of human judgement about this primal encounter. Judgement on the meaning of God's Word, the making of theology, however, is never final and never perfect. The final word of judgement belongs to God at the end of time.[36] Thus, the task of theologising is a humble one and is always mediated by imperfect instruments in imperfect times. This is one important context, supported by her knowledge of the history of Christianity, within which Ruether's views on creation and salvation are to be understood.

The second context for understanding Ruether's position on theology is her claim that distortions in the relationality of Christian life indicate distortions in theology. Creation and salvation theologies are particularly relevant to the distortions on which she focuses. In the case of the distortion represented by the duality of body and soul, a reading of the creation narratives through the lens of both Hebrew and Greek conceptions of the relationship between spirit and matter has led to an association of women with body and men with soul. Such an interpretation was exacerbated by the focus on rationality during the Enlightenment. This is a typical feminist critique, but Ruether painstakingly lays out the historical and theological developments that support a patriarchal system in which women are oppressed. She confronts any indications of essentialist differences between men and women and sees the origin of men's power over women in the social constructions of history, re-enforced by religio-cultural perceptions such as body and soul, spirit and matter, rationality and emotionality, and subjectivity and objectivity. These same dualities also result in an emphasis in salvation theology on redeeming humans "out of" this world, soul "out of" body.

Patriarchy is just one (though a primary one for Ruether) of the distortions of relationality that is buoyed up by Christian theological interpretations. Over the corpus of her work, Ruether also brings this critique to questions of religious and class relations of power: Christian perceptions of Jews, and of Palestinians, colonialism and imperialism and human relationship to the earth. Her own theological contribution lies in her attempts to show the breadth and ambiguity of the Christian tradition and to recover resources for a reconstruction of Christian theology to support a reformed relationality. She sees two major threads within the Christian tradition: the official interpretations supported by Christian hierarchies and the prophetic stream that has continued to challenge and change the tradition toward greater authenticity charity, justice and liberation. Ruether sought to contribute to the latter stream but going beyond the organic process of change to one in which radically new symbols and meanings can emerge. This she sees as necessary and probable as women's experience (and that of other oppressed groups) becomes a voice and a ground in theology.

---

[36] Ruether (1967), 226-277.

The Reconstruction of Creation Theology

In the reconstruction of creation theology, Ruether presents two concerns: earth-human relationship and human-human relationship. Both of these are ultimately concerned with the human-divine relationship. Earth is "good" in the sense of Genesis 1 because it participates in being, and God is the ground of all being. In *Women and Redemption*, human relationship to the rest of creation is described as "biophilic mutuality".[37] Biophilic mutuality applies both within and across species. The ontological grounding of all creation in God is also the ground of all ethical behaviour in humans. When humans were created, they were imbued with an intelligence; this was not to separate humans from the rest of the creation or to give them special privilege to lord over other species, but rather to define their role in maintaining the mutuality within creation. The lording over nature by humans is a disruption or distortion of relationality, a misuse of power, a sinful condition.

Given her historical-critical method, her knowledge of ancient mythology and her understanding of the Bible as human words about God's Word, Ruether has no problem endorsing new scientific accounts of the emergence and evolution of the cosmos. Her focus on the Genesis creation narratives is on the construction of the notions of good and evil they contain. She reconstructs these from the point of view of contemporary feminism. Having traced the long tradition of associating women with the initiation of evil into the world and women's bodies with the embodiment of evil, Ruether defines original sin as distorted relationality. The authenticity intended by God for both men and women is compromised. Sexism is a key instance of this. The possibility of a genuine I-Thou relationship is meagre. On the one hand, women are defined and come to experience themselves as objectified, deficient, sub-humans in a system that demonises them. On the other, the controlling male is also distorted by its normative role in brutality and heightened rationality that denies him the authentic expression of his humanity. Both males and females are caught in a vast system of inauthenticity. This is radical distortion of relationality, a degrading of the integrity of the personal centre of our being and of all beings and thus, the original sin.

Ruether is also insistent on the sacramental nature of creation, which stems not only from the understanding of God as Creator and ground of all being, but also in her understanding of Christ. In *Women and Redemption*, she asserts that Christ "as redeemer is not over against this cosmological source of cosmic life, but is the re-manifestation of Word and Wisdom of God which is the source and ground of life for the whole creation".[38] This accommodation and adaptation of the Greek idea of the cosmic soul is evident, she points out, in the New Testament letter to the Colossians (1:15-20) and was an idea central to the early church even up until the scientific revolution and the Enlightenment. It is a view that provides a resource for and has resonance with contemporary ecotheology.

The Unity of Creation and Redemption

Like many Christian ecotheologians and ecofeminists, Ruether laments the division in

---

[37] Ruether (1998), 223.

[38] Ruether (1998), 191.

Christian tradition between creation and salvation. The anthropomorphic and androcentric emphases have both influenced such a reading of the tradition and been enforced by it. The implication of this division in theology is that the destiny of the human is not an integral part of this bodily world, as she claims in *Gaia and God*. The real redemption (her preferred term for the perhaps too generic "salvation") happens in the destruction of this world and the reign of another.

With regard to the creation mythology in the book of Genesis, Ruether holds that nature, or the sum of cosmic life, was never paradisiacal from a human perspective; it was never totally benign to humans. Nor is nature capable of fulfilling human hopes for authentic personal or community life (Ruether's definition of "the good" or human ideal). Humans have not fallen, nor has nature, in the sense that some primal act of disobedience has destroyed the human capacity to work toward authentic mutuality in all relationships. Sin arose as a condition as humans became socialised into systems of domination and oppression and developed ideologies to maintain them. In the case of gender relations, salvation for woman is not a matter of faithfulness to the teachings of a male dominated system – church or otherwise. Rather, it is a transformation of gender relations toward restored mutual respect and equality. While humans are entrapped within oppressive systems of their own creation, they have not lost their power to overturn them, even if that will never be totally accomplished.

While Ruether, especially in her later works, leaves open the real meaning of redemption within Christian feminism, she does make some assertions about hopeful directions for redemption theology and its union with creation theology. In the conclusion to *Women and Redemption*, she gives a summary of the positions of many Christian feminists and ecofeminists, drawing out both the inadequacies and the strengths of their positions. On the one hand, for instance, the fact of a male saviour can be reconciled with feminist theology; it is the quality of Jesus' humanity and not his gender that is normative. On the other hand, she later concludes, this does not fully overcome "the basic social-symbolic structure in which Jesus, a male, opts for women as objects of concern".[39] Furthermore, the emphasis on the suffering and death of Jesus as redemptive has been a problem for women. Some parallel the suffering of women as victims with that of Jesus, but does this not celebrate the passive suffering of women? Suffering is also a factor in liberation, but not a redemptive factor; rather it is part of the risk of change. For Ruether, redemption occurs as conversion, the restoration of open and enriching systems through life-giving relationships in community, "not getting oneself tortured to death".[40] Patriarchy as well as other oppressive systems (all of which are entwined) subvert creation and resist salvation.

Just as creation and salvation are moments in the action of a single God, nature and society cohere in a single community under the sovereignty of God. The God of creation is the God of salvation. There is no new agenda. For Ruether, salvation is always mediated and accessible to our understanding only in the realities of life itself. This, as she consistently demonstrates in her historical presentations, has been neglected in the dominant interpretations of both creation and salvation. Hence for her there are no valid meanings to creation and salvation that do not have an impact on the systems of

---

[39] Ruether (1998), 278.

[40] Ruether (1998), 279.

liberation or oppression which Christians strive to influence and live by. The Creator imbued the creation with a desire for a mutuality that enhances both individual and community capacities for a full and creative life. Sin is the hindrance to the perfection of this claim. Yet it has never been totally destroyed. Redemption, encapsulated in the entire life, death and resurrection of Jesus Christ, broke through the oppression of gender, race, class, slavery and ethnicity. For Ruether, the paradigmatic text for the understanding of redemption is the early baptismal formula from Galatians (3:28): "In Christ, no more male or female, Jew or Greek, slave or free". This is never fully achieved. But the real "fruits of redemption" (to use a traditional phrase) are not immortality and a perfect world to come. Rather, according to Ruether, they are the work of this world. The in-breaking of the kingdom confronts the cycles and systems of sin in enabling the formation of earth communities of liberation, the fulfilment of creation.

References and Recommended Reading

Bouma-Prediger, Steven (1995), *The Greening of Theology: The Ecological Models of Rosemary Radford Ruether, Joseph Sittler, and Jürgen Moltmann*, Atlanta: Scholars Press.

Chopp, Rebecca (1989), "Seeing and Naming the World Anew: The Works of Rosemary Radford Ruether", *Religious Studies Review*, Vol. 15, 1, 8-11.

Eaton, Heather (2009), "Reflections on the Contribution of Rosemary Radford Ruether", *Feminist Theology*, Vol. 17, 2, 152-157.

Hilkert, Mary Catherine (1995), "Feminist Theology: Key Religious Symbols, Christ and God", *Theological Studies*, Vol. 56, 2, 341-352.

--- (1997), "Feminist and Womanist Theologies", in: David F. Ford (ed.), *The Modern Theologians* (second edition), Oxford: Blackwell, 389-404.

Ramsay, William M. (1986), *Four Modern Prophets: Walter Rauschenbusch, Martin Luther King, Jr., Gustavo Gutiérrez, Rosemary Radford Ruether*, Atlanta: John Knox.

Ruether, Rosemary Radford (1967), *The Church against Itself*, New York: Herder and Herder.

--- (1998), *Women and Redemption: A Theological History*, Minneapolis: Augsburg Fortress.

Snyder, Mary Hembrow (1988), *The Christology of Rosemary Radford Ruether: A Critical Introduction*, Mystic: Twenty-Third Publications.

Anne Marie Dalton

Elizabeth Johnson (1941-) – The Creator Spirit Vivifying Life

Elizabeth Johnson is one of the foremost American feminist theologians. She was born on 6 December 1941 in New York. In 1959 she entered the Sisters of St. Joseph of Brentwood, Long Island, a Catholic religious congregation. This was three years before the beginning of the Second Vatican Council (1962-1965) and her religious formation was a very traditional semi-cloistered experience. In contrast, her life as a feminist theologian has been radically open to the "signs of the times", especially the situation of women.

Her theological studies were done at Manhattan College in New York where she earned an M.A. in 1970 and at the Catholic University of America in Washington, DC, where she was awarded a Ph.D. in theology in 1981, the first woman to receive this degree. She was on the faculty of the Catholic University of America from 1980 to 1991 and is currently distinguished professor of theology at Fordham University in New York. She was president of the Catholic Theological Society of America.

Her writings include *Consider Jesus: Waves of Renewal in Christology* (1990), *She Who Is: The Mystery of God in Feminist Theological Discourse* (1992), *Women, Earth, and Creator Spirit* (1993), *Friends of God and Prophets* (1998), *Truly Our Sister: A Theology of Mary in the Communion of Saints* (2003) and *Quest for the Living God: Mapping Frontiers in the Theology of God* (2007).[41]

Pneumatological Ecofeminism

Johnson's approach to the interrelationship of creation and salvation is rooted in her explication of the fundamental connection between the degradation of creation, the oppression of women and the Spirit of God. Her thesis is "that the exploitation of the earth, which has reached crisis proportions in our day, is intimately linked to the marginalisation of women, and that both of these predicaments are intrinsically related to forgetting the Creator Spirit who pervades the world in the dance of life".[42]

In her groundbreaking study of God as Trinity in female language, *She Who Is*, she stresses that all of life mediates "the dialectic of presence or absence of divine mystery".[43] This includes the natural world, personal and interpersonal experience and social structures. She traces the neglect of the Spirit in the Western theological tradition and makes the connection between its marginalisation and that of women.

Drawing on the Wisdom tradition of the Scriptures, Johnson names the Spirit as Spirit-Sophia. For example, the Book of Wisdom describes Sophia as "a pure radiance of the glory of the Almighty" (Wisd. 7:25). Spirit-Sophia vivifies, renews, empowers and graces. Because the Spirit is life-giver, "the whole universe comes into being and remains in being through divine creative power, *Creator Spiritus*".[44] The Spirit's breath has given life to all and continues to do so. From the moment of the Flaring Forth, more than fourteen billion years ago, "she hovers like a great mother bird over her egg, to hatch the living order of the world out of primordial chaos (Gn 1:2)".[45] Johnson asserts, "The Creator Spirit is the unceasing, dynamic flow of loving power that sustains the world, brings forth life, weaves connections between all creatures, and repairs what gets damaged. Instead of sitting beyond the point of the pyramid of privilege, the divine Spirit encircles and indwells the universe."[46]

As astronomers tell us, the universe is still expanding into the furthest reaches of deep space and the Spirit is there as the "creative origin of all life"[47] – whose presence is deeper embedded in creation than human language can describe. Johnson asserts that "if she were to withdraw her divine presence everything would go back to no-

---

41 In March 2011 the Committee on Doctrine of the United States Conference of Catholic Bishops issued a very negative judgement of *Quest for the Living God*, calling into question its coherence with Catholic teaching. This critique was strongly countered by statements of support by the Catholic Theological Society of America and other bodies. In October 2011 the same Committee on Doctrine issued another strong negative interpretation of the book.

42 Johnson (1993), 2.

43 Johnson (1992), 124.

44 Johnson (1992), 133.

45 Johnson (1992), 134.

46 Johnson (2008), 9.

47 Johnson (1993), 42.

thing".[48] This union is described in female language: "the pregnant female body provides a good metaphor"[49] for this mutual abiding of the Spirit and creation.

Johnson uses the scriptural theme of glory to deepen her interpretation of the presence of the Spirit. Glory "is a category of divine immanence perceived through the world's participation in divine beauty".[50] To speak of the "glory of God" is to maintain "that the incomprehensible holy mystery of God indwells the natural and human world as source, sustaining power and goal of the universe".[51] Humanity's response must be both awe and prophetic action.

Spirit-Sophia renews and empowers all creatures. This is seen in fertility – human, animal and in nature – and also in human creativity and the works of liberation and justice. In nature the earth is renewed each year in spring with the signs of new life. Even though human action is having such a damaging effect on the earth, "the resilience of earth's systems, within finite limits, is one sign of the Spirit's efficacy".[52] Johnson points out that our current ecological crisis, caused by human action and inaction, illustrates Paul's image of all of creation "groaning" (Rom. 8:22).

To renew the earth, to preserve life and to work for justice and liberation are all acts of prophecy, efforts of cosmic and social renewal. Thus any attempt to "spiritualise" and restrict the presence and power of the Spirit to a person's relationship with the divine is a radical misunderstanding of who the Spirit is and what the Spirit does. All of creation – nature, humans, social structures – are to be renewed and empowered by Spirit-Sophia.

In describing the work of the Spirit as gracing, Johnson explicitly links the Spirit to other religious traditions. The work of grace is universal but it is made concrete in religious practice, "thereby clearly focusing on the Spirit's deeds of drawing all of creation towards the holiness of God".[53]

Because the Spirit is both personal and universal, many metaphors have been used to speak of her. In the Christian tradition, the Spirit has often been described as love and gift. Building on both Augustine's and Aquinas's reflections on the Trinity, Johnson expands their interpretations in feminist categories. Love "has strong affinities with the model of relationship most prized by feminist thought",[54] but in terms of the Spirit it "cannot be used to legitimize patriarchal structures but signals a migration towards reciprocity in community as the highest good".[55] To speak of the Spirit as gift can be problematic if it refers to the "gifts of women's service", the result of their socialisation in all cultures to give and not receive. Johnson emphasises that the very nature of gift is gratuitous – it cannot be owed. Spirit-Sophia is free and liberating. Feminist theology uses additional metaphors for the Spirit such as friend, sister and the maternity of the Spirit.

---

48 Johnson (1992), 134.

49 Johnson (2008), 9.

50 Johnson (1996), 89.

51 Johnson (1996), 91.

52 Johnson (1992), 135.

53 Johnson (1992), 139.

54 Johnson (1992), 143.

55 Johnson (1992), 143.

Johnson summarises her view of the Spirit: "Spirit-Sophia, friend, sister, mother and grandmother of the world builds relationships of solidarity, not antithesis, between God and human beings and among human beings with each other and the earth."[56]

Ecofeminist Perspectives

Johnson's pneumatology is thus the foundation for her ecofeminism. She roots our current ecological crisis in the continuing bitter fruits of hierarchical dualism, the heritage of Greek philosophy extrapolated into contemporary experience. Dualism is premised on binary opposites: spirit and matter, men and women, humanity and nature. The second in the pairs is understood to be of less importance and value.

Johnson describes the practical meaning of this dualism: "... men are linked with a transcendent, spiritual principle beyond nature, while women and the earth embody the lower, material principle, existing within a natural inferiority for which there is no remedy."[57] Women and nature are both assigned only instrumental value and their continuing exploitation "has a common ideological root: men's separation from and supposed superiority to material femaleness".[58] Thus sexism and ecological degradation have grown and lamentably flourished together.

The sexism which continues to permeate the Christian tradition also has resulted in a sense of cosmic alienation. How can humanity see worth and value in the natural world – in the earth, our only home – when this ideology continues to insist that women and nature are lower than men and their life of the intellect?

Johnson lists a litany of the components of our ecological crisis: "global warming, holes in the ozone layer, clear-cut forests, drained wetlands, denuded soils, polluted air, poisoned rivers, overfished rivers and the threat of nuclear conflagration".[59] The perils of our planet impact most starkly on women: "... poor women whose own biological abilities to give birth are compromised by toxic environments, and whose nurturing of children is hampered at every turn by lack of clean water, food and fuel."[60]

The theological root of this dire situation is seen in the neglect of the Spirit in Christian theology. Dualism is a danger to all on earth. But "a theology of the Creator Spirit overcomes the dualism of spirit and matter with all of its ramifications, and leads to the realization of the sacredness of the earth".[61] Her felicitous phrase "Dualism has trouble with threes"[62] is particularly striking.

Johnson describes three models of humanity's relation with the earth. She rejects two and affirms the third. The kingship model, based on hierarchical dualism with male humanity in charge, ranks creatures and assigns them value according to how valuable they are for humans. Thus a spider is less important than a cow. The stewardship model at first appears more friendly to the earth since it mandates that humanity

[56] Johnson (1992), 147.
[57] Johnson (1993), 12.
[58] Johnson (1993), 15.
[59] Johnson (2007), 186.
[60] Johnson (2007), 187.
[61] Johnson (1993), 59-60.
[62] Johnson (1993), 20.

must guard and take care of the earth and all who share this planet with us. But it omits the dependence and connection that humanity has with all of creation. We are not separate from those we care for. The model of kinship avoids the deficiencies of the other two models. Kinship "sees human beings and the earth with all its creatures intrinsically related as companions in a community of life" and thus "the flourishing or damaging of one ultimately affects all".[63] For example, the continuing extinction of species of flora and fauna is escalating and the loss of any species impoverishes all of creation, including humanity.

The Creator Spirit as life itself thus gives all of created reality a sacramental character. Centring ecological theology, particularly ecofeminism, in the Spirit leads to an image of God "not at or beyond the apex of the pyramid of being as in modern theism, but within and around the emerging, struggling, living, dying and renewing circle of life and the whole universe itself".[64] Creator Spirit loves the material, and thus all of creation is holy – the physical world, nature, bodies and especially women's bodies.

Johnson stresses that an ecological theology rooted in the Spirit has two important benefits. "First, it opens doors to new forms of relationship with the all-holy God present and active throughout the whole world" and second "this theology motivates an ethic of care for the Earth"[65] with many implications. To understand the earth as a sacrament of divine presence presents a multitude of challenges to people of faith who need "to become prophetic and challenging, promoting care, protection and healing of the natural world even if these go counter to powerful economic and political interests – and they do".[66]

Johnson outlines three forms of action required by the ecological crisis. The first is sacramental. Because of the Spirit's life-giving presence "matter bears the mark of the sacred, being imbued with spiritual radiance".[67] We are called to gaze on the world contemplatively "with the eyes of love rather than with an arrogant, utilitarian stare"[68] and in doing so to experience the sacramental character of Earth and all of creation.

The second is a new form of asceticism which removes "what blocks our sensitivity to divine power and presence" by working "to restore right relations between humankind and otherkind distorted by hubris and greed".[69] This is an arduous task, because humankind has become enslaved by consumerism and greed. Thus Johnson suggests that new forms of fasting, retreats, wilderness experiences, almsgiving – all part of the Christian ascetic tradition – need to be developed so that Christians can experience a greater freedom in relation to the personal and social forms of slavery.

The third response is prophetic "action on behalf of justice for the Earth"[70] which also extends to all with whom we share this one planet. One criterion guides this prophetic word and action: "whether or not these contribute to a sustainable Earth com-

[63] Johnson (1993), 30.
[64] Johnson (2007), 189.
[65] Johnson (2008), 19.
[66] Johnson, (2007), 197.
[67] Johnson (2008), 17.
[68] Johnson (2001), 121.
[69] Johnson (2001), 122.
[70] Johnson (2001), 123.

munity".[71] Social justice and ecological devastation are deeply intertwined, and it is women and children who suffer the most as their environment deteriorates. For example, poor women in Asia, Africa and Latin America have to walk increasingly long distances to find the water and firewood needed to sustain their families. Today, Johnson asserts that "social justice has an ecological face".[72]

Conclusion

Elizabeth Johnson's feminist interpretations of the mystery of God are the foundation of her ecofeminism. Her development of a theology of the Trinity in female language includes naming the Spirit as Spirit-Sophia, who is love, gift, friend and sister to all of created reality. The Spirit as the vivifier of all life overcomes the hierarchical dualism which is a philosophical and theological cause of our current ecological crisis. Women and nature both continue to suffer from its pernicious effects.

The Spirit who dwells in all of reality loves all of creation, not just part of it. Women who have been named as of lesser value in the Christian tradition are equally loved and empowered by the Spirit. Johnson's ecofeminist perspective thus brings together a renewed pneumatology, a theology of the intrinsic connections of all of reality in the web of life and ethical implications for how humanity, with all of creation, will live or die together.

References and Recommended Reading

Johnson, Elizabeth A. (1990), *Consider Jesus: Waves of Renewal in Christology*, New York: Crossroad.

--- (1992), *She Who Is: The Mystery of God in Feminist Theological Discourse*, New York: Crossroad.

--- (1993), *Women, Earth, and Creator Spirit*, New York: Paulist Press.

--- (1996), "Heaven and Earth are Filled with Your Glory", in: Michael J. Himes and Stephen J. Pope (eds.), *Finding God in All Things: Essays in Honor of Michael J. Buckley, SJ*, New York: Crossroad, 84-101.

--- (1999), *Friends of God and Prophets: A Feminist Theological Reading of the Communion of Saints*, New York: Continuum.

--- (2001), "Passion for God, Passion for the Earth", in: Mary Hombrow Snyder (ed.), *Spiritual Questions for the 21st Century: Essays in Honor of Joan D. Chittister*, Maryknoll: Orbis, 118-125.

--- (2003), *Truly Our Sister: A Theology of Mary in the Communion of Saints*, New York / London: Continuum.

--- (2007), *Quest for the Living God: Mapping Frontiers in the Theology of God*, London / New York: Continuum.

--- (2008), "Creative Giver of Life: An Ecological Theology of the Holy Spirit", The Spirit in the New Millennium: The Duquesne University Fourth Annual Holy Spirit Lecture and Colloquium, <www.duq.edu/holy-spirit/2008.cfm>, retrieved 9 August 2011.

Rakoczy, S. (2008), "The Theological Vision of Elizabeth A. Johnson", *Scriptura*, Vol. 98, 137-155.

Susan Rakoczy

---

71 Johnson (2001), 123.

72 Johnson (2001), 124.

Grace Jantzen (1948-2006) – "They Shall Flourish as a Garden"[73]

> At the heart of her work was a concern for the way in which a preoccupation with death and violence had distorted the Western cultural imagination ... In particular she regarded Christianity's veneration of a transcendent, disembodied, dispassionate God (and) its institutionalisation of a desire for other-worldly salvation as flight from immanent, material existence ...[74]

The question which runs through the writings of Grace Jantzen (1948-2006) for at least the last ten years of her life is this: why are we so preoccupied with death rather than life? She notes that this preoccupation with death is gendered, entwined with violence and leads to an aversion for bodies (especially female bodies), the material world and beauty. This question and the alternative she sought to explore, namely an imaginary which focuses on natality and the flourishing of the earth and all its creatures, shape her discussion of creation and salvation.

The Earth as the Body of God

Jantzen's most extended theological work is *Becoming Divine* (1998) in which she set out to write a feminist philosophy of religion. She explains how the philosophers of religion in the Christian West have constructed a god who looks suspiciously like "his" creators – an omnipotent patriarch who, removed from his creation, presides over it, who is rational, male and disembodied. By way of a corrective she seeks, therefore, to describe a "god according to our gender";[75] a God who is "a disruption of the dualistic and hierarchical western symbolic",[76] a God who could be described as "the horizon of our becoming"[77] and whose desire is natality and "a flourishing of the earth and those who dwell upon it".[78] This understanding of God has its roots in her earlier book *God's World, God's Body* (1984), in which she challenged the dualist assumptions of Western theological thought that separate God from creation, spirit from material and soul from body. Instead, she instead proposed that we should view God as embodied – not reduced to the universe, just as human beings are not reduced to our bodies, but are co-extensive with it.

In her last work, the third in a proposed six-volume project which was never completed because of her death, she insists on the co-inherence of God and the material universe. Again she notes the theme which runs through the Western philosophical enterprise from Plato onwards, through Augustine, and into modern theology, in which the divine is divorced from material creation. In *A Place of Springs* (2010), as indeed in the other two volumes, she seeks to retrieve a theology which foregrounds beauty as a way of disrupting the violence and deathly obsession of the West. She notes how for Plato and the neo-Platonists beauty has to do with the soul rather than the body.[79]

---

73 Jantzen (1998), 156.

74 Graham, 2.

75 Jantzen (1998), 254.

76 Jantzen (1998), 275.

77 Jantzen (1998), 274.

78 Jantzen (1998), 274.

79 Jantzen (2010), 132.

Indeed it is not even in the body that we perceive beauty, says Plato, but in the inner sight.[80] These ideas were taken up in early Christianity and especially by Augustine, who, "even though he wrote with deep appreciation of the beauties of creation and the blessings these beauties confer", also asserted that God must be separate from the physical world.[81] Augustine's insistence on the doctrine of creation *ex nihilo* is just such an attempt to keep God and the created order separate. Jantzen critiques this doctrine which "goes well beyond scriptural pronouncement"[82] on the basis that the strict separation of God from the material universe precludes an understanding of God's action in the world. Furthermore, it suggests that human beings cannot encounter God within the world of material things.[83] This in turn leads to a disregard for creation and the idea that salvation entails escape from the physical world, including an escape from the body. Jantzen notes that one of the consequences of this strict separation of God and the universe is "the obliteration of the sense of kinship in the whole web of life …"[84] – kinship she felt closely. She describes the privilege of living "in the heart of the beautiful Lake District", "the endlessly various beauty" of her surroundings which she describes as sacramental.[85] In contradistinction, Jantzen therefore contends that "the universe *is* divine, not in the sense that God is reducible to atomic particles but in the sense that sacredness is one way of characterizing the universe …"[86] Although she does not explicate the idea in detail, in her last book, *A Place of Springs*, she begins to consider what it might mean to know "animals, plants, maybe even rocks and stars … not just for … utilitarian ends but as part of a living world where beauty and goodness had as great a part as truth …"[87]

Sin, Salvation and Flourishing

Always alert to the gendered nature of Christian theological formulation, Jantzen points out that much theological reflection on what constitutes sin is described by men who hold a dominant position in the church and society, and that ideas of salvation which derive from these gendered notions of sin are not life-giving, especially for women (to which we might add the poor and the earth).[88] For Jantzen, sin and its remedy is perhaps best articulated when she cites, with approval, the early Quaker leader Margaret Fell:

> It is the denial of this life, the endeavour to limit the Spirit of the living God, which has caused the ungodliness and death dealing of the age, says Fell, and it is by returning to the life of God and finding in oneself that welling up of divine light which is the remedy, because it brings the possibility of radically new insight and action.[89]

---

[80] Jantzen (2010), 134.
[81] Jantzen (2010), 142.
[82] Jantzen (2010), 143.
[83] Jantzen (2010), 147.
[84] Jantzen (1998), 151.
[85] Jantzen (2010), 1.
[86] Jantzen (2010), 148.
[87] Jantzen (2010), 117.
[88] Jantzen (1998), 159
[89] Jantzen (2010), 82, 83.

Rather than sin, however, Jantzen uses the language of illness, especially psychological illness, to describe the human condition. She diagnoses that "a constitutive feature of the western symbolic is a preoccupation with death, and with it, a longing for other worlds".[90] Mortality is perceived "not as a human fact but as a fundamental philosophical category".[91] For example, we describe human beings as mortals rather than natals. Our language betrays us. She also draws attention to Christianity's emphasis on the afterlife and especially the terrors of hell.[92] She asks, therefore, "what if we were to begin with birth ... how if we were to treat natality and the emergence of *this* life and *this* world with the same seriousness and respect which had traditionally been paid to mortality and striving for other worlds?"[93] It is this question which shapes her way of considering religion and which impacts her rethinking some traditional questions for a philosophy of religion. For example, she notes that a standard topic in philosophy of religion is the question as to whether people of religions other than Christianity may be "saved". But, she asks, is there not something "grievously amiss" with a discussion of the salvation of immortal souls, when many of those "souls" would find salvation in food, clean water and shelter now? "Yet about this the philosophy is deafeningly silent."[94] The investment in mortality rather than natality is apparent.

However, she goes further than simply suggesting that salvation be understood in the way advocated by liberation theologians, namely, the salvation of the poor here and now. She suggests that the very language of salvation is so embedded in theology that we do not recognise it as a *metaphor*.[95] The metaphor has become a literal perception, a dogmatic theological truth.[96] Consequently Christian theology has become premised on our need to be rescued from this fallen and evil world by God who intervenes from outside to take us to our true home which is a place we go to after death. When these attitudes are linked to the prevailing sexist attitudes that link women to the body and men to the rational mind, the result is a deeply gendered "deathly symbolic"[97] in which, as many liberation theologians have noted, the focus on life after death distracts from engaging with daily struggles of women, the poor and the earth. She thus suggests that the metaphor of salvation needs to be balanced with another metaphor, namely that of flourishing.[98]

The promise of flourishing is a theme of both the biblical prophets and the Wisdom literature (for example Zechariah 9:10-17, Hosea 14:3-7, Psalm 92:12 and Proverbs 14:4). In the New Testament writings, although the specific vocabulary of flourishing is absent, there the idea is still manifest, for example in Ephesians 3:19-20, 2 Corinthians 9:8 and the Fourth Gospel in particular. However, despite the presence of this theme of flourishing in the Bible, the focus in Christian theology has shifted almost

---

90 Jantzen (2004), 5.
91 Jantzen (1998) 2.
92 Jantzen (2009), 179.
93 Jantzen (1998), 2.
94 Jantzen (1998), 146.
95 Jantzen (1998), 161.
96 Jantzen (1998), 160.
97 Jantzen (2004), 12.
98 Jantzen (1998), 156-170.

entirely to the metaphor of salvation, particularly from the Reformation theologians onwards. She therefore suggests a retrieval of that balancing metaphor of flourishing. When this is linked to her suggestion that we pay attention to natality rather than mortality, there are rich possibilities, which can only be briefly surveyed here.

Firstly, flourishing is a positive concept which suggests verdant life. By way of contrast, salvation implies rescue from a crisis.[99]

Secondly, the metaphor of flourishing calls for a love of this world and its creatures rather than seeing the material world as evil or, at best, a vale of tears though which we must pass. Furthermore, as ecologists remind us, the entire ecosystem is interdependent so that flourishing does not imply that one group or species should flourish at the expense of others. If salvation is rescue of a (select) group of people for some kind of heavenly existence, flourishing calls for a careful fostering of connectedness and care that every species blossom.[100]

Thirdly, one of the consequences of the metaphor of salvation is that we require rescue by someone outside the crisis situation. We come thus to value saviour figures, reducing the rest of us to helpless creatures in need of ruling and rescuing. This is precisely the basis for ideologies such as patriarchy, racism and colonialism. The metaphor of flourishing, instead, suggests an inner dynamic of growth and mutual commitment and responsibility to one another's flourishing. We depend on others just as much as they depend on us. There is no room here for rescuers and dependents.[101] Drawing on the work of Emmanuel Levinas, Jantzen thus develops what she calls an "ethics of natality".[102] Though she critiques his masculinist approach, she argues with him both against the reduction of the other to an ontological category, and for the recognition of the other as a face who calls forth justice. This "justice in the face of the natals" is the way in which the divine is called forth: "God can only be defined through human relations."[103] The other is not to be ruled, saved, or categorised in any way, but always to be responded to with sympathy and love, allowing her to make fresh and unexpected new beginnings in relationship.

Fourthly, salvation is more often than not an individualistic concept, especially when it is linked to individual belief and because it is rescue from this world, there is no concern for others or the ecosystem. As Jantzen dramatically expresses it – "personal salvation whilst the rest of the world goes up in flames".[104] On the other hand, flourishing is impossible by oneself alone. It implies interconnectedness, just as earth and sun and rain together lead to the blossoming of a plant. Furthermore, whilst salvation tends towards a static once-for-all image, flourishing is dynamic.[105]

Finally, salvation too often (with the significant exception of some of the liberation theologies) implies rescue of the soul with little concern for the body. This mind / body dualism, theologically justified by a dualism between God of ultimate value and

[99] Jantzen (1998), 160.
[100] Jantzen (1998), 165, 166.
[101] Jantzen (1998), 160.
[102] Jantzen (1998), 231-248.
[103] Jantzen (1998), 250.
[104] Jantzen (1998), 165.
[105] Jantzen (1998), 165.

the material universe which has little or no worth, leads inevitably to the ecological crisis we face.[106] Flourishing "does not make sense unless bodiliness is taken into account ... (and) involves thriving, luxuriant growth, diversity, obvious and exuberant good health".[107] In turn this leads back to Jantzen's proposition that the material universe should not be conceived as separate from God.

It is impossible to do justice to the complexity of Jantzen's ideas on beauty, its denial in the Western symbolic and the possibilities for redemption which its retrieval offers. However, we may simply note here her contention that an imbalanced emphasis on truth and ethics and the denial or repression of beauty may be seen as part of the problem of violence and the obsession with death and other worlds, which in turn have led to domination of or disregard for the material universe.[108] The world, she asserts, is in need of redemption.[109] Her suggestion is that reclaiming an appreciation of beauty, both natural and artistic, is the way to "release the springs of creativity by which newness can enter the world".[110] Far from an escape from the world through death, reclaiming beauty enables us to encounter the divine in the world and each other, in Jantzen's own words, "to redeem the present".[111]

The purpose of her balancing metaphor of flourishing may be summarised as a way of seeking to "safeguard the fragile beauty of the created universe and its inhabitants ... to instill a love of this world by promoting an ideal of just and loving subjects".[112]

References and Recommended Reading

Graham, Elaine L. (2009), "Redeeming the Present", in: Elaine L. Graham (ed.), *Grace Jantzen: Redeeming the Present*, Aldershot: Ashgate, 1-19.

Jantzen, Grace (1984), *God's World, God's Body*, Philadelphia: Westminster.

--- (1995), "Healing our Brokenness: The Spirit and Creation", in: Mary Heather MacKinnon and Moni McIntyre (eds.), *Readings in Ecology and Feminist Theology*, Kansas City: Sheed and Ward, 284-298.

--- (1998), *Becoming Divine: Towards a Feminist Philosophy of Religion*, Manchester: Manchester University Press.

--- (2004), *Foundations of Violence*, London: Routledge.

--- (2009), *Violence to Eternity* (edited by J. Carrette and Morny Joy), London / New York: Routledge.

--- (2010), *A Place of Springs* (edited by J. Carrette and Morny Joy), London / New York: Routledge.

Joy, Morny (2009), "Grace Jantzen and the Work of Love", in: Elaine L. Graham (ed.), *Grace Jantzen: Redeeming the Present*, Farnham: Ashgate, 23-39.

Janet Trisk

[106] Jantzen (1995).

[107] Jantzen (1998), 167.

[108] Jantzen (2010), 51.

[109] Jantzen (2004), 3.

[110] Jantzen (2004), 5.

[111] Jantzen (2004), 6.

[112] Joy, 31.

Further Developments

These essays on five significant feminist theologians who have engaged with ecological issues demonstrate the breadth of theological reflection on the ways that ecofeminism informs a renewed understanding of creation and salvation.

A pervasive theme is a critique of the philosophical and theological dualism which has permeated Christian theology like a virus, infecting every aspect of theological reflection from the earliest centuries of Christian faith. This dualism has opposed man-woman, mind-matter, body-spirit, with the second of the pair judged by male theologians as inferior to the first. Through the identification of woman with nature, both have been objectified, to be used at will by men. An individualistic, anthropocentric view of creation has led to the degradation of creation and has placed all who share this planet in peril.

In response, these women propose images of connection and connectedness: of humanity and creation, of the intrinsic relatedness of creation and salvation / redemption, of humanity in relationship with each other as men and women, no longer in dualistic opposition.

These essays have shown how each of the theologians has done ground-breaking work in ecofeminism. Catherina Halkes's writings are distinguished by the ways she joins the themes of conversion and transformation. The primary Christian doctrines of creation and salvation are interwoven and expressed in sacramental language by Sallie McFague and Elizabeth Johnson. The cosmos and all of creation are permeated by the presence of God, by Spirit-Sophia in Johnson's language. Bodies – all bodies, including women's bodies – are holy. The metaphor of the body of Christ assumes new meaning when it is connected to the holiness of all that is created. Christ is indeed the cosmic Christ of Colossians and Ephesians (Col. 1:15-20; Eph. 1:20-22) and our understanding of the universe as ever-expanding stretches Paul's language to embrace the dynamism of constant creation.

Rosemary Radford Ruether wrote some of the first significant essays on ecofeminism and although she reflects from a North American perspective, she demonstrates a focused interest in the ecological challenges of poor women around the world. Sallie McFague's image of the earth as the body of God has begun to shape our ecological theological imagination. Grace Jantzen provocatively asks why we are so concerned with death and not with the flourishing of life.

In the foundational work of ecofeminism, the paradox of women and nature as objects to be used and not reverenced has been extensively analysed. This area raises the question of human agency: how can women and men both "use" the gifts of creation and not "misuse" them? Women's goodness as fully created in the image of God is now a theological precept. But still humanity abuses creation. How will the next step be taken?

One of the strengths of ecofeminism is that it invites theological reflection which connects many theological themes. Creation and salvation are primary, but ecofeminism also has implications for other areas of theology. What is the nature of the human person who lives and acts on this one planet? What can we hope for as humanity – for ourselves, for the future? How might an ecofeminist eschatology describe this hope? What resources does the Christian tradition, in dialogue with other world religions, provide for an ecofeminist spirituality, a spirituality which is premised on "life to the full"?

Ecofeminisms are rooted in their particular social and political contexts. Ruether and Johnson both stress that care for creation must include action for liberation from oppression. It is this perspective that can build theological bridges between these North American and European theologians and their sister theologians in Asia, Africa and Latin America. The facts of ecological damage are different in the North and South. The writings of women such as Denise Ackermann (South Africa), Sophie Chirongoma (Zimbabwe), Gabriele Dietrich (India), Celia Deane-Drummond (United Kingdom), Heather Eaton (Canada), Ivone Gebara (Brazil), Aruna Gnanadason (India), Lorna Hallahan (Australia), Teresia Hinga (Kenya), Maria Jansdotter (Sweden), Chung Hyun Kyung (Korea), Fulata Lusungu Moyo (Malawi), Mercy Oduyoye (Ghana), Anne Primavesi (England), Kwok Pui-Lan (China) and Susan Rakoczy (South Africa) stress that ecofeminist theological reflection must also lead to transformative ecofeminist praxis.[113]

The foundations of ecofeminism have been laid, but much more work lies ahead. What areas might the emerging generation of ecofeminist theologians engage? The "new cosmology" with its extraordinary vision of the place of the earth including humanity invites wonder and awe. But as we recognise with utter dismay how the earth is in ever-increasing danger from global warming and climate change because of the activities of humanity, theologians are challenged to begin to connect the "new universe story" with the imperative to care for this earth, our only home.

Injustice and inequality describe the world in the early 21st century. How can ecofeminist insights contribute to an ethic of co-responsibility for creation?

There is much talk of "spirituality" by persons both within and outside religious traditions. Ecofeminist theologies hold rich resources for spirituality in reference to embodiment and the interrelationship of prayer and ecological praxis in a panentheistic perspective.

Ecofeminism is indeed an unfolding theological project and many more women and sympathetic men are invited to the table for reflection which leads to action.

References and Recommended Reading

Ackermann, Denise M. (1997), "Earth-Healing in South Africa: Challenges to the Church", *Ecotheology*, Vol. 2, 48-58.

Deane-Drummond, Celia E. (2008), *Eco-Theology*, London: Darton, Longman and Todd.

Dietrich, Gabriele (1998), "Dalit Feminism and Environment", *Religion and Society*, Vol. 45, 4, 89-98.

Eaton, Heather (1996), "Ecological-Feminist Theology", in: Dieter T. Hessel (ed.), *Theology for Earth Community: A Field Guide*, Maryknoll: Orbis, 77-92

--- (2005), *Introducing Ecofeminist Theologies*, London / New York: T & T Clark.

Hallahan, Lorna (2004), "Beautiful Lies and the Dung Heap", in: Denis Edwards and Mark Worthing (eds.), *Biodiversity and Ecology: An Interdisciplinary Challenge. Interface: A Forum of Theology in the World*, Vol. 7, 1, 118-123.

Kwok, Pui-Lan (1999), "Mending of Creation: Women, Nature and Eschatological Hope", in: Serene

[113] Many of these contributions are explored in other chapters. For references to contributions from the perspective of "Western ecofeminist theologies", see the section on recommended reading.

Jones and Margaret A. Farley (eds.), *Liberating Eschatology: Essays in Honor of Letty M. Russell*, Louisville: Westminster John Knox, 144-155.
Rakoczy, Susan (2004), *In Her Name: Women Doing Theology*, Pietermaritzburg: Cluster.

Susan Rakoczy

9. North American Perspectives from the Margins

Edited by Willis Jenkins

Introduction

Ecotheology produced in North America sometimes elides its own context, making for the odd impression that a theological movement to reclaim creation has little connection to its own habitat. Beyond the irony of this apparent displacement in ecotheology, the disconnection from context can cause two serious problems. First, readers who come to such texts looking for Christian teaching on how to live faithfully in their land can read theologies that treat nature, ecology and creation as cosmological abstractions rather than lived relations. In those cases, the work of theology seems obtuse to the struggle of churches to offer witness to life as communities participating in particular places.

Second, the elision of context by North American writers can permit ecotheologies to develop without self-reflective acknowledgement of their contextual impact. That becomes especially problematic when North American theologians evade critical engagement with the political ecologies of power within which their work is situated. Then theologies that do engage with political ecologies – such as liberationist approaches to ecological debt in South American ecotheology – become "contextual" theologies, operating (one may suppose) on a subsidiary scale to the more general doctrinal register of ecotheology proper. The churches of the western hemisphere badly need to conduct a theological conversation between South America and North America. Yet the conversation remains thin because North American ecotheologies tend not to understand themselves as contextual theologies, and so rarely recognise or respond to the criticism from South American churches.

The three theological movements included here represent important exceptions. Each is profoundly shaped by the experience of living in North America and each self-consciously cultivates an understanding of creation and salvation shaped through lived negotiation with this continent. Agrarian theologies take up a strand of North American thought, strong from the founding of the American colonies, that roots personal freedom and civic virtue in agricultural relations to the soil. Environmental liberation theologies confront ecological mediations of social violence, begun in the genocide and slavery of the colonial era, and continued through structures of environmental racism. North American Catholicism, more extensively than any other denomination on the continent, has worked to articulate a theological ethic for a regional common good informed by pluralist experience, which is represented in a series of pastoral letters from and for particular bioregions.

The three theologies obviously lie in some tension with one another. For example, whereas agrarian theologians celebrate emplacement, environmental justice theologians interrogate displacements. Urban environments often seem alienating and destructive to agrarian thinkers, while environmental justice movements interpret the city as habitat and community. Southern United States agrarianism is historically entwined with racist ideologies, making environmental justice theologians concerned to first protect persons from romances of identity and geography. Catholic social teaching measures both agrarian and liberationist commitments against an integrating account of the common good, which neither agrarian nor environmental-justice thought seems interested in developing.

So this chapter does not present a consistent North American way of connecting creation and salvation. Instead, by its variety, it shows the dynamic importance for doctrines of creation and salvation of theological engagement with the North American experience. Arising from the experience of cultivating soil, agrarian theologies reclaim the centrality of land expressed in ancient Hebrew covenantal understandings of relationship with God. In a time of ecological distress, Norman Wirzba shows, agrarians make a point of insisting that salvation cannot be sought apart from our bodily participation in particular local communities. Salvation can therefore be experienced as healing and restoration – for land and people.

Arising from the experience of ecological mediations of political violence, environmental justice movements show how liberation comes to persons embodied in creation. So they expand liberation to account for ecologically embedded persons and to confront the way that dominating power flows through environments. By starting from liberation and following its ecological implications, I argue, environmental justice responses begin to reclaim creation for their understanding of salvation, which in turn begins to expand in order to bring more of creation within its scope.

Arising from a series of pastoral responses to regional political ecologies, North American Catholic theologies have developed the key themes of nature and grace in Catholic social thought in order to interpret North America as what John Hart calls a "sacramental commons". In that concept, Hart brings together the concepts of solidarity, the common good, a preferential option for the poor, human dignity, and stewardship of creation that shape the relation of natural law and sanctifying grace in modern Catholic thought. Hart shows how that relation takes shape in North America according to the church's engagement with regional political ecologies.

Willis Jenkins

North American Agrarian Theology

The roots of agrarian thought and practice extend deep into humanity's ten-thousand-year history of agriculture. It is a diverse history in which people have sought to secure livelihood through the growth of food (a complex process that presupposes the domestication of plants and animals), the production of fibre and the harvesting of energy. As a work of culture, it has sometimes made important contributions to the way we understand economic, political and social order, the refinement of human character and the nature of reality.[1] On occasion it has also prompted profound reflection on what it means to be responsible to God for the well-being of land, creatures and fellow human beings.

Like other cultures, the history of North American settlement cannot be understood apart from its complex relationship to this agrarian heritage. Encounters with indige-

[1] See Hanson.

nous forms of agriculture, the displacement and genocide of indigenous peoples, the distribution of lands, the development of a slave economy, the Jeffersonian ideal of the yeoman citizen, and the growing divide between an industrialising north and an agrarian south – all of these developments raised deep questions about how people should live on the land. It is not until the Second World War and the implementation of industrialised agriculture that we see a growing migration of people from farms to cities, and thus the gradual cultural eclipse of an agrarian sensibility.

Today's urbanisation amounts to a profound transformation in what we experience and know as our place in the world. It needs to be contrasted with the fact that, for millennia, the vast majority of people calibrated life's meaning and significance, but also personal expectations and fulfilment, to ecological and agricultural realities. Alongside fellow human beings, fields, streams, forests and animals played vital roles in the minds and imaginations of most people, and gave direction and purpose to their living. Human identity and vocation, in other words, were daily and practically intertwined with the well-being of the world's diverse living and non-living creatures. The "land", by which I mean the world's diverse habitats and the many creatures that live on them, was deeply compelling and a constant focus of individual and communal care, because it was so inextricably tied to personal and social livelihood. The insular character of much recent urban and suburban design, however, means that most people have little appreciation for or direct contact with (and thus limited intelligent concern for) ecological and agricultural matters.

Today's urbanisation is also of tremendous theological significance, because it contributes to an abstract understanding of creation and limits our appreciation for the ecological scope of God's salvation purposes. Not having sustained relationships with the land – through food and fibre production, energy capture, or waste management – people find it difficult to understand themselves as vulnerable and embodied creatures necessarily, beneficially and responsibly joined together with other creatures, all dependent upon God. Put simply, it is hard to appreciate God as the one who daily sustains life and invites humanity to participate in the work of nurturing creation if one's relationship to the world is primarily that of a consumer.

North American Agrarianism

A stream of agrarian writing, flowing from Thomas Jefferson, Liberty Hyde Bailey, Aldo Leopold and Wes Jackson (among several others), has accompanied distinctly North American agrarian ways of life. Chief among the writers, however, has been Wendell Berry (1934-), a Kentucky farmer, poet, novelist and essayist. In his work we find a clear articulation of agrarianism as a comprehensive cultural vision that holds the health of the land and people together: human well-being cannot be long sustained at the expense of the land. Agrarianism is not simply about protecting a farming way of life, and thus of interest to a very small segment of the population. Instead, it is about developing the affections and practices – and thus also the appropriate economic, political, educational, social and religious institutions – that will lead *all* people into ways of life that respect, nurture and celebrate God's gift of creation.

According to Berry, "no matter how urban our life, our bodies live by farming; we come from the earth and return to it, and so we live in agriculture as we live in flesh".[2] This position reflects the practical truth that we are bodies that eat, drink and breathe. The daily demands of digestion and respiration, but also building and creating, provide constant confirmation of the fact that our life is utterly dependent on the well-being of the many created bodies – ranging from micro-organisms in the soil to the ozone layer in the atmosphere, as well as the full range of plants, insects and animals that live between them – that intersect with and nurture our own. Creation consists of an indescribably vast and interconnected membership of creatures in which each member both receives and contributes to the nurture and movement of the whole. This fundamental, lived insight has been largely forgotten by today's urban populations. Much of Berry's work has been an exploration of why and how a remembering of creaturely interdependence is vital to the healing and sustainability of any culture.

Agrarian Theology

The Hebrew and Christian scriptures presuppose an agrarian orientation that has the health of relationships between God, humanity and land constantly in view. Biblical scholar Ellen Davis writes: "[T]he Hebrew Scriptures are land-centered in their theological perspective … there is no extensive exploration of the relationship between God and humanity that does not factor the land and its fertility into that relationship."[3] Creation is not engaged as an abstraction, commodity, or scenic view but as a dynamic, practical and fully sensible expression of God's love and care. God is constantly looking after the land. God is the essential gardener (Gen. 2:8) and the good shepherd (Ps. 23:1) who daily provides for the material needs of all creatures and works to bring about their renewal and *shalom* (Isa. 65). "The eyes of the LORD your God are always on [the land], from the beginning of the year to the end of the year" (Deut. 11:12). In Jesus the fullness of this God dwells and is made incarnate. He is the one through whom and for whom "all things in heaven and on earth are created", and it is through his cross that God is reconciling all creatures to himself (Col. 1:15-20).

Both creation accounts in Genesis provide a theological articulation of an agrarian view. Genesis 1 presents a poetic visioning of the ordering of the world, an ordering in which the diverse members of creation, though clearly dependent upon God as the ultimate source of their life, also depend on each other to produce and maintain life. The earth sprouts out plants that seed themselves and bear fruit that can then be food for others. God creates a fruitful world in which waters "bring forth swarms of living creatures" (1:20) and the earth brings forth "living creatures of every kind" (1:24). God's declaration of the goodness of creation stems, at least in part, from its astounding fertility and its ability to provide for the needs of each other.

Humanity is created as one member within this fecund membership. People are charged by God to be fruitful and subdue and have dominion over all the creatures (1:26-28). The interpretation of this much-invoked command has often failed to take into account its priestly (and exilic) perspective that knew the land to be a vulnerable and morally complicated possession. People can fail to live properly in the land – most obviously by undermining the ecological and socio-economic conditions necessary for

---

2 Berry (1977), 97.

3 Davis, 8.

continuing fruitfulness and nurture – and so come to know the pain of hunger and displacement. Human dominion, understood in an agrarian way, bears little resemblance to recent forms of industrial power that are unparalleled in their geographical reach and destructive potential or that premise human success on the exploitation of creation's members. Instead, it refers to a constellation of practices and responsibilities that promote long-term fertility and plant and animal health. Davis wisely recommends that we translate this passage not as "dominion over" but as "mastery among" creatures, thereby communicating clearly that what is at stake is not only human flourishing but the flourishing of all creatures together.[4]

In Genesis 2 the matrix of God's creativity is a garden, or more specifically, the soil that is its material foundation. God creates human (2:7), plant (2:9) and animal life (2:19) from out of the ground. Soil is the common origin and also the end of all earthly life (3:19). There is no escape from the potential and the limits of soil. That we live at all is only because God is present to the ground like a gardener or farmer (Ps. 65) who cultivates the land. As the psalmist understands it, the day God turns away is also the day creatures "die and return to their dust" (Ps. 104:29).

Again, human beings are presented as having a unique responsibility: "The LORD God took the man and put him in the garden of Eden to till it and keep it" (Gen. 2:15 and 3:23). This description gives an agrarian stamp to human identity and vocation, because it suggests that who we are and what we are to do must circulate through this responsibility to take care of the soil. Coming from the soil (*adamah*), humans (*adam*) must constantly turn their attention toward it as the focus of their concern and work. "For the Yahwist, the human being from primordial time has been destined to farm the land from which he himself was formed."[5] Though we may not all be "professional" gardeners or farmers, the nature of our humanity as embodied, earthy creatures bound to each other through relationships of nurture and eating means that none of us are exempt from the responsibilities of maintaining healthy soil, clean water, vigorous plant growth and animal contentment. Even as urbanites, people must find ways – in their shopping, eating and voting, for instance – to calibrate their desires and expectations to meet the needs of the land.

An agrarian theological imagination pictures creation as a complex, dynamic, interdependent, comprehension-defying, embodied realm in which God's vivifying presence is constantly being made known. Creation is not a storehouse of "natural resources" or an amoral, value-neutral mass waiting for us to appropriate it. Far from being a deistic once-and-for-all act completed long ago, creation is the scene through which God's love is daily made beautiful, fragrant and delectable.[6]

This depiction of creation has important implications for the way we characterise salvation. To begin, salvation cannot amount to a repudiation of or escape from creation, because such a view denies God's affirmation of and commitment to the world. Nor can it affirm a teaching like the immortality of the soul, because this view presupposes a denigration of material reality and bodily life.

4 Davis, 55.

5 Hiebert, 35.

6 See Wirzba (2003b).

In the essay "Christianity and the Survival of Creation" Berry argues that the dualisms between Creator and creature, spirit and matter, body and soul, religion and nature, religion and economy, and worship and work are "the most destructive disease that afflicts us".[7] The effect of dualisms of this sort is that they turn us against the world rather than toward it as the aim of our affection and work:

> By dividing body and soul, we divide both from all else. We thus condemn ourselves to a loneliness for which the only compensation is violence – against other creatures, against the earth, against ourselves. For no matter the distinctions we draw between body and soul, body and earth, ourselves and others – the connections, the dependencies, the identities remain ... The willingness to abuse other bodies is the willingness to abuse one's own. To damage the earth is to damage your children. To despise the ground is to despise its fruit; to despise the fruit is to despise its eaters. The wholeness of health is broken by despite.[8]

Agrarians object to an other-worldly characterisation of salvation, because it violates both the goodness of creation and denies God's desire to draw near to us, a desire made most clear in the incarnation of God in the body of Jesus Christ.[9] Creation and salvation are neither separable from each other nor opposed to each other. If they were, it would be very difficult to account for God's constant abiding with the earth and its creatures (even God's delight in creation's wildness – see Job 38-41) and God's promise to make a new world of the places that are being ravaged and destroyed by human sin. The prophet Isaiah's vision of a new heaven and a new earth does not amount to a plucking out of human souls from the earth. Instead, it points to God's creation of a joyful dwelling place, a distinct geographical place marked by the absence of weeping and distress and the construction of houses and vineyards productive of good food and peaceful life together (Isa. 65). In this time to come, God promises to the faithful that God will "plant them upon their land, and they shall never again be plucked up out of the land that I have given them" (Amos 9:15). It represents an agrarian future insofar as it is a vision of the care, well-being and celebration of all creatures living in their lands.

This conception of salvation as the healing and transformation of the material, created world is amplified in the ministry of Jesus Christ. His work of feeding, healing, exorcism and reconciliation point to the "new creation" that is made possible "in him" (2 Cor. 5:17). Jesus' ministry does not abandon bodies but rather addresses them, making them whole. From an agrarian point of view, this means that his ministry also addresses all the ecological and agricultural bodies that touch and nurture them. It makes no sense to limit God's transforming and reconciling ways to individual souls. It must, as the early Christians knew, include "all things in heaven and on earth" (Col. 1:16). It must end in the movement of heaven to earth, a movement in which God – in an agrarian type of dwelling – brings all creatures to their full and glorious life (Rev. 21).

---

7 Berry (2002), 313.

8 Berry (1977), 106.

9 See Wirzba (2003a).

References and Recommended Reading

Berry, Wendell (1977), *The Unsettling of America: Culture and Agriculture*, San Francisco: Sierra Club Books.
--- (2002), *The Art of the Commonplace: The Agrarian Essays of Wendell Berry* (edited by Norman Wirzba), Washington, DC: Counterpoint.
Davis, Ellen F. (2009), *Scripture, Culture, and Agriculture: An Agrarian Reading of the Bible*, New York: Cambridge University Press.
Hanson, Victor Davis (1999), *The Other Greeks: The Family Farm and the Agrarian Roots of Western Civilization* (second edition), Berkeley: University of California Press.
Hiebert, Theodore (1996), *The Yahwist's Landscape: Nature and Religion in Early Israel*, New York: Oxford University Press.
Wirzba, Norman (2003a), "Placing the Soul: An Agrarian Philosophical Principle", in: Norman Wirzba (ed.), *The Essential Agrarian Reader: The Future of Culture, Community, and the Land*, Lexington: The University Press of Kentucky, 80-97.
--- (2003b), *The Paradise of God: Renewing Religion in an Ecological Age*, New York: Oxford University Press.

Norman Wirzba

North American Environmental Liberation Theologies

Violence against creation is reshaping the meaning of liberation in some North American communities. If liberation includes the whole embodied experience of persons in a community, then its meaning encompasses dehumanising ecological degradation. Over the past few decades a groundswell of movements has emerged across the continent in order to confront the communication of social violence through ecological relations. Justice extends as far as harm, which in an age of ecological degradation, means that justice must, for example, follow toxins through soil and water via political decisions into particular wombs. Liberationist reflection on the ecological dimensions of justice may then recover the importance of creation to liberation theologies by starting from places of human suffering.

Formal theological reflection on the meaning of those movements for understanding of liberation still lags, however, in part because environmental liberation tropes have been shaped by an uneasy relationship between two groups of movements: the environmental justice movements that confront injustice in vulnerability to harms and access to resources, and the wilderness movements that seek to preserve North American lands from industrial development in order to preserve a geography of spiritual freedom. There are similar movements and tensions in other regions, but the North American context is distinct for the importance of race in understanding environmental injustice and the significance of the idea of wilderness in American social imaginaries. Moreover, ideas of race and wilderness inflect one another, charging the relationship between ideas of liberation and creation.

The sparse theological attention to environmental justice movements lags behind extensive sociological studies and overlooks significant involvement from churches and faith-motivated groups. Because sociology has taken the lead, the role of faith commitments and theological ideas often remains implicit and underdeveloped. Yet some community movements clearly carry innovative trajectories of theological recovery and reform that expand received notions of liberation. The future of thinking about God's creation within liberation theologies, I will show, may be emerging in hemispheric networks of indigenous networks, and emerging connections of South and North American theological communities.

Environmental Racism and Liberation Theology

One of the most influential involvements of Christian churches in US environmental thought remains one of the least theologically developed. The idea of "environmental racism" may be traced to the protest of a predominately black North Carolina community attempting to stop a federal toxic waste dump in their county. Environmental racism quickly became a powerful tool for correlating risk exposures with other forms of social injustice, and thereby initiating new interpretations of the American landscape.

The role of key civil-rights organisations, including Martin Luther King's Southern Christian Leadership Council (SCLC), helped transform what appeared to be "not-in-my-backyard" opposition to a locally unwanted land use into an extension of the struggle for racial justice. The (unsuccessful) Warren County protest began to depict how even environmental policies could exacerbate an unnoticed form of racial injustice. In this case, a progressive hazardous waste regulation led to the disposal of chemicals in a politically weak community. The drama of trucks carrying toxic soils into a predominately African-American community made visible the environmental dimensions of structural racism.

Christian churches did not take the lead in this struggle, but their participation was important from the start and they quickly authorised this extension of social justice. At Warren County the protests were first made possible by the coalition of a white church and a black church. Following the method of SCLC civil-rights efforts, protests were organised from mass meetings held in the churches, and sometimes accompanied by sermons and songs. And when the charge of environmental racism was made, empirical proof was first established by a report commissioned by the United Church of Christ: *Toxic Wastes and Race in the United States* (1987). (A follow-up report twenty years later depicts even stronger evidence of environmental racism.)[10]

Showing that race is the most significant statistical factor in the geography of toxic waste sites, the report was a landmark not only for the emergence of a new kind of environmentalism, but also for a deeper understanding of racism. By showing how land becomes a resource in civic processes that maintain white power, the report demonstrated that struggles against racism must understand and investigate ecological relations as forms of political relations. If soil and water communicate the deathly discharge of political decisions and economic processes, then liberation after Warren County must encompass the environmental vulnerability of human embodiment. It must confront racism not only in personal consciousness and political institutions, but the racism indirectly maintained through protection of inherited landscapes and distribution of environmental risks.

Faith communities that preach salvation as liberation must, after the Warren County protests, discover how God liberates humans from ecologically mediated violence.

---

[10] See Bullard et al.

North American black liberation theologies have begun to reflect this discovery. Womanist theologians have been especially prominent in naming the ecological dimensions of racist violence. Emilie Townes condemns environmental racism as contemporary form of "lynching a whole people" and she calls for "the yoking of civil and environmental rights" in the development of a holist account of justice.[11] Delores Williams has developed an interpretation of sin as defilement of black bodies, signifying defilement of nature in general.[12] Condemning environmental racism thus becomes a way of reclaiming the embodiment of humanity within creation, and connecting the violence that threatens that embodiment to violence against all creation.

So notions of salvation begin to include and overcome hitherto unnoticed dimensions of sin. Rooted in the embodied experience of those suffering ecologically mediated violence, liberation begins to extend to the cosmos that sustains human bodies. For example, Williams writes that womanist theologies develop a notion of salvation that drives "active opposition to all forms of violence against humans (male and female), against nature (including nonhuman animals), against the environment and against the land".[13] Karen Baker-Fletcher observes that historically, for black women, "hope and salvation are experienced in connection with God as Spirit within creation – in skies, trees, water, land, birds, family, friends, humanity, the body".[14]

Womanists are routinely credited for developing black liberation theology in these directions, which otherwise leaves ecological issues as a minor topic. The disproportionate interest from womanists may reflect the fact that active leadership in environmental justice movements is often carried by women of colour, many of whom are motivated by faith.[15] Dwight Hopkins has noted this holistic trajectory in the black environmental liberation theologies arising from anti-racist movements, and has begun to sketch the sort of cosmic soteriology it seems to require. The "holistic disease" of ecologically mediated racism, Hopkins observes, requires the "holistic health and healing" of the sort found in the cosmic Christologies of Ephesians and Colossians.[16]

Black environmental liberation theology challenges racism in the received body of North American ecotheology in terms of both content and method. Ecotheology has been methodologically racist, argues James Cone, when it has started from ideas of creation rather than the experiences of creation in oppressed communities.[17] The resulting doctrines of creation inevitably reflect a dominant culture's ecological experience, and in North America that means the Euro-American experience of establishing white supremacy over the continent. That project continues through contemporary environmentalist attempts to preserve landscapes that prioritise the memory of the Euro-American experience on the continent at the expense of projects to make all communities at home in a decent habitat.

Put formally, Cone implies that doctrines of creation should be constructed from

[11] Townes, 55, 60.

[12] Williams (1993).

[13] Williams (1997), 118-119.

[14] Baker-Fletcher, 63 and 115.

[15] See Kaalund; Taylor.

[16] Hopkins.

[17] Cone, 30.

within soteriology, and specifically from within the struggles for liberation by communities confronting the racism of their inherited lands. By developing theologies of creation from the experiences of those on the geographic margins, the guiding metaphors for our imagination of "creation" begin to shift from wilderness to the sustaining habitats in which we live, work and play. Environmental justice movements often disdain the emphasis of mainstream environmentalism on far-away iconic species and on wilderness. The objection is not simply anthropocentric, although it is often interpreted that way. It is rather anthropo-cosmic: environmental concern should begin from the first environment of one's body and then incorporate all the sustaining relations of one's habitat, extending out toward the rest of the living earth. Liberation comes to all earth, this view implies, as humans learn to create just and sustaining habitats for all their relations.

Environmental Liberation as North American Land Theology

An emergent alliance of environmental justice movements, including those working in Hispanic and Native American communities, gathered in 1992 at the First National People of Color Environmental Leadership Conference, which was funded in part by the United Church of Christ. This event produced the "Principles of Environmental Justice", the first of which "affirms the sacredness of Mother Earth".[18] That phrase indicates a still wider scope of liberation, beyond safe habitat to sacred creation.

The idea of environmental racism has facilitated shared theological reflection among African American and native American communities. Although their primary experience of the continent differs – the diasporic experience of slavery on an unknown land and genocidal displacement from the lands that shape identity – they share oppression abetted by a reflexive relation of race and nature. In his *American Indian Liberation* (2008), George Tinker notes that ideas of race were constructed by colonising Euro-Americans to facilitate white control of North American land. The "one drop" rule of African inheritance required to classify one as "black" created a mass of slave labour to work a seized continent, while the rule that marriage of an Indian to a Euro-American made one "white" allowed Euro-Americans to gain control over native land titles, including reservation land. In both cases, constructions of race served a dominant culture's bid for control over the North American continent. Tinker and other native theologians have criticised dominant cultural ideas of nature and culture, land and justice, that shape the Euro-American worldview.[19]

Chief among the liabilities of the dominant worldview is a subordination of the created world. Indigenous peoples across the continent and, indeed, around the world, tell stories about their relation to each other and to God through their stories of place. Doing so, they recover the moral and theological significance of creation for understandings of relation to God. This may be a gift, Tinker suggests, that indigenous cultures can have for their colonisers, who now find themselves in jeopardy of "unsustainability". However, for Euro-Christianity to hear the importance of recovering creation, native theologians hold, their ideas of salvation must cease from trying to convert Indians to European religious culture, from trying to save the souls of First Peoples by

---

18 See <www.ejnet.org/ej/principles.html>, retrieved 14 October 2011.

19 Tinker (2008), 21.

transforming them in the image of a white God.[20] In addition to its obvious spiritual violence, that sort of proselytising suppresses the priority of creation contextually known by imposing a faith in which grace overshadows experiences of nature.

Native witness to the way spiritual identities are shaped through long-lived relations with particular lands thus challenges any ideas of creation that do not reflect intimate, storied experience with a particular place. "Creation" is not a general concept or world picture, warn native theologians; it is a lived relation with a definite place, known through stories told by one's community.[21] The emergence of a common "Mother Earth" figure among many different North and South American indigenous peoples might mislead non-native theologians to see a general religious account of Earth's sacred value. But this emergence should probably be interpreted as a self-consciously paradoxical global indigeneity: sharing in common the threat of a globalising industrial economy to contextual ways of life, a network of indigenous communities posits a shared symbol of sacred creation in order to protect their many different ways and stories of living in a place. A common theological symbol of creation is thus forged from a liberationist need – to inhabit lands and bioregions in freedom.

Conclusion

North American environmental liberation theologies are distinct from the political ecology movements in other regions in that they emphasise the significance of racism more than class exploitation in shaping views of nature and freedom. By exploring new dimensions of liberation through interrogation of the colonial experience of North America, these theologies seek to liberate American lands and peoples from unjust legacies of settlement, including the injustices perpetuated by contemporary environmental conservation policies. They therefore recover creation for theology through liberationist solidarity with suffering, which serves to open critical space for re-imagining the meaning of creation.

References and Recommended Reading

Baker-Fletcher, Karen (1998), *Sisters of Dust, Sisters of Spirit: Womanist Wordings on God and Creation*, Minneapolis: Fortress.

Bullard, Robert, Mohai, Paul, Saha, Robin and Wright, Beverly (2007), *Toxic Wastes and Race at Twenty: 1987-2007: Grassroots Struggles to Dismantle Environmental Racism in the United States*, United Church of Christ Justice and Witness Ministries.

Cone, James (2007), "Whose Earth is it Anyway?", in: Dieter Hessel and Larry Rasmussen (eds.), *Earth Habitat: Eco-Injustice and the Church's Response*, Minneapolis: Fortress, 23-32.

Deloria, Vine (1973), *God is Red: A Native View of Religion*, New York: Putnam.

Hopkins, Dwight (2008), "Holistic Health and Healing: Environmental Racism and Ecological Justice", in: Stephanie Y. Mitchem and Emilie M. Townes (eds.), *Faith, Health, and Healing in African American Life*, Westport: Praeger, 16-32.

Kaalund, Valerie Ann (2004), "Witness to Truth: Black Women Heeding the Call for Environmental Justice", in: R. Stein (ed.), *New Perspectives on Environmental Justice: Gender, Sexuality, and Activism*, New Brunswick: Rutgers University Press, 78-92.

Taylor, Dorceta (1997), "American Environmentalism: The Role of Race, Class, and Gender in Shaping Activism 1820-1995", *Race, Gender and Class*, Vol. 5, 1, 16-62.

[20] Deloria.

[21] Weaver.

Tinker, George (1996), "An American Indian Theological Response to Ecojustice", in: Jace Weaver (ed.), *Defending Mother Earth: Native American Perspectives on Environmental Justice*, Maryknoll: Orbis, 153-176.
--- (2008), *American Indian Liberation: A Theology of Sovereignty*, Maryknoll: Orbis.
Townes, Emilie Maureen (1995), *In a Blaze of Glory: Womanist Spirituality as Social Witness*, Nashville: Abingdon.
Weaver, Jace (1996), "Introduction: Notes from a Miner's Canary", in: Jace Weaver (ed.), *Defending Mother Earth: Native American Perspectives on Environmental Justice*, Maryknoll: Orbis, 107-121.
Williams, Delores (1993), "Sin, Nature, and Black Women's Bodies", in: Carol Adams (ed.), *Ecofeminism and the Sacred*, New York: Continuum, 24-29.
--- (1997), "Straight Talk, Plain Talk: Womanist Words About Salvation", in: Emilie Maureen Townes (ed.), *Embracing the Spirit: Womanist Perspectives on Hope, Salvation, and Transformation*, Maryknoll: Orbis, 97-121.

Willis Jenkins

North American Catholicism: Sacramental Commitments to Creation and Community

Introduction

In the waning years of the 19th century, the Roman Catholic Church began to express a serious commitment to social justice, particularly in terms of the rights of working people and the poor. The impetus was Pope Leo XIII's 1891 encyclical, *Rerum Novarum* (On the Condition of Labour). In the last quarter of the 20th century, North American Catholic bishops began to link care for creation with social justice for the human community. Concern for planetary and biotic well-being complemented concern for the "common good". Bishops' socio-ecological documents emerged first in the United States of America as regional statements and then as a national pastoral letter, *Renewing the Earth: An Invitation to Reflection and Action on Environment in Light of Catholic Social Teaching*[22] (1991), inspired by the regional statements and by John Paul II's World Day of Peace Message, *The Ecological Crisis: A Common Responsibility* (1990).[23] Thereafter, US and Canadian bishops issued periodic regional and national statements.

A key statement in John Paul's peace message is that "Christians, in particular, realize that their responsibility within creation and their duty toward nature and the Creator are an *essential part of their faith*" (par. 15; emphasis added). That is an innovative teaching with far-reaching implications. Since "faith" includes "duty toward nature", Christians writing about and working for environmental respect and responsibility were not expressing and implementing a new doctrine or morality, but being faithful to and elaborating existing tradition. North American bishops subsequently inculcated a deeper awareness of Catholic tradition and doctrine with their socio-ecological teachings.

In their elaboration of responsibility to community *and* creation in what might be

[22] United States Catholic Bishops (1991a).
[23] See John Paul II, Pope.

called an "ecological era" because of significantly increased global awareness about and concern for environmental impacts by humans on their Earth home and on Earth's flora and fauna (including on the poor, the most vulnerable segment of the global human family), the bishops included in their documents consideration of traditional doctrines: "sacrament", "sin", "salvation" and "mission". Christ, church, community and creation were integrated, and adapted to current consciousness and contexts. Commitment to a "preferential option for the poor" was complemented by consciousness of a "sacramental universe".

Ecojustice

Linking the Church's social teaching with environmental theology has a scriptural basis in Jesus' last-judgement story (Matt. 25:31-43). In the narrative, people's "last chance" for salvation depends on whether or not they have fed the hungry, given drink to the thirsty, clothed the naked, sheltered the homeless and visited the sick and the imprisoned. The passage teaches that Earth's natural goods, and human-produced goods, are intended to provide for both individual as well as community needs. The human common good cannot be sustained without the contributions of abiotic Earth (soil for agriculture, water for agriculture and household use, and clay for building construction) and biotic Earth beings (agricultural produce, including plants that provide food – orchards, vines, trees and ground crops; medicinal herbs to heal the sick; animals that provide meat; and plants and animals that provide fibre for clothing – cotton from the soil and wool from sheep; and building materials from trees). The "Son of Man", the divinely commissioned judge, invites into God's presence those who have been compassionate toward the poor (implication: those who have used Earth's and humans' goods to succour the poor); and the "Son of Man" condemns to exile from divine presence those who have ignored or disparaged the poor (those who have not used the goods at their disposal to help their neighbour). In the Catholic tradition, the narrative is the basis for the traditional moral teaching exhorting "corporal works of mercy".

When natural or processed goods are hoarded and not properly distributed, or are poisoned, polluted or otherwise harmed by human action, the needs of the poor – and of all people and other living creatures – cannot be met. Both care for community and care for creation are essential for human (and other) life, and for human livelihood.

The relationship between care for creation and compassion for the poor is expressed particularly well in ten "Principles of Land Stewardship" described in *Strangers and Guests: Toward Community in the Heartland* (1980),[24] and in ten "Considerations for Community Caretaking" elaborated in *The Columbia River Watershed: Caring for Creation and the Common Good* (2001),[25] an international, bioregional pastoral letter issued by the bishops of Western Canada and the US. These complementary lists weave together Catholic concerns for creation, community and church. Both documents originated at the initiative of lay Christians.

Strangers and Guests focuses on agricultural stewardship, saving owner-operated family farms, mining practices and equitable distribution of land and wealth. The first

[24] Midwestern Catholic Bishops.

[25] Columbia River Watershed Catholic Bishops.

two principles, "The land is God's" and "People are God's stewards on the land", assert basic biblical understandings that "Earth is God's" and that people are to care for God's land – which includes what is described in civil law as public or private "property". The third and tenth principles, "The land's benefits are for everyone" and "The land's mineral wealth should be shared", require equitable distribution of Earth's natural goods. The document expresses biblical jubilee-year provisions: land ownership and land (re)distribution in the fourth and ninth principles, "The land should be distributed equitably" and "The land's workers should be able to become the land's owners"; and responsible use of land in the fifth through seventh principles: "The land should be conserved and restored", "Land use planning must consider social and environmental impacts" and "Land use should be appropriate to land quality".[26] The document also promotes a progressive land tax, and the rights of (Native American) Indians[27] to land and goods.

The US-Canada bishops' *Columbia River Watershed* letter focuses on environmental pollution, species extinction, loss of community, Indian treaty rights, ethnic minority rights and well-being, and equitable and responsible land ownership and use. Among its "Considerations for Community Caretaking", the first two promote the "common good"; the third urges conservation and protection of "species of wildlife"; the fourth requires respect for "the dignity and traditions of the region's indigenous peoples" and the ninth advocates respect for "ethnic and racial cultures, citizens and communities"; the fifth promotes "justice for the poor, linking economic justice and environmental justice"; the seventh promotes "social and ecological responsibility" by mining, manufacturing and forestry enterprises, among others; and the eighth urges energy conservation and "environmentally integrated alternative energy sources".[28] The letter states that "God's presence is discernible in all creation"; God has called all creation "very good"; God "loves the community of all life"; and "God intends the earth's goods to be equitably shared.[29] Human well-being and planetary well-being are intertwined and interdependent.

Sacraments

Extended understandings of the traditional Catholic understanding of "sacrament" helped link ecological responsibility and economic well-being.

Pope Paul VI, in his address to the Second Latin American Bishops' Conference, in Medellín, Colombia (1968), expanded the concept of "sacrament", implicitly linking it to "salvation". When discussing the last-judgement story, he declared that "the poor are the sacrament of Christ". The revelatory poor mediate the Son of Man, an immanent divine presence who requires compassion and justice; this divine judge will hold accountable those who respond neither to the suffering poor nor to biblical prophets' voices urging compassion and justice, and threatening retribution if these are not practiced.

---

26 For elaboration of the complete list of principles, see Hart (2004), 41.

27 Although the asserted "politically correct" term is "Native Americans", the majority of traditional native people in the US prefer "Indian" over "Native American".

28 For elaboration, see Hart (2006), 216.

29 Hart (2004), 52-53.

In *Renewing the Earth: An Invitation to Reflection and Action on Environment in Light of Catholic Social Teaching* (1991), the US bishops link creation and traditional church teachings on sacraments. The concept of a "sacramental universe" extends understandings of "sacrament" beyond seven church rituals to include creation as a whole: "[T]he environmental movement has reawakened appreciation of the truth that, through the created gifts of nature, men and women encounter their Creator. The Christian vision of a *sacramental universe* – a world that discloses the Creator's presence by visible and tangible signs – can contribute to making the earth a home for the human family once again" (par. 6; emphasis added). Effectively, ecclesial sacraments in church are complemented by natural sacraments of creation. Such a sacramental creation consciousness enables Christians to perceive signs of the Creator in creation, and to experience what the Appalachian bishops describe in *At Home in the Web of Life*[30] (1995): "In this magnificent work of God's creation, misty mountain haze is holy incense, tall tree trunks are temple pillars, sun-splashed leaves are stained glass, and song-birds are angelic choirs".[31] The bishops of Alberta, Canada, express similar sentiments in *Celebrate Life: Care for Creation* (1998): "Catholics see creation in a 'sacramental' way … God is present and speaks in the dynamic life forces of our universe and planet as well as in our own lives. Respect for life needs to include all creation … Ecological destruction and the loss of biodiversity obscure our ability to see and experience God and are an affront to the Creator."[32]

The poor and creation, then, are "sacramental" in complementary ways: they are revelatory of the presence of God on Earth, and present a divine invitation to responsibly meet community needs and utilise well creation's common goods.

Sin, Service and Salvation

In their regional statements, the bishops present ways in which John Paul's "essential part of Christian faith" should be considered theologically and ethically, and embodied in Church principles and practice. "Essential" is a key concept: care for creation is not an option, selectively adopted and operative as the believer chooses. It defines for people in the pew and in the pulpit the obligation to serve Creator and creation. Concern for "salvation" becomes, then, not solely a hope for a better future in an other-worldly spiritual realm, but a stimulus to effect a better present and future in the material Earth world.

Service to God and to Earth – in all Earth's totality, abiotic and biotic – is required. There is a unique reversal, here, of anthropocentric attitudes and adverse interpretations of Scripture evident previously in Church teachings: that all creation is created for "man" [*sic*], and is in "his" service. Rather, humans are to serve Earth, to care for the abiotic context of their existence and for biotic beings with whom they are interdependent and interrelated. The extent to which people fulfil this responsibility will determine the extent to which Earth returns the favour: if people harm creation, then creation will be unable to provide a context in which human needs will be met. "Essential" means that not only will humans be held accountable for their ecological sin-

[30] Appalachian Catholic Bishops.

[31] Paragraph 15, quoted in Hart (2004), 44-45.

[32] Catholic Bishops of Alberta, Canada.

fulness in a future spiritual dimension, as narrated in the last-judgement story; human environmental sin will be punished here and now. People hope to be "saved" through God's mercy from the just consequences of their personal and communal sins; creation is groaning to be "saved" from the unjust consequences of people's ecological sins: when they exploit Earth and extinct biota (species "become extinct" when they disappear through natural evolutionary processes; species are "extincted" when human practices cause their disappearance). If humans care for Earth and Earth's biota, all will benefit.

Native Peoples: Social Justice and Spirituality

The bishops' documents advocate righting the injustices perpetrated against Indian nations in the US and First Nations in Canada, and celebrate their culture and Earth-related spirituality. The bishops' enhanced understanding of "mission" enables them to fulfil Jesus' command to "teach all nations" in a dramatically different way than evident in traditional Christian missionaries' attitudes and actions. The bishops advocate reciprocity, not domination, in discussions of religion and spirituality related to Creator and creation; and affirm the rights of Indians to sovereignty over territory, natural goods and cultural integrity.

The *Statement of US Catholic Bishops on American Indians* (1977),[33] after noting that early missionaries did not respect native cultures, states in an ecumenical spirit that "faith finds expression in and through the particular values, customs and institutions of the people who hear it. ... American Indian peoples had developed rich and diverse cultures long before the first Europeans came to the American continent." The bishops acknowledge their "responsibility to join with our American Indian sisters and brothers in their ongoing struggle to secure justice", including through the "speedy and equitable resolution of treaty and statute questions" (paragraphs. 8, 12, 16, 20, 25).

The US bishops' statement entitled *1992: A Time for Remembering, Reconciling and Recommitting Ourselves as a People: Statement of the National Conference of Catholic Bishops on Native Americans* (1991)[34] describes the relationship between Earth and Indian / Native American traditions, and notes the bishops' incorporation of native insights in their own documents. The bishops affirm native spirituality – "The coming of religious faith in this land began not five hundred years ago, but centuries before in the prayers, chants, dance and other sacred celebrations of Native people" – and call for respectful reconciliation between "the essential traditions of Catholic faith and the best of the traditions of Native American life". The bishops state that "Native Americans have the right to be self-determining, to decide the ways their land and natural resources on those lands are used for the benefit of their people and for the broader common good" (paragraphs 27, 28, 29, 30).

The bishops of Alberta, Canada, state that "we can learn much from the spiritual traditions of our aboriginal brothers and sisters which celebrate our kinship with the rest of creation and seek to strengthen the sacred circle of all creation".[35] The Alaskan bishops' *A Catholic Perspective on Subsistence: Our Responsibility toward Alaska's*

---

[33] United States Catholic Bishops (1977).

[34] United States Catholic Bishops (1991b).

[35] Hart (2004), 47.

Bounty and Our Human Family (2002)[36] advocates "respect and honor for the culture and traditions of indigenous peoples" and "the right of Alaska native people to preserve their cultures", including their "Earth-related spirituality".[37]

North American Catholic bishops' contextual considerations of traditional doctrines, commingled with their consciousness of contemporary ecological conditions, promote care for the "least of these" and for Earth and Earth's biota. Their implicit expectation is that as God's will is increasingly done "on Earth as it is in heaven", the commonwealth of God gradually will be realised.

References and Recommended Reading

Alaskan Catholic Bishops (2002), A *Catholic Perspective on Subsistence: Our Responsibility toward Alaska's Bounty and Our Human Family*, <www.archdioceseofanchorage.org/a_catholic_ perspective_on_subsis.htm>, retrieved 18 October 2011.

Appalachian Catholic Bishops (1995), *At Home in the Web of Life: A Pastoral Message on Sustainable Communities in Appalachia*, Webster Springs: Catholic Committee of Appalachia.

Catholic Bishops of Alberta, Canada (1998), *Celebrate Life: Care for Creation*, <www.wcr.ab.ca/bin/eco-lett.htm>, retrieved 18 October 2011.

Christiansen, Drew and Grazer, Walter (eds.) (1996), *"And God Saw That It Was Good": Catholic Theology and the Environment*, Washington, DC: United States Catholic Conference.

Columbia River Watershed Catholic Bishops (2001), *The Columbia River Watershed: Caring for Creation and the Common Good: An International Pastoral Letter by the Catholic Bishops of the Region*, Seattle: Washington State Catholic Conference, <www.columbiariver.org>, retrieved 18 October 2011.

Hart, John (2004), *What Are They Saying About ... Environmental Theology*, Mahwah: Paulist Press.

--- (2006), *Sacramental Commons: Christian Ecological Ethics*, Lanham: Rowman and Littlefield.

John Paul II, Pope (1990), *The Ecological Crisis: A Common Responsibility*, Washington, DC: United States Catholic Conference.

Midwestern Catholic Bishops (1980), *Strangers and Guests: Toward Community in the Heartland*, Des Moines: National Catholic Rural Life Conference, <www.cooperativeindividualism.org/catholic-bishops-statement-1980.html>, retrieved 18 October 2011.

United States Catholic Bishops (1977), *Statement of US Catholic Bishops on American Indians*, Washington, DC: United States Catholic Conference.

--- (1991a), *Renewing the Earth: An Invitation to Reflection and Action on Environment in Light of Catholic Social Teaching: A Statement of the US Catholic Bishops*, Washington, DC: United States Catholic Conference.

--- (1991b), *1992: A Time for Remembering, Reconciling and Recommitting Ourselves as a People: Statement of the National Conference of Catholic Bishops on Native Americans*, Washington, DC: United States Catholic Conference.

John Hart

Towards the Theological Rediscovery of North America

In a remarkable meditation on the cultural and biological violence visited on North America by the European "discovery" and colonising search for wealth, Barry Lopez invites its current residents to find in one another cultural possibilities for "the rediscovery of North America". Even while bearing knowledge of the loss of unimaginable

---

[36] Alaskan Catholic Bishops.

[37] Hart (2004), 56.

wealth – of species, languages, peoples – Lopez summons its impoverished inhabitants to begin anew in shaping our languages and social imagination to the search for the real wealth of this continent. Insofar as theology searches for the treasure without price, it has its role to play and its peculiar witness to offer.

The movements discussed in this chapter represent a kind of theological rediscovery of the continent, each wrestling in its own way with legacies of violence, injustice, diminishment, and each seeking to open possibilities of inhabiting the land in peace and justice. Their common conviction is that how North Americans live in their place matters for how North American Christians talk about life with God. From three distinctive margins of North America's market society, they imagine what salvation means for a people still so captive to the pursuit of false wealth that they cannot see the glories around them, or hear the tongues that know how to hymn these places as home.

These three schools of contextual North American ecotheology represent only the most robust examples of a broader turn toward bioregional context in the field of religion and ecology. Working from Europe, Sigurd Bergmann has helped theorise a "spatial turn" that interprets the rising theological interest in place. Theologies of place as well as religious-studies approaches to interpreting the meaning of a locality, site or enactments of place now regularly appear in anthologies and journals. A number of emerging scholars are currently writing their first books on the ethics, theology and / or spirituality of specific bioregions or political ecologies.

The emergence of such work represents not only interest in the *topos* of ecotheology, but increased attention toward the way that religious practice shapes modes of human participation in particular ecological economies. Sarah McFarland Taylor's *Green Sisters: A Spiritual Ecology* (2007) is one of the most interesting such examples. Analysing a (mostly) North American network of female Catholic monastic communities, Taylor makes "re-inhabitation" a mutually interpretive metaphor for how their tradition informs restorative environmental ethos and how their ecological practice drive their revision of the tradition. Re-inhabiting their lands and buildings, the sisters re-inhabit the Catholic faith. (It works as a pun as well: re-in*habit*ing the nun's habit.)

Anna Peterson's *Seeds of the Kingdom: Utopian Communities in the Americas* (2005) investigates the different styles of religious utopianism in the land communities of North American Amish and Central American Catholic base communities. It thus represents one of the only works to conduct comparative interpretation of contextual ecotheologies across geographical boundaries. Moreover, Peterson's final chapter attends to some of the soteriological implications of utopian land communities. Their enactments of sustaining, peaceful community of creation stand against styles of political realism (in the tradition of Reinhold Niebuhr) that suppose that grace cannot meaningfully shape group life.

In theological ethics, a turn toward particular ecological problems recovers North American context in another way. Kevin O'Brien's *An Ethics of Biodiversity* (2010) develops a sacramental approach through broad engagement with ecotheology and the global literature of conservation biology. Yet by writing intentionally for a North American audience, discussing policy options and conservation priorities for a US context, O'Brien successfully "places" his theological ethic. O'Brien makes a point of showing how ecotheology can engage multiple scales of the problems at hand by working from regional and national issues toward the global dimensions of the problem and its general theological features.

Finally, through critical methodological attention to the field of religion and ecology, the contributors to *Inherited Land* (2011) show how intellectual currents within North America and beyond have shaped work in the broader field and in ecotheology. Their inquiries implicitly show how attending to the received fields of ecological inquiry in religious studies and in theology (the first sense of "inherited land"), can help theologians begin to attend more creativity and intimately with the many inherited lands of creation.

This chapter has shown how inhabiting theological and geographical margins can bring into view the obscured North American context of much ecotheology. Dominant ecotheological discourse can sometimes treat ruptures of nature and grace as abstractions rather than lived relations. As theology rediscovers North America, it is opened to inflection by the creatures of its habitat and oriented to critical engagement with the political ecologies from which it is produced. As it gets nearer to its habitat, ecotheological narrations of salvation become more incarnate in the flesh of a particular land and its peoples.

References and Recommended Reading

Bauman, Whitney, Bohannon, Richard and O'Brien, Kevin (2011), *Inherited Land: The Changing Grounds of Religion and Ecology*, Eugene: Wipf and Stock.

Bergmann, Sigurd (2007), "Theology in its Spatial Turn: Space, Place, and Built Environments Challenging and Changing the Images of God", *Religion Compass*, Vol. 1, 3, 353-379.

Lopez, Barry (1992), *The Rediscovery of North America*, New York: Vintage.

O'Brien, Kevin (2010), *An Ethics of Biodiversity: Christianity, Ecology, and the Variety of Life*, Washington, DC: Georgetown University Press.

Peterson, Anna (2005), *Seeds of the Kingdom: Utopian Communities in the Americas*, New York: Oxford University Press.

Taylor, Sarah McFarland (2007), *Green Sisters: A Spiritual Ecology*, Cambridge: Harvard University Press.

Willis Jenkins

10. Latin American Theologies

Edited by Guillermo Kerber

Introduction: The Context of Liberation Theologies

In reflecting on the contribution of Latin American theologians to a discussion of the relationship between creation and salvation, avoiding the impact of liberation theology is impossible. Indeed, the phenomenon of liberation theology stands out in theological contributions from Latin America in the last fifty years.

Liberation theology started in the 1960s and 1970s in Latin America. At that time, the continent was experiencing highly significant processes of social and political transformation. Social movements were developing rapidly and were aimed at structural change in society. At the same time and in some cases related to the former, revolutionary movements emerging throughout the region clamoured for immediate political change and opted for an armed struggle to seize power. In this turbulent context intellectual production had a close link with social and political action in various areas. Firstly, at that time, Latin American social sciences developed the concepts both of dependency and of liberation as a description of what was going on in the region. Authors like Theotonio dos Santos and Orlando Fals Borda greatly contributed to a better understanding of unusual developments widespread through the region. Secondly, various disciplines incorporated the notion of liberation in their discourses. A pedagogy of liberation was elaborated by Paulo Freire and a philosophy of liberation was proposed by Enrique Dussel, for example.

The Roman Catholic Church, the majority church in the region, representing more than 80% of the population at the time, contextualised the outcomes of the Second Vatican Council at the General Conference of Latin American Bishops in Medellin in 1968. The conference issued quite challenging documents concerning justice, peace and the centrality of the poor in evangelisation.

In summary, the 1960s and 1970s was a time troubled by a multiplicity of social, political, theoretical and ecclesial developments.

It is in this context, in this *humus*, that liberation theology was, or better, liberation theologies were, born. Though liberation is a leitmotiv of many productions, there are differences among the various authors. Since they were concerned with liberation from a theological perspective, which differs from a social or political perspective, they addressed diverse topics over the decades as the historical reality evolved.

Of the first generation of liberation theologians some names became quite well known in the continent and beyond it. We can mention, without trying to be exhaustive, the Peruvian Gustavo Gutiérrez, the Brazilian Leonardo Boff, the Spaniard-Salvadorian Jon Sobrino and the Uruguayan Juan Luis Segundo. Although these and other Catholic thinkers are the better known because their works have been translated into several languages, it is worth also mentioning the significant contribution of Protestant theologians to the development of liberation theology since its origin. These include for instance the Brazilian Rubem Alves, the Argentinian José Miguez Bonino and the Uruguayan Julio de Santa Ana.

If there are differences among the various liberation theologies, what is the common denominator among them? Gustavo Gutiérrez wrote in an article in the 1980s: "In liberation theology there are two central intuitions that were also the first chronologically and still constitute its dorsal spine: we refer to the theological method and the perspective of the poor."[1]

The method of liberation theology and the perspective of the poor (a theological consequence of the option for the poor) continue today to be crucial insights for understanding the reflection coming from that continent. The method of liberation theology may be presented as a refinement of the methodology of Catholic Action groups: See – Judge – Act. These three moments refer to the knowledge of reality with a suitable set of instruments, especially from the social sciences (see), the confrontation of reality with God's Word, where biblical hermeneutics plays a key role (judge) and, finally, the action consistent with the interpretation of reality (act). For Latin American theologians, theology is a secondary moment, while reality, life, history has a certain priority. Theology as a secondary moment entails re-flection, a return to reality. But as Gutiérrez warned: "Theology, as critical reflection on the historical praxis illuminated by the Word, not only does not replace other functions of theology like wisdom and rational knowledge, but also presupposes and needs them."[2]

The perspective of the poor is an attempt to locate oneself, from a social and epistemological standpoint, in the poor's place. In the first generation of liberation theologians, the notion of the poor is not mainly an economic but a sociological one. In his *A Theology of Liberation* (1988; Spanish original 1971), Gutiérrez wrote: "The poor, today, is the oppressed, the marginalized by the society, the proletarian who struggles for his basic rights, the social class exploited and stripped, the nation that fights for liberation."[3] Only some decades later, theologians like Jung Mo Sung, working closely with economists like Franz Hinkelammert, spoke of the interaction between economy and liberation theology.

In addition to these two elements, a few others help in understanding the matrix of liberation theologies: the community dimension, expressed, among other ways, through Christian base communities ("Comunidades Eclesiales de Base", or CEBs), a driving force behind a new way of being church; the so-called popular reading of the Bible, a crucial component of CEBs where Protestant biblical scholars like Milton Schwantes have made important inputs; and last but not least, spirituality, a component which is quite often forgotten when describing liberation theology. But as Leonardo Boff wrote: "Liberation theology was born of a profound spiritual experience: sensitivity and love for the poor who make up the large majorities of our continent."[4] The spirituality of liberation is explicitly addressed, for instance, in the writings of Gutiérrez and Leonardo Boff.

Creation and Salvation

Over the decades liberation theology has expanded, reflecting on various other topics

1 Gutiérrez (1982), 257.

2 Gutiérrez (1971), 38 (translation – GK).

3 Gutiérrez (1971), 38 (translation – GK).

4 Boff (1975), 14.

but keeping to this matrix. It is within this context that we need to pose the question "How have Latin American theologians addressed the relationship between creation and salvation?"

The theme of liberation is obviously a key component of liberation theology and liberation is one concept that may be used to describe salvation. For instance, the English edition of Gutiérrez's *Teología de la liberación* (1971) has as title *A Theology of Liberation: History, Politics, and Salvation*. The "of" in this title begs further questions that are common to all forms of genitive theology, namely whether liberation is an adjective describing liberative theological reflection (see Segundo's notion of "the liberation of theology"), or whether theological reflection focuses on the processes and struggles for "liberation". By contrast, the topic of creation was not one of the main concerns for Latin American theologians in their early writings. Christology, anthropology and ecclesiology were among the priorities. Only later, when they were trying to present a more holistic theological approach and, in some cases, because of the analysis of the ecological crisis, did creation become a key concern for these authors.

The first two sections of this chapter, with its focus on Latin American contributions, present the work of two of the founders of liberation theology, Gustavo Gutiérrez and Leonardo Boff. More recent and significant developments are introduced through the work of ecofeminist theologian Ivone Gebara and indigenous theological perspectives.

Douglas Lawrie passionately presents Gustavo Gutiérrez's insights, which stress the interaction between liberation and salvation, justice and peace, creation and history. With a theology strongly based in biblical interpretation, Gutiérrez invites the reader to a contemplative experience. This is the experience of God's gratuitous love that foreshadows the full communion of the new creation.

Guillermo Kerber follows Leonardo Boff's path to show how creation has increasingly played a key role in his theology. Showing how salvation relates to integral liberation and its components, he then presents the increasing influence of ecological thought and panentheism in Boff's understanding of creation.

Pauliina Kainulainen introduces the work of Brazilian Catholic sister Ivone Gebara on creation and salvation, highlighting how her ecofeminist perspective leads her to present human beings, God and creation as immersed in the mystery of relatedness. At the same time, Kainulainen stresses that, for Gebara, the concept of salvation is markedly this-worldly. Without denying the transcendent dimension of salvation, she is more interested in the immanent and concrete expressions of it, stressing how Jesus' life and his tenderness to the earth open the way for an ecological salvation.

Maria Chavez, an Aymara theologian, closes the chapter with what is perhaps one of the most challenging aspects that theology has to deal with in Latin America today: indigenous theologies. Chavez shows how indigenous theologies in the region, despite their variety, share a common thread as political theologies committed to the liberation of indigenous peoples' communities and their land, contributing to the deconstruction of the Western andro-anthropocentric and white hegemonic theology. In this sense, indigenous theologies criticise the dominant understanding of creation rooted in Enlightenment rationality and the current logic of the market and consumerism.

The four authors show through their contributions how liberation theology has developed over the decades and has addressed issues such as creation and salvation. The intimate relationship between systematic theology and ethics in Latin American theologians is evident in the four sections. Furthermore, the importance of spirituality, as stated above, is evident from all these contributions.

References and Recommended Reading

Boff, Leonardo (1975), *Teología desde el cautiverio*, Bogotá: IAPS.

--- (1997), *Cry of the Earth, Cry of the Poor*, New York: Orbis

Boff, Leonardo and Hathaway, Mark (2009), *The Tao of Liberation: Exploring the Ecology of Transformation*, Maryknoll: Orbis.

Ecumenical Association of Third World Theologians (2011), "Ecology and Religion: In This Hour of Planetary Emergency", *Voices*, Vol. 24, Special issue 2011-1, <http://internationaltheologicalcommission.org/files/Voices2011-1.pdf>, retrieved 31 August 2011.

Groody, Daniel (2011), *Gustavo Gutiérrez: Spiritual Writings*, Maryknoll: Orbis.

Gutiérrez, Gustavo (1971), *Teología de la liberación: Perspectivas*, Lima: CEP. English translation (1988), *A Theology of Liberation: History, Politics, and Salvation*, Maryknoll: Orbis.

--- (1982), *La fuerza histórica de los pobres*, Salamanca: Sígueme.

Koinonia (2011), *Revista Electrónica Latinoamericana de Teología*, <http://servicioskoinonia.org/relat>, retrieved 31 August 2011.

Segundo, Juan Luis (1975), *Liberación de la teología*, Buenos Aires: Lohlé. English translation (1976), *The Liberation of Theology*, Maryknoll: Orbis.

Sung, Jung Mo (1994), *Teologia e economia: Repensando a teologia da libertação e utopias*, Petropolis: Vozes.

--- (2000), "Economics and Theology: Reflections on the Market, Globalization, and the Kingdom of God", in: P. M. Zulehner, A. Tausch and A. Müller (eds), *Global Capitalism, Liberation Theology and the Social Sciences*, New York: Nova Science.

Susin, Luiz Carlos and Dos Santos, Joe Marçal G. (eds.) (2011), *Nosso planeta, Nossa vida: Ecologia e teologia*, Sao Paulo: Paulinas.

Guillermo Kerber

Gustavo Gutiérrez (1928-) – From Gratuitousness to Community

Introduction

Gustavo Gutiérrez, often called the father of liberation theology, is usually remembered for phrases such as "solidarity with the poor" and "history from the underside". Yet such innovations do not exhaust his theology, which is broad in scope and in the best sense traditional. In his liberation theology both terms carry emphasis. Gutiérrez does not use "liberation" as a slogan to sell theology or theology as one instrument among others to achieve liberation. Because he is hostile to any "reductionism", he wishes to do justice to "the great themes of all true theology".[5] If, nevertheless, his theology emphasises salvation and awards to creation a subsidiary role, this requires explanation.

Gutiérrez was born in Lima on 8 June 1928 of mestizo (part Hispanic, part Quechuan) parents. His family, though not desperately poor, was far from wealthy. After initial medical studies, he decided that he was destined for the priesthood. He pursued undergraduate studies in Peru and Chile and postgraduate studies at Louvain and Lyon

[5] Gutiérrez (1983), 61.

before being ordained in 1959. Afterwards he combined teaching at the Catholic University in Lima with extensive travels and ministering to the poor parish of Rímac, where he founded and directed the Bartolomé de Las Casas Institute. Thus three worlds, the academic, the global and ecumenical, and that of poor Peruvians, intersect in his work. The influence of theologians, both Catholic (Congar, Rahner, etc.) and Protestant (Moltmann, Bonhoeffer, von Rad, etc.), and secular thinkers (Marx, Althusser, etc.), stands alongside that of ordinary people caught between the reality of oppression and the promises of the gospel.

Liberation and Salvation; Justice and Peace

When Gutiérrez wrote of the 16th-century Dominican Bartolomé de Las Casas that he "had historical perspective and political vision, but the driving force in his life was faith in Christ",[6] he could have been speaking of himself. Those who ignore this, ludicrously misinterpret him. As an explicitly theocentric theologian, he does not seek a new, radicalised gospel, but reveals the radicality of the gospel. He does not use theology to justify any prevailing human praxis – the opposite is true. Far from overlooking the influence of sin, which he interprets as the turning away from God and others, he shows how pervasive it is. He does not replace spiritual salvation with political, social and economic liberation, but rejects, on theological grounds, precisely the separation implicit in such formulations.

Salvation, the communion of people with God and among themselves,[7] implies God's new creation, which fulfils rather than replaces this world. Salvation depends on God's gratuitous love in Christ, not on human efforts or natural processes. Humans cooperate in the broader plan of salvation in that God gives them freedom to enter into communion. Since sin, individual or structural, robs people of this positive freedom, turning them into "non-persons", liberation is a prerequisite for salvation. Christ is ultimately both saviour and liberator, because humans by themselves cannot overcome sin, yet, since Christ *incarnate* did this, we are empowered to free ourselves and others. Salvation is a gift outright; liberation a gift and a task (though Gutiérrez does occasionally conflate liberation and salvation).

As liberation of the whole, concrete person relates to salvation, so comprehensive justice relates to peace. Peace without justice is a travesty; true communion cannot flourish within oppressive relationships. Humans cannot simply proclaim peace, but should *do* justice – wherever injustice prevails. Therefore solidarity with the poor is, in the Latin American context, the primary calling of the church. Though *logically* justice comes before peace, and liberation before salvation, Gutiérrez knows that we enjoy elements of true communion and peace now, in the Eucharist, for instance. Without such incursions of God's gratuitous love, "even the struggle for justice would be crippled".[8] They provide the hope that sustains faithful and loving action.

Creation as Salvation and Creative Love

The above explains why Gutiérrez consistently calls creation "God's first act of salva-

[6] Gutiérrez (1993), xvi.
[7] Gutiérrez (1973), 151.
[8] Gutiérrez (1984), 110.

tion". Though von Rad's influence on his view of creation is patent (and acknowledged), his own theology demands it. Creation is God's gratuitous act of self-communication, of establishing communion. Gutiérrez stresses the close relationship between creation and salvation: if the creation of the world is a salvific act, all subsequent salvific acts manifest God's creativity. "Creation and salvation have a christological import."[9] In that gratuitousness – a key term for Gutiérrez – is closely related to creativity, the theme of creation is not slighted.

Yet Gutiérrez uses the word "creation" seldom and the word "history" very frequently. God is primarily revealed in history – as liberator, doer of justice, maker of covenants. Belief in God as Creator is the product of secondary theological reflection (as in von Rad): in the Old Testament it is understood from the Exodus, in the New Testament, from Christ. The Saviour is also the Creator, an order that cannot be reversed without danger. *Creatio*, the ongoing creativity of God and humans, is prominent; *creatura* hardly features. In early works, for instance, Gutiérrez mentions "land" often, but only in connection to human ownership. Later, he does speak of "the natural world" in less anthropocentric terms, while maintaining the "privileged place" of humans.[10]

Gutiérrez speaks of "life" or "the world" in historical terms, as dynamic processes rather than static entities. He defends "a dynamic and historical conception of man, oriented definitively and creatively toward his future".[11] If Gutiérrez learned about the importance of history from Marx, his own view is thoroughly theological (and owes more to von Rad and Moltmann). History is "open-ended" precisely because it remains open to God's creative acts and to human action. Liberation, far from replacing salvation, stands opposed to "development", particularly if this means "unfolding according to natural laws". Such laws, even if they emanate from some creator, rule out subversive incursions of gratuitous divine and human love. If "whatever is is good", both the gospel and Christian praxis lose their validity.

Poverty and Oppression: Not God's Creation

Interpreting the world through the lens of Genesis 1:31 leads to the justification of poverty and oppression. Interpreting it through the lens of the Exodus or the crucified Jesus leads to "a denunciation of the existing order".[12] It also places the poor, the oppressed, the enslaved, "the scourged Christs of the Indies" at the centre of theology. Theology is done about, for and by them. Whereas "the gospel of creation", seen in isolation, is no gospel to them, the gospel of liberation is already latent in their own struggles. This is the nub of Gutiérrez's new way of doing theology "from below", from the concrete place where gospel and human experience and practice meet.[13]

Theology as critical reflection is a secondary but indispensible step. Without its critical edge ("in the light of the Word"), human practices are indiscriminately justified, hence Gutiérrez's fears about "baptizing the revolution". Therefore, the doctrine of

---

9 Gutiérrez (1984), 32.

10 Gutiérrez (1991), 82.

11 Gutiérrez (1973), 32.

12 Gutiérrez (1973), 233.

13 Gutiérrez (1990), 48.

creation, a typical theological construct, reminds believers that the world, however perverted by sin, remains God's property and has to be reclaimed, not abandoned. Theology then feeds back into praxis: liberation entails changing the world, not fleeing it. Similarly, "solidarity with the poor" is a necessary theological construct, based on reading the Bible within a concrete situation, that guides subsequent action. Unless theology inspires action, it is worthless.

Poverty, as opposed to spiritual poverty, is "a scandalous condition"[14] not to be tolerated or idealised (as if the poor are "privileged", while others have to bear the burden of their wealth). Since "poverty means death",[15] "the God of life" opposes it. The privilege of the poor lies solely in God's preferential care for them. This "predilection",[16] far from excluding universality, flows precisely from God's universal love, which cannot tolerate the relegation of some to the status of "non-person". If the God who was present in Job's suffering is present today in the "world of the poor", that is where the church, if it is to be faithful, has to be in its praxis *and* its theologising. "Solidarity with the poor" is thus no dramatic pose; it requires acting, reading the Bible and reflecting on it in communion with the poor.

Since Gutiérrez uses the Bible more frequently than most systematic theologians, his hermeneutics deserves attention. He has been blamed both for making poverty "the key in his reading of Scripture" and for suggesting that the Bible has a clear basic meaning and that "he knows what this is".[17] In both cases the result may be superficial exegesis. But, Gutiérrez suggests, worse than superficiality that remains open to correction is learned triviality in pursuit of academic reputations.[18] In von Rad's view of the Bible as a record of people's struggles to come to terms with God in ever-new contexts, he found a biblical theology of salvation that invites preaching and action. Moreover, he knows that the Bible also reads its readers.[19] Can academic exegesis escape these tensions and still inform church practice?

Encountering God: Spirituality and Contemplation

Had Gutiérrez made the experience of the poor an absolute starting point, his hermeneutics and theology would have been open to question. But the Christian praxis of the poor is always already a response to God's word / act: "everything begins with an encounter".[20] Without the encounter with God, there can be neither theology nor *Christian* praxis. First God's love reaching out to us; then our twin response of adoration and doing God's will; then intellectual reflection and talk about God in the twin languages of prophecy and contemplation.[21] At this deep level, salvation and creation are conjoined, for God's word / act and our words / acts are all both salvific (loosening debilitating ties) and creative (realising new possibilities). The truth is not encapsulat-

---

14 Gutiérrez (1973), 291.

15 Gutiérrez (1990), 9.

16 Gutiérrez (1987), 94.

17 Siker, 69f.

18 Gutiérrez (1983), 3f., 208.

19 Gutiérrez (1990), xvii.

20 Gutiérrez (1991), 80.

21 Gutiérrez (1990), 5ff.

ed in a ("correct") term or construct: "[T]he truth that liberates is Christ himself".[22]

Contemplation or spirituality, far from being an appendix to liberation theology, is as integral to Christian living as commitment to action is. Nor is contemplation merely the motive force driving the quest for justice; it also imposes a limit on "justice thinking", with its language of merit and retribution.[23] Gutiérrez's frequent references to the great contemplatives of the church (St John of the Cross, etc.) demonstrates that he is fully serious in this regard. Although he emphasises that spirituality, being the incursion of the Spirit into people's concrete lives, is not divorced from the material, he does not reduce the spiritual to the political. Instead, he expands traditional academic theology in two directions: towards concrete political action (in his broad sense) and towards mystical contemplation.

The encounter with God reveals God's gratuitous love and thereby provides liberation with its goal. Liberation frees people for communion, not for an abstract "autonomy". The experience of love as gratuitousness (not based on lovability) foreshadows the full communion of the new creation. Gutiérrez believes that communion always involves an element of the gratuitous that goes beyond natural ties or inclination (gracious affiliation, not natural affinity). Sadly these aspects of Gutiérrez's theology, barely touched on here, are often overlooked by both his critics and his Western admirers. They call for deep reflection and add depth to his view of salvation, but they do not directly reveal his view on creation, except in as much as it is rooted in the creativity of love. The focus is eschatological rather than protological.

Conclusion: Loss or Salutary Warning?

Though creativity (*creatio*) is crucial in Gutiérrez's theology, creation as *creatura* undoubtedly plays a secondary role. Arguably, some themes in his theology (human dignity and rights, the inherent striving for liberation, the value of science, "the world" and "fulfilment") require a more thorough treatment of the topic. Because he starts "from below", amidst the struggles of the poor, liberation and salvation appears first in his field of vision and are more thoroughly conceptualised. The gaps in his account do not necessarily imply any devaluation of God's initial creative act, though they may become problematic – for instance, when he speaks of "mastering the earth" and in his account of the natural and the supernatural.

Yet one cannot overlook the distinct merits of Gutiérrez's approach. Those who "hunger and thirst for justice" do not *first* ask about cosmology or the relationship between science and the Bible. "God the Creator" can be seen as author of the order that marginalises them; the suffering Christ, however, is "God become poor", God with them and for them. Afterwards they can approach creation Christologically, as Gutiérrez does by using John 1.[24] If Gutiérrez's theology is theocentric, his hermeneutics is Christocentric.[25] In Christian theology this can hardly be otherwise.

Secondly, whereas *creatio* implies the gratuitous giving of love, *creatura* can be in-

---

22 Gutiérrez (1990), 97.

23 Gutiérrez (1991), 162f.

24 Gutiérrez (1991), 80ff.

25 Gutiérrez (1983), 61; (1990), 3f.

terpreted as an assembly of fixed properties interacting according to laws. In this there can be neither love nor hope, only mechanical progression. Nor can there be loving (gratuitous) communion, only ties of dependence or exploitation determined by "nature". Gutiérrez's reflections on Job show how clearly he saw the dangers of mechanistic schemas, which deny the freedom of God and thus also the freedom of God's people.

Finally, on the pages of his books Gustavo Gutiérrez appears as a supremely magnanimous, compassionate, flexible man, modestly admitting that he has not thought through everything, eagerly assimilating new perspectives (he increasingly emphasises the oppression of women). Gaps in his thinking are surely not cold-blooded exclusions, for his liberation theology is pre-eminently open. And it was he who reminded us that such "non-academic" considerations are also relevant to doing and assessing theology.

References and Recommended Reading

Brown, Robert McAfee (1990), *Gustavo Gutiérrez: An Introduction to Liberation Theology*, Maryknoll: Orbis.

Cadorette, Curt (1988), *From the Heart of the People: The Theology of Gustavo Gutiérrez*, Oak Park: Meyer-Stone.

Ellis, Marc H. and Maduro, Otto (eds.) (1989), *The Future of Liberation Theology: Essays in Honor of Gustavo Gutiérrez*, Maryknoll: Orbis.

Gutiérrez, Gustavo (1973), *A Theology of Liberation* (translated by C. Inda and J. Eagleson; revised edition, 1988), Maryknoll: Orbis.

--- (1983), *The Power of the Poor in History* (translated by R. B. Barr), Maryknoll: Orbis.

--- (1984), *We Drink from Our Own Wells* (translated by M. J. O'Connell), Maryknoll: Orbis.

--- (1987), *On Job* (translated by M. J. O'Connell), Maryknoll: Orbis.

--- (1990), *The Truth Shall Make You Free* (translated by M. J. O'Connell), Maryknoll: Orbis.

--- (1991), *The God of Life* (translated by M. J. O'Connell), Maryknoll: Orbis.

--- (1993), *Las Casas: In Search of the Poor of Jesus Christ* (translated by R. B. Barr), Maryknoll: Orbis.

--- (1997), *Sharing the Word through the Liturgical Year* (translated by C. J. Dees), Maryknoll: Orbis.

Gutiérrez, Gustavo and Shaull, Richard (1977), *Liberation and Change*, Atlanta: John Knox.

Siker, Jeffrey S. (1996), "Uses of the Bible in the Theology of Gustavo Gutiérrez: Liberating Scriptures of the Poor", *Biblical Interpretation*, Vol. 4, 1, 40-71.

Douglas G. Lawrie

Leonardo Boff (1938-) – Towards the Liberation of the Whole Creation

Leonardo Boff is one of the best-known Latin American theologians. One of the fathers of liberation theology in the seventies, for more than twenty years he has been writing significantly on issues related to environment and ecology and their relationship with theology and spirituality.

Towards the Liberation of the Whole Creation

One of his first writings, *Jesus Christ Liberator*, published in 1972, started a process, common to other Latin American theologians, which tries to develop the notion of liberation and its theological implications. The late 1960s and early 1970s in Latin America was a time when several liberation movements were struggling to change the political situation in their respective countries. From a theological perspective, which differs from sociological or political ones, liberation should be understood in a comprehensive way or, as Boff and others call it, as "integral liberation".

From this perspective, liberation is closely related to salvation. For Boff, there is no eschatological salvation, which equates to integral liberation, without historical mediations. But how then can eschatological salvation be articulated with its historical manifestations, namely economic, social and political liberations? For Boff there are four models of articulation:

- The Chalcedonian model: Just as in Christ divinity and humanity relate to the point of forming a dual unit without division or separation, but also without confusion or mutations, so eschatological salvation intrinsically includes historical liberations.
- The sacramental model: Just as, according to the principle of sacramentality, grace is mediated by a reality of this world to which it is joined, so historical liberations are not dissociated from salvation, even if salvation is not realised only in historical liberations.
- The agapaic model: According to the Christian concept of love, there is an identification between love of God and love of the neighbour, so that anyone who loves the neighbour loves God. Just as God is found in the neighbour, so salvation is found in historic liberations.
- The anthropological model: The unity and difference of the two principles (body and soul) that constitute the human being can help to illuminate the difference between historic liberations and eschatological salvation.

No matter which model is chosen, the reality for Boff is that Christian salvation cannot exist without economic, political, social and ideological liberation as visible signs of the dignity of the human being.

Especially in Boff's early writings we can see a tendency towards an anthropocentric approach to salvation, which is also reflected in some of his later writings. But in these a more holistic understanding of salvation and liberation is expressed. This is also the case for the notion of creation, as we will see below.

Creation and Liberation

Since the 1970s, Boff has addressed what he calls the "transcendental and eschatological vocation of the whole of creation". Some of his affirmations at that time are cast in a clearly anthropocentric language, for instance when he stated in a chapter title of one of his books: "Man is a being called to dominate nature and to be its Master."[26]

For Boff, a theology of creation has been subjugated to the dominant theology, which for historical and institutional reasons has concentrated much more on the mystery of redemption. A renewed theology of creation, for him,[27] should be deeply rooted in the thinking of Origen and St Augustine, enriched by the experience of St Francis as developed by the Franciscan school (St Bonaventure, Duns Scotus and William of Ockham), enriched by the theology of the Orthodox Church and able to incorporate the

[26] Boff (1980), 48.
[27] Boff (1995), 46.

new cosmology. This theology of creation, or ecotheology, emphasises creation as the dance of God's love, as the mirror of both God and all created things. From that perspective, human beings are not above but within creation. And the world does not belong to humans but to God, its Creator. However, the world is given to humans as a garden to cultivate and tend, and they thus have a relationship of responsibility towards it. In contrast to a destructive, dominating involvement, Boff calls for a deeply ecological involvement, directed at maintaining the balance of creation, as it advances and is transformed by human work.

This theology of creation will then, according to Boff, help us to find the significance of a theology of salvation. Redemption implies tragedy, the fall of creation and humankind's failure to fulfil its vocation, and a breakdown affecting all humans and their cosmic environment. Because humans have not preserved the creation, it is wounded and groans and cries out for liberation (Rom. 8:22). But this cry is not for it to be replaced but for it to be redeemed. The creation has basically retained its status as a good creation. Human beings do not have such absolute power over God's work as to damage it at its heart, but they can inflict grievous wounds on it. God's work of salvation gathers up creation, redirects the arrow of time, and heals the bleeding wounds.

Panentheism, Perichoresis and Spirituality

From this ecotheological perspective there is derived a deep sense of the sacramentality of all things. Boff adopts, recognising process theology and ecofeminist thought, a panentheistic standpoint: God is in all and all is in God. The sacramentality of the created universe remains open to new possibilities, in the acknowledgment that the process of evolution is incomplete. Only at the end will there be a Sabbath rest for all of creation.

The Trinity as the interplay of perichoretic relationships between Father, Son and the Holy Spirit[28] receives a new understanding with the ecological perspective to which Boff subscribes. Ecology stresses the study of relationships and, in classic Christian teaching on the Trinity, the three persons are constituted by their relationship. But the trinitarian God is not an exclusively Christian doctrine. There is a trinitarian thread running through the other great religious traditions of humankind. The coexistence of unity and diversity in the universe stressed by ecological discourse helps us to understand the communion within the divine Trinity. God in Trinity is par excellence relationality. *Perichoresis* enables us to overcome tritheism by affirming the communion and complete relationality among the divine persons who are what they are by their essential and intrinsic communion and inter(retro)relating.

From a panentheistic point of view, if God is communion and relationships, then everything in the universe lives in relationship and everything is in communion with everything else. Thus the Trinity emerges as one of the most suitable representations of the mystery of the universe. And *perichoresis* can also be applied to the mutual relationship between God and creation. Yet further, the world is complex, diverse and one, intertwined and interconnected, because it is a mirror of the Trinity. God emerges in every being, can be glimpsed in every relationship, and breaks into every ecosys-

[28] Boff (1997), 154.

tem. And, most of all, God becomes sacrament in the life of each human being. Thus the sacramentality of the created universe takes on a new dimension as it incorporates the new cosmology and the concept of panentheism.

If God is in all and all is in God, as panentheism proclaims, that is due to the third person of the Holy Trinity, the Holy Spirit. The Christian doctrine of the Holy Spirit, Boff reminds us, incorporates the religious tradition of seeing the world as inhabited by spirits, a place where vital energies are experienced, which is systematised in animism, a cosmology that is the primitive mentality reaching down into the depths of our psyche. The spirit in the Judaeo-Christian tradition (*ruah*) is an expression and extension of this vital space. Though the Holy Spirit was for centuries sidelined in Western churches, since the 1970s the Spirit has become highly relevant in the search for a new spirituality, an experience of the Spirit transcending the various religious confessions, and not only those that are Christian.

Boff asks: How does the Holy Spirit of the Christian Trinity tie in with creation? Through *perichoresis* the creation is by nature trinitarian. The Father creates *through* the Son *in* the Holy Spirit. The cosmos is shown to be an interplay of relationships, because it is created in the likeness and image of the triune God. The Spirit has from the beginning entered the universe, made it her dwelling and furthermore has left self behind to dwell within the creation.

The Spirit, Boff reminds us, being a feminine noun in Hebrew and having attributes like sustaining life processes, gestation, protection and expansion of life, complements the male attributes normally given to God the Father and to the Son (Jesus).

Boff's thinking on the previous topics drives him to reformulate Christology.[29] Just as the spiritual principle was at work in creation, so was the Christic principle. Boff follows Teilhard de Chardin's approach, which has been a reference point for him since Boff's *O Evangelho do Cristo cósmico* ("The Gospel of the Cosmic Christ", 1971), in describing the evolutionary process in this way: cosmogenesis – Christogenesis – Christ of faith – historical Jesus (including incarnation, life, passion, death and resurrection). For Boff, "Christ" is not a noun but a qualifying adjective. The Christic dimension accompanies the process of cosmogenesis and anthropogenesis and becomes Christological through the incarnation of the Son. That is part of an evolutionary process of the whole of creation that moves eschatologically towards the Omega point, the point towards which the whole of creation converges. The Christ of faith is located in the Jesus of history. The incarnation roots Jesus in the cosmos. Moreover, the passion and death of Jesus are an expression of the crucifixion of the cosmic Christ. Finally, in the resurrection life, Christ comes back transfigured at an incomparably higher level. Boff here concludes by quoting Moltmann: "In the Risen one evolution becomes revolution in the original meaning of the word."[30]

Conclusion: The Cry of the Earth, the Cry of the Poor

The interaction between creation and liberation in Boff's thought leads to a revision of dogmatic theology, but also to a re-examination of ethics and spirituality.

The ethical aspect, he suggests, is to be seen in the emergence of liberation theo-

[29] Boff (1997), 174-186.
[30] Moltmann, 303, quoted in Boff (1997), 182.

logy. Liberation theology was set in motion by ethical indignation in the face of the dire poverty of the masses, especially in the Third World. It is this actual, sociological and ethical presence of the poor in the work of liberation theology that gives it an epistemological status: the poor constitute the point from which one attempts to conceive of God, Christ, history, the mission of the churches, creation and salvation. Confronted with the cry of the oppressed and the excluded, social justice is most urgently sought in order to assure life and the human dignity that goes along with it. But social justice, Boff states, is not enough. Ecological justice entails more than social justice, as it refers to a new covenant between human beings and other beings, a new gentleness toward what is created, and the fashioning of an ethic and mystique of kinship with the entire cosmic community. The earth, Boff concludes, is also crying out under the predatory and lethal machinery of our models of society and development. To hear these two interconnected cries and to see the same root cause that produces them is to carry out integral liberation.

To explore the relationship between creation and salvation would therefore mean to widen the meaning of the option for the poor, which has been a key component of Boff's theology and of liberation theologies in general. This option, Boff affirms, should include an option for the most threatened of other beings and species. These include, for Boff, the poorest human beings, those whose way of life is threatened with extinction, such as the Kaiapo, the Yanomani, and other tribes, and animal species like the golden micalion, the iruapuro and the panda. Without forgetting these species, Boff recalls that the most threatened being in creation is planet Earth itself as a whole.[31] Thus the need to assure the sustainability of planet Earth in the short, medium and long term is primary.

In summary, for Boff, the relatedness of creation and salvation is necessary, owing to the new paradigm, the paradigm of the "re-ligation" (connectedness) of all with all. A new paradigm, he declares, calls for a new language, a new imagination, a new politics, a new pedagogy, a new ethics, a new discovery of the sacred and a new process of individuation (spirituality). The cry of the poor should be listened to together with the cry of the earth, and the whole of humanity should respond effectively to such cries.

References and Recommended Reading

Boff, Leonardo (1971), *O Evangelho do Cristo cósmico*, Petrópolis: Vozes.
--- (1978), *Jesus Christ Liberator*, Maryknoll: Orbis.
--- (1980), *El destino del hombre y del mundo*, Santander: Sal Terrae.
--- (1995), *Ecology and Liberation: A New Paradigm*, Maryknoll: Orbis.
--- (1997), *Cry of the Earth, Cry of the Poor*, Maryknoll: Orbis.
Boff, Leonardo and Hathaway, Mark (2009), *The Tao of Liberation: Exploring the Ecology of Transformation*, Maryknoll: Orbis.
Gibellini, Rosino (1988), *The Liberation Theology Debate*, Maryknoll: Orbis.
Moltmann, Jürgen (1993), *The Way of Jesus Christ*, Minneapolis: Fortress.

Guillermo Kerber

[31] Boff (1997), 113.

Ivone Gebara (1944-) – No More Violence towards the Earth and Humans

Postdogmatic Feminism and a Revision of Christianity's Metaphysical Groundings

> Analyses using gender as well as the contributions of contemporary science have given us enough indication about the impossibility of maintaining traditional theological discourse unchanged. Traditional discourse has been, like other knowledge, directly or indirectly complicit in the planetary destruction we are witnessing today.[32]

These words by the Brazilian ecofeminist philosopher and theologian Ivone Gebara take us to the core of her task as a theologian. Her starting points in theological reflection are the concern for the poor women in her urban surroundings in north-east Brazil and the concern for the earth. In other words, Gebara engages in ecofeminist theology. Ecofeminism is a multifaceted academic and social movement that brings together gender perspectives and ecological awareness. A focal insight of ecofeminism is that historical, symbolic, political and economic relationships exist between the denigration of the natural world and the oppression of women. This is the case at least in Western cultures.[33]

Gebara is a Catholic nun, a Sister of Notre Dame. She holds doctorates in philosophy and religious studies, and has taught for many years at the Theological Institute of Recife (ITER). Gebara has published various books; those translated into English include *Mary: Mother of God, Mother of the Poor* (1989), *Longing for Running Water: Ecofeminism and Liberation* (1999), and *Out of the Depths: Women's Experience of Evil and Salvation* (2002).

Gebara views critically the complicity of Christian theology in the systems that have proved to be destructive of the well-being of the most vulnerable. She wants to raise a discussion about our whole Western cosmological vision. Her aim is to dismantle this patriarchal cosmology of dualist hierarchies that sustains ideologies and systems of domination of some (Christian white, male, ruling-class humans) over others (non-Christians, non-whites, women, the poor, and the earth).[34] In a word, Gebara wants to renew Christian thinking so that it does not perpetuate violence anymore.

Gebara aims at taking care of the earth through a thoroughgoing revision of Christianity's metaphysical groundings. She criticises the dominant mechanistic worldview and its ties with the dominion of the earth. Gebara wants to replace it with a holistic cosmology that appreciates mutual, non-hierarchical relationships among people and among species.

In order to achieve this transformation, Gebara deems it necessary to deconstruct theological claims and doctrines. According to Gebara, it is important to dare to ask questions arising from daily life and concrete experiences, seeking new ways of speaking. This process begins with a deconstruction of theology, revealing its reality as anthropology. All theology and also the Bible are human constructs.

---

[32] Gebara (2002), 171.

[33] See Eaton, 4.

[34] See Gebara (1999a); Ruether, 250-251.

Gebara wants to do post-patriarchal and post-dogmatic, but not post-Christian, theology. She sees her way of doing theology in the continuum of the mystical tradition – one could call it Wisdom theology – that appreciates the personal and cosmic dimension of faith and relativises the importance of dogma.

A Critique of the Traditional Doctrine of Creation

"Patriarchal theology, and especially creation theology, legitimises both the oppression and the domination of nature and the existence of hierarchical relationships among all beings."[35] Gebara is highly critical of the way in which creation theology has often held the view that God stands above nature as Creator and lawgiver. The need to stress God's discontinuity with all the powers of the cosmos, the earth, human beings and animals appears to be of fundamental importance in maintaining the hierarchical organisation of our societies.[36] Gebara refers to the habit of appealing to the so-called orders of creation, which has often meant oppression for women and other denigrated groups of people. She also interprets the image of God as Creator as a masculine image.[37]

In *Longing for Running Water*, Gebara, from her anthropological and ecofeminist perspective, wants to persuade her readers that the human person is relatedness and that God too is better understood as a great relational mystery. Gebara has difficulties with the use of personal metaphors in speaking about God, she prefers cosmic and other metaphors like Mystery, Relationship or Energy. Gebara re-theologises the idea of evolution and sees the world as a great evolutionary process (with some influences of process theology).

So Gebara does not have much to say about creation. She prefers to speak about the magnificent creativity that manifests itself in the universe. Gebara de-theologises the doctrine of the Trinity so that it becomes a symbolic way of speaking about our deep sense of unity in multiplicity in the cosmos, in the earth and in our own person. In this multiplicity of the cosmos there is amazing creativity: the cosmos is not static. For Gebara, the Trinity is not a distant separate God living someplace else, but a symbolic expression of the basic dynamic of life itself in a process of vital interrelational creativity.[38]

With this kind of de-theologising Gebara seeks ways to rescue the old theological words so that they can again convey meaning. She may be right in her opinion that too much of Christian theological language and symbols have become so petrified that they are no longer able to move people's hearts. Whether Gebara's solution to deconstruct theology to anthropology can enliven the meanings remains to be discussed.

Salvation as Small Everyday Resurrections

Regarding salvation, Gebara has much more to offer. Gebara's theological background is in the Latin American liberation theology of the 1970s and 1980s. But in her later

[35] Gebara (1999a), 16.

[36] See Gebara (1999a), 114.

[37] See Gebara (2002), 159.

[38] See Gebara (1999a), 145; Ruether, 252.

writings Gebara distances herself from the – as she sees them – somewhat mechanistic and patriarchal elements of liberation theology. She is not convinced by the promises of liberation theology about a perfect future state of justice and happiness. Gebara wants to look at the present moment and the possibilities of salvation / happiness in it.

Gebara uses a phenomenological method to analyse suffering. In *Out of the Depths* her focus is on women's suffering that has taken different forms in history. She picks up as examples stories of women's lives where evil is present as poverty, loss, marginalisation, denial of access to knowledge and education, in a word, violence in many forms. She includes in her analysis the evil women themselves do. Gebara wants to re-theologise these experiences.

The anthropological basis of this theology is that human beings are a mixture of good and evil. Gebara does not find meaningful the traditional metaphysical way of describing a perfectly good original state, then the fall and later an eschatological state of perfection again. She prefers referring to the life of Jesus and his saving acts as the most meaningful theological basis for a contextual theology. As her concept of the human being involves a mixture, so also does her concept of salvation. Salvation is for Gebara not a "once and for all solution" but something fragile, ephemeral, corporeal and concrete in the daily life.[39]

Gebara's concept of salvation is markedly this-worldly. Gebara does not deny the transcendent dimension of salvation, but she is interested in the immanent and concrete expressions of it:

> Salvation is more than a promise, even if it is already a way out of heading toward salvation. Salvation is a get-together, an event, a sentiment, a kiss, a piece of bread, a happy old woman. It is everything that nourishes love, our body, our life. It is more than happiness in the hereafter, even if we hang on to the right to dream of our eternal tomorrow.[40]

According to Gebara, this kind of "mini-salvation" does not exclude struggling for better conditions of life for all. There is the well-known dialectic between the "already" and the "not yet". But the moments of salvation are small, everyday resurrections.[41] Gebara is keenly aware of the transitory character of human life. Therefore she stresses that "because we are going away, it is necessary to have tender embraces; because we are going away, people who are hungry must eat today, and I must share my bread".[42] Gebara's conception of salvation is in some aspects similar to the old Hebrew this-worldly view of salvation.

This kind of immanent salvation has no need of an external saviour. Gebara finds the traditional doctrines of atonement hardly useful anymore. Nevertheless, she appreciates Jesus' life as a redemptive paradigm. Salvation thus comes close to the idea of liberation. Rosemary Radford Ruether has summarised the meaning of the life of Jesus for feminist theology as follows: "dissent against oppressive religious and political structures; taking the side of the oppressed, particularly women; living a praxis of

[39] See Gebara (2002), 126-127, 180.

[40] Gebara (2002), 125.

[41] See Gebara (2002), 121-125; Gebara (1999a), 147.

[42] Gebara (2002), 130.

egalitarian relations across gender, race, class, and other status differences imposed by the dominant society; pointing toward a new time when these hierarchies will be overcome and anticipating redeemed relations in a community of celebration here and now."[43] This description fits Gebara's theology quite well, but Gebara puts even more emphasis on the dimension of salvation here and now.

Like many other feminist theologians, Gebara does not want to stress the role of Jesus as the only salvific person. But Jesus has a lot to offer, not least in the way he expressed tenderness towards the earth. According to Gebara, this tenderness between human beings and the earth is mutual.[44] To the still rather anthropocentric message of Jesus must today be added an ecological awareness: Gebara uses the concept of "ecological salvation" and she wants us to open ourselves up to a "more biocentric understanding of salvation":

> This new way of doing things seems to me perfectly justified, because it maintains not only the most fundamental aspects of Jesus's perspective but also the understanding that we are a living body in constant evolution. Theology has repeated many times that Jesus did not proclaim himself; using an ecofeminist perspective, we could say that he proclaimed respect for the life of every being and abundant life for all.[45]

The Meaning of the Cross

In feminist theology generally, the cross of Jesus tells about the risk, or the cost of discipleship. Feminist theologians are critical of the doctrines of atonement that are centred on Jesus' suffering sacrifice on the cross as a surrogate for sinful humanity. Doctrines of this kind are instrumental in maintaining patterns of submission to violence, reinforcing often the unjust suffering of women and other already oppressed groups. Instead, the cross must be seen as a symbol of evil, something bad imposed by an imperial power. It is a rejection of Jesus' ministry of life as good news to the poor by the powerful who sought to silence him. The cross is a symbol of the risk that anyone struggling against oppression may experience at the hands of those who want to keep the system of domination intact. What is redeeming is not Jesus' death but his life. The resurrection of Jesus shows that the powers of violence lost the battle.[46]

In this feminist theological vein, Gebara de-theologises the theme of the cross of Christ. Instead, she wants to talk about crosses in the plural. These are the sufferings of ordinary people, their daily burdens, mixed with moments of hope and salvation. Gebara states that salvation is not outside, but mixed with suffering; it is present where one would not think to find it.[47]

Salvation denounces cruelty and is expressed in tiny everyday events of redemption, like those narrated in the gospels. According to Gebara, this kind of salvation is what especially women find attractive in the gospel of Jesus. The simplicity of the saving

---

[43] Ruether, 276-277.

[44] See Gebara (1999b), 184.

[45] Gebara (1999b), 183-184. See also Gebara (2002), 121, 143.

[46] Ruether, 233-234.

[47] Gebara (2002), 126.

acts in the gospels should be remembered. These acts are instances of raising to life, restoring sight and life and relationships of justice. In daily moments of encounter one shares one's bread, fish or wine; one heals a sick person or draws near to a prostitute. All these acts are actual, temporal and corporeal.[48]

Gebara's critique of the traditional doctrines about the cross is crystallised in the claim that many interpretations of the cross have been developed by socio-religious systems as a veil to cover up unjust crosses. This veil does not allow one to distinguish between suffering caused by the wrongdoing of others and the existential anguish present in every human life.

Conclusion

It is practically impossible to define the relationship between creation and salvation in the "post-dogmatic" theology of Ivone Gebara. Her doctrine of creation is nearly non-existent despite her ecofeminist approach. Nevertheless, Gebara makes a valuable contribution to the discussion about salvation. Gebara's conception of salvation is strongly immanent, but as such it presents an important corrective to traditional conceptions that have more or less forgotten the immanent, concrete and everyday aspects of salvation in the gospel narratives about Jesus' life. Gebara takes them seriously and creates touching images of "everyday resurrections". Her conception of salvation also integrates an ecological awareness.

Gebara shows that too often in the history of Christian communities and their theologies, dogmatism has led to violence towards other people and the earth. But in her need to reject this, Gebara underplays the positive meaning of doctrine for the integrity of the Christian tradition. If the sense of continuity with the core of Christian tradition (mystical and doctrinal) gets very thin, does this kind of theology have the persuasive power to transform actual Christian communities? The ecological and other global challenges facing Christians are huge and all the sources of transforming power are needed.

References and Recommended Reading

Eaton, Heather (2005), *Introducing Ecofeminist Theologies*, London / New York: T & T Clark.

Gebara, Ivone (1999a), *Longing for Running Water: Ecofeminism and Liberation* (translated by David Molineaux), Minneapolis: Fortress.

--- (1999b), "Quién es el 'Jesús liberador' que buscamos?", in: J. J. Tamayo Acosta, (ed.), *Palabras claves sobre Jesús de Nazaret*, Estella: Verbo Dei, 149-188.

--- (2002), *Out of the Depths: Women's Experience of Evil and Salvation* (translated by Ann Patrick Ware), Minneapolis: Fortress.

Gebara, Ivone and Bingemer, Maria Clara (1989), *Mary, Mother of God, Mother of the Poor*, Tunbridge Wells: Burns and Oates.

Ruether, Rosemary Radford (1998), *Women and Redemption: A Theological History*, Minneapolis: Fortress.

Pauliina Kainulainen

[48] Gebara (2002), 128.

Land as Mother: An Indigenous-Theology Perspective

From Abya Yala

Abya Yala is the "mature land, fertile and abundant". It is the indigenous name for what is called Latin America and the Caribbean by outsiders. Although each indigenous group uses a different name according to its language, the name Abya Yala, of Kuna origin, became very popular after 1992, the year in which the five hundredth anniversary of the arrival of the Spanish conquistadores was commemorated. On the one hand, the name is used mostly in the space of political demands for self-determination; on the other hand, it helps to reaffirm the cultural identity of the new indigenous generations. In this century the term testifies to the capacity for generating life amidst suffering, exploitation and marginalisation. New paradigms of civilisation arise from Abya Yala and many of them come from the cultural matrix of the descendants of the original nations of Abya Yala.

Since the 1970s, indigenous peoples have expressed their protests and proposals in international and ecumenical forums. They protest against injustices, the continued attempts at genocide and cultural assimilation, dispossession of lands and territories, rivers, mountains, sacred sites, natural resources, etc. These protests are shaped by the use of different languages, in a creative combination of political and spiritual concepts and symbols. This entails the explicit elaboration of indigenous theologies and a focus on the different worldviews and spiritual values that the indigenous cultures have maintained for centuries, despite subjugation. It also involves proposals to enrich the world and the church with their traditional ancestral wisdom and their particular experiences of Christianity, in the context of dialogue with other Christian theologies as equals. In recognising the deep crisis in which the capitalist system finds itself, indigenous proposals are directed towards the whole world, the complex web of life on earth, to try to ensure life and its possibilities by suggesting a different form of relationship, a distinct worldview and an earth-centred spirituality.

The word "indigenous" here refers to the indigenous populations oppressed by colonialism and capitalism, who recognise themselves as heirs and successors to the great civilisations that existed prior to the North Atlantic process of colonisation and Christianisation and who join with other oppressed and excluded sectors of their societies in search of joint liberation. The category "indigenous" or "Indian" is an external imposition that "has gathered our peoples in pain, resistance and in theological reflection".[49] The category "peoples" in the plural refers to the amazing diversity of indigenous peoples, and especially to the Latin American experience of rebellions, where huge social transformations have been initiated and carried out by human conglomerates. Such peoples are established in certain territories and recognise themselves as bound together by certain cultural and social factors, worldview, origin and destiny. From a declared situation of death, indigenous peoples are arising and with them the hope for a better possible world where so many other worlds are present.

[49] López Hernández, 31.

Rooted in the Daily Life and Religious Experiences

The daily life of indigenous communities, both urban and rural, informs the theological reflection about a history of pain which is also full of grace. Religious experiences bear witness to a creative way to express both Christianity and indigenous religions. The Christian faith has been welcomed in the cultural matrix of indigenous peoples and a creative mutual challenge is shaping the current forms of indigenous culture and religious expression. The welcoming of indigenous cultures into mainline Christianity and theological reflection has not happened as yet. Despite such negation, new approaches and processes of theological dialogue are strengthening the search for and envisioning of a new understanding of and for life, in both Catholic and Protestant circles.[50]

Indigenous theology is plural and diverse, depending on the region and culture of such peoples.[51] Affirming its contextual character, it also claims universality because of its sources, resources, approach and the theological themes that are addressed. It is a political theology committed to the liberation of communities among indigenous people, their land and its resources, and engaged in the decolonisation, deconstruction and depatriarchalisation of occidental, andro-anthropocentric and white hegemonic theology.

Indigenous theology criticises the dominant understanding of creation that is rooted in Enlightenment rationality, the logic of the (free?) market and the culture of consumerism. The "Enlightenment paradigm of euro-centric modernity rooted in the conquest of nature is the major root causes of today's world crisis. Christian theologies have played its role in justifying exploitation of mother earth."[52] Reductionist scientific methods have taken the personal and a sense of mystery out of a comprehension of the land. Accordingly, land is understood as merely material and never as alive or the Mother of Life. Enlightenment rationality entails a reinforcement of the already hegemonic Hellenic comprehension of life in the European context. Platonic Hellenism was already hegemonic in its theological interpretations and marked further interpretations of person, nature, history, creation and salvation.

This dominant understanding of creation is hierarchical in nature. A hierarchical order was applied not only to human society but also to nature, so that some were subordinated to others and condemned to serve and to be used. Material nature and non-human creatures were protected only in order to serve human needs and definitely not for all human beings. Another criticism raised by indigenous theology is directed at an anthropocentric view of creation. The human being is the centre and point of reference for everything. Accordingly, creation exists for the sake of realising God's covenant in Jesus Christ with humanity, and in consequence creation has no spirit or history, nor is

---

50 There have been five symposiums on *Teología India* held by the Catholic Conference of Bishops in Latin America and the Caribbean. The World Council of Churches and the Latinoamerican Council of Churches started a process of theological dialogue among and with indigenous theologians in order to continue raising the theological voice of indigenous peoples.

51 It is possible to name three major trees with many branches: *Teología India* in Central America, *Teología Andina* in the Andean region and, in its initial stages, *Teología Amazónica* in the Amazonas region.

52 Longchar, 2.

it capable of being redeemed. Salvation is mostly understood in relation to human history and usually without relation to the complexity of life surrounding humanity.

Finally, a linear comprehension of history limits the possibilities of understanding the relationship between creation and salvation. In the case of Andean cultures, time is not understood in a linear sense. Cycles of time divide each stage of history and time cannot be understood separately of space.[53] The work of God is found throughout time and space and not merely in the beginning or at the last moment. Other theologies tend to understand creation and salvation from a linear conception of time: creation as the origin, and eschatological salvation as the final moment in history. Focusing on these edges of linear time somehow undermines the necessity of taking responsibility in the present, right here and now.

Indigenous peoples, women, black peoples and other minorities were typically associated with nature and therefore subjugated. This same logic of domination is associated with an Enlightenment rationality, the functioning of the market and a culture of consumerism. This logic is still employed to justify oppression, even slavery and annihilation, as well as the exploitation and devastation of nature, which also affects actual climate change. It is within indigenous theologies that one may therefore find a sensitivity for the impact of this logic of domination.

Creation and Humankind

One of the core themes for indigenous theology has to do with with the land and creation, in association with political vindication and spiritual connotations. For indigenous theology, land is loaded with political significance. From the concrete experience of suffering, hope and resistance, indigenous theologies denounce land dispossession, the exploitation and misuse of natural resources, foreign and national oppression of indigenous nations, cultural breakdown, threats associated with the tourism industry, the massive violation of the human rights of indigenous peoples, specially of indigenous women and children, etc. The life and destiny of humanity and the earth are deeply interconnected. Threatening and violating human dignity also affects the land / earth and vice versa. In this context, salvation appears as the possibility to overcome oppression, not only for humanity but also for creation (as *creatura*). Salvation is clearly linked to liberation from oppressive structures: socio-economic and cultural ones and the rationality which leads to the devastation of nature.

By drawing from indigenous worldviews and traditional wisdom, indigenous theology opens space to consider the earth as sacred. Earth / Creation is not conceived only as material nature but as a living reality with whom relationships characterised by mutual care are possible. Creation is considered as a web of life where the human being is not the apex or superior but just part of the whole living organism. The whole cosmos is perceived as connected and integrated. Earth is at the centre of religious experience. This relationship with Earth is deeply spiritual. An earthly spirituality sustains the daily experience of life of indigenous peoples, particularly of women, including their attitudes and discourses. Relations of reciprocity and solidarity between persons, families, and communities, ways of self-organisation for survival and reli-

53 The Aymara word *pacha* means "time and space", both together, and implies a non-linear understanding of history.

gious rituals to ensure the balance of life alike are based on this earthly spirituality and form part of daily experience. This spirituality provides a fertile ground in which a different logic can develop that offers alternatives to the current consumerist way of life. An earthly spirituality is also a way of replying to the feeling of an increasing loss of a sense of life among younger generations.

For indigenous peoples, life is considered possible because of a delicate balance, which needs to be nurtured and respected. The fracturing of this balance affects all kinds of life on Earth and threatens the Earth herself, ergo, the possibility of life itself. To affect the natural balance is a suicidal attitude. While recognising and celebrating the improvement in the quality of human life during the past centuries, indigenous theologies identify and denounce the kind of rationality behind the ideas of unlimited progress and technocratic civilisation. Indigenous theology proposes walking a step further in order to recover the spiritual relation to the Earth / creation so as to heal the fractures following from our spiritual separation from creation. In this context, salvation means to heal relationships among all the elements in creation and to rebalance the fluid energy of life in creation. To go back to the loving arms of Mother Earth is an answer to the current crisis for human civilisation that is expressed dramatically by climate change and financial problems. It is also a qualitative step towards a new level of human conscience.

Even though the human being is not the centre of creation, humanity has a big responsibility to rebalance relationships in creation. This responsibility stems from the recognition of the relational aspect of humanity, its capacity for being in relationships, therefore from conscience, spirit and energy. As an integral part of creation, a portion of Earth herself, humanity participates in the creative work of God in creation for the salvation of creation.

Mother Earth

In recognising the hegemonic Enlightenment rationality and current logic of consumerism as root causes of the separation between humanity and creation, indigenous theology proposes to reconnect to creation and to the spiritual energy of the Earth as Mother. The view of Earth as Mother and as sacred is the major contribution of this theological perspective. For the vast majority of indigenous peoples, Earth is more than material nature; it is Mother Earth. She is the giver and sustainer of life. This is born from religious experiences through which indigenous communities refer to themselves as children of Mother Earth. In the Andes in particular, they are the "children of the Pachamama".[54] All religious practices and moral prescriptions are related to maintaining the balance of life and guaranteeing the reproduction of life within the Earth community.

Apart from challenging a monotheistic comprehension of God, typical of Christianity and other main religions, indigenous theologies reinforce a panentheistic compre-

[54] *Pachamama* is an Aymara word of which the primary meaning is "Mother Earth". The word has not only been used in theological reflections in the Andes region. Its international use comes from the negotiations before the United Nations where indigenous peoples have a strong voice. See the proposals of the Plurinational State of Bolivia regarding the rights of Mother Earth, presented at international negotiations on climate change.

hension of God. Owing to a cyclical comprehension of time in the Andean cultures, the emphasis does not fall on the beginning or origin of creation but on the maintenance of the balance in creation. Therefore, God is not mainly the Creator but the Maker of order or the Sustainer of the balance and possibility of life. God cannot be understood only from the two opposite edges of time: creation as origin and escatological redemption. God is part of everything, is in the Earth and in the cosmos. God is the universal system of relations itself. For theology and Christianity, it means the possibility of opening doors to welcome other experiences of God which can broaden and deepen the religious (*re ligare*) experience of the mystery of life, to whom we refer as God / Goddess. A pluralistic experience of God was always present in the human religious experience as is also evident from the Hebrew Bible.

In dialogue with the biblical witnesses, indigenous theologies discover the revelation of God in creation and in the incarnation. As a result, creation is seen to be the first act of God's revelation. Incarnation, on the other hand, shows the possibilities of fullness of grace for – but not only for – humankind. In the biblical creation narratives, God reveals himself / herself as co-creator with the earth (Gen 1:9), so that Earth / creation (as *creatura*) participates actively in the creation (as *creatio*) of life on the same earth. God has never been alone in her / his creative work. By the same logic, through its own mechanisms of rebalancing, Earth / creation also participates in the salvific work of God.

For indigenous theologies, creation and salvation are intertwined all the time, where and when needed, because they are understood as the continuing work of God. For Andean cultures, everything happens in the same *Pacha*, in the same creation / cosmos where we share life and where human history is possible. God, the sustainer of life, guarantees the continuation of life on Earth and performs salvation whenever the balance is re-established.

By Way of Conclusion

Indigenous peoples understand themselves as "peoples of the walk", walking peoples towards their utopias and in a permanent process of re-creating and assessing their projects. In Abya Yala, indigenous theology is articulated mainly by "theologians of daily life" who do not have theological degrees, but who have own extraordinary experiences of inclusive faith. The daily faith of these lay theologians expresses the deep confidence in the grace of God who has always been accompanying the indigenous walking and who promises the healing of the broken balance of life. With courage and faith indigenous theologies affirm that the God of our ancestors, the God of creation and the God of salvation are the same, manifested in Jesus, the Christ of all peoples.

References and Recommended Reading

Estermann, Josef (ed.) (2006), *Teología Andina: El tejido diverso de la fe indígena* (volumes 1 and 2), La Paz: ISEAT / Plural.

Longchar, Wati (no date), "Green Theology: A Tribal Perspective", Mimeo (unpublished).

López Hernández, Eleazar (2000), *Teología India, Antología*, La Paz: Verbo Divino.

Quispe, Maria Chavez (ed.) (2010), "Perspectives on Indigenous Theologies and Spiritualites", *The Ecumenical Review*, Vol. 62, 4, 333-436.

Maria Chavez Quispe

Further Developments

While salvation as liberation has been, as already stated, a key focus since the early writings of liberation theologians, creation is a topic that only more recently entered into the scope of Latin American theology. Interesting developments in the last decades on creation and salvation can be found in various domains.

The first one is related to the emergence of a Latin American ecotheology since the late 1980s. The consequences of the ecological crisis in the region provoked, indeed, a deeper analysis on creation and salvation. Concrete expressions of the crisis, such as the deforestation of the Amazon, the growth of megacities and their pollution, land and water grabbing and the scarcity and privatisation of water, offered new challenges to theological work. Responding to these challenges, institutions like the Departamento Ecuménico de Investigaciones (DEI) in Costa Rica or the Centro de Investigación y Promoción Franciscano y Ecológico (CIPFE) in Uruguay have done significant research on the link between ecology and theology.

A second area of reflection has been the work done on indigenous theologies. The overview Maria Chavez gives in her section reflects a trend that needs further comment. The increasing participation of indigenous peoples' movements in the social and political struggles of some regions in Latin America, especially the Andean region and Central America, has been accompanied by a form of theological reflection, which, based on indigenous worldviews, has held together creation and salvation as key concepts. A particular focus of theological reflection has been on land issues.

Related to this second area of reflection, the theology done by Afro-Brazilian and other Afro-Latin American scholars, also suggests a non-Western way of relating to the land and the earth. As Maria Albenize Farias Malcher states, "The land (territory) becomes a life value, a space of experienced relationships, the fruit of memories and personal, shared experience. In this context the land for these communities is not built only as a territorial extension. It is a portion of geographical space where material production occurs as a production of symbolic and cultural meanings for the community."[55] Indigenous and Afro-Latin American theologies have also contributed in recent years to theological reflection on religious pluralism in the region. Here, too, issues related to creation and salvation are being addressed. The various editions of the World Forum on Theology and Liberation have helped to systematise such contributions.

Although some books and articles have been translated into English, most of them continue to be available only in Spanish or Portuguese, as can be seen in the bibliography provided below and in the four previous sections. Some websites have addressed creation, salvation and related topics and offer updated contributions to the ongoing theological debate, for example *Revista Electrónica Latinoamericana de Teología*.

References and Recommended Reading

Barros, Marcelo and de Caravias, José Luis (1988), *Teología de la tierra*, Madrid: Paulinas.
Ecoteología, <http://ecoteologiapuj.blogspot.com/>, retrieved 31 August 2011.
Farias Malcher, Albenize Maria (2009), "Identidade quilombola e territorio", Paper presented at the

[55] Farias Malcher (2009), 13 (translation – GK).

World Forum on Theology and Liberation, Belem, Brazil, 2009, <www.wftl.org/pdf/ 046.pdf>, retrieved 16 October 2011.

Hedström, Ingemar (1990), *Volverán las golondrinas? La reintegración de la creación desde una perspectiva latinoamericana*, San José (Costa Rica): DEI.

--- (1993), *Somos parte de un gran equilibrio: La crisis ecológica en Centroamérica*, San José (Costa Rica): DEI.

Hedström, Ingemar, Perez, Aguirre L., Merino, A. et al. (1990), *Cultura, ética y religión frente al desafío ecológico*, Montevideo: CIPFE.

Kerber, Guillermo (2006), *O ecológico e a teologia latinoamericana*, Porto Alegre: Sulina.

Kerber, Guillermo, Peixoto, J., Dussel, E. et al. (1991), *Crisis, ecología y justicia social*, Montevideo: CIPFE.

May, Roy H. (1990), *Tierra: Herencia o mercancia? Justicia, paz e integridad de la creación*, San José (Costa Rica): DEI.

Revista Electrónica Latinoamericana de Teología, <www.servicioskoinonia.org/relat/>, retrieved 31 August 2011.

Susin, Luiz-Carlos (ed.) (1999), *Mysterium creationis: Um olhar interdisciplinar sobre o Universo*, Sao Paulo: Paulinas

Vigil, José Maria (2006), *Teologia do pluralismo religioso*, Sao Paulo: Paulus. *World Forum on Theology and Liberation*, <www.wftl.org/>, retrieved 31 August 2011.

Guillermo Kerber

11. African Theological Perspectives

Edited by Ben-Willie Kwaku Golo

Introduction

It is widely acknowledged that there has been a shift in the centre of Christianity towards Africa in the 20th century. This is characterised by a growth of diverse expressions of African Christianity and innovative theological reflection. While the African theological landscape was dominated by an incessant engagement with theologies of indigenisation and inculturation in the 1970s, there is now a diversity of constructive theological approaches. These include evangelical, inculturation, liberation, reconstruction, feminist and Pentecostal theologies. This chapter provides a survey of such approaches in terms of the following questions: Do these strands of African theology configure the God of salvation as the God who is continually involved in and sustaining the creation? Is our communion with this God of both creation and salvation, by extension, our communion with God's creation?

African Christian theology is dominated by engagements with the person of Christ. John Pobee observes that Christology is at the heart of the encounter between Christianity and culture in Africa.[1] This engagement with Jesus Christ seems to suggest a certain priority attached to the message of salvation among African theologians. The central Christian conviction, namely that "God has decisively wrought salvation for all in and through Jesus Christ",[2] correlates with the aspirations of African Christians. However, this message of salvation has also been radicalised in African theologies in the light of contextual challenges in Africa.

In African theologies salvation not only entails spiritual redemption from the "forces of darkness" (which is crucial in the African context because of the belief in pervasive evil forces and spirits), the experience of forgiveness of sins, and a new relationship with God for the "saved" in Christ. African theologies also presuppose a notion of salvation that encompasses redemption from physical powers and social structures that induce an identity crisis, poverty and mediocrity among Africans and the oppression of women, children and other vulnerable groups – all of which tend to render the experience of "being saved" meaningless and doubtful. Each of the strands of African theology may therefore be understood as a quest for a contextualised African brand of the Christian faith and as an elucidation of the message of salvation in the African context. This typically leads to a radicalisation of the received message of salvation by African theologians, for example in terms of cultural wholeness, liberation, healing, reconstruction or exorcism.

Therefore, for African Christians salvation through Jesus Christ means freedom not only from spiritual oppression and bondage, but also from the unfettered shackles of an identity crisis, economic deprivation and political bondage. Such experiences of salvation are spontaneously expressed by ordinary Christians and are not always ver-

---

1 Pobee (1979). See also Stinton; Nyamiti; Mugambi and Magesa.

2 Bosch, 393.

balised and documented in the form of academic reflection. These shackles are constituted by the legacy of Christian mission in association with sustained forms of imperialism, on the one hand, and by oppressive social and cultural (mostly, patriarchal and class-defined) norms and traditions that are portrayed as natural, on the other. In academic theological reflections, such notions of salvation are expressed in different ways in the theologies of inculturation, liberation, feminism, reconstruction, and the emerging prosperity theologies that have dotted the landscape of African theology. In African ecotheology such a notion of salvation is extended to also address the environmental problems ravaging Africa today.

In African theology before the turn of the century, with a few exceptions,[3] there has been a lack of theological reflections on the complex but crucial connection between creation and salvation. It has seldom been recognised that the fallen state of the entire creation, including the rebellious and prodigal state of humankind, serves as the context for understanding God's salvific grace. However, salvation "can only take place within the realm of creation".[4] In his survey of an emerging environmental awareness in African theologies, Mante observes that "there has been a negligible or almost non-existent theological response to this severe crisis in African Christianity"[5] even though "African theologians reveal that when they are engaged in formulating traditional thought-forms, the nonhuman environment always plays a large role".[6] This correlates with the assertion of Marthinus Daneel that "Black African theologians have done little towards producing a comprehensive Africanised theology of the environment".[7] However, the tide is turning through an increasing number of postgraduate theses, monographs and edited volumes.[8] In a thorough survey of the available literature, Conradie manages to identify four dominant approaches to discourse on Christianity and the environment in (South) Africa, namely in terms of the stewardship of resources (nature conservation), the restoration of ancestral land, sustainable development (seeking a rich blessing) and the quest for environmental justice.[9]

In a nutshell, environmental concerns have not been addressed in African reflections on salvation as adequately as cultural, social or economic concerns. As a result, notions of salvation have tended to remain rather anthropocentric.[10] This has rendered African theologies impoverished at a time when global environmental problems such as climate change have impressed upon the human consciousness the need for an alternative way of looking at experiences of salvation.

In the light of an emerging global environmental awareness, and theological fermentation in the African context, the questions raised by Ogbu are pertinent: "Why is evil waxing strong in the midst of such massive religious ferment? Does the church

---

3 Here one may mention the early contributions by Pobee, Sindima, Asante and Obeng, respectively.

4 Conradie (2005), 19.

5 Mante, 23.

6 Mante, 42.

7 Daneel (2001), 175.

8 See especially Mugambi and Vähäkangas.

9 See Conradie (2007).

10 This is the assessment of Mante.

see? Does it hear the cry or possess the power to unmask the predatory powers?"[11] It is rather perplexing that African theologians can ignore creation in their reflections on the message of salvation in the African context.

The essays in this chapter depart from the premise that the vibrancy that has characterised African Christianity may provide fertile ground for understanding the relationship between creation and salvation and also for safeguarding the integrity of creation. The sections included here gather insights from some of the diverse theological strands that are dominant in Africa today:

Robert Agyarko explores the relationship between faith in God as Creator (in continuity with African traditional religion and culture) and God as Saviour (the message about Jesus Christ that came with missionaries) from the perspective of African inculturation theology. Jesse Mugambi addresses the same problem from the perspective of liberation and reconstruction theologies in Africa in order to understand the impact of environmental degradation on the plight of poor, marginalised, oppressed and abused creatures. Fulata Lusungu Moyo explores the link between the violation of women's bodies and ecological destruction from an ecofeminist perspective, retrieving the spirituality of indigenous cults in Malawi that were traditionally led by women. Finally, Ben-Willie Kwaku Golo comments on the vibrancy of neo-Pentecostal notions of salvation, but observes an underlying tension between other-worldly notions of salvation and preaching a gospel of prosperity in neo-Pentecostal churches in Africa. This tension inhibits an earthkeeping ethos and praxis among such churches. Together these essays indicate the vibrancy of contemporary African Christian theologies.

References and Recommended Reading

Asamoah-Gyadu, Kwabena J. (2005), *African Charismatics: Current Developments within Independent Indigenous Pentecostalism in Ghana*, Leiden: Brill.

Asante, Emmanuel (1994), "Ecological Crisis: A Christian Answer", *Trinity Journal of Church and Theology*, Vol. 4, 2, 9-19.

Bosch, David J. (1991), *Transforming Mission: Paradigm Shifts in Theology of Mission*, Maryknoll: Orbis.

Conradie, Ernst M. (2005), *An Ecological Christian Anthropology: At Home on Earth?* Aldershot: Ashgate.

--- (2007), "Christianity and the Environment in (South) Africa: Four Dominant Approaches", in: Len Hansen (ed.), *Christian in Public: Aims, Methodologies and Issues in Public Theology*, Beyers Naudé Centre Series on Public Theology, Stellenbosch: SUN Press.

Daneel, Marthinus L. (2001), *African Earthkeepers: Wholistic Interfaith Mission*, Maryknoll: Orbis.

Mante, J. O. Y. (2004), *Africa: The Theological and Philosophical Roots of Our Ecological Crisis*, Accra: Sonlife.

Mugambi, Jesse N. K. and Magesa, Laurenti (eds.) (1989), *Jesus in African Christianity: Experimentation and Diversity in African Christology*, Nairobi: Initiative.

Mugambi, Jesse N. K. and Vähäkangas, Mika (eds.) (2001), *Christian Theology and Environmental Responsibility*, Nairobi: Acton.

Nyamiti, Charles (1999), "African Christologies Today", in: Jesse N. K. Mugambi and Laurenti Magesa (eds.), *Jesus in African Christianity: Experimentation and Diversity in African Christology*, Nairobi: Initiative, 17-39.

Obeng, Emmanuel A. (1999), "Healing the Groaning Creation of Africa", in: Mary N. Getui and Emmanuel A. Obeng (eds.) (1999), *Theology of Reconstruction: Exploratory Essays*, Nairobi: Acton.

[11] Ogbu, 193.

Ogbu, Kalu O. (2000), *Power, Poverty and Prayer: The Challenges of Poverty and Pluralism in African Christianity, 1960-1996*, Frankfurt am Main: Peter Lang.
Pobee, John (1979), *Towards an African Theology*, Nashville: Abingdon.
--- (1985), "Creation Faith and Responsibility for the World", *Journal of Theology for Southern Africa*, Vol. 50, 16-26.
Sindima, Harvey (1990), "Community of Life: Ecological Theology in African Perspective", in: Charles Birch, William Eakin and Jay B. McDaniel (eds.), *Liberating Life: Contemporary Approaches in Ecological Theology*, New York: Orbis, 137-148.
Stinton, Diane (2004), *Jesus of Africa: Voices of Contemporary African Christology*, Maryknoll: Orbis.

Ben-Willie Kwaku Golo

Inculturation Theologies – Is the God Who Saved Us the Same As the One Who Created Us?

Introduction

One may identify especially three main types of African Christian theology, namely liberation theology, inculturation theology and African women's theology, often included under the rubric of liberation theology. African liberation theology, as seen in the writings of Jean-Marc Ela, Engelbert Mveng, Laurenti Magesa and others, approach African economic and political struggles from a theological perspective. The inculturation approach takes Africa's pre-Christian and pre-Muslim religious experience seriously. It seeks to integrate the Christian faith with African cultural life and thought forms, as shown in the works of John Mbiti, Harry Sawyerr, Bolaji Idowu, Edward Fashole-Luke, Kwesi Dickson, Kwame Bediako and others.

How is the relationship between creation and salvation – with special reference to the redemption of nature, understood in African inculturation theologies? Mercy Amba Oduyoye's question "Is the God of our redemption the same God of our creation?"[12] encapsulates and raises the need to relate the themes of creation and salvation in African theology. As Conradie rightly notes:

> This question is born from the African quest for identity. What is the continuity between a pre-Christian African notion of the Creator God (the "Supreme Being") and the Christian message of redemption that took root in Africa following the work of Western missionaries? Because the earliest Bible translators have used the same word and name for the God of our ancestors and for the God of Christian proclamation, there appears to be some continuity, but given the legacy of colonialism the deep tensions are all too obvious.[13]

The God of Creation and Redemption in African Christian Theology

Looking at African theological discourses, one may conclude that the concept of God as Creator and Sustainer of the universe is encountered all over Africa and that there is no debate anymore with regard to the originality of the concept. More importantly, it is

[12] Oduyoye, 75.
[13] Conradie (2011), 13.

also clear that African theologians see the Supreme Being in Africa as none other than the God proclaimed by Christianity. However, this equation raises further questions on the relationship between the "God of creation" in the African context and the "God of redemption", namely the triune God, in a Christian context. This issue becomes crucial in the context of the relationship between God and lesser divinities (as well as the ancestors) in African belief, on the one hand, and the relationship between God and lesser divinities (as well as the ancestors) in Christianity, on the other.

Is the Christian God of salvation the same as the African God of creation? The answer to this question is knotty; it is affirmed amidst tensions. Bolaji Idowu contends that the Creator God of the African tradition is not intrinsically different from the God of creation and salvation proclaimed and experienced by Christians.[14] He rejects any such distinction, affirming that Africans, especially African Christians, recognise only one God, the Supreme Universal God, One and the same God, the Creator of all the ends of the earth. For Idowu, "God" means *Olodumare*, God known and experienced in the Yoruba pre-Christian religious tradition. He argues that of the three religions in Nigeria – Traditional Religion, Islam and Christianity – there is not one which has the right to speak as if there are many creator gods from which each religion or nation may select one option. Idowu also contends that the basic theology of traditional religion (as of Islam and Christianity) in each locality has always insisted on one God, one universe. Idowu follows the argument that because the Creator God is one, the traditional religious worshippers in Africa serve the same God worshipped by Christians and Muslims, but with different approaches. Idowu further affirms that the Yoruba people do not only know God; they even worshipped him before the advent of the missionaries. He admits that there is some abuse of such forms of worship but maintains that that happens only when a person makes the image an end in itself. He laments that by a miscarriage of purpose, the church has succeeded in preaching to, and in teaching Africans about, a strange God whom they have nevertheless come to identify as the God of their forefathers.

John Mbiti contends that the Creator God did not only reveal himself to Abraham and other Old Testament fathers but also to our African forefathers.[15] Kwesi Dickson, Kwesi Sarpong and Kwame Bediako also affirm this view. By contrast and from an African evangelical perspective, Byang Kato admits that African traditional worshippers have an awareness of the Supreme Being who is none other than God, the Father of our Lord Jesus.[16] However, he holds that the knowledge that Africans had of God was only enough to convict them of their sin, and that God was not known enough to be worshipped in Africa.[17]

The above theologians represent the broad spectrum of African Christian theologies. Thus for many, if not most, African theologians, the Creator God in African culture is the same as the Creator God proclaimed in Christianity. However, this equation raises further theological questions on the relationship between God and the lesser divinities (as well as the ancestors) in African belief systems and in Christianity.

---

[14] Idowu, 147.

[15] Mbiti (1969), 29-30.

[16] Kato, 113.

[17] Kato, 29.

The "God of our Ancestors" and the God Proclaimed by Missionaries

In Christianity, God tends to be isolated from the ancestors and the lesser divinities who Africans (traditionally) have believed to be closely related to the Supreme Being. Meanwhile, many African societies have identified their traditional concept of the Supreme Being with the Christian God. This is clear from Bible translation, as the various African names for the Supreme Being is used for the Christian God. Nonetheless, this is done in the midst of theological confusion. For instance, Onyame (the Akan name for the Supreme Being) is not only completely cut-off from the ancestors and the *abosom* (the lesser divinities), but is also considered as a competitive enemy. The Christian Akan concept of Onyame the Saviour clearly cannot be the traditional Akan concept of Onyame the Creator who regularly dines with the lesser divinities and the ancestors (in libation rituals). In other words, if Onyame is not only seen by the Akan as closely related to the ancestors (as well as the lesser divinities), but if the latter also serve as intermediaries between Onyame and human beings, then such a concept of the Supreme Being definitely cannot be regarded as the same as the Christian God by Christians. There are three main ways that African theologians approach this problem.

Firstly, there is a contention that the lesser divinities were not only closer to the Supreme Being, but that they also served as intermediaries between him and human beings.[18] However, in Christianity, Jesus has replaced the intermediary role of the ancestors and the lesser divinities.[19] This, however, raises a question: What is the current position of the ancestors and lesser divinities in relation to God, and how should Christians relate to these intermediaries?

Secondly, there is a denial of any cordial relationship between the Supreme Being and the ancestors (as well as the lesser divinities), so that the latter do not serve as intermediaries between the Supreme Being and human beings in African traditional belief.[20] This approach also betrays the common understanding of the cordial relationship between the Supreme Being and ancestors (as well as lesser divinities) in African traditional belief. However, with regard to the question whether or not the lesser divinities serve as intermediaries, it has to be noted that this is not clear in African traditional belief.

Thirdly, there is a widespread contention that the lesser divinities do still have a place in Christianity. One may, for example, on theological grounds identify their role as similar to that of the angels as portrayed in biblical literature.[21]

Looking at the first two approaches, we are still left with the unanswered question of why the ancestors and *abosom*, who enjoyed a cordial relationship with Onyame, have turned to become Onyame's enemies. Such an unanswered question genuinely raises problems with regard to the identification of Onyame the God of our ancestors with the Christian God of redemption. From the analysis of the above approaches, it is evident that the first approach is not consistent. In asserting that the lesser divinities

---

[18] Theologians who hold this view include Idowu, Mbiti, Nyamiti, Sarpong and Bediako.

[19] This view is represented especially by Kwame Bediako.

[20] This is a popular view held by many members of missionary churches in West Africa.

[21] This view is represented especially by S. N. Ezeanya and Kwesi Sarpong.

serve as the intermediaries between God and human beings in African belief, there is the need to determine when their services were terminated; otherwise, there may be two Onyame (Supreme Beings), the one who hates the lesser divinities and the other who works with them. The third approach makes an attempt to maintain theological consistency by adopting and adapting into Christianity the Supreme Being who is known to people traditionally. This is done by identifying the ancestors with Christian saints and the lesser divinities with the biblical angels. Nevertheless, whether or not there are adequate theological grounds to justify these identifications is an issue that requires further reflection, especially since the ancestors and the lesser divinities were demonised by the missionaries – a judgement still largely accepted among African Christian leaders.

In a nutshell, African theologians by and large identify the African God of creation with the Christian God of redemption despite the tensions that remain. Another important issue that needs to be explored in connection with these debates may be posed as follows: how does the relationship between the "God of our ancestors" and the God proclaimed by missionaries affect the non-human environment?

God's Redemption of Creation in African Christian Theology[22]

The significance of the non-human environment is widely recognised by scholars of African traditions. More interestingly, such recognition is also emerging in African Christian theology. Nyamiti says that "all creatures are meant to work and co-operate together to reach this final goal".[23] While the eschatological perspective is distinctively Christian, it is important to recognise that the sense of human responsibility for the natural environment can be identified in the African cultural context. The concept of co-creativity may be applied to the participation of all created things in the fulfilment of God's purpose.[24] Dickson contends that all things in the natural world are regarded as being interconnected, and this includes humans as well as animals, plants and inanimate objects. In this respect, Dickson is able to speak of a "kinship with nature", a theme which captures Akan ecotheology.[25] Nyamiti and Dickson make a distinction between human and non-human, and uphold the human to be superior to non-human animals. For Nyamiti, human dignity consists in its nearness to God and sharing in God's life and power. The human is the soul of the universe.[26]

Pobee also argues that if creation is by the decisive will of God, as affirmed in both African tradition and Christian faith, then human beings must seriously consider the intention and will of God in creating the world in their interaction with non-human creation. Pobee therefore says, "The careless and irresponsible use of creation can only be regarded as assault on God".[27] Bujo states in a similar vein: "We cannot claim to be

---

[22] Peter Fulljames offers an excellent discussion in this regard.

[23] Nyamiti, 65

[24] Nyamiti, 65.

[25] Dickson, 49.

[26] Such a distinction is necessary for the development of an African ecotheology. It will help to set a buffer against an over-reaction to "correct" the wrong attitude towards non-human creation.

[27] Pobee, 19.

Christians if we engage in destruction of God's creation like deforestation".[28] Pobee and Bujo have therefore widened sin to include actions that are harmful to other created things.

Despite this recognition of the significance of the non-human environment, African theologians are yet to take up ecology as a vital theological issue to be addressed. In particular, the question how creation is to be redeemed requires further reflection. What is clearly and largely seen in African theological discourses is human responsibility towards non-human creation. This is captured by Dickson with the notion of "kinship with nature". That is, both human and other creatures were created by God, so that such other creatures have their distinct purpose. From this follows the contention that a careless and irresponsible use of resources can only be regarded as sin against God. This is championed by many African theologians including Pobee and Bujo.

Of course, African theologians argue that a biblical understanding of salvation can only make sense if it embraces their total world, both physical and spiritual. Mbiti comes closer in relating "our ancestors' God of creation" to the "Christian God of redemption" by asserting that God is ultimately the Saviour of people and of all things, since God is their Creator.[29] Interestingly, he also notes that in traditional Akamba culture there is a belief of "rising from the dead" which involves not only human beings but animals as well.[30] On may expect Mbiti to relate creation to salvation by developing this insight, but he has not yet done so. Thus, on the whole, the views of soteriology among African Christian theologians have little place for non-human creatures; humans may be saved without reference to their ecosystems. Human beings are stewards of non-human creation but eschatological salvation is limited to humans.

Conclusion

African culture assumes a holistic worldview, integrating the world within an ordered cosmos. Human society is part of nature and humankind works and communicates with nature. Nature does not belong to humankind, but humankind to nature. With such a background, one may expect that ecotheology should not be difficult to develop further in the African context. However, the deep-seated dualism which underpinned Western theology still influences African Christian theology. It undermines any efforts to think about humans in, with, and as part of nature. Dualism also frustrates any effort to think of God as radically other and outside of this world. As a result, Western theological discourses have tended to keep the doctrine of creation and salvation apart from each other. While new perspectives have been added to what constitutes salvation (liberation, reconstruction, overcoming evil), attempts to bring the two together are not fully developed in African Christian theologies. If African theology develops following a Western pattern, one would expect nothing radically different from such a Western approach. This is still evident from the African theologians whose works have been surveyed above. They still operate from an anthropocentric perspective without stressing ontological relations between humans and their environment; they fail to take

[28] Bujo (1998).

[29] Mbiti (1997), 167.

[30] Mbiti (1971),157-158.

advantage of the ecological redemptive ideas in African traditional religion. The task that now remains for African theologians is to articulate what kind of doctrinal / ethical lenses might emerge from a (re-)reading of biblical texts and from the African cultural context in order to develop an indigenous African ecological theology.

References and Recommended Reading

Bujo, Bénézet (1998), *The Ethical Dimension of Community, the African Model and Dialogue between North and South*, Nairobi: Paulines.
Conradie, Ernst M. (2011), *Creation and Salvation, Volume 1: A Mosaic of Selected Classic Christian Theologians*, Berlin: LIT.
Dickson, Kwesi (1984), *Theology in Africa*, London: Darton, Longman and Todd.
Fulljames, Peter (1993), *God and Creation in Intercultural Perspective: Dialogue between the Theologies of Barth, Dickson, Pobee, Nyamiti and Pannenberg*, Frankfurt am Main: Peter Lang.
Idowu, Bolaji E. (1965), *Toward an Indigenous Church*, London: Oxford University Press.
--- (1973), *African Traditional Religion: A Definition*, London: SCM.
Kato, Byang H. (1975), *Theological Pitfalls in Africa*, Kisumu: Evangelical Publishing House.
Mbiti, John (1969), *African Religions and Philosophy*, New York: Heinemann.
--- (1971), *New Testament Eschatology in an African Background*, Oxford: Oxford University Press.
--- (1997), "God, Sin, and Salvation in African Religion", in: William R. Barr (ed.), *Constructive Christian Theology in the Worldwide Church*, Grand Rapids: Eerdmans, 162-167.
Nyamiti, Charles (1976), *African Tradition and Christian God*, Eldoret: Gaba.
Oduyoye, Amba (2000), *Hearing and Knowing: Theological Reflections on Christianity in Africa*, Maryknoll: Orbis.
Pobee, John (1985), "Creation Faith and Responsibility for the World", *Journal of Theology for Southern Africa*, Vol. 50, 16-26.

Robert Owusu Agyarko

Theologies of Liberation and Reconstruction

Introduction

The theologies of liberation and reconstruction are historical initiatives. Events of human history occur between the parentheses of divine creation and salvation. As human initiatives liberation and reconstruction are conditioned by the divine initiatives of creation and salvation. God creates and God saves. Humans propose, but God disposes (Prov. 16:19, 19:21; Jer. 10:23).[31] In time sequence, creation precedes history, while salvation succeeds history. Thus the two notions of creation and salvation are not historical facts, nor are they scientific hypotheses. These two notions are outside the scope of history, presented and inculcated as religious doctrines central to the three "Abrahamic" religions (Judaism, Christianity and Islam), providing some answers to the three intractable ontological questions about ultimate origin, ultimate purpose and ultimate destiny.

The temptations of Jesus at the beginning of his public ministry (Matt. 4:1-11) provide insights into the relationship between creation and salvation, on the one hand, and

[31] See Thomas à Kempis, *Of the Imitation of Christ:* "For the resolutions of the just depend rather on the grace of God than on their own wisdom; and in Him they always put their trust, whatever they take in hand. For man proposes, but God disposes; neither is the way of man in his own hands" (Book 1, chapter 19).

liberation and reconstruction, on the other. Likewise, the opening verses of John's Gospel offer a concise presentation of God as Creator, Author of Life and Master of History. The first miracle in the narratives of John's Gospel is turning fresh water into seasoned wine during a wedding feast at Cana in Galilee. This first miracle is instructive of John's perception of the relationship between creation and salvation. The divine Creator's authority (Logos) permeates the whole of creation (turning fresh water into seasoned wine) and the whole of human history (history as the appreciation of human joys and sorrows, hopes and fears, achievements and failures). Humankind is a product and beneficiary of divine benefaction. Thus liberation and reconstruction are impossible without divine oversight – without creation and salvation.

This insight is discernible in Paul's epistle to the Romans (Rom. 8:18-25). Paul's articulation of the doctrines of creation and salvation is punctuated with his exhortations for the apostles and all Christians to take responsibility in building the new Christian community transcending ethnicity (neither Jew nor Gentile), status (neither slave nor free), and gender (neither male nor female). This message is especially lucid in the Epistle to the Galatians (Gal. 3:28), which echoes the consensus reached during the Council of Jerusalem (Acts 15). Paul's exhortations are pointers to reconstructive theology. In Romans 12:2 he urges: "Do not be conformed to this world, but be transformed by the renewing of your minds, so that you may discern what is the will of God – what is good and acceptable and perfect."

For Christians, Jesus is the unique manifestation of divine authority within history – through his entire public ministry of healing, teaching, miracles, presence and relationships. In John's Gospel Jesus is presented as "the bread of life" (John 6:35, 48); "the way, the truth and the life" (John 14:6), "the true vine" (John 15:1). John's Gospel is the most articulate in illustrating the links between the theologies of liberation and reconstruction; between the doctrines of creation and salvation; between birth through water and birth through the Spirit (John 3:5). In John's Gospel water is turned into wine (John 2:1-11), the impotent are restored to wholeness (John 5:1-9), the blind see (John 9:1-7), the deaf hear; the dead are raised to life (John 11:38-44). Through symbolism the author of John's Gospel illustrates the link (and the contrasts) between history and eternity; between creation and its Creator; between God and humankind.

The Doctrines of Creation and Salvation as Ontological Themes

The doctrine of creation attributes the ultimate origin of everything to the divine Creator, who brings "everything" into being "out of nothing" through divine authority. The divine Creator is self-accountable – which does not apply to creatures; their well-being can be attributed the divine Creator. The narratives in the Pentateuch are artistic attempts to express this doctrine from various perspectives. In the Eden narrative (Gen. 1-3), the divine Creator is portrayed as the ultimate originator of all things. Humans are expected to respect and appreciate this divine authority. Humility on the part of humans is prescribed in the "Abrahamic" doctrine of creation as the ideal relationship between humans and their Creator, between humans and the rest of creation, and also among the humans themselves. Humans, though intelligent and crafty, cannot supersede their Creator. The greatest human offence against the divine Creator is that of pride (blasphemy), which estranges the creature from its Creator. Human creativity is subject to divine originality. Thus the capacity of humans for creativity, innovation and invention is derived from the power emanating from the divine Creator. The doctrine of creation contrasts human finitude with divine infinitude. The divine Creator is the Nameless One, from whom all names are derived. The Psalmist attests to this sense of awe, in which the human individual is overwhelmed by the magnificence and beneficence of the Creator.

The doctrine of salvation affirms that human history is neither the beginning nor the end of life – that human life precedes birth and continues after death. Thus the doctrine of resurrection qualifies the doctrine of salvation, emphasising that physical death is the beginning of a new mode of existence, disembodied and freed from the confines of matter, duration and space. The ultimate purpose of humans within history is to live in harmony with the rest of creation (with other humans, other species and future generations) so that the divinely created order is sustained. Human disruption of the divinely created order implies human disobedience against the divine Creator. The consequence of that disobedience is experienced both within and beyond history. The Book of Revelation contains graphic visions of scenarios beyond the present age (aeon). These visions are more symbolic than actual, since the visionary has not physically experienced them. Religious notions are expressed mostly in idiom, symbol and ritual. The apocalyptic visions in the Book of Revelation are much more than the narratives of a dreamer. More contextually, they are critiques of the present order, contrasting it with the anticipated new order free from the agonies experienced by the present generation. Apocalyptic visions are visions of hope, comparable to the utopias of the dreamers of the European Renaissance.[32] Revelation 21:1-8 articulates such a positive vision of the future within the context of an apparently hopeless present as a vision for a new heaven and a new earth.

Ultimate Origin and Ultimate Destiny as Affirmations of Faith

The answer to the puzzling question of ultimate destiny can only be anticipated as a matter of faith. It cannot be confirmed empirically in advance. Historical notions are expressed mostly in actions, reflections, documents, movements, monuments and institutions. Thus the theologies of liberation and reconstruction, as historical movements, respond to social and ecological challenges variously, depending on the variable factors in specific circumstances and contexts. Movements focused on the struggles for liberation tend to be ecologically destructive, because the political interests of activists often override the necessity to preserve and protect ecology. For this reason, struggles for liberation must of necessity be followed up with reconstructive initiatives, restoring the ravages of conflict. The ecological crisis in this millennium is the culmination of centuries of human destruction of creation by successive civilisations. Ecological balance and harmony is the key to sustainable livelihoods. Mahatma Gandhi famously cautioned that in creation there will be more than enough for the need of all humans, but not enough for even one person's greed. Likewise, Jesus advises that sustainable livelihood is possible for all humans, provided that basic needs take precedence over luxurious wants (Matt. 6:25-33). The theologies of reconstruc-

[32] The European Renaissance inspired many authors to write and publish alternative visions of the future. These include Thomas More's *Utopia*, Erasmus's *In Praise of Folly* and Thomas Hobbes's *Leviathan*.

tion focus on reconstructive hermeneutics with regard to both economy and ecology.

African Ontology and the Trinitarian Doctrinal Formula

Hebrew ontology resonates with African ontology. Both are neither otherworldly nor futuristic.[33] The strong influence of neo-Platonism in early Christian thought eventually yielded the trinitarian doctrinal formulations which do not correspond with African notions of past, present and future. John Mbiti in his book *New Testament Eschatology in an African Background* (1971) suggested that the fascination, excitement and preoccupation of many African Christians with futuristic and otherworldly concerns may be attributed to the novelty of neo-Platonic notions encrypted in the Nicene and Chalcedonian formulations of Christian doctrine. From the perspective of ontology, African Christianity seems to fit within at least three broad categories of doctrinal interpretation: (a) mainstream denominations implanted from Europe and North America via the modern missionary enterprise; (b) African Instituted Churches which arose as reactions against missionary tutelage and (c) Pentecostal and Charismatic movements which emphasise otherworldly and futuristic rewards (or punishments) for past and present conduct. These three broad categories are not mutually exclusive. There are African expressions of Christianity striding across the categories. Generally, however, it is interesting to observe the almost total absence of neo-Platonic doctrinal formulations in the creeds of African Instituted Churches.[34] This echoes the doctrinal conflicts during the early church, which led to the marginalisation of African churches by the imperial church centred in Rome.

African ontology is neither trinitarian nor salvationist.[35] It is communally pragmatic and existentialist. The African worldview is presupposed with varying degrees of emphasis in all three the categories of African Christianity listed above. Although African Christianity is overtly excited about the message of salvation, this excitement is neither transcendentalist nor futuristic. African Christians are excited about "salvation" because they see in Jesus of Nazareth the possibility of overcoming the constraints and limitations imposed by imperial and local politics, economics, ethics, aesthetics, kinship and religion.[36] The apocalyptic and messianic tendencies in some strands of African Christianity camouflage the existentialist urgency with which African Christians associate with the gospel. African Christianity includes the whole demographic spectrum – old and young Africans, men and women, schooled and unschooled, high and low, poor and rich, rural and urban, professional and lay, powerful and powerless. The dynamism of African Christianity is rooted in the "instant appeal" of the gospel, depending on the mode of presentation and the social disposition of both the pastors and their congregations. To African Christians the brief Gospel of Mark is the most appealing narrative of the impact of Jesus in their lives. African Christians find it easy to identify themselves with Jesus, the rural rabbi from Nazareth, whose teaching resonates with their worldview. African Christianity can echo the songs of praise in many of the psalms.

[33] See Kibicho.

[34] See, for example, Anderson.

[35] See Magesa.

[36] See Stinton.

Creation and Salvation in Theologies of Reconstruction

In African languages, as in Hebrew, there is no semantic differentiation between liberation from "political and economic" bondage, on the one hand, and deliverance from "religious and inner" bondage, on the other. In the Old Testament the notions of "deliverance" and "liberation" include freedom from all limitation and restriction – both external and internal; both individual and communal; both religious and politic. In my book *African Christian Theology: An Introduction* (1989), I have written:

> In the African context and in the Bible salvation as a theological concept cannot be complete without liberation as a socio-political concept. Thus Jesus, proclaiming his mission, quoted from the book of Isaiah [Isa. 61: 1-2] to indicate the concreteness and relevance of his concern ... That the fundamental concern of African Christian Theology has been liberation-salvation has been manifested in the activities of many African Christians and in the growth of [tens of thousands] of 'independent churches in the continent of Africa. Most African Christians have not felt it necessary to theorize about Christian theology, because to them religious faith is practical living expressed most effectively through experience, not through words. The time has come when it is necessary to analyze the premises of African Christian experience and study it in relation to that of peoples in other parts of the world. This systematic analysis and study, however, will be realistic and relevant as African Christian Theology if Africans themselves will be the analysts and students of their own experience. Liberation, of course, has many aspects and in the various countries and sub-regions of Africa it has different historical manifestations ... What is important to point out in this context is that while liberation both as concept and as a historical struggle in Africa today takes on different emphasis in different parts of Africa, it must be the over-arching goal—the historical project—out of which and for which an African Christian Theology must emerge.[37]

Numerically, Christianity is expanding in tropical Africa in inverse proportion to the rate at which it is shrinking in Europe and North America. This situation is not new. Saul of Tarsus (St Paul) already observed it at Corinth – a city in the 1st century which would compare favourably with any cosmopolitan town in the 21st century.

The canonical texts comprising the sacred scriptures of Judaism, Christianity and Islam affirm the doctrinal paradox that powerful and wealthy regimes eventually crumble under the persistent struggles of the poor and weak whose ultimate strength comes from the divine Creator and Author of history. The challenge is always that when the struggle for liberation has been won, the victors become conformed to the norms entrenched by their former oppressors, and the resulting regimes often become more oppressive than the former ones. Such is the tragedy of leadership depicted in the canonical sacred texts of the "Abrahamic" religions. In my book *From Liberation to Reconstruction* (1995), I proposed that the theology of liberation ought to be succeeded by a theology of reconstruction in conceptual, logical and programmatic sequence:

> New language will be needed for the "New World Order". With the end of the Second World, it no longer makes sense to talk of the "Third World". After all, God created one world, which we have tended to truncate for our own convenience – or

[37] Mugambi (1989), 12-13.

> inconvenience. The 'New World Order" will require a new understanding of the Church and a new corresponding theology. This theology should be reconstructive rather than destructive; complementary rather than competitive; integrative rather than disintegrative; programme-driven rather than project-driven; people-centred rather than institution-centred; deed-oriented rather than word-oriented; participatory rather than autocratic; regenerative rather than degenerative; future-sensitive rather than past-sensitive; co-operative rather than confrontational; consultative rather than impositional. The end of the old order is the beginning of the New Order, in which all the peoples of the world can participate without being branded with either one ideological label or the other.[38]

The theology of reconstruction will have to take ecological concerns seriously, restoring and rehabilitating the habitats which humankind has destroyed under the pretexts of "civilisation", "progress", "development" and "economic growth".

Conclusion

In my book *Christian Theology and Social Reconstruction* (2003), I emphasise the instructive role of the New Testament in shaping our theological hermeneutics:

> Using the paradigm of Reconstruction, it should be clear that the New Testament is a collection of reconstructive texts, with Jesus as the leader of a movement of social reconstruction. His twelve disciples are invited to form the vanguard of a reconstructive movement. They are so successful that within a short time they distinguish themselves as a community whose norms differ from those of the disciples of John and of the Pharisees. The early Church makes a similar impact in Graeco-Roman cities, to the extent that it supplants the Roman Empire. Starting as a tiny and persecuted minority, the early Church emerges from the ruins of Roman Empire as the heir to the Roman throne. Unfortunately, it falls into the temptations of temporal power, and becomes both intolerant and oppressive. The paradigm of Reconstruction helps to provide a critique on Euro-American church history, both within the North Atlantic region and in the areas where the modern missionary enterprise has been operative.[39]

The Nicene Creed affirms God as creator and the risen Christ as judge. After Chalcedon, however, the doctrine of creation fades from the centre to the periphery of ecclesial thought, while the promise of salvation becomes restricted to the confines of the church: outside the church no salvation! The destructive crusades were conducted in the name and blessing of Christianity. So was the dehumanising and depopulating trade in African slaves, the imperial expansion and colonial settlement in Africa and the Americas. The Christian missionary enterprise was premised upon spreading the message of "salvation" to the "heathens" and "pagans". But "salvation" in the missionary teachings meant indoctrination and induction of the converts into the denominations implanted in the imperial colonies, all in the service of Empire.

From the European Renaissance onwards, the ideals of modernity and progress have been portrayed as the sacrificing of culture and nature at the altars of technology and

---

[38] Mugambi (1995), xv.

[39] Mugambi (2003), 129.

imperial power. The demographic shift of Christianity from the North Atlantic to Africa, South America and Asia is inevitably contributing new hermeneutical insights about creation and salvation, derived from non-European cultural and religious traditions which take for granted the unbroken cord between nature and culture, liberation and reconstruction. It is paradoxical that at the beginning of the third millennium imperial, technological and economic power is concentrated in nations where active adherents to Christianity are a minority.

This paradox is instructive. Jesus of Nazareth, within the prophetic tradition, teaches us that God as author of creation and salvation cannot be domesticated into any religion, denomination, sect or cult. Humans, as God's creatures, must discern divine guidance in creation, ensuring that culture resonates with nature. Failure to abide by this principle will lead to more alienation between nations, peoples, cultures and religions. The current ecological crisis is a consequence of profligate exploitation of nature for short-term gain. Restoration of ecological balance will be costly and long. The principles of precaution, mitigation and adaptation are enshrined in the Earth Charter.[40] These principles resonate with the prophetic exhortation on humans to care for creation rather than to plunder it. Here is the preamble to the Earth Charter, which is a fitting conclusion to this section:

> We stand at a critical moment in Earth's history, a time when humanity must choose its future. As the world becomes increasingly interdependent and fragile, the future at once holds great peril and great promise. To move forward we must recognize that in the midst of a magnificent diversity of cultures and life forms we are one human family and one Earth community with a common destiny. We must join together to bring forth a sustainable global society founded on respect for nature, universal human rights, economic justice, and a culture of peace. Towards this end, it is imperative that we, the peoples of Earth, declare our responsibility to one another, to the greater community of life, and to future generations.

References and Recommended Reading

Anderson, Alan H. (2001), *African Reformation: African Initiated Christianity in the 20th Century*, Trenton: Africa World.

Kibicho, Samuel G. (2005), *God and Revelation in an African Context*, Nairobi: Acton.

Magesa, Laurenti (1997), *African Religion*, Maryknoll: Orbis.

Mbiti, John (1971), *New Testament Eschatology in an African Background*, Oxford: Clarendon.

Mugambi, Jesse N. K. (1989), African Christian Theology: An Introduction, Nairobi: Heinemann.

--- (1995), *From Liberation to Reconstruction*, Nairobi: East African Educational Publishers.

--- (2003), *Christian Theology and Social Reconstruction*, Nairobi: Acton.

Stinton, Dianne (2004), *Jesus of Africa: Voices of Contemporary African Christology*, Maryknoll: Orbis.

Jesse N. K. Mugambi

[40] See <www.earthcharterinaction.org/content/pages/Read-the-Charter.html>, retrieved 31 August 2011. The Earth Charter is a declaration of fundamental ethical principles for building a just, sustainable and peaceful society in the 21st century, seeking to inspire in all people a new sense of global interdependence and shared responsibility for the well-being of the whole human family, the greater community of life, and future generations. It is a product of a decade-long worldwide, cross-cultural dialogue on common goals and shared values.

Women as Guardians of Mother Earth

The Bodies of African Women and the Body of Mother Earth

Since time immemorial, women have been very closely associated with nature as Mother Earth. In times and within cultures where the attitude toward nature is one of reverence and awe, this association yields benefits for women. However, when the attitude is one of abuse, plunder and rape, as is often the case today, this association translates into the abuse of women. This suggests a shift from a time when women and Mother Earth were respected and God was viewed as immanent, to a time where men seek to control and subdue women and the earth, and God is regarded as transcendent and remote.

There exist widespread perceptions that women may be valued primarily as hospitable, sexually reproductive beings instead of as companions. The same can be said about the valuing of Mother Earth for her mineral resources. These misconceptions add to women's vulnerability as the "subdued" and "controlled" mothers of their communities. For Mother Earth, the endless plunder and exploitation of her body has led to irreversible environmental degradation as well as to endless wars, mainly fuelled by the powerful and greedy with their unquenchable desire to control these resources.

Such perceptions are expressed through a story told in Kenya on the matriarchal powers of Mumbi that were eroded when power hungry men conspired to impregnate her eight formidable daughters in order to overthrow them in their vulnerable state of motherhood.[41] This may serve as a parable for the way in which men have exercised control over the earth and over women, instead of being their companions.

That this has devastating consequences both for environmental degradation and for the plight of women may be briefly illustrated with observations from Malawi. In Malawi, agriculture forms the backbone of the national economy. Approximately 70% of the work on small agricultural holdings is done by women.[42] Yet women in Malawi face a dreadful plight: some 32% of households are headed by women and they represent about 46% of the poor in Malawi. Some women are forced to engage in prostitution as a means of livelihood not only for themselves but also for their dependants. Research carried out on the prevalence of HIV among commercial sex workers in 1997 revealed that in the urban areas of Malawi an estimated 75% of the sex workers were divorced women whose only available commercial commodities were their own bodies. According to a baseline survey carried out by the Evangelical Association of Malawi in Christian households, a high number of women involved in commercial sex work do it for providing basics (like food) to their children..[43]

Likewise, ecological degradation in Malawi is there for everyone to see. In lay person's terms, if ecological degradation continues at current rates, one can predict that in less than fifty years to come, more than half of the lakeshore villages will be flooded by Lake Malawi; Zomba Mountain will be bare of half of its trees and probably most of the slopes heavily eroded; half of Lake Chilwa will turn into a swamp; and women

---

[41] See Kenyatta.

[42] Nkhoma and Kirwan, 13.

[43] Evangelical Association of Malawi.

in the rural villages, without tap water, will have to walk twice the distances they cover now to fetch water for household chores.

How can churches in Malawi respond to such forms of self-destruction? Will they muster the courage to engage prophetically with unjust systems of power (outside and inside the country) that aggravate such degradation?

The problem is that churches have been trapped in the same spirit of control that causes such destruction. They reflect the patriarchal structures that reinforce a spirit of control over nature and women's bodies alike. Moreover, Christian theology seems to be trapped in various forms of dualism that have denigrated the body as sinful or trivial, while uplifting the mind as superior. The connection of the body with women (through motherhood), and of the mind to men, seems to justify a disengagement of the masculine from embodiment and reinforces forms of dualism. Such dualism is also expressed theologically in an understanding of the divine being. Such disembodiment justifies the bias that the divine cannot be feminine nor can the feminine be divine.

In this contribution I will explore the question: what may Christian theology learn from indigenous women's spirituality in such a context? I will first share three case studies of women acting as guardians of Mother Earth. Then I will employ an ecofeminist analysis of the relationships between humanity and the environment, and between creation and Creator, in order to seek relationships characterised by mutual vulnerability rather than domination and control. Finally, I will conclude by drawing lessons from these guardians of Mother Earth for our own ecumenical process of addressing the current ecological and economic injustices.

Instances of Indigenous Women's Spirituality

In most African cultures one finds oral histories and narratives of egalitarian societies where matriarchs were rulers of their communities and co-nurturers together with sacred Earth. Various examples can be cited:

In southern Malawi, the subsistence of the matrilineal Mang'anja (Nyanja / Chewa) and Yao, as agriculturalists, totally depends on the rainy season. As such, their religio-cultural life focuses on ensuring that rains are regular. According to James Amanze, "religious beliefs exercise great power over a people living under an agricultural subsistence economy left to the mercy of ecological forces".[44] The Mang'anja and Yao believe in a Chauta God ("the Big Bow" for "Rainbow"), the Supreme Being conceived as Rain-giver, who is accessible through the ancestral spirits. The Mang'anja were known for their well-organised rain cults from 1400 to 1600. Schoffeleers argues that up to the last century, in the Lower Shire region of southern Malawi[45] "territorial mediumships were almost exclusively female".[46] These women were guardians who protected Mother Earth (the land) as the home that their communities depended on. Their status in society was that of guardians of Mother Earth. They played a significant role in decision making regarding land use and the production of food, and in wealth creation.

---

[44] Amanze, 10.

[45] See Schoffeleers; Schoffeleers and Roscoe.

[46] Phiri, 28.

According to Schoffeleers, the M'bona cult among the Mang'anja centred around a shrine believed to be visited by a spirit of the High God in the form of a great snake.[47] The M'bona cult is associated with the Lundu kings who are said to have built up their own Maravi kingdom alongside that of Kalonga and Undi in the Lower Shire region.[48] At this shrine a human "wife", who was known as M'bona, acted as an intermediary with the High God, prophesying God's commands to the Mang'anja people. The title of M'bona for this spirit "wife" was taken from the Mang'anja (Chewa) word *wona* which means "to see". As such, M'bona was a seer, which refers to her powers as a spirit medium. According to Schoffeleers, she shared these powers with the other spirit "wives" among the Chewa. Amanze explains this in terms of a division of labour among the Mang'anja matriclans: "The Phiri, to whom the traditional chiefs belonged, retained political power and the Banda maintained a close relationship with the land and were credited with the power of making rain."[49]

Another example is found in the case of Makewana among the Chewa in central Malawi. Makewana, as a spiritual wife, was given the title of God (Chisumphi) because she was the High God's representative and when possessed, she spoke in a voice that people recognised as God's.[50] Makewana's divine powers seem to have been eroded by the coming of Christian missionaries with their patriarchal and hierarchical inclinations that seemed to condemn indigenous cultures and religions as pagan.

Within the Chisumphi cult (Chisumphi = God as giver of rain) where Mangadzi or Makewana was the keeper of the rain shrine, the role of the intermediary was also exclusively in the hands of women. According to Isabel Phiri, "... it was believed the (Makewana) controlled the rain. ... [S]he was responsible for ceremonies to bring rain, as well as to utter prophecies and make divination. It is said that Makewana would disappear into the sacred pool of Malawi for three days at a time in order to call down the rain."[51]

In his monograph *African Theology in Images* (2000), Martin Ott offers "an anthropological and theological evaluation and analysis" of the images of inculturation presented at Mua Mission, a Roman Catholic mission centre that houses the KuNgoni Arts Centre. In his analysis, he looks at the image of Makewana, as a high priestess and rainmaker. According to Ott, the image depicts a powerful woman who would measure up to the image of a goddess, "... a woman with long swirling dark hair, a spiral shell suspended around her neck, a calabash of water in one hand, and a long stick in the other", and "rain prophetesses ranked among the most important figures of the Malawian rain cults".[52] Isabel Phiri, acknowledging Makewana's great influence, argues that her connection to the High God might also suggest that the Chewa recognised the feminine nature of God as nurturer. She argues that the term *makewana* (literally, "mother of children") suggests nurturing connotations attached to the concept of God (as Leza). Phiri refers to the work of J. C. Chakanza who states:

---

[47] Schoffeleers, 148.

[48] Schoffelleers, 162.

[49] Amanze, 152.

[50] See Phiri, 31.

[51] Phiri, 30.

[52] Ott, 277.

> Leza, from the verb *kulera* in Chewa and Tonga means one who rules or rears. Leza, then, refers to God as the one who nurtures rears or rules creation. ... Makewana means mother of all children and by implication, mother of all people. A mother has characteristics of nurturing and rearing children.[53]

A further example: While both the M'bona and the Chisumphi cults seem to have receded from the contemporary public religious and cultural life, the Bimbi cult in the Upper Shire has an active rainmaking shrine among the Chewa of the southern region. Just like the M'bona seers, the Bimbi are climatic religious specialists "well versed in rainmaking ceremonies and rituals. They are a remnant of a complex religious system, which in the past constituted the Maravi religion".[54] Since the Bimbi cult's inception around the 1400s, its rituals were mainly intended to ensure at least two important agricultural functions, namely the availability of rain and the enhancement of the fertility of the land.

The name Bimbi is derived from the title given to the cult figure, which is indicative of the function of this personage. Bimbi is a person who, depending on what is required by the ancestral spirits, comes under the inspiration of the spirits of the departed, making her or him talk while in a trance. She or he is a mouthpiece, a prophet, as well as a symbol of fecundity. Her or his primary duty is to bring the oracles of the spirits about rain to the people so that they can respond to them through prayers and avoid or eliminate personal or impersonal spiritual forces, like witchcraft, that could hinder the blessings of rain and land fertility as punishment from angry ancestors.[55]

Interestingly, because of the alternative governing system of this cult, the Bimbi can be either a woman or a man, depending on who the previous person was. If it is a woman, she is given the title of Mtsamila. *Mtsamila* comes from the Mang'anja word *tsamila*, which means "lean upon or against" so as not to fall off. There are at least two explanations of this title. The first conveys a soteriological meaning: one upon whom the whole world leans. The second is related to the first: the one who is in control of rain. She is the one who controls the "bags" of rain, which is given by God through the ancestral spirits. The understanding is that without this female Bimbi's role to gauge what the ancestors are saying, the rains would be uneven and chaotic.[56] This indicates the significance of her rainmaking role as guardian of life. Through her ritual activities, Bimbi saves the land (earth) and the lives of the people by protecting them from dangers such as droughts, famines and witchcraft.[57]

While Amanze claims that the Chewa world is a man's world, Isabel Phiri's analysis suggests that, before the coming of Scottish missionaries, the Chewa world was more of a woman's world. Women had significant influence when it came to decision making in their communities, where progeny was not only traced through the mother; connectedness to Mother Earth was also traced through the mother not the father. That the personage of Bimbi alternates between a man and a woman seems to bring into question Amanze's assumption that the Chewa world is a man's world.

---

53 Chakanza in Phiri, 31.

54 Amanze, 12.

55 Amanze, 16.

56 Amanze, 17.

57 Amanze, 16.

Accordingly, the Malawian concept of God as Leza / Mlezi / Lezi (God the sustainer of humanity and the rest of creation) suggests one who creates and nurtures all creation as her / his own children.[58] Despite the fact that indigenous religions in Malawi seem to present themselves as if they were androgynous, Leza has characteristics of both mother and father. The qualities of creating and nurturing are therefore both included.

Care for Mother Earth: Ecofeminist Perspectives

As an exercise in African women's theology I will now employ an ecofeminist analysis in search for ecological and economic justice (ecojustice) for women and their communities. For ecofeminists the two aspects of the struggle for ecojustice are intrinsically linked. It is a holistic struggle against the web of oppression that systemically destroys the environment (Mother Earth) and discriminates against women, denigrating them to utter poverty and social oppression. How does an ecofeminist perspective enrich women's struggle for ecojustice?

The basis of ecofeminism is the connection between ecojustice and the liberation of women. It entails a call for gender- and ecojustice amidst patriarchal cultural realities. The ecofeminist search for ecojustice challenges the traditional perspective that values women and the environment in terms of their usefulness rather than as having intrinsic worth. The ecofeminist search for ecojustice is therefore a women's struggle for freedom, self-determination and equality, contextually expressed in each culture and all biological systems. This perspective also seeks to transform society from subjugation and exploitation to an environment of justice and care based on the feminist principles of interconnectedness and interdependence.

An ecofeminist perspective assumes that we are interdependent as humans (male and female) and dependent upon Mother Earth. Theologically, this may draw from the creation stories in the first book of the Hebrew Bible suggesting that both male and female were equally created in the image of God: God created human beings in God's own image and created them male and female (Gen. 1:27). Likewise, Genesis 2 affirms God's design of mutuality as the basis for marital relations. On this basis ecofeminism draws from women's struggle for freedom, equality and economic as well as ecological justice. As a form of praxis, it aims at the preservation of life for present and future generations.

Constructively, the role of women who occupy positions of spiritual leadership have been recognised in ecofeminist theologies. However, patriarchal influence has resulted in amnesia about such possibilities. Women, as a result, have lost the power of the erotic, what Audre Lorde would call "women's holistic embodied spirituality and being". According to Lorde, pressured by patriarchal cultural contexts, women have been socialised to suspect, vilify, abuse, distrust and even devalue this power which rises from the non-rational knowledge within them:

> The erotic is a resource within each of us that lies in a deeply female and spiritual plane, firmly rooted in the power of our unexpected or unrecognized feelings … The erotic is a measure between the beginnings of our sense of self and the chaos of

[58] See Van Breugel, 29-30.

> our strongest feelings. It is an internal sense of satisfaction to which, once we have experienced the fullness of this depth of feeling and recognized its power, in honour and self-respect we require no less of ourselves.[59]

In response, ecofeminist theologians seek to reclaim the beauty and glory of the body – especially the bodies of women. For example, in *Sister Outsider* (1994) Audre Lorde explores the power of the erotic which stems from the beauty of the body. Sandra Rushing, acknowledging that spirituality and sexuality are deeply interwoven, argues for a Christian theology that is embodied. Fulata Lusungu Moyo argues for a theological understanding of incarnation as God becoming bodied-self. This implies that "apart from other salvific revelations, [it] would unveil something about God's affirmation of the goodness of the body as well as God's enjoyment of beauty".[60] For ecofeminists, the reclaiming of the goodness of the body refers to both the bodies of humans and of Mother Earth that are so often subjugated and exploited by the greedy and powerful.

Creation and Salvation: The Quest for Ecojustice

In a disembodied hierarchical theology, humanity is given the divine mandate to control and subdue the rest of creation. By contrast an ecofeminist reading of God's good creation is that it is interconnected. The relationship between creation and humanity is therefore not hierarchical, following a logic of control. It is one of interdependence, requiring the human virtues of compassion and respect.

According to Felix Chingota, biblical accounts testify that humanity was made from the same essence as the earth (Gen. 2:4-7, 1 Cor. 15:47), and that, apart from being from the same essence, they depend on each other for life.[61] Because of such a relationship, Chingota suggests the need for the church in Africa to adopt a more holistic theology that challenges human beings to be good stewards of the earth. This could be construed as a call to ecotheology. The call to good stewardship is an improvement over the problematic kingship model based on control. However, it still originates from a dualistic and hierarchical understanding of the relationship between humanity and the environment. As long as this relationship is conceived in terms of dualism and hierarchy, possibilities of further abuse cannot be ruled out, because the call to stewardship is based on the goodwill of the powerful.

The ecological and economic exploitation of Mother Earth and of women is sustained by hierarchical relationships that give the powerful uncontrolled access to exploit the less powerful. Notions of stewardship or care, despite the emphasis on the common good, still leave the onus of such care at the mercy and goodwill of the powerful. By contrast, the interconnectedness, and therefore the interdependence of women and men, of humanity and Mother Earth are stressed in ecofeminist theologies all over the world and also in the African context. Thus the care and respect of one another and of Mother Earth can no longer be seen as an available option of those of goodwill, but a necessary requirement for living together in a just community of women and men within God's own creation.

---

59 Lorde, 53, 54.

60 Moyo (2004a), 74.

61 Chingota, 10.

References and Recommended Reading

Amanze, James (2002), *African Traditional Religion in Malawi: The Case of Bimbi Cult*, Blantyre: Christian Literature Association in Malawi.

Chingota, Felix (2003), "Bible Study Notes on Creation", in: Fulata Lusungu Moyo and Martin Ott (eds.), *Christianity and the Environment*, Blantyre: CLAIM, 10-18.

Evangelical Association of Malawi, Programme on HIV / AIDS (2002), "The Baseline Survey on HIV / AIDS in Malawi", Unpublished report, Lilongwe: EAM.

Kenyatta, Jomo (1938), *Facing Mount Kenya: The Tribal Life of the Gikuyu* (edited by J. Kariuki), Nairobi: Heinemann.

Lorde, Audre (1984), *Sister Outsider: Essays and Speeches*, Trumansburg / New York: The Crossing Press.

Moyo, Fulata L. (2004a), "Religion, Spirituality and Being a Woman in Africa: Gender Construction within the African Religio-Cultural Experiences", *Agenda: Empowering Women for Gender Equity*, Vol. 61, 72-78.

--- (2004b), "Sex, Gender, Power and HIV and AIDS in Malawi: Threats and Challenges to Women Being Church", *Journal for Constructive Theology*, Vol. 10, 1, 85-102.

Nkhoma, Matiya H. and Kirwan, Moira (1997), "Social Change and Widowhood: The Experience of the Tonga People of Northern Malawi", *Religion of Malawi*, Vol. 7, 12-18.

Ott, Martin (2000), *African Theology in Images*, Blantyre: Christian Literature Association in Malawi.

Phiri, Isabel. A. (1997), *Women, Presbyterianism and Patriarchy*, Blantyre: Christian Literature Association in Malawi.

Schoffeleers, J. M. (ed.) (1999), *Guardians of the Land*, Gweru: Mambo.

Schoffeleers, J. M. and Roscoe, A. (1985), *Land of Fire: Oral Literature from Malawi*, Limbe: Dzuka.

Van Breugel, J. W. M. (2001), *Chewa Traditional Religion*, Blantyre: Christian Literature Association in Malawi.

Fulata Lusungu Moyo

Creation and Salvation in African Neo-Pentecostalist Theology

Introduction

Referred to by Asamoah-Gyadu as the "third wave of Pentecostal Christianity"[62] which is currently enjoying massive growth in Africa, and by Kalu as "the third dimension of African response to the gospel, a 'setting to work' of missionary message and a reconstruction of Christian experience in Africa",[63] the label "neo-Pentecostal" is used here as "an umbrella term to encompass Pentecostal renewal phenomena associated with trans-denominational fellowships, prayer groups, ministries and independent churches which came into existence or prominence from about the last three decades".[64]

According to Asamoah-Gyadu, neo-Pentecostals emphasise that "the experience of the Spirit, following conversion, not only empowers the believer to be an effective witness, but also opens the door to the reception of ministry gifts of the Spirit including those of healing, discernment and prophecy".[65] Here neo-Pentecostalism refers to those independent churches or organised groups popularly known as charismatic churches.

---

[62] Asamoah-Gyadu, 26.

[63] Kalu, 86.

[64] Asamoah-Gyadu, 26; see also Mwaura.

[65] Asamoah-Gyadu, 27.

Labelling them as "Independent Neo-Pentecostal Charismatic Churches" or "Charismatic Ministries", Omenyo notes that they have emerged consequential to the evangelical and charismatic renewal of the late 1960s and early 1970s.[66] I have referred to them elsewhere as "neo-evangelicals".[67] Examples of these churches include the International Central Gospel Church (ICGC) and Christian Action Faith Ministries (CAFM) in Ghana; the Living Faith Church (Winners Chapel) and Christ's Embassy in Nigeria; and Jabula New Life Ministries in Zimbabwe.

One striking phenomenon of these neo-Pentecostal churches is their radical (re)definition of the doctrine of "true" salvation, which reflects what Asamoah-Gyadu calls their "key soteriological goals".[68] The urgency with which neo-Pentecostals in Africa explore such a (re)definition and how this correlates with their teachings about creation within the context of climate change and growing environmental destruction will be explored in this section. The sources come mainly from my ongoing research on the perceptions and responses of Ghanaian Christians to global environmental problems gathered through interviews, informal discussions, and observations as an insider. Notwithstanding contextual interpretations and the localisation of practices, the cosmological orientations, beliefs and theologies of neo-Pentecostalists are usually similar in Africa compared to elsewhere in the world. This results from their networking, transnationalism and collaboration,[69] more especially with their American progenitors, as well as from the globality of the phenomenon. However, where necessary, I will offer examples from my own context, namely Ghana.

Creation in African Neo-Pentecostal Theology

The ways in which neo-Pentecostals in Africa (or for that matter elsewhere in the world) approach a theology of creation remains relatively unexplored. However, as with African Christianity in general, African neo-Pentecostals regard creation as the handiwork of God. They acknowledge God as the sole creator of everything on earth, under the earth and in the sky (heavens), including humankind. They affirm, with Christians generally, drawing from biblical evidence in Genesis and the Psalms, that God created the heavens and the earth in the beginning, that God is the absolute originator and owner of creation, and that the creation is good for human habitation and sustenance. Interviews with neo-Pentecostals in Ghana, including church leaders, reflect such a generally accepted Christian notion of creation.

What is more particular to neo-Pentecostal theology is the notion that creation is dominated by evil spirits and archangels and that African societies are saturated with demonic and wicked spirits that are at the root of all misfortunes and failures.[70] As in indigenous African thought, these malevolent spirits are always considered as working against humans and preventing them from enjoying an abundant life and prosperity and fulfilling their God-given destinies.[71]

---

[66] Omenyo.
[67] Golo.
[68] Asamoah-Gyadu, 133.
[69] See Ojo.
[70] See Ayegboyin.
[71] See Larbi; Asamoah-Gyadu.

However, in neo-Pentecostal theology, the cosmos is not only infused with evil and wicked powers and spirits but is equally infused with benevolent and good spirits, especially the Spirit of God. The conception is that God is involved in the daily activities of the righteous and that the Spirit and presence of God is encountered within creation, protecting and empowering the righteous against wicked spirits. It is in creation that the Christian encounters and interacts with God's presence and power. It is the place where the divine drama takes place. Indeed, there is a panentheist conception of creation among neo-Pentecostals who believe that they are able to encounter the presence of God in the natural environment. This belief is expressed in forest prayer movements, and the purchase of mountains and sublime and remote places far outside urban areas in order to have spiritual encounters. However, it is important to note that, in neo-Pentecostal theology, this does not imply that creation is equated with God. Creation is not to be worshipped.

African Neo-Pentecostals and Salvation

The notion of the triumph of creation and order over chaos, understood as interventionist acts of God, if not as a cosmic war between God and the forces of evil, seems to underpin the concept of salvation among neo-Pentecostals in Africa. I suggest that their concept of salvation is twofold: (a) salvation as deliverance of the human soul and (b) salvation as prosperity and wealth (including health and fertility). Larbi describes these dimensions in terms of "otherworldliness" and "this-worldliness" respectively.[72]

Firstly, for neo-Pentecostals in Africa, salvation basically entails the conversion, transformation and empowerment that is wrought in one's life through an encounter with Jesus Christ, leading to the redemption and forgiveness of sin, the transformation into a new person (rebirth or to be "born-again") and an empowerment through the Holy Spirit to live a new life. However, salvation from the perspective of Africa's neo-Pentecostals will mean salvation not only from sin but also "from one's spiritual enemies, that is the devil, evil spirits, witchcraft and other such inimical forces who are only out to 'steal, kill and destroy' (John 10:10)".[73] This is related to the belief that human persons are exposed to malevolent spirits which are more powerful than human beings and which require any human person to search for what Larbi calls a "balance of power" in order to tilt power in the realm of the spirit for the benefit of that person.[74] It is this radicalisation of salvation as rebirth of the soul from sin and the whole being from demonic forces and oppression that is plausible to neo-Pentecostals – not only the abstract confession of sins and baptism in the Holy Spirit, possibly leading to the experience of speaking in tongues. Salvation also entails liberation and / or the redemption of the individual from demonic spirits and their manipulations and the ability to have authority over these spirits and overpower them in the name of Jesus Christ.

Secondly, for most neo-Pentecostals, salvation implies empowerment through the Spirit to prosper. Failure to realise this is explained in terms of evil powers running

[72] Larbi, 378.
[73] Asamoah-Gyadu, 134.
[74] Larbi.

amok. This reflects another radicalisation of their notion of salvation. Wealth and prosperity are understood as the consequence of the first form of salvation. Among neo-Pentecostals in Africa, God's redemption must yield or trigger the blessings of prosperity. With reference to several portions of the Bible such as Proverbs 10:22; Joshua 1:8; Deuteronomy 8:17-18; and especially 3 John 2, neo-Pentecostals maintain that it is the will of God for the righteous to prosper, for it is a covenanted blessing based on a Christian's Abrahamic ancestry.[75] Ayegboyin agrees that "they start from the premise that *Jehovah Jireh* 'our provider', is a God of abundance. He owns the silver and the gold. He has placed us in the world of abundance and it is His perfect will for Christians to prosper."[76] While such prosperity is understood broadly, and surely includes spiritual prosperity, the teachings and lifestyles of the prosperity teachers demonstrate an emphasis on material and financial prosperity.

As noted by Asamoah-Gyadu, what "constitutes 'alienation' and 'transformation' depends not only on the theological presuppositions of the religions concerned, but also on the religio-cultural contexts of religious practitioners and devotees".[77] The conclusion one can draw from neo-Pentecostals in Africa is that their "story of the incarnation is thus their good news of salvation – salvation from fear of evil spirits, from sickness and disease, from economic and social deprivation, from ignorance from who they are, and above all, salvation from total and complete alienation from the Father of all flesh: God".[78]

Neo-Pentecostalism, Creation and Salvation – A Brief Environmental Appraisal

The neo-Pentecostal notions of salvation as "this-worldliness" and "otherworldliness", sketched above, reveal a somewhat interrelated but contradictory position with regard to environmental sustainability. The emphasis on "otherworldliness" has the tendency of justifying Christian irresponsibility and inactivism to protect God's creation. It also justifies the need to subdue and have dominion in order to overcome the demonic spirits inherent in creation, thereby opening the floodgates to a life free from suffering and misfortunes – for that is the will of God for humankind, that which has been spiritually sanctioned from above. Consequently, the prosperity messages across the pulpits of neo-Pentecostal churches are replete with dominion language. However, as Heim suggests, this understanding of salvation is inversed for it sees salvation as "the state achieved when the evils and estrangements of human life are overcome".[79] It is also important to bear in mind some of the following questions in the quest for salvation: are creation and salvation related? Is the God who saves the same as the God who created the earth? If this is the same God, how is creation linked to salvation? What place does creation have in our covenant relationship with the Creator God, offered through the grace of salvation?

It is important to note that just as disorder and chaos (forces of darkness) in creation have been overcome and transformed by the liberating and transforming power of God, so human beings have been redeemed from the forces and oppression of evil

75 Asamoah-Gyadu.
76 Ayegboyin, 159.
77 Asamoah-Gyadu, 133.
78 Larbi, 380.
79 Heim, 322.

spirits and sin that degrade human nature, and by extension, the created order. This implies the remoulding of humankind into a new being to participate in the "earth community" for its revitalisation and flourishing from decay – a process of continuous creation through redemption. Thus Conradie submits that "creation could be viewed as God's continuous redemptive acts towards the *telos* of creation, while redemption could be understood as a creative process in which God allows something new to emerge out of a world infected by sin".[80] Therefore, we see that the grace of re-creation and rebirth from decay and degradation is intrinsic to salvation. Thus creation and salvation are mutually inclusive and not exclusive. The salvation (re-creation) of the human being, who forms part of creation, may be understood as an ongoing redemptive and transformative work of God. Consequently, one would think that salvation as God's grace of renewal and transformation places a responsibility on individual human beings. To the contrary, this is not quite the gist of neo-Pentecostal theologies. What neo-Pentecostals do is to depict God's concern for creation (both human and non-human) and its protection against decay as merely a spiritual redemption and / or a deliverance from the bondage of evil forces and spirits. In my view, Christians who have been redeemed, rebirthed and transformed by the same grace and power of God, are to work to overcome the deep-seated forms of chaos in contemporary society that have degraded God's creation. Any theology that supports a flight from the earth should therefore be seen as irresponsible to God's creation.

Furthermore, with a renewed dominion theology, it is not surprising that neo-Pentecostals show little interest in curbing lifestyles and attitudes that exacerbate the destruction of creation, but rather encourage affluence and an enchantment with modern technology, forms of mobility, consumption and the quest for more. Evidently, the prosperity preached by contemporary neo-Pentecostals, seeking for more than a decent living,[81] is inimical not only to the integrity of creation, but also to the quest for justice, peace and dependence on God in society. Against this background, one can hardly argue that such attitudes are in line with salvation through Jesus Christ, especially when one considers how creation has been subjected to degradation (Rom. 8:14) through thoughtless acts of materialism, affluence and consumption.

Conclusion

Neo-Pentecostals in Africa do not factor the redemption of the earth into their theology of salvation, since they do not relate the degradation of creation to the sins of humanity. The reason for that is their refusal to appreciate the intrinsic relationship between the violation of creation and the violation of the nature of humanity by the same enemy – sin and the ruling powers. Consequently, humanity and the rest of creation continue to be violated by sin. This calls for a recursive and holistic reflection on the grace of salvation so that the redemption of creation is not jeopardised.

In light of debilitating global environmental problems, one would think that neo-Pentecostals would be attentive to the salvation of the created order and be able to resist the "principalities" of a runaway consumerism – which is simply unsustainable. This would follow from their radical theology of salvation understood as "rebirth" and

[80] Conradie, 19.

[81] As suggested by Larbi.

"new creation",[82] since such salvation, although not exclusively, "encompasses relations with the rest of creation: harmony with nature and eternal life".[83] As depicted in Isaiah 44:21-23, the salvation and / or redemption of humankind cannot exclude that of creation.

References and Recommended Reading

Asamoah-Gyadu, Kwabena J. (2005), *African Charismatics: Current Developments within Independent Indigenous Pentecostalism in Ghana*, Leiden: Brill.

Ayegboyin, Deji (2011), "New Pentecostal Churches and Prosperity Theology in Nigeria", in: Afe Adogame (ed.), *Who is Afraid of the Holy Ghost? Pentecostalism and Globalization in Africa and Beyond*, Trenton: Africa World, 150-179.

Conradie, Ernst M. (2005), *An Ecological Christian Anthropology: At Home on Earth?* Aldershot: Ashgate.

Golo, Ben-Willie K. (2011), "Reconciling the Groaning Earth Too: Making a Theological Ethical Case for a Radical Neo-Evangelical Environmentalism in Ghana and Its Implication for Mission in 21st Century Ghana", Paper presented at the International Conference on the Church and the Environment in Africa, Baptist University College, Kumasi, Ghana, April 2011.

Heim, S. Mark (2004), "Salvation as Communion: Partakers of the Divine Nature", *Theology Today*, Vol. 61, 322-333.

Kalu, Ogbu (2011), "Who is Afraid of the Holy Ghost? Presbyterians and Early Charismatic Movements in Nigeria, 1966-1975", in: Afe Adogame (ed.), *Who is Afraid of the Holy Ghost? Pentecostalism and Globalization in Africa and Beyond*, Trenton: Africa World, 83-109.

Larbi, Emmanuel Kingsley K. (1995), "The Development of Ghanaian Pentecostalism: A Study in the Appropriation of the Christian Gospel in the 20th Century Ghana Setting with Special Reference to the Apostolic Church, the Church of Pentecost and the International Central Gospel Church", Doctoral dissertation, University of Edinburgh.

Mwaura, Philomena Njeri (2008), "The Role of Charismatic Christianity in Reshaping the Religious Scene in Africa: The Case of Kenya", in: Afe Adogame, Roswith Gerloff and Klaus Hock (eds.), *Christianity in Africa and the African Diaspora: The Appropriation of a Scattered Heritage*, London: Continuum, 180-192.

Ojo, Mathews A. (2008), "Transnational Religious Networks and Indigenous Pentecostal Missionary Enterprises in the West African Coastal Region", in: Afe Adogame, Roswith Gerloff and Klaus Hock (eds.), *Christianity in Africa and the African Diaspora: The Appropriation of a Scattered Heritage*. London: Continuum, 167-179.

Omenyo, Cephas N. (2006), *Pentecost Outside Pentecostalism: A Study of the Development of Charismatic Renewal in the Mainline Churches in Ghana*, Zoetermeer: Boekencentrum.

Ben-Willie Kwaku Golo

Further Developments

The sections in this chapter explore the relationship between creation and salvation from the perspectives of diverse strands of African theology. They reflect the strengths and opportunities available to African theologies for placing creation and the natural world on the theological agenda and addressing them head-on. They underscore the importance of relating the earth's history to the salvation history of humankind. This would preclude a notion of salvation from the earth – which would logically imply a corrupted and degraded creation in need of salvation. This is especially the case since

[82] See Omenyo.

[83] Heim, 329.

care for creation is not an option for Christians but an injunction (Genesis 2:15).

Notwithstanding the neglect of creation theology in various African theologies, the essays in this chapter typify the current and emerging trends in African ecotheologies. From the turn of the century there has emerged a number of African theologians that have addressed ecological concerns from different perspectives and orientations. Such contributions include a number of edited volumes, special issues of journals and ecclesial statements that were published in Africa itself.[84] In addition, there are also some monographs that either deal with typically African contexts and issues or with global themes:

- Marthinus Daneel's trilogy reflects some fermentation in inculturation theology that does not only show emerging trends in ecotheology in Africa but also reflect how the theologies emerging from Africa are not always systematised and articulated in academic discourse. In *African Earthkeepers: Interfaith Mission in Earth-Care, Volume 1* (Pretoria: Unisa, 1998), Daneel explores the interfaith environmental partnership with traditional leaders among the Shona of Zimbabwe towards restoring the land. In *African Earthkeepers: Environmental Missions and Liberations in Christian Perspective, Volume 2* (Pretoria: Unisa, 1999), Daneel explores the environmental motivations and activities of diverse African Instituted Churches (AICs) in a consortium known as the Association of African Earthkeeping Churches (AAEC). In an abridged version of these two volumes, entitled *African Earthkeepers: Wholistic Interfaith Mission* (Maryknoll: Orbis, 2001), Daneel further develops an African theology of the environment around three themes – theocentrism, Christology and pneumatology.
- Samson Gitau's *The Environmental Crisis: A Challenge for African Christianity* (Nairobi: Acton, 2000) explores African and biblical worldviews and constructs an African Christian theological basis for environmental conservation, using some Christian attitudes towards the environment in Kenya as a case study.
- In *Africa: Theological and Philosophical Roots of Our Ecological Crisis* (Accra: Sonlife, 2004), Mante explores the theological and philosophical bottlenecks that have rendered African theologians unable to address ecological problems head-on, irrespective of the problems impacting on Africa. He proposes some ecological guidelines for Africans today.
- In *An Ecological Christian Anthropology: At Home on Earth*? (Aldershot: Ashgate, 2005) Ernst Conradie explores some theological underpinnings of human creatureliness and the place and vocation of humans on earth.
- Ben-Willie Golo's doctoral dissertation *Towards an African Earth Theology of Liberation: A Study of Deforestation in Ghana in a Globalised World* (Trondheim; NTNU, 2006) explores the environmental situation in Ghana and the responses of the churches to that, in the light of globalised environmental problems. He develops a constructive African eco-Christological framework of relatedness within the biotic community of created beings.

---

[84] For a selection of such contributions, see the entries below under "References and Recommended Reading".

While this list of such monographs is not exhaustive, these contributions, together with the essays in this chapter, reflect some emerging trends in attempts to do theology in Africa that takes into consideration the intrinsic connection between the redemption of humankind and the whole of God's creation. A theology that loses this connectedness in our context today is not only faulty but also oppressive and, indeed, irrelevant.

References and Recommended Reading

Conradie, Ernst M., Mtetwa, Sipho and Warmback, Andrew (eds.) (2002), *The Land is Crying for Justice: A Discussion Document on Christianity and Environmental Justice in South Africa*, Stellenbosch: Ecumenical Foundation of Southern Africa.

Diakonia Council of Churches (2006), *The Oikos Journey: A Theological Reflection on the Economic Crisis in South Africa*, Durban: Diakonia Council of Churches.

Getui, Mary N. and Obeng, Emmanuel A. (eds.) (1999), *Theology of Reconstruction: Exploratory Essays*. Nairobi: Acton,

Kanyoro, Musimbi R. and Njoroge, Nyambura J. (eds.) (1996), *Groaning in Faith: African Women in the Household of God*, Nairobi: Acton.

MacGarry, Brian (ed.) (1995), *Waste or Want? Environment and Poverty Seminar Papers*, Gweru: Mambo / Harare: Silveira House.

Moyo, Fulata L. and Ott, Martin (eds.) (2002), *Christianity and the Environment*, Kachere Test 13, Blantyre: Christian Literature Association in Malawi.

Mugambi, Jesse N. K. and Vähäkangas, Mika (eds.) (2001), *Christian Theology and Environmental Responsibility*, Nairobi: Acton.

Vorster, Willem S. (ed.) (1987), *Are We Killing God's Earth?* Pretoria: University of South Africa.

Warmback, Andrew E. (ed.) (2002), "Church, Environment and the World Summit on Sustainable Development", *Bulletin for Contextual Theology in Africa*, Vol. 8, 2-3, 1-134.

Ben-Willie Kwaku Golo

12. Asian Theological Perspectives

Edited by Lee Yeong-Woo

Introduction

This chapter does not offer an integrated discussion of Asian Christian perspectives on the relationship between creation and salvation. Given the relatively brief period in which theological institutions have been established in East Asia, it would be hard to imitate the secondary scholarship found in other chapters. Instead, five constructive contributions from a number of distinct contexts, namely India, China, Japan and South Korea, are simply juxtaposed.

Lai Pan-chiu offers a survey of the ways in which the relationship between creation and salvation is understood in Chinese Catholicism, Chinese Protestantism and among cultural (liberal) Christians. He argues that Chinese culture, particularly Confucianism, may offer useful resources for Chinese Christian theology to formulate a more unifying view of creation and salvation. The continuing divine action of creation-salvation manifests the same virtue of God as benevolence as Confucianism, and bears the same characteristics of creativity with due respect to the freedom as well as the integrity of creatures.

Kohara Katsuhiro reflects on the nuclear disasters associated with Hiroshima, Nagasaki and Fukushima. He contrasts the light created by God and the expanding human needs for light (energy). On this basis he offers a critique of the insatiable desire of humans fuelled by the advancement of science and technology and the impact of that on Japanese society. He calls for theological reflection on the relation between God's work and God's rest in order to resist the fallacy of discussing nuclear energy solely in terms of safety and efficiency, of considering its benefits to the current generation only. Instead, if the full life cycle of products is recognised, responsibilities towards future generations have to be taken into account. He suggests that solidarity with future generations may be explored through traditional Japanese notions of family and ancestral veneration.

Lee Jeong-Woo explores the history of Korean Christianity, recognises that Christianity in Korea is deeply associated with Western industrialisation and argues that the tendency towards dualistic thinking among conservative Protestant churches in Korea may well be criticised as lying at the root of environmental degradation. He commends the notion of *Donghak* as a way of emphasising the interdependent relationship between the divine, humanity and nature.

Grace Ji-Sun Kim offers perspectives on creation and salvation on the basis of the experience of Asian women, with particular reference to the South Korean context. She suggests that a theology emphasis the role of Spirit / *Chi* can help to overcome alienating dualisms between body and spirit, women and men and creation and salvation.

George Zachariah articulates subaltern perspectives from the margins in the Indian sub-continent. He observes the links between the groaning of creation in terms of ecological destruction and the plight of the marginalised. In this context there is a need for the redemption *of* the earth and a thorough theological integration of the doctrines of creation and salvation. Drawing from the Ashur myth that envisions the earth as the household of all creatures, a vision emerges of a God who hears the cry of also of non-human beings.

Together these perspectives offer a sample of the creative theological engagements that are currently taking in the Asian context – where te Christian convictions have to be explained with reference to other religious traditions as a matter of necessity.

Creation and Salvation in Chinese Perspective

Introduction

The development of a Chinese Christian understanding of creation and salvation has been shaped by its theological inheritence, as well as by its cultural, historical and sociopolitical contexts. Since the "luminous religion" (*jing jiao*), which was pejoratively and incorrectly labelled as Nestorian Christianity, flourished in China rather briefly and left no significant impact on the subsequent development of Chinese Christian theology, Catholicism and Protestantism are the two major forms of Christianity in China. The prevalent theological legacy inherited by Chinese Christianity is thus mainly from the Latin / Western tradition rather than the Greek / Orthodox / Eastern tradition. As we will see, the traditional Chinese culture challenges this theological legacy and may provide important resources for reconsidering the relationship between creation and salvation.

Challenges and Resources from Chinese Culture

In the Judeo-Christian tradition, the word "creation" seems to imply the view that the world is a work or a product of a personal agent or agents. The term *ktisis* used by early Christian theologians is associated with images of craftsmanship or of building and raising an edifice. Radically different from this understanding, the Chinese religions regard the world as a living system. With its key metaphor for "creation" referring to the growth and development within the actual process of nature, creation is understood as analogous to the growth of an organism and does not presuppose an external and personal agent of creation. Creation is thus a continuous process taking place here and now, rather than a single act that happened once upon a time and was completed a long time ago. Though some Chinese philosophers considered nothingness (*wu*) as the source of being (*you*), mainstream Chinese culture understands the universe as endless or eternal. Its conception of creation is closer to the biblical understanding of creation out of chaos (*hun dun*) than to that of *creatio ex nihilo* in classical Christian theology.

Both Confucianism and Daoism emphasise that creation is a natural and non-interventionist process. According to Daoism, the Dao (or Tao) is universally present, life-giving and life-sustaining, but its "action" is characterised by "non-intervention" or "without action" (*wu wei*). In other words, it "brings forth" a harmonious universe spontaneously, effortlessly, and in accordance with the natural courses of all things. Similarly, Confucianism understands the universe as a living system characterised by the production, renewal and reproduction of life, which embodies the metaphysical principle of creativity or the virtue (*de*) of heaven or God, which / who brings forth an orderly and harmonious universe silently and spontaneously in accordance with its / his / her own nature.

Confucianism emphasises that this virtue or metaphysical principle underlying the universe as a harmonious and orderly cosmos is benevolence (*ren*), rather than the divine intelligence or sovereignty highlighted by some Christian theologians. Similar to the Christian understanding of the *imago Dei*, Confucianism suggests that the human being is endowed with the highest capacity for *ren* which constitutes human nature as well as the goal of spiritual cultivation. For Confucianism, the aim of salvation or spiritual cultivation is not to escape from nature. On the contrary, based on the idea of "forming one body with the myriad things of Heaven and Earth", which is shared by Daoism and Buddhism, Confucianism suggests that human and non-human beings are united in one body in creation and / or salvation. In this cosmic process of creation-salvation, the human being is entrusted the role of "created co-creator" assisting the *creatio continua*, which refers to the renewal or transformation of lives as well as maintaining the order and harmony of the universe. To a certain extent, the perfection or salvation of the universe relies on human salvation or participation. For Confucianism, the destiny of a human being is not only in terms of attaining sagehood, full actualisation of human nature, or participation in the divine virtue of benevolence, but also participation in the divine economy. In this sense, the Confucian understanding of human salvation comes closer to the Christian concept of deification or sanctification, rather than that of the remission of sin. The divine action of creation as well as of salvation is persuasive, non-coercive and cooperative, and manifests the same virtue of benevolence.

A Chinese Catholic Perspective

When the Catholic missionaries entered into China in the 16th century, they disseminated both the Christian religion and Western science and technology. The Christian doctrine of creation was interpreted mainly with regard to how God had created the universe once upon a time and out of nothing, which embodied God's intelligence and sovereignty to be discovered by science. The creation of non-human beings was understood as a means for the goal of the creation of humankind, which was regarded as the apex of creation. A corollary of this anthropocentric understanding of creation was an even more anthropocentric view of salvation, which was interpreted mainly in terms of original sin, penal substitution / satisfaction and the ultimate destiny of the human soul in either heaven or hell. The participation of non-human beings in salvation was largely ignored or denied. Some missionaries upheld human uniqueness in creation and criticised the Chinese understanding of forming one body with the myriad things of heaven and earth. They also made use of the metaphor of a building constructed by a builder to support the Christian understanding that the universe cannot exist by itself and must have a creator external to the world. They argued against the traditional Chinese view, which seemed to imply a universe coming into existence by itself. Given the divergences between the Chinese and Christian views of creation and salvation, conflict seemed to be inevitable.[1]

---

[1] See Gernet.

In spite of these divergences, Chinese Christians such as Yang Tingyun (1562-1627), combined the Confucian and Christian views in their theologies. Yang accepted the Christian doctrine of creation, but he made use of Chinese philosophical concepts to formulate his cosmology without making reference to the story of creation in seven days and Adam and Eve as the first man and woman. Instead, Yang's interpretation of creation is ethically and soteriological orientated. Through identifying the triune God as our "Great Father-Mother" (*da-fu-mu*), instead of the gender-biased expression "our Heavenly Father", Yang took filial piety, a cardinal Confucian virtue, as the cornerstone to forming a theology which linked up with piety (revere heaven as a filial child), ethics (love other people as brothers and sisters) and spirituality (overcoming one's self in order to serve God and fellow creatures). Yang seldom mentioned the doctrine of original sin and tended to assume the goodness of human nature. For him, God loved the people so much that he / she endowed human nature with good-conscience (*liang zhi*) so that human beings could serve God and love people. This is what Yang called "teaching by nature" (*xing-jiao*), which is to be supplemented by "teaching by book" (*shu-jiao*), for example the books of Moses, and fulfilled in the "teaching by grace" (*en-jiao*) of Jesus Christ.[2] It is quite noticeable that Yang's theology, which unifies human creation with salvation, bears many Confucian characteristics.

A Chinese Protestant Perspective

When Protestantism entered into China, most of its pietistic missionaries tended to take the salvation of individual Chinese souls as the highest, if not the only, goal of missionary work. This overwhelming concern for salvation was by no means particular to the Christian churches in China. Owing to the political turmoil, social unrest and cultural crisis in modern China, many Chinese intellectuals took "saving the nation" (*jiu guo*) as their "ultimate concern" and the sole criterion for evaluating the adequacy of different cultural, religious and ideological traditions.

In response to the rise of nationalism and scientism, some Chinese theologians, particularly those influenced by liberal theology or the theology of social gospel, attempted to defend the Christian doctrine of creation against scientific challenges and to reinterpret the Christian doctrine of salvation in terms of the salvation of the nation. Most of them tended to adopt a Christocentric approach to theology and focused on the personality of Jesus or the kingdom of God as an ideal society in Jesus' preaching.[3] Although Zhao Zichen (= T. C. Chao, 1888-1979) and Wu Leichuan (= Wu Zhenchun, 1870-1944) did make some comparisons between the Christian and traditional Chinese ideas of cosmos / creation / nature, the cosmic dimension of salvation remained ignored and the doctrine of salvation largely disconnected from the doctrine of creation in their theologies.

In response to the sociopolitical situation of Communist China, Ding Guangxu (= Bishop K. H. Ting, 1915-) articulated a theology focusing on the concept of the "cosmic Christ". His major ideas include the following:

(1) Agape is as an attribute of God's essence expressed in the divine creation, providence, redemption and sanctification;

---

2 See Standaert.

3 See Lam Wing-hung.

(2) All good things originated from God and therefore Christians should learn to appreciate all the good things taking place outside the church;

(3) All things will be redeemed, renewed and reconciled in Christ;

(4) The activities of the Holy Spirit are universal and not to be restricted to the visible church;

(5) Human beings are created in the image of God, which was corrupted during the fall but not totally lost; and

(6) "Glorifying God and serving fellow human beings" is the supreme principle for Christian living.[4]

No matter whether it was influenced by his Anglican background or his political motivation of affirming the role of the Communist Party, Ding's interpretation of the concept of the cosmic Christ offers an important attempt at integrating the doctrines of creation and salvation.

Among the "cultural Christians", who engage in theological activities without being church members, the relationship between creation and salvation is rather problematic. Liu Xiaofeng, the best-known "cultural Christian", started his theological inquiry with a comparative study of the attitudes of Chinese and Western poets towards the world, through focusing on the Daoist idea of "free wandering" (*xiao yao*) and the Christian idea of salvation (*zheng jiu*).[5] Liu argues that, facing the suffering, meaninglessness and absurdity of this world, one has to make an existentialist decision choosing either the Daoist attitude of seeking and enjoying one's own happiness, or the Christian attitude of entering into human society and bearing the burden of the cross. It is very clear that the question of salvation was right at the heart of Liu's theology from the very beginning. However, his subsequent interpretation of salvation is individualistic and disconnected from the doctrine of creation.

Among the Chinese theologians outside Mainland China, Yang Mugu (= Arnold M. K. Yeung, 1945-2002) took the doctrine of creation as the foundation of his theology as well as his responses to the social, political and ecological issues. He attempted to criticise and rectify the Chinese churches' "escapist" attitude towards sociopolitical issues, an attitude partially based on the misconception that creation was under the control of Satan after the fall so that any attempt to improve the society is thus futile and meaningless. In order to refute this misconception, Yang, following the theologies of Irenaeus and Athanasius, emphasises the unity between creation and salvation and the message that "This is My Father's World".[6] Facing the issue of Hong Kong's returning to China in 1997, especially the confrontation between the citizens of Hong Kong and the Chinese government, Yang proposed a contextual theology of reconciliation. Based on his exposition of the doctrine of salvation as reconciliation in the Bible, on patristic theology (especially Irenaeus and Maximus the Confessor) and on some modern theologians, Yang argued that as a model for salvation, reconciliation was more comprehensive and adequate than liberation. After the events of 4 June

[4] See Ting and Li.

[5] See Liu Xiaofeng.

[6] See Yang Mugu (2007).

1989, Yang's theology of reconciliation was ignored or rejected by most of the Hong Kong Christians mainly due to Yang's mediating or reconciling political position derived from his theology. However, Yang's theology of reconciliation is in principle separable from his political position, and remains an important attempt to link up the doctrine of creation and the doctrine of salvation through the concept of the reconciliation of the whole creation in Christ.[7]

Conclusion

The Chinese culture may offer useful resources for Chinese Christian theology to formulate a more unifying view of creation and salvation. According to this view, creation and salvation are not two distinct or separate actions – one natural and applying to all creatures and the other supernatural and applying to humankind only. Both the divine creation and salvation include rather than exclude or undermine human participation. This continuing divine action of creation-salvation manifests the same virtue of God as benevolence, and bears the same characteristics of creativity with due respect to the freedom as well as the integrity of creatures.

In recent years, some Chinese theologians, such as Li Jingxiong (= Peter K. H. Lee), attempted to use resources from Chinese culture to articulate a theology of creation in response to the ecological challenge.[8] One of these attempts is to use the Confucian framework to emphasise the unity of God's creation and salvation.[9] It may be concluded that Chinese Christian theology might not have properly established a fully developed and distinctive view of creation and salvation, but with its own cultural resources, it has the potential to make a significant contribution to this area of theological discussion.

References and Recommended Reading

Fällman, Fredrik (2008), *Salvation and Modernity: Intellectuals and Faith in Contemporary China* (revised edition), Lanham: University Press of America.

Gernet, Jacques (1985), *China and the Christian Impact: A Conflict of Cultures* (translated by Janet Lloyd), Cambridge: Cambridge University Press, 208-213.

Lai, Pan-chiu (1998), "Christian Ecological Theology in Dialogue with Confucianism", *Ching Feng*, Vol. 41, 3-4, 309-344. Reprinted in *Dialogue and Alliance* (2003), Vol. 17, 1, 61-90.

Lai, Pan-chiu and Lam, Jason (eds.) (2010), *Sino-Christian Theology: A Theological Qua Cultural Movement in Contemporary China*, Frankfurt am Main: Peter Lang.

Lam, Wing-hung (1983), *Chinese Theology in Construction*, Pasadena: William Carey Library.

Lee, Peter K. H. (2000), "A Christian Chinese Version of Eco-Theology: Goodness, Beauty, and Holiness in Creation", in: Dieter T. Hessel and Rosemary Radford Ruether (eds.), *Christianity and Ecology*, Cambridge: Harvard University Center for the Study of World Religions, 337-356.

Li, Jieren (2008), *In Search of the Via Media between Christ and Marx: A Study of Bishop Ding Guangxun's Contextual Theology*, Lund: Lund University.

Liu, Xiaofeng (1988), "Salvation and Free Wandering" (in Chinese), Shanghai: Renmin Chubanshe.

Malek, R. (ed.) (2002), *The Chinese Face of Jesus Christ* (5 volumes), Nettetal: Steyler.

Standaert, N. (1988), *Yang Tingyun, Confucian and Christian in Late Ming China: His Life and Thought*, Leiden: Brill.

Ting, K. H. (1989), *No Longer Strangers: Selected Writings of Bishop K. H. Ting* (edited with an

---

7 See Yang Mugu (2003).

8 See Lee.

9 Lai Pan-chiu.

introduction by Raymond L. Whitehead), Maryknoll: Orbis.
Wickeri, Philip L. (2007), *Reconstructing Christianity in China: K. H. Ting and the Chinese Church*, Maryknoll: Orbis.
Yang, Huilin and Yeung, Daniel H. N. (eds.) (2006), *Sino-Christian Studies in China*, Newcastle: Cambridge Scholar Press.
Yang, Mugu (2003), "Theology of Reconciliation and Church Renewal" (in Chinese), Hong Kong: Seed Press.
--- (2007), "This is My Father's World: A Study of Creation" (in Chinese), Hong Kong: Ming Feng.

Lai Pan-chiu

Creation and Apocalyptic Crises in Japan: A Theological Lesson Learned from the Hiroshima, Nagasaki and Fukushima Disasters

> In those days people will no longer say, "The fathers have eaten sour grapes, and the children's teeth are set on edge." Instead, everyone will die for his own sin; whoever eats sour grapes, his own teeth will be set on edge. (Jer. 31:29-30)

Light Created by God and Light Created by Humans

The Hebrew Bible starts off with the account of the creation of the world and of human-beings. It also describes humanity's sin. However, regarding a definition of "sin", the Bible offers only various hints. Some passages of the Bible can be interpreted to imply that human beings are born with original sin, while other passages seem to deny this notion. The above verses from the book of Jeremiah tell us clearly that we cannot attribute our sin to others, including our ancestors, or hold others responsible for our sin. In other words, sin is not something to be inherited, and we should accept responsibility for what we have done on our own.

In Japan, Christians account for less than 1% of the total population. Accordingly, the above verses from the Book of Jeremiah are known to very few Japanese people. Whether believing in the idea of the inheritance of sin or not, an overwhelming majority of Japanese people have now recognised anew a grave problem that affects us and will continue to affect our descendants as well. On 11 March 2011 the eastern part of Japan was struck by a huge earthquake and tsunami, which resulted in severe damage to the Fukushima Daiichi Nuclear Power Plant and caused radiation to leak into the atmosphere. The most serious threat of radiation exposure is the harmful effects on the health of people, both those currently living and those yet to be born. It is true that nuclear power has enhanced the comfort and convenience of our lives to a certain extent, but it has also led to a daunting problem that will impose staggering costs on future generations. Today, many Japanese people have begun to understand the grave implications of the passage, "The fathers have eaten sour grapes [cesium and other radioactive materials], and the children's teeth are set on edge."

Needless to say, this is not the first time for Japan to face the negative consequences of nuclear energy. In the wake of the atomic bombings of Hiroshima and Nagasaki, the deadly terror of radiation was etched in the minds of Japanese people so deeply that post-war Japanese society regards nuclear weapons as an "absolute evil", which is in contrast to the view of the nuclear-armed nations that nuclear weapons are a "necessary evil". Even in Japan, however, the government and the business community turned to the promotion of nuclear energy as a "necessary evil", emphasising the "virtues" of nuclear power and trying to shed its evil image as much as possible. As a result, most Japanese people came to accept nuclear energy as a good thing. It is against this backdrop that the disaster hit Japan on 11 March 2011.

We may gain new insights into this situation by trying to answer the following question. What is the difference between the light that appeared when God said, "Let there be light" at the beginning of Creation (Gen. 1:3) and the light that exploded above Hiroshima and Nagasaki in 1945 or the light that burst inside the reactors of the nuclear power plant in Fukushima in 2011? The blessings of nature and the laws of nature behind them have supported the lives of God's creatures, including humans. Without the blessings of nature, no creatures can sustain life on earth. At the same time, however, we know that the tools provided by nature may be used in diverging ways. For example, fire is a useful tool that can bring light to the darkness of night and keep us warm, but it can also spell disaster, destroying humans and property. The tools and energy that men have discovered in and taken from nature, ranging from fire to nuclear energy, can serve two contradictory purposes – sustaining human society, on the one hand, and destroying it, on the other.

While the light that exploded above Hiroshima and Nagasaki meant triumph to those involved in the development of atomic bombs, it meant death to the people beneath it. The same light brought joy to some and despair to others. The fatal effects of radiation caused post-war Japanese society to suffer serious psychological trauma. At the same time, the tragedies of Hiroshima and Nagasaki led Japan to pledge to never again engage in war, and this pledge has taken root deeply in Japanese society. However, the 3/11 tragedy indicates that we have another story to tell about nuclear energy.

This does not mean that Japan did not make enough effort to communicate to new generations the sheer magnitude of the tragedy caused by war, but post-war Japanese society gave the highest priority to economic growth and turned to nuclear energy for its ability to constantly generate a huge amount of electricity. As a result, many people chose to turn a blind eye to the potential danger of nuclear energy, and the Japanese government and industry stressed how safe and usable nuclear energy could be, as if to offset the danger inherent within it. In addition, more recently, the need to prevent global warming has often been cited as a justification for promoting nuclear power plants. It has been widely argued that we can reduce CO_2 emissions by promoting nuclear power generation and thus contribute to environmental preservation, and environmental organisations have not always been explicitly opposed to this argument.

However, the insistent claim of the Japanese government and industry that Japan's nuclear power plants were absolutely safe (this insistence is known as the "safety myth" in Japan) was falsified entirely upon the occurrence of the Fukushima incident, and the safety myth was completely debunked. As it turned out, the light we wanted to see in nuclear fission generated a power that kills humans and animals. Did the light we saw at Hiroshima, Nagasaki and Fukushima stem from the light that appeared at the beginning of God's creation? Or did we just fail to use the light properly, and, if managed in an appropriate manner, would the light have caused no problem? While the Fukushima incident has forced Japan and the rest of the world to rethink conventional energy policies, it has also posed to theologians a question about the meaning of creation for modern society.

In the Garden of Eden, God said to Adam and Eve, "You are free to eat from any tree in the garden; but you must not eat from the tree of the knowledge of good and evil, for when you eat of it, you will surely die" (Gen. 2:16-17). However, "the woman saw that the fruit of the tree was good for food and pleasing to the eye, and also desirable for gaining wisdom" (Gen. 3:6). Similarly, the fruit brought by nuclear energy appeared "good for food and pleasing to the eye, and also desirable for gaining wisdom". We will need some more time before we can determine whether nuclear energy is the fruit of the tree of knowledge of good and evil that God forbade us to eat. However, at least, today's Japanese society knows that the fruit that looked so good to eat brought fatal consequences, and reflects on this fact again and again while at the same time recalling the scenes of devastation caused by the atomic bombings. The light that appeared at the beginning of creation was recognised as "good" by God. It supported various kinds of creatures that were given life. On the other hand, the light that caused massive damage to Hiroshima, Nagasaki and Fukushima was not a blessing of God – it brought destruction to humans and all other creatures. How should we distinguish between the fruit that may be eaten and that which must not? This is the very first question that God posed to humanity, to which we have not yet been able to find an answer. However, it is certain that we cannot discuss the issue of salvation in the 21st century without addressing this question in earnest from the perspective of ecotheology. In this light, this contribution explores a sense of direction for Japanese ecotheology while taking into consideration the historical background of Japan.

Creation and Eschatology

Since ancient times, Japan has given us many stories that suggest close relationships between humans and nature. While nature offers many benefits to us at all times, we know that unpredictable natural disasters such as earthquakes and tsunamis can instantly destroy all that we have created and achieved. For this reason, the Japanese people have developed a mind set accepting the idea that "everything is ephemeral" and seeing aesthetic value in something or someone doomed to perish against a polytheistic background. Moreover, the development of Japanese Buddhism was significantly affected by the idea of the "last age of the dharma", a belief that the world would eventually enter the final period when correct Buddhist teachings would no longer be practiced. In this light, we may say that an eschatological mood in a broad sense of the word has been inherent in the mental climate of Japanese people. In fact, this mood is expressly reflected in many contemporary Japanese novels and in anime (animation movies) as well as manga (comics).

Of course, Japan is not the only nation that harbours serious concerns over the collapse of the existing order. If addressed incorrectly, global warming and the other environmental problems that face us today could trigger a food crisis, which may result in conflicts and could eventually even endanger the survival of humanity. However, the fear of extinction is not new to our time. Instead, trauma over extinction has been preserved in myths since primordial times. While one of the most well-known examples of this is the biblical story of Noah's flood, similar myths about a flood that cleansed humanity in preparation for rebirth were held by many peoples, from the Sumerian tribes to the indigenous peoples of Asia, Africa, Oceania, North America and South America. In any case, many ancient myths contain archetypal stories regarding the awe of nature among ancient peoples and the lessons they learned from it.

While we can still learn many things from these myths, today's environmental crisis has aspects that are quite different from the extraordinary natural phenomena that caused fear among people in the past. Unlike past natural disasters, much of the crisis that faces us today is attributable to human activity. Needless to say, the Fukushima nuclear power plant accident is a typical example of such a crisis. The combination of a natural disaster (the tsunami) and a human-made disaster (the blind reliance on the safety of nuclear power plants) resulted in unprecedented damage.

We may even say that most environmental problems have resulted from the insatiable desire of humans fuelled by the advancement of science and technology. In the past, people could expect that a flood, however devastating, would naturally come to an end when the rainy season was over. Today's environmental crisis, however, is most likely to become aggravated and could eventually threaten the survival of human societies if left to take its own course. Thus, ongoing environmental devastation may be considered to be closely connected to the experiences that prompted eschatological reflections in various religious traditions.

When considering the theme of creation in the Japanese context, we cannot disregard its connection with eschatology. In Christianity, biblical apocalypticism has often been regarded as unacceptable or inappropriate, because it is incompatible with the mental climate of the Japanese people.

First, let me briefly mention how apocalypticism is viewed by contemporary biblical scholars in Japan. Takashi Onuki, a Japanese New Testament scholar, suggests that on the one hand, apocalyptic literature contributes to the establishment of personal individuality. On the other hand, he points out some negative influences and places special emphasis on how apocalyptic prophecy can be associated with the rationalism of natural science.[10] Meanwhile, he also offers important insights that can help us to understand the root causes behind such tragedies as the sarin gas attack in the Tokyo subway carried out by the Aum Shinrikyo cult in 1995. Takashi Onuki maintains that the apocalyptic-literary way of thinking tends to regard history as an object of observation and that this can easily resonate with a scientific way of thinking that regards the physical world as an object of observation. Viewing history in terms of determinism and fatalism may sometimes drive radical apocalyptic believers to anti-social behaviour – an aspect that should not be overlooked.

Apocalyptic forms of eschatology are characterised by a sharp dualistic distinction between the chosen people, who are eligible for salvation exclusively, and others, who are to be subject to the judgement of the last days. Behind this view is an equally dualistic, if not antagonistic, contrast between life and death. In general, Japanese religions tend to deny the view that life and death are in conflict with each other. Such views are emerging in Christian theology as well. For example, according to Rosemary Radford Ruether, the notion that after the apocalyptic destruction of the world we will be freed from our death and given eternal life is highly problematic from an ecological point of view.[11]

---

[10] Takashi Onuki, 21-28.

[11] Ruether, 83.

The earth's ecosystems that nurture and maintain our lives have a history of about 4500 million years behind them, and we are allowed to exist within this complex network of life that is beyond human understanding. Simply put, ecotheology must help us to recognise the value of what we have taken for granted as being a blessing. It must stir within us a deep empathy for nature, and thus help us to foster solidarity among different generations.

Creation and Sabbath in a Sustainable Society

Terms such as "creativity" and "creative ability" are positively accepted at all times in modern society. Creating something new simply means offering additional usability and values. In terms of 21st-century ecotheology, however, the value of creating something may be admitted only to a limited extent, as creation without regard to consumption and disposal is a crime in the context of the ideal recycling-oriented sustainable society to be realised in the future. For example, nuclear power generation that requires the disposal of radioactive waste may be profitable in terms of energy, but does not deserve to be called "creative" when seen from the perspective of ecotheology, however high the energy efficiency may be. Today, we are no longer permitted to discuss the value of products without considering its full life cycle, namely how it is produced, consumed and recycled. The religious overtones of the "creation" of a product and the "end" of its "life" cycle now need to be recognised.

Put theologically, we need to consider creation and "rest" (Sabbath) together. Just as "God rested from all the work of creating that He had done" (Gen. 2:3) on the seventh day after the creation of the world, all beings must take a rest to avoid affecting ecosystems unnecessarily. We are entering an age when production (a form of creation) that pays no heed to the final disposal, redistribution and recycling of resources is frowned upon. Nuclear energy should be evaluated theologically from this perspective as well. We should avoid the fallacy of discussing nuclear energy solely in terms of safety and efficiency, of considering its benefits to the current generation only. In this light, we as theologians now assume an important responsibility to communicate the significance of God's rest that follows upon God's creative work. If we pay no heed to intergenerational solidarity, waste finite resources in pursuit of only our own interests, and postpone responding to current risks, then future generations will suffer disadvantages one-sidedly.

To prevent such a situation from arising, attempts have been made to establish an ethics for future generations on the basis of utilitarianism, intergenerational contracts, and the rights of future generations. However, a final solution has not yet been found. In the West, the notion of social contracts among the present generation has become mainstream, but little attention has been directed to forms of ethics that span a longer period of time than just one generation. In Asia, on the contrary, intergenerational connections that span the past, present and future still play an important role, as shown by the traditional concept of "family." This concept is deeply rooted in Asian culture, for example in the form of ancestor veneration. We should not hastily dismiss this concept as being pre-modern and feudalistic from the perspective of Western ethics. Of course, we have good enough reasons to critically examine the repressive nature of traditional notions of "family" and ancestor veneration. Nevertheless, ancestral veneration may be significant in attempts to renew our understanding of the intergenerational ethics immanent in Asian religious traditions from the perspective of ecotheology.

Jesus said, "Therefore do not worry about tomorrow, for tomorrow will worry about itself" (Matt. 6:34). These words of Jesus do not release us from our responsibilities to future generations. We know that if we eat sour grapes (radiation, ultraviolet rays, endocrine-disrupting chemicals, etc.), not only *our* teeth but also our children's teeth are set on edge. Therefore, we should have as much awareness as possible of our responsibilities towards future generations. We are no longer allowed to postpone performing our responsibilities towards "tomorrow".

References and Recommended Reading

Takashi, Onuki (1996), "Eschatology of the Ancient Apocalypse: Natural Science and the End Prophecy" (in Japanese), in: S. Hasumi and M. Yamauchi (eds.), *The Mediterranean: Eschatological Temptations*, Tokyo: University of Tokyo Press, 16-30.

Ruether, Rosemary Radford (1994), *Gaia and God: An Ecofeminist Theology of Earth Healing*, San Francisco: Harper.

Kohara Katsuhiro

Creation and Salvation in the Context of Korean Christianity

Introduction

This section will consider how the theme of creation and salvation can help Korean Christianity enhance its ecological awareness and praxis. I will also offer some insights from Korea's cultural and religious heritage to enrich an ecological understanding of creation and salvation.

A Brief History of Korean Christianity

According to the 2005 Korean census, Buddhism (22.8%) and Christianity (Protestantism 18.3%; Catholicism 10.9%) are the two major religions in Korea. Confucianism (0.2%) is not necessarily regarded as a religion, but still plays a significant role in Korean society in many ways. Shamanism, as a form of indigenous religious practice of the Korean people, has been deeply influential in contextualising these forms of organised religion imported from other countries into Korean culture. Among the new religious movements, Chondogyo (Teachings of the Heavenly Way) should be mentioned, since it emerged from Donghak (Eastern Learning), a peasant movement that has made a significant impact on modern Korean history.

Roman Catholic missionaries arrived in Korea in 1794. Soon after they arrived, a number of Koreans converted to Catholicism since they were attracted to its egalitarian ethics. However, the Chosun Dynasty responded to that with severe persecution mainly because the converts refused to perform the ancestor worship that had been at the centre of Chosun culture. This kind of revolt was regarded as a sociopolitical challenge to a strongly stratified Chosun Dynasty that had lasted for approximately five centuries.

Most Western Protestant missionaries entering Korea during the 1880s were able to begin their missionary work without encountering serious persecution. This was made possible because Chosun intellectuals were willing to absorb Western Christianity as a way to learn Western science and technology so that they could make their country strong enough to defeat foreign threats in the midst of a rapid decline of the dynasty. Christianity was welcomed especially by lower class people and women who had been deprived of basic human rights and who experienced the benefits of modern education and Western style hospitals built by missionaries. It should be noted that, despite such social services provided by Western missionaries, their extremely conservative theological views lie at the root of the conservatism of contemporary Korean Christianity. From the beginning, Korean Christianity was moulded to pursue Westernisation eagerly.

During the thirty-five-year imperialist occupation (1910-1945) under Japan, Korean Christianity was able to gain credibility by participating in the struggle for national independence. Unfortunately, liberation from Japanese rule at the end of World War II led to the division of the Korean peninsula and the tragic Korean War (1950-1953) which was also the first full-scale conflict during the cold war. Most Christians in North Korea had to flee to South Korea to escape from communist persecution. This tragic experience further enhanced the conservatism among Korean Christians.

As South Korea's economy began to rise from the ashes of the war, with aid from Western countries, during the 1960s, Korean Christianity's pro-Western attitude and anti-communist sentiments were significantly strengthened. The Protestant sector of the Korean population increased until the 1990s. However, during that time, some Christians began to raise issues of social justice as they saw the many victims of government-driven industrialisation and urbanisation. They also began to appreciate a sense of cultural identity as they realised that Western missionaries devalued the significance of the Korean cultural heritage. This new awareness inspired Korean theologians to develop various forms of Korean theology, such as Minjung theology (Korean liberation theology), and theological reflection on Korean culture and on Korean religions. Such progressive theologies, however, seem to have had little impact on Korean churches because of the latter's strict conservatism.

Creation and Salvation in Korean Theology

While Korean Christianity, a successful example of the missionary efforts of Western churches in Asia, has been known for its rapid growth, it is evident that Korean Christianity has shown little interest in integrating ecological concerns into the life and mission of the church. In these days, many Korean Christians have come to realise that the destruction of the environment poses a spiritual problem. The question is: who are we as human beings living within various ecosystems? Christianity, which came to Korea from the industrialised West, is thus regarded as part of the problem. In response, some Korean theologians[12] tend to draw ecological insights from non-Christian resources rather than to attempt to reconstruct a Korean understanding of the Christian faith in the form of a Korean ecotheology.

How then may the theme of creation and salvation be addressed in such a context? The theme of creation has seldom been at the centre of modern theology, especially because of the Protestant tendency to reject "natural theology" through an emphasis on

[12] See, for example, Park Jong-Chun.

the Word of God. Korean Christianity has been deeply influenced by this perspective. In addition, a literal understanding of the creation stories in Genesis is one of the most powerful hindrances preventing Korean churches from engaging in dialogue with an ecological understanding of creation since this would require an embrace of evolutionary views. In fact, modern theology has generally failed to interpret the implications of modern science for the doctrine of creation and reduced the cosmological dimension of this doctrine into a personal belief in the Creator. In this situation, Korean churches tend to respond to the ecological crisis on the basis of a theology of stewardship without involving a comprehensive revisioning of the Christian doctrine of creation in relation to contemporary scientific views of reality. For Korean churches to be ecological, it is necessary to restore an organic view of reality to overcome the modernist positioning of humans over nature. This would require interpreting the contemporary scientific view of reality in the light of the biblical faith in the triune God as Creator. This will offer an opportunity to overcome the prevailing anthropocentric understanding of creation as providing merely the stage for human history.

As observed above, Korean Christianity has played a significant role in the critical moments in Korean modern history. It was introduced as a "new power" when the Chosun Dynasty began to collapse at the end of the 19th century, and offered a "new energy" for rebuilding the country out of nothing after the totally devastating war. Korean people were desperately seeking for a way to develop their economy at all costs. The urgent goal was to achieve Westernised industrialisation. There was no room for any ecological considerations.

What kind of ecological wisdom could be drawn from this reflection on the role of Korean Christianity in the process of modern industrialisation? Can we affirm that pursuing industrialisation is inevitably doomed to end up with ecological destruction? I agree with those ecotheologians who regard Lynn White's famous accusation of human dominion over nature as an unwarranted oversimplification of the biblical creation story. However, I wonder if there is any intrinsic relation between the idea of creation as divine project and economic development as human project. If not, I suppose that Korean Christianity should have paid deeper attention to the notion of stewardship in order to differentiate between necessary attempts to overcome poverty and the insatiable desire for material wealth. Instead, it simply praised economic growth as God's blessing. While this may be important to overcoming poverty, it is crucial to find a more sustainable form of economic development. Economic growth should be governed by concerns for social justice so that its fruits can be shared with all people and especially by concerns for ecological justice so that the evolving web of life can be enhanced. Needless to say, excessive consumerism may be regarded as an ecological sin.

An even more deadly non-ecological attitude in Korean Christianity is related to the extreme emphasis on other-worldly salvation, namely of human soul from this world. Indeed, a preoccupation with "life after death" or "eternal life in heaven" has been widely criticised as one of the most anti-ecological aspects of Christian faith. In reality, the belief in life after death for the human soul is very popular also among East Asian cultures and religions where it has functioned as a source of wisdom to enhance communal aspects of life. By contrast, the Christian emphasis on life after death seems to entail contempt for the present life on earth. Such a difference, I suppose, stems from a dualistic understanding of God and world. In spite of its constant emphasis on God's presence in the world, as long as the world is understood in terms of contingency or transience and in opposition to God's eternity, it is likely that Christians will conclude that this earth is not our home and that the material world has no intrinsic value. As Paul Santmire suggests, one may identify both an "ecological motif" and a "spiritual motif" in the history of Christianity.[13] It seems obvious that, as ardent admirers of Westernisation, the individualistic emphasis on "life after death" and "salvation of the human soul into heaven" among Korean churches can be criticised as a pervasive ideology that has destroyed a sense of community in Korean culture and society.

However, I believe that the Christian emphasis on the transcendent God as "the Wholly Other" can offer an opportunity to resist human arrogance, as Karl Barth showed against the 19th-century liberal optimism based on pride in human possibilities. Even in the context of the ecological crisis, the transcendent God can be understood as the ultimate source of ecological *metanoia* if we do not ignore the biblical teaching that the transcendent God, as the Radical Other, is also the Lord of the earth. This may be complemented by Christological and pneumatological ways to affirm the intrinsic value of this evolving universe. However, this remains incomplete without the Christian hope for cosmic redemption – which affirms the intrinsic value of our bodily existence on earth and the necessity of the salvation of the earth as well. Here Moltmann's affirmation of the earth as God's home through the indwelling of the Spirit will be helpful in widening the individualistic, other-worldly, anti-bodily understanding of Christian salvation among conservative Korean churches. Indeed, all of us are called to renew our fragmented and distorted vision of reality to befriend this fragile planet in the midst of ecological collapse.

Korean Cultural Insights for Christian Ecological Theology

As H. Richard Niebuhr's famous typology in *Christ and Culture* suggests, the encounter between Western Christianity and Korean religions prompts much theological reflection. It has been said that Korean shamanism served as the fertile soil for transforming various foreign religions into Korean religions when they were introduced into Korea. When Daoism, Buddhism and Confucianism came to Korea, they were able to coexist without serious conflicts, although there were some periods of tensions among these religions caused by changing political regimes. Such a peaceful coexistence is possible mainly on the basis of the emphasis on harmony in shamanism. However, one may also argue that this coexistence was possible because all these religions have a non-dualistic view of reality.

Such a peaceful coexistence is possible mainly because of shamanism's emphasis on harmony among people. However, one may also argue that this coexistence was possible because harmony is a core value in all these religious traditions. While these East Asian religions have a sense of the Ultimate or Supreme Being as the source of life, their emphasis on harmony provides a non-dualistic view of reality so that people can pursue harmony with one another and with nature as well.[14]

When Christianity arrived in Korea, shamanism again played a significant role in

[13] See Santmire.

[14] See Kim Sung-Hae.

fostering a Korean form of Christianity, although most Korean Christians may not be aware of the deep dynamism of this underlying inter-religious encounter. As I have observed above, since Korean Christianity has functioned as a driving force for Western industrialisation, it has easily acquired a contact point with Korean people deeply influenced by a shamanistic understanding of earthly well-being as a divine blessing.[15] However Korean Christianity has been criticised as a foreign power that destroys traditional values and community life. I believe that Christianity's apparently dualistic understanding of the relationship between God and the world might be the main cause of conflict between Christianity and other Korean religions.

Korean religions may, therefore, be useful resources for enhancing theological attempts to articulate a non-dualistic understanding of the relationship between God and the world. Although most conservative churches have condemned traditional religions as forms of idolatry, some progressive theologians such as Kim Kyoung-Jae and Keel Hee-Sung have begun to engage in interreligious dialogue to explore the possibility of mutual enhancement. Given increasing public awareness of environmental degradation, Korean Christians have come to realise the lack of an "ecological motif" (Santmire) in the ways that they practise their faith. They may thus appreciate a Buddhist compassion for all forms of life, a Taoist humble respect for the holiness of nature and a Confucian emphasis on the unity of heaven and humanity, suggesting a harmonious relation between humans and non-human nature. Through such insights from Chinese religions, Korean traditional religion offers considerable ecological wisdom for the daily practising of the Christian faith. For instance, the promotion of "Korean food for Korean people" recognises the significance of local food. This does not necessarily imply a form of nationalism, but an awareness of our bodily rootedness in the land. The human body and the earth are not separate entities. Indeed, Korean Christianity is challenged to rediscover the folk wisdom in Korean culture and to integrate that into Christian practice in order to overcome the dualistic emphasis on the human soul over the body that has been received from Western Christianity.

Finally, I commend the indigenous Korean notion of *Donghak* (Eastern Learning) founded by the Korean Confucian scholar Ch'oe Che-U around 1860. It grew out of radical social reform movement by the poor peasant class in the 19th century, attempting to integrate Confucian, Buddhist, Taoist, shamanistic and even Catholic influences as a way of protest against sociopolitical corruption based on the stratification system and Western imperialistic invasion. This notion of *Donghak* is derived from their labelling of Western Catholics as *Seohak* (Western Learning). *Donghak* emphasises the immanence of Hanullim (the heavenly God) and the role of humans as *sich'onju* (bearing or serving God) and as *innaech'on* (human being is God). It also underlies the significance of the unity of the human will with the divine (cosmic) will as a way of saving humans from the disease that is associated with all forms of evil in the universe. Thus the notion of *Donghak* signifies interdependent and harmonious relationship among the divine, humanity and nature.[16]

This may be regarded as very similar to a form of panentheism. Panentheism is commonly employed by trinitarian forms of ecological theology and by process theo-

---

[15] See Lee Jung-Young

[16] See Chung Ki-Yul.

logy alike to emphasise both God's transcendence and God's immanence. In addition, *Donghak* combines this religious dimension with social justice and feminist concerns. I believe the notion of *Donghak* may provide rich resources to bridge East Asian religious traditions and Western Christianity in the context of the ecological crisis.

Conclusion

If Christian ecological theology wishes to affirm the intrinsic value of the earth, it seems necessary to resist the dualistic splitting of God from the world in order to allow for a more integrative vision. Of course, this does not mean that the idea of the transcendent God should be totally renounced. Its prophetic vision should be retained as a subversive call to transform human sinful arrogance. In this sense, a Christian understanding of creation and salvation and Korean religious traditions can mutually challenge and enhance each other.

References and Recommended Reading

Chung, Ki-Yul (2007), *Donghak Concept of God / Heaven*, New York: Peter Lang.

Keel, Hee-Sung (1989), "Salvation according to the Korean Zen Master Chinul and Karl Barth", *Buddhist-Christian Studies*, Vol. 9, 13-23.

Kim, Kyoung-Jae (1994), *Christianity and the Encounter of Asian Religions: Method of Correlation, Fusion of Horizons and Paradigm Shifts in the Korean Grafting Process*, Zoetermeer: Boekencentrum.

Kim, Sung-Hae (1988), "Religious Reality and Coexistence in Present-Day Korea", *Korea Journal*, Vol. 28, 3, 4-17.

Lee, Jung-Young (1996), "Relationship between Christianity and Shamanism in Korea: A Historical Perspective", *Asian Journal of Theology*, Vol. 10, 2, 333-347.

Park, Jong-Chun (1998), *Crawl with God, Dance in the Spirit: A Creative Formation of Korean Theology of the Spirit*, Nashville: Abingdon.

Santmire, H. Paul (1985), *The Travail of Nature: The Ambiguous Ecological Promise of Christian Theology*, Philadelphia: Fortress.

Lee Jeong-Woo

Creative Word: Asian Women's Perspective on Creation and Salvation

Religious History in Korea

Korea is a multi-religious country where different world religions have existed side by side during various periods of its history.[17] There is much evidence of syncretism. Pungryudo was the henotheistic religion of the ancient Han people who believed in the heavenly God, the God of light and life, called Hananim. When Pungryudo and Shamanism met, an integration occurred.[18] Most Christians in Korea have been highly resistant to syncretism even though their religious practices indicate an implicit or unconscious syncretism. The horizons of Shamanism, Buddhism and Confucianism have not only changed and developed within themselves, but have also integrated with

[17] Suh Nam-dong uses the term "confluence" to describe the syncretistic activity in Korea. Confluence is the coming together of two religions, much like two rivers flowing into each other to form one river. See Suh Nam-dong, 177.

[18] See Kim Kyoung Jae, 105, 107.

each other over many centuries to create a syncretic religio-cultural society.[19] There are components of Confucian filial piety and recognisable behavioural roles for men and women found in Korean Christianity today. There are also elements of Shamanism's emphasis on physical, emotional and spiritual healing, and Buddhist styles of meditative prayer.[20] Despite these elements of syncretism, Korean Christians tend to deny its reality in their lives and their practice of Christianity. However, this syncretistic reality is key to how they understand creation and salvation for themselves and in particular for Asian women.

The appearance of Roman Catholicism in Korea occurred without the help of Western priests, but through certain Korean neo-Confucianists who were convinced through their own study that Roman Catholicism was true. Then in the late 19th century, when Protestant missionaries entered Korea, they focused on the working class. Christianity evidently fed the spiritual hunger of many Korean people and helped them to resist the oppression they suffered from the local elites.[21] Spirituality and religious understandings of Mahayana Buddhism, Shamanism and Confucianism all helped the Korean people to receive the gospel.[22]

Korean women were forced to provide "comfort to foreign troops" as sex slaves for the Japanese. They were considered "war supplies" and although the Japanese government has adamantly withheld military documents, a study conducted by a Korean feminist group estimated that more than two hundred thousand Korean women became comfort women between 1932 and 1945.[23] They were repeatedly raped every day with reports stating an average of fifty times a day. Many of the women were tortured and killed. This type of cruelty is inconceivable. In the midst of this suffering and inconceivable pain, how could Asian women view themselves as created by God and saved by God?

Asian women live amidst patriarchy and colonialism. As colonised people they become "othered" in many ways. In this "othering" the desire to dominate gains its end. Empire-building is therefore all about power-building by creating a devalued other. Asian women are colonised not only by Western imperialist power but also by Asian kyriarchal domination.[24] Thus Asian women are dominated by two forms of destructive forces which subjugate and subordinate them. In the midst of this it becomes crucial for women to understand their own subordination and subjugation. With this recognition, Asian women can begin to reconstruct themselves by re-imagining what creation and salvation means for them.

Creation

A creation story forms an important part of every culture, society and tradition. Religions also have their own creation stories to make sense of how they came into existence. Koreans have their own creation myth called the Tangun myth to help them

[19] See Kim Kyoung Jae, 106.

[20] See Wells, 60.

[21] Kim Kyoung Jae, as cited in Wells, 64.

[22] Kim Kyoung Jae, 118, 119.

[23] Orevillo-Montenegro, 85.

[24] Kang Namsoon, 218, 219.

describe how they got to this place, where they are supposed to be going and what their role is in this life. Creation stories are the key to the meaning and place of the nation's history. It gives birth to history. We see evidence of this also in the Genesis account of creation.

Creation is where everything got started. It is God who brought all nations and peoples – all things – into existence. From the beginning to the end, God is fully and entirely present.[25] God the Creator desired to give birth to the created world. God is all in all. Ecofeminist theologians like Sallie McFague understand the earth as God's body. Since it is God's body, we need to take care of it, be mindful of how we treat it and recognise that we need it to exist for future generations. We cannot continue to take and rape the earth as our modern contemporary culture has begun to do. We need to give back and allow the earth to heal and grow. Otherness leads to misusing and abusing the world.

Creation is thus seen as bringing light into darkness, turning chaos into order and overcoming death with life. A hymn of creation from the *Rigveda*, composed between 1500 and 1200 BCE in India, was strangely similar to the book of Genesis in its description of the primordial state of the universe.[26] Many Christians believe that the Genesis creation story is a very unique account, but similarities to the *Rigveda* reveal that it is a story shared by many cultures and peoples.

God who created all things shows how God is the mover of the universe. God is the ultimate source of the universe who creates life and gives life to all things. It is within this place that Asian women gain strength through faith in a God who creates and breathes new life to those who are broken and burdened by sexism, domination and subjugation. This is a huge difficulty for many women to overcome. This is what the Creator God means as God liberates Asian women. In turn, this will help in the work towards salvation. Women need salvation from the pain experienced in this world as well as from the eternal life hereafter. As we compare the domination of the earth with the domination of women, especially Korean women, who suffered under patriarchy more severely than Western women (given that Asian patriarchy is more destructive), we need to grasp that the domination of the source of life and the sustenance of life are destructive. We need to recognise that women and earth are important aspects of creation. Women are a creation of God and not a by-product to be thrown away.

Salvation

History is the product of God's saving intervention. It is where God meets people in divine power and love. Many turn to Exodus as they remind themselves how the river Jordan stopped its flow to let their ancestors cross from the wilderness into the land of promise. They visualise how God fought for them to secure a foothold in an alien land.[27] God hears the cry of God's people and saves us. God is the Saviour and will continue to save us as we reach out to God.

The time-honoured dictum that there is "no salvation outside the church" is untrue.

---

25 Song Choan-Seng (1982), 54, 55.

26 Song Choan-Seng (1979), 36.

27 Song Choan-Seng (1979), 38.

The Christian church, in its totality – its teachings, institutions, liturgies, even sacraments taken together – cannot be equated with salvation. Salvation is a miracle of God's grace. Christians cannot confine it to themselves. Salvation becomes a grace to all people and cannot be limited. God's saving grace cannot be institutionalised. The ultimate test of salvation is not subscription to particular creeds and confessions or adherence to dogmatic formulations and orthodoxy. The key to salvation is found in what Jesus himself declared: "Not everyone who says to me 'Lord, Lord' will enter the kingdom of Heaven, but only those who do the will of my heavenly Father" (Matt. 7:21; Luke 6:46). This must be why Jesus went on to say: "When the day comes, many will say to me, 'Lord, Lord, did we not prophesy in your name, drive out demons in your name, and in your name perform many miracles?' Then I will tell them plainly, 'I never knew you; out of my sight, you and your deeds are evil!'" (Matt. 7:22-23). The church has turned salvation into something totally "spiritual" and has treated it as a monopoly to which only priests and pastors have direct access. Jesus never tired of driving home the point to the religious authorities that salvation has little to do with God if it has little to do with people in need and pain. Salvation begins with the life people live on earth socially, politically and religiously. It does not begin with eternal life in heaven.[28]

For Asian women, salvation needs to be intricately tied to the everyday events of their lives. As so many are sexually exploited, politically dismissed and culturally dominated, they need salvation now. It cannot be something that happens in the afterlife. As women suffer under the religious burdens of Confucianism, Buddhism and Christianity, which continue to subordinate women by assigning them a secondary status, they seek to experience salvation in the present.

In many ways, the story of creation is in a true sense the story of salvation, loaded with cosmic and historical implications. You cannot have a creation story unless you have experienced such salvation. The Israelites who were saved during the Exodus reflected back on their liberation and then needed to describe their origins, leading them to write down their creation story. Creation is God's response to this cosmic groaning. God's work of salvation leads to the emergence of a new creation. Thus creation and salvation are in reality two sides of the same coin. Where there is creation, there is salvation. Creation is God's redeeming act, while redemption is God's creating act. The whole cosmos, and human beings in particular, is sustained and renewed by this creating and redeeming God until the time of fulfilment.

God's creative and redemptive involvement with the world is not entirely foreign to Asian spirituality. It is reflected in Gautama Buddha's resolve to set out on a mission to preach the truth upon attaining his enlightenment. Buddhist culture imbued with Buddhist spirituality became predominant in the mind and life of hundreds of millions of people in Asia.[29] It is within this context and understanding of spirituality that many Asian women are living. This syncretistic understanding of creation and salvation may empower Asian women as they are able to draw on their rich history of religious spirituality, which was not just imported through Christianity, but has existed in much of their history. Chung Hyun Kyung argues that Asian women need to move away from

[28] Song Choan-Seng (2002), 315- 317.

[29] Song Choan-Seng (1979), 40, 41.

the attempted doctrinal purity of Christian theology, as there is no pure doctrine. Rome claims to have it; Eastern Orthodoxy claims to have it, and then there are the biblical fundamentalists who also think they know what that entails. Additionally, among all of the Presbyterian groups in Korea, questions are raised concerning theological orthodoxy (which is strongly upheld). What matters to Asian women's survival is liberation for themselves and their communities. Furthermore, it is the life force that will empower them to claim their full humanity. Asian women need to selectively choose life-giving elements of their culture and religions and weave new patterns of religious meaning that will liberate them from oppression and hardship.[30] They need life-affirming aspects for their life here on earth rather than being told to wait until they die.

Spirit / Chi

One aspect of the divine that they can turn to for salvation is the Spirit. A notion of Spirit is found in many cultures, and in Asia it is commonly understood as *Chi*, which is a life force that gives and sustains life.[31]

It is necessary to be open to other religious and cultural traditions to gain insight into the words used when others talk about the divine and the Spirit. This openness can lead to further dialogue, acceptance and the welcoming of strangers. As we search the globe, we discover global understandings of the Spirit such as *Chi*, *prana* and *ha*, which are all versions of the life-giving Spirit. These various terms all point to the same Spirit that is life giving and life sustaining. *Chi* is found throughout the world in various ethnic groups, and this commonality between cultures and people will aid us in our attempt to embrace the other. This process of embracing the other – or reconciliation – is central to salvation / redemption. As Christians from different social locations begin to recognise a common thread, understanding *Chi*, *prana*, *ha*, Holy Spirit and other terms for the Spirit as interrelated can be experienced as salvific for us as Christians and in our relationships with others.[32]

Spirit / *Chi* is salvific in that it saves us, within us and among us and with others. It is a spirit that bonds us and draws humanity closer to all other living creatures. It will sustain us and keep us aware of our interconnectedness and inter-reliance (to each other, the world and all of creation), without which we will not survive. Hence Spirit-*Chi* is essentially what keeps humanity alive, as it is the life-giving force within us. Spirit / *Chi* is salvific and negotiates a space to save those who are living in the liminal spaces between us.[33] This will include the Asian women who are falling between the cracks.

The dualism of spirit and body has had detrimental results for a Western Christian understanding of the Spirit, but the notion of *Chi* reminds us to balance the two. It will move us closer to the New Testament understanding of body and spirit where the two are closely connected, much like in an Asian understanding. If we examine Mark 5:34, it can be translated "your faith has made you well" or "your faith has saved you". In

---

30 Chung Hyung Kyung, 113.

31 For a more detailed discussion on Spirit and Chi, see my *The Holy Spirit, Chi and the Other* (2011).

32 See Grace Ji-Sun Kim, 145.

33 See Grace Ji-Sun Kim, 134, 135.

Greek, the verbs "made well" and "saved you" are the same. The original Greek reveals a similarity between healing and saving. It demonstrates that the body and Spirit are more interconnected than a modern Western understanding seems to suggest. Healing the body and saving the Spirit are one and the same.[34] Asian women have been broken by physical, spiritual and emotional abuse. For Asian women to be saved, it would entail that they are made well and that their battered and broken bodies are healed.

Christianity needs to emphasise a togetherness of the body and spirit. This will in turn help to eliminate the marginalisation of women, minorities and anyone that is described as "the other". This requires more than avoiding distinctions between Spirit and matter; it builds a unity between the two. It is a movement to reclaim the body as good and show that Spirit and body are one. A holistic notion of salvation requires both body and spirit working together to bring meaning and wholeness to humanity.[35] This offers courage and strength to those women who have been denigrated, denied equality, hidden from view and lacking a voice in the public sphere. In other words, the God of salvation is the Creator who saves us all. The salvation of our spirit also includes our body, in the present and in the future. If the Creator of all life pronounces it to be good, who are we to say otherwise?

References and Recommended Reading

Chung, Hyun Kyung (1990), *Struggle to be the Sun Again*, New York: Orbis.

Kang, Namsoon (2008), "Re-constructing Asian Feminist Theology", in: Sebastian C. H. Kim (ed.), *Christian Theology in Asia*, Cambridge: Cambridge University Press, 205-226.

Kim, Grace Ji-Sun (2002), *The Grace of Sophia: A Korean North American Women's Christology*, Cleveland: Pilgrim.

--- (2011), The Holy Spirit, Chi and the Other: A Model of Global and Intercultural Pneumatology, New York: Palgrave Macmillan.

Kim, Kyoung-Jae (1994), *Christianity and the Encounter of Asian Religions: Method of Correlation, Fusion of Horizons and Paradigm Shifts in the Korean Grafting Process*, Zoetermeer: Boekencentrum.

Orevillo-Montenegro, Muriel (2006), *The Jesus of Asian Women*, Maryknoll: Orbis.

Song, Choan-Seng (1979), *Third-Eye Theology: Theology in Formation in Asian Settings*, Eugene: Wipf and Stock.

--- (1982), *The Compassionate God*, Maryknoll: Orbis.

--- (2002), *Jesus in the Power of the Spirit*, Eugene: Wipf and Stock.

Suh, Nam-dong (1983), "Historical References for a Theology of Minjung", in: *Minjung Theology* (edited by The Commission on Theological Concerns of the Christian Conference of Asia), Maryknoll: Orbis, 155-182.

Wells, Harold (1988), "Korean Syncretism and Theologies of Interreligious Encounter: The Contribution of Kyoung Jae Kim", *Asia Journal of Theology*, Vol. 12, 56-76.

Grace Ji-Sun Kim

[34] See Grace Ji-Sun Kim, 141.

[35] See Grace Ji-Sun Kim, 148.

Towards a Redeemed Earth: Subaltern Social Movements in India

Shifts in Theological Perspective

Theological reflections are always the products of specific contexts, and the attempt to apply them to different contexts, by claiming universality, is problematic. Dominant theologies have the tendency to project what is particular to them as universal to all, whereby particular experiences, values and symbols are being made normative for doing theology and making ethical decisions everywhere. This has resulted in the theological colonisation of peoples and communities all over the world. The awareness of the danger of universalisation has led to the emergence of social location and lived experience of the community as the loci for doing theology. The objective realities of the subjects thus have become important categories in theological and ethical discourses. However, contextual articulations of theology, in general, tend to ignore the methodological significance of the collective politics of the subjects and lead to an apolitical essentialism. We see this approach in mainstream ecotheology where dominant readings of the crisis of the earth, viewed from nowhere, are presented as meta-narratives and where panaceas are prescribed, claiming universal validity and applicability. This is the context in which a view from the grassroots, reiterating the interrelationship between theology and political praxis, becomes paradigmatic. It calls for methodological transgressions that reject the universal categories and instead affirm the mediation of the oppositional gaze from the grassroots, affirming the agency of the subaltern social movements.

We see the above-mentioned methodological shifts and transgressions in Indian Christian theologies. Theological reflections in India have always been attempts to make sense of Christian faith and practices in relation to religio-cultural contexts and socio-political realities. In the early phase of the Christian theological constructions in India, the protagonists were the converts from Brahmanical Hinduism, and the theological problem for them was to present Christianity in relation to Hindu scriptural and philosophical traditions. In this process, their social embeddedness in the caste hierarchy with its supremacy and exclusion of Dalits became incorporated into their theological constructions. The first half of the 20th century witnessed India's struggle against British colonialism and that inspired Indian Christian theologians to reflect theologically on freedom and social revolutions. The main thrust of the theological reflections in the post-independent India was to facilitate Christian participation in nation building. As post-colonial India became incorporated into the bandwagon of neo-liberal globalisation, theological engagement became a liberative praxis of radical social interventions in solidarity with the struggles of the people. Along with the struggles for economic justice, India witnessed the insurrection of marginalised identities like Dalits, tribals, adivasis and women, affirming their difference and demanding self-determination, recognition and dignity. Several contextual theologies such as Dalit theology, tribal theology and adivasi theology came into being during this phase.

These shifts in theological perspectives became possible thanks to the radical discernment of new sources in the theological engagement with context. When the bodily mediated experiences of the victims – the tortured body and the altered earth – became the primary source for doing theology, they became the hermeneutical lenses for reading Scripture and tradition. In the pluralistic context of India the need to recognise the plurality of Scripture was realised. Orality, folklore, traditional wisdom of indigenous communities, prudential practices of creation care and the like became important sources in constructing theology. Subaltern social movements are also considered "texts" that can inform the construction of liberative theology in India today.

The Groaning of Creation and Subaltern Ecotheological Reflections

Before we begin to explore contemporary ecotheological discourses in India, particularly emerging from such social movements, it is important to listen to the groaning of creation that we hear in India today. Rain forests are denuded, rivers are dammed and ocean beds are raped. The commons are being snatched away from the communities and are now on sale for corporate plunder. In the name of the "common good" and "national interest", millions have been uprooted from their abodes. Suicide seems the only dignified option for those who used to live in communion with nature. But in the midst of this reign of death we also see a new celebration of life in the affirmation that another world is possible. Such affirmations continue to arise in the small pockets of resistance in the villages and small towns and the metropolises where people gather together to resist the reign of death. This polyphony of new harmonies is a contemporary experience of epiphany, one which not only invites but inspires us to do theology differently. A view from the grassroots – the standpoints of those who are uprooted from life – forms the key to experiencing this epiphany.

Ecotheological reflection from the grassroots, hence, is the vision of an engaged collectivity of the subaltern communities about their lives on earth in communion with all other living beings. Such a perspective from the grassroots affirms the very subalternity of earth, and describes how the otherness of nature and the otherness of the subordinated others are correlated. It depicts how the subordinated others at the grassroots perceive the realities that continue to make them powerless and reduce all life forms to commodities to be plundered and exploited. Subaltern ecotheology envisions the interconnectedness between social justice, differences and environmental degradation. It unmasks the brutal face of development and globalisation. A host of social, environmental and political theories are being analysed and used as resources in this constructive endeavour. It recognises and retrieves the liberative strands in the religious traditions, scriptures, rituals and cosmogonies of the communities, and uses them as resources in their struggles. Subaltern ecotheology, therefore, is a vision and praxis for interpreting the reality and changing it radically from the subaltern standpoint, so that a different world may become a contemporary reality.

Creation and Salvation in Indian Christian Theologies

Indian Christian theological reflections, in general, do not approach creation and salvation as two distanced doctrines. Rather, we find creative attempts to understand creation and salvation as closely interrelated experiences. Pandippedi Chenchiah (1886-1959) understood salvation not as a return to the pristine beauty of Eden, but rather as a cosmic creative evolutionary movement towards a new humanity, society and cosmos. For him this cosmic evolution is the creative act of God, which can be interpreted as the continuation of creation. Through incarnation, God in Jesus Christ became an earthly being to facilitate the cosmic evolution – salvation. For M. M. Thomas (1916-1996), incarnation is the continuation of creation. Struggles for the transformation of sinful and unjust social structures are human participation in the ongoing divine act of creation. Reflecting upon the struggles for equality, justice and dignity of the oppressed communities, Thomas interpreted salvation as humanisation: "if the final destiny of human beings is ultimately an incorporation into Christ's glorified humanity ... salvation itself could be defined as humanization in a total and eschatological sense."[36] In the context of the distress of the earth which we mourn today, salvation could be interpreted as the redemption of the earth.

Ecosophy from the Scriptures of our Neighbours

Studies on the historical roots of the ecological crisis have exposed the "huge guilt" of the Judeo-Christian tradition, particularly medieval Christianity, and its attitudes towards nature in turning God's creation into commodities for profit and wealth accumulation.[37] That means the dominant theological perspective on earth is violent and life-negating, and it is incapable of enabling us to experience the divine in the terrestrial. As a result, nature is being perceived as creatures without intrinsic worth, created to serve the needs and greed of human beings. This is the context in which Indian expressions of Christian ecotheology, emerging from the grassroots, look for ecosophia in the scriptures and oral traditions of our neighbours of other faiths. Hence Sebastian Kappen observes that "for a wisdom that would save us from the ecological crisis, we have to return to the matriarchal traditions".[38]

The *Bhumisukta* in *Atharvaveda*, proclaims: "The Earth is my Mother, I am son of the Earth. The Rain-giver is my father; may he shower on us blessings. All creatures born from you move round upon you. You carry all that has two legs, three or four. To you O Earth belong the five human races" (*AV* 12.1). The affirmation that the earth is our common mother enables us to understand the community of creation as a family around Mother Earth. Kappen observes that this understanding of creation has its impact on human attitudes towards nature in the Vedic community: "They also worked; they sowed and reaped. But all this was done in the spirit of reverence. To them cultivation was also cult, an act of worship. Labor did not render the earth sterile, much less bring ruin upon her. Rather, it helped her to come to her own, to become fecund and bear fruit."[39] This is the cosmic ethical behaviour of *rita* which is inscribed in the whole community of creation. Creation in this sense helped the Vedic community to merge itself into the wider community of creation.

That the "world is the body of God" is a theological metaphor developed by Ramanuja, the 11th-century Hindu philosopher-saint. Along with Sallie McFague, Indian Christian ecofeminist theologians have appropriated this metaphor to construct ecotheological reflections. This metaphor has the potential to inspire us to go beyond the anthropocentric doctrine of creation on the basis of dominion and stewardship towards an ecological doctrine of creation. As Gabriele Dietrich rightly observes: "The body is the whole, human beings cannot subjugate nature but human community also

---

[36] Thomas, 18.

[37] See White.

[38] Kappen, 51.

[39] Kappen, 68.

cannot be subsumed under nature."[40] To see the world as the body of God creates a culture of reverence in the community of creation which is antithetical to the prevailing culture of dominion, plunder and accumulation. Commenting on the theological attempt to redeem the biblical command to have dominion over the rest of the creation and to subdue them (Gen. 1:28), Orthodox theologian Metropolitan Paulose Mar Gregorios observes that "Replacing the concept of domination with the concept of stewardship will not lead us very far, for even in the latter there lies the hidden possibility of the objectification and alienation which are the root causes of the sickness of our civilization. Nature would remain some kind of property, owned not by us, of course, but by God, given into our hands for efficient and productive use.[41] Again, the metaphor, "the world is the body of God" becomes a corrective to the Christian doctrine of creation here.

Cosmogony as Source of Liberative Praxis

The modern market economy is a world of disembeddedness. The ecological challenge in our times is to re-embed the human in the land and the community, and it is here we need to turn to the subaltern ecological ethnicities. Ecological ethnicities are communities which have developed "a certain respectful use of the bounty of nature and, consequently, a commitment to create and preserve a technology that interacts with the place and its nonhuman collectivity in a sustainable manner".[42] In the Indian context, ecological ethnicities are the Dalits, adivasis, fisher folk, tribals and other subsistent communities that are being displaced from their commons by global corporations and the state. Reclaiming their commons, their traditional wisdom, practices and rituals are essential to create a world devoid of violence and ecological destruction. These subaltern communities and their movements, as they fight back against the Goliaths of neoliberal globalisation and development with their slings, take inspiration from their cosmogonies. The Ashur myth from the Munda tribe in Central India is one of these cosmogonies which can inspire us in our times.

Ashurs were the industrialists of the early days. They used furnaces for smelting iron, and they continued to do it without any break. That led to the warming up of Earth, the home of all creatures. When the animals, the insects, the trees and all other creatures felt the warming of the earth as unbearable, they approached Singboga, the Sun God, for his intervention to persuade the Ashurs to stop iron smelting. God heard their cry and sent birds as messengers to the Ashurs. So the birds went and told them that God wants the Ashurs to do iron smelting either in the day or in the night only. That was God's compromise to keep the industry going without affecting the creatures. But the Ashurs, who, just like our techno-capitalists, were confident in their ability to discern what was good for all and arrogant enough to believe that God would not think any different from them, did not listen to God's messengers. Finally the Sun God himself came down to Earth as a boy. One day he came to the Ashurs and requested them to stop iron smelting either in the day or night. They got angry, caught him and put him into the furnace. But to their surprise, the boy came out of the furnace

[40] Dietrich, 200.

[41] Gregorios, 87.

[42] Parajuli, 560.

with gold and diamonds on his body and in his hands. The Ashurs wanted to grab all the precious metal from the furnace. So they all jumped into the furnace and asked their wives to bellow faster. Shortly, the wives realised that their husbands had all burnt to ashes. So they wanted to take revenge on the boy, but by that time the boy was being lifted up into the sky. The wives tried to get hold of the hands and feet of the boy. But they all fell back down to the burning earth.

The Ashur myth envisions the earth as the household of all creatures. Human beings are not given any special privileges in this assembly of creation. Rather, they all strive together for the welfare of all. The vision of God in the Ashur myth reveals a God who hears the cry of even the non-human beings. The messengers of the Sun God – the prophets – are the birds. In response to the cry of creation, God incarnates in their midst as a young child – the subaltern one – to redeem the earth and its children from global warming. In that redemptive incarnation and praxis, God shares the pain and agony of his beloved creation and is burnt alive by the forces of death and destruction. But God transcends the shackles of death and emerges as the reigning symbol of eternal hope and life by facilitating the self-destruction of the agents of death. The forces of greed and accumulation take away the creativity of science and technology and make it subservient to the interests of Mammon. But the divine ecosophy has the creative potential to transform the very furnace of global warming into a site for a new politics and spirituality of resistance and victory over death and destruction. This resistance against the powerful is led by a young child with the support and solidarity of the assembly of creatures. Such an absurd vision of transforming the furnace of death into a resource pool for the prosperity and well-being of the whole inhabited earth offers a powerful vision for us to believe in the possibility of a world redeemed of climate injustice. This is the meaning of creation and salvation emerging from the subaltern ecological ethnicities and their social movements.

In the biblical narratives, we also find the visions of creation and new creation emerging from the subaltern communities. The vision of the new heaven and new earth narrated in the book of Revelation is soaked with the blood and sweat of the communities in the colonies of the Roman Empire who were stripped of their dignity, rights and freedom, and transformed into tools for the ends of Empire. What we find in Revelation is the insurrection of the subjugated knowledge of the dispossessed, the displaced and the enslaved, envisioning creation and salvation outside the logic of the prevailing imperial system. As God's creation, all created beings share the trans-systemic being of the absolute Other. The theological anthropology of the first creation story where human beings are created in the image of God needs to be understood from this perspective. For the exiled community, the confession of God the Creator and the affirmation of human beings as created in the image of God is more than a creation story. It is the subaltern theological foundation for resisting the colonisation of their life world.

The book of Revelation emerged in the context of the imperial totalising claims of the Roman Empire. The apocalyptic vision of the new heaven and the new earth is therefore the longings of a community and their landscape objectified by the imperial desire for accumulation, affirming the possibility of a "redeemed earth" beyond the totality. A closer analysis reveals that the apocalypse is a poetics of testimony, a vision that is born out of the determination of a community that refused to attribute the worth to receive "power and wealth and wisdom and might and honor and glory and blessing" to the imperial system. Rather, the dispossessed and the enslaved proclaim: "Worthy is the Lamb that was slain." Said differently, in the absurd poetics of dreaming visions that are illogical to the colonised imaginations, the Other becomes the site for a new discourse and praxis that envision a redeemed earth beyond the logic of the imperial system.

References and Recommended Reading

Abraham, K. C. (1992), *Eco-Justice: A New Agenda for Church's Mission*, Bombay: BUILD.

Dietrich, Gabriele (2001), *A New Thing on Earth*, Delhi: ISPCK.

Gnanadason, Aruna (2005), *Listen to the Women: Listen to the Earth*, Geneva: WCC.

Gregorios, Paulos Mar (1978), *The Human Presence: Ecological Spirituality and the Age of the Spirit*, New York: Amity House.

Kappen, Sebastian (1994), *Tradition, Modernity, Counterculture: An Asian Perspective*, Bangalore: Visthar.

Nalunnakkal, George Mathew (1999), *Green Liberation*, Delhi: ISPCK.

Parajuli, Pramod (2001), "Learning from Ecological Ethnicities: Toward a Plural Political Ecology of Knowledge", in: John A. Grim (ed.), *Indigenous Traditions and Ecology: The Interbeing of Cosmology and Community*, Cambridge: Harvard University Press, 559-589.

Thomas, M. M. (1971), *Salvation and Humanization*, Madras: CLS.

White, Lynn Jr. (1967), "The Historical Roots of Our Ecological Crisis", *Science* 155, 10 March 1967, 1203-1207.

Zachariah, George (2011), *Alternatives Unincorporated: Earth Ethics from the Grassroots*, London: Equinox.

George Zachariah

13. Oceanic Readings on Creation and Redemption

Clive Pearson

On Becoming an Icon

The present situation in critical parts of Oceania entails an ecotheological imperative. The level of ecological threat is widely acknowledged. The tendency of international scholarship is to highlight the vulnerability to rising sea levels of low-lying islands like Kiribati and Tuvalu. For the "seawater peoples" of the region as a whole, the symptoms of ecological degradation are much more extensive. For Ama'amalele Tofaeono, the "eco-dangers" facing Oceania include the depletion of fishing stocks, deforestation, the loss of biodiversity, mining, changed agricultural practices and nuclear-waste dumping and nuclear testing.[1] These matters become theological, owing to the level of Christian profession in Oceania. It is as if the life of faith is embedded in cultural practice and memory. Writing out of the Solomon Islands, Cliff Bird refers to a religio-cultural reading of the household of life where the religious and the cultural are intimately intertwined in a localised manner.[2] Bird describes their "meeting" in a way in which the symbolic world of culture and the gospel cannot function and be understood without each other.[3]

The level of environmental risk is now such that Jione Havea has argued that the "existential predicament" arising must indeed lead to a rethinking of beliefs and understanding.[4] This rethinking weaves together the life of faith with long-established cultural practice. Bird writes of a theological synthesis. Havea considers what this predicament might mean in terms of an Oceanic worldview. He makes reference to the grief associated with the unearthing of the remains of ancestors from beach-front graves and the loss of homes and gathering sites which are no longer secure.

The ecological threat is such that Havea suggests destiny is at hand. It is a common refrain in one form or another. The case was put rather vividly by the former prime minister of Tuvalu, Kamuta Laatasi: "It seems that the world does not care what happens to my people; they want to see everybody floating before they respond."[5] The relatively common response is to look beyond the region and ask the rest of the world a question full of resonances for a "Bible-conscious" people: "Are we not your neighbours? What did we do to deserve this?"[6] The Tuvaluans are destined to become a nation of environmental refugees. Their future prospects shot to global prominence for a brief moment at the Copenhagen climate change conference (COP 15) at the end of 2009. Tuvalu was in the headlines of the world's media because of its proposal that the rise in temperature should be held to no more than 1.5 degrees Celsius. For the Alliance of Small Island States (AOSIS) this level was their bottom line; it was non-

---

1 See Tofaeono.

2 See Bird (2008), 32-102.

3 Bird (2008), 202.

4 Havea (2011).

5 Quoted in Halapua, 38

6 See Horner and Le Gallic.

negotiable.[7] The "Tuvalu Protocol" led to chants and placards of "Tuvalu is the real [or new] deal", "Stand with Tuvalu".[8] For a moment Tuvalu became a global symbol which "interrupted" the discussions of much larger, much more powerful nations; its representatives "drove a wedge" between the islands of the Pacific and the Caribbean and developing nations like India and China. Out of necessity Tuvalu has become highly attuned to matters to do with timing on a world stage.

The capacity of these low-lying atolls to become an icon has not been lost on Pacific theologians. Winston Halapua, for instance, discerns a revelatory dimension in this destiny Havea has named. Tuvalu becomes an Oceanic icon "in which there is the potential to see ourselves". This epiphany is like an ecojustice principle giving voice to the earth. The present-day story of islands like Tuvalu and Kiribati illustrate "our falling short as humans and our abuse of the precious gifts of creation; the ocean is robbed of its potential to give life".[9]

There is a risk in this iconic status and the claim made by Mark Hayes that "we are all Tuvaluans".[10] It can become all too easy for the particular threat and the experience of the most vulnerable to be co-opted into other agendas. The difficulty with which the global community must contend is that the imminent loss of low-lying islands is not the fault of a low consumption people. Halapua is mindful of how the Tuvaluans are "the first victims of global warming".[11] Surveying the region, Tofaeono draws out how rising sea levels "alter not only the existing social and physical structures, but also [damage] the moral and spiritual relations and value-systems of communities".[12] These island sites are not places of privilege.

There is a world of difference between Hayes's global appropriation of Tuvalu and the dissertations written by locals like Tafue Lusama and Maina Talia. Rather than reportage, what one finds here is the authentic voice of the most vulnerable, who will seldom be given the opportunity to speak in venerated theological locations. The thick description of "dangerous effects" of rising sea levels is an account now of everyday living. It bears the mark of an authenticity not so readily conveyed by timelines of impending disasters and statistics – nor always by academic theological discourse. The land is faced with being "re-colonised by the sea"; the people's cry is that "we are trapped". The theological agenda is saturated with questions to do with how the biblical story of Noah is to be read now. Are the "end times" drawing nigh? Where is salvation to be found? Faced with the prospect of relocation and the fragmentation of culture, Talia asks "how can we sing our *fatele* [a traditional song / dance] in a foreign land"?[13]

The implications for theology are far-reaching. The issue at stake is not simply one of how an authentic and viable ecotheology might be constructed and appropriated. There is also a matter of complicity to be addressed. The thesis of Lynn White Jr.

---

7 See Vidal (2009a, 2009b).

8 See Vidal (2009a).

9 Halapua, 38

10 Hayes.

11 Halapua, 36-39.

12 Tofaeono, 41-42.

13 See Talia; Lusama.

concerning Christianity's "huge burden of guilt" for the current ecological crisis is well known to Oceanic writers. In their context the problem for faith is manifested in a two-fold way. Its origins lie in the way in which religion and culture come together and permeate each other. Tofaeono refers to "religio-cultural lifeways".[14] That is the foundation. The heart of the "theo-ecological problems" in the region, Tofaeono argues, are to be found in "the detachment of the traditional doctrines of the indigenous religion ... from the teachings of the Christian religion".[15]

The distinctive nature of this location invites reflection on the nature of voice. Havea insistently refers to the politics of climate change. Who speaks on the matter and in whose interests do they do so? Will the subaltern / local voice be heard? Havea is, in effect, asking where does the story, the telling and conversation – the *talanoa* – of primarily oral cultures, fit within the high-powered politics and economics of climate change?[16] How can this cultural practice secure a space in the midst of the technical expertise of a well-constructed Christian theology and ethics that follows a classical pathway?

The Oceanic writers in the field of ecotheology engage with key biblical ideas and metaphors and make use of prevailing doctrinal constructs. Where they differ, it lies in a sensitivity to cultural ways of knowing, relating and communicating. Bird especially highlights the significance of local forms of epistemology.[17] Tofaeono is adamant that this Euro-American manner of doing theology must be complemented with a subjective-participatory method that will allow for story-telling, oratory and a poetical approach.[18] There is always in the foreground a prophetic dimension because of the level of risk. What is done biblically and theologically cannot be detached from the level of compromise to the "sacred bio-physical whole" in which creation and salvation is discussed.[19]

The Gift of Creation

The coming together of environmental risk and Christian conviction is evident in a number of public statements made by churches in the region. The Pacific churches' consultation on climate change in 2004 released the *Otin Taai Declaration*. The sense of urgency could not be ignored. This ecumenical gathering strove to address "all countries" with regard to the Kyoto Protocol as well as to put pressure on companies that are major producers or consumers of fossil fuels to move towards a less carbon-intensive economy. Other Christians throughout the world were invited to act in solidarity. In practical terms the consultation recommended a concerted education programme throughout the islands and across generations. The pastors were encouraged to equip themselves with an appropriate ecotheology that would help their people "fully understand the relationship of God, nature and the people". The organising theological script was grounded in the participants' belief that the church in Oceania

---

14 Tofaeono, 29.

15 Tofaeono, 18.

16 See Havea (2010); Havea (2011), 46-49; also Halapua, 54-66.

17 Bird (2008), 189.

18 Tofaeono, 21.

19 Tofaeono, 245.

was called by God to affirm their commitment to care for the earth as their response to God's love for creation.[20]

This *Otin Taai Declaration* was developed further at an assembly of the Pacific Conference of Churches in late 2007. One of the opening additional paragraphs embraced a relatively new development in an island hermeneutic. The link was made between Oceania and the indigenous concept of *moana* (meaning "ocean" or "sea"). Now there is an explicit connection made with the doctrine of creation: "Our *Moana*, our Oceania is our gift from God". It is "a part of God's creation". The churches in the Pacific are part of the whole body of Christ. In this place, standing at this *turanga wae wae*, these "dwellers of this ocean" are, in effect, the representatives for the worldwide community. It is "our duty to be stewards of this gift".[21]

What is distinctive about this reading of a doctrine of creation is the primary role assigned to the third day of the Priestly narrative in Genesis 1:6-8. The emphasis is not so much on the creation of humankind in the image of God. There is no desire to balance an anthropocentric interpretation of the text through a balancing act of identifying the seventh day, the Sabbath, as the crown of creation. It is the ocean that commands attention. It does so in a way which is at odds with the way in which the Hebrew people associate the sea and all its depths with chaos.

Such an ecotheological strategy should come as no surprise. Several decades ago, theologians in the region had elected to think in terms of Oceania rather than the Pacific.[22] Far too often the latter designation was co-opted by the much larger countries on the Pacific Rim. The effect was to render the islands small, insignificant, invisible. With respect to a global understanding of climate change, Halapua would argue the islanders then become "powerless people".[23] What had already been proposed was that the region should think of itself as the Liquid Continent. The islands might be small but the ocean which embraced them was large.

Halapua has taken this idea a step further. His theological initiative for critical times such as these is to offer a theology which bears the name *theomoana*. The comparison is with the "landlocked" theologies of the Euro-American West and its doctrinal constructs. The preference is for a wrestling with the formative metaphor of the ocean with its symbols of waves, currents, interconnectedness, rhythms, surfaces and depths, and hence mystery.[24] Rather than seeing the waters as a source of threat, Halapua argues that the ocean is a "gift and it has the capacity to be a life-giver". For Tofaeono, Oceania is indeed "a home created and given by the Creator God" for those who inhabit this watery part of planet Earth.[25] It furnishes a way of life for the *tangata moana*, the people of the sea.[26] The very heart of a *theomoana* is to recognise creation's gift and resist instrumental values which have so often exploited and commodified the ocean in the service of colonialism and globalisation.

---

[20] The *Otin Taai Declaration* (2004) was subsequently published by the World Council of Churches.

[21] Halapua, 96.

[22] Tuwere (1995), 9; Kamu, 15.

[23] Halapua, 76.

[24] Halapua, 3-5, 79.

[25] Tofaeono, 58

[26] Halapua, 44.

This "embrace of the waves" also has the capacity to weave in the history and future prospects of its people. Both Halapua and Havea look back to a mythic past in which these "seawater peoples" navigated the unknown in their *waka* [canoes] and established formative patterns of culture. The metaphor of *moana* allows for a connection to be made between home and migration and being diasporic. It thus offers an ancestral link to myths and stories for communities confronting the likelihood of imminent relocation. Havea wonders whether these people "are destined to return to the deep from which they came".[27] Tofaeono notes that home becomes fluid and flexible.[28] Unlike in the case of other indigenous theologies, their understanding of temporal cycles is not only circular, but allow for a narrative of migration patterned on the oceanic currents and not only upon the waves. Their relationship to the Liquid Continent, God's gift, an act of creation, is very different, then, from the experience of others facing rising sea levels and the inundation of deltas in lands with abundant hinterlands. The tendency to place Kiribati and Tuvalu in a list which includes Bangladesh, for instance, is too generic and plays down the significance of an oceanic hermeneutic.

There is an earthy, landed side to this watery way of life, of course. The threat to sedentary habitable places, sacred spaces, gathering locations spawns the prophetic urgency of concern. It is evident that in an Oceanic setting the land cannot be seen apart from the *moana*. The two are part of the whole. The vision lying behind the *Otin Taai Declaration* bound the land (*vanua*, *whenua*, *fonua*, *enua*) and the ocean into an interrelated, holistic view of life.

The most notable island description of land and its symbolic place is Sevati Tuwere's ground-breaking work on the Fijian *vanua*.[29] For Bird the land is a key starting point to a theology that is contextual. It bears witness to the "life-giving presence" of the self-transcendent life of the triune God. The land "stands open to divine premonition and providence". In his *pepesa* theology the land becomes sacramental. It possesses *mana* (esteem, reverence): its rhythms, cycles and processes are occasions for celebrating and remembering. It is "the open house of God".[30]

From the perspective of a Christian doctrine of creation what becomes especially pertinent for ecological reasons is the place assigned to humankind. There is not the same anthropocentric primacy which has so often characterised the dominant theological trajectories of the Christian faith. The distinction between the sacred and the secular that is so familiar in the West is not prevalent. For Bird, the land is woven together in a relationship with all beings into a continuity and community of life. There is interdependence and reciprocity.[31]

Creation and Salvation

The Oceanic perspective on an ecotheological reading of creation and salvation presupposes a holistic view of these religious and cultural lifeways. It recognises the ambiguous ecological effect of the mission-shaped Christian faith that accompanied

---

[27] Havea (2011), 36-38.

[28] Tofaeono, 37

[29] See Tuwere (2002),

[30] See Bird (2008), 193-197.

[31] See Bird (2001).

colonialism. It is standard practice for those writing in the field to cite well-documented reports on Tofaeono's "eco-dangers". It is not uncommon for a raft of biblical stories and selected doctrines to emerge which then becomes an organising text for the sake of reading these "signs of the times".

There is no wholesale borrowing of an ecological hermeneutic of Scripture from somewhere else. There is nevertheless astute insight. Havea is gifted in intertexuality and can place an event, a text in its own right, alongside a biblical narrative. The separation of the waters and the sky on the third day and the construction of a dome pose a disturbing question: "Is God's creation falling apart? Has the force that moved the waters away from the face of the Earth failed?"[32] The *Otin Taai Declaration* was at pains to "say a word about God's promise to Noah not to flood the earth again". This covenantal confession possesses an understandably popular attraction, but is also a liability in the light of Havea's queries above. The critical reply for the shapers of the *Otin Taai Declaration* is that the sea's rising is "not an act of God". For a *theomoana* this is not a possibility. The integrity of God's gift of the watery creation and its capacity to be a giver of life must be preserved. The onus is placed on humankind and its failure to be a representative guardian. There is no ostensible invocation of the rhetoric of a fallen creation or a doctrine of sin. The *Otin Taai Declaration* prefers to use the public language of human economic and consumer activities. It calls for its readers to respond to God's covenant with Noah and "act in love towards creation".

The practical situation in which the islanders find themselves is such that the need for an ecological rendering of the theological reflection on the theodicy problem becomes an imperative. The technical syllogisms of this problem to do with the goodness and power of God are not named. Lusama believes the matter presents itself in the tendency for these atoll-dwellers to blame themselves and look upon God as punitive. For a people inclined towards a literal (what Tofaeono elsewhere calls an "ordinary"[33]) interpretation of Scripture, it is critical to create some hermeneutical distance from the Noah story itself. The problem lies not in the promise highlighted in the *Otin Taai Declaration*, but in the co-opting power of too close an identification with a sinful generation. The most pressing task is to present an alternative script and take issue with a theory of retribution. For Lusama, the most appropriate biblical paradigm to place alongside Noah, a symbol of hope, is in this instance the innocent suffering of Job. The integrity of lament and cry of the heart is preserved. The salvific, redemptive love of God is manifested in and through the suffering, cross-bound Christ whose public ministry draws him to the least for the sake of good news. There is no formal cosmic or wisdom Christology here. The redemptive significance lies in the release of the innocent from a punitive text and a retaliatory God. The Christian vocation and mission, then, is to work in solidarity with innocent victims.[34]

In terms of doctrinal constructs, the common practice is to opt for a model of God that is self-consciously panentheistic. Halapua and Bird both argue that this line of approach furnishes a "pervading presence" of God[35] and establishes a better balance

---

32 Havea (2011), 39.

33 Tofaeono, 148.

34 Lusama, 77-110.

35 See Bird (2008), 166-169.

between transcendence and immanence. It It enables cultures to understand the nature and being of God in a way that is more immediate and yet not animistic. The primary benefit of this redress lies in the degree to which it makes room for traditional customs, a holistic view of the world and that flowing sense of relationality and connection which pervades the religio-cultural lifeways of islanders. The translational model of mission which accompanied the arrival of the Christian faith in the islands – and became formative as a result – was inclined too far towards the otherness of God. The redemptive effect of panentheism, then, is to overcome the separation of a received Christian tradition and indigenous beliefs.

The Oceanic writer most overtly concerned with the theological axis of creation and salvation is Tofaeono. The two belong together. The biblical theme of creation cannot stand apart from the soteriological side of faith and act as if it is simply a prologue to history. The purpose and goal of creation is itself attributed to Christ. It is now time to "redefine the relationship between God, humanity and the whole of creation" with the purpose of minimising ecological destruction in mind. For Tofaeono, creation and salvation must be the central *locus* for the mission of God. They must be "contextually realised" and "authentically interpreted".[36]

There is a panentheistic tendency in Tofaeono's theology as well. Of seminal significance for the case he mounts is a difference in the way God is viewed. He argues that the Euro-American optic is more likely to emphasise the human-like attributes of God. For his context in *fa'Samoa*, God – or Atua – is both a Being and a Thing. In a similar vein Bird will speak of a plurality of spirits which pervade the household of life and which a panentheistic reading of God might recognise as apprehensions or anticipations of the divine.[37] This Oceanic alternative lends itself to an understanding of God which is communal, interrelational and interdependent. Tofaeono is wishing to take leave of what he terms "distorted views" of God, so often established upon the attribute of power.[38] Here Tofaeono is critiquing theologies that are essentially anthropocentric and established upon the primacy of the male voice and experience.

This tendency towards panentheism leads itself in turn towards making use of the cultural concept of the *aiga* or "household". The term can be extended metaphorically to include more than a place and an extended family. Tofaeono's reading of the *aiga* mirrors the familiar theological notion of creation as the *oikonomia* of God. The household becomes the *aiga o Atua* (the household of God). It is also the household of life across time and space; it is thoroughly communal, including the natural world as well as ancestors and those who lie before us in the future. Participation in the *aiga* is mediated through a diversity of attributes in keeping with a panentheist emphasis. This framework furnished by the *aiga* thus allows for a "local symbol" to speak in a manner which includes "the origins and locus of one's identity". It allows for the integration and weaving together of theological ideas and indigenous experience.[39] It enables an ecotheological exposition to happen.[40]

[36] Tofaeono, 19-20.

[37] See Bird (2008), 192.

[38] Tofaeono, 235.

[39] Tofaeono, 234.

[40] Tofaeono, 187.

It is not surprising that thinking on the *aiga* leads rather easily into trinitarian thinking. For Tofaeono the triune God is looked upon both as "Creator and an intimate part of the community of creation". This is a communal God who "creates by relating and participating". Such is the nature of the metaphor of the *aiga* that God is conceived of as a "family in God's self by ways of relating to each other, but also through relational ties to creation, the world with all its parts become inseparable members of the single whole".

This focus on the Trinity has become an emerging pattern under pressure of the ecological risk. The earlier Pasifikan biblical and theological strategies have been occasioned by the desire to rethink the missionary legacy and find a distinctive Oceanic hermeneutic with respect to Scripture and, theologically, a distinct Christological voice. The pattern described by Tofaeono is replicated – with variations – by Bird and Taipisia Leilua. What is most striking about Bird's reading of the relational Trinity is how this understanding of God precedes first (in terms of experience and knowing) from God the Father / Creator and the Spirit. It is a religio-cultural perspective of the Trinity which will lead into the "determinative revelation and knowledge of God" in and through Jesus who "is the culmination of life".[41] In a way which is not yet thought through sufficiently, Bird draws a distinction between "present salvation" and salvation that is more eschatological.

The strength of these Oceanic readings lies in the attention given to the doctrine of creation. Their panentheistic tendencies enable a strong connection to be made with those cultural lifeways. There is an obvious sense of urgency facing the theological task. There is a need for this to be communicated to a people, the majority of whom Tofaeono describes as being "not interested in reading and writing books". These are "story-oriented communities".[42] There is less of an overt focus on naming salvation in formal theological categories. The intimations of such salvation are hidden away in talk of home, belonging, the rhythms of waves, land, and in a selection of biblical texts. In recent times there has been an increasing recourse to the doctrine of the Trinity in association with indigenous religio-cultural symbols. Leilua looks forward to a new covenant, a new creation in Christ: that Oceanic heaven, he declares, "must have a sea".[43]

References and Recommended Reading

Bird, Cliff (2001), "A Theological and Ethical Exploration of Pepesa [Land] as Community in the Marovo Context, Solomon Islands", M.Th. thesis, Pacific Theological College, Suva.

--- (2008), "Pepesa – The Household of Life: A Theological Exploration of Land in the Context of Change in the Solomon Islands", Unpublished Ph.D. thesis, Charles Sturt University, Sydney.

Halapua, Winston (2008), *Waves of God's Embrace: Sacred Perspectives for the Ocean*, Norwich: Canterbury.

Havea, Jione (2010), "The Politics of Climate Change: A Talanoa from Oceania", *International Journal of Public Theology*, Vol. 4, 345-355.

--- (2011), "Rising Seas, Drifting Bones, Dispersing Homes", in: Norman Habel and Peter Trudinger (eds.), *Water: A Matter of Life and Death*, Adelaide: ATF, 35-48.

[41] Bird (2008), 195.

[42] Tofaeono, 21.

[43] Leilua, 289-292.

Hayes, Mark (2006), "We Are All Tuvaluans", *Griffith Review*, Winter, 173-186.
Horner, Christopher and Le Gallic, Gilliane (2004), *The Disappearing of Tuvalu: Trouble in Paradise* (DVD), Watertown: ETC Production.
Kamu, Lalomilo (1995), "A Response to Sevati Tuwere", *Pacific Journal of Theology*, Series 2, 15-18.
Leilua, Taipisia (2011), "Covenant for a New Oceania: A Theological Response to the Environmental Crisis From a Samoan Perspective", Ph.D. thesis, Melbourne College of Divinity.
Lusama, Tafue (2004), "Punishment of the Innocent: The Problem of Global Warming with Special Reference to Tuvalu", M.Th. thesis, Tainan Theological College and Seminary.
Otin Taai Declaration (2004), Geneva: WCC.
Talia, Maina (2009), "Towards Fatele Theology: A Contextual Theological Response in Addressing Threats of Global Warming in Tuvalu", M.Th. thesis, Tainan Theological College and Seminary.
Tofaeono, Ama'amalele (2000), *Eco-Theology Aiga – The Household of Life: A Perspective from the Living Myths and Traditions of Samoa*, Erlangen: Verlag für Mission und Ökumene.
Tuwere, Sevati (1995), "An Agenda for the Theological Task of the Church in Oceania", *Pacific Journal of Theology*, Series 2, 13, 5-14
--- (2002), *Vanua: Towards a Fijian Theology of Place*, Suva: Institute of Pacific Studies.
Vidal, John (2009a), "Copenhagen Deal Breaks Down as Developing Nations Split Over 'Tuvalu Protocol'", *The Guardian*, 9 December 2009.
--- (2009b), "Vulnerable Nations at Copenhagen Summit Reject 2C Target", *The Guardian*, 10 December 2009.

Clive Pearson

14. Global Ecumenical Theology

Martien E. Brinkman

In this contribution I will first discuss two methodological questions, namely the question of the relation between a global ecumenical theology and concrete contexts and the question of its subjects: who is doing global ecumenical theology where? Secondly, I will analyse the relationship between creation and salvation in the bilateral dialogues of the last four decades. Thirdly, I will sketch the state of the current debate on an ecumenical creation theology. Finally, I will link the implied idea of creation to that of salvation. A critical sacramental approach to creation provides this link.

Two Methodological Reflections

What could that be, a global ecumenical theology? Do we really presume a global theology like a global economy or a global market? It will be one of the main challenges of world Christianity not to manifest a form of ecumenism that is just a stained-glass version of the cosmopolitanism of the current political and economic empires of the world. Their cosmopolitanism is in reality not more than a bleak kind of universalism and a badly hidden form of imperialism. What we need is not a universal theology in abstraction of concrete contexts. True universality does not arise through abstraction but through the apparently unlimited possibility of recognising the authenticity of particular experiences in different parts of the world. Authentic universality (or catholicity) always concerns a particularity that transcends its own limits.[1]

The well-known story of Martin Luther King's "I have a Dream" speech at the end of the march on Washington in 1963 illustrates this nicely. At a specific place and at a specific time, King articulated his dream of the end of racial segregation between black and white. This particular experience by King has since then been recognised by millions of people all over the world because they had similar experiences of racial segregation and they too longed passionately for the end of it. A bridge could be built between King's dream and the dreams of others and therefore it could acquire universal significance. The same holds true for the letters from prison of Dietrich Bonhoeffer and the diaries of Anne Frank and Mahatma Gandhi. The universal recognition of their authenticity is still impressive up to now. Therefore, our conclusion must be that a global ecumenical theology does not per definition need to be an abstract theology, detracted from concrete contexts.

The next question is "Who is doing global ecumenical theology and where can it be found?" Confronted with this question many will immediately point to the World Council of Churches (WCC), but only one-third of World Christianity is represented in this ecumenical body. The WCC represents, thus, a minority in world Christianity. The WCC does not include the Roman Catholic Church, most of the Pentecostal and Evangelical churches and many recently founded large regional indigenous churches.[2] The

---

1 Eboussi-Boulaga (1981), 114.

2 Brinkman (1995), 145-166.

WCC Commission on Faith and Order, however, has the Roman Catholic Church as official member and in the Global Christian Forum the WCC is in a continuous dialogue with Pentecostals and Evangelicals. Moreover, there are, in almost all parts of the world (in Europe, Africa, Asia, the Middle East, Latin America, the Pacific, North America, etc.), regional Councils of Churches supported by the WCC with a broader membership than the WCC. So, although Geneva is no longer the unique ecumenical centre of the world – there are nowadays other centres elsewhere in the world as well (Rome, Lausanne, Singapore, Hong Kong, Jerusalem, etc.) – the WCC is still one of the main catalysts of ecumenical reflection. Current ecumenism has become more and more a regional enterprise focused on the main issues of specific parts of the world,[3] but in spite of this regionalisation WCC publications still play their (modest) role as antennas of ecumenical developments on a worldwide scale. That is the reason why I still use them as point of reference in this contribution.

Creation and Salvation in Bilateral Ecumenical Dialogues

The official bilateral dialogues between the main church traditions express a wide variety of concepts of salvation. This variety mirrors the variety of salvation concepts in the New Testament. Although many traditions foster a certain preference for one or two concepts, they, generally speaking, do not deny the legitimacy of other concepts. It is for example clear that the Lutherans opt for justification as their central concept of salvation, the reformed opt for justification in relation to sanctification, the Orthodox for *theosis*, the Anglicans for incarnation, the Roman Catholics for incarnation in connection with sacrifice, the Methodists for renewal and the Pentecostals for holiness. Among these traditions the Lutherans and the Orthodox are often the most reluctant to recognise the rough equivalence of the different concepts of salvation.[4]

Unavoidably, these dialogues express the special attention given to the role that the church plays in the process of applying these different concepts of salvation in human life, because the aim of the dialogues is often an official agreement in which the interaction between the churches involved is structured officially. That explains their ecclesiological focus. Between the lines, however, the implications for the relation between creation and salvation are clearly recognisable.

Among the different church traditions four approaches regarding the relation between creation and salvation can be discerned: a strong focus on justification and its juridical terminology, on sanctification and personal renewal and its "physical" terminology (rebirth, renewal, growth, etc.), on liberation and freedom and its political terminology and on communion and its relational and participatory terminology.

Especially in the first approach, creation is more or less a precondition for salvation. It is the "fallen" creation that makes salvation necessary. So, creation and salvation can clearly be distinguished from each other. In the second approach creation has more to do with the eschaton than with the proton, more with the future than with the world's past. Creation becomes mainly re-creation and cannot be distinguished clearly from salvation anymore. To the contrary, it is the core component of the idea of salvation. The same holds true for the third approach. It may be regarded as the societal

[3] Tsetsis, 461-468.

[4] Rodger and Vischer, 53.

variant of the more individualistic second approach. Here, too, creation means re-creation and points to the divine initiative and the human involvement in this initiative. In the fourth approach creation is again a precondition of salvation. In this case, unlike the first approach, the reference to creation does not function as an explanation of the need of salvation, but as a guarantee of the material substance of salvation. It offers the opportunity to be incorporated into something that already exists substantially. None of these four approaches, however, offers an instructive insight into the interconnectedness of creation and salvation as two interwoven but still discernible concepts.[5]

A Sketch of the State of the Debate on Ecumenical Creation Theology

Since the sixth Assembly of the WCC in Vancouver in 1983, the concept of the "integrity of creation" has been introduced in ecumenical circles, eliciting a substantial corpus of literature.[6] From a dogma-historical point of view, this concept is of long standing. It was frequently employed in the history of doctrine to indicate the paradisiac condition (*status integritatis*), upset by the fall (*status corruptionis*) and again restored by the redemption in Christ (*restitutio in integrum*). An echo of this classic scheme could still be heard in the way the official report of the seventh World Assembly of the WCC in Canberra (Australia) in 1991 relates the groans of creation exclusively to the consequences of sin and not, for example, also to the capriciousness and cruelty of evolution – as geologists and biologists have taught us. It speaks romantically and naïvely about an original "ecological equilibrium" and points to the covenant with Noah that has been broken![7]

Far more promising is the development of a "theology of life", since 1994, by leading ecumenical theologians such as Julio de Santa Ana, Martin Robra and Larry Rasmussen.[8] The first presupposition of this theology, in which ecology and ethics are integrated, is the presupposition that belief in God the Creator implies a certain independence for the earth. At the moment that God calls the earth into existence, God is distinguished from the earth. The earth is different from God, but is the work of God's hands. The image of the relation of the artist to her or his work can be useful here. The artist has to be distinguished from his work. She can even distance herself from it. But she always remains connected with it. She can be recognised in it. Hence, several medieval Christian thinkers – among others Nicholas of Cusa – spoke simultaneously of the *aliud* and *non-aliud* (other and non-other) character of creation in relation to its Creator. This duality implies that radical transcendence and radical immanence are no real options for creation theology. Like the relation between an artist and her work there remains a relation between Creator and creation, but it is always an indirect relation, never automatically given. It needs interpretation. Theologically speaking, creation can never be considered a totally closed book and also never a totally open book.

[5] With his consent, I derived this division into four approaches from Rienk Lanooy's almost concluded Ph.D. manuscript on the idea of salvation in the bilateral dialogues of the last four decades of the former century.

[6] See, for example, the contribution from an African perspective by Jesse Mugambi (1987).

[7] Report of Section I: "Giver of Life –Sustain Your Creation!" in Kinnamon, 54-57. For the inviolability of the covenant with Noah, see Genesis 9:8-17.

[8] See Santa Ana; Robra; Rasmussen.

The Gospel according to John speaks about God who in Christ enters his own realm, but was not received by his own (John 1:11). The tension between recognition ("his own") and non-recognition ("not received") requires a great measure of differentiation in the relationship between God and the world.

The second presupposition of a theology of life is a twofold concept of nature: nature as an encompassing, more or less neutral concept and as a normative concept. When nature is interpreted as a neutral concept, human existence is considered primarily to be just part of a broader natural world. Nature can then be equated with concepts such as "world" and "earth". However, "nature" is actually an ambivalent concept. It points as much to tsunamis, hurricanes, earthquakes and all kinds of horrible diseases as to majestic mountains, fertile valleys, magnificent birds and miraculous recoveries.

In spite of such experiences of the ambivalence of the surrounding natural world, Jews, Christians and Muslims continue to speak about the destination of the world in association with God's providence. Such divine providence does not exclude, but includes human freedom (free will) and natural contingency. Traditional concepts such as *causa prima* and *secunda*, *concursus* and *cooperatio* are nowadays often replaced by images like those of the servant, steward, trustee, tiller and keeper. Nature then becomes a more normative concept. It is no longer understood only as a given entity, but as an ongoing historical process, a *creatio continua*. Nature is here equated with the essence of everything that exists, including its potentialities. These potentialities refer to a destination. And this idea of destination allows us to speak about human responsibility. It introduces the ethical aspect into every kind of creation theology.

The third presupposition of a theology of life is therefore the integration of eco-theology and ethics. This integration can be called the main characteristic of this theology. One of the problems that previously arose in international ecumenical discussions of environmental questions was the tendency of people from the South to see this as a luxury problem posed by people from Northern industrialised countries. However, this tendency has changed dramatically over the past two decades. While contexts and starting points radically differ, it is now agreed that environmental issues are indeed global ecumenical issues. Dwindling natural resources have been recognised as posing problems to the countries in the South as well. Access to and use of the natural resources and global life-support systems is distributed very unevenly over human populations. This "colonisation" of the biosphere is mainly due to the high per capita environmental impact in the North. If the inequality in the level of exploitation of the biosphere persists and if overall levels of environmental pressure will remain above the buffering capacities embedded in the biosphere, then the consequences will manifest themselves particularly in the poorest parts of the world where population growth is the highest. Nowadays resource scarcity coupled with social inequality leads to conflicts over natural resources such as fertile land, water and oil.

Hence, environmental concerns can no longer be regarded as in conflict with social concerns. Social justice cannot be done apart from a healthy environment, and a sustainable environment will not come about without greater social justice. The biblical concept of social justice includes healthy relationships in creation as a whole. So, there is a clear link between poverty, powerlessness, social conflict and environmental degradation. One of the great merits of a theology of life that emerged in the 1990s is to have established this link firmly.

When we start from the presupposition that (a) the earth is the work of God's hands, but is not divine, (b) "nature" understood as "earth" or "world" is an ambivalent concept, but understood as "essence" is a normative concept and (c) environmental and social concerns are intrinsically intertwined, we are still confronted with a number of unresolved questions. Let us explore only the most important of these.[9]

If humans are created in the image of God, how do they, as participants in God's creative work, find an adequate balance between mystery and mastery? The mystery character of all created things confronts us with their intrinsic value. The mastery character of our calling to be image of God confronts us with the necessity to indicate priorities. Psalm 8 expresses this tension nicely. On the one hand, it articulates the humble position of humans in God's creation. It asks: "What is mankind that you are mindful of them, human beings that you care for them?" (NIV). On the other hand, it is fully aware of the high position attributed to humans as image of God: "You made him a little lower than the heavenly beings and crowned him with glory and honour" (Ps. 8:4 and 5, NIV). It is clear that humans take a special position in God's creation, but what does this special position imply exactly? We all know about the historical abuse of Genesis 1:28-30 with its command to humans to "subdue" the earth and to "rule" over the animals and to consider all the products of the earth as theirs. Where, then, can one find the balance between our unique position as image of God and the command to take the lead and our humble position just as dust among all God's other creatures and to be fully aware that a (hu)man's life is like grass: "[H]e flourishes like a flower of the field; the wind blows over it and it is gone, and its place remembers it no more" (Ps. 103:15-16, NIV).

A second intriguing question is whether creation's natural order is altered by sin. Much traditional theology assumed that the entry of sin into the world brought predation, decay and physical death to the natural world. The Faith and Order report "God in Nature and History"(1967) denied the existence of such an unambiguous state of original perfection, the so-called *status integritatis*, although we have observed (see above) that there are still allusions to it in the report of the seventh World Assembly of the WCC in Canberra in 1991.[10] Geologists and biologists have taught us that death belongs to life. The lifetime of everything on earth is limited. The genes of all that lives on earth have an expiry date. Life is unthinkable without the recurring cycles of growth and decay. These cycles belong to the goodness of God's creation. We are, however, also fully aware of the disturbance of these cycles through human activities. Sometimes the traces of these disturbances are centuries old. Sometimes they are also the result of irresponsible human behaviour. So, in a certain sense, human sin has indeed changed ecosystems and consequently the structure of God's created order. The question whether sin has altered the natural order therefore requires a nuanced answer.

A third question pertains to a theology of place (on earth). Traditional Western theology follows an agenda of time, asking when God's action in history was initiated and will be completed in history. Some non-Western cultures, however, focus instead on questions of place. Where is God's reign to be discovered in relation to the soil, the mountains, the water and the sky? If justice means the fullest possible flourishing of

9 For some of these questions, see Granberg-Michaelson.

10 For the text of the impressive report "God in Nature and History", see Vischer, 7-31.

all aspects of human life within given natural constraints, then nothing is more basic to this idea of justice than the space to live. It is the basic condition of all human communities. This leads the North American theologian Sallie McFague to remark that geography will be one of the most crucial aspects of creation theology in future: "Where is the best land and who has access to it? What good space is available on this planet and who controls it? Who cares for it? Who will inherit the land?"[11]

How can these questions about (a) the relation between mystery and mastery, (b) the corrupting influence of sin and (c) space on earth, be related to the question of salvation (redemption)?

Creation and Salvation in Global Ecumenical Theology

Creation and salvation are not the same, but they can also not be separated. In the section on creation and salvation in bilateral dialogues, I referred to the different concepts of salvation applied in these dialogues. Sometimes the meaning of salvation here comes very close to that of creation, but creation is then primarily understood as re-creation. It is not meant with reference to the current, ambivalent, empirical world. Creation as re-creation is a normative concept and has everything to do with the restoration of the destination of nature in Christ. Creation as re-creation is almost a synonym for salvation. Creation is more or less absorbed by salvation. However, the two concepts, creation and salvation, can no longer be properly distinguished on this basis. Then creation (including the empirical earth) disappears behind the soteriological horizon.

The word "salvation" presupposes that one is saved from something. It is an indication of an act of liberation (redemption) in an already existing world. In Christian theology that world always preserves its own value. Hence, salvation can never be a substitute for creation. To say it in the words of Joseph Sittler at the third World Assembly of the WCC in New Delhi in 1961: "A doctrine of redemption is meaningful only when it swings within the larger orbit of a doctrine of creation. For God's creation of earth cannot be redeemed in any intelligible sense of the word apart from a doctrine of the cosmos which is man's home, his definite place, the theatre of his selfhood under God, in cooperation with his neighbor, and in caring-relationship with nature."[12] And in one of the sections of the report of the Fourth World Conference of Faith and Order at Montreal in 1963 one finds the following question: "If Christ was flesh and blood and if he is to be the Lord of all creation, how can we, his followers, so often flee into a spirituality that divorces God from earth and its possibilities?"[13]

Every answer to this question has to deal with the relationship between creation and salvation. For the Christian faith there cannot be a contrast between the Creator God who gives everything its place and the Saviour God who, through the cross and resurrection of Jesus Christ, liberates us from the harmful impact of our bondage to sin. The Father of Jesus Christ is the same as the Creator God who does not abandon the works of his hands (Ps. 138:8; 146:6; 148:6). It is especially in an ecumenical doctrine of the

---

[11] McFague, 101.

[12] See the report on Sittler's address to the assembly, with the title "Called to Unity", in WCC (1962), *The New Delhi Report*, 15.

[13] Rodger and Vischer, 44.

sacraments that both creation and salvation can find their proper place. The materiality, the earthliness, of the sacraments indicates that we do not rise beyond the bounds of our daily, earthly existence in the salvific experience given through the sacrament. It is not only the symbolic language we use during the celebration of the sacraments that connects us with the earth. The elements of the sacraments themselves – water, bread, wine, oil, salt and incense – time and again bring us to the centre of creation. The sacraments touch and are also touched by all aspects of human life. As tools of God's redemptive activity the sacraments have an exemplary and critical function towards the use and abuse of nature. They contribute to the transformation of the world according to God's purpose for humanity and creation.[14] The interaction between word and action in the sacraments qualifies the "elements" and turns their use into a salvific experience. In Christian worship the sacraments make use of the elements of the created world to manifest the presence of the triune God among us and in us.[15]

All earthly symbols have an intrinsic ambivalence. They never express a simple transparency. Their transparency depends fully upon the setting in which they are placed. The "elements" of the sacraments provide an excellent illustration of such a need for a setting. The sacraments offer this setting. In the sacraments our daily earthly existence is not pushed aside or shattered forever but put in such a light that it is seen from another, less ambivalent, perspective.

Creation and sacrament do not simply overlap. Our earthly existence is not automatically a sacramental existence either. Rooted in our daily existence, the sacraments offer a salvific sense of direction to our ambivalent existence. Christian theology traditionally emphasised that the Holy Spirit makes us participants in this salvific event. It is the Holy Spirit that relates the fragility and vulnerability of our earthly existence to the essence of Jesus' life, his cross and resurrection, revealing the perspectives contained in the relation between creation and sacrament for the sake of the whole of creation in all its parts.[16]

Creation and sacrament are, hence, not primarily connected because of the incarnation, but because of Jesus' cross and resurrection. An incarnational, sacramental approach always runs the risk of an uncritical sacralisation of earthly existence. The emphasis, however, on cross and resurrection, creates the space for a catharsis, a purification. The linking pin between creation and sacrament is here the preparedness to die and rise with Jesus in his cross and resurrection. So, it is never a self-evident relation. It is a relation based upon faith, upon the preparedness for self-sacrifice. It is the way from negation to confirmation.

At the basis of this relation there is no self-evident transparency but a dynamic event of absence and presence, given in all the earthly symbols. This dynamic event can be interpreted as identical with the dynamic dialectics of the relation of cross and

---

[14] WCC (1982), 146

[15] Kinnamon, 57.

[16] For the emphasis on the work of the Holy Spirit in relation to the sacraments, see one of the main publications of the Groupe des Dombes, "The Holy Spirit, the Church and the Sacraments". The influence of this informal French-speaking ecumenical group left its traces clearly in the Reformed-Roman Catholic dialogue document "Towards a Common Understanding of the Church". For the text of this document, see Gross, Meyer and Rusch (2000), 780-818, especially 804-805.

resurrection. Therefore, the dynamics of cross and resurrection form a more adequate "model" for the relationship between creation and sacrament than the model of incarnation. That is a too static model to account adequately for the dialects of absence and presence that is characteristic of Christian experience. This dialectical view of Christ's presence in the sacraments leaves more room for Christ's real path of life through death to resurrection as formulated in the old baptismal and eucharistic prayers.[17]

It is this real-life experience that connects us with all the earthly realities as well. The sacraments of baptism and Eucharist are impressive symbols of the efficacy of this link between sacrament and creation. The WCC's so-called Lima text, *Baptism, Eucharist and Ministry*, of 1982 calls baptism "the sign of the new life through Jesus Christ" and underscores that it makes Christians partakers of the mystery of Christ's death and resurrection. This participation gives them a new ethical orientation under the guidance of the Holy Spirit. And the same Lima text states that the Eucharist is the great thanksgiving to the Father on behalf of the whole of creation, for the world which God has reconciled in Christ is present in the bread and wine of every Eucharist. Bread and wine, fruits of the earth and human labour, are presented to the Father in faith and thanksgiving. "The Eucharist thus signifies what the world is to become: an offering and hymn of praise to the creator, a universal communion in the body of Christ, a kingdom of justice, love and peace in the Holy Spirit."[18]

The relationship between creation and sacrament shows us that the relationship between creation and salvation has to be a nuanced one. When we speak about God's salvation in creation, it means predominantly "blessing". God the Creator grants salvation in the form of an affirmative act, and we call that act a blessing. The salvation that God in Christ grants is primarily salvation as redemption – redemption from the bondage of sin. It is a critical, dialectical act that presumes negation (dying with Christ) and confirmation (rising with Christ). The result is purification, a real catharsis. And finally the salvation that God through the Holy Spirit grants is mainly empowerment, inspiration to sustenance and to renewal. It is again an affirmative, sanctifying act. None of these acts can be separated from the other. They mutually presume each other. No redemption without blessing and empowerment, no blessing without redemption and empowerment and no empowerment without redemption and blessing. Their interconnectedness prevents any one-sided interpretation of salvation with an exclusive emphasis on either material blessing or merely subjective or objective forgiveness or (internal or external) spiritual renewal. All the above-mentioned aspects of the concept of salvation are incorporated in the sacraments. The sacraments presume all three these aspects of salvation. Therefore, they offer an instructive illustration of what the relationship between creation and salvation really encompasses.

References and Recommended Reading

Briggs, John, Oduyoye, Mercy Amba and Tsetsis, Georges (eds.) (2004), *A History of the Ecumenical Movement, Volume. 3: 1968-2000*, Geneva: WCC.

Brinkman, Martien E. (1995), "Ecumenicals and Evangelicals", in: Martien E. Brinkman, *Progress in*

[17] It was especially the French liturgist Louis-Marie Chauvet who asked attention for the role of cross and resurrection instead of incarnation in his sacramental approach to the relatedness of creation and salvation. See his classic work *Symbol and Sacrament* (1995).

[18] WCC (1982), 10-11 (E4) and 2 (B4).

Unity? Fifty Years of Theology within the World Council of Churches: 1945-1995: A Study Guide, Louvain: Peeters / Grand Rapids: Eerdmans, 145-166.

--- (1999a), "Horizon of an Ecumenical Creation Theology", in: Martien E. Brinkman, *Sacraments of Freedom: Ecumenical Essays on Creation and Sacrament – Justification and Freedom*, Zoetermeer: Meinema, 11-31.

--- (1999b), "An Ecumenical Sacramentology", in: Martien E. Brinkman, *Sacraments of Freedom: Ecumenical Essays on Creation and Sacrament – Justification and Freedom*, Zoetermeer: Meinema, 71-90.

Chauvet, Louis-Marie (1995), *Symbol and Sacrament: A Sacramental Reinterpretation of Christian Existence*, Collegeville: Liturgical Press.

Codina, Victor (1994), "Sacraments", in: Ignacio Ellacuria and Jon Sobrino (eds.), *Mysterium Liberationis: Fundamental Concepts of Liberation Theology*, Maryknoll: Orbis, 654-676.

Conradie, Ernst M. (2006), *Christianity and Ecological Theology: Resources for Further Research*, Stellenbosch: SUN Press.

Eboussi-Boulaga, Fabian (1984), *Christianity Without Fetishes: An African Critique and Recapture of Christianity*, Maryknoll: Orbis.

Granberg-Michaelson, Wesley (1994), "Creation in Ecumenical Theology", in: David G. Hallman (ed.), *Ecotheology: Voices from South and North*, Geneva: WCC / Maryknoll: Orbis, 96-106

Gross, Jeffrey, Meyer, Harding and Rusch, William G. (eds.) (2000), *Growth in Agreement II: Reports and Agreed Statements of Ecumenical Conversations on a World Level 1982-1998*, Faith and Order Paper 187, Geneva: WCC / Grand Rapids: Eerdmans.

Groupe des Dombes (1980), "Holy Spirit, the Church and the Sacraments", *One in Christ*, Vol. 18, 234-264.

Kinnamon, Michael (1991), *Signs of the Spirit: Official Report Seventh Assembly WCC*, Geneva: WCC / Grand Rapids: Eerdmans.

McFague, Sallie (1993), *The Body of God: An Ecological Theology*, Minneapolis: Fortress.

Meyer, Harding and Vischer, Lukas (eds.) (1984), *Growth in Agreement: Reports and Agreed Statements of Ecumenical Conversations on a World Level*, Faith and Order Paper 108, New York: Paulist Press / Geneva: WCC.

Mugambi, Jesse N. K. (1987), *God, Humanity and Nature in Relation to Justice and Peace*, Geneva: WCC.

Rasmussen, Larry (1994), "Theology of Life and Ecumenical Ethics", in: David G. Hallman (ed.), *Ecotheology: Voices from South and North*, Geneva: WCC / Grand Rapids: Eerdmans, 112-129

Robra, Martin (1996), "Theology of Life – Justice, Peace, Creation: An Ecumenical Study", *The Ecumenical Review*, Vol. 48, 1, 28-37.

Rodger, Peter C. and Vischer, Lukas (1964), *The Fourth World Conference on Faith and Order: The Report from Montreal 1963*, London: SCM.

Santa Ana, Julio de (1995), *Elements for a Theology of Life*, Geneva: Xerox.

Tsetsis, Georges (2004) "The Significance of Regional Ecumenism", in: Briggs, Oduyoye and Tsetsis (eds.), 461-468

Vischer, Lukas (1968), *New Directions in Faith and Order: Bristol 1967 Reports, Minutes, Documents*, Faith and Order Paper 50, Geneva: WCC.

WCC (1962), The New Delhi Report: The Third Assembly of the World Council of Churches 1961, London: SCM.

--- (1982), *Baptism, Eucharist and Ministry*, Faith and Order Paper 111, Geneva: WCC.

--- (1990), *Baptism, Eucharist* and *Ministry 1982-1990: Report on the Process and Responses*, Faith and Order Paper 149, Geneva: WCC.

Martien E. Brinkman

The Crystal of Salvation *in* Creation – A Postscript

Sigurd Bergmann

"Why is it so difficult to do justice to God's work both of creation and of salvation?", asked Ernst Conradie in his introduction to this volume. Meandering through the many and surprisingly rich contributions to this book, one can state that the difficulties have now definitively been overcome, owing to the cooperative efforts of the many authors. Indeed, these authors have turned the difficulties into highly useful tools. On this basis, the theme addressed in this book can serve as productive challenge not only to eco-theologians but to Christian theology in general. The task to not only relate, but to integrate the doctrines of creation and salvation in a comprehensive vision of God's work has deeply involved theologians in different periods of the history of Christianity and in different regions of its expansion. The various chapters of this book clearly demonstrate how such a task elicits an immense flow of creativity also amidst contemporary challenges.

At the end of the book, the editor's introductory question may even be reformulated: why is it so tremendously fruitful to explore the relation between and integration of creation and salvation? However, one also needs to raise the question: why is it necessary to reconstruct the theological past for the sake of the theological future in the context of a late modernity that shimmers in the colourful manifold of transcultural and translocal exchanges at the same time as it suffers under increasing social, environmental and spatial injustice?

Both volumes on the theme of creation and salvation show how the interaction between an understanding of the world as creation and the experience of and hope for salvation has served as a central driving force, a systematic steam "locomotive" in the history of theology. Creation and salvation need to be related, at every place and in every time anew, and both need to be embedded in each other in order to keep the inner dynamic of Christian life and work together. Separating creation and salvation implies substantial risks. One could easily regard the Christian faith exclusively as belonging to those who regard themselves as the primary objects of God's work of saving his own and thus as co-workers with God. Alternatively, one could universalise the adoration of nature and thus mystify God's identity. As Bonhoeffer once observed, God cannot exist in general but only in particular as the God of the here and the now.

As the editor noted in his introduction, the Christian message about salvation through the historical (and thus the earthly and bodily) Christ must not be understood as salvation *from* creation but as the salvation *of* creation. One may also mine this insight deeper to explore how God's work of creation implies *the creation of salvation*. Can and should one regard the work of salvation and liberation in itself as a part of the triune God's ongoing creation? Obviously yes, I would say.

Following the classical paths of trinitarian theology, such a deep integration makes sense because it does not allow one to attribute creation to the Father and salvation to the Son and the Spirit. A truly trinitarian perspective would identify the three in one and would approach both creation and salvation in terms of a directed movement "in the Spirit through the Son to the Father". A reduction of the Christian creed as a symbolic expression of faith in the triune God to a simple triality of articles does essential harm to the heart of the Christian faith. It encourages a split between creation and salvation, which history has revealed as one of the most fatal abysses for theological reflection. Since these two volumes now offer the interested reader an extensive and differentiated exploration of the relationship between creation and salvation through the ages and in different geographic contexts, one can only hope that these publications will serve as a durable antidote against splitting creation and salvation, and will help to prevent shallow ways of connecting them arbitrarily.

For me as series editor – and I trust this would also be true for other readers – the various chapters of the two volumes act as a stimulating crystal, a glass that in surprisingly many ways refracts the divine light in the light of contextualised and historicised, defective-but-justified human attempts to keep and tie together our experiences, images and rhetorical artefacts about God's liberative work in, with and through creation. One can twist and turn the crystal around in order to gain many different perspectives, contemplating how the triune Creator liberates in a diversity of cultural, geographical and natural habitats and how the triune Liberator creates new forms of life, hope and countervailing power.

One can hold the crystal in different forms of light to see what patterns may emerge from that. One kind of example is the disciplined investigations concerning the strengths and limitations of theological systems in the large community of theologians – who sometimes play their games of re-reading, re-figuration and re-construction in inspiring and creative ways, surprising even themselves with the figures that emerge from the potter's clay, but sometimes also in painfully narrow-minded ways. One can hold the crystal to contemplate how theological creativity becomes accelerated when it enters into a deep exchange with other reflexive systems, including ancient philosophy, feminism or various modes of environmentalism. One can also spin the crystal around quickly just for a breath of fresh air in order to gain unfamiliar insights, to cast an eye on new maps and metaphors. For Westerners familiar with our common patristic and medieval past, it will indeed be refreshing to dwell with the perspectives offered in the chapters on non-Western contexts.

One common conclusion about the inner dynamic of Christian theology can be drawn from the various chapters in the two volumes. Whether one departs from the need for liberation or from nature (interpreted as God's beloved creation), one will find that the one refers to the other and that they sometimes interpenetrate each other. Many paths lead from the one to the other and back in a circular flow. Contemplating the beauty and righteousness of creation, where the sun shines and rain falls equally for all, will necessarily lead to a perception of the suffering of creatures and their hope and struggle for justice. Thirsting for salvation cannot be limited to the individual, but necessarily leads to questions regarding the liberation of everything that exists between heaven and earth. The historical Christ will always remain the bodily and earthly Christ, imagined as a microcosm of all life and a liberating mediator. Believing that the earth, our home, is embraced by the triune God as a sacred creation necessarily implies the pain of eschatological anticipation, the tension between the already-here-and-now and the still-not-yet-fully.

Finally, for the sake of the self-understanding of the church, the church needs to learn that it will scarcely survive without seeking, steadily afresh, an integrated understanding of God's work of creation and salvation. A time of dangerous anthropogenic environmental change, when physical and philosophical pain is steadily increasing, in different religious traditions as well as among so-called secularists, is perhaps best captured in the question how we can continue to believe in anything – be it God, humanity, reason, money or power. For the Christian community of faithful, there appears to be a burning need to construe what it means to believe that God works as a liberating creator and a creative liberator among those who suffer under human sin. How does the life-giving Spirit "take place" in the midst of a community of divine icons hoping and "groaning in the pains of childbirth"? My hope is that readers will not stop twisting the crystal of salvation in creation after putting aside these two volumes.

Sigurd Bergmann

Series Editor: *Studies in Religion and the Environment* (LIT Verlag)

List of Contributors

The following persons contributed to the volume. An email address is indicated in each case.

Robert Owusu Agyarko teaches at the Ghana Baptist University College in Kumasi, Ghana. <revagyarko@yahoo.com>

Pauli Annala teaches systematic theology in the Department of the Systematic Theology at the University of Helsinki in Finland. <pauli.annala@helsinki.fi>

Nikolaos Asproulis is a Ph.D. student in systematic theology at the Hellenic Open University in Greece. <asprou@acadimia.gr>

Matthew Baker is a Ph.D. student in systematic theology at Fordham University in the United States of America. <lkb77@juno.com>

Sigurd Bergmann is professor of religious studies at the Norwegian University of Science and Technology in Trondheim, Norway. He is the series editor of *Studies in Religion and the Environment* (LIT Verlag). <sigurd.bergmann@ntnu.no>

Steven Bouma-Prediger teaches theology and ethics at Hope College in Holland, Michigan, in the United States of America. <boumapred@hope.edu>

Martien E. Brinkman teaches ecumenical and intercultural theology in the Faculty of Theology at the VU University Amsterdam in the Netherlands. <m.brinkman9@kpnplanet.nl>.

Bo Claesson works as a theologian at the University of Gothenburg's Department of Literature, History of Ideas and Religion. <bo.claesson@lir.gu.se>

Ernst M. Conradie teaches systematic theology and ethics in the Department of Religion and Theology at the University of the Western Cape in South Africa. <econradie@uwc.ac.za>

Henry Cöster is professor of religious studies and Theology at Karlstad University in Sweden. <henry.coster@kau.se>

John Culp teaches philosophy of religion in the Department of Theology and Philosophy at Azusa Pacific University in the United States of America. <jculp@apu.edu>

Anne Marie Dalton is professor of religious studies at Saint Mary's University, Halifax, in Canada. <annemarie.dalton@smu.ca>

Celia E. Deane-Drummond is professor in theology, concurrent between the College of Arts and Letters and the College of Science, at the University of Notre Dame in the United States of America. <Celia.Deane-Drummond.1@nd.edu>

Heather Eaton is professor at Saint Paul University in Ottowa, Canada. <heaton@ustpaul.ca>

Denis Edwards is associate professor of historical and systematic theology in the Department of Theology of Flinders University in South Australia. <denis.edwards@flinders.edu.au>

Hans S. A. Engdahl is extraordinary professor in the Department of Religion and Theology at the University of the Western Cape in South Africa and is currently based in Sweden. <hengdahl@uwc.ac.za>

Mickey Gjerris teaches bioethics and philosophy of science at the University of Copenhagen in Denmark and is a member of the Danish Ethical Council. <mgj@life.ku.dk>

Ben-Willie Kwaku Golo is lecturer in the Department for the Study of Religions at the University of Ghana, Accra. <bgolo@ug.edu.gh>

Mary Grey is professor emerita of the University of Wales, Lampeter, and visiting professor at St Mary's University College, Twickenham, London, in England. <m.grey@surfwise.co.uk>

John Hart is professor of Christian Ethics at Boston University School of Theology in the United States of America. <drjhart@bu.edu>

Willis Jenkins is Margaret Farley associate professor of Social Ethics at Yale Divinity School in the United States of America. <Willis.Jenkins@yale.edu>

Pauliina Kainulainen holds a doctorate in theology from the University of Joensuu, Finland. <pauliina.kainulainen@uef.fi>

Guillermo Kerber, originally from Uruguay, presently coordinates the work on Care for Creation and Climate Justice at the World Council of Churches, Geneva, Switzerland. <GKM@wcc-coe.org>

Dirk van Keulen is a postdoctoral researcher at the Protestant Theological University in the Netherlands. <dirkvankeulen@planet.nl>

Grace Ji-Sun Kim is associate professor of doctrinal theology at the Moravian Theological Seminary in Bethlehem, Pennsylvania. She is originally from South Korea. <gjskim@moravian.edu>

Kohara Katsuhiro teaches systematic theology, religious ethics and the comparative study of monotheistic religions at the School of Theology at the Doshisha University, Kyoto, Japan. <katsuhiro@kohara.ac>

Akke van der Kooi is senior lecturer in systematic theology at the Protestant Theological University, location Groningen, in the Netherlands. <avanderkooi@pthu.nl>

Lai Pan-chiu teaches at the Department of Cultural and Religious Studies at the Chinese University of Hong Kong. <pclai@cuhk.edu.hk>

Douglas G. Lawrie teaches Old Testament in the Department of Religion and Theology at the University of the Western Cape in South Africa. <dlawrie@uwc.ac.za>

Lee Jeong-Woo teaches systematic theology, worship and congregational development at the Institute of Doctor of Ministry, related to the Presbyterian Church in the Republic of Korea. <jwemmanuel@hotmail.com>

Michael Lodahl is professor of theology and world religions at Point Loma Nazarene University in San Diego, California, in the United States of America. <MichaelLodahl@pointloma.edu>

Christo Lombard teaches systematic theology and ethics in the Department of Religion and Theology at the University of the Western Cape in South Africa. <clombard@uwc.ac.za>

Dan Martin is a Ph.D. candidate in theology at the University of Dayton in Dayton, Ohio, in the United States of America. <martind @ndapandas.org>

Fulata Lusungu Moyo, originally from Malawi, is Programme Executive for Women in Church and Society for the World Council of Churches, where she coordinates women's voice, participation and perspectives in Unity, Mission, Justice and Diakonia. <Fulata.Mbano_Moyo@wcc-coe.org>

Jesse Mugambi teaches in the Department of Philosophy and Religious Studies at the University of Nairobi in Kenya. <jnmugambi@gmail.com>

Daniel Munteanu, originally from Romania, is assistant professor at the Otto-Friedrich University of Bamberg, Germany. <daniel.munteanu@web.de>

Ådne Njå obtained a doctorate in theology from the Faculty of Theology at University of Oslo and serves as a pastor in the Brønnøy parish of the Church of Norway in Norway. <adne.nja@bronnoykirke.no>

Aristotle Papanikolaou is associate professor of theology and co-founding Director of the Orthodox Christian Studies Program at Fordham University in the United States of America. <papanikolaou@fordham.edu>

Clive Pearson, originally from New Zealand, is associate professor and principal of the United Theological College in Sydney, Australia, and Head of the School of Theology at Charles Sturt University in Australia. <cpearson@nsw.uca.org.au>

Stephen J. Plant is dean and Runcie fellow at Trinity Hall, Cambridge, in the United Kingdom. <sjp27@cam.ac.uk>

Maria Chavez Quispe is an Aymara theologian from La Paz, Bolivia, and currently serves in the World Council of Churches as consultant for the Indigenous Peoples'

Programme. <Maria.Chavez_Quispe@wcc-coe.org>

Susan Rakoczy is professor of systematic theology and spirituality at St Joseph's Theological Institute, Cedara, and the School of Religion, Philosophy and Ethics of the University of KwaZulu-Natal, South Africa. <srakoczy@sjti.ac.za>

Svein Rise is professor of systematic theology at the School of Religion, Education and Intercultural Studies, Bergen, in Norway. <Svein.Rise@NLA.no>

Norman Russell teaches early church history at Heythrop College, University of London in England. <normanvrussell@hotmail.com>

John Sanders is professor of religious studies in the Department of Religious Studies at Hendrix College in Conway, Arkansas, in the United States of America. He may be contacted at <sandersj@hendrix.edu>.

Oliver Smith is lecturer in Russian at the University of St Andrews in Scotland. <olgs@st-andrews.ac.uk>

Christopher Southgate is research fellow in theology at the University of Exeter in England and vice principal, South West Ministry Training Course. <C.C.B.Southgate@exeter.ac.uk>

Elizabeth Theokritoff, Elizabeth Theokritoff is an Orthodox Christian independent scholar and theological translator based in New Jersey in the United States of America. <e.theokritoff@ some.oxon.org>

Janet Trisk is an honourary lecturer at the University of KwaZulu Natal, rector of St David's Prestbury in Pietermaritzburg, South Africa and director of theological education for the diocese of Natal. <triskj@telkomsa.net>

Mika Vähäkangas is professor of mission studies and ecumenics at Lund University in Sweden and adjunct professor of dogmatics at Helsinki University in Finland. <mika.vahakangas@teol.lu.se>

Annalet van Schalkwyk is associate professor in the Department of Christian Spirituality, Church History and Missiology, University of South Africa, Pretoria in South Africa. <vschaa@unisa.ac.za>

Anné H. Verhoef teaches philosophy and ethics at the North-West University in Potchefstroom, South Africa. <Anne.Verhoef@nwu.ac.za>

Norman Wirzba is research professor of theology, ecology, and rural life at Duke Divinity School in the United States of America. <nwirzba@div.duke.edu>

George Zachariah serves Gurukul Lutheran Theological College and Research Institute, Chennai, India, in the Department of Christian Theology and Ethics. <gzachariahk@gmail.com>

Index of Personal Names